Exchange of Information and Data Protection in Cross-border Criminal Proceedings in Europe

Ángeles Gutiérrez Zarza
Editor

Exchange of Information and Data Protection in Cross-border Criminal Proceedings in Europe

Springer

Editor
Ángeles Gutiérrez Zarza
The Hague
The Netherlands

ISBN 978-3-642-40290-6 ISBN 978-3-642-40291-3 (eBook)
DOI 10.1007/978-3-642-40291-3
Springer Heidelberg New York Dordrecht London

Library of Congress Control Number: 2014947123

Printed on acid-free paper

Springer is part of Springer Science+Business Media (www.springer.com)

Foreword

With the entry into force of the Lisbon Treaty and the adoption of the Stockholm Programme, the processing and protection of personal data has become one of the most relevant matters in the area of Freedom, Security and Justice of the European Union.

The Charter of Fundamental Rights of the European Union, which recognised the protection of personal data as a separate fundamental right in its Article 8, has become legally binding not only for EU institutions, bodies, offices and agencies, but also for Member States when acting within the scope of EU law.

Article 16 of the Treaty on the Functioning of the European Union (TFEU) and the abolition of the three-pillar structure provide for the possibility of replacing Directive 95/46/EC and other existing instruments with a comprehensive legal framework on data protection. In accordance with this new legal framework, in January 2012 the Commission issued a legislative package for an overall reform of the data protection rules, including a Communication setting out its main objectives and two legislative proposals: a draft Regulation establishing a general EU framework for data processing and protection (the General Data Protection Regulation), and a draft Directive covering the processing and protection of personal data in the areas of police and judicial cooperation, and national criminal proceedings (the Data Protection Directive).

In the context of the General Data Protection Regulation, a relevant issue currently under discussion is the revision of the traditional principles, rights and procedures on data protection, in order to make them more effective in practice and to deal with new challenges. New phenomena like cloud computing, social networks and geo-location devices are gradually becoming a part of the daily life of the citizens, who have the right to be adequately protected against any breaches of data protection rules.

On the other hand, the Stockholm Programme has also encouraged relevant discussions in the field of data protection. Although the principle of availability would continue to give "important impetus" to the collecting, processing and sharing of information in the area of Freedom, Security and Justice, the European Council has stressed the need to assess the existing information systems and criminal databases—especially those set up in the past years on the basis of the principle of availability—and integrate them into the framework of a coherent and overall EU Information Management Strategy (IM Strategy). More coherence in the multitude of information systems and databases created for law enforcement purposes, most of which are based on the need to fight against terrorism, is absolutely necessary. New databases should not be created without a prior evaluation of the existing information systems and a real privacy and data protection impact assessment of the new proposal.

The fight against terrorism continues to be a major concern, also for third countries enjoying close relations with the European Union. To tackle this phenomenon, the United States (of America) (US), Canada and Australia have signed individual agreements with the European Union, in order to receive information collected by EU air carriers operating flights from and to their countries, for the prevention, detection, investigation and prosecution of terrorist offences and serious (transnational) crime.

In the framework of such agreements, a considerable amount of personal data is provided to law enforcement authorities of the US, Canada and Australia. These data are provided by passengers to carriers when booking a flight or checking in, and include names, travel dates, travel itinerary, ticket information, contact details, travel agent at which the flight was booked, means of payment used, seat number and baggage information.

Moreover, in application of the EU–US Agreement on the Transfer of Financial Messaging Data for purposes of the Terrorist Finance Tracking Program (TFTP), the US Treasury Department is receiving personal data related to financial payments made by European citizens and companies.

The EU-US Agreement on TFTP is closely monitored by the EU institutions. Following intensive discussions on the US surveillance revelations and data protection, the work has been resumed as to the development of a general transatlantic framework with adequate safeguards for the sharing of personal data for law enforcement purposes.

Judges and prosecutors of the Member States should be aware of the practical consequences of this challenging context. They have a particular obligation to protect privacy and personal data of the citizens in the current information society. Both are fundamental rights of the citizens, expressly recognised in the Charter of Fundamental Rights of the European Union and in most of the legal systems of the Member States, and thus enforceable before the national courts.

Furthermore, the new technologies have created useful tools for police and judicial authorities. The appropriate balance will need to be found between the efficiency of the criminal investigation (when gathering, processing and exchanging criminal data) and the rights of privacy and data protection of persons who may be targeted or otherwise be involved in those investigations, in order to avoid any risk of inadmissibility of evidence at trial stage.

Some databases (criminal records, arrested persons, land registers, taxes and revenues) may be directly accessible by judges and prosecutors, simply by introducing a password in their computers located at court. In the near future, the exchange of information with Eurojust through the Eurojust National Coordination System, as well as access to databases on criminal records of other Member States of the European Union, will be a reality.

Since 2007, the members of the project entitled "Data Protection in Criminal Proceedings" have worked closely with different institutions and bodies of the European Union and of some Member States (mainly Spain, Germany, the Netherlands and the UK) with the main objective of providing awareness and specialised training on the processing and protection of personal data to judges and prosecutors of the Member States.

The European Data Protection Supervisor has actively supported and participated in the activities organised in the framework of this project, with a view to encouraging an exchange of professional experience and expertise in this new and dynamic environment. I hope that this handbook will provide incentives to its readers to continue in the same spirit and to benefit from the enormous possibilities of the EU databases, information systems, channels and agencies set up for the purposes of preventing and combating crime with full respect of the fundamental rights of the individuals concerned.

Brussels, Belgium
December 2013

Peter Hustinx

Rationale

The idea of the DPiCP Project originated in a seminar held at the Faculty of Law of Toledo on 24 and 25 May 2007. In a meeting room of this ancient Convent of the Dominican Order, data protection experts from different European institutions and agencies, as well as Spanish judges, prosecutors and university professors had the opportunity to discuss the implications, in the area of cross-border criminal proceedings, of two main topics closely related to each other: the increasing exchange of information for the purposes of investigating and prosecuting criminal offences, including the setting up of new databases and information systems, on the one hand, and the impact of these phenomenon in privacy and other fundamental rights of suspects and other individuals concerned, including the protection of their personal data, on the other hand.

The discussion ran in parallel to the debate on the most appropriate methodology for providing training on this complex matter. This training was considered necessary because most judges and prosecutors of the Member States were not familiar with the enormous possibilities that come from having access to databases and information systems storing cross-border information that might be crucial in national investigations and proceedings. Moreover, judicial authorities considered mostly the rules on data processing, data protection and data security as a purely set of administrative rules with a minimum impact in ongoing investigations and prosecutions.

Following discussions in the Toledo seminar, from 12th to 14th September 2007 the Council of Europe hosted a workshop for judges and prosecutors on "Data protection in criminal proceedings", with special focus on Spain, the Netherlands and the United Kingdom. This workshop, with a practice-orientated approach, was based on a case study related to a criminal investigation of drugs, organised crime and money laundering coordinated by the United Kingdom with the support of Europol and Eurojust. In order to progress in the investigation, the UK national competent authorities requested relevant information stored in databases and information systems of other Member States (The Netherlands, and Spain) and a third State (Russia). In the different sessions of this workshop, the role of Eurojust and Europol was promoted, the possibilities of the EU information systems explored, and the applicable legal instruments analysed. The importance of the administrative rules governing data quality, data protection and data security was highlighted.

The institutions involved in the Toledo seminar then presented a proposal to the Commission, under the "Criminal Justice Programme 2008", for the organisation of a set of training courses on data protection in criminal proceedings. The proposal was entitled "Data Protection in Criminal Proceedings" (DPiCP) Project.

The Commission awarded a grant to the DPiCP Project and, with its support and co-financing, a another workshop on data protection in criminal proceedings was hosted by the Council of Europe, in Strasbourg, on 7–9 October 2009. This training activity combined a theoretical and practical approach, in order to provide law enforcement and judicial authorities with the necessary basic knowledge, competences and skills to prevent and combat cross-border criminality through the efficient use of the EU agencies and information systems mentioned above. The European Judicial Training Network (EJTN) actively promoted this training activity.

EJTN also supported another two training courses organised in Madrid, at the Spanish General Council of the Judiciary (on 14–16 July 2010), and in Barcelona, at the Spanish Judicial School (on 24–26 October 2011). A considerable number of judges attended both training courses, which focused on the impact of the EU framework for exchange of information in national criminal proceedings.

Discussions during these training courses resulted in the publication in 2012 of a handbook for Spanish judges and prosecutors, covering both the European dimension and the national legal system of Spain.[1]

This book has a more reduced scope and defined purpose. In scope, it mainly covers the European dimension of the information systems and rules for the processing and protection of personal data, although some references are also made to the impact of those rules in domestic investigations and criminal proceedings. As for its purpose, the book intends to be a useful tool for trainers and practitioners in the preparation of training activities related to cross-border cooperation and exchange of information in the fight against organised crime.

During the drafting of this book, I have given special consideration of the Communication "Building trust in EU-wide Justice: a new dimension to European Judicial Training" issued by the Commission in September 2011,[2] as well as discussions taken place at the Conference "Stimulating European Judicial Training" organised by the Commission on 10 April 2013, in Brussels.[3]

---

[1] *Nuevas tecnologías, protección de datos y proceso penal*, coordinated by Ángeles Gutiérrez Zarza, edit. Wolters Kluwer, Madrid 2012.

[2] COM(2011) 551 final.

[3] All information, including the Agenda and materials of the conference, are available at http://ec.europa.eu/justice/events/judicial-training-2013/index_en.htm. See, in particular, Le Bail, F.: "The European added value: the EU role in Judicial Training"; Berlinguer, L.: "The EP Pilot Project on European Judicial Training"; Goldsmith, J.: "The European training platform: the e-Justice portal as entry point for finding a training session".

In the above-mentioned Communication, judicial training is considered a crucial element of the creation of a European judicial culture, as it enhances mutual confidence between Member States, practitioners and citizens and ensures the efficient functioning of the European Judicial Area.

This Communication confirmed the importance of providing legal practitioners with appropriate training on EU law, including, among other priority areas, judicial cooperation in criminal matters and data protection.

Another relevant document considered carefully during the preparation of this book has been the Communication "Establishing a European Law Enforcement Training Scheme" (LETS) adopted by the Commission on 27 March 2013.[4] According to this Communication, training for police, customs, border guards and other police authorities is essential to create a common European law enforcement culture and ensure effective cross-border cooperation against serious crime.

This book offers guidance to those dealing with the challenging task of providing training for law enforcement and judicial authorities in the complex topic of cross-border exchange of information and data protection in criminal matters. While the book has been drafted with those objectives in mind, the author is conscious that the matter is extremely complex, the legal instruments are dispersed, and the databases and information systems are constantly evolving.[5] I am confident, however, that the content of the book will be of help to both trainers and legal practitioners seeking to become more familiar with the new possibilities of the EU in fighting cross-border crime effectively and protect EU citizens, whilst respecting privacy and fundamental rights of the suspects and accused persons.

---

[4] COM(2013) 172 final. Brussels, 27.3.2013.

[5] The reader will find updated information and documents related to the content of this book at www.idee.ceu.es/en-us/home.aspx.

Acknowledgements

I would like to express my most sincere gratitude to the European Commission, the Council of Europe, the Spanish Ministry of Science and Education, and both the University of Castilla-La Mancha and the Regional Government of Castilla-La Mancha, for the constant support and co-financing of the Data Protection in Criminal Proceedings (DPiCP) Project. Special thanks should also be given to the Spanish General Council of the Judiciary, the Spanish Judicial School, the Spanish Data Protection Agency, the Spanish General Prosecutor's Office, and the European Judicial Training Network for their collaboration and commitment in the organisation of the training activities for judges and prosecutors organised in the framework of the DPiCP Project and in other activities to follow-up this project.

I am also extremely grateful to the team of experts who provided training and shared their extensive knowledge on data protection and/or criminal proceedings during this project, in particular, to Diana Alonso Blas, Joaquín Bayo Delgado, Giovanni Butarelli, Jose Antonio del Cerro, Elena Domínguez, Daniel Drewer, Antonio Frías, Laraine Laudati, Carlos Lesmes, Miguel Marcos, Peter Michael, Angelika Möhlig and Graham Sutton. We all are extremely grateful to Peter Hustinx for his inspiring support during the DPiCP Project. Many thanks as well to the participants in these training activities, most of them judges and prosecutions from the Member States and experts from EU institutions and bodies, who exchanged practical experiences and provided fresh perspectives on this complex topic.

The book would not have been possible without the determination of Anke Seyfried and the enormous patience and great professionalism of Athiappan Kumar, both from Springer. Thanks are also extended to Professor Tim Wilson of the University of Northumbria Law School, who kindly assisted at the proof stage.

The book was finished on 15 December 2013.[6] All the good ideas it contains are from the above-mentioned experts. Mistakes are mine.

The Hague, The Netherlands Ángeles Gutiérrez Zarza
15 December 2013

[6] The reader will find updated information and documents related to the content of this book at www.idee.ceu.es/en-us/home.aspx.

Abbreviations

AFSJ	Area of Freedom, Security and Justice
ARO(s)	Asset Recovery Office(s)
AWF	Analysis Work File
CAHDATA	Ad hoc Committee on Data Protection (of the Council of Europe)
CARIN	Candem Asset Recovery Inter-Agency Network
CATS	Coordination Committee in the Area of Police and Judicial Cooperation in Criminal Matters (*Comité de l'article trente-six*)
CEPOL	European Police College
CFrD	Council Framework Decision
CIS	Customs Information System
CMS	Case Management System
CoE	Council of Europe
COM	Commission Document
Coreper	Committee of Permanent Representatives (*Comité des repré sentants permanents*)
COSI	Standing Committee on Operational Cooperation on Internal Security
DAPIX	Information Exchange and Data Protection (Working Party of the Council of the EU)
DHS	Department of Homeland Security
Dir.	Directive
DL	Deprivation of Liberty
Doc.	Document
DPiCP	Data Protection in Criminal Proceedings (Project)
EAFS	European Academy of Forensic Science
EAW	European Arrest Warrant
EC3	European Cybercrime Centre
ECHR	European Convention of Human Rights and Fundamental Freedoms
ECIM	European Crime Intelligence Model

ECOFIN	European Council of Financial Affairs
ECRIS	European Criminal Records Information System
ECtHR	European Court of Human Rights
EDPS	European Data Protection Supervisor
EEA	European Economic Area
EEW	European Evidence Warrant
EIO	European Investigation Order
EIS	Europol Information System
EIXM	European Information Exchange Model
EJN	European Judicial Network
EJTN	European Judicial Training Network
ENCS	European National Coordination System
ENFSI	European Network of Forensic Science Institutes
ENISA	European Network and Information Security Agency
ENUs	Europol National Units
EP	European Parliament
EPE	Europol Platform for Experts
EPOC	European Pool against Organised Crime
EPRIS	European Police Records Index System
EU	European Union
EUCPN	European Crime Prevention Network
Eu-LISA	European Agency for the Operational Management of Large-scale IT systems in the area of Freedom, Security and Justice
EUR	Euro
Eurofisc	European Network of national officials to detect and combat new cases of cross-border VAT fraud
Europol	European Police Office
FIDE	Customs Identification Database (*Fichier d'identification des dossiers d'enquête douanière*)
FIU(s)	Financial Intelligence Unit(s)
FRA	European Union Agency for Fundamental Rights
Frontex	European Agency for the Management of Operational Cooperation at the External Borders of the Member States of the European Union
GPS	Global Positioning System
IberRed	Iberoamerican Network of International legal Cooperation
IM Strategy	Information Management Strategy
ISS	Internal Security Strategy
IT	Information Technology
IXP	Information Exchange Platform
JHA	Justice and Home Affairs
JIT(s)	Joint Investigation Team(s)
JSB	Joint Supervisory Body
LETS	European Law Enforcement Training Scheme

LIBE	Standing Committee of the European Parliament on Civil Liberties, Justice and Home Affairs
MLA	Mutual Legal Assistance
MoU	Memorandum of Understanding
OCC	On-Call Coordination
OCTA	Organised Crime Threat Assessment
OECD	Organisation for Economic Cooperation and Development
OfPE	Order freezing property or evidence
OJ	Official Journal of the European Union
OLAF	Anti-Fraud Office of the European Union
p.	Page
parr.	Paragraph
PIES	Prüm Implementation, Evaluation and Strengthening of Forensic DNA data exchange (Project)
PIF	Protection of the Financial Interests of the European Union (*Protection des intérêts financiers*)
PIU	Passenger Information Unit
PNR	Passenger Name Record
SEC	Commission working documents
SFD	Swedish Framework Decision
SIENA	Secure Information Exchange Network Application
SIS	Schengen Information System
SIS-II	Second Generation System Information System
SOCTA	Serious Organised Crime Threat Assessment
SPOC(s)	Single Point(s) of Contact
SWD	Staff Working Document (of the Commission)
SWIFT	Society for Worldwide Interbank Financial Transfers
TCM	Terrorism Conviction Monitor
TE-SAT	Terrorism Situation and Trend Report of the European Union
TEU	Treaty on European Union
TFEU	Treaty on the Functioning of the European Union
TFTP	Terrorist Financing Tracking Program
TFTS	Terrorist Financing Tracking System
THB	Trafficking in Human Beings
TTIP	Transatlantic Trade and Investment Partnership
TWF	Temporary Work File
UMF2	Universal Messaging Format 2
UN	United Nations
US	United States (of America)
VAT	Value Added Tax
VIS	Visa Information System

Contents

Part I
Introduction

Chapter 1
Like Mushrooms After a Rainy Autumn Day

In the past 10 years, the Member States of the EU have experienced an increasing exchange of information for the purposes of preventing and fighting serious cross-border crime. Several elements have contributed to this intensive workflow in the area of Freedom, Security and Justice of the EU.

Firstly, there has been an intensive period of policy and legislative work to create an adequate framework to enable law enforcement and judicial authorities from different Member States to work together in ongoing investigations and criminal proceedings, regardless of the existence of different jurisdictions and legal systems in the EU.

In order to tackle the criminal organisations and networks threatening the security of the EU in the most effective and efficient manner, some innovative principles (mutual recognition, availability) and concepts (Information Management Strategy, European Information Exchange Model) have been adopted.

In accordance with the principle of mutual recognition, which was officially proclaimed by Tampere conclusions, the Issuing and executing judicial authorities are entitled to contact each other directly to exchange information and relevant documents. Obviously this exchange of information and documents must still be undertaken under specific legal instruments and through the appropriate channels, but such cooperation is no longer not longer in the hands of the diplomatic services of Member States: judicial authorities can speak to each other directly and discuss details of common investigations and prosecutions. This constant dialogue will ensure a fruitful collaboration in a particular criminal investigation or prosecution.

The recognition of the principle of availability by The Hague multiannual programme initiated a culture of mutual cooperation and sharing of information across the European Union. According to this principle, a law enforcement officer who needs information in order to perform his duties should be able to obtain that information from another Member State, and the law enforcement office holding

---

The opinions expressed by the author are personal and do not necessary coincide with those of the institution she is working for.

Á.G. Zarza (ed.), *Exchange of Information and Data Protection in Cross-border Criminal Proceedings in Europe*, DOI 10.1007/978-3-642-40291-3_1,

the information should make it available, for the stated purpose, taking into account the requirements of ongoing investigations in that Member State.

The implementation in practice of this principle has resulted in a proliferation of information systems, channels and tools for the exchange of information, which motivated the need for a comprehensive, integrated and well-structured Information Management (IM) Strategy for the Internal Security of the EU. Following a thoroughly assessment of the implementation of the most relevant existing legal instruments, the Commission has designed a European Information Exchange to guide the Union and the Member States in cross-border exchange of information for operational purposes.

There has also been a proliferation of rules governing the processing and protection of personal data in the area of Freedom, Security and Justice of the EU. In 2005, Mr Charles Elsen pointed out that "the data protection rules were growing like mushrooms after a rainy Autums day",[1] and certainly this situation has steadily increased.[2] As Directive 95/46/EC[3] excluded from its scope of application the areas of police and judicial cooperation in criminal matters, the setting up of each information system and databases has been accompanied by its own set of principles, rights and proceedings on data protection.

The Treaty of Lisbon was envisaged by the Commission as a unique legal basis for the adoption of common rules for the processing and protection of personal data in both private and public sectors, including police and justice matters. Although the Commission has issued two different initiatives on this matter (the General Data Protection Regulation and the Data Protection Directive, the later focused on criminal matters), there is a consistent and common approach on this matter.

From a more practical point of view, the Commission has continued working on several initiatives aimed at promoting the exchange of information for the purposes of preventing and fighting cross-border crime. The initiatives of the Commission on the Terrorism Finance Tracking System (TFTS) in the European Union and of the EU Passenger Name Record (PNR) Scheme are some of the most innovative tools in this area.

In this policy and legal framework, we cannot forget the Council of Europe. It was the pioneer European institution regulating the processing and protection of personal data and now, it is sharing this role with the EU.

A second element motivating the increasing exchange of information for the purposes of preventing and fighting serious cross-border crime is the gradual

[1] "Police information systems in the European Union", *The rights of the individual vis-à-vis police information systems*, published by the *Comissao Nacional de Proteccao de Dados*, Lisbon, 1999, p. 114.

[2] Mr HUSTINX mentioned more recently that, "since 2005, about 40 percent of Commission proposals analysed in EDPS opinions on new legislation were closely connected to the Area of Freedom, Security and Justice" (eucrim 1/2013, p. 1).

[3] Directive 95/46/EC on the protection of individuals with regard to the processing of personal data and on the free movement of such data. OJ L 281, 23.11.1995, p. 31.

consolidation of the EU agencies and bodies (Eurojust, Europol, OLAF) with competences in this field.

As neither Europol nor Eurojust have any investigative power (meaning that they cannot generate their own investigations and, in the case of Eurojust, prosecutions), both EU agencies completely rely on the information received from the national competent authorities. For the appropriate development of their tasks, the National Members of Eurojust are in permanent contact with the national prosecution services of their countries of origin, to identify how to best disrupt and dismantle cross-border criminal organisations.

This constant dialogue generates a workflow in the form of a fluent exchange of information between all the actors involved. Europol and Europol are governed by strict rules for the processing and protecting of personal data. OLAF, the contact points of the networks with competences in the area of Criminal Justice also exchange relevant information related to ongoing investigations and proceedings.

The third element contributing to an increasing exchange of information is the setting up of important EU information systems and databases (Prüm, SIS-II, ECRIS) enabling law enforcement authorities access, through appropriate channels (SIENA, Swedish Council Decision) and tools (of police cooperation, of judicial cooperation as the confiscation order), the information needed to get a clear picture of criminal phenomena and organisations.

As it has been mentioned, the setting up of these information systems and databases has been accompanied by their own rules for the processing and protection of personal data. These administrative rules should be strictly observed during the collection, transmission, processing and exchange of information at police level. However, when a criminal investigation has started, the application of the rules for the processing and protection of personal data becomes more complicated, mainly because criminal proceedings have their own rules for the management of judicial activities and the protection of the fundamental rights of the individuals concerned (suspects, victims, witnesses).

The confluence of the rules on data protection and those governing criminal proceedings has many practical implications. As an example, in domestic investigations, some lawyers tend to exercise the right of access to the judicial file in accordance with the rules on data protection, whilst the right to information in criminal proceedings has been, and still is, one of the fundamental rights protecting suspects and accused persons in the context of investigations and criminal proceedings. Regardless of which the prosecutor is introducing the information about the case in a manual file or in a case management system, the right to information in criminal proceedings as regulated in the national Codes of criminal proceedings would be applicable. In cross-border cases, the Directive 2012/13/EU of 22 May 2012 on the right to information in criminal proceedings[4] would be more appropriate than the Council Framework Decision 2008/977/JHA of 27 November 2008 on the protection of personal data processed in the framework of police and judicial

[4] OJ L 142, 1.6.2012, p. 1.

cooperation in criminal matters. These examples do not mean that the rules for the processing and protecting of personal data do not have any relevance in the area of criminal proceedings: they prove that the limits between both set of rules are not always clear and that the same interest of the suspects (to be informed on the existence of an investigation against him) may be protected by one or another set of rules, depending mainly on whether there is a formal investigations or not against this individual. If there is such formal investigation, the Codes of criminal proceedings apply.

The new proposal for a Data Protection Directive in cross-border criminal proceedings[5] is flexible enough to allow different scenarios and possibilities for regulating the interaction between the rules on data protection and those of the criminal proceedings at national level.

Another relevant element to consider is that, in most of cases, the exchange of information between police or judicial authorities precedes, but does not replace, the issuing and execution of request for police and judicial cooperation in criminal matters. As example, automated searches in Prüm system may result in a match between a DNA sample and a DNA profile, however, the name of the individual concerned will be only provided in response to known following a request for mutual legal assistance sent by a police or judicial authority.

We can find another relevant example in the case of PNR information transmitted to United States. The information transmitted through this system is very valuable for the prevention or investigation at police level of serious forms of crime, however, if a formal criminal investigation starts in any Member State of the EU, the EU- US Agreement on Mutual Legal Assistance should apply to the receipt of such information from US authorities through the appropriate channels and its insertion in the judicial file.

As cross-border criminality evolves, the EU bodies must improve their operational capacities to prevent and combat criminal offences in the most effective manner. This has been the main reason for the proposals of new Regulations about Europol[6], Eurojust[7] and the European Public Prosecutor's Office[8]. The proposals for exchange of information among them, as well as with the judicial authorities of the Member States is one of the most innovative and interesting matters under

[5] Proposal for a Directive on the protection of individuals with regard to the processing of personal data by competent authorities for the purposes of prevention, investigation, detection or prosecution of criminal offences or the execution of criminal penalties, and the free movement of such data. Document COM(2012) 12 final.

[6] Proposal for a Regulation of the European Parliament and of the Council on the European Union Agency for Law Enforcement Cooperation and Training (Europol) and repealing Decisions 2009/371/JHA and 2005/681/JHA. COM(2013) 173 final. Brussels, 27.3.2013.

[7] COM(2013) 535 final. Brussels, 17.7.2013.

[8] COM(2013) 534 final. Brussels, 17.7.2013.

consideration in the area of police and judicial cooperation in criminal matters.[9] New legal instruments and tools, as the proposal for the European Investigation Order,[10] and the possibility to exchange requests of judicial cooperation through e-Justice portal[11] are innovative too.

Despite the existence of a great number of policy strategies, legal instruments, tools and channels for the exchange of information in the EU, all of them should be better aligned to support the common goal of protecting the EU citizens in an area of Freedom, Security and Justice. This has been the approach taken by the Lithuanian and Greek Presidencies of the Council of the EU in view of the next Multiannual Action Plan for the period 2014–2018. No more mushrooms, but the existing crop needs to be better quality, more healthy. The importance of the new initiatives under discussion at EU level in order to facilitate the exchange of cross-border information for law enforcement and judicial authorities is analysed in the last chapter of the book.

A final remark is needed, related to the scope of the book. This is focused on the "operational" information gathered, processed and exchanged for the purposes of preventing and combating serious cross-border crime. "Strategic" information is not analysed in this work, although some references are made to the strategic information processed by Eurojust and Europol, or to the EU policy cycle for serious and international crime. We hope this operational approach will be of interest for the reader, and will provide a clear view on the efforts being made by both the EU institutions and Member States to protect the EU citizens in an Area of Freedom, Security and Justice.

[9] Regulation of the European Parlaiment and of the Council concerning investigations conducted by the European Anti-fraud Office (OLAF) repealing Regulation (EC) No. 1073/1999 of the European Parliament and of the Council and of the Council Regulation (Euratom) No 1074/1999. Council document 17427/12 GAF 29 FIN 1022 CODEC 2955 OC 728.

[10] Initiative of the Kingdom of Belgium, the Republic of Bulgaria, the Republic of Estonia, the Kingdom of Spain, the Republic of Austria, the Republic of Slovenia and the Kingdom of Sweden for a Directive of the European Parliament and the Council regarding the European Investigation Order in criminal matters. Council document 9288/10 COPEN 117 EUROJUST 49 EJN 13 PARLNAT 13 CODEC 384. Brussels, 21 May 2010.

[11] https://e-justice.europa.eu/home.do.

Part II
European Policy and Legal Framework

Chapter 2
The Area of Freedom, Security and Justice of the EU

2.1 Direct Contacts Between Judicial Authorities in Accordance with the Principle of Mutual Recognition

In the past, the national judicial authorities conducting investigations and criminal proceedings did not maintained contacts with their colleagues in other Member States. The traditional requests for judicial cooperation (e.g., extradition, rogatory letters) were channelled through the Ministries of Justice and of External Affairs and involved as intermediaries the diplomat and consular services of the requesting and requested countries.

The system, quite uneffective and slow in practice, required certain changes when the free movement of citizens started to became a reality in an Area of Freedom, Security and Justice.[1]

The European countries that signed the 1990 Convention implementing the 1985 Schengen Agreement were committed to protect its citizens against serious cross-border crime by improving and simplifying, among others, the mechanisms of judicial cooperation in criminal matters. In this context, Art. 53 of the 1990 Convention stated that, without prejudice of the possibility of sending requests through the Ministries of Justice or Interpol (parr. 2), "requests for assistance may

The opinions expressed by the author are personal and do not necessary coincide with those of the institution for which she working.

[1] On this Area and on the principle of mutual recognition, see Flore (2009), pp. 24 and 366; Monar (2010), p. 21; Elsen (2010), p. 255; Peers (2011), pp. 4 and 655; Klip (2012), pp. 13 and 362; Gutierrez Zarza et al. (2004).

On the changes introduced by the Treaty of Amsterdam, see Labayle (2002) and Bruti Liberati (2002).

On the principle of mutual recognition, see also Gless (2005), p. 121.

Á.G. Zarza (ed.), *Exchange of Information and Data Protection in Cross-border Criminal Proceedings in Europe*, DOI 10.1007/978-3-642-40291-3_2,

be made directly between judicial authorities and returned via the same channels" (parr. 1).[2]

In the EU Context, the Treaty of Maastricht proclaimed very timidly that judicial cooperation was one of the "matters of common interest" of the Member States. However, this short sentence was relevant enough to serve as legal basis for the adoption by the Council of two joint actions aimed at facilitating contacts between the judicial authorities of different Member States:

- First, the Joint Action 96/277/JHA of 22 April 1996 adopted on the basis of Article K.3 of the Treaty of European Union concerning a framework for the exchange of liaison magistrates to improve judicial cooperation between the Member States of the EU.[3] In accordance with its Art. 1(3), the aim of this Joint Action was "to increase the speed and effectiveness of judicial cooperation and to promote the pooling of information on the legal and judicial systems of the Member States and to improve their operation". Under specific arrangements between the home Member State and the host Member State, liaison magistrates may also handle "the exchange of information and statistics designed to promote mutual understanding of the legal systems and legal data bases of the States concerned" [Art. 2(2)].
- Second, the Joint Action 98/428/JHA of 29 June 1998 adopted on the basis of Article K.3 of the Treaty of European Union on the creation of a European Judicial Network.[4] In accordance with one of its recitals:

  > Effective improvement of judicial cooperation between the Member States requires the adoption of structural measures at European Union level to enable the appropriate direct contacts to be set up between judicial authorities and other authorities responsible for judicial cooperation and judicial action against forms of serious crime, within Member States.

  With this spirit, the contact points of EJN were conceived as "active intermediaries with the task of facilitating judicial cooperation between the Member States", enabling judicial and other competent authorities to establish the most appropriate direct contacts and provide them with the necessary information "to prepare an effective request for judicial cooperation or to improve judicial cooperation in general" (Art. 4).

The possibility of the requesting and the executing judicial authorities to provide the necessary information and discuss with liaison magistrates or EJN contact points the difficulties encountered in cross-border investigations and prosecutions was a major step in the area of judicial cooperation. Another relevant change was that, following this exchange of information and views, formal requests for mutual

[2] See Annex to the Protocol integrating the Schengen acquis into the framework of the EU. This Protocol was annexed to the Treaty on European Union and to the Treaty establishing the European Community by the Treaty of Amsterdam. OJ C 340, 10.11.1997.

[3] OJ L 105, 27.4.1996, p. 1.

[4] OJ L 191, 7.7.1998, p. 4.

legal assistance and extradition could be sent and returned directly—in certain cases—between the competent judicial authorities.

In the particular area of money laundering and in accordance with Art. 4 of the Joint Action 98/699/JHA of 3 December,[5] Member States should "encourage direct contacts between investigators, investigating magistrates and prosecutors of Member States making appropriate use of available cooperation arrangements" (parr. 1). In case of difficulties, the requested State should endeavour to satisfy the request in some alternative way "after appropriate consultation with the requesting State" (parr. 2).

The Convention of 27 September 1996 relating to extradition between the Member States of the EU privileged the role of the central authorities for the transmission and reception of extradition requests and supporting documents (Art. 13). However, the judicial authorities of the Member States which had submitted a declaration to Art. 14 were entitled to send requests for supplementary information directly to the judicial authorities or other competent authorities responsible for criminal proceedings. In practice, most of the Member States which adopted the Convention submitted such declaration.[6]

The Treaty of Amsterdam reinforced notably the importance of judicial cooperation in criminal matters in the EU. This Treaty proclaimed that one of the objectives of the Union—i.e., not a mere common interest of the Member States—should be "to provide citizens with a high level of safety within an area of freedom, security and justice by developing common action among the Member States in the field of police and judicial cooperation in criminal matters and by preventing and combating racism and xenophobia". A Protocol Annexed to the Treaty integrated the Schengen *acquis*, including its legal provisions on judicial cooperation, into the legal framework of the EU.

The new Treaty consolidated the previous achievements, and created the appropriate legal framework for some new elements developed by the Action Plan on how best implement the provisions of the Treaty of Amsterdam in an Area of Freedom, Security and Justice (Vienna Action Plan). Among these new elements, the Vienna Action Plan announced the need to start "a process with a view to facilitating mutual recognition of decisions and enforcement of judgements in criminal matters",[7] and the convenience "of extending and possibly formalising the exchange of information on criminal records".[8]

In line with the Treaty of Amsterdam and the Vienna Action Plan, the Tampere European Council stated that a joint mobilisation of police and judicial resources

[5] Joint Action 98/699/JHA of 3 December 1998 adopted by the Council on the basis f Article k.3 of the Treaty on European Union, on money laundering, the identification, tracing, freezing, seizing and confiscation of instrumentalities and the proceeds of crime. OJ 333, 9.12.1998.

[6] See Gutierrez Zarza et al (2004), p. 1291.

[7] P. 12 and 13.

[8] Cit., p. 14.

was needed to guarantee that there were no hiding place for criminals or the proceeds of crime within the Union.[9]

As it is well known, Tampere also proclaimed the principle of mutual recognition as "the cornerstone of judicial cooperation in both civil and criminal matters within the Union". This principle entails that a judicial decision adopted in a Member State should be executed in other Member State as if this decision was taken by a judicial authority of that later State. Mutual recognition is based on the assumption that, despite the diversity of criminal law systems in the EU, the Member States are all part of a European judicial culture founded on common values, including the respect of human rights and fundamental freedoms, and that judicial authorities take their decisions in accordance with such common values. All judicial authorities must be confident in the structure and functioning of the legal systems, and in the ability of all Member States to ensure a fair trial.

Following the Tampere conclusions, a comprehensive programme of measures to implement the principle of mutual recognition in criminal matters was adopted by the Council and the Commission in 2001. In accordance with this Action Plan, the principle of mutual recognition must be sought at all stages of criminal proceedings, including pre-trial stage, conviction and post-sentencing follow-up decisions.[10]

Although the Council had given priority to the adoption of measures with a view to the freezing and further confiscation of the proceeds of crime,[11] the terrorist attacks in New York and Washington in 2001 accelerated the dossier of the European Arrest Warrant (EAW), which was adopted at the JHA Council meeting of 13 June 2002.[12] So far, the EAW is the most representative and frequently applied EU legal instrument based on the principle of mutual recognition. When the location of the individual concerned is known, the issuing judicial authority is entitled to transmit the EAW directly to the executing judicial authority. Difficulties faced during the issuing, transmission or execution of the EAW, as well as during the surrender of the person arrested, can be discussed and solved directly between both judicial authorities. There is also the possibility to ask for the assistance of EJN, or in certain cases Eurojust, in order to overcome such difficulties and obstacles.

Eurojust, also mentioned in the Tampere Conclusions,[13] was set up by Council Decision of 28 February 2002 as the new actor in the EU landscale with the main objectives of providing support and assistance to the judicial authorities of the Member States in complex investigations and prosecutions against serious cross-

[9] Tampere Conclusions, p. 2.

[10] Programme of Measures to implement the principle of mutual recognition of decisions in criminal matters. OJ C 12, 15.1.2002, p. 10.

[11] Action Plan of 2001, p. 14.

[12] Council Framework Decision 2002/584/JHA of 13 June 2002, on the European Arrest Warrant and the surrender procedures between the Member States of the EU. OJ L 190, 18.7.2002.

[13] See point (46).

border crime. In cases of organised crime, money laundering, drugs trafficking, or trafficking of human beings, Eurojust maintains frequent contacts and permanent exchange of information with the national competent authorities, in order to tackle these criminal offences of the most coordinated manner.

The Council Framework Decision on freezing and confiscation was adopted in 2003. In most of the cases, the judicial authorities of the Member States continued requesting the freezing and further confiscation of criminal assets on the basis of the Convention on Mutual Legal Assistance between the Member States of the EU of 29 May 2000. Among other reasons, the freezing order required the previous identification of the properties or criminal assets, which is not always possible. Moreover, another request for confiscation on the basis of the Convention of 2000 or the Council Framework Decision on confiscation was needed afterwards.

The Convention of 2000 simplified notably the freezing and further confiscation of criminal assets, because both requests could be submitted in the same rogatory letter. Moreover, requests for mutual assistance and spontaneous exchange of information could be made directly between the requesting and the requested competent judicial authority [Art. 6(1)].

Tampere Council Conclusions were replaced by a new multiannual programme, the so called The Hague Programme for the period 2005–2009.[14] This Programme established a clear link between mutual recognition and mutual trust, and included a set of measures to be implemented in order to increase trust between the judicial authorities of the Member States.

The Hague Programme also urged the EU institutions to work on a common core of fundamental rights for suspects and accused persons. In particular:

> The further realisation of mutual recognition as the cornerstone of judicial cooperation implies the development of equivalent standards for procedural rights in criminal proceedings, based on studies of the existing level of safeguards in Member States and with due respect for their legal traditions. In this context, the draft Framework Decision on certain procedural rights in criminal proceedings through the European Union should be adopted by the end of 2005.[15]

In the genuine EU area of Justice identified as one of the ten priorities for the next 5 years, the Action Plan of The Hague Programme included an ambitious list legal instruments to ensure the implementation of the principle of mutual recognition in all steps of criminal proceedings. The Council Framework Decisions on

[14] The Hague Programme: strengthening Freedom, Security and Justice in the European Union. OJ C 53, 3.3.2005, p. 1.

[15] The Hague Programme: strengthening Freedom, Security and Justice in the European Union. OJ C 53, 3.3.2005, p. 12.

financial penalties,[16] confiscation,[17] custodial sentences,[18] probation[19] and supervision measures[20] were adopted accordingly.

A Council Framework Decision on taking account convictions in other criminal procedures was also adopted. To ensure the exchange of information on criminal records, two Council Decisions on ECRIS were adopted too.

The Treaty of Lisbon has provided a solid legal basis for the achievements made by the Union in the field of Criminal Justice. A comprehensive Title devoted to the Area of Freedom, Security and Justice has been introduced in Chapter V of the Treaty on the Functioning of the EU (TFEU), including a chapter on Judicial Cooperation in Criminal Matters (Arts. 82–86 TFEU). In accordance with this legal framework, the Union constitutes "an area of freedom, security and justice with respect for fundamental rights and the different legal systems and traditions of the Member States" [Art. 67(1)]. Judicial cooperation in criminal matters is based on the principle of mutual recognition in criminal matters [Art. 82(1)], and includes the approximation of the laws and regulations of the Member States in certain areas including, inter alia, mutual admissibility of evidence and the rights of individuals in criminal procedure [Art. 82(2)(a) y (b)].

On the principle of mutual recognition, the most relevant legal instruments on the table of the European legislator are the European Investigation Order and the European Freezing and Confiscation Order.

Combating crime effectively requires a close cooperation and dialogue between the judicial authorities of the Member States and the involvement, when necessary, of the contact points of EJN and other networks as the European Network of experts in Joint Investigations Teams. In complex cases requiring coordination, Eurojust continues providing support and strengthening coordination and cooperation between national investigating and prosecuting authorities. In accordance with Art. 85(1), Eurojust can be entitled to initiate criminal investigations and propose the initiation of prosecutions conducted by competent national authorities, "particularly those relating to offences against the financial interests of the Union". The Commission has decided to wait the results of the sixth round of mutual

[16] Council Framework Decision 2005/214/JHA of 24 February 2005 on the application of the principle of mutual recognition to financial penalties. OJ L 76, 22.3.2005, p. 16.

[17] Council Framework Decision 2006/783/JHA of 6 October 2006 on the application of the principle of mutual recognition to confiscation orders. OJ L 328, 24.11.2006, p. 59.

[18] Council Framework Decision 2008/909/JHA of 27 November 2008 on the application of the principles of mutual recognition to judgements in criminal matters imposing custodial sentences or measures involving deprivation of liberty for the purpose of their enforcement in the European Union. OJ L 327, 5.12.2008, p. 27.

[19] Council Framework Decision 2008/947/JHA of 27 November 2008 on the application of the principle of mutual recognition to judgements and probation decisions with a view to the supervision of probation measures and alternative sanctions. OJ L 337, 16.12.2008, p. 102.

[20] Council Framework Decision 2009/829/JHA of 23 October 2009 on the application, between the Member States of the European Union, of the principle of mutual recognition to decisions on supervision measures as an alternative to provisional detention. OJ L 294, 11.11.2009, p. 20.

recognitions to decide whether the existing powers of Eurojust as an intermediary between the national judicial authorities can be extended further to give Eurojust an active role with direct impact in national criminal procedures.

Based on Art. 86 TFEU, a new actor has appeared in the Union scale: the European Public Prosecutor's Office (EPPO), responsible for investigating, prosecuting and bringing to judgement the perpetrators of, and accomplices in, offences against the financial interests of the Union. The EPPO will not be a mere intermediary between the national authorities of the Member States, but will assume the investigations and further steps of the national criminal proceedings in the particular field of the protection of the financial interests of the EU. For the appropriate performance of its tasks, the EPPO will need to work closely, maintain permanent contacts and exchange information with the national prosecution services and other relevant EU actors, including Eurojust, Europol and OLAF.

In this context the Stockholm Programme—the third multiannual programme for the Area of Freedom, Security and Justice of the EU—gave priority to the citizens and the protection of its fundamental rights for the period 2010-2014. El Roadmap of the Commission on the rights of the suspects of criminal offences was gradually developed. The Directive 2010/64/EU of 20 October 2012 on the right to interpretation and translation in criminal proceedings and the Directive 2012/13/EU of 22 May 2012 on the right of information in criminal proceedings were adopted by the Council. The proposal for a Directive on the strengthening of certain aspects of the presumption of innocence and the right to be present at trial in criminal proceedings, the proposal for a Directive on provisional legal aid, and the proposal for a Directive on safeguards of children suspected and accused in criminal proceedings were presented by the Commission in December 2013.

If we consider now the area of judicial cooperation in criminal matters, it seems that all the elements envisaged in the previous Treaties and multilateral programmes are present. The principle of mutual recognition has been implemented in different stages of the criminal proceedings, and the approval in the near future of both the European Investigation Order and the Order for freezing and further confiscation will improve consistency and efficiency in the fight against serious cross-border crime. The competent judicial authorities can easily approach national contacts points of different networks in order to solve practical problems or difficulties during the issuing, transmission or execution of requests for judicial cooperation. In complex cases, judicial authorities may ask for the support and assistance of Eurojust. When applying the legal instruments based on the principle of mutual recognition, judicial authorities should respect the fundamental rights of the citizens, in particular the rights of the victims and of the suspects of criminal offences in cross-border cases.

Well aware of these achievements, the ongoing reflection process with a view to the adoption of the next multiannual programme is focused on the consolidation of the progress made, rather than in the introduction of new elements in the area of Freedom, Security and Justice of the EU. Among other key elements, discussions during the Lithuanian Presidency of the EU have highlighted the role of the JHA agencies in the implementation of the legal instruments of judicial cooperation and in the collection of knowledge, the increased use of innovative tools and channels for the exchange of information, and the need to provide appropriate training on new technologies for EU practitioners.[21]

2.2 The increased Exchange of Information Among Law Enforcement Authorities in Accordance with the Principle of Availability

For many decades, cross-border police cooperation and exchange of information was not very frequent among the law enforcement authorities of different Member States: law enforcement authorities mostly focused on the national dimension of serious forms of criminality, and were very reluctant to facilitate this information to police authorities of other Member States.

The situation evolved gradually with the suppression of the internal borders and the need to establish some compensatory measures to the free movement of persons in the Schengen area. Initially conceived and developed in the margins of the EU project, the 1990 Convention implementing the 1985 Schengen Agreement promoted a close cooperation between police authorities of different countries and set up one of the most relevant tools for the exchange of law enforcement information: the Schengen Information System (SIS).[22] Article 39(1) of the 1990 Convention referred to the need of police authorities to "assist each other for the purposes of preventing and detecting criminal offences, in so far as national law does not stipulate that the request has to be made and channelled via the judicial authorities". The operation and use of SIS, as well as the rules applicable for data protection and data security, were laid down in a specific Title of the 1990 Convention.

In 1993, the Treaty of Maastricht proclaimed that "combating" serious forms of international crime was one of the matters of common interest of the EU.

Based on Art. k.3 TEU, the Council recommended to the Member States the adoption of the Convention on the establishment of a European Police Office (Europol Convention).[23] The Convention was drawn up with the common objective "of improving police cooperation in the field of terrorist, unlawful drug trafficking and other serious forms of international crime through a constant, confidential and intensive exchange of information between Europol and Member States's national units" and considering that, in the field of police cooperation, "particular attention must be paid to the protection of the rights of individuals, and in particular to the protection of their personal data".[24]

[21] See Part V "New Developments".

[22] See Genson (2002), p. 125.

[23] Council Act of 26 July 1995 (95/C 316/01), OJ C 316, 27.11.1995, p. 1.

[24] Convention based on Art. K.3 TEU, on the establishment of a European Police Office (Europol Convention), Annexed to the Council Act of 26 July 1995 mentioned in the previous note, p. 3.

As in the area of judicial cooperation, police cooperation was reinforced notably after the entry into force of the Treaty of Amsterdam and the creation of an Area of Freedom, Security and Justice. Jointy with the Protocol integrating the Schengen acquis in the EU, this Treaty highlighted the importance of ensuring the security of the EU citizens by enhancing a close cooperation between the law enforcement authorities of the Member States. In words of the Vienna Action Plan, "freedom loses much of its meaning if it cannot be enjoyed in a secure environment and with full backing of a system of justice in which all Union citizens and residents can have confidence".[25] The Vienna Action Plan also included, among other measures, "examine Europol access to SIS",[26] and "study the possibility of setting up a system of exchanging fingerprints electronically between Member States".[27]

The Tampere Council Conclusions called on the Council "to provide Europol with the necessary support and resources" to ensure that, in the near future, its role would be strengthened "by means of receiving operational data from Member States and authorising it to ask Member States to initiate, conduct or coordinate investigations, or to create joint investigative teams in certain areas of crime".[28]

In the particular are of the EU actions against money laundering, the Tampere conclusions promoted the operational exchange of information between the units specialised in the identification and communication of suspicious transactions:

> With due regard to data protection, the transparency of financial transactions and ownership of corporate entities should be improved and the exchange of information between the existing financial intelligence units (FIU) regarding suspicious transactions expedited. Regardless of secrecy provisions applicable to banking and other commercial activity, judicial authorities as well as FIUs must be entitled, subject to judicial control, to receive information when such information is necessary to investigate money laundering.

The Hague Programme[29] recognised officially that the exchange of information among law enforcement authorities should be governed by the principle of availability. The European Council considered that the strengthening of the area of Freedom, Security and Justice required "an innovative approach to the cross-border exchange of law-enforcement information" and declared that, with effect from 1 January 2008, the exchange of such information should be governed by the principle of availability

> Which means that, throughout the Union, a law enforcement officer in one Member State who needs information in order to perform his duties can obtain this from another Member State and that the law enforcement agency in the other Member State which holds this

[25] Doc. cit., p. 2.

[26] Vienna Action Plan, cit., p. 11.

[27] Cit., p. 14.

[28] Cit., parr. 45.

[29] The Hague Programme: strengthening freedom, security and justice in the European Union, Council document 16054/04 JAI 559. Brussels, 13 December 2004.

> information will make it available for the stated purpose, taking into account the requirement of ongoing investigations in that State.[30]

The Hague Programme invited the Commission to present, by the end of 2005, legislative proposals for the practical application of the principle of availability, in which certain key conditions related to the exchange of information, data integrity, data protection and data security should be observed.[31]

This Programme also stated that:

> The methods of exchange of information should make full use of new technology and must be adapted to each type of information, where appropriate, through reciprocal access to or interoperability of national databases, or direct (on-line) access, including for Europol, to existing central EU databases such as the SIS.

In the specific area of management of migration flows, including the fight against illegal immigration, mentioned the need to "maximise the effectiveness and interoperability of EU information systems in tackling illegal immigration and improving borders controls as well as the management of these systems", including the Schengen Information System (SIS), Visa Information System (VIS) and EURODAC, "taking into account the need to strike the right balance between law enforcement purposes and safeguarding the fundamental rights of individuals".[32]

The Hague programme also made a short reference to "the proposal for a common EU approach on the use of passengers data for border and aviation security and other law enforcement purposes",[33] and acknowledged the particularities of the exchange of information between the security and secret services of the EU Member States, as follows:

> The exchange of information between security services should be maintained and improved, taking into account the overall principle of availability and giving particular consideration to the special circumstances that apply to the working methods of security services, e.g. the need to ensure the methods of collecting information, the sources of information, and the continued confidentiality of the data after the exchange.[34]

The internal bodies of the Council had long discussions on the meaning and scope of the principle of availability,[35] and identified different modalities of access to information.

The first modality was the direct access by the requesting law enforcement authority to the databases located in another Member State. This modality, advocated by the Commission, faced some reluctances from the Member States due to several factors: language problems, information technology problems, financial

---

[30] The Hague Programme, p. 18.

[31] The Hague Programme, p. 18.

[32] The Hague Programme, p. 7.

[33] In line with Declaration on Combating terrorism adopted on 25 March 2004, doc. 7906/04, point 6. The Hague Programme, cit., p. 8.

[34] The Hague Programme, p. 8.

[35] Also the academia discussed the principle of availability and its interaction with other key principles as interoperability, equivalence and mutual recognition. See in particular Bigo et al. (2007). See also Jones (2007).

costs, and the lack of sufficient guarantees to ensure the protection of principles and rights of data protection.

A second modality was the indirect access to information upon request and under the same conditions as the law enforcement authorities of the requested Member State. The principle of "equivalent access" to available information guided the Commission Proposal for a Council Decision on the exchange of information based on the principle of availability. The Member States did not receive it with enthusiasm, mainly because another initiative had been discussed in parallel and was finally considered more feasible: the Council Framework Decision on simplifying the exchange of information and intelligence between law enforcement authorities of the Member States of the European Union (the so-called Swedish initiative).[36]

Another modality was indirect access to information from another Member State through European or national central indexes. A search on the index would reveal whether some information on the person or object concerned was available, using a hit-no hit mechanism. Following a positive match in the index, the requesting Member State should apply the legal instruments on law enforcement or judicial cooperation in criminal matters to receive relevant information and personal data. This modality inspired the searches in the DNA and dactyloscopic databases of the Treaty of Prum. During the implementation of The Hague Programme, the provisions of this Treaty were integrated into the EU framework.

The Council and Commission Action Plan implementing the Hague Programme on strengthening freedom, security and justice in the European Union stated that this legislative proposal should be accompanied by a proposal about principles and fundamental rights in the field of police and judicial cooperation in criminal matters.[37]

Following the entry into force of the Treaty of Lisbon, Title V of the TFEU includes a particular chapter on Police cooperation in criminal matters (Arts. 87–79).

Although the principle of availability is not expressly recognised in these legal provisions, Art. 87(2)(a) states that, for the purposes of prevention, detection and investigation of criminal offences, the European Parliament and the Council may establish measures concerning "the collection, storage, processing, analysis and exchange of relevant information". The Court of Justice of the EU will have to interpret soon this legal provision, as result of the action for annulment presented by the Commission against *Directive 2011/82/EU of 25 October 2011 facilitating the cross-border exchange of information on road safety related traffic offences*[38] (in this section, the Directive).

The Commission considers that Art. 87(2) TFEU is not the appropriate legal basis, as the Directive aims at introducing a mechanism for the exchange of

---

[36] See Bose (2007).

[37] Document (2005/C 198/01), DO C 198, 12.8.2005, p. 10.

[38] OJ L 288, 5.11.2011, p. 1.

information between Member States that covers road trafficking offences of an administrative or criminal nature, while Art. 87 only refers to police cooperation against criminal offences. In Commission's view, the appropriate legal basis would be Art. 91(1) TFEU because the purpose of the Directive is to improve road safety, which is one of the common transport policy areas provided for in this legal provision.

Although the judgement of the Court in this case is still pending,[39] the Opinion of the Advocate General has made some relevant statements not only on the appropriate legal basis, but also in relation to the area of Freedom, Security and Justice of the EU, the important of the exchange of information in this area, and the functional interpretation of the "police authorities" as they are referred to in Art. 87 (1) TFEU.[40]

The Advocate General mentions that "the development of the free movement of persons in the territory of the Union is, quite frequently, a synonymous of impunity in the area of road traffic offences". This is particularly relevant when such offences are committed by a vehicle immatriculate in a Member State other than those where the offence has been committed, especially when the offence has been registered automatically with the assistance of cameras, without any direct contact between the driver and the law enforcement authority.

Hence, the exchange of information among law enforcement authorities in this particular field is envisaged as a counter measure to fight against the impunity of road trafficking offences committed in a different country, and specially in relation with those offences detected through surveillance cameras.

On the other hand, the Court decision mentions that Articles 4 and 5 of the Directive "have instaured a typical mechanism of police cooperation", as it is *a system for the exchange of police information between competent authorities in order to ensure results in the investigations related to road trafficking offences and allow the prosecution of this criminal offences by the identification of the infractors.*

On the scope and meaning of "police cooperation", the General Advocate mentions that Article 87(1) is broad enough to involve "all the Member States' competent authorities" including, among others, "police, customs and other specialised law enforcement services in relation to the prevention, detection and investigation of criminal offences". The General Advocate states that police cooperation can also take place in the framework of Article 87 TFEU between competent authorities with a different role that the application of criminal law among the Member States when they carried out police cooperation in a broader sense, including administrative police or judicial police. The General Advocate concludes that police cooperation should be interpreted in a functional matter, thus covering police cooperation among all the authorities of the Member States responsible for the prevention, investigation and prosecution of offences.

[39] Action brought on 30 January 2012. European Commission v European Parliament and Council of the European Union, Case C-43/12.

[40] Conclusions of the Advocate General Mr Yves Bot of 10 September 2013.

On the other hand, the Stockholm Programme has mentioned that the principle of availability should continue giving "important impetus" to the work of the European Union in the creation of an extensive toolbox for collecting, processing and sharing information between national authorities and other European players in the area of Freedom, Security and Justice.[41] It also made some references to some other relevant concepts related to the security of the European Union, namely the Information Management Strategy for the EU internal security, the European Information Exchange Model, the Union Passenger Names Record (PNR) system.

In the context of the ongoing discussions in view of the next multiannual programme for the area of Freedom, Security and Justice of the EU, the Lithuanian Presidency of the EU suggested focusing on the quality of the implementation of the Union acquis and the consolidation of the achievements, with particular attention to the expertise gained by the EU agencies operating in this area, the external dimension of the JHA policies, the reinforcement of internal security against organised crime, and the benefits of the most recent scientific and technological developments, "at the same time respecting privacy and fundamental rights".[42]

2.3 Common Rules for Processing and Protecting Information and Personal Data

2.3.1 Directive 95/46/EC as the Centrepiece... But Not in Criminal Matters

In the EU, the processing and protection of personal data is mainly governed by Directive 95/46/EC of 24 October 1995 on the protection of individuals with regard to the processing of personal data and on the free movement of such data (DP Directive).[43] The DP Directive, which is considered "the centrepiece of existing EU legislation on personal data protection", was adopted in the framework of the then so-called "first pillar" and become applicable in the areas related to Community Law.

Therefore, police and judicial cooperation in criminal matters were excluded from the scope of Directive 95/46/EC. That was clearly indicated in its Art. 3(2), first indent, according to which the DP Directive will not be applicable to the processing of personal data:

> In the course of an activity which falls outside the scope of Community law, such as those provided for by Titles V and VI of the Treaty of European Union and in any case to

---

[41] On this matter vid. Section 4.2.2 of the Stockholm Programme, doc. cit., p. 18.

[42] Council doc. 13340/13. Brussels, 5 September 2013.

[43] OJ L 281, 23.11.1995, p. 51.

processing operations concerning public security, defence, State security (...), and the activities of the State in areas of criminal law.

As result, the information systems and databases created in the EU for the purposes of preventing and combating crime were all accompanied by their own set of rules for the processing and protection of personal data. The 1990 Convention implementing the 1985 Schengen Agreement devoted a title to the SIS,[44] including legal provisions on "Operation and use of the Schengen Information System" (Arts. 93–101) and on "Protection of personal data and security of data in the Schengen Information System" (Arts. 102–118). More than half of the legal provisions of the Europol Convention of 1995 were devoted to the Europol Information System, its Analysis Work Files and the rules for the processing and protection of personal data.[45]

Every set of rules mentioned the Council of Europe Convention for the protection of individuals with regard to automatic processing of personal data (Convention 108), as well as the Recommendation No. R(87)16 of the Committee of Ministers to Member States Regulating the use of personal data in the police sector. As in many other fields of law, the Council of Europe was the pioneer institution setting up rules to ensure proper balance between the rights of the individuals and the use of the technologies by both public and private sectors. Being aware of the complexity of ensuring such balance in the area of police investigations, the abovementioned Recommendation was issued in this specific sector.[46]

The Vienna Action Plan of 1998 mentioned that "another fundamental freedom deserving special attention in today's fast-developing information society is that of respect for privacy and in particular the protection of personal data". Moreover,

> When, in support of the development of police and judicial cooperation in criminal matters, personal data files are set up and information exchanged, it is indeed essential to strike the right balance between public security and the protection of individual's privacy.[47]

From this perspective, the Vienna Action Plan included a specific action in order to study "the possibilities for harmonised rules on data protection".[48]

The drafting of common rules for the processing and protection of personal data in criminal matters is being a long-running process. In 1998, Italy presented a

[44] Title IV, Arts. 92 to 119.

[45] See inter alia Arts. 7–9 ("Information system"), Arts. 10–12 ("Work files for the purposes of analysis), Arts. 13–25 ("Common provisions on information processing") and Art. 38 ("Liability for unauthorized or incorrect data processing").

[46] On the Convention 108, its Protocol, the Recommendation No. R(87) 15, the Case-Law of the European Court of Human Rights on this matter, and the ongoing work in the Council of Europe with a view to update Convention 108, see SUTTON G(2012), p. 3.

[47] Vienna Action Plan, cit., p. 3.

[48] Cit., p. 13.

discussion paper on the protection of personal data in the third pillar[49] in 1998, which was followed by a draft Resolution on this matter in 2001. This Resolution was not finally submitted to the Council, but served as basis for the proposal by the Greek Presidency of the EU (during the fist semester of 2003) of a set of common standards for the processing and protection of personal data in the third pillar of the EU.[50]

The Hague Programme of 2004 confirmed the need to adopt common standards fo the processing and protection of personal data in the areas of police and judicial cooperation and invited the Commission to submit a proposal on this matter, which should come hand-in-hand with a proposal for exchange of information in accordance with the principle of availability. As result, in October 2005, the Commission presented its *Proposal for a Council Framework Decision on the protection of personal data processed in the framework of police and judicial cooperation in criminal matters* (in this section, the *Proposal)* as the legal instrument complementary to those implementing in practice the principle of availability. The proposal expressly stated that exchange of cross-border information for law enforcement purposes was estimated to increase and needed to be complemented by consistent rules for the processing and protection of personal data.[51]

The abovementioned Council Framework Decision was adopted on 27 November 2008[52] (DP Framework Decision). It includes a set obligations for the actors who process personal data of individuals (data processing), and a set of rights of those individuals (data protection). It also includes some rules related to the confidentiality and security of the information (data security), as well as judicial remedies, rules on liability, supervisory authorities, and the setting up of a specific working party on this matter. Common rules for the transmission of personal data to third countries have been foreseen too.

However, its scope is rather limited. The DP Framework Decision is not directly applicable to most of the EU information systems and databases (SIS, CIS, among others), neither the agencies (as Eurojust and Europol, having their own tailor-made set of rules on data protection (Recital 39). The specific provisions for the processing and protection of personal data applicable to some other EU information systems and databases take precedence over the provisions of the DP Framework Decision. Finally, the DP Framework Decision is not applicable for the processing and protection of personal data at national level [Recital (7)].

The Treaty of Lisbon introduced some relevant provisions into the EU Treaties that facilitated a comprehensive approach for the processing and protection of personal data in the European Union.

---

[49] Council doc. 8321/98 JHA 15.

[50] JHA Council meeting on 5-6 June 2003. Council doc. 9845/03 (Presse 150), p. 32.

[51] Proposal for a COUNCIL FRAMEWORK DECISION on the protection of personal data processed in the framework of police and judicial co-operation in criminal matters. COM(2005) 475 final. Brussels, 4.10.2005, p. 8.

[52] OJ L 350, 30.12.2008, p. 60.

2.3.2 Article 16(2) TFEU: A Strong Legal Basis for Processing and Protecting Personal Data in the EU

Art. 16(2) of the Treaty of Functioning of the EU (TFEU) provides a stronger basis for a common framework of data protection applicable to the EU institutions and bodies and, in certain circumstances, to the Member States. This stronger basis has been possible only with the abolition of the so-called three-pillar structure of the European Union by the Treaty of Lisbon.[53] This legal provision is as follows:

> 2. The European Parliament and the Council, acting in accordance with the ordinary legislative procedure, shall lay down the rules relating to the protection of individuals with regards to the processing of personal data by Union institutions, bodies, offices and agencies, and by the Member States when carrying out activities which fall within the scope of Union law, and the rules relating to the free movement of such data. Compliance with these rules shall be subject to the control of independent authorities.
>
> The rules adopted on the basis of this Article shall be without prejudice to the specific rules laid down in Article 39 of the Treaty of the European Union.

There are also two other relevant provisions to take into consideration, both also inserted in the EU Treaties following the entry into force of the Treaty of Lisbon.

On the one hand, Art. 39 TEU, which is applicable in the field of Common Foreign and Security Policy:

> In accordance with Article 16 of the Treaty of the Functioning of the European Union, and by way of derogation from paragraph 2 thereof, the Council shall adopt a decision laying down the rules relating to the protection of individuals with regards to the processing of personal data by the Member States when carrying out activities which fall within the scope of this Chapter, and the rules relating to the free movement of such data. Compliance with these rules shall be subject to the control of independent authorities.

On the other hand, the Declaration N. 21 Annexed to the final Act of the Intergovernmental Conference which adopted the Treaty of Lisbon. This Declaration, on the protection of personal data in the areas of judicial cooperation in criminal matters and police cooperation, reads as follows:

> The Conference acknowledges that specific rules on the protection of personal data and the free movement of such data in the fields of judicial cooperation in criminal matters and police cooperation based on Article 16 of the Treaty on the Functioning of the European Union may prove necessary because of the specific nature of these fields.

The combination of these three legal provisions has resulted in a legislative package proposed by the Commission in January 2012. The package proposes a Regulation of general application,[54] and a Directive on the protection of individuals with regard to the processing of personal data by competent authorities for the

---

[53] See Hijmans (2010), p. 219; De Hert and Riehle (2010), p. 159. See also the foreword written by Hustinsx (2010), p. 1.

[54] Proposal for a regulation on the protection of individuals with regard to the processing of personal data and on the free movement of such data (General data protection Regulation). COM (2012) 11 final. 2012/0011 (COD). Brussels, 25.1.2012.

purposes of prevention, investigation, detection or prosecution of criminal offences or the execution of criminal penalties, and the free movement of such data[55] (DP draft Directive).

The DP draft Directive is intended to cover the exchange of information among the police authorities and judicial competent authorities at national level. Conversely, this Directive will not apply to the processing of personal data "(a) in the course of an activity which falls outside the scope of Union law, in particular concerning national security", neither to the processing of personal data "(b) by the Union institutions, bodies, offices and agencies" [Art. 2(3) DP draft Directive].

This legislative package is under discussion at the internal bodies of the Council and of the European Parliament at the time of writing.

2.3.3 *Article 16(1) TFEU: The Protection of Personal Data as a Fundamental Right of Citizens, Including Suspects and Accused Persons*

Art. 16(1) TFEU states:

> Everyone has the right to the protection of personal data concerning them.

With a very similar wording, Art. 8 of the Charter of Fundamental Rights of the EU[56] (EU Charter) proclaims the protection of personal data as one of the fundamental rights of the individual. It is distinguished from respect for private life and family life, which are recognised in Art. 7 thereof. Both provisions are as follows:

> Article 7. Respect for private life and family life
>
> Everyone has the right to respect for his or her private and family life, home and communications.
>
> Article 8. Protection of personal data
>
> 1. Everyone has the right to the protection of personal data concerning him or her.
> 2. Such data must be processed fairly for specific purposes and on the basis of the consent of the person concerned or some legitimate basis laid down by law. Everyone has the right of access to data which has been collected concerning him or her, and the right to have it rectified.
> 3. Compliance with these rules shall be subject to control by an independent authority.

According to its Article 51, the EU Charter applies to the institutions, bodies, offices and agencies of the European Union, and therefore all their acts, legislative or

[55] COM(2012) 10 final. Brussels, 25.1.2012. See REDING V (2010), p. 25. On the DP draft Directive see Chap. 17 of this book.

[56] The EU Charter was signed and solemnly proclaimed by the Presidents of the European Parliament, the Commission and the Council at the European Council on 7 December 2000, in Nice. It reflects the general principles enshrined in the European Convention for the Protection of Human Rights and Fundamental Freedoms of 1950, and those derived from the case law of both the European Court of Human Rights and the Court of Justice of the European Union. With the entry into force of the Treaty of Lisbon on 1st of December 2009, the EU Charter was given binding effect equal to the Treaties, as is clearly stated in Article 6(1) of Treaty of the European Union (TEU).

non-legislative, must be in full conformity with it. The EU Charter only applies to the Member States when they implement EU law. As recognised by Article 52(1), any limitation on the exercise of the rights and freedoms recognised by the Charter, including the protection of personal data, must be provided by law and respect both the essence of those rights and freedoms and the principle of proportionality.

Also the Stockholm Programme underlined the importance of the fundamental rights on privacy and data protection. Among the political priorities established in this multiannual programme, the European Council has emphasized the promotion of the European citizenship and the fundamental rights, including the protection of personal data[57]:

> European citizenship must become a tangible reality. The area of freedom, security and justice must, above all, be a single area in which fundamental rights and freedoms are protected. The enlargement of the Schengen area must continue. Respect for the human person and human dignity and for the other firths set out in the Charter of Fundamental Rights of the European Union and the European Convention for the protection of Human Rights and fundamental freedoms are core values. For example, the exercise of these rights and freedoms, in particular citizen's privacy, must be preserved beyond national borders, especially by protecting personal data (. . .).

The importance of the fundamental right of data protection is reiterated in Sect. 2.5, on "Protecting citizen's rights in the information society", as follows:

> When it comes to assessing the individual's privacy in the area of freedom, security and justice, the right to freedom is overarching. The right to privacy and the right to the protection of personal data are set out in the Charter of Fundamental Rights. The Union must therefore respond to the challenge posed by the increasing exchange of personal data and the need to ensure the protection of privacy. The Union must secure a comprehensive strategy to protect data within the Union and in its relations with other countries. In that context, it should promote the application of the principles set out in relevant Union instruments on data protection and the 1981 Council of Europe Convention for the Protection of Individuals with regards to Automatic Processing of Personal Data as well as promoting accession to that Convention. It must also foresee and regulate the circumstances in which interference by public authorities with the exercise of these rights is justified and also apply data protection principles in the private sphere.

Among other tangible consequences of the recognition of data protection as a fundamental right, the EU institutions must take account of this fundamental right when proposing new policy and legislative initiatives. In this respect the Commission,[58] the Parliament[59] and the Council[60] expressed their commitment to establish the necessary internal mechanisms guaranteeing that new legislative

---

[57] See Hijmans (2010), p. 222

[58] Commission Communication on the Strategy for the effective implementation of the Charter of Fundamental Rights by the European Union, COM(2010) 573 final. Brussels 20.10.2010. See in particular the "Check List" included in the Strategy thereto.

[59] European Parliament Resolution of 15 December 2010 on the situation of Fundamental Rights in the European Union (2009).

[60] See Council Conclusions on the role of the Council of the European Union in ensuring the effective implementation of the Charter of Fundamental Rights of the European Union, adopted at JHA Council Meeting of 24 and 25 February 2011, in Brussels.

proposals and amendments to the existing legal instruments will be submitted with full respect for fundamental rights, including the fundamental right of protection of personal data. As far as the Commission is concerned, new proposals must be accompanied by an assessment on privacy and data protection, conducted either as a separate assessment or as part of the general fundamental rights' impact assessment carried out by the Commission.[61] The EU institutions also have been invited to consult, where appropriate, with the European Union Agency for Fundamental Rights on the development of policies and legislation with implications for fundamental rights.[62]

Among other examples, the Impact Assessment of the Proposal for a Directive of the European Parliament and of the Council on the use of Passenger Name Record (PNR) data for the prevention, detection, investigation and prosecution of terrorist offences and serious crime[63] included a particular section on data protection. On 15 June 2011, following a request by the European Parliament, the European Union Agency for Fundamental Rights presented its Opinion on the fundamental rights compliance of a Proposal for a Directive on the use of PNR data.[64]

A second relevant consequence is the ability of judicial authorities to refer some questions related to the interpretation of Art. 8 of the Charter to the Court of Justice of the EU, for a preliminary ruling. We can find some cases admitted by the Court already (still pending at the time of writing) such as the Case C-293/12,[65] Case C-372/12,[66] Case C-446/12,[67] Case C-594/12,[68] the Case 46/13,[69] and the Case C-101/13,[70] as well as the Judgment of the Court of 17 October 2013 on the Case C-291/12, Michael Schwarz v. Stadt Bochum.[71]

See also Council Conclusions on the Council's actions and initiatives for the implementation of the Charter of Fundamental rights of the European Union, adopted at the General Affairs Council Meeting of 23 May 2001, in Brussels.

[61] See Commission's Impact Assessment Guidelines, document SEC(2009)92, 15.1.2009. On this matter, in general terms, see Clarke (2011), p. 111, and more recently Wright and De Hert (2012).

[62] Section 2 ("Promoting citizen's rights: a Europe of rights"), Sect. 2.1 ("A Europe built on Fundamental Rights") of the Stockholm Programme.

[63] Document COM(2011) 32 final. Brussels, 2.2.2011. On the impact assessment, see document SEC(2011) 132 final, p. 19.

[64] In October 2008, this Agency issued a previous opinion on the matter. Both are available at www.fra.europa.eu/fraWebsite/research/opinions/op-passenger-name-record_en.htm

[65] OJ C 258, 25.8.2012, p. 11.

[66] OJ C 303, 6.10.2012, p. 18.

[67] OJ C 26, 2.1.2013, p. 16. See also Cases C-447/12, C-448/12 and C-449/12 (all published in the same OJ C 26, 2.1.2013).

[68] OJ C 79, 16.3.2013, p. 7.

[69] OJ C 147, 25.5.2013, p. 3.

[70] OJ C 156, 1..2013, p. 19.

[71] *See* an extract of the most relevant paragraphs of this Judgement in Sect. 2.5 of this book.

2.4 The EU Policy on Information Exchange and Management

2.4.1 The EU Information Management Strategy

The EU Information Management (IM) Strategy is a policy concept developed gradually from the principle of availability, to overcome the difficulties created by the proliferation of information systems, channels, tools and legal instruments created at EU level and by the Member States for the purposes of preventing and fight against crime. It is also intended to improve functionality for and coordination between the actors involved in the gathering, analysis and exchange of information.

This Strategy was first recommended in the Report of the Informal High Level Advisory Group on the Future of European Home Affairs Policy in June 2008, in preparation for the Stockholm Programme, to remedy what was described as an "uncoordinated and incoherent palette of information systems and instruments" which have "incurred costs and delays detrimental to operational work". The need for this policy concept was confirmed by the Council's conclusions on the principle of convergence and the structuring of internal security,[72] and the follow-up on the outcome of the Informal JHA ministerial meeting in the field of Modern Technologies and Security.[73] The Stockholm Programme confirmed the need for coherence and consolidation in developing information management and exchange, and invited the Council to adopt and implement an EU Information Management Strategy, entailing business driven development, a strong data protection regime, interoperability of IT systems and rationalisation of tools as well as overall coordination, convergence and coherence.

The EU IM Strategy is underpinned by some key concepts of the area of Freedom, Security and Justice, including the Internal Security of the EU. The later relies on effective mechanisms for the exchange of information between national authorities and other European players, and the aim of achieving closer cooperation between them in order to increase efficiency in the fight against cross-border crime. In this context, the exchange of information is considered a precondition, or an essential tool, to realise the objectives of the Internal Security of the EU.

The EU IM Strategy is also considered complementary to the EU's priorities in the fight against serious cross-border crime. While the IM Strategy states "how" to ensure the good management of the existing databases and information systems, EU's priorities set out "what" (which types of criminality) should be tackle through proper cooperation and exchange of information among all the actors involved.

The IM Strategy was adopted by the Council of the EU at its JHA Meeting in December 2009. It provides a methodology, based on eight focus areas, to ensure that decisions about the need for managing and exchanging data are taken in a

[72] Council document 14069/08 JAI 514 CATS 78.

[73] Council document 10143/09 JAI 324 CATS 55 ASIM 54 ENFOPOL 145 CRIMORG 85.

coherent, efficient, cost-effective way, that is accountable and comprehensible to both the citizens and the professional users. As expressed in the Council Conclusions on an Information Management Strategy for EU internal security:

> Effective and secure cross border exchange of information is a precondition to achieve the goals of internal security in the European Union.
>
> This requires the right information to be available at the right time, for the right person and in the right place.

The IM Strategy is based on a multidisciplinary approach, as it embraces all EU bodies and national authorities with competences in preventing and fighting against crime:

> The authorities concerned will be essentially law enforcement authorities, authorities responsible for border management and judicial authorities dealing with criminal matters.[74]

The EU IM Strategy and related documents (mainly IMS Actions)[75] are focused on the tasks to be performed by the law enforcement authorities of the Member States (and Europol), although the national judicial authorities and Eurojust are also mentioned.

The following eight focus areas determine the application of the IM Strategy[76]:

1. Needs, requirements and added value should be assessed as a precondition for development.

   Any initiative for the setting up of a new information exchange system should be based on an in-depth analysis of the existing solutions at EU level and in the Member States, covering the definition of needs, requirements and added value of such initiative, as well as a assessment of its legal, technical and financial impact. This assessment exercise should involve end-users, who will mainly be the law enforcement and judicial authorities of the Member States.
2. Development follows agreed workflows and criminal intelligence models.

   Business processes must allow the quick, efficient, user friendly and cost-effective exchange of information and criminal intelligence. Moreover, the work flows must be described in detail, well-known and accessible.
3. Development should serve both data protection requirements and business operational needs.

   The security of the information systems and the rights of the EU citizens, specially the right to data protection, should be ensured in parallel to the practical implementation of the principle of availability, so that the correct information is made available to the competent authorities of the Member States.
4. Interoperability and coordination must be ensured both within business processes and technical solutions.

---

[74] Council Conclusions on the EU IM Strategy, p. 3.

[75] An Action list has been set up for the implementation of the EU IM Strategy.

[76] These eight focus areas are developed in the "Annex to the Annex" of the Draft Council Conclusions on an Information Management Strategy for the EU (Council document 16637/09 JAI 873 CATS 131 ASIM 137 JUSTCIV 249 JURINFO 145, p. 9 et f.).

In line with the European interoperability strategy, solutions should be interoperable from a legal, semantic, business and technical perspective. Technically, the IT solutions adopted should comply with commonly agreed standards and principles.

5. Re-utilization is the rule: do not re-invent the wheel.

   The sharing and re-utilization of solutions that have proved to be successful and sustainable should be the guiding principle for any new improvement or development. With this approach, the IM Strategy can be seen as "a critical review of instruments currently in use for information exchange that should assess their efficiency and effectiveness in order to provide for the rationalization of existing arrangements before starting to develop new tools". As we will see in the next sections, an assessment of the existing instruments for information exchange was undertaken by the Commission with its Overview on information management in the area of Freedom, Security and Justice, the Information Mapping Project and, more thoroughly, the European Information Exchange Model (EIXM).
6. Member States must be involved from the very start of the process.

   The authorities of the Member States who are responsible for the implementation of the workflows at national level (including law enforcement authorities as key users) should be involved from the beginning of the development process.
7. There is a clear responsibility for each part of the process, ensuring competence, quality and efficiency.

   The roles and responsibilities of each actor involved must be clear and well defined. The necessary systems should be in place to ensure that all parties concerned are involved at the right level and at the right stage of the process, but also to guarantee that there is overall coordination and coherence.
8. Multidisciplinary coordination must be ensured.

   All the relevant authorities and key users need to interact and be involved in the development and further use of the information systems. Regardless the different national structures that exist in the Member States, the competent authorities should ensure availability and exchange of information. IT support and standardisation must be as horizontal as possible and based on common principles.

2.4.2 Overview of Information Management in the Area of Freedom, Security and Justice

In July 2010, the Commission presented its "Overview of information management in the area of freedom, security and justice"[77] (hereinafter, Overview). With this Overview, the Commission provided a full picture of the legal instruments,

[77] COM(2010) 385 final. Brussels, 20.7.2010. See Lodge (2010), p. 2.

information systems and channels adopted at EU level for the collection, processing and exchange of information for law enforcement and migration management purposes.

The Overview referred to other initiatives that, as mentioned by the European Council in the Stockholm Programme, should be developed (or studied in view of their feasibility) by the Commission: an EU PNR system for the prevention, detection and prosecution of terrorism and serious crime; an Entry/Exit System, and a Registered Travellers Programme, the possible introduction of an EU terrorist financing tracking system equivalent to the US TFTP, the potential establishment of an Electronic System of Travel Authorisation, and the possible setting up of a European Police Records Index System (EPRIS).

The EDPS reasoned that this overview should be only considered a first step in the evaluation process of the existing EU systems and databases, and that it should be followed by more concrete measures on how to align them in order to ensure a "comprehensive, integrated and well-structured EU policy on information exchange and management".[78]

2.4.3 *The Information Mapping Project of the Commission*

In 2010 and during the first quarter of 2011, the Commission channelled the assessment of the existing legal instruments, information systems, channels and tools through an Information Mapping Project[79] consisting of three phases: an information mapping exercise as such an assessment of the relevant element identified and the elaboration of recommendations on how to consolidate the cross-border exchange of information and criminal intelligence. The scope of the project covered the EU Member States and Norway, Iceland, Switzerland and Liechtenstein [all within the European Economic Area (EEA)].

An Information Mapping Project Team, including representatives of the Trio Presidency, interested Member States, Europol, Eurojust, the European Data Protection Supervisor and the European Network of Information Security Agency, met regularly and reported to the Ad Hoc Working Group on Information Exchange. The main sources of information were the answers to the questionnaires distributed to Member States and other stakeholders, the study drawn up by a private consultancy firm who were granted a contract by the Commission,[80] and the regular meetings of the members of the Project.

The final report of the Information Mapping Project Team provided a full picture of the processes for the exchange of information and criminal intelligence in the

[78] Opinion of the EDPS on the cited Overview, OJ C 355, 29.12.2010, p. 16 (parr. 19).

[79] Council document 5046/10 JAI 5 CATS 4 ASIM 4.

[80] See http://ec.europa.eu/dgs/home-affairs/e-library/documents/categories/studies/index_en.htm.

EU, by covering four main areas: relevant enacted legislation, communication channels, information flows, and technological solutions.[81]

The results of this mapping exercise facilitated the evaluation of the Swedish Framework Decision and the Prüm Decisions, and the elaboration of the European Information Exchange Model (EIXM).

2.4.4 *The European Information Exchange Model*

On the basis of the Information Mapping Project conducted in 2010 and 2011, the Commission published its Communication on "Strengthening law enforcement cooperation in the EU: the European Information Exchange Model (EIXM)" on 7 December 2012.[82]

The EIXM was accompanied by a Report on the implementation of the Council Decision 2008/615/JHA of 23 June 2008 on the stepping up of cross-border cooperation, particularly in combating terrorism and cross-border crime (the "Prüm Decision").[83] The Commission had reported on the evaluation of the Swedish Council Decision in 2011.[84] The EIXM makes constant references to both legal instruments, but it has a broader scope.

In words of the Commission, the Communication on the EIXM "takes stock of how the resulting cross-border information exchange in the EU works today, and makes recommendations for how to improve it".[85] Through these recommendations, the Commission provides a "model" for guiding the EU and the Member States in the implementation of the existing legal instruments and in streamlining of the communication channels used. It also stressed the Commission's commitment to supporting training on information exchange and funding for Member States.

The EIXM is based on the following elements:

1) In the EU, cross-border exchange of information among the EU bodies and national competent authorities "generally works well".[86]

---

[81] The interim results and the final report of the Information Mapping Project are frequently referred to in Part IV, Chap. 7.

[82] COM (2012) 735 final. Brussels, 7.12.2012. See Council Conclusions following the Commission Communication on the European Information Exchange Model (EIXM). Justice and Home Affairs Council meeting. Luxembourg, 6 and 7 June 2013. See also Opinion of the European Data Protection Supervisor on the Communication from the Commission to the European Parliament and the Council entitled "Strengthening law enforcement cooperation in the EU: the European Information Exchange Model (EIXM)".

[83] On the Prüm Decision, see Part IV, Chap. 7, Sect. 7.2, of this publication.

[84] SEC(2011) 593. On the Swedish Council Decision, see Part III, Chap. 8, Sect. 8.2 of this publication.

[85] COM(2012) 735 final, p. 1.

[86] COM(2012) 735 final, p. 2.

The exchange of information has become a crucial tool for ensuring the Internal security of the EU through efficient collaboration and cooperation between the competent authorities of the Member States.

2) No new databases or information systems are necessary in the near future. Although there are some new systems envisaged by the EU institutions or certain Member States, an in-deep assessment in accordance with the focus areas proposed in the EU IM Strategy should be carried out before taking any decision on the setting up new systems.
3) The existing EU instruments governing EU databases and information systems (and specially the "Prüm Decision") need to be implemented better by the Member States.
4) Existing communication channels should be also streamlined particularly in SIRENE Bureaux, Europol National Units (ENUs), and Interpol National Central Bureaux.

The EDPS has expressed some concerns as regards the use of a single channel default channel, for three main reasons. Firstly, from the point of view of the purpose limitation principle, there is a diversity of instruments, channels and tools and each one has been designed for different purposes: "the use of a channel designed for a specific purpose should not lead to the possible use or collection of the data transmitted on this channel for other purposes. This poses the risk of what is often described as "function creep", namely, a gradual widening of the use of a system or database beyond the purpose for which it was originally intended". Secondly, the use of a particular channel has direct implications in terms of data protection and security of the authority (or the agency) managing this channel. And finally, from a technical point of view, mechanisms that are designed for information exchange for a specific purpose are not necessarily appropriate to other purposes. As example:

> The communication tool SIENA developed by Europol has been tailored for specific exchange of information between the competent authorities of Member States and third parties for police cooperation. Thus specific functionalities of SIENA have been developed and implemented based on the needs identified at the moment of the creation of such tool. These functionalities require amongst others the users to enter certain types and amount of information. The EDPS points out that SIENA's functionalities are not necessarily appropriate for the exchange of information in a different context and for different purposes.[87]

5) There is an interaction between the different instruments, channels and tools. As mentioned in this Communication:

> A criminal investigation can involve parallel or sequential use of more than one instrument. In a cross-border case of serious or organised crime, a person or object could be checked against both the Europol Information System and SIS, and where there are "hits" follow-up requests could be made via Europol or SIRENE channels, respectively. A biometric trace could be the subject of a Prüm exchange followed by a post-hit Swedish Initiative request using the SIENA tool.[88]

---

[87] Opinion of the EDPS on the EIXM, parr (28) and (29).

[88] COM(2012) 735 final, p. 6.

6) The existing role of Europol as key player for the exchange of information at police level is enhanced. As reiterated in the Proposal for a new Regulation on Europol, it is stated in EIXM that:

> Europol should become a hub for information exchange between the law enforcement authorities of the Member States not excluding the possibility to use other reliable channels of law enforcement information exchange among the Member States.[89]

7) The judicial authorities of the Member States are also frequently involved in information exchange for the purposes of a criminal investigation or further steps of a criminal proceeding. In some cases, specially when the information is sensitive or has been gathered by coercive investigative measures, the exchange of information among law enforcement officers might require judicial authorisation.

   In other situations, namely when the investigation is conducted by a prosecutor or investigating judge, information is exchange through the issuing and execution of rogatory letters and other instruments of judicial cooperation in criminal matters.

   It is also important to take in mind that some EU information systems (Prüm Decision) and legal instruments (Swedish Framework Decision) foresee both police and judicial follow-up of initial requests.

   The Communication mentioned that "law enforcement experts perceive differing rules [on the legal instruments of judicial cooperation] rules as a source of delay in cross-border investigations". To overcome such delays, the added value of involving Eurojust in transnational judicial investigations and prosecutions, as well as the future role to play by the European Investigation Order should be considered.
8) Cross-border exchange of information should take place with full respect of three key elements: data quality, data security, and protection of privacy and personal data.
9) To ensure full coordination of the existing databases and systems at national level, the Commission supported the setting up of Single Points of Contact (SPOCs) at a national level.

> A Single Point of Contact (SPOC) is a "one-stop shop" for international police cooperation, operating 24/7, in which a Member State bring together its SIRENE Bureau, ENU and Interpol National Central Bureaux, and contact points for other channels.[90]

On this point, the EDPS recalls that "a database may only be accessed by duly authorised staff in the performance of their tasks and for the purposes for which the database has been created. Therefore, the composition and the

[89] Council Conclusions, p. 4.

[90] COM(2012) 735 final. Brussels, 7.12.2012, p. 1. The setting up of SPOc was one of the conclusions of the third round of mutual evaluations. This proposal was reiterated in the Council Conclusions on 7–8 June 2012, Council document 10333/12.

modalities of SPOCs should b carefully analysed and defined in order to ensure that the rules applicable to each database are complied with".[91]

10) EIXM also refers to the importance of providing training to the competent authorities involved cross-border exchange of information in the framework of the European Law Enforcement Training Scheme (LETS),[92] particularly for specialist officers as those working in SPOCs. As highlighted by the EPDS, training should also cover information security and data protection rules.[93]

    The Commission has committed itself to providing funding for the organisation of such training activities and exchange programmes under the 2014–2020 EU Internal Security Fund.

11) Finally, the Commission stresses the importance of gathering and processing high quality statistics on exchange of information and intelligence. In particular, Prum statistics (including Prum hits that helped investigations) should be improved and developed further.

The EIXM presented by the Commission has been welcomed by the Member States and the EDPS. However, both have expressed their wishes to go beyond a description of the existing systems and how to apply them in practice. The EIXM should have also proposed strategic perspectives to overcome identified gaps concerning cross-border information exchange. The EDPS suggested the Commission making an inventory of data protection problems and risks, and of possible improvements within the current legal context (including, as example, ongoing discussions on the distinction processing of data of suspects and non suspects).[94]

2.5 Relevant Case-Law of the Court of Justice of the European Union

The number of judgements of the Court of Justice of the EU related to the Area of Freedom, Security and Justice of the EU is rather limited. This is mainly because, prior to the entry into force of the Treaty of Lisbon, national courts could only submit questions for preliminary rulings to the Court of Justice if the respective Member State had agreed on it and made a formal declaration under Art. 35 of the Treaty of the European Union.

Under this limited competence, the judgments were mostly related to EAW, Schengen, the rights of the victims, and of the suspects of terrorist offences included in EU terrorist lists. Such matters were not related directly to this book and are not discussed below.

[91] Opinion of the EDPS on the EIXM, parr (31).

[92] On the LETS see the Rationale of this publication.

[93] Opinion of the EDPS on the EIXM, parr (36).

[94] See Opinion of the EDPS on the EIXM, parr (38).

However, in the following pages we have reviewed some cases considered relevant from a different perspective, because they referred to questions on data processing and protection that are relevant for criminal matters in general (as the Lindqvist Case) or because they were related to criminal proceedings at national level.

Following the entry into force of the abovementioned Treaty, the Court has full competence with respect to any new legal instrument adopted in the area of Freedom, Security and Justice. In relation to the legal instruments adopted previously, the Court will also have competence as from 1 December of 2014, which is the date of expiration of a transitional period of 5 years.

Under this transitional jurisdiction, the Court has issued some relevant decisions on matters related to exchange of information, data protection and national criminal proceedings in the EU. An extract of the most relevant Judgements are reproduced bellow, whilst other decisions on criminal matters are briefly mentioned in different sections to this book.

2.5.1 *Case C-101/01 v* **Lindqvist** *[2003] I-ECR 12971. Judgment of the Court of 6 November 2003*[95]

Directive 95/46/EC—Scope—Publication of personal data on the internet—Place of publication—Definition of transfer of personal data to third countries

In the course of the criminal proceedings against Mrs Lindqvist, the Göta Hövratt (Court of Appeal, Sweden) referred to the Court for a preliminary ruling several questions concerning *inter alia* the interpretation of some provisions of Directive 95/46/EC.

Mrs Lindqvist was charged with breach of the Swedish legislation governing the protection of personal data for publishing on her internet site personal data on a number of people working with her on a voluntary basis in a parish of the Swedish protestant church (parr. 2).

In 1998, Mrs Lindqvist set up internet pages at home on her personal computer in order to allow parishioners preparing for their confirmation to obtain information they might need. At her request, the administrator of the Swedish Church's website set up a link between those pages and that site (parr. 12). These pages contained information about Mrs Lindqvist and other 18 colleagues, sometimes including their full names, and described in a mildly humorous manner the jobs held by their colleagues and their hobbies. In many cases family circumstances and telephone numbers were mentioned. She also stated that one colleague had injured

---

[95] Judgment ECLI:EU:C:2003:596. Opinion (C-101/01) ECLI:EU:C:2002:513.

het foot and was working half-time on medical grounds (parr. 13). Mrs Lindqvist colleagues had not given their consent to the publication of the information in those pages, nor had the Datainspektionen (supervisory authority for the protection of electronically transmitted data) had been informed on her activity. She removed the pages in question as soon as she become aware they were not appreciated by some of her colleagues (parr. 14).

Mrs Lindqdvist was fined by the Eksjö tingsrätt (District Court, Sweden) and appealed against that sentence to the Götta Court of Appeal (parr. 16).

Among the questions referred for a preliminary ruling, the Götta Court of Appeal asked whether the act of mentioning, on an internet page, various persons and identifying them by name or by other means, for instance by giving their telephone number or information regarding their working conditions and hobbies, constituted the "processing" of "personal data" "wholly or partly by automatic means" within the meaning of Article 3(1) of Directive 95/46) (parr. 19).

On this question, the Court ruled that:

- According to the definition in Article 2(a), the term "personal data" used in Article 3(1) of Directive 95/46 covers any information relating to an identifier or identifiable natural person: therefore, *this term undoubtedly covers the name of a person in conjunction with his telephone coordinates or information about his working conditions or hobbies* (parr. 24);
- According to the definition in Article 2(b) of Directive 95/46, the term "processing of such data" used in Article 3(1) covers any operation or set of operations which are performed upon personal data, whether or not by automatic means. This provision also gives some examples of such operations, including disclosure by transmission, dissemination or otherwise making data available: this follows that *the operation of loading personal data on an internet page must be considered to be such processing* (parr. 25)
- Placing information on an internet page entails, under current technical and computer procedures, the operation of loading that page onto a server and the operations necessary to make that page accessible to people who are connected: *such operations are performed, at least in part, automatically* (parr. 26).

Another question submitted to the Court was whether these processing of personal data was covered by one of the exceptions in Article 3(2) of Directive 95/46/EC. Mrs Lindqvist had alleged that private individuals who make use of their freedom of expression to create internet pages in the course of a non-profit-making or leisure activities were not carrying out an economic activity and were thus not subject to Community law. Otherwise, the question of the validity of Directive 95/46/EC would arise as, in adopting it, the Community legislator would have exceed the powers conferred on it by Article 100a of the EC Treaty (at that time, Article 95 EC). She therefore considered that the approximation of laws, which concerns the establishment and functioning of the common market, cannot serve as a legal basis for Community measures regulating the right of private individuals to freedom of expression on the internet (parr. 30).

- The Court ruled that recourse to Article 100a of the Treaty does not presuppose the existence of an actual link with the free movement between the Member States in every situation or activity referred to by the measure founded on that basis. A contrary interpretation would make the limits of the Directive particularly uncertain, which would be contrary to its essential objective of approximating the laws, regulations and administrative provisions of the Member States in order to eliminate obstacles to the functioning of the internal market deriving precisely from disparities between national legislations (see Joined Cases C-465/00, C-138/01 and C-139/01 Österreichischer Rundfunk and Others [2003] ECR I-4989, parr. 41 and 41). Therefore, the Court concluded that the expression "activity which falls outside the scope of Community law" cannot be interpreted in each individual case by analysing whether the specific activity at issue directly affects the freedom of movement between the Member States (parr. 42).
- On the specific exceptions provided for in Article 3(2) of Directive 95/46/EC, the Court considered that the first indent (in other words, the activities provided for by Titles V and VI of the Treaty on European Union and processing operations concerning public security, defence, State security and activities in areas of criminal law), are, in any event, activities of the State or of State authorities and unrelated to the fields of activity of individuals (parr 43). The exception applies only to the activities which are expressly listed there or which can be classified in the same category (*ejusdem generis*) (parr. 44).
- As per the second indent, the 12th recital of the preamble cites, as examples of the processing of data carried out by a natural person in the exercise of activities which are exclusively personal or domestic, correspondence and the holding of records of addresses (parr. 46): that exception must therefore be interpreted as relating only to activities which are carried out in the course of private or family life of individuals, which is clearly not the case with the processing of personal data consisting in publication on the internet so that those data are made accessible to an indefinite number of people (parr. 47).

The fifth question submitted to the Court was related to the transfer of personal data to third countries. In particular, the Swedish Court of Appeal asked if the act in Sweden of using a computer to load personal data onto a home page stored on a server in Sweden—with the result that personal data become accessible to people in third countries—constituted a transfer of data to third countries within the meaning of Article 25 of Directive 95/46/EC (parr. 52).

The Court considered it necessary to take into account the both the technical nature of the operations carried out and the purpose and structure of Chapter IV of that Directive where Article 25 appeared.

- After considering the technical nature of the operations, the Court concluded that "personal data which appear on the computer of a person in a third country, coming from a person who has loaded them onto an internet site, were not directly transferred between those two people but through the computer infrastructure of the hosting provider where the page was stored.
- According to the Court, Chapter IV sets up a complementary regime to the general regime set up by Chapter II of that Directive concerning the lawfulness

of processing of personal data (parr. 63). Its objective, as defined in the 56th to 60th recitals, is to limit transfers of personal data to third countries which ensure an adequate level of protection. The adequacy of such protection must be assessed in the light of all the circumstances surrounding the transfer operation or the set of transfer operations: where a third country does not ensure an adequate level of protection the transfer of personal data to that country must be prohibited (parr. 64). Chapter IV of Directive 95/46/EC does not contain any provision concerning use of the internet. In particular, this chapter does not lay down any criteria fr deciding whether operations carried out by hosting providers should be deemed to occur in the place of establishment of the service or at its business address or in the place where the computer or computers constituting the service's infrastructure are located (parr. 67).

Therefore, the Court ruled that given, first, the state of development of the internet at the time the Directive 95/46/EC was drawn up and, second, the absence in Chapter IV of any criteria applicable to the use of Internet, one cannot presume that the Community legislator intended the expression "transfer [of data] to a third country" to cover the loading, by an individual in Mrs Lindqvist's position, of data onto an internet page, even if such data are thereby made accessible to persons in third countries with the technical means to access them (parr. 68).

2.5.2 *Case C-317/04 European Parliament v Council and Case C-317/04 European Parliament v Commission. Judgment of the Court (Grant Chamber) of 30 May 2006*[96]

Protection of individuals with regard to the processing of personal data—Air transport—Decision 2004/496/EC—Agreement between the European Community and the United States of America—Passenger Name Records of air passengers transferred to the United States Bureau of Customs and Border Protection—Directive 95/46/EC—Article 25—Third countries—Decision 2004/535/EC—Adequate level of protection

In the final stage of the negotiations of the *Agreement between the European Community and the United States of America on the processing and transfer of PNR data by Air Carriers to the United States Department of Homeland Security, Bureau of Customs and Border Protection (CPB)*, the European Parliament presented two actions for annulment. The first action (Case C-317/04) was for the annulment of the Council Decision 2004/496/EC of 17 May 2004 on the conclusion

[96] Judgment ECLI:EU:C:2006:346 Opinion (C-317/04) ECLI:EU:C:2005:710.

of the Agreement.[97] The second action (Case C-318/04) was for the annulment of the Commission Decision 2004/535/EC of 14 May 2004 on the adequate protection of personal data contained in the Passenger Name Record of air passengers transferred to the United States Bureau of Customs and Border Protection (the decision on adequacy).[98]

The negotiations about this Agreement had stated as result of the legislation passed by the United States in November 2001 providing that air carriers operating flights to or from the United States or across United States territory had to provide the United States competent authorities with electronic access to the data contained in their automated reservation and departure control systems (Passenger Name Records, PNR data). As results of the concerns expressed by the Commission on the possible conflict of the obligation imposed to EU air carriers with the European and national laws of the Member States on data protection, the United States postponed the entry into force of this Agreement. However, some months later United States refused to waive the right to impose penalties on airlines falling to comply with the legislation on electronic access to PNR data after 5 March 2003. As result, certain European airlines started granting United States access to PNR data.

The United States issued a document containing undertaking of the part of CBP, on the basis of which the Commission issued the Decision on adequacy pursuant to Art. 25(6) of Directive 95/46/EC. The Decision on adequacy, as well as the proposal for a Council Decision concerning the conclusion of the Agreement with the United States, were submitted by the Commission to the European Parliament.

The European Parliament contented that Commission Decision 2004/535/EC of 14 May 2004 was *ultra vires* because it was adopted on the basis of Directive 95/46/EC, which expressly excludes operations concerning public security, defence, State security (including the economic wellbeing of the State when the processing operation relates to State security matters) and the activities of the State in areas of criminal law from its scope of application in Article 3(2).

The Commission and the UK argued that the air carriers' activities fell within the scope of Community law because they involved activities of private parties (the air carriers), rather than activities of the Member States, and since the air carriers' aim in processing PNR data was simply to comply with Community law.

In the course of both proceedings, the European Data Protection Supervisor (EDPS) sought leave to intervene in supporting the position of the European Parliament. In line with EDPS observations, the Court considered that the Supervisor was responsible not only for monitoring and ensuring the application of the provisions of Regulation (EC) No 45/2001 and any other Community act relating to the protection of the fundamental rights and freedoms of natural persons with regard to the processing of personal data by Community institution or body, but also for advising Community institutions and bodies on all matters concerning the processing of personal data. That advisory task does not cover only the processing of personal data by those institutions or organs. For those purposes, the Supervisor

[97] OJ 2004, L 183, p. 83, and corrigendum at OJ 2005, L 255, p. 168.

[98] OJ 2004, L 235, p. 11.

carries out the duties provided for in Article 46 of that Regulation and exercises the powers conferred on him by Article 47 of the Regulation. As result, the Court issued two orders granting the EDPS leave to intervene in Case C-317/04 and in Case C-318/04 in support of the form of order sought by the European Parliament (see parr. 2 and 18 of the Case C-317/04 [2005] I-02457, Order of the Court (Grant Chamber) of 17 March 2005).

Given the connection between the Cases, the Court considered appropriate to join them for the purposes of the judgment (parr. 49).

In Case 318/04, the European Parliament considered that the first indent of Article 3(2) of Directive 96/45/EC, relating to the exclusion of the activities which fall outside the scope of Community law, was infringed (ultravires action) (parr. 51).

In view of the European Parliament, the processing of PNR data after transfer to the United States authorities would be carried out in the course of activities of the State mentioned in Article 3(2) first indent. As stated in parr. 43 of the judgement in Case C-101/01 Lindqvist [2003] ECR I-12971), these activities were excluded from the scope of Directive 95/46/EC (parr. 52).

The Commission's point of view, supported by United Kingdom, was that the activities of the air carriers clearly felt within the scope of Community law (parr. 53).

The Court found that, while PNR data are initially collected by airlines in the course of an activity which falls within the scope of Community law, namely the sale of an aeroplane ticket which provides entitlement to a supply of services, the data processing which is taken into account in the decision on adequacy is, however, quite different in nature (parr. 57).

According to the seventh recital in the preamble, the United States legislation in question concerns the enhancement of security and the conditions under which persons may enter and leave the country. The eight recital states that the Community is fully committed to supporting the United States in the fight against terrorism within the limits imposed by Community law. The 15th recital states that PNR will be used strictly for purposes of preventing and combating terrorism and related crimes, other serious crimes, including organised crime, that are transnational in nature, and attemps to evade warrants or escape from custody for those crimes (parr. 55).

Hence, the transfer of PNR data falls within a framework established by the public authorities that related to public security and the activities of the State in areas of criminal law (parr. 56 and 59). The Court concluded that these argument of the European Parliament was well founded and that the decision on adequacy must consequently be annulled.

In Case C-317/04, the European Parliament contested Article 95 EC as the legal basis for Decision 2004/496.

The Commission considered that the Agreement concerns the free movement of PNR data between the Community and the United States under the conditions which respect the fundamental freedoms and rights of individuals, in particular privacy. It is intended to eliminate any distortion of competition, between the Member States' airlines and between the latter and the airlines of third countries, which may result from the requirements imposed by the United States, for reasons relating to the protection of individual rights and freedoms. Moreover, the Commission also observed Art. 95 EC as "the natural legal basis" for the Decision because the Agreement concerns the external dimension of the protection of personal data when transfered within the Community. It also mentioned that the initial processing of the data by the airlines is carried out for commercial purposes. The use of which the United States authorities make of the data does not remove them from the effect of the Directive (parr. 66).

The Court concluded that Art. 95 EC, read in conjunction with Art. 25 of Directive 95/46/EC cannot justify Community competence to conclude the Agreement (parr. 67). The Agreement related to the same transfer of data as the decision on adequacy and therefore to data processing operations which, as has been stated above, are excluded from the scope of the Directive (parr. 68). Consequently, Decision 2004/496 was also annulled by the Court (parr. 69 and 70).

2.5.3 *Case C-275/06* **Promusicae** *[2008] ECR I-00271. Judgement of the Court (Grand Chamber) of 29 January 2008*[99]

Information society—Obligations of providers of services—Retention and disclosure of certain traffic data—Obligation to disclosure—Limits—Protection of confidentiality of electronic communications—Compatibility with the protection of copyright and related rights—Right to effective protection of intellectual property

In the course of proceedings between Productores de Música de España (Promusicae) and Telefónica de España SAU (Telefónica), the *Juzgado de lo Mercantil* Number 5 of Madrid, Spain, referred to the Court for a preliminary ruling a question related to the interpretation of the following three Directives:

- Directive 2000/31/EC of 8 June 2000 on certain legal aspects of information society services, in particular electronic commerce, in the internal market (Directive on electronic commerce)[100];
- Directive 2001/29/EC on the harmonisation of certain aspects of copyright and related rights in the information society,[101] and
- Directive 2004/48/EC on the enforcement of intellectual property rights.[102]

[99] Judgment ECLI:EU:C:2008:54. Opinion ECLI:EU:C:2007:454.

[100] OJ L 178, 17.7.2000, p. 1

[101] OJ L 167, 22.6.2001, p. 11

[102] OJ 2004, L 157, p. 45 and corrigendum, OJ L 195, 2.6.2004, p. 16.

The proceedings started following the refusal of Telefonica to disclose the identities and physical addresses of certain persons whom it provided with internet access services, whose IP address and data and time of connection were known. According to Promusicae, those persons used the KaZaA file exchange program (peer-to-peer to P2P) and provided access in shared files of personal computers to phonograms in which the members of Promusicae held the exploitation rights (parr. 30). Promusicae claimed before the national court that the users of KaZaA were engaging in unfair competition and infringing intellectual property rights, and therefore requested the disclosure of the above information in order to be able to bring civil proceedings against the persons concerned (parr. 31). The Juzgado de lo Mercantil initially ordered the preliminary measures requested by Promusicae, however, Telefónica appealed against that order stating that the abovementioned Directives allowed such disclosure only in the framework of criminal proceedings or for the purpose of safeguarding public security and national defence, not in civil proceedings or as a preliminary measure in the framework of such civil proceedings.

The question submitted to the Court was basically whether, in light of the abovementioned Directives and of Arts. 17 and 47 of the Charter of Fundamental Rights of the EU, the obligation to communicate personal data is also applicable, in order to ensure effective protection of copyright, in the framework of civil proceedings.

Starting with Directive 2002/58, the Court stated that the general obligation of confidentiality imposed by its Art. 5 admits some exceptions in accordance with Art. 15(1) as soon as they constitutes a necessary, appropriate and proportionate measure within a democratic society to safeguard national security (i.e. State security), defence, public security, and the prevention, investigation, detection and prosecution of criminal offences (parr. 49). None of these exceptions appeared to relate to situations that call for the bringing of civil proceedings (parr. 51).

Hence, as first conclusion, the Court ruled that neither Directive 2000/31/EC nor Directives 2001/29/EC and Directive 2004/48/EC required the Member States to lay down, in a situation such as that in the main proceedings, an obligation to communicate personal data in order to ensure effective protection of copyright in the context of civil proceedings.

However, the Court acknowledged that Article 15(1) ended the list of these exceptions with an express reference to Article 13(1) of Directive 95/46, which also authorises the Member States to adopt legislative measures to restrict the obligation of confidentiality *where that restriction is necessary for the protection of the rights and freedoms of others* (parr. 56 to 60). Moreover, recital 2 in the preamble to Directive 2002/58/EC seeks to respect the fundamental rights and observes the principles recognised in the Charter, including full respect for the rights set out in Arts. 7 and 8 thereof: Article 7 substantially reproduces Art. 8 of the European Convention for the Protection of Human Rights and Fundamental Freedoms signed at Rome on 4 November 1950, which guarantees the right to respect for private life, and Article 8 of the Charter expressly proclaims the right to protection of personal data (parr. 64).

Therefore, as second conclusion, the Court ruled that the Member States, when transposing those Directives, should take care to rely on an interpretation of them which allows a fair balance to be struck between the various fundamental rights protected by the Community legal order, as well as with the general principles of the Community law, including the principle of proportionality (parr. 70).

2.5.4 Case C-301/06, Ireland v. Parliament and Council, 10 February 2009[103]

Action for annulment—Directive 2006/24/EC—Retention of data generated or processed in connection with the provision of electronic communications services—Choice of legal basis

Ireland requested that the Court annul Directive 2006/24/EC on the retention of data generated or processed in connection with the provision of publicly available electronic communication services or of public communication networks,[104] *on the grounds that it was not supported by an appropriate legal basis. The Commission submitted the proposal for a Directive on the basis of Article 95 of the Treaty of the European Community. Ireland's main argument was that the predominant objective of the Directive was to facilitate the investigation, detection and prosecution of crime, including terrorism. Therefore, Ireland contended that the legal basis of the Directive should have been Title VI of the EU Treaty, in particular Articles 30 EU, 31(1)(c) EU and 34(2)(b) EU, rather than the cited Article 95 TEC.*

The Court did interpret the sole or principal objective of Directive 2006/24/EC as being the investigation, detection and prosecution of crimes. Article 95(1) TEC enables the Council to adopt measures for the approximation of laws. Furthermore, the purpose of the Directive was to harmonise disparities between national provisions governing data retention by service providers, particularly regarding the nature of the retained data and the length of their retention periods. It covers the activities of service providers in the internal market, and thus does not govern access to data or use thereof by police or judicial authorities of the Member States.

The Court affirmed the adequate legal basis for Directive 2006/24/EC.

[103] Judgment ECLI:EU:C:2009:68. Opinion ECLI:EU:C:2008:558.

[104] OJ L 105, 13.4.2006, p. 54.

2.5.5 *C-524/06, Huber v. Germany, 16 December 2008*[105]

Protection of personal data—European citizenship—Principle of non-discrimination on grounds of nationality—Directive 95/46/EC—concept of necessity—General processing of personal data relating to citizens of the Union who are nationals of another Member State—Central register of foreign nationals

In December 2008, the European Court of Justice entered a preliminary ruling on the application of Articles 12(1), 17 and 18 of Directive 95/46/EC. This ruling was entered to address issues raised by Mr Heinz Huber, an Austrian national residing in Germany, who pressed charges against the Federal Office for Migration and Refugees (*Bundesamt für Migration und Flüchtlinge*).

The preliminary ruling was triggered by Mr Huber's request to the Federal office for Migration and Refugees for the deletion of his personal data from the "Ausländerzentralregister" (AZR), a centralised register storing certain personal data on foreign nationals residing permanently in Germany. On 22 July 2000, Mr Hubert requested the deletion of his personal data from this database arguing that he was being discriminated against because the database did not track German nationals.

Per the German authorities, the cited database was used for statistical purposes only, and its data was only available to security and police services, and the judicial authorities, when investigating and prosecuting criminal activities which threatened public security.

As a preliminary observation, the Court pointed out that "the processing of personal data for the purposes of the application of legislation relating to the right of residence and for statistical purposes falls within the scope of application of Directive 95/46", but the situation is quite different "when the objective of processing those data is connected with the fight against crime".

Regarding the primary purpose of the database, the Court declared that "as Community law presently stands, the right of free movement of a Union citizen in the territory of a Member State of which he is not a national is not unconditional, but may be subject to the limitations and conditions imposed by the Treaty and by the measures adopted to give it effect". In this sense, it could logically be necessary for a Member State to have information and documents readily available to determine whether a national of another Member State has the right of residence within its territory, and to confirm that no justifications for restricting that right exist. However, "such register must not contain any information other than what is necessary for that purpose". As to the statistical function of the register, the Court stated that "Community law has not excluded the power of Member States to adopt

[105] Judgment ECLI:EU:C:2008:724. Opinion ECLI:EU:C;2008:194.

measures enabling the national authorities to precisely monitor population movements affecting their territory", but the storage of individualised personal information in a general register is another matter.

Therefore, the Court concluded that

> a system for processing personal data relating to Union citizens who are not nationals of the Member State concerned, such as that put in place by the Law on the central register of foreign nationals, of 2 September 1994, and having as its object the provision of support to the national authorities responsible for the application of the law relating to the right of residence, does not satisfy the requirement of necessity laid down by Article 7(e) of Directive 95/46/EC . . ., interpreted in the light of the prohibition on any discrimination on grounds of nationality, unless:
>
> - It contains only the data which are necessary for the application of the national laws by the authorities of that jurisdiction; and
> - Its centralised nature enables legislation relating to the right of residence to be more effectively applied to Union citizens who are not nationals of the Member State.
>
> It is for the national court to ascertain whether those conditions are satisfied in the main proceedings.
>
> The storage and processing of data containing individualised personal information in a register, such as the Central Register of Foreign Nationals, for statistical purposes cannot, on any basis, be considered to be 'necessary' within the meaning of Article 7(e) of Directive 95/46/EC.

Regarding the processing of the personal data contained in the cited database for the purposes of fighting crime, the Court considered that the objective was legitimate, but the systematic processing of personal data restricted to the data of the non-nationals constitutes discrimination which is prohibited by Article 12(1) of the European Community Treaty.

2.5.6 *Case T-194/04, Bavarian Lager Co. Ltd v. Commission, Judgment of the Court of First Instance of 8 November 2007*[106]

Access to documents—Regulation (EC) No. 1049/2001—Documents relating to proceedings for failure to fulfil obligations—Decision refusing access—Protection of physical persons in relation to processing of personal data—Regulation (EC) No. 45/2001—Concept of private life

The applicant requested that the Court annul the Commission's decision of 18 March 2004, rejecting its request for access to the minutes of a meeting held

[106] Judgment ECLI:EU:T:2007:334.

by the Commission in 1994, which was attended by officers of the Director General for the Internal Market and Financial Services, officials of the UK's Department of Trade and Industry, and representatives of the *Confederation de Brasseurs du marche Commun* (CBMC) in the context of an infringement proceeding against the UK under Article 169 of the (former) Treaty of the European Community.

The Commission denied the applicant access to the names of the meeting participants, invoking the exception provided in Article 4(1)(b) of Regulation No. 1049/2001 of 30 May 2001 regarding public access to European Parliament, Council and Commission documents. The cited provision allows the institutions to refuse access to a document where disclosure would undermine the protection of "privacy and the integrity of the individual, in particular in accordance with Community legislation regarding the protection of personal data".

The Court reasoned that Regulation No. 1049/2001 of 30 May 2001 "is designed to ensure the greatest possible transparency of the decision-making process of the public authorities and the information on which they base their decisions", and to promote "good administrative practices". Access to documents containing personal data falls under Regulation No. 1049/2001, according to which, in principle, all documents of the institutions should be accessible to the public, except for cases covered by the regimen of exceptions in Article 4, including the need to protect privacy and integrity of individuals, and the fundamental right of data protection.

According to the Court, there was "no reason in principle to exclude professional or business activities from the concept of 'private life'". In accordance with the case law of the European Court of Human Rights, "private life" is a broad concept that does not lend itself to an exhaustive definition; it protects the right to identity and personal development as well as the right of any individual to establish and develop relationships with other human beings and with the outside world.

However, the Court declared that exceptions to the principle of access to documents must be interpreted restrictively. In this case, the Court highlighted that the text of the minutes refers not to physical persons but to the agencies that the individuals worked for and represented via their attendance, such as the CBMC or the Directorate General for the Internal Market and Financial Services, among others. The Court concluded that

> disclosure of the names of the CBMC representatives is not capable of actually and specifically affecting the protection of the privacy and integrity of the persons concerned. The mere presence of the name of the person concerned in a list of participants at a meeting, on behalf of the body which that person represented, does not constitute such interference, and the protection of the privacy and integrity of the persons concerned is not compromised.

Therefore, the Court decided to annul the Commission's decision of 18 March 2004, which rejected the applicant's request for access to the full minutes of the meeting of 11 October 1996, including the names of all participants.

2.5.7 *Case C-28/08, European Commission v. Bavarian Lager Co. Ltd., Judgment of the Court, 29 June 2010*[107]

Appeal—Access to the documents of the institutions—Document concerning a meeting held in the context of a procedure for failure to fulfil obligations—Protection of personal data—Regulation (EC) No. 45/2001—Regulation (EC) No. 1049/2001

The Commission appealed the Judgment of the Court of First Instance of the European Communities in the case *European Commission v. Bavarian Lager Co. Ltd.*

The Court pointed out that Regulations 45/2001 and 1049/2001 were adopted on dates very close in time to each other, and do not contain any provisions granting one regulation primacy over the other. "In principle, their full application should be ensured". The particular and restrictive interpretation that the Court of First Instance gave to Article 4(1)(b) of Regulation No. 1049/2001 does not correspond to the existing balance between both regulations. The Court held that the Commission was right to verify whether the data subjects had given their consent to the disclosure of their personal data. "...[B]y releasing the expurgated version of the minutes of the meeting of 11 October 1996 with the names of five participants removed therefrom, the Commission did not infringe the provisions of Regulation No 1049/2001 and sufficiently complied with its duty of openness". Furthermore, the Court reasoned that the Commission has not yet been able to weigh up the various interests of the parties concerned, as Bavarian Lager has not provided any express and legitimate justification demonstrating why the transfer of that personal data was necessary. Under these circumstances, the Court concluded that the Commission was right to reject the application for access to the full minutes of the 11 October 1996 meeting.[108]

2.5.8 *T-259/03, Nikolaou v. Commission, 12 September 2007*[109]

Ms Nikolaou brought an action before the Court of First Instance of the European Communities, requesting compensation for the non-material damage and harm to her health suffered as a consequence of notices that appeared in the European press about an ongoing investigation conducted by OLAF, in which she was involved.

[107] Judgment ECLI:EU:C:2010:378. Opinion ECLI:EU:C:2009:624.

[108] *See, however,* Opinion of the Advocate General Sharpston of 15 October 2009.

[109] Judgment ECLI:EU:T:2007:254.

OLAF also issued a press release concerning this investigation, including a reference to it in its Annual Report and, although in both cases her name was not mentioned, the applicant contended that the provided information made it particularly easy to identify her. On the other hand, the applicant requested that OLAF be granted access to her file, the final report and any other information concerning its findings after investigating the allegations against her, which OLAF also refused to disclose to her.

As a preliminary issue, the Court stated that the burden of proof in this case, and similar cases of non-contractual liability, is on the applicant, who must establish whether an institution acted illegally and the extent of the damages suffered. On the contrary, the burden of proof shifts to the institution when a fact giving rise to damages could have resulted from any number of potential causes, and the institution has not introduced any proof as to which was the true cause, even though it was best placed to do so. The Court concluded that an OLAF staff member leaked information, including personal data, to a journalist for publication, and that OLAF's press release confirmed the veracity of the leaked facts by publishing another press release and including references to the case in its Annual Report. The information published in the press release was personal data, because the individual concerned was easily identifiable: the fact that the applicant was not named did not protect her anonymity.

The leak of this information, by transmitting personal data to a journalist, and the subsequent publication of the information in a press release, constituted the unlawful processing of personal data, violating Article 5 of Regulation 45/2001. OLAF was in the best place to prove how the leak occurred and, in the absence of such proof, OLAF and the Commission must be held responsible.

The publication of the press release was unlawful under Articles 5(a) and (b) of Regulation 45/2001, because the public did not need to know the information published in the press release at the time of its publication, before the competent authorities had decided whether or not to pursue judicial, disciplinary or financial remedial measures.

2.5.9 *Case C-291/12* Michael Schwarz v Stadt Bochum *[2003] I-ECR 12971. Judgement of the Court (Fourth Chamber) of 17 October 2013*[110]

Reference for a preliminary ruling—Area of Freedom, Security and Justice—Biometric passport—Fingerprints—Regulation (EC) No. 2252/2004—

(continued)

[110] Judgment ECLI:EU:C:2013:670. Opinion ECLI:EU:C:2013:401.

Article 1(2)—Validity—Legal basis—Procedure for adopting—Articles 7 and 8 of the Charter of Fundamental Rights of the European Union—Right to respect for private life—Right to the protection of personal data—Proportionality

In the course of proceedings between Ms Schwarz and the Stadt Bochum (city of Bochum), the *Verwaltungsgericht Gelsenkirchen (Administrative Court, Gelsenkirchen, Germany)* referred to the Court of Justice for a preliminary ruling the question on the validity of Art. 1(2) of Council Regulation (EC) No 2252/2004 of 13 December 2004 on standards for security features and biometrics in passports and travel documents issued by Member States, as amended by Regulation (EC) No 444/2009 of the European Parliament and of the Council of 6 May 2009.

Mr Schwarz had applied to the Stadt Bochum for a passport, but refused to have his fingerprints taken at that time. Following the refusal of the Stadt Bochum to deliver the requested passport without fingerprints, Mr Schwarz brought an action before the abovementioned Court. Among other reasons, Mr Schwarz considered that Art. 1(2) of Regulation 2252/2004, which imposes the obligation to take fingerprints of persons applying for passports, infringes the right to the protection of personal data ldi down in Arts 7 and 8 of the Charter of Fundamental Rights of the EU.

The Court examines whether taking fingerprints and storing them in passports, as provided for in Art. 1(2) of Regulation No. 2252/2004, constitutes a threat to the rights to respect for private life and the protection of personal data and, in that case, whether such threat can be justified.

On the first point, the Court concludes that, from a joint reading of Arts. 7 and 8 (1) of the Charter, "the taking and storing of fingerprints by the national authorities (. . .) constitutes a threat to the rights to respect for private life and the protection of personal data" (parr. 29).

As regards the justification of this twofold threat, the Court refers to Art. 8(2), according to which personal data cannot be processed except on the basis of the consent of the person concerned or "some other legitimate interest laid down by law". On this second exception, the Court states that "the rights recognised by Arts. 7 and 8 of the Charter are not absolute rights but must be considered in relation to their function in society (see to that effect *Volker und Markus Schecke and Eifert, parr. 48, and Case C-543/09 Deutsche Telekom [2011] ECR I-3441, parr. 51)*" (parr. 33).

In light of Art. 52(1) of the Charter, limitations of the exercise of those rights are possible so long as those limitations (a) area provided for by law, (b) meet an objective of general interest recognised by the Union, and (c) are proportionate to the aims pursued by Regulation No 2252/2004 and, by extension, to the objective of preventing illegal entry into the European Union (parr. 34).

(a) On the first point, it was clear that limitations arising from the taking and storing of fingerprints when issuing passports were provided for by Art. 1(2) of Regulation No 2252/2004 (parr. 35).

(b) Concerning the objective of general interest, Art. 1(2) read in the light of recitals 2 and 3 has two specific aims: to prevent the falsification of passports, and prevent its fraudulent use or the use of persons other than their genuine holders (parr. 36).

(c) On the proportionality principle, the Court considered whether the measures implemented by that regulation are appropriate for attaining those aims and do not go beyond what is necessary to achieve them (*Volker und Markus Schecke and Eifert, parr. 74).*

The Court concluded that the storage of fingerprints on a highly secure storage medium as provided for by that provision requires sophisticated technology, thus reducing the risk of passports being falsified and to facilitate the work of the authorities responsible for checking the authenticity of passports at EU borders.

In assessing whether such processing is necessary, the Court examined whether it was possible to envisage measures which could interfere less with the rights recognised in Arts. 7 and 8 of the Charter but still contribute effectively to the objectives of Regulation No. 2252/2004.

The Courts considered that an action involves no more than the taking of prints of two fingers", was not an operation of an intimate nature. Although fingerprints are taken in additional fo the facial image, the combinations of these two operations cannot be considered as a relevant threat to the rights recognised by Arts. 7 and 8 of the Charter. Moreover, the only real alternative to the taken of fingerprints would be an iris scan, but nothing suggested that the later procedure would interfere less in the rights recognised by Arts. 7 and 8 of the Charter, and it is commonly considered that iris-recognition is not yet as advanced as fingerprint-recognition technology (parr. 52).

Lastly, the Court considered it crucial "that the processing of any data fingerprints taken pursuant to that provision should not go beyond what is necessary to achieve that aim". In accordance with Art. 4(3) of Regulation No. 2252/2004, fingerprints may be used "only for verifying the authenticity of a passport and the identity of its holder", and cannot be used for purposes other than those provided for by that Regulation". On this particular issue, the Court made the following statements:

> (...) it is true that fingerprints play a particular role in the field of identifying persons in general. Thus, the identification techniques of comparing fingerprints taken in a particular place with those stored in a database make it possible to establish whether a certain person is in that particular place, whether in the context of a criminal investigation or in order to monitor that person indirectly (parr. 59).
>
> However, is should be borne in mind that Art. 1(2) of Regulation No 2252/2004 does not provide for the storage of fingerprints except with the passport itself, which belongs to the holder alone (parr. 60).
>
> The Regulation not providing for any other form or method of storing those fingerprints, it cannot in and of itself, as in pointed out by recital 5 of Regulation No 444/2009, be interpreted as providing a legal basis for the centralised storage of data collected thereunder or for the use of such data for purposes other than that of preventing illegal entry into the European Union (parr. 61).
>
> In those circumstances, the arguments pu forward by the referring court concerning the risks linked to possible centralisation cannot, in any event, affect the validity of that

regulation and would have, should the case arise, to be examined in the course of an action brought before the competent courts against legislation providing for a centralised fingerprint base (parr. 62).

References

Bigo D, Gruggeman W, Burgess, Mitsilegas V (2007) The principle of information availability. Working paper for the Commission funded Challenge Project, May 2007. www.libertysecurity.org

Bose M (2007) Der Grundsatz der Verfugbarkeit von Informationen in der stratrechtlichen zusammenarbeit in der Europaischen Union. Gottingen

Bruti Liberati E (2002) Les difficultés de la cooperation. In: Criminal justice cooperation in the European Union after Tampere, Series of publications by the Academy of European Law in Trier, vol 33, p 115

Clarke R (2011) An evaluation of privacy impact assessment guidance documents. Int Data Privacy Law 1(2):111

De Hert P, Riehle C (2010) Data protection in the area of freedom, security and justice – a short introduction and many questions left answered. ERA Forum 11:159

Elsen C (2010) Personal reflections on the institutional framework of the Area of Freedom, Security and Justice. In: Monar J (ed) The institutional framework of the AFSJ, Brussels

Flore D (2009) Droit Pénal Européen. Les enjeux d'une Justice Penal Europeenne, edit. Larcier, Brussels, pp 24 and 366

Genson R (2002) La cooperation policiere pratique sous Schengen: quels enseignements pour l'avenir? In: Criminal justice cooperation in the European Union after Tampere, Series of publications by the Academy of European Law in Trier, vol 33, p 125

Gless S (2005) Mutual recognition, judicial enquiries, due process and fundamental rights. In: Vervaele J (ed) European evidence warrant. Translational judicial inquiries in the EU. Intersentia, Cambridge/Antwerpen/Oxford, p 121

Gutierrez Zarza A et al (2004) El espacio judicial europeo. Cooperacion judicial civil y penal. Código de normas/The European judicial area. Judicial cooperation in civil and criminal matters. Code of rules. Colex, Madrid

Hijmans H (2010) Recent developments in data protection at European Union level. ERA Forum 11:219

Hustinsx P (2010) Eucrim 1:1

Jones C (2007) Implementing the 'principle of availability': the European Criminal Records Information System, the European Police Records Index System, and the Information Exchange Platform for law enforcement authorities. www.statewatch.org

Klip A (2012) European criminal law. An integrative approach. Intersentia, Cambridge/Antwerp/Portland, p 13 y 362

Labayle H (2002) Les nouveaux instruments juridiques du Traité d'Amsterdam: problemes d'interprétation. In: Criminal justice cooperation in the European Union after Tampere, Series of publications by the Academy of European Law in Trier, p 67

Lodge J (2010) Quantum surveillance and 'shared secrets'. A biometric step too far? Centre for European policy studies, Brussels, p 2

Monar J (2010) The institutional framework of the AFSJ. Specific challenges and dynamics of change. In: The institutional dimension of the EU's area of freedom, security and justice, Brussels

Peers S (2011) EU justice and home affairs law. Oxford EU Law Library, p 4 y 655

Wright D, De Hert P (2012) Privacy impact assessment. Law, Governance and Technology Series 6, Springer

Part III
Eurojust, Europol and OLAF. EU Networks for Administrative, Police and Judicial Cooperation on Criminal Matters

Chapter 3
Eurojust

3.1 Mission

Eurojust is the body of the European Union created in 2002 and reinforced in 2009[1] in order to work in close cooperation with the judicial authorities of the Member States conducting investigations and prosecutions against serious forms of cross-border crime.[2]

Although it is based in The Hague, The Netherlands, Eurojust maintains daily contact and undertakes a regular exchange of information with investigating judges and prosecutors in Member States responsible for the conduct of complex cases requiring the practical application of legal instruments of judicial cooperation in criminal matters.

In an Area of Freedom, Security and Justice without internal borders, the members of criminal organisations and networks can move easily from one to another Member State of the EU. Police and judicial authorities responsible for the prevention and combating of serious cross-border crime have limited jurisdiction and are not entitled to undertake any investigative measure or judicial decision beyond the limits of their Member States of origin. Eurojust was created to fill the gap between the continuity of criminal activities committed across the European Union and the fragmented ability of national judicial authorities to investigate and prosecute them.

The scope of competence of Eurojust covers a wide range of criminal offences of a serious nature and cross-border dimension, which are listed in the Annex to the Council Decision of Europol. The list includes inter alia unlawful drug trafficking,

The opinions expressed by the author are personal and do not necessary coincide with those of Eurojust.

[1] See Eurojust legal framework in Sect. 3.2.

[2] Gutierrez Zarza (2010), p. 71.

Á.G. Zarza (ed.), *Exchange of Information and Data Protection in Cross-border Criminal Proceedings in Europe*, DOI 10.1007/978-3-642-40291-3_3,

illegal money-laundering activities, illegal immigrant smuggling, trafficking in human beings, motor vehicle crime, computer crime, corruption and environmental crime.

The field of competence of Eurojust also covers "other types of offences" at the request of a competent authority [Art. 4(2) EJ Decision]. In accordance with this legal provision, Eurojust is entitled to provide support in cases of new types of criminality not expressly listed in the Annex to the EP Decision (maritime piracy), or other types of criminality requiring a coordinated action at EU level (genocide suspects who, after committing crimes in third countries, are residing in the Member States).

Eurojust is a driven-demand body. This means that, within its scope of competence, Eurojust provides support upon request of the national authorities of the Member States. The number of cases initiated on the basis of the information provided by Europol is very reduced.

In this context, the mission of Eurojust is twofold:

- Eurojust promotes and ensures the *coordination among judicial authorities of different Member States who are combating the same criminal organization or phenomenon.*

  This can range, for instance, from criminal organisation involved in drug trafficking in Spain, France, The Netherlands and Denmark, to a mobile itinerant group that originate in Albania and is committing thefts in Slovenia, the Czech Republic, Germany and Austria.

  In these cases, judicial authorities would not have any possibility to succeed and dismantle the whole organisation if they worked in isolation and without taking into consideration the transnational implications of the domestic investigations or prosecutions. In order to combat cross-border criminal activities successfully, judicial authorities are compelled to align their actions: they have to ensure that the suspects are arrested in different Member States simultaneously, that bank accounts and proceeds from crime are frozen in all the Member States at the same time, and that house searches and seizures in different places are synchronised. Only with these coordinated actions at judicial level, is the total dismantling of a criminal organisation possible.

  Eurojust promotes and ensures an expeditive exchange of information and proper coordination among the judicial authorities of the Member States threatened by the same criminal organisation or network. We will see in the following sections how the tasks, powers and tools of Eurojust are aimed at facilitating the exchange of information and the coordination between of investigations and prosecutions.
- Eurojust also *facilitates cooperation and assist in the removal of obstacles that judicial authorities may face when issuing and/or executing legal instruments of judicial cooperation in criminal matters.*

  For example, a Italian prosecutor investigating a case of corruption at national level, may need certain information from bank accounts located in Germany or from Spanish land registers. Assistance might also be sought to deal with a case of murder that has been committed by a citizen of another Member State.

Quite frequently, judicial authorities conducting investigations or prosecutions against serious cross-border crime need the gathering of certain information in another Member State (witnesses testimonies, forensic reports, DNA profiles, criminal records), or the arrest and further surrender of (some of) the suspects. In these cases, the issuing and/or execution of the legal instruments on judicial cooperation in criminal matters (rogatory letters, European arrest warrants) can be subject to delay or encounter difficulties (e.g. unclear drafting, or several requests for additional information).

Eurojust ensures better communication and exchange of information among the issuing and executing judicial authorities, and assist in the removal of obstacles and in optimising execution of the legal instruments on judicial cooperation in criminal matters.

In practice, the abovementioned investigations frequently evolve towards more complex scenarios requiring both coordination and cooperation. For instance, in cases of child pornography Eurojust could be initially asked to provide support in the issuing of rogatory letters for the interception of communications in another Member State. In a later stage, the information gathered from the computer of the suspect may result in a need for close cooperation between the Member States where other collaborators of the victims are residing.

There are also three other scenarios in which support from Eurojust is foreseen:

- Investigations and criminal proceedings involving a Member State and the Commission (mainly cases affecting the financial interests of the EU) [Art. 3(3) EJ Decision];
- Investigations and criminal proceedings conducted by a Member State and requiring the execution of requests of judicial cooperation in a third State [Art. 3(2) and 27b(3) EJ Decision];
- Investigations and criminal proceedings conducted by a third State and requiring the execution of requests for judicial cooperation in at least two Member States [Art. 27b(1)].

In all these scenarios, Eurojust does not have any investigative or prosecutorial power. It works in close cooperation with the national prosecutors and investigation judges and assist them in with the transnational dimension of criminal proceedings. However, the all investigative and prosecutorial powers remain in the hands of the national judicial authorities, and the judicial files remain on their desks. This is one of the most relevant elements of the Area of Freedom, Security and Justice of the EU: the existence of 28 Member States, each of them with its own jurisdiction and national legal system(s), without any supranational body entrusted with the fight against serious crime affecting to several Member States. The Member States are responsible for combating cross-border criminality, with the support and assistance of Eurojust as a "facilitator" or a "mediator".

3.2 Legal Framework

Eurojust was established by Council Decision 2002/187/JAH of 28 February 2002 setting up Eurojust with a view to reinforcing the fight against serious crime (EJ Decision 2002).[3]

The EJ Decision 2002 has been amended twice. First, by Council Decision 2003/659/JHA[4] (EJ Decision 2003) in order to bring certain provisions of EJ Decision 2002 into line with the Financial Regulation applicable to the general budget of the European Communities. Second, by Council Decision 2009/426/JHA of 16 December 2008 on the strengthening of Eurojust (EJ Decision 2008).[5] The later focused on the following main areas: (1) the setting up of an On-Call Coordination (OCC) system in order to enable Eurojust to provide support in urgent situations, by ensuring the availability of the National Members at any time (Art. 5a); (2) the extension of the powers of the College to situations in which the national authorities were not able to reach an agreement on how to solve a conflict of jurisdiction [Art. 7(2)] or were confronted by recurrent refusals or difficulties on judicial cooperation [Art. 7(3)]; (3) the introduction of a common basis of equivalent judicial powers for all the National Members, although mitigated by a "national safeguard clause" (Art. 9a–9f); (4) the establishment in each Member States of a Eurojust National Coordination System (ENCS), conceived as a flexible structure in order to create a link between Eurojust, EJN and the contact points of other networks of judicial cooperation in criminal matters, and facilitate the transmission of operational information to Eurojust; (5) the introduction of the obligation imposing the national authorities to provide Eurojust with information related to specific types of crime, investigative measures or difficulties on judicial cooperation; (6) certain amendments confirming the complementarity and mutual partnership between Eurojust and EJN, and (7) in the area of external relations, the possibilities of Eurojust to second liaison magistrates to third countries, and to coordinate the execution of requests from third countries addressed to more than one Member State.[6] These legal provisions have configurated Eurojust as a "body" of the EU with legal personality (Art. 1 EJ Decision). Therefore, Eurojust is not an

[3] OJ L 63, 6.3.2002, p. 1. Previously to the setting up of Eurojust a provisional unit, called Pro-Eurojust, developed its functions at the premises of the Council.

[4] OJ L 245, 29.9.2003, p. 44. The purpose of this Council Decision was to bring certain provisions of the Council Decision of 2002 into line with the Council Regulation (EC, Euratom) No. 1605/2002 of 25 June 2002 on the Financial Regulations applicable to the general budget of the European Communities. It is therefore not relevant for the purposes of this handbook.

[5] OJ L 138, 4.6.2009, p. 14. The consolidated version of the Council Decision of 2002, as amended by the cited Council Decisions of 2003 and 2008, shall be hereinafter referred to as "Council Decision of Eurojust". See Council Document 5347/3/98 REV 3 COPEN 9 EUROJUST 3 EJN 2. Brussels, 15 July 2009.

[6] See Explanatory memorandum to Council Decision on EJN and to Council Decision on the strengthening of Eurojust. Council doc. 5038/08 COPEN 2 EUROJUST 2 EJN 2.

Agency of the EU strictu sensu, although it is considered "de facto" as one of the agencies of the Area of Freedom, Security and Justice. As result, Eurojust is included within the scope of the "Common approach on EU decentralised agencies" endorsed by the European Parliament, the Council and the Commission in July 2012, and the Roadmap on the follow-up of the Common approach with concrete timetables for the planned initiatives. In line with the Common approach and in accordance with Art. 41a EJ Decision, an independent external evaluation of Eurojust will be conducted in 2014.

In order to assist in the implementation of the EJ Decision 2009, an Informal Working Group met regularly, at Eurojust premises, under successive presidencies of the Council of the EU. The Strategic Seminar "Building new bridges between Eurojust and the Member States", organised jointly by the Swedish Presidency of the EU and Eurojust on 7–8 September 2009, in Stockholm, focused on the implementation of the EJ Decision 2009 in the Member States.[7]

The sixth round of mutual evaluations deals with "The practical implementation and operation of the Council Decision 2002/187/JHA of 28 February 2002 setting up Eurojust with a view to reinforcing the fight against serious crime and of the Council Decision 2008/976/JHA on the European Judicial Network in criminal matters". In December 2013, the reports of Sweden, Lithuania, Belgium, Estonia, Slovak Republic, Denmark, Finland, Hungary, Austria and France had been adopted and made public.

The abovementioned legal framework is developed further by the Rules of Procedure of Eurojust[8] and, in the area of personal data, by the Rules of Procedure on the processing and protection of personal data at Eurojust.[9]

A specific legal provision on Eurojust was introduced by the Treaty of Lisbon into the Treaty on the Functioning of the European Union (TFEU). In accordance with this legal provision (Art. 85 TFEU), in June 2013 the Commission submitted a Proposal for a Regulation on the European Union Agency for Criminal Justice Cooperation (Eurojust).[10]

Besides this legal framework and the national laws implementing the abovementioned Council Decisions, Eurojust operates in a complex legal context that includes international conventions and treaties, EU legal instruments of judicial cooperation and national implementing laws, national Codes of criminal law and of criminal proceedings. One of the tasks of Eurojust is precisely to ensure that the different legal systems (and Codes) at stake in a particular investigation or prosecution coordinated by Eurojust are compatible to each other so that, for instance, the

[7] See Council doc. 16925/09.

[8] OJ C 286, 22.11.2002, p. 1.

[9] Text adopted unanimously by the College of Eurojust during the meeting of 21 October 2004 and approved by the Council on 24 February 2005. OJ C 68, 19.3.2005, p. 1. See also Additional rules defining specific aspects of the application of the rules on the processing and protection of personal data at Eurojust to non-case-related operations, adopted by the College of Eurojust on 27 June 2006, at www.eurojust.europa.eu/about/legal-framework.

[10] COM(2013) 535 final. Brussels, 17.7.2013. On the EJ draft Regulation, see Part V, Chap. 13.

information and evidence gathered in a Member State can be admissible in Court in another Member State of the EU.

Another relevant challenge for Eurojust is to ensure compliance with the rules for the processing and protection of personal data applicable at Eurojust premises, in the exchanges of information with the Member States, and at national level, without compromising the investigations and prosecutions supported by Eurojust.

3.3 Structure and Governance

3.3.1 National Members and National Desks

The structure of Eurojust is unique.[11] Eurojust is composed of 28 National Members, being each of them a prosecutor, investigating judge or police officer of equivalent competence seconded by the respective Member State in accordance with its legal system.

The National Members are the heads of the respective National desks, or national offices, located all of them in different floor of the same Eurojust building in The Hague.

The National desks are also composed of one or more Deputies and/or Assistants and, in many cases, Seconded National Experts. All of them are experienced practitioners (mainly prosecutors) very well known in their Member States of origin. This proximity and permanent contacts with the national judicial authorities is the real added value of Eurojust, as it facilitates enormously the work of national authorities conducting complicated cross-border investigations who do not hesitate to contact their colleagues in The Hague and ask for support in the transnational implications of such investigation.

National Members, Deputies and Assistants are subject to the respective national laws as regards their status. Some common rules regarding the minimum term of office of the National Members are set out in Art. 9(1) EJ Decision, to ensure continuity of the work of Eurojust and of national members themselves.

The National members receive their salaries and emoluments from the Member State of origin, with the exception of work relating to the development of Eurojust's tasks, which is considered as operational expenditure and covered by Eurojust budget (Art. 33 EJ Decision).

[11] See Labayle and Nilsson (2010), p. 195.

3.3.2 *The College*

The 28 National Members form the College of Eurojust, which is responsible for the organisation (management board) and the operation (casework related matters) of Eurojust. For many years the College has met every week to discuss operational, management, strategic and policy matters. Following an internal reflection session of the College held in October 2012, operational, policy and strategic matters are now being handled jointly, in the so-called Operational meetings of the College. The College meets separately as a Management Board.[12] The College elects a President from among the National Members, and two vice-Presidents. At the time of writing the President of Eurojust is Ms Michele Coninsx, National Member for Belgium. The Vice-Presidents of Eurojust are Francisco Jiménez-Villarejo, National Member for Spain, and Mr Ladislav Hamran, National Member for the Slovak Republic.

Although not yet implemented, the College is empowered to appoint liaison magistrates to third States, for the purposes of facilitating judicial cooperation with such State, in accordance with Article 27a of the Council Decision of Eurojust.

3.3.3 *The Administration*

The National Members and the National desks are supported by a Secretariat, or Eurojust Administration, headed by an Administrative Director. Different Units and Services (including the Case Analysis Unit, Legal Service, Human Resources) comprise the Administration of Eurojust. Staff Members are subject to the Staff Regulations and internal implementing rules.

The Data Protection Officer (DPO) is also part of the staff of Eurojust. Although he/she is under the direct authority of the College, the performance of his/her tasks is guaranteed to be independent [Art. 17(1) EJ Decision].

The Joint Supervisory Body (JSB) is an external and independent body with the main tasks of monitoring the activities of Eurojust involving the processing of personal data, and ensuring compliance with the rules for the processing and protection of personal data. The JSB is entrusted with the examination of appeals by individuals in order to verify whether data are processed by Eurojust in a lawful and accurate manner, and provides advice during the negotiations of agreements with third States and bodies.[13]

---

[12] Report from the Eurojust Seminar on the new draft Regulation on Eurojust: "An improvement in the fight against cross-border crime?", The Hague, 14–15 October 2013. Council doc. 17188/13 EUROJUST 135 COPEN 226, p. 6.

[13] An overview of the activities of the Eurojust JSB can be found in the Activity Report of the Joint Supervisory Body for the year 2012. Council doc. 12129/13 EUROJUST 55.

3.3.4 The Secretariats of the Networks

The internal structure of Eurojust also includes the Secretariats of different networks involved in judicial cooperation in criminal matters, namely the Secretariat of the European Judicial Network, the Secretariat of the Network for Joint Investigation Teams, and the Secretariat of the European Network of contact points in respect of persons responsible for genocide, crime against humanity and war crimes. The Secretariats are part of the staff of Eurojust but function as separate units (Article 25a(1)(a) and (2) and (3) EJ Decision).

3.4 Tasks, Powers and Tools

3.4.1 The Double Dimension of the National Members

It is traditionally considered that the National Members of Eurojust have a double dimension or 'hat', in particular:

- The National Members are part of a European body with legal personality and a crucial role in the fight against serious crime within the area of Freedom, Security and Justice of the EU. From this perspective, both the National Members and the College have been empowered with certain "tasks" related to promote the exchange of information on cross-border investigations and prosecutions, ensure coordination, and facilitate cooperation between the judicial authorities conducting such investigations and prosecutions;
- The National Members are also called to work in close cooperation with the investigating judges and prosecutors of thir own Member States, covering the transnational implications of the national criminal proceedings. From this point of view, the National Members are entrusted with a common core of "powers" enabling them to carry out certain investigative measures and acts with a direct impact and effects in national criminal proceedings of their Member State of origin.

3.4.2 Tasks of Eurojust Acting Through Its National Members or as a College

National Members are usually contacted by home authorities in complex cross-border cases requiring support in the issuing, transmission or execution of several requests for judicial cooperation in criminal matters. The support can also be requested, in urgent cases, through the OCC system (Art. 5a(3) EJ Decision). The "actions" that the National Members can undertake to provide such support are enumerated in Article 6 ("Tasks of Eurojust acting through its National Members").

Under particular circumstances, and especially when the investigations or prosecutions can have repercussions at Union level or might affect Member States other than those directly concerned, the College of Eurojust can undertake the tasks enumerated in Article 7 Eurojust Council Decision ("Tasks of Eurojust acting as a College").

Acting through its National Members, Eurojust may ensure that the judicial authorities exchange relevant information [Art. 6(1)(b)], coordinate their investigations and prosecutions [Art. 6(1)(c)], and cooperate closely [Art. 6(1)(d)]. In bilateral cases, the National Members should consider whether the case is complex enough to require the involvement of Eurojust. Otherwise, the case should be referred to the European Judicial Network. In this respect, Art. 6(1)(e) states that the National Members of Eurojust "shall cooperate and consult with the European Judicial Network, including making use of and contributing to the improvement of its documentary database".

The National Members of Eurojust are also entitled to issue formal requests addressed to the national judicial authorities of his/her Member State for the following purposes:

- To undertake an investigation or prosecution in specific acts.

  Eurojust may not initiate investigations or prosecutions against serious cross-border crime. However, some complex cases might require the involvement of Member States other than those that initially conducted investigations and prosecutions against the criminal organisation. Likewise, some complex cases might require the involvement of Member States other than those that initially conducted investigations and prosecutions against the criminal organisation. In those cases, the respective National Member may request his/her home authorities to initiate an investigation.
- To accept that a judicial authority may be in a better position to undertake an investigation or to prosecute specific acts.

  This task is very relevant in cases of existing or potential conflicts of jurisdiction, and especially then judicial authorities of different Member States could prosecute the same criminal organisation on the basis of the same facts. To safeguard the principle "non bis in idem" and avoid unnecessary costs and efforts, Eurojust may request the national authorities of one of the Member State involved, to consider that the judicial authorities of other Member State are in a better position to continue with the criminal proceedings.
- To coordinate action between the competent authorities of the Member States concerned.

  As we have mentioned already, one of the objectives of Eurojust is to ensure the best possible coordination among judicial authorities combating the same criminal phenomenon. To do so, Eurojust has relevant tools that will be analysed in further sections.
- To set up a joint investigation team in keeping with the relevant cooperation instruments.

Joint Investigation Teams enables police and judicial authorities from different Member States to work together on a daily basis "as a team" regardless the borders of the Member States concerned: competent authorities can easily move from one territory to another, and exchange information and evidence without the need (under certain conditions) to issue and execute rogatory letters and other formal requests of mutual regal assistance.

– Provide any information that is necessary for it to carry out its tasks.

  In order to ensure transmission of information, cooperation and coordination between judicial authorities, Eurojust needs to get a proper view of the criminal phenomenon and of the transnational dimensions of the case. Eurojust receives very frequently only a copy of the European Arrest Warrant or a short email requesting assistance and support: additional information on the cross-border elements of the case might help the National Member to understand the difficulties of the case and assist to overcome them. To this aim, Art. 1(a)(v) enable the National Member to issue a request for information.

– Take special investigative measures, or any other measure justified for the investigation or prosecution.

  The expertise acquired by Eurojust in the last 10 years is frequently relevant to identify the best manner to approach a particular criminal investigation or prosecution. For instance, innovative investigative methods for the interception of communications in real time can be proposed to the national judicial authorities in cases of cybercrime.

Although responses to these requests are not mandatory, the Member States should ensure "that competent national authorities respond without undue delay to requests made under this Article" (Article 6(2) EJ Decision).

Some of the tasks that Eurojust can undertake acting as a College are similar to the tasks just mentioned, although the following differences would merit particular attention.

Firstly, Article 7(1)(f) entitles the College to assist Europol "in particular by providing it with opinions based on analyses carried out by Europol". This is an area of common work not fully explored by both bodies. So far, the Europol analysis reports are particularly relevant in the framework of the coordination meetings. Conversely, during its operational meetings Europol could benefit from Eurojust opinions inter alia on the legal instruments applicable for the arrest and surrender of a suspect; on the safeguards and fundamental rights of the persons concerned by a EAW; on the rules for gathering information and evidence in a Member State to be admissible in court in other Member State.

Secondly, Article 7(2) and (3) empowers Eurojust to issue written non-binding opinions in two particular situations:

• "Where two or more National Members cannot agree on how to resolve a case of conflict of jurisdiction", "provided that the matter could not be resolved through mutual agreement between the competent national authorities concerned".

- Recurrent refusals or difficulties concerning the execution of requests and decisions on judicial cooperation, where the situation could not be resolved through mutual agreement between the competent national authorities or through the involvement of the National Members concerned.

In both cases, the opinion of Eurojust has to be promptly forwarded to the Member State(s) involved.

Should a competent national authority decide not to comply with a request issued by their National Member or the College (Articles 6(a) and 7(a)), or with a non-written opinion of the College (Article 7(2) and (3)) it must inform Eurojust "without undue delay of their decision and of the reasons for it", in accordance with Art. 8 EJ Decision. This legal provision states that

> where it is not possible to give the reasons for refusing to comply with a request because to do so would harm essential national security interests or would jeopardise the safety of individuals, the competent authorities of the Member States may cite operational reasons.

These reasons ("harm essential national security interests" or "jeopardise the safety of individuals") seems closer to a police investigation than to a judicial investigation or criminal proceeding in which is Eurojust is providing assistance or support. A reference to the risk to "undermine ongoing investigations prosecutions or court proceedings" or the "fundamental rights of suspects, accused persons or victims" would be more appropriate.

3.4.3 Powers Granted to the National Members in Their Capacity as Competent National Authorities

In accordance with the "double dimension" of the role of National Members of Eurojust, Articles 9 to 9f EJ Decision recognise a common core of powers to be exercised by the National Members "in their capacity as national judicial authorities". Such common core of powers had already been foreseen in the EJ Decision of 2002, but was drafted in such general terms[14] that this resulted in a "variable geometry" of the powers granted to their National Members by the Member States of origin.

Arts. 9–9f EJ Decision intend to ensure that at least some powers are conferred to all National Members, whilst the level of recognition of others will depend on the particularities of the constitutional rules, criminal justice systems and structures of each Member State.

---

[14] Article 9(3) of the Council Decision of 2002 stated: "Each Member State shall define the nature and extent of the judicial powers it grants its national member within its own territory. It shall also define the right for a national member to act in relation to foreign judicial authorities, in accordance with its international commitments (. . .)".

The "ordinary powers" mentioned in Art. 9b, as well as the modalities of access to certain national databases listed in Art. 9(3), should be conferred to all National Members.

Conversely, the "powers exercised in agreement with a competent national authority" regulated in Art. 9c, and the "powers exercised in urgent cases" regulated in Art. 9d should be granted as far as those powers are not contrary to the constitutional rules, fundamental aspects of the criminal justice system, or the federal structure of the Member State concerned (Art. 9e). If the later (and in accordance with the so-called "national safeguarding clause"), the National Member should be at least competent to submit a request to the national competent authority in pursuance of the powers mentioned in Arts. 9c and 9d.

- In the exercise of ordinary powers, National Members should be entitled "to receive, transmit, facilitate, follow up and provide supplementary information" of requests and decision of judicial cooperation in criminal matters (Article 9b (1)). In case of partial or inadequate execution, the National Members should be entitled "to ask for supplementary measures in order for the request to be fully executed" (Article 9b(2)).
- In agreement with the competent national authority, of at its request, the National Members may, under their capacity as competent national authorities, "issuing and completing", as well as "executing", requests and decisions of judicial cooperation. They may also "order in their Member State investigative measures considered necessary at a coordination meeting organised by Eurojust", and authorising and coordinating controlled deliveries. (Article 9(1)(a) and (c)).
- In urgent cases and in so far as it is not possible for them to identify or to contact the competent national authority in a timely manner, the National Members may be granted powers "to authorise and coordinate controlled deliveries in their Member State", and to execute requests and decisions on judicial cooperation in criminal matters (Article 9(d)).

The powers conferred to the National Members i could be also exercised, without undue delay, in relation to the execution of the requests received from other Member State through the OCC system [Art. 5a(3) EJ Decision].

Art. 9(3) EJ Decision confers the National Members the power to have equivalent access, or at least be able to obtain the information contained in certain databases. The information retrieved or received by a Member State from these databases may help inter alia to determine whether this person has committed similar offences in other Member States. This could be used in the case of a perpetrator of child pornography which has been convicted previously in other Member States and whose criminal records are stored in ECRIS. This can also be the case of a member of a violent itinerant group which has committed previous murders in other Member States, and whose DNA profile is stored in Prüm system.

In order to maximise the possibilities of these searches, the National Members should be granted access (or be able to receive information from) the national databases and, through the national contact points, of the interconnected databases from other Member States. This does not seem controversial, as far as Art. 9(3)

EJ Decision states that the National Member should have the same level of access "as would be available to him in his role as a prosecutor, judge or police officer", and the later authorities have (direct or indirect) access to Prüm and ECRIS systems, among others.

It is unclear whether relevant information extracted from those databases and sent to a National Member could be transmitted to other National Member(s) and, through them, be inserted in the national judicial files. Otherwise, the information should be further transmitted formally between the Member States concerned through legal instruments of judicial cooperation in criminal matters.

The particular powers conferred to the National Members in the context of Joint Investigation Teams (Art. 9f EJ Decision) are analysed in the next section.

3.4.4 *Eurojust Tools*

3.4.4.1 Coordination Meetings

Eurojust has developed some tools to provide the necessary support and assistance to the national judicial authorities conducting investigations and prosecutions against serious cross-border crime.

One of the most relevant tools are the coordination meetings. In those meetings, judicial authorities from different Member States are able to sit down together, round a big table, in order to share information about the state of play of investigations and prosecutions, and discuss the best manner to coordinate their actions in at national level, and the requests for assistance in other Member States. Meetings are convened by the relevant National Members in agreement with the national judicial authorities. Eurojust provides support in the planning of the journey to The Hague and will cover travel costs. Eurojust also provides simultaneous translation, so that judicial authorities can explain the details of ongoing investigation in their own language.

The preparation and conduction of the meetings are actively supported by the Case Analysis Unit. Among other tasks, this Unit has the challenge to group the different pieces of information provided by the national judicial authorities and, on the basis of such information and the data and support provided by Europol, compose the overall picture of the criminal phenomena. This overall picture is provided, and completed, during the coordination meeting.

In many coordination meetings, the main objective is to design and agree on a common Action Plan including actions and investigative measures to be adopted simultaneously (and in a coordinated manner) in the different Member States with a view to tackle and dismantle the criminal organisation in question.

3.4.4.2 The Coordination Centres

The days agreed to take action simultaneously in different Member States against the same criminal organisation, the National Members concerned and Eurojust analysts arrive at Eurojust in the early morning. They monitor in real time the execution of domiciliary searches, the freezing of criminal assets and the arrest of the suspects, among other measures. They also assist the judicial authorities to overcome the difficulties derived from the existence of different legal instruments, or if certain additional information is needed before the execution of a rogatory letter or any other instrument of judicial cooperation in criminal matters.

3.4.4.3 The Joint Investigation Teams

A Joint Investigation Team (JIT) is a team of police and judicial authorities from different Member States and/or other parties, including third States, set up on the basis of a written agreement, for a specific purpose and a limited period of time.[15] JITS are mainly governed by Art. 13 of the Convention on Mutual Assistance in Criminal Matters between the Member States of the EU[16] and by the Council Framework Decision 2002/465/JHA of 13 June on Joint Investigation Teams [OJ L 162, 20.6.2002, p. 1].

The creation of a JIT is highly advisable where criminal organisations operate in several Member States and closely coordinated actions are required on-the-spot to tackle them. In particular, JITs have demonstrated a clear added value in cases of drug trafficking, trafficking in human beings, fraud and corruption.

Within the framework of a JIT Agreement and in accordance with specific operational action plans, JITs members are able to discuss and agree on common strategies, undertake specific investigative measures, exchange and gather information in real time, and share specialised knowledge. Practitioners participating in JITs enjoy an appropriate legal framework to discuss matters related to the disclosure and confidentiality of documents and the admissibility of evidence. This new working method also promotes the interaction between police and judicial authorities from different legal systems and judicial cultures.

Based on the practical experience gained over the years, Eurojust provides advice to judicial authorities on the potential benefits of setting up a JIT in a particular case and, if decided so, can also support the setting up and running of a JIT.

The potential advantages of setting up a JIT and, if decided so, the negotiation of the JIT Agreement and the drafting of the operational action plan are frequently discussed during coordination meetings organised at Eurojust premises.

---

[15] On this matter, see more in detail Eurojust News, Issue No. 9—June 2013.

[16] OJ C 197, 12.7.2000, p. 1.

Apart from this type of support and assistance, the National Members of Eurojust are entitled to participate in JITs, including the possibility of being leaders or members of a JITs supported by EU budget (Art. 9f EJ Decision).

In 2012[17], 78 JITS involving Eurojust were active. National Members participated in 47 newly created JITs, either in their capacities as national competent authorities or on behalf of Eurojust. The JITs were created to tackle inter alia cases of drug trafficking, money laundering, trafficking in human beings and fraud.

Eurojust also provides logistical and financial support to JITs, including the reimbursement of travel expenses, accommodation, translation and interpretation, and loans of equipment such as mobile telephones, laptops, mobile printers and scanners. These costs have been covered by EU budget through two consecutive grants administered by Eurojust under the "Prevention of and Fight against Crime" Programme of the Commission (the JIT Funding Projects). Since the second project ended, Eurojust has issued two additional calls for proposals in order to cover the operational needs of JITs from the Eurojust regular budget.

Of 143 funding applications received in 2012 (Figures extracted from Eurojust Annual Report 2012, p. 35), Eurojust provided financial support to 62 JITs involving 22 Member States. Most of the JITs financially supported by Eurojust were related to drug trafficking and trafficking in human beings.

3.5 Exchange of Information with National Judicial Authorities and Between National Members

3.5.1 Initial Information About the Case

Judicial authorities requiring the support of Eurojust to address the transnational implications of their investigations and prosecutions are able to contact directly the National Member from their own Member State (Art. 9(2) EJ Decision). This initial contact usually marks the beginning of a close cooperation and a fluent exchange of casework information between the prosecutor or investigating judge and the respective National Member of Eurojust.

National Members are easy reached via mobile phone or e-mail. In order to ensure and facilitate the contacts with the national desks in urgent cases, as we have seen previously Eurojust has set up a On-Call Coordination System (Article 5a EJ Decision). This tool allows the national judicial authorities requiring the assistance of Eurojust to phone to a general number, which identifies the State of origin of the phone call and forwards it to the person "on call" in the relevant National desk.

[17] Figures extracted from Eurojust Annual Report 2012, p. 34.

3.5.2 Immediate Exchange of Information Among the National Members

Once the National Member has an overall picture on the investigation or prosecution conducted at national level and on the possible role to be played by Eurojust in a case, he/she is empowered to contact the National Members whose countries are also involved (or present some links) with that investigation or prosecution. As expressly stated in Article 13(3) in fine EJ Decision, "National Memers should be promptly informed on the case which concerns them".

The fact that all the National Members have their regular place of work at the seat of Eurojust (Art. 2(2)(a) EJ Decision) and are based in the same building facilitates enormously a close cooperation and the speedy exchange of information between them on investigations and prosecutions involving several Member States.

National Members are able to discuss details of the case by dialing an extension, taking the lift and visit another desk, or meeting briefly in any of the Eurojust meeting rooms. However, as this is part of formal national investigations and prosecutions, such initial contacts among the desks should be followed by formal meetings convened in accordance with Arts. 14–17 EJ Rules of Procedure.

In accordance with these legal provisions, the College analyses the status of its operational matters at least once a month. In the College operational meetings, the National Member who has been approached by his/her home authorities to assist in an ongoing investigation or criminal proceeding should report to the College regarding the opening of the Eurojust case. The College is also briefed about the closure of the case when Eurojust support and assistance has come to an end. Reports to the College on the opening and closure of cases is considered to be as "Operational work of the College (level I)" (Art. 15 EJ Rules of Procedure).

Following a College operational meeting, the National Members concerned with the same Eurojust case usually convene an ad hoc meeting to analyse the case carefully. Discussions during those meetings are considered as "Operational work of the College (level II)" (Art. 16 Ej Rules of Procedure).

Lastly, the National Members concerned by complex cases requiring extensive discussions with home authorities convene coordination meetings. These meetings, which have been described previously, are considered to be as "Operational work of the College (level III") (Art. 17 EJ Rules of Procedure). The Action Plans agreed during coordination meetings are monitored, the days of action, through the Eurojust coordination centre.

Following the opening of a Eurojust case, the National Members are entitled to carry out the tasks listed in Article 6 EJ Decision. For instance, they may ensure proper exchange of information between the national authorities, or facilitate the issuing, transmission or execution of requests of judicial cooperation in criminal matters. The National Members can also exercise the powers listed in Art. 9–9f in accordance with the national law of his/her Member State of origin.

If it is a case of the College, Eurojust may perform any of the tasks of Art. 7 EJ Decision which includes, inter alia, the possibility to ask a judicial authority to consider that another one may be in a better position to continue with the investigation or prosecution.

3.5.3 ...Without Prejudice to Direct Contacts Between National Judicial Authorities

The involvement of Eurojust in a particular investigation or prosecution, supporting the national authorities of different Member States in the transnational implications of the case, should not prejudice or impede "direct contacts between competent judicial authorities as provided for in instruments on judicial cooperation, such as Article 6 of the Convention on Mutual Assistance in Criminal Matters between the Member States of the European Union" (Article 12(7) Council Decision of Eurojust).

3.5.3.1 Mandatory Transmission of Information to Eurojust According to Article 13(5)–(7) EJ Decision. The Eurojust template

To ensure that Eurojust receives operational and strategic information, the Eurojust Council Decision of 2008 introduced in Article 13(1), last indent, the obligation of the national judicial authorities to transmit to Eurojust "at least" the information referred to in paragraphs (5)–(7) and specified further in the Annex to the Eurojust Council Decision. In particular:

- Information on the setting up, legal framework applicable and results of the work of the Joint Investigation Teams (JITs) (Article 13(5)). For those situations, the following types of information should be transmitted to Eurojust:

  (a) "participating Member States,
  (b) type of offences concerned,
  (c) date of the agreement setting up the team,
  (d) planned duration of the team, including modification of this duration,
  (e) details of the leader of the team for each participating Member State,
  (f) short summary of the results of the Joint investigation teams" [parr. (1) of Annex].

- Information on investigations and prosecutions involving at least three Member States, in the framework of which some requests or decisions on judicial cooperation have been transmitted to at least two Member States, and provided that the criminal offences under investigation or prosecution fulfil one of the following three criteria:

- The offence is punishable by a custodial sentence or a detention order for a maximum period of at least 5 or 6 years, and is one of the following criminal offences: trafficking in human beings, sexual exploitation of children and child pornography, drug trafficking, trafficking in firearms, their parts and components and ammunition, corruption, fraud affecting the financial interests of the European Communities, counterfeiting of euro, money laundering, or attacks against information systems (Article 13(6)(a)); or
- "There are factual indications that a criminal organisation is involved" (Article 13(6)(b)); or
- "There are indications that the case may have a serious cross-border dimension or repercussions at European Union level or that might affect Member States other than those directly involved" (Article 13(6)(c)).

  In these situations, the following information should be transmitted to Eurojust:

  (a) "data which identify the person, group or entity that is the object of a criminal investigation or prosecution
  (b) Member States concerned,
  (c) the offence concerned and its circumstances,
  (d) data related to the requests for, or decisions on, judicial cooperation including regarding instruments giving effect to the principle of mutual recognition, which are issued, including:

    (i) data of the request,
    (ii) requesting or issuing authority,
    (iii) requested or executing authority,
    (iv) type of request (measures requested),
    (v) whether or not the request has been executed, and if not on what grounds" (parr.(2) of Annex)

- Information on "cases where conflicts of jurisdiction have been arisen or are likely to arise" (Art. 13(7)(a). In these situation, the following information should be transmitted to Eurojust:

  (a) "Member States and competent authorities concerned,
  (b) data which identify the person, group or entity that is the subject of a criminal investigation or prosecution,
  (c) the offence concerned and its circumstances" [parr. (3) of Annex]

- Information on "controlled deliveries affecting at least three States, at least two of which are Member States" [Art. 13(7)(b)]. In this case, the following information should be transmitted to Eurojust:

  (a) "Member States and competent authorities concerned,
  (b) data which identify the person, group or entity that is the object of a criminal investigation or prosecution,
  (c) type of delivery,

(d) type of offence in connection which the controlled delivery is carried out." [parr. (4) Annex].

- Information related to "repeated difficulties or refusals regarding the execution of requests for, and decisions on, judicial cooperation, including regarding instruments giving effect to the principle of mutual recognition" [Art. 13(7)(c)]. Under those circumstances, the following information should be transmitted to Eurojust:

  (a) "requesting or issuing State,
  (b) requested or executing State,
  (c) description of the difficulties" [parr. (5) Annex]

The supply of these categories of information to Eurojust constitutes a legal obligation for the national judicial authorities, excepting when the such supply would mean "(a) harming essential national security interests; or (b) jeopardising the safety of individuals" [Art. 13(8) EJ Decision]. As mentioned previously, the drafting of both exceptions seems to be closer to police investigations than to judicial investigations and proceedings. Another wording would be preferable.

As the information should be transmitted "in an structured way" (Article 13(11)), Eurojust has elaborated a "Template for the transmission of information ex Article 13(5)–(7) of the Council Decision of Eurojust", which has been reproduced in the Annex of this publication.

The template includes a general part related to all the situations foreseen in paragraphs (5)–(7), followed by a special part about the information to be provided for the particular situations of the cited paragraphs.

Jointly with the type of information mentioned in the Annex to the Council Decision of Eurojust, the judicial authorities can also provide other types of information considered relevant for the case, by filling in the empty boxes included in different sections of the template.

The template is available electronically in the 23 languages of the EU. The electronic version includes drop-down lists in many sections, to facilitate the filing of the form and further storage of the information in the Case Management System of Eurojust.

Once the template has been filled it, it should be send to the corresponding National Member for Eurojust.

In principle, any modification of the information transmitted should be notify to Eurojust by using the same template.

The number of templates received by Eurojust is rather low, mainly because the judicial authorities do not always see the added value of providing such information to Eurojust. Depending on the type of situation confronted by the national authority, the added value of filling the Eurojust template and send it to Eurojust could be as follows:

- The transmission of the Eurojust template will be interpreted as a request for assistance in the case concerned "only if so specified by a competent authority". In this case, the respective National Member would have received the necessary information, in an structure manner, to start providing assistance and support to home authorities.
- In cases where the Eurojust template is transmitted without requesting the assistance of Eurojust, the National Member might consider that such assistance may result in a more effective investigation or prosecution of the case. If so, he or she will approach the national authority who sent the template and suggest Eurojust involvement. The National Member is also entitled to exercise the tasks of Art. 6 and powers of Art. 7 in this case.
- When Eurojust is not providing operational support to the case described in the template, the information is analysed carefully from a strategic point of view and will be a crucial source of information for the strategic meetings and reports of Eurojust.

3.5.3.2 Mandatory Transmission of Information to Eurojust According to Council Decision 2005/671/JHA of 20 September 2005 on the Exchange of Information and Cooperation on Terrorist Offences

The different scenarios for the exchange of information envisaged in Article 13 of the Council Decision of Eurojust should be considered "without prejudice to other obligations regarding the transmission of information to Eurojust, including Council Decision 2005/671/JHA of 20 September on the exchange of information and cooperation concerning terrorist offences".

Article 2(2) of the Council Decision mentioned above states the obligation of each Member State no nominate a national correspondent for Eurojust for terrorist matters, with the main tasks of having access to and collect all relevant information concerning prosecutions and convictions for terrorist offences and sent it to Eurojust. The type of information that should be transmitted to Eurojust is listed in Article 2(4) of that Council Decision.

For the purpose of this publication, it is important to underline that Article 2(6) of Council Decision 2005/671/JHA establishes the obligation of the Member States to make available to the judicial authorities of other Member States relevant information on ongoing terrorist offences. This information might be exchange among the judicial authorities during a coordination meeting organised at Eurojust premises. In that case, the information will be exchanged among the judicial authorities "in accordance with national law and relevant international legal instruments". This paragraph is as follow:

> Each Member State shall take the necessary measures to ensure that any relevant information included in documents, files, items of information, objects or other means of evidence, seized or confiscated in the course of criminal investigations or criminal proceedings in connection with terrorist offences can be made accessible as soon as possible, taking

account of the need not to jeopardise current investigations, to the authorities of other interested Member States in accordance with national law and relevant international legal instruments where investigations are being carried out or might be initiated or where prosecutions are in progress in connection with terrorist offences.

To ensure the transmission of information on the basis of this provision, Eurojust elaborated a template and distributed it among the national correspondents for Eurojust for terrorist matters.

The purpose of the transmission of this information to Eurojust is twofold. On the one hand, Eurojust can develop a more proactive role in the cases transmitted to it, thus suggesting coordination among the national authorities of different Member States investigating the same terrorist organisation.

On the other hand, on the basis of such information, Eurojust drafts its contribution to the Te-SAT report of Europol. This information is also a valuable source of information for the drafting of the Terrorist Conviction Monitor of Eurojust.

3.5.4 The Feedback to the Competent National Authorities

According to Article 13a(1) EJ Decision, "Eurojust shall provide competent national authorities with information and feedback on the results of the processing of information, including the existence of links with cases already stored in the Case Management System". This legal provision can give the impression that the feedback is provided by Eurojust at the end of the Case. However, Eurojust feedback to the national authorities could be interpreted in a wider sense in order to include all type of support and assistance provided by Eurojust during the development of a Case (tasks of the National Members, tasks of the College, powers of the National Members, among others).

3.6 The Case Management System of Eurojust

3.6.1 Concept and General Structure

The Case Management System (CMS) is the electronic database set up at Eurojust premises to ensure the proper management of operational information, and support the operational work of the National Members and the College (Article 16(2)(a) Council Decision of Eurojust).

It also facilitates the access to information on ongoing investigations and prosecutions (Article 16(2)(b)), and promotes the interaction between the National Members involved in the same operational case, and makes possible the production of the necessary statistics on casework.

The CMS is also intended to "facilitate and monitoring of lawfulness and compliance with the provisions of this Decision concerning the processing of personal data" (Article 16(2)(c) Council Decision of Eurojust). It allows the DPO to ensure and verify the application of the data protection rules applicable to Eurojust. Lastly, the CMS also supports the exchange of structured data between Eurojust and the Member States by establishing connections between the CMS and the ENCS.

As it is clearly stated in Article 16(6) of Council Decision of Eurojust, "for the processing of case related personal data, Eurojust may not establish any automated data file other than the Case Management System".

From a technical point of view, the CMS makes use of a software tool developed in the framework of the European Pool against Organised Crime (EPOC) established in 2002 at the initiative of the Italian Ministry of Justice, with the support and co-financing of the Commission within the Criminal Justice Programme. Subsequent editions of that EPOC have allowed the progressive improvement of the functionalities of the CMS, including the registration of cases, the storage and sharing of case-related documents and personal data, the automated detection of possible links between the cases, and the preparation of casework statistics. This tool also facilitates the planning of coordination meetings and the completion of the corresponding minutes. The last edition of this Project (the EPOC IV) is intended to ensure the interoperability between the national judicial information systems and the CMS of Eurojust and facilitate the exchange of information through the ENCS.

The CMS "is composed of temporary work files and of an index which contain personal and non-personal data" (Article 16(1) thereto).

3.6.2 The Link of the CMS with the Member States: The Eurojust National Coordination System (ENCS)

Article 12(2) of Council Decision of Eurojust establishes the obligation of the Member States to setting up a Eurojust National Coordination System (ECNS),[18] with two main objectives: ensuring the coordination at national level of the different actors of judicial cooperation in criminal matters, and facilitating the carrying out of the tasks of Eurojust within the corresponding Member State.

Firstly, with the setting up of the ENCS the European legislator intends to provide certain coherence at national level to the work of the contact points, national correspondents and National Members of Eurojust. The idea behind this

[18] The Informal Working Group for the implementation of the new Eurojust Decision decided to create the so-called "Fiche suedoise" for collecting information on the setting up of the ENCS in the 27 Member States. The "Fiche suedoise" are updated regularly and distributed among the participants of Eurojust meetings related to the implementation of the Eurojust Council Decision 2008.

task is to promote synergies among all of them, so that they can work in close cooperation and not in competition to each other.

The interest of the European legislator of ensuring this close cooperation at national level is particularly clear regarding EJN and Eurojust. The Council Decision of Eurojust of 2009 has reiterated this idea in many of its paragraphs. Article 25a(1) declares that both entities should maintain "privileged relations with each other, based on consultation and complementarity, *especially between the national member, the European Judicial Network contact points of the same Member State and the national correspondents for Eurojust and the European Judicial Network*". Therefore, the National Member should inform the EJN contact points, on a case-by-case basis, "of all cases which they consider the Network to be in a better position to deal with" (Article 25a(1)(a)).

Also with this spirit of consultation and complementarity, Article 12(5) entrusts ENCS with the tasks of "assisting in determining whether a case should be dealt with the assistance of Eurojust or of the European Judicial Network" (paragraph (b)), and "assisting the national member to identify relevant authorities for the execution of requests for, and decision on, judicial cooperation, including regarding instruments giving effect to the principle of mutual recognition" (paragraph (c)).

Secondly, the ENCS is expected to improve the carrying out of the tasks of Eurojust within that Member State, ensuring, among other measures, "that the Case Management System referred to in Article 16 receives information related to the Member State concerned in an efficient and reliable manner" (Article 12(5)(a)). Certainly, one of the major difficulties of Eurojust in its first decade has been the lack of enough information, from a qualitative and quantitative point to view, to performance its tasks properly. However, the drafting of this paragraph is not providing details on how, in which manner, could the actors involved in ENCS—and mainly the national correspondent for Eurojust designated to that purpose—contribute to increasing the amount and quality of the information storaged in CMS.

Considering that the information storage in CMS is related to ongoing investigations and prosecutions initiated at national level, it seems that the main role of the national correspondent for Eurojust (and other actors involved in CMS at national level) would be to *assist and support* the national authorities conducting investigations and prosecutions in the provision of relevant information to Eurojust. This is confirmed by Recital (11) of the Council Decision of Eurojust, according to which "the Eurojust National Coordination System *should not have to be responsible for actually transmitting information to Eurojust*, Member States should decide on the best channel to be used for the transmission of information to Eurojust".

Certainly, most of the Member States are discussing and drawing at this moment the possible flow of information among the competent judicial authorities and the National Members, as well as the best channel to be used to transmit information to Eurojust. They will have to take in mind that, in order to ensure the reception of information in an structured manner, Eurojust has adopted the template to be filled in cases of Article 12(5)–(7).

The national correspondents for Eurojust will probably have a relevant role to play in ensuring that judges and prosecutions fill in that Eurojust template properly.

To this aim, it is more than advisable that the Member States designate, as national correspondents for Eurojust, prosecutors and investigating judges located in strategic offices and courts, from which they could easily be aware of ongoing investigations and prosecutions with a transnational dimension.

The internal flow of information, the channels decided at national level to transmit information to Eurojust and the particular role assigned in this context to the national correspondents for Eurojust are without prejudice to the existing particularities in the fight against terrorism, in accordance with the Council Decision 2005/671/JHA of 20 September 2005 on the exchange of information and cooperation concerning terrorist offences. In this particular field, the national correspondents for Eurojust for terrorist matters do have the obligation to transmit information to Eurojust, making use of the corresponding template.

3.7 Processing and Protection of Personal Data by Eurojust

The processing and protection of personal data by Eurojust are governed by Arts 14–25 of EJ Decision, developed further by the Rules of procedure on this matter adopted by the College on 21 October 2004 and approved by the Council on 24 February 2005[19] (EJ DP rules).

A first relevant element of the abovementioned rules is its scope of application. It is clear that the rules on data protection should apply to the operational information and personal data stored in the CMS for the purposes laid down in Art 14(1) EJ Decision. However, it is not so clear whether such rules should also apply to the exchange of information with the national judicial authorities, and more specifically to the information transmitted by the competent authorities to Eurojust. We have seen in previous sections that the daily operational work of the College members with the national judicial authorities generates a constant exchange of information and personal data related to ongoing investigations and prosecutions. From the perspective of the national judicial authorities, information is exchanged with Eurojust in the context of requests for judicial cooperation that are (at least also) covered by the Council Framework Decision 2008/977/JHA on the protection of personal data processed in the framework of police and judicial cooperation in criminal matters. This is the legal instrument applicable for the transmission of information between the law enforcement authorities and Europol. Therefore, the same legal framework seems to be applicable mutatis mutandis to the exchange of information between national judicial authorities and Eurojust.

Closely related to this matter, a second relevant question is whether all the information and documents received by Eurojust are subject to the EJ DP rules as soon as they are received by the National desks. Also in this case, the answer is rather complex mainly because the amount and quality of the information received

[19] OJ C 68, 19.3.2005, p. 1.

by the desks in quite different. Eurojust has not adopted yet common guidelines on the type of information to be transmitted and on how to process such information internally. Such rules, which are under discussion at the moment, will be extremely useful from two different perspectives.

First, the rules will ensure the insertion in the CMS of consistent data thus improving the identification of links between the cases and the provision of appropriate feedback to the national judicial authorities in accordance with Art. 13a EJ Decision.

Second, both Eurojust and the national judicial authorities of the Member States will have a common understanding on which type of information and documents should be transmitted to Eurojust for the appropriate development of its tasks. Eurojust does not need to receive the entire judicial file that is in the hands of the national prosecutor or investigating judge: the support of Eurojust is focused on the transnational dimension of national investigations and proceedings, and therefore only the documents and information related to this transnational dimension should be transmitted to this EU body. In the specific cases where Eurojust is providing a very punctual support (for example, to overcome obstacles for the execution of an European Arrest Warrant), the respective College member only needs certain details of the investigation: those related to the suspect or convicted person who is the subject of the arrest and further surrender. The data that are not necessary for the purposes for which Eurojust is carrying out its tasks and powers should not be processed by this agency, but deleted from CMS and/or sent back to the national authority who provided them.

A third relevant element, also closely link to the previous paragraphs, is whether all the information provided by the national judicial authorities to the national desk and on the basis of which Eurojust is providing support and assistance should be inserted in CMS, or only the entities listed in Art. 15 EJ Decision. The CMS allows for the insertion of pdf documents and other relevant attachments provided to the College members by national judicial authorities, but this technical possibility cannot be a valid argument to conclude that all information received by the desks should be included in CMS: it is, as mentioned, only a technical possibility. On this relevant matter, the National desks maintain different approaches: some of them includes any single document into CMS, whilst others insert only the data (of some of the data) enumerated in Art. 15 EJ Decision.

Article 15 EJ Decision contains two lists of personal data that can be processed by Eurojust. The first list, more extensive, enumerates the information and personal data related to suspects of convicted persons. The second list is applicable to witnesses or victims in a criminal investigation or in criminal proceedings supported by Eurojust. The lists should be applied restrictively: both paragraphs clarify that Eurojust can "only" process such data, although "in exceptional cases" and "for a limited period of time" Eurojust may also process "other data relating to the circumstances of an offence where they are immediately relevant to and included in ongoing investigations which Eurojust is helping to coordinate" [Art. 15(3) EJ Decision]. Those personal sensitive data "revealing racial or ethnic origin, political opinions, religious or philosophical beliefs, trade union membership, and data concerning health or sex life" could be processed by Eurojust "only when such data are necessary for the national investigations concerned as well as for coordination within Eurojust". In both cases, the Data Protection Officer should be informed on the processing such personal data.

In Eurojust's view, EJ rules on data protection rules constitute a robust, effective and tailor-made regime absolutely necessary to ensure proper execution of the tasks of Eurojust. When Eurojust was established in 2002, the then existing structure of the three pillars motivated that Eurojust could not be governed by Directive 95/46/EC, neither by Regulation 45/2001, and therefore a specific set of rules were adopted. Eurojust also considers that the very comprehensive data protection rules in place are necessary in view of the specific nature of the work done in the field of judicial cooperation.[20]

The need for a strong set of rules for the processing and protection of personal data is true as soon as no other rules are applicable for the tasks undertaken by this agency in the area of judicial cooperation in criminal matters. If other rules regulated the rights of the suspects, the management of the case from a procedural point of view, it wouldn't be the case. In fact, in the areas of judicial cooperation properly covered by EU legal instruments (for instance the right of the suspect to access to the judicial file), such legal instruments should prevail, and not the rules on data protection.

Apart from the considerations described above, the EJ Decision regulates in detail the principles for the processing of information by Eurojust, the rights of the individuals concerned, and the supervision scheme of the processing of information carried out at Eurojust premises.

With regard to the principles, the necessity principle in embedded in Art. 14(1) EJ Decision, according to which Eurojust may process personal data "insofar as it is necessary to achieve its objectives, (. . .) within the framework of its competence and in order to carry out its tasks". The principles of proportionality, lawfulness and proportionality are referred to in Art. 14(3) EJ Decision. According to the first, "personal data processed by Eurojust shall be adequate, relevant and not excessive in relation to the purpose of the processing". According to the second, "personal data processed by Eurojust shall be processed fairly and lawfully".

Time limits for the storage of personal data are laid down in Art. 21 EJ Decision. The guiding principle of this legal provision is that personal data can not remain in CMS, neither on paper at the national desks, if Eurojust is not longer providing support to this investigation and/or prosecution. Eurojust maintains a restrictive interpretation of the situations listed in Art. 21(2) and the College members receive a reminder on the need to delete personal data when any of the time limits is approaching. The main consequence of the application of this legal provision is that, when a case is closed, all the information related to the case that has been stored in CMS is deleted. This includes not only personal data, but also other data that are extremely important for other purposes (strategic, statistics) as the

[20] Alonso Blas (2012), p. 6.

description of the criminal offence(s) committed at national level, a brief description of the investigation in the framework of which the support of Eurojust has been requested, or the type of support provided (including for example legal problems analysed during a coordination meeting). Whilst it is clear that the name of the suspect and other personal data cannot remain in CMS when they are not necessary, other type of information included in CMS should be kept, either in CMS or in a separate repository. As this has not been the case so far, Eurojust does not have a memory of the cases solved. To start building such memory, in January 2013 the College approved a pilot project on Case illustrations that is still ongoing.[21]

The rights of the individuals concerned by an investigation or a criminal procedure supported by Eurojust are regulated in Arts. 19 and 20 EJ Decision. It is important to take into consideration that those rights can be exercised by the citizens with regard to the information and personal data received, processed and/or exchanged by Eurojust, but not with regard to the specific investigative measures, preventive measures and/or other acts of judicial cooperation that are supported by Eurojust. For the later, the rules of criminal procedure and the rules for the protection of suspects in the area of judicial cooperation should apply. This would be for instance the case of the "control deliveries" supported by Eurojust. Being the control delivery an investigative measure, the fundamental rights protecting the suspect subject to this measure should be those contained in the criminal code and/or the rules of judicial cooperation. From the point of view of the rules on data protection, we cannot consider that investigative measures are an exception to the general rule of the right of information: it rather seems that the rules on data protection are not applicable to the specific investigative measures adopted in a criminal case. This can be the reason why the EJ Decision did not foresee the right to be informed. The confusion arrived because the EJ DP rules included "ex novo" such fundamental right.

Security of the data processed by Eurojust is governed by Art. 22 EJ Decision, Arts. EJ DP rules and related internal provisions adopted by Eurojust in accordance with parr. (2) thereto.

Eurojust has a two-level system of supervision of compliance with the existing rules for the processing and protection of personal data. First, the Data Protection Officer (DPO) is a Eurojust staff member under the direct authority of the College, although acting independently in the performance of its duties [Art. 17(1) EJ Decision]. DPO has to ensure Eurojust compliance with the rules on the processing and protection of personal data [Art. 17(2) EJ Decision]. Secondly, the Joint Supervisory body has the main tasks of monitoring and ensuring that Eurojust activities comply with the rules governing the processing and protection of personal data (Art. 23 EJ Decision).

[21] See Council document 13880/13 LIMITE EJUSTICE 65. Brussels, 20 September 2013.

3.8 Cooperation with EU Partners

In accordance with Art. 26(1) EJ Decision, Eurojust maintains "cooperative relations" with the Commission, the Council and the European Parliament, as well as with other EU institutions set up by the Treaties (Court of Auditors).

The Commission is "fully associated with the work of Eurojust" and participate in that work "in the areas within its competence" [Art. 11(1) EJ Decision]. From an operational point of view, the Commission "may be invited to provide its expertise" in the context of investigations and prosecutions supported by Eurojust [Art. 11(2) EJ Decision]. Conversely and based on Eurojust's expertise, the Commission may seek Eurojust's opinion on all draft instruments prepared in the area of police and judicial cooperation in criminal matters [Art. 32(3) EJ Decision].

In July 2012, the Commission and Eurojust signed a Memorandum of Understanding with the purposes of improving cooperation and establishing a mechanism for efficient, regular and transparent contacts and exchange of information between them. A separate Memorandum of Understanding on the management of financial transfers was concluded on 11 January 2010.

Eurojust also maintains a close relation with the Council of the EU. Relevant decisions adopted by the College need further confirmation and/or approval by the Council, as it is the case of the elections of the President and Vice-Presidents of Eurojust. Important documents (Rules of Procedure, Annual Reports, Agreements of Cooperation and Memorandums of Understanding) should be submitted to the Council for approval as well. Eurojust informs the Council "of any plans it has for entering into any negotiations and the Council may draw any conclusions it deems appropriate" [Art. 26(2) EJ Decision].

Representatives from Eurojust attend different working parties of the Council in order to provide its expertise during discussions and benefit from the experience and knowledge of the Member States and the General Secretariat of the Council.

The relations and cooperation with the European Parliament is fluent and mutually beneficial, especially following the entry into force of the Treaty of Lisbon.

In October 2009, Eurojust and Europol signed an Agreement of Cooperation in the framework of which both units, located in The Hague, work in close cooperation to coordinate police and judicial investigations against cross-border crime and facilitate the setting up and running of JITs. To ensure the mutual exchange of relevant information, Eurojust is connected to SIENA and associated to most of Europol AWFs (Focal points). As mentioned, Europol attends many of the coordination meetings organised by Eurojust and, in an spirit of reciprocity, Eurojust is also informed and have the possibility of participating in some of the operational meetings financially supported by Europol.

It also coordinate national police investigations against serious cross-border crime.

In the framework of a formal criminal investigation, the analysis provided by Europol can help enormously to identify the links between the members of the criminal organisation and therefore to tackle them with the most effective approach. Obviously, in practice, judicial authorities and law enforcement authorities, as well as Europol and Eurojust, must work together and in close cooperation to fight against serious crime.

At strategic level, Eurojust contributes to the (TE-SAT) Reports and SOCTA Reports and participate actively in the EU policy cycle for serious and organised crime in order to enhance its judicial dimension.

Eurojust has also nominated a representative as member of the Programme Board of the Europol Cybercrime Centre (EC3), and seconded an expert to EC3 on part time basis.

The Eurojust–Europol exchange programme has increased notably the understanding of the structure and the working methods of the respective organisations.

OLAF and Eurojust should also cooperate and work closely, in the particular area of the protection of the financial interests of the EU. To this aim, a Practical Agreement on Arrangements of Cooperation between Eurojust and OLAF was signed in September 2008. OLAF, as an administrative unit of the Commission, is in an optimal position to discover irregularities affecting the budget of the EU. However, when OLAF has complited the administrative investigation and the file is transmitted to the judicial authorities of the Member States involved, the information would have to be transmitted also to Eurojust, specially—but not only—in cases with a cross-border dimension. We say "not only" because Article 3(3) EJ Decision expressly recognises Eurojust competence to develop its tasks in cases involving only a Member State and the Community. In both situations, the Eurojust request to initiate a criminal investigation or prosecution, although not mandatory, could contribute to the initiation of criminal investigations at national level, as a follow-up of OLAF administrative investigations. As regards the EU networks involved in judicial cooperation in criminal matters, Eurojust and EJN enjoy privileged relations based on "consultation and complementarity" [Art. 25a(1) EJ Decision].

At operational level, both bodies were created to provide support and assistance to the judicial authorities of the Member States in cross-border cases. In general terms, EJN contact points are in the best position to deal with specific questions in bilateral cases, whilst the involvement of Eurojust is more useful in bilateral complex cases, and in multilateral cases. Although in practice it is nos always easy to identify whether a case should be dealt by Eurojust or by EJN, a fair distribution of roles and a good communication between both bodies is crucial.

In order to ensure a fair distribution of roles, the National Members of Eurojust have to inform the EJN contact points, on a case-by-case basis, "of all cases which they consider the Network to be in a better position to deal with" [Art. 25a(1)(a)].

With the aim of facilitating a good communication, the National Member, EJN contact points, and national correspondents of Eurojust and EJN are involved in ENCS [Art. 12(2) EJ Decision]. The Eurojust CMS should be accessible by EJN contact points and national correspondents [Art. 16b(1) EJ Decision], and this CMS may be linked to EJN secure telecommunications connection [Art. 16(3) EJ Decision].

If considered appropriate, the EJN contact points of the Member States concerned by a case can be invited to participate in a coordination meeting organised by Eurojust. With a more general character, Art. 25a(1)(c) EJ Decision states that EJN contact points "may be invited on a case-by-case basis to attend Eurojust meetings", which could have an operational or strategic nature.

Lastly, the Secretariats of EJN, of the JITs Experts Network and of the so-called Genocide Network form part of the staff of Eurojust, although they function as separated units [Art. 25a(1)(b) and (2) EJ Decision].

3.9 Cooperation with Third States, and International Organisations and Bodies

Criminal organisations and networks operating in the area of Freedom, Security and Justice do not limit their criminal activities to the territory of the 27 Member States: very frequently, serious cross-border crime originates from and/or has third States as main destiny. Some practical examples extracted from the EU Organised Crime Threat Assessment (OCTA) 2011[22] can illustrate better this situation.

Although cocaine from Colombia still has Spain and Portugal as main entry points, it has been partially routed via some parts of the Sahel region, including Mali, and is possibly controlled by terrorist cells linked to Al Qaeda in the Islamic Maghreb or other rebel groups.[23] To ensure the dismantling of criminal organisations using these routes and be able to bring suspects to court, Eurojust needs to work closely not only with the judicial authorities of the Member States, but also with Colombia and other Iberoamerican countries where cocaine is produced, as well as with African countries recently involved in these criminal activities.

Another relevant new trend in the relocation of illegal immigration flows from the Mediterranean maritime routes to the borders between Greece and Turkey.[24] To tackle this criminal phenomenon, a close cooperation with Turkish authorities is crucial.

A considerable number of Russian-Albanian speaking groups have increased their activities related to carbon credit fraud, payment card fraud and commodity counterfeiting.[25] To ensure the arrest of the suspects and the freezing and further confiscation of their criminal assets, Eurojust needs fluent relations with Russia and the Western Balkan countries that are not yet part of the EU.

Internet has become a fantastic tool for everybody, including criminal organisations involved in high-tech cybercrime, audiovisual piracy, recruitment of

[22] Available at www.europol.europa.eu/latest_publications/31.

[23] OCTA 2011, pp. 8–9 and 13.

[24] OCTA 2011, p. 8.

[25] OCTA 2011, pp. 8 and 30.

victims of trafficking in human beings, or child pornography, among many others[26]: in these cases, the victims can be citizens of the European Union, the suspects can have their residence in United States and service providers can be located in India: permanent contacts and a close cooperation with US and Indian authorities will be absolutely necessary to bring the suspects to jail.

These are only some practical examples of the need to involve third countries in the daily work of Eurojust.[27] Some figures can also provide a better view. In 2011, third States were involved in more than 211 operational cases of Eurojust: the most frequently requested third State was Switzerland, followed by Norway, Croatia, US, Turkey, Bosnia and Herzegovina, Serbia, Morocco, and Liechtenstein.[28] In 2012, Third States participated in 49 coordination meetings, with Norway (10), Switzerland (9), Turkey (6), US (5), Albania (5), the former Yugoslav Republic of Macedonia (3), Croatia (2) and Serbia (2) as the most frequently involved parties[29].

To be more effective in fighting crime involving third States, in certain cases Eurojust may conclude an Agreement of cooperation in accordance with Article 26a(1) EJ Decision, or request the third State for the nomination of a contact point among its competent judicial authorities. Eurojust can also sign a Memorandum of Understanding, or become observer before certain organisations or networks.

As mentioned before, the College has also the possibility of posting liaison magistrates to third countries on behalf of all Member States. This possibility, introduced by the EJ Decision of 2008, has not been implemented in practice yet, although discussions on the tasks, functions and professional status of such Liaison Magistrates are ongoing.

3.9.1 Agreements of Cooperation, Liaison Prosecutors and Contact Points

According to paragraphs (2)–(9) of Article 26a EJ Decision, the signature of an Agreement of cooperation provides the appropriate legal framework to the exchange of operational information, including personal data, related to ongoing investigations and prosecutions. It also facilitates the attendance of competent authorities from the third State to coordination meetings organised by eurojust, because the information and personal data can be easily shared with them. In 2011, judicial authorities from third States participated in approximately a quarter of the total number of coordination meetings organised by Eurojust.[30]

---

[26] OCTA 2011, pp. 9 and 45.

[27] See Labayle and Nilsson (2010), p. 206.

[28] Eurojust Annual Report 2011, p. 41.

[29] Eurojust Annual Report 2012, p. 36.

[30] See Eurojust Annual Report 2011, p. 41.

This circumstance (the exchange of personal data and sensitive information on ongoing investigations and prosecutions) requires, among other measures, an exhaustive verification of the level of protection of personal data in the third State with whom Eurojust pretends to start negotiations.

At the moment, Eurojust has signed Agreements of cooperation with Norway, Iceland, US, former Yugoslav Republic of Macedonia, Switzerland and Liechtenstein.[31] The draft Agreement of Cooperation between Eurojust and the Republic of Moldova was submitted to the Council by letter of the President of Eurojust in December 2013.

Norway has seconded a Liaison Prosecutor working regularly at Eurojust premises and can register its own casework. A new Liaison Prosecutor from US will be nominated soon.

The negotiation of cooperation agreements with the Russian Federation and Ukraine being a top priority for Eurojust. Contacts to explore the possibilities of initiating negotiations on cooperation with the State of Israel, Albania, Bosnia and Herzegovina, Montenegro, Serbia and Turkey, among others, are ongoing.[32]

Eurojust promotes strategic discussions with third States on the practical application of legal instruments on judicial cooperation in criminal matters, including problems identified and best practices. With this approach, a *Seminar on Judicial Cooperation in Criminal Matters between the EU Member States and the Southern Neighbours of the EU* was organised in Limassol, Cyprus, on 4–5 October 2012,[33] and a *Workshop on the application of the Mutual Legal Assistance and Extradition Agreements between the European Union and the United States of America* took place on 25–26 October 2012 at Eurojust premises.

Lastly, approximately 30 third States (including Argentina, Canada, Egypt, India, Korea and the Russian Federation) have designated one or more national competent authorities as contact points for Eurojust.

---

[31] These Agreements are available at http://www.eurojust.europa.eu/doclibrary/Eurojust-framework/Pages/agreements-concluded-by-eurojust.aspx.

[32] See Eurojust Annual Report 2011, p. 53.

[33] The Seminar was co-organised by Eurojust, the Cyprus Presidency of the EU, the Attorney General of the Republic of Cyprus and the European Commission (DG Enlargement—TAIEX). It focused on the current legal and practical issues, obstacles and best practices in four areas of judicial cooperation (mutual legal assistance, extradition, transfer of criminal proceedings and transfer of sentenced persons) between the EU Member States and the Southern neighbours of the EU (Algeria, Egypt, Israel, Jordan, Lebanon, Libya, Morocco, Palestinian Authority, Syria and Tunisia). The questionnaire that served as a basis for the preparation of this Seminar is Council Document 13425/12 COPEN 190 USA 26 JAIEX 64 (Brussels, 7 September 2012). The replies of the questionnaire are marked as a LIMITE Council Document.

3.9.2 Memoranda of Understanding. Eurojust as Observer in Certain International Institutions and Bodies

The Memorandums of Understanding are generally signed between Eurojust and international organisations and bodies with relevant tasks and initiatives in the area of criminal justice, including the analysis of analyse new trends and modus operandi, evaluation of the implementation of policies and legal instruments in this field, and/or facilitation of contacts and proposal of good practices on judicial cooperation in a particular region.

So far, Eurojust has signed Memorandums of Understanding with the Iberoamerican Network of International Legal Cooperation (IberRed), the United Nations Office of Drugs and Crime (UNODC), Interpol and Frontex.[34]

In the framework of the Memorandum of Understanding with Iber-Red, the Eurojust National Member for Spain and the Secretariat of this network are in permanent contact, thus facilitating the identification of the judicial authorities competent to dismantle criminal organisations operating in both regions, and facilitating enormously the execution of requests for mutual legal assistance and extradition.

Eurojust has also designated contact points for the International Criminal Court and Interpol and the Maritime Analysis and Operations Centre.

Following an exchange of letters between both organisations, the Financial Action Task Force (FATF) agreed to accept Eurojust as an observer organisation at its Plenary meeting in June 2009. Contact details of the Eurojust contact point were provided to FATF immediately afterwards. FATF is an intergovernmental body focused on the development and promotion of legal, regulatory and operational standards and measures for combating money laundering and terrorist financing.[35] The *FATF 40 Recommendations against Money Laundering*, originally adopted in 1996 and last revised in 2012, and the *9 Special Recommendations on Terrorist Financing* adopted in 2001, have been endorsed by many States and regions around the world. FATF also monitors the progress of its members in the implementation of the implementation, and examines new trends and risks affecting the international financial system. The Eurojust contact point for FATF actively participates at the plenary meetings of this body and, based on the practical experience of Eurojust, provides valuable contributions in the annual typologies meetings on new trends and risks.

[34] The Memorandums of Understanding are also available at http://www.eurojust.europa.eu/doclibrary/Eurojust-framework/Pages/agreements-concluded-by-eurojust.aspx.

[35] Website of FATF is www.fatf-gafi.org.

References

Alonso Blas D (2012) Data protection at Eurojust: a robust, effective and tailor-made regime. Leaflet published by Eurojust, p 6

Gutierrez Zarza A (2010) Delincuencia organizada, autoridades judiciales desorganizadas y el aún poco conocido papel de Eurojust. In: Aranguena Fanego C (dir) Espacio de Libertad, Seguridad y Justicia: últimos avances en cooperación judicial penal, p 72

Labayle M, Nilsson GH (2010) The role and organisation of Eurojust. Added value for judicial cooperation in criminal matters. In: Monar J (ed) The institutional dimension of the European Union's area of freedom, security and justice. P. Lang, Brussels, p 195

Chapter 4
Europol

4.1 Mission

Europol is an agency of the EU based in The Hague (The Netherlands). Its task is to support the law enforcement authorities of the Member States in the investigations and operations aimed at preventing and fighting serious cross-border crime.

At operational level, Europol acts as a hub for the collection and analysis of intelligence and police information received from the Member States. This information is crucial to identify the modus operandi and movements of existing criminal organisations and networks, and agree on common actions and operations by the Member States concerned to tackle them. Europol provides assistance and support to the law enforcement authorities during such common actions and operations, including those carried out through JITs.

At a strategic level, the intelligence and police information collected and analysed by Eurojust is extremely useful for the identification of new trends of criminality or existing criminal organisations threatening the security of the EU citizens. The results of this analysis are reported to both the EU institutions (the Council, the Counter-Terrorist Coordinator, among others) and Member States in order to coordinate preventive and repressive actions in response to such threats.

4.2 Legal Framework

As agreed by the Treaty of Maastricht and on the basis of its Art. k. 3, the Convention on the establishment of an European Police Office (Europol Convention) was adopted in 1995 and came into force in 2007.[1]

[1] OJ C 316, 27.11.1995, p. 2.

Á.G. Zarza (ed.), *Exchange of Information and Data Protection in Cross-border Criminal Proceedings in Europe*, DOI 10.1007/978-3-642-40291-3_4,

In order to improve Europol's effectiveness, the Europol Convention was amended by three successive Protocols. The "Money laundering Protocol"[2] extended the competences of Europol to money laundering activities. The "JITs Protocol"[3] provided the legal basis for the participation of Europol in Joint Investigation Teams and enabled Europol to request national police authorities to initiate criminal investigations. The "Danish Protocol"[4] improved the legal provisions on the processing and protection of personal data, conferred further powers to the European Parliament and extended the scope of competences of Europol. When these Protocols came into force in 2007, the EU institutions had prepare the initiative of the Commission for a new Europol legal framework.[5]

Council Decision 2009/371/JHA establishing the European Police Office (Europol), was adopted on 6 April 2009[6] with the following main objectives: (1) the establishment of Europol as an entity of the Union funded from the EU general budget; (2) the enhancement of the role of the European Parliament in the democratic control of Europol (through the adoption of its budget and the discharge in respect of the implementation of such budget for each financial year, among others); (3) the reinforcement of the tasks of Europol in the support of national police investigations; (4) an extension of competency, so that Europol may assist the Member States in combating specific forms of serious crime, regardless the existence or not of an established or proven link with organised crime; (5) the participation of Europol staff in JITs; (6) new powers for Europol to create and manage information processing systems, (7) improved legal provisions for the processing and protection of personal data, including the setting up of a Europol Data Protection Officer, (8) clear rules for the establishment and maintenance of cooperative relations between Europol and other EU institutions and bodies, including Eurojust, (9) clear rules for the exchange of information and cooperation with third States and international organisations, and (10) some simplification of the procedures and tasks of the Management Board. The EP Decision entered into force on 1 January 2010.

Following the entry into force of the Treaty of Lisbon and in accordance with Art. 88 TFEU, a Proposal for a Regulation on the European Union Agency for Law Enforcement Cooperation and Training (Europol) and repealing Decision 2009/

---

[2] Protocol drawn up on the basis of Article 43(1) of the Europol Convention amending Article 2 and the Annex to that Convention ("the Money Laundering Protocol"), OJ C 358, 13.12.2000, p. 2.

[3] Protocol amending the Europol Convention and the Protocol on the privileges and immunities of Europol, the members of its organs, the deputy directors and the employees of Europol (the JIT Protocol), OJ C 312, 16.12.2002, p. 2.

[4] Protocol drawn up on the basis of Article 43(1) of the Europol Convention amending that Convention ("the Danish Protocol"), OJ C 002, 6.1.2004, p. 3.

[5] COM(2006) 817 final. 2006/0310 (CNS). Proposal for a Council Decision establishing the European Police Office (Europol), COM(2006) 817 final, SEC(2006) 1682 and SEC(2006) 1683. Brussels, 20.12.2006. For a general view on the Commission proposal, see Peers (2007).

[6] OJ L 121/37, 15.5.2009. *See* De Moor (2010), p. 1089.

371/JHA and 2005/681/JHA was presented by the Commission in March 2013.[7] At the time of writing this Proposal is under discussion within the internal bodies of the Council and the European Parliament.

4.3 Structure and Governance

Europol is staffed by officials recruited from the Member States among all existing public bodies that are responsible under national law for the preventing and combating criminal offences. Member States may second national experts to Europol (Art. 39(5) EP Decision).

Europol liaises with a single national unit for each Member State [Arts. 1(2) and 8 EP Decision]. These national units second one or more liaison officers to Europol headquarters. The liaison officers constitute the national liaison bureaux and are instructed by their national units to represent the national interests within Europol (Art. 9 EP Decision).

The Europol Director is appointed by the Council and accountable to the Management Board in respect of the performance of his duties. Assisted by three Deputy Directors, he is responsible for the performance of the tasks assigned to Europol and its day-to-day administration (Art. 38 EP Decision).

The external Management Board of Europol is composed of one representative of each Member State and one Commission representative. The Chairperson of the Management Board is supported by a Secretariat (Art. 37 EP Decision).

4.4 Tasks

Europol has been entrusted with many important tasks in the area of police cooperation in criminal matters (Arts 5–7 EP Decision).

The principal functions of Europol are related to:

- The collection and analysis of intelligence and police information, and the reporting of analysis results to the competent authorities of the Member States through the Europol National Units, including the cases of major international events;
- The provision of support to the law enforcement authorities of the Member States in police investigations and operations, including requesting the initiation, conduct or coordination or investigations, and the setting up of JITs, and

[7] COM(2013) 173 final. Brussels, 27.3.2013. 2013/0091 (COD).

– The preparation of threat assessments, strategic analyses and general situation reports relating to its objectives, including organised crime threat assessments.

Europol has also been designated as the Central Office for combating euro counterfeiting (Art. 5(5) EP Decision) and is also responsible for the European Cybercrime Centre (EC3).

Among its additional tasks, Europol provides advice on police investigations on the basis of its specialised knowledge in investigative methods and innovative techniques [Art. 5(3)(a) EP Decision].

Subject to the availability of enough human and budgetary resources, Europol is also responsible for providing training to police authorities, in close cooperation with the European Police College (CEPOL), facilitating technical support between the Member States, developing crime prevention methods, and improving technical and forensic methods and analysis, as well as investigative procedures [Art. 5(4)(d) EP Decision].The Prüm helpdesk is based at Europol premises.

4.5 Exchange of Information with the Europol National Units

The Europol National Units are the liaison body between Europol and the competent authorities of the Member States. They are tasked with the supply of relevant information and intelligence to Europol, including information for storage in its databases and information that has resulted from the evaluations undertaken by the Europol National Units. They are also responsible for responding to requests for information, intelligence and advice from Europol [Art. 8(4) EP Decision].

Direct contacts between Europol and police national authorities, although possible, are subject to conditions determined by the Member States, including the prior involvement of the Europol National Units [Art. 8(2) EP Decision].

In order to ensure the frequent and secure exchange of information with the Member States, Europol has established a Secure Information Exchange Network Application (SIENA).

4.6 The Europol Information System, Analysis Work Files and Focal Points

The Europol Information System is the tool set up by Europol in order to process relevant information and personal data necessary for the performance of Europol's tasks (Art. 11 EP Decision). This system allows the entry of specific types of information (entities) listed in Art. 12(2) to (4) EP Decision. The Europol National Units have direct access to the system (Art. 13 EJ Decision).

In specific areas of crime involving at least two Member States, Europol opens Analysis Work Files (AWFs) for the purposes of analysing information to assist criminal investigations.[8] Quite recently, Europol has introduced a new AWF concept aimed at reorganising the AWF system and making it a more flexible and useful tool for the Member States. The new concept integrates three main elements: the existing AWF, the Focal Points (FP), and the Target Group (TG).

The AWFs are the Europol specific tools enabling the storage, modification and use of data concerning specific areas of crime. Within an AWF, a FP is focused on certain phenomenon that are commodity based (e.g. euro counterfeiting), thematic based (e.g. VAT fraud) or a regional angle (Baltic Sea). The TGs are particular projects intended to support international criminal investigations or criminal intelligence operations against a specific suspects or organised crime groups.

4.7 Processing and Protection of Personal Data by Europol

As the analysis of intelligence and police information one of the main tasks of Europol, this EU agency receives, processes and exchanges a huge amount of information and personal data with the Member States, other EU agencies and, under more restrictive conditions, third countries and international institutions and bodies.

The reception, processing and exchange of information and personal data is subject to strict and tailor-made rules on data protection,[9] which are contained in the EP Decision (Arts. 10–35, 40, 41, 46 and 52), and developed further by Council Decision 2009/936/JHA of 30 November 2009, adopting the implementation rules for Europol analysis work files,[10] the Council Decision 2009/968/JHA of 30 November 2009 adopting the rules on the confidentiality of Europol information[11] and the Council Decision 2009/934/JHA of 30 November 2009 adopting implementing rules for Europol's relations with partners, including exchange of personal data and classified information.[12]

The principles of the Council of Europe Convention for the Protection of Individuals with regard to Automatic Processing of Personal Data of 28 January 1981, and those of the Recommendation No R(87)15 of the Committee of Ministers

[8] See Council Decision 2009/936/JH A of 30 November 2009 adopting the implementing rules for Europol analysis work files. OJ L 325, 11.12.2009, p. 14.

[9] The observance by Europol of strict rules for the processing and protection of personal data has been one of the reasons for the setting up of the European Cybercrime Centre (EC3) at Europol premises. On this matter see Drewer and Ellermann (2012), pp. 381–395.

[10] OJ L 325, 11.12.2009, p. 14.

[11] OJ L 332, 17.12.1009, p. 17.

[12] OJ L 325, 11.12.2009, p. 6.

of the Council of Europe of 17 September 1987 (Article 27 Europol Council Decision) must be strictly observed by Europol (Art. 27 EP Decision).

The transfer of information from the Member States to Europol (through the National Units) is governed by the Council Framework Decision on the protection of personal data processed in the framework of police and judicial cooperation in criminal matters, and related implemented provisions adopted by the Member States. According to the principle of purpose limitation, personal data provided by Europol can only be used by the Member States "in order to prevent and combat crimes in respect of which Europol is competent, and to prevent and combat other serious forms of crime" (Art. 19 EP Decision).

The rights of access, correction and deletion of personal data are recognised by Arts 30 and 31 EP Decision.

The supervision scheme of Europol is based on the existence of an internal Data Protection Officer (DPO) who is a member of Europol staff (Art. 28 EP Decision), and an external Joint Supervisory Body composed of representative from the national data protection authorities of the 28 Member States (Art. 34 EP Decision).

4.8 Cooperation with EU Partners

Europol maintains good relations, regularly exchanges information and is engaged in close cooperation with EU institutions, bodies and agencies with competences in the area of Freedom, Security and Justice of the EU.

As mentioned, the Europol Decision enhanced the control of the European Parliament over Europol "in order to ensure that Europol remains a fully accountable and transparent organisation, due account being taken of the need to safeguard the confidentiality of operational information" [Recital (29) EP Decision].

In line with Art. 5, Europol engages intensive cooperation with the Council, chiefly with the Standing Committee on Operational Cooperation on Internal Security (COSI), in ensuring the Internal Security of the European Union. Together with COSI and the Member States, Europol is responsible for the implementation of the EU Policy Cycle for organised and serious international crime. The Serious Organised Crime Threat Assessment (SOCTA) Report issued by Europol in March 2013, was the basis for the adoption by Council of its Conclusions on setting up the EU's priorities for the fight against serious and organised crime between 2014 and 2017,[13] and the following steps of the cited EU Policy cycle.

For the appropriate performance of its tasks, Europol may conclude agreements or working arrangements with the EU bodies, offices and agencies, including Eurojust [Article 22(1)(a) EP Decision]. As mentioned above, in June 2004 Europol

[13] Adopted at JHA Council Meeting, Luxembourg, 6 and 7 June 2013.

and Eurojust signed an Agreement of cooperation that provides a framework for improving mutual understanding and complementary activities.

Cooperation between both institutions, particularly in respect the exchange of information, could be improved further through a clearer delimitation of the analytical capabilities of Europol and Eurojust, and further reflection on the type of information that Eurojust could gather, process and exchange with the national authorities of the Member States without overlapping with the analysis of intelligence and police information that is the core business of Europol.

From a temporal point of view, in most of cases the intelligence and preliminary information collected in an investigation would be better processed and analysed by Europol. This information and intelligence is based on mere suspicious and suppositions requiring further analysis and, in most of cases, additional police investigative measures. In this context, Europol can provide a real added value by composing the overall picture of the criminal organisation or network, or the movements of a small group of individuals moving quickly from one to another Member State of the EU. Europol can support and ensure coordination of the investigative techniques and operations undertaking on the ground and continue composing the overall situation of the investigation. "Before making a request for the initiation of a criminal investigation, Europol shall inform Eurojust accordingly" [Art. 7(2) EP Decision].

The opening of an investigation by a national prosecution office requires more accurate information and data. When such information, contrasted enough, has been included in the judicial file, could be transmitted to Eurojust in order to request its assistance with the transnational dimension of the investigations and/or prosecutions. The National Members of Eurojust, with the support of the Case Analysis Unit where appropriate, will facilitate the identification of the legal instruments of judicial cooperation applicable in this particular case, provide assistance in the removal of obstacles of judicial cooperation in criminal matters, and ensure a good communication and a fluent exchange of information among the judicial authorities of the Member States concerned by the formal investigation or prosecution.

Lastly, Europol provides technical support and/or host the secretariat of several networks and platforms of practitioners. As example, the secretariat of the Camden Assets Recovery Inter-Agency Network (CARIN) is hosted by Europol.

4.9 Cooperation with Third States, International Organisations and Bodies

For the appropriate performance of its tasks, Europol is entitled to conclude strategic and operational arrangements with third states and organisations, which "may concern the exchange of operational, strategic or technical information, including personal data and classified information".

To ensure consistency with the general policy of the EU in respect of third States, the Council has determined with which third States and organisations Europol may conclude agreements [Article 26(1)(a) EP Decision]. These are listed in Council Decision 2009/935/JHA of 30 November 2009.[14]

On the other hand, in the context of the Agreement between the EU and US on the processing and transfer of financial messaging data for the purposes of the Terrorist Financing Tracking Programme (TFTP), Europol has been entrusted with the verification on whether the requests of the US Treasury Department comply with the principles of necessity and proportionality, among others, listed in Art. 4 of the Agreement.[15]

References

De Moor A (2010) The Europol decision: transforming Europol into an agency of the European Union. Common Mark Law Rev 47(4):1089

Drewer D, Ellermann J (2012) Europol's data protection framework as an asset in the fight against cybercrime. ERA Forum 13:381–395

Peers S (2007) Europol: the final step in the creation of an "Investigative and operational" European police force. In: Statewatch analysis. Human Rights Centre, University of Essex. www.statewatch.org/news/2007/jan/europol-analysis.pdf

[14] OJ L 325, 11.12.2009, p. 12.

[15] OJ L 195, 27.7.2010, p. 5. *See* in more detail Europol Report, "Europol Activities in Relation to the TFTP Agreement. Information note to the European Parliament. 1 August 2010 – 1 April 2011".

Chapter 5
The European Anti-Fraud Office (OLAF)

5.1 Mission

The European Anti-Fraud Office (OLAF) is a service of the European Commission with a special independent status for conducting internal and external administrative investigations against fraud, corruption and any other illegal activity detrimental to the financial interests of the Union. OLAF was established in 1999 on the basis of Article 280 of the former EC Treaty.

5.2 Legal Framework

OLAF was established by Commission Decision 1999/352/EC, ECSC, Euratom of 28 April 1999.[1] The investigations conducted by OLAF were regulated further in the following three EU legal instruments:

- Regulation (EC) No. 1073/1999 of 25 May 1999 concerning investigations conducted by the European Anti-Fraud Office[2];
- Council Regulation (EURATOM) No. 1074/1999 of 25 May 1999 concerning investigations conducted by the European Anti-Fraud Office[3];
- Interinstitutional Agreement of 25 May 1999 between the European Parliament, the Council of the European Union and the Commission of the European Communities concerning internal investigations by the European Anti-Fraud Office.

---

[1] OJ L 136, 31.5.1999, p. 20.

[2] OJ L 136, 31.5.1999, p. 1.

[3] OJ L 136, 31.5.1999, p. 8.

Á.G. Zarza (ed.), *Exchange of Information and Data Protection in Cross-border Criminal Proceedings in Europe*, DOI 10.1007/978-3-642-40291-3_5,

Following a lengthy and challenging legislative process that started in 2006,[4] the legal framework of OLAF has been amended quite recently by the following instruments:

- The Regulation (EU, Euratom) No. 883/2013 of 11 September 2013 concerning investigations conducted by the European Anti-Fraud Office (OLAF) (OLAF Regulation)[5] has repealed both the Regulation (CE) No. 1073/1999 and the Council Regulation (Euratom) No. 1074/1999;
- Following the entry into force of the OLAF Regulation, the Commission Decision 2013/478/EU of 27 September 2013[6] (OLAF Decision) introduced relevant changes in the Decision 1999/352/EC, ECSC, Euratom establishing the European Anti-Fraud Office.

It should be noted, however, that recital (5) OLAF Decision states that, in the event that a European Public Prosecutor's Office is established, the Commission "should assess the need for revision of this Decision". A Communication on "Improving OLAF's governance and reinforcing procedural safeguards in investigations: A step-by-step approach to accompany the establishment of the European Public Prosecutor's Office"[7] was submitted by the Commission jointly with the Proposals for a Eurojust draft Regulation[8] and a EPPO draft Regulation.[9]

5.3 Structure and Governance

OLAF is composed of staff members from all the Member States with specialised expertise in the prevention and fight against irregularities affecting the financial interests of the EU and related matters, and are recruited from custom authorities, police officers, judicial authorities and experts on information technology and data protection matters.

---

[4] See Commission proposal for amending Regulation 1073/1999 (COM(2006) 244); Resolution of 20 November 2008 of the European Parliament (P6_TA_PROV(2008) 553); Reflection paper on the reform of the European Anti-Fraud Office (OLAF) (SEC(2010) 859); Amended Proposal for a Regulation amending the Regulation (EC) No. 1073/1999 concerning investigations conducted by the European Anti-Fraud Office and repealing Regulation (Euratom) No. 1074/1999 (COM(2011) 135 final). On the relevant changes suggested by the Commission in 2006 and the Parliament Resolution of 2008 see Staicu (2008), p. 117.

[5] OJ L 248, 18.9.2013, p. 1.

[6] OJ L 257, 28.9.2013, p. 19.

[7] COM(2013) 533 final. Brussels, 17.7.2013.

[8] Proposal for a Regulation on the European Union Agency for Criminal Justice Cooperation (Eurojust). COM(2013) 535 final. Brussels, 17.7.2013.

[9] Proposal for a Council Regulation on the establishment of the European Public Prosecutor's Office. COM(2013) 534 final. 2013/0255 (APP). Brussels, 17.7.2013.

A Supervisory Committee is responsible "for the regular monitoring of the discharge by the Office of its investigative function" (Art. 4 OLAF Decision and Art. 15 OLAF Regulation).

OLAF is headed by a Director-General appointed by the Commission. In exercising OLAF investigative powers, the Director-General neither seeks nor takes instructions from the Commission, any government or any other institution or body [Arts. 3 and 5(1) OLAF Decision and Art. 17 OLAF Regulation].

5.4 Tasks

The tasks of OLAF are focused on the initiation and conduction of internal and external administrative investigations "for the purpose of strengthening the fight against fraud, corruption and any other illegal activity adversely affecting the Union financial interests, as well as any other act or activity by operators in breach of Community provisions" [Art. 2(1) OLAF Decision].

In the context of internal administrative investigations, OLAF's tasks also cover "serious facts linked to the performance of professional activities which may constitute a breach of obligations by officials and servants of the Communities likely to lead to disciplinary and, in appropriate cases, criminal proceedings", as well as analogous breach of obligations of members of EU institutions, bodies and agencies not submitted to the Staff Regulations and the Conditions of Employment of Other Servants of the Communities [Art. 2(1)(b) OLAF Decision].

OLAF is also tasked with the preparation of legislative acts and regulatory provisions in the areas of activity of the Office, including relevant instruments under Title V TFUE and instruments on the protection of the euro against counterfeiting [Art. 2(4) OLAF Decision]. This Office is also responsible for the organisation of training courses and the provision of technical assistance for the protection of the euro against counterfeiting [Art. 2(2) OLAF Decision].

As regards external administrative investigations, before taking any decision on whether opening or not an investigation, OLAF is entitled to inform the Member State concerned on the existence of certain information which suggest that has been certain irregularities against EU Budget within its territory [Art. 3(6) OLAF Regulation]. The irregularities can be related to fraud, corruption or any other illegal activity affecting the financial interests of the EU, including those connected with a grant agreement, a decision or a contract concerning Union funding.

The decision to open an external investigation is taken by the Director-General, on his own initiative or upon request, on the basis of the information also provided by any third party or anonymous information [Art. 5(1) and (2) OLAF Regulation].

Following an OLAF request, the competent authorities of the Member States are requested to take appropriate precautionary measures under their national law, including those aimed at freezing and safeguarding evidence [Art. 7(7) OLAF Regulation].

External investigations are conducted by the OLAF staff members designated by the Director-General and under his direction. The designated OLAF staff members are entrusted with the carry out of on-the-spot checks and inspections in the Member States, including access to all information and documents relating to the matter under investigation (Art. 3 OLAF Regulation). These checks and inspections are subject to Council Regulation (Euratom, EC) No. 2185/96 of 11 November 1996 and the sectorial rules referred to in Art. 9(2) of that Regulation.[10]

OLAF staff members should conduct investigations in an objective and impartial manner, with full respect of the principle of presumption of innocence and the procedural guarantees laid down in Art. 9 OLAF Regulation. A person within the scope of an investigation has *inter alia* the rights to avoid self-incrimination, to be assisted by a person of his choice during an OLAF interview, and to use any of the official languages of the EU, as well as to receive a copy of the record of such interview [Art. 9(2)]. When the investigation is completed and before the drawing up of the conclusions, the person concerned should be given the opportunity to comment on facts concerning him [Art. 9(4)].

On completion of an OLAF investigation, a report should be drafted under the authority of the Director-General. According to Art. 11(1) OLAF Regulation

> the report shall give an account of the legal basis for the investigation, the procedural steps followed, the facts established and their preliminary classification in law, the estimated financial impact of the facts established, the respect of the procedural guarantees in accordance with Article 9 and the conclusions of the investigation.

The report should be accompanied by some recommendations on whether any disciplinary, administrative, financial or judicial action should be taken by the Member State(s) concerned. It should also "specify in particular the estimated amounts that should be recovered, as well as the preliminary classification in law of the facts established".

The reports are sent to the competent authorities of the Member State (s) concerned by the OLAF investigation. OLAF is entitled to follow-up measures taken at national level on the basis of its reports (see below).

OLAF commitment in the investigations and prosecutions against fraud and other criminal offences affecting the financial interests of the EU goes beyond its involvement in the possible initiation of a criminal investigation. According to Art. 12(4) OLAF Regulation, "the Office may provide evidence in proceedings before national courts and tribunals in conformity with national law and the Staff Regulation".

Art. 11(2) OLAF Regulation states the evidential value of OLAF reports,[11] as follows:

---

[10] OJ L 312, 23.12.1995, p. 1.

[11] On this matter, see Gonzalez-Herrero and Madalina Butincu (2009), p. 90.

> In drawing up such reports and recommendations, account shall be taken of the national law of the Member State concerned. Reports drawn up on that basis shall constitute admissible evidence in administrative or judicial proceedings of the Member State in which their use proves necessary, in the same way and under the same conditions as administrative reports drawn up by national administrative inspectors. They shall be subject to the same evaluation rules as those applicable to administrative reports drawn up by national administrative inspectors and shall have the same evidentiary value as such reports.

5.5 Exchange of Information with the Competent Authorities of the Member States Concerned

When undertaking its tasks, OLAF is entitled to transmit to the competent authorities of the Member State(s) concerned the information obtained in the course of an external investigation. The provision of such information will enable the national competent authorities to take appropriate action and provide the necessary assistance and support to OLAF.

Following receipt of an OLAF report and its recommendations, the competent national authorities should inform OLAF "in due time, on their own initiative or at the request of the Office, of the action taken on the basis of the information transmitted to them under this Article" [Art. 12(3) OLAF Regulation]. Although action in response to OLAF reports and recommendations is not mandatory, follow-up decisions taken at national level following receipt of such material is expected to improve the protection of the financial interests of the EU by the Member States. The transmission of OLAF reports and recommendations to Eurojust could also contribute to a more effective fight against fraud and related criminal offences. On the basis of this information, Eurojust may request the initiation of a criminal investigation at national level. Compliance with a request is not mandatory, but should the judicial authorities decide not to comply with such Eurojust request, they must report to Eurojust "without undue delay of their decision and of the reasons for it" (Art. 8 EJ Decision).

5.6 The OLAF Case Management System and the Anti-Fraud Information System

The CMS of OLAF was created to provide a reliable register of OLAF cases. The case-specific part of the CMS, which includes case files for new, ongoing and closed cases, allows case handlers to record case-related documents at any time during the life cycle of the case. It is also used to create official documents from OLAF work form templates, and it supports system searches and allows for visualisation and arrangement of scanned case documents.

Several modules run alongside the case-specific part of the CMS. The Intelligence Request Module is used to manage requests from within OLAF and from its external partners for case support to the intelligence units. The Mutual Assistance Module includes the capacity to organise and record the information that OLAF sends to the Member State authorities, and shows the progress of investigations that take place in the Member States. It also includes an address book with the names and details of various contact persons in the Member States and third countries. The Legal and Judicial Advice Module is used to manage and record requests for legal advice. It enables case handlers to request advice on specific cases and gives the legal experts access to the relevant case files, thereby ensuring that advice is based on a full understanding of all the issues concerned.

To prevent, detect and prosecute operations leading to breaches of customs or agricultural legislation, the competent authorities need to exchange high-quality data in a secure manner and within a well-defined framework. The Anti-Fraud Information System (AFIS) provides the organisational and technological platform for a rapid dissemination of information. AFIS enables a better exchange of information among the competent national authorities, and between them and OLAF. It also allows for the carrying out of monitoring procedures and more effective cooperation.

5.7 Processing and Protection of Personal Data by OLAF

As one of the services of the Commission, OLAF is subject to Regulation (EC) 45/2001 on the protection of individuals with regard to the processing of personal data by Commission institutions and bodies (DP Regulation).[12]

In principle, DP Regulation should govern the processing and protection of the information and personal data processed by OLAF mainly through its Case Management System. However, OLAF has experienced an extensive application of such rules that, at the moment, are regulating every step of OLAF administrative proceedings.[13] This situation is a good example of the tendency of the data protection rules to cover areas of law that have not been properly covered by administrative or criminal legislation. In the case of OLAF, the rules governing the administrative investigations are hardly developed in OLAF legal instruments, and have been developed further through "guidelines" (mainly through the "Guidelines on investigation procedures for OLAF staff"). In parallel to this "soft law", a strong set of rules for the processing and protection of personal data has been developed progressively and at the moment, as mentioned, is governing every step of OLAF administrative proceedings. As it has been also mentioned in other sections to this book, the extensive application of the rules on data protection to areas of law traditionally covered by procedural rules is a valid option: however, it seems rather paradoxical that a set of rules adopted to regulate the use of a tool for OLAF

[12] OJ L 8, 12.1.2001, p. 1.

[13] See Laudati (2013), p. 14.

investigations (mainly CMS) are in currently governing the entire investigations and the work of OLAF staff.

Another possible element for further reflection is the fact that OLAF investigations are not subject to tailor-made rules on data protection (as it is the case of Eurojust and Europol), but to the rules applicable to the EU institutions and bodies (DP Regulation). The daily application of the DP Regulation by OLAF constitutes a good example of how the general legal framework of data protection (including supervision by EDPS) is flexible enough and offers workable solutions for the particular needs of the (administrative) investigations without generating undue administrative burdens.[14] In other words, OLAF experience shows that EU general rules on data protection are flexible enough to provide an adequate legal framework for the processing and protection of personal data in the area of investigations, without the need to create tailor-made rules for individual agencies or services.

5.8 Cooperation with EU Partners

Article 13 OLAF Regulation is devoted to the relations of OLAF with Eurojust and Europol. The administrative arrangements signed between OLAF and Eurojust, and between OLAF and Europol, have been mentioned in previous sections of this publication.

On the relations between OLAF and Eurojust, it might be relevant to mention that Art. 13(2) expressly recognises OLAF obligation to transmit Eurojust relevant information on the reports sent to the national judicial authorities with a view to the initiations of criminal investigations and prosecutions.

Lastly, OLAF manages some IT platforms supporting exchange of information in matters related to the protection of the financial interests of the Union, as the Customs Information System (CIS) and the Custom Files Identification Database (FIDE).

Eurofisc was established on the basis of Eurocanet, a pilot initiative involving OLAF (Eurocanet).[15] OLAF also supports the European Partners Against Corruption (EPAC), on the basis of which the Network of contact points against corruption was established by Council Decision 2008/852/JHA of 24 October 2008.[16]

---

[14] See Laudati (2013), p. 14.

[15] *See* in this Part III, Chap. 6, Sect. 6.3.

[16] OJ L 301, 12.11.2008, p. 38.

5.9 Cooperation with Third States and International Organisations and Bodies

OLAF is entitled to agree administrative arrangements with the competent authorities of third States and with international organisations and bodies. "Such arrangements may concern exchange of operational, strategic or technical information, including, on request, progress reports". Proper alignment with the policies and priorities of the Commission and of the European External Action Service should be ensured [Art. 14(1) OLAF Regulation].

References

Gonzalez-Herrero J, Madalina Butincu M (2009) Eucrim 3:90
Laudati L (2013) Data protection at OLAF. Eucrim 1:14
Staicu A (2008) The reform of OLAF. Legal framework and the proposal for a Regulation amending the OLAF Regulation. Eucrim 3–4:117

Chapter 6
EU Networks for Administrative, Police and Judicial Cooperation in Criminal Matters

6.1 The Financial Intelligence Units (FIUs)

A Financial Intelligence Unit (FIU) is a national office or body responsible for receiving, processing and reporting on suspicious or unusual transactions that may be relevant to combating money laundering and terrorism financing.

When creating their FIUs, countries around the world have adopted different models. Some FIU are empowered to directly exchange of information with law enforcement and/or competent judicial authorities, while according to other models, the type of information the FIUs collect can only be shared with other FIUs.

In 1995, a group of FIUs met at the Egmont Arenberg Palace in Brussels to establish an informal group to facilitate international cooperation in the fight against money laundering and terrorism financing. Since then, the so-called Egmont Group has met regularly to improve cooperation between FIUs in the areas of information exchange, training, and to share expertise and best practices.[1]

The Egmont Group has created a secured encrypted capability for sharing operational information in accordance with its "Principles of information exchange" adopted in The Hague in June 2001.

Based on a Finnish initiative, the European Union adopted Decision 2000/642/JHA of 17 October 2000 concerning arrangements for cooperation between Financial Intelligence Units (FIUs) of the Member States in exchanging information.[2] Under this umbrella, some Member States established fiu.net in 2002 (www.fiu.net), a decentralised network application allowing EU FIUs to exchange information

---

This section has been drafted by Ángeles Gutiérrez Zarza. The opinions expressed by the author are personal and do not necessary coincide with those of the institution she is working for.

[1] *See* www.egmontgroup.org.

[2] OJ L 271, 24.11.2000, p. 4.

Á.G. Zarza (ed.), *Exchange of Information and Data Protection in Cross-border Criminal Proceedings in Europe*, DOI 10.1007/978-3-642-40291-3_6,

among themselves. The network currently operates with the support of the Commission's s-TESTA, but ongoing discussions suggest that Europol's secure SIENA application may be used in the future to operate the network instead.[3]

Since 2005, in the framework of Directive 2005/60/EC (Third Anti-Money Laundering Directive),[4] EU FIU's receive, analyse and disseminate reports on suspicious transactions related to money laundering and terrorism financing.

In 2006, the Commission set up an informal "EU Financial Intelligence Unit Platform", which in April 2008 issued a report titled "Confidentiality and data protection in the activity of FIUs".[5] The report stresses the importance of striking an adequate balance between the detection, disclosure and analysis of suspicious transaction reports for the purposes of combating money laundering and terrorism financing, and granting necessary respect for data protection safeguards and rights. Particular attention is given to the data protection rights of individuals and the confidentiality requirements applicable to the activities of FIUs.[6]

The Proposal for a Directive on the prevention and use of the financial system for the purpose of money laundering and terrorist financing gives an important role to the FIUs in this particular area. Recitals (40) and (40a) are as follows:

> (40) Improving the exchange of information between FIUs within the EU is of particular importance to face the transnational character of money laundering and terrorist financing. The use of secure facilities for the exchange of information, specially the decentralised computer network FIU.net and the techniques offered by that network should be encouraged by Member States. The initial exchange between the FIUs of information related to money laundering or terrorist financing for analytical purposes and which is not further processed or disseminated should be allowed unless it would compromise the legitimate interests of the Member State or of a natural or legal person.
>
> (40a) In order to be able to respond fully and rapidly to enquiries from FIUs, obliged entities need to have in place effective systems enabling them to have full and timely access through secure and confidential channels to information about business relationships that they maintain or have maintained with specified legal or natural persons. Member States could, for instance, consider putting in place systems of banking registries or electronic data retrieval systems which would provide FIUs with access to information on bank accounts. Member States should also consider establishing mechanisms to ensure that competent authorities have procedures in place in order to identify assets without prior notification to the owner[7].

[3] Commission Communication, "Overview of information management in the area of Freedom, Security and Justice", COM(2010) 385 final, p. 14.

[4] OJ L 309, 25.11.2005, p. 15.

[5] Available at http://ec.europa.eu/internal_market/company/docs/financial-crime/fiu-report-confidentiality_en.pdf.

[6] See Study on "Best practices in vertical relations between the Financial Intelligence Unit and (1) law enforcement services and (2) Money Laundering and Terrorist Financing Reporting entities with a view to indicating effective models for feedback on follow-up to and effectiveness of suspicious transaction reports", available at http://ec.europa.eu/dgs/home-affairs/e-library/documents/categories/studies/index_en.htm.

[7] Council doc. 16775/13 EF 239 ECOFIN 1063 DROIPEN 147 CRIMORG 152 CODEC 2698.

6.2 The Asset Recovery Offices (ARO)

Most Member States have created or designated national Asset Recovery Offices (AROs) to promote and coordinate the location, freezing and further confiscation of the proceeds and benefits of transnational crimes.

The main instrument governing AROs is Council Decision 2007/845/JHA of 6 December 2007 concerning cooperation between Asset Recovery Offices of the Member States in the field of tracing and identification of proceeds from, or other property related to, crime.[8] This Decision stresses the need to promote direct communication, the frequent exchange of information and the adoption of best practices among AROs, either upon request or spontaneously,

> for the purposes of the facilitation of the tracing and identification of proceeds of crime and other crime related property which may become the object of a freezing, seizure or confiscation order made by a competent judicial authority in the course of criminal or, as far as possible under the national law of the Member States concerned, civil proceedings.[9]

The AROs exchange information in accordance with Swedish Framework Decision 2006/960/JHA of 18 December 2006 on simplifying the exchange of information and intelligence between law enforcement authorities of the Member States of the European Union,[10] using the form Annexed thereto. When filling out this form, the initiating ARO must specify "the object of and the reasons for the request and the nature of the proceedings", as well as "details on property targeted or sought (bank accounts, real estate, cars, yachts and other high value items), and the natural and/or legal persons presumed to be involved (e.g., names, addresses, dates and places of birth, date of registration, shareholders, headquarters)" (Article 3(2) of the Council Decision on AROs).

The Council Framework Decision on AROs contains a provision on data protection (Article 5). It states that *the use of information* which has been exchanged directly or bilaterally under this Decision "shall be subject to the national data protection provisions of the receiving Member State, where the information shall be subject to the same data protection rules as if they had been gathered in the receiving Member State". The *personal data processed* should be protected "in accordance with the Council of Europe Convention of 28 January 1981 (...) and, for those Member States who have ratified it, the Additional Protocol of 8 November 2001 to that Convention, regarding Supervisory Authorities and Transborder Data Flows". Additionally, personal data obtained under the Decision by law enforcement authorities should be handled with respect for the principles of Recommendation No R(87) 15 of the Council of Europe Regulating the Use of Personal Data in the Police Sector.

---

[8] OJ L 332, 18.12.2007, p. 103.

[9] Articles 1(1) and 2(1) of the Council Decision on AROs.

[10] OJ L 386, 29.12.2006, p. 89.

The Commission also actively supports an informal EU Asset Recovery Offices Platform, created in 2009, that organises high-level conferences and financing projects. Most of the innovative projects supported by the Commission in this area are dedicated to managing former criminal assets, reusing them for the benefit of society.

The abovementioned platform works in close cooperation with Camden Assets Recovery Inter-Agency Network (CARIN), an informal and global network for practitioners and experts offering support to judicial authorities determined to remove the illicit wealth from the criminal organisations. CARIN was formally created in 2004 to promote cross-border and inter-agency cooperation, exchange of information, and innovative methods and techniques to ensure the identification and further confiscation of the proceeds from crime. CARIN secretariat is located at Europol's headquarters.[11]

6.3 The European Network of National Officials to Detect and Combat New Cases of Cross-Border VAT Fraud (Eurofisc)

Eurofisc is a decentralised network of national officials who are responsible for the detection and prosecution of cross-border VAT frauds. Eurofisc was established in alignment with the Conclusions of the Economic and Financial Affairs Council on 7 October 2008 and the experiences of Eurocanet; it was officially created via the Council Regulation (EU) No 904/2010 of 7 October 2010.[12]

Eurofisc's main responsibility is to ensure that VAT is correctly applied in cross-border transactions taxable in a Member State other than the one where the supplier is established, and to take swift and targeted action when VAT fraud does occur. Eurofisc's main tool is an information exchange system that includes an early warning mechanism, permitting the rapid and accurate storage and sharing of information.[13]

The exchange of information should respect the rights and obligations laid down by Directive 95/46/EC of 24 October 1995 on the protection of individuals with regard to the processing of personal data and on the free movement of such data, although some limitations are envisioned in order to combat VAT fraud effectively.

[11] The 2nd edition of CARIN handbook is accessible at www.europol.europa.eu/sites/default/files/publicatoins/carin-manual_0.pdf.

[12] Council Regulation (EU) No 904/2010 of 7 October 2010 on administrative cooperation and combating fraud in the field of value added tax (recast), OJ L 28, 12.10.2010, p. 1.

[13] *See* www.eurofisc.eu.

6.4 The National Cybercrime Alert Platforms, the European Cybercrime Platform, and the European Cybercrime Centre (EC3)

In line with the corresponding JHA Council Conclusions adopted in October 2008,[14] most of the Member States have established national cybercrime alert platforms in order to collect, analyse, and exchange information about offences committed on the internet. The offences identified at national level were initially reported to the European Cybercrime Platform (ECCP) managed by Europol, which analysed the information and exchanged it with the competent authorities in the framework of its mandate.

A major step forward in the prevention and fight against cybercrime was done in January 2013 with the official setting up of the European Cybercrime Centre (EC3) at Europol. EC3 is conceived as the focal point in the EU to ensure efficient preventive measures and operations to tackle different categories of serious crimes committed on-line, including crimes:

- Committed by organised groups to generate large criminal profits (online fraud)
- Causing serious harms to victims (online child pornography)
- Affecting critical infrastructures and information systems in the EU (the so call "cyber attacks")

EC3 is expected to facilitate the detention and prosecution of criminal organisations, networks and individuals related to the criminal offences mentioned above. It will also develop forensic tools and innovative investigative measures, provide specialised training in this field, and promote a close cooperation with the private sector and the research community. The centre will issue threat assessment reports on cybercrime.[15]

6.5 The European Judicial Network (EJN)

The European Judicial Network in criminal matters (EJN) was created in 1998 to facilitate the practical application of the legal instruments on criminal justice cooperation. The contact points of the network are experienced judges, prosecutors and representatives of the Ministries of Justice, committed to help other practitioners involved in transnational investigations and criminal proceedings. Each

[14] Council Conclusions on setting up national alert platforms and a European alert platform for reporting offences on the Internet, JHA Council of 24.10.2008. *See also* Council Conclusions concerning an Action Plan to implement the concerted strategy to combat crime, General Affairs Council, 26.4.2010.

[15] See more in detail https://www.europol.europa.eu/ec3.

Member State has also nominated a "tool correspondent". The Commission has appointed a contact point for the matters within its competence.

The EJN has created an impressive set of tools facilitating, among other matters, the identification of the competent authority to whom a particular request for mutual legal assistance should be addressed, and the identification of the legal instrument applicable in a specific situation. Another tool allows the issuing of the request online that can be downloaded into the computer of the user. EJN tools are available through the website of this network.[16]

For the appropriate development of their tasks, the contact points are entitled to receive and exchange information on a particular investigation and prosecution, including personal data, through the secure communication connection mentioned in Article 9 of the Council Decision 2008/976/JHA of 16 December.[17] The possibilities of this connection, specially with regard to its use by the national correspondents for Eurojust, national correspondents for Eurojust for terrorist matters, National Members of Eurojust and liaison magistrates appointed by Eurojust (referred to in Article 9(4)) are not fully developed yet.

6.6 The Joint Investigation Team (JIT) Experts Network

The Joint Investigation Team Experts Network was established in July 2005, in accordance with The Hague Programme, "with a view to encouraging the use of JITs and exchanging experiences and best practices"[18]. The Network also promotes and assists in the setting up, running and evaluation of JITs. It is composed of practitioners designated as contact points by the Member States. Eurojust and Europol have also nominated a JIT contact point for the Network.

The JIT Experts Network Secretariat forms part of the staff of Eurojust, although it functions as a separate unit [Art. 25a(2) EJ Decision].[19]

6.7 The Genocide Network

The European Network of contact points in respect of persons responsible for genocide, crimes against humanity and war crimes (Genocide Network) was set up by Council Decision 2002/494/JHA of 13 June[20]. According to Art. 2 of this Decision:

[16] www.ejn-crim.europa.eu.

[17] OJ L 348, 24.12.2008, p. 130.

[18] The Hague Programme, p. 13.

[19] See more information in Eurojust News. Issue No 9—June 2013 and at www.eurojust.europa.eu/Practitioners/networks-and-fora/jitsnetwork/Pages/JITs-network.aspx.

[20] OJ L 167, 26.6.2002, p. 1.

> (1) Each contact point's tasks shall be to provide on request, in accordance with the relevant arrangements between Member States and applicable national law, any available information that may be relevant in the context of investigations into genocide, crimes against humanity and war crimes (. . .), or to facilitate cooperation with the competent national authorities.
>
> (2) Within the limits of the applicable national law, contact points may exchange information without a request to that effect.

The Secretariat of the Genocide Network forms part of the staff of Eurojust, although it functions as a separate unit [Art. 25a(2) EJ Decision].

6.8 The Contact-Point Network Against Corruption

The Contact-point Network against Corruption was created by Council Decision 2008/852/JHA of 24 October 2008[21], with two main objectives: the setting up of a forum for the exchange of best practices and experiences concerning the prevention and fight against corruption, and the facilitation of the communication between its members at both operational and strategic level.

Upon request of this network, its Secretariat could form part of Eurojust staff [Art. 25a(3) EJ Decision].

[21] OJ L 301, 12.11.2008, p. 38.

Part IV
Exchange of Information and Cooperation Between the Member States

Chapter 7
EU Information Systems and Databases

7.1 Searching for Individuals and Vehicles. The New Schengen Information System (SIS-II)

The Schengen Agreement was originally signed in 1985 between France, Germany, Belgium, Luxembourg and the Netherlands for the abolition of the internal borders and the free movement of their citizens in the common internal territory. A Convention on the implementation of the Schengen Agreement was signed on 19 July 1990, permitting the expansion of the Schengen territory to include other Member States and the establishment of common rules regarding visas, rights of asylum and checks at external borders.

At the moment 26 European countries are signatories to the Convention of Application of the Schengen Agreement, including 22 Member States[1] and Norway, Iceland, Switzerland and Liechtenstein. The UK and Ireland participate in some aspects of Schengen, particularly in police and judicial cooperation in criminal matters, the fight against drugs and SIS. Denmark can decide whether to apply any new measure constituting a development of the Schengen *acquis*. Bulgaria and Romania, which fulfil the criteria to apply in full the Schengen acquis, are waiting at the time of writing for a Council decision on the lifting of controls at their internal borders.

In 1997, a Protocol attached to the Treaty of Amsterdam integrated the Schengen Agreement into the EU *acquis*.

The Schengen Agreement included some "compensatory measures" to ensure the security of citizens in an area without internal borders[2], mainly by reinforcing

---

The opinions expressed by the author are personal and do not necessary coincide with those of Eurojust.

[1] Namely Belgium, France, Germany, Luxembourg, The Netherlands, Portugal and Spain (1995); Italy and Austria (1997); Greece (2000), Denmark, Sweden and Finland (2001); Czech Republic, Estonia, Hungary, Lithuania, Latvia, Malta, Poland, Slovakia and Slovenia (2007).

[2] According to Article 23 of the Schengen Borders Code, a Member States may exceptionally reintroduce border controls at its internal borders where there is a serious threat to public policy or

Á.G. Zarza (ed.), *Exchange of Information and Data Protection in Cross-border Criminal Proceedings in Europe*, DOI 10.1007/978-3-642-40291-3_7,

cooperation and coordination among administrative, law enforcement and judicial authorities of the Member States in the fight against crime.[3] To facilitate the practical application of these "compensatory measures", the signatories agreed to the establishment of the Schengen Information System (SIS).

SIS is a joint centralised information system operational since 1995, including a national section in each participating Member State (N-SIS) and a technical support function (C-SIS) initially located in Strasbourg, France. This IT system is supplemented by the Supplementary Information Request at the National Entry (SIRENE) network.

The Member States can issue different types of alerts for persons and goods, namely:

- Persons wanted for arrest for extradition purposes (Article 95);
- Nationals of third countries for the purposes of refusing entry (Article 96);
- Missing persons (Article 97);
- Witnesses or persons summoned to appear before the judicial authorities in connection with criminal proceedings to account for acts for which they are being prosecuted, or persons who face a criminal judgement or a summons to report to serve a penalty of deprivation of liberty (Article 99); and
- Certain objects sought for the purposes of seizure or for use as evidence in criminal proceedings (i.e., motor vehicles, trailers and caravans, stolen firearms, blank official documents, identity papers and banknotes) (Article 100).

The competent authorities of the Member States participating in SIS may carry out automated searches, which produce a "hit" when the details of the person(s) or goods sought match those of an existing alert. In those cases, the law enforcement authority may request supplementary information about particular person(s) or goods via the network of SIRENE bureaux.

Law enforcement and judicial authorities, among others, can access SIS in accordance with the Member State's internal rules. Europol has access to the alerts for persons wanted for arrest for extradition purposes, and to the alerts for persons subject to special surveillance measures, while Eurojust has access to the alerts for

---

internal security (see Regulation (EC) No. 562/2006 establishing a Community Code on the rules governing the movement of persons across borders (Schengen Borders Code), as amended by Regulation (EU) No. 610/2013).

[3] Although not directly related to the exchange of information, see on Schengen the Judgment of the Court of Justice of the EU of 5 September 2012, annulling Council Decision 2012/252/EU of 26 April 2010 supplementing the Schengen Borders Code as regards the surveillance of the sea external borders in the context of operational cooperation coordinated by the European Agency for the Management of Operational Cooperation at the External Borders of the Member States of the EU, Case C-335/10 *European Parliament v. Council of the EU*. The Court ruled that the cited Council Decision contained "essential elements of external maritime surveillance" that go beyond the scope of the additional measures that could be implemented by the comitology procedure, and therefore only the EU legislation was entitled to adopt them.

persons wanted for arrest for extradition purposes, and to the alerts for witnesses and persons summoned to appear before the court.[4]

At the request of the Member States[5], in 2001 the Commission began to develop the second generation SIS (SIS II) in order to extend the operational capacity of SIS and simplify its functionality.[6] SIS-II entered into operation on 9 April 2013. Following the migration of data from SIS I+ to SIS-II, the European Agency for the operational management of large-scale systems in the Area of Freedom, Security and Justice (eu-LISA)[7] took over responsibility for the day-to-day running of the central system on 9 May 2013.

The new system provides for the storage of fingerprints, photographs and copies of European Arrest Warrants attached directly to alerts for persons wanted to be arrested, and the identification of links between different types of information recorded (i.e., an alert for a person and a vehicle). It has also inserted new types of alerts (stolen aircrafts, boats, containers, means of payment). The Fourth bi-annual report on the functioning of the Schengen area (covering the period 1 May–31 October 2013) mentions that, although SIS-II started functioning smoothly, the number of alerts stored in the system constantly increases and, "thanks to its enhanced functionalities and overall performance, the system contributes significantly to safeguarding both the security and the free movement of persons in the Schengen area"[8].

---

[4] Council Decision 2005/211/JHA of 24 February 2005 concerning the introduction of some new functions for the Schengen Information System, including the fight against terrorism. OJ L 8, 15.3.2005, p. 44.

[5] The idea of developing a SIS II was already mentioned in the Action Plan on how best to implement the provisions of the Treaty of Amsterdam on an Area of Freedom, Security and Justice (Vienna Action Plan), adopted by JHA Council of 3 December 1998, p. 6.

[6] The new system was established by Regulation (EC) No 1987/2006 of 20 December 2006 on the establishment, operation and use of the second generation Schengen Information System (SIS II) (OJ L 381, 28.12.2006, p. 4) and by Council Decision 2007/533/JHA of 12 June 2007 on the establishment, operation and use of the second-generation Schengen Information System (SIS II) (OJ L 205, 7.8.2007, p. 63).

The instruments setting up the responsibilities of the Commission and the Member States for the migration are laid down in Council Regulation (EC) No 1104/2008 of 24 October 2008 (OJ L 299, 8.11.2008, p. 1) and in Decision 2008/839/JHA of 24 October 2008 (OJ L 299, 8.11.2008, p. 43), later amended by Regulation (EC) No 541/2010 of 3 June 2010 (OJ L 155, 22.6.2010) and by Regulation (EC) No 542/2010 of 3 June 2010 (OJ L 155, 22.6.2010), respectively.

[7] OJ L 286, 1.11.2011, p. 1.

[8] COM(2013) 832 final. Brussels, 28.11.2013, p. 6.

7.2 DNA Analysis Files, Dactyloscopic Data, Vehicle Registration Data, Mass Disasters and Serious Accidents, and Prevention of Terrorism. The Prüm System

7.2.1 Background

On 27 May 2005, seven EU Member States (Belgium, Germany, Spain, France, Luxembourg, the Netherlands and Austria) signed in Prüm (Germany) the *Convention on the stepping up of cross-border cooperation, particularly in combating terrorism, cross-border crime and illegal immigration* (the Treaty of Prüm), with the main goal of ensuring the automated access by the law enforcement authorities of those countries to information stored in specific national databases of other Member States, for the purposes of prevention and fight against terrorism and organised crime. The Treaty of Prüm, which entered into force on 1 November 2006, was complemented by an Implementing Agreement of 5 December 2006.[9]

Although the Treaty of Prüm was adopted outside the legal framework of the EU, the participating Member States expected to bring this provisions within the EU *acquis* after an evaluation of its practical application, which was to take place within 3 years following its entry into force. There was not need to wait for the results of this evaluation. The Treaty of Prüm was certainly welcomed by other Member States (namely Finland, Italy, Portugal and Slovenia) who expressed soon their interest in acceding to it. Moreover, in the first semester of 2007 the then German Presidency of the EU promoted in different fora "that the promising model offered by the Prüm Treaty (. . .) should be considered at EU level as soon as possible".[10] These type of statements were accompanied by relevant figures on the exchange of DNA data between Germany and Austria.[11]

---

[9] See on this Convention the public hearing at LIBE Committee on "The Prum Convention: Integration or fragmentation of European Justice and Home Affairs?", Brussels, 22 June 2006. Council doc. 11130/96, PE 233 CRIMORG 114 ENFOPOL 140 MIGR 97. Brussels, 30 June 2006.

[10] About the steps and negotiations taken place at police level to integrate the Treaty of Prüm into the EU legal framework, see Burgess (2007), p. 1.

[11] "German searches of Austria's DNA database apparently turned up 1.510 matches of "hits" (enabling a request for further information from the searching state), with the Austrian authorities able to connect 710 'open' criminal cases in Germany with known suspects. The hits in the Austrian database were made in connection with 14 homicides, 885 thefts, and 85 robberies or instances of extortion" (Burgess 2007, p. 3).

However, certain Member States,[12] European institutions[13] and academics[14] were concerned about the procedure followed for the adoption of this Treaty, the absence of a comprehensive legal framework for the protection of personal data applicable in addition to the particularities on data protection laid down in the Treaty, and the risk of breaching the fundamental rights of the citizens by making an extensive use of massive searches of criminal data (data mining or data profiling techniques). Concerns about the lack of standardised criteria for the collection and processing of DNA profiles was also frequently raised. Legislative work for the integration of the Prüm Convention into the Union *acquis* started in early 2007.[15]

7.2.2 Legal Framework

In February 2007, 15 Member States presented a proposal for a *Council Decision on the stepping up of cross-border cooperation, particularly in combating terrorism and cross-border crime*,[16] with the aim of incorporating the substance of the provisions of the Prum Treaty into the legal framework of the European Union.

The proposal was virtually identical to the Treaty of Prum, except for the exclusion of measures to improve cooperation with combating illegal immigration, the use of air marshals on aircraft[17] and the "hot pursuing" legal provision allowing officers to cross from one State into another without prior consent (excluded measures, not incorporated in the EU Council Decision, the Treaty of Prum remains applicable among the signatories to the Treaty of Prüm). The provisions of the Treaty of Prüm allowing the automatic searching of DNA profiles, dactyloscopic data and vehicle registration data (VRD), those regulating the supply of information relating to major events and in order to prevent terrorist offences, and the rules governing data protection, were incorporated in the draft Council Decision.

---

[12] UK was particularly reluctant to some aspects of the Treaty of Prum. See the Report with evidence of the House of Lords, European Union Committee, 18th Report of Session 2006–2007: "Prum: an effective weapon against terrorist and crime?".

[13] The concerns of the EDPS were expressed with the occasion of the examination of witnesses to the UK report mentioned in the previous footnote. See in particular the Memorandum by Mr Peter HUSTINSX, p. 31, and the answers provided by Mr Joaquin BAYO DELGADO and Mr Hielke HIJMANS to the European Union Committee on 25 March 2007 (minutes of evidence, questions 119–139 and 140–141), available at: http://www.publications.parliament.uk/pa/ld200607/ldselect/ldeucom/90/7032205.htm.

See also Working Document on a Council Decision on the stepping up of cross-border cooperation, particularly in combating terrorism and cross-border crime, Committee on Civil Liberties, Justice and Home Affairs of the European Parliament (rapporteur CORREIA, F.).

[14] See Burgess (2007), p. 1.

[15] See Council doc. 6220/07 CRIMORG 29 ENFOPOL 19. Brussels, 9 February 2007.

[16] OJ C 71, 28.3.2007, p. 35.

[17] Both were first pillar measures and therefore impossible to be regulated by Council Decision (as third-pillar instrument).

The *Council Decision 2008/615/JHA on the stepping up of cross-border cooperation, particularly in combating terrorism and cross-border crime*, was adopted by the Council at its JHA Meeting on 23 June 2008.[18] It was accompanied by the Council Decision 2008/616/JHA of 23 June 2008 establishing the indispensable provisions allowing the administrative and technical implementation of the forms of cooperation set out in the Council Decision mentioned above.[19]

The Annex of the Decision 2008/616/JHA includes further details concerning its technical and administrative implementation. A manual has been also prepared and is kept updated by the General Secretariat of the Council, on the basis of the information and notifications provided by the Member States in accordance with Article 18(2) thereto.

An Agreement on the application of certain provisions of both Council Decisions was signed between the EU and Iceland and Norway in November 2009 and further concluded by Council Decision of 26 July 2010.[20]

7.2.3 Guiding Principles

In general terms, the Council Decisions of Prüm are based on the principle of availability, according to which a law enforcement officers in one Member State who needs information in order to carry out his duties can require it from another Member State, whose law enforcement authorities of the Member State holding that information has to make it available.

However, comparing these legal instruments with others inspired on the principle of availability,[21] the Council Decisions of Prum have adopted a different and more cautious approach for the exchange of information. In words of the EDPS, "the initiative can be qualified as a step towards availability, but does not *strictu sensu* implement the principle of availability".[22] This is especially clear regarding the files containing biometric data. In cases of DNA datafiles and dactiloscopic datafiles, law enforcement authorities of one Member State are not entitled to have direct access, but indirect access through reference data. Only when a match has been identified, can further data might be requested in accordance with follow-up procedures.

---

[18] OJ L 210, 6.8.2008, p. 1.

[19] OJ L 210, 6.8.2008, p. 12.

[20] OJ L 238, 9.9.2010, p. 1.

[21] On the principle of availability, See Sect. 2.2 of this book.

[22] Opinion of the EDPS on the initiative of the Kingdom of Belgium (. . .), with a view to adopting a Council Decision on the stepping up of cross-border cooperation, particularly in combating terrorism and cross-border crime. OJ C 169, 21.7.2007, p. 5.

7.2.3.1 Automated Access to Reference Data from DNA Files

The Prüm Council Decision 2008/615/JHA establishes an obligation on the Member States to keep national DNA analysis files for the investigation of criminal offences, and to ensure the availability of reference data from those files. According to Article 2(2), "reference data shall only include DNA profiles established from the non-coding part of DNA and a reference number", and they shall not contain any data from which the data subject can be directly identified. The processing of DNA should be carried out "in compliance with the national law applicable to the processing" (Article 2(1)).

The Member States are also obliged to nominate a contact point for the purposes of supplying the information requested by law enforcement authorities of other Member States. "The powers of the national contact points shall be governed by the applicable national law" (Article 6(1)).

The law enforcement authorities nominated as contact points are entitled to have access to the reference data of the DNA analysis files of other Member States, for the purpose of conducting automated searches of DNA profiles in individual cases (Article 3(1)), or to undertaken automated comparison of unidentified DNA profiles with the reference data of DNA analysis files of other Member State (Article 4(1)).

The comparison of DNA data works on a "hit/no-hit" basis. When an automated comparison result in a match (or "hit") in the database, the related personal data can be provided in response to a separate follow-up request. In accordance with Article 5 of the Council Decision 2008/615/JHA, regulating the supply of further personal data and other information:

> Should the procedures referred to in Articles 3 and 4 show a match between DNA profiles, the supply of further available personal data and other information relating to the reference data shall be governed by the national law, including the legal assistance rules, of the requested Member State.

In order to ensure the follow-up of matches at police level, Europol has issued several UMF2[23] Standardised forms. At this stage, whether the information gathered through these forms can be included directly in the judicial file in order to be assessed as evidence would depend on the law governing criminal proceedings in the requesting Member State.

At judicial level, personal data following a Prüm hit can be obtained through the issuing and execution of mutual legal assistance requests (mainly through the 2000 Convention on Mutual Legal Assistance between the Member States). Eurojust can provide advice on the judicial follow-up of the Prüm matches, accelerate the execution of the corresponding requests, and assist national prosecutors in overcoming possible obstacles for obtaining the information requested.[24]

---

[23] UMF is the abbreviation of Universal Messaging Format.

[24] Discussions on the police and judicial follow-up of Prüm matches are taking place in the framework of the Project for the Implementation, Evaluation and Strengthening of Forensic DNA data exchange (PIES Project), coordinated by the *Nationaal Instituut voor Criminalistiek*

The distinction between a police and a judicial follow-up of the Prüm matches, and the possibilities of using the Swedish initiative at police level (instead of the UMF2 Standardised forms mentioned above) are referred to in the EIXM, as follows:

> Where follow-up information is needed as evidence before a court, a judicial cooperation request will normally be required. However, where use as evidence is not or not yet needed, systematic use of the Swedish Initiative as legal basis and SIENA as communication tool should be promoted so as to make full use of the advantages of each and to align Member States with a single best practice.[25]

7.2.3.2 Automated Access to Referenda Data from Dactyloscopic Files

As with DNA files, the Prüm Council Decision 2008/615/JHA introduces an obligation on Member States to allow indirect access to reference data from the national fingerprint identification systems. Such reference data will only include "dactyloscopic data and a reference number" (Article 8), whilst reference data which is not attributed to any individual (unidentified dactyloscopic data) must be recognisable as such.

The contact point nominated by the respective Member State is allowed, in particular cases and for the prevention and investigation of criminal offences, to have access to the reference data of the automated fingerprint identification system established in another Member State, and conduct automated searches by comparing dactyloscopic data.

When the searching has showed a match between dactyloscopic data, the supply of further available personal data and other information relating to the reference data "shall be governed by the national law, including the legal assistance rules, of the requested Member State" (Article 10). Therefore, further information containing personal data may only be transmitted to the investigating Member State in application of the legal instruments of police and judicial cooperation in administrative and criminal matters.

7.2.3.3 Direct Access to Vehicle Registration Data

The Council Decision of Prüm allows direct access to data relating to owners and operators, as well as data relating to vehicles, both stored in vehicle registration databases.

The major difference between the access given to DNA profiles and fingerprints databases, on the one hand, and the access given to vehicle registration data, on the other hand, is that access to the later is not limited to reference data: direct access to data is allowed because the processing of vehicle data provided is not considered as intrusive as the processing of biometric data.

---

en Criminologie (NICC) of Belgium with the support and co-financing of the European Commission under the ISEC programme.

[25] COM(2012) 735 final, p. 8.

Another difference is the purpose for which the access is granted. For DNA profiles and fingerprints, access is limited to criminal offences, while access to vehicle registration data is made available for the prevention and investigation of administrative and criminal offences, and in order to maintain public security. The Directive 2011/82/EU of 25 October 2011 facilitating the cross-border exchange of information on road safety related traffic offences[26] relies inter alia on the software application especially designed for the purposes of Art. 12 of Decision 2008/615/JHA.

7.2.4 Data Protection Rules

Chapter 6 (Articles 24–32) of the Council Decision 2008/615/JHA contains certain provisions applicable for the processing and protection of personal data. It includes some relevant definitions (Article 24), the obligation of the Member States to guarantee a level of protection of personal data in its national law at least equivalent to that resulting from the Convention 108 of the Council of Europe and related instruments (Article 25), the need to respect the principles of purpose limitation and accuracy of the information (Articles 26 and 28), a description of the competent authorities for the processing of the information supplied (Article 27), and some technical and security measures (Articles 29 and 30). The Chapter recognises the right to information and damages of the data subject (Article 31) and the obligation of the receiving Member State to inform the supplying Member State "on the request of the processing of supplied data and the result obtained" (Article 32).

In an Opinion to the Council Decision 2008/615/JHA, the EDPS stressed the need for a general framework for data protection in the third pillar,[27] also applicable in addition to the rules on data protection contained in the Council Decision of Prüm:

> (...) the provisions of Chapter 6 of the initiative are intented to build on a general framework for data protection (see Article 25 of the initiative). The provisions must be seen as lex specialis applicable to the data supplied pursuant to this Council Decision. Unfortunately, the present general framework of Council of Europe Convention 108 and related documents is unsatisfactory. However, the intention in itself illustrates that an appropriate general framework laid down in a Council Framework Decision is needed (...).[28]

Another relevant matter pointed out by the EDPS was that, if the searches in DNA and dactyloscopic databases resulted in a "hit", personal data should be provided in accordance with the national law including, if necessary, the legal instruments on judicial cooperation in criminal matters:

[26] OJ L 288, 5.11.2011, p. 1.

[27] Document cited, p. 9.

[28] Document cited, p. 10.

> (. . .) the nature of the provisions on data protection in Chapter 6 themselves, as far as they build on the traditional notion of mutual legal assistance in criminal matters, are an illustration of the need for a general framework. Information sharing presupposes a minimum-harmonisation of basic rules on data protection or at least the mutual recognition of national law, as to avoid that the effectiveness of cooperation is harmed by differences between the laws of the Member States.

The EDPS has also called for a simplification of the multiple legal instruments applicable:

> "(. . .) Although the initiative provides for harmonisation on some important matters of data protection law, on other important matters, the provisions on data protection in Chapter 6 do not harmonise national law nor they prescribe mutual recognition. Instead, they build on the simultaneous applicability of two (or more) legal systems:" supply of data is quite often only allowed if the laws of both the supplying Member State and the receiving Member State are observed. In other words, on those matters the initiative does not contribute to an area of freedom, security and justice without internal borders, but they give substance to the traditional system of mutual legal assistance in criminal matters, based on sovereignty.[29]

Lastly, the EDPS considered the provision in the Council Decision on Prüm about the right of information to the data subject without prior request. The first sentence on Article 31(1) thereof is as follows:

> At the request of the data subject under national law, information shall be supplied in compliance with national law to the data subject upon production of proof of his identity, without unreasonable expense, in general comprehensive terms and without unacceptable delays, on the data processed in respect of his person, the origin of the data, the recipient or groups of recipients, the intended purpose of the processing and, where required by national law, the legal basis for the processing.

According to the EDPS, "this requirement is contrary to an essential element of data protection, namely that the data controller provides a data subject from whom data relating to himself are collected with some basic information on this collection, without being requested to do so by that data subject". The EDPS recognises that this right can be subject to certain exceptions, conditions and limitations, "for instance to protect the interest of an ongoing criminal investigation, but that may not result in the right itself being deprived of its substantive content, by requiring as a general rule a request from the data subject".[30]

The convenience of recognising the right of information of the individual concerned in the context of police and judicial investigations should be examined carefully. A automatic recognition of this principle could compromise the purpose for which a particular information and/or database has been set up (in most of the cases, the need to safeguard the security of the citizens, prevent and combat serious criminal offences).

---

[29] Document cited, p. 11.

[30] Document cited, p. 12.

7.2.5 Implementation and Evaluation

Article 25(2) of Council Decision 2008/615/JHA establishes an important pre-condition for the exchange of information among the Member States, according to which:

> The supply of personal data provided for under this Decision may not take place until the provisions of this Chapter have been implemented in the national law of the territories of the Member States involved in such supply. The Council shall unanimously decide whether this condition has been met.

The unanimous decision of the Council is taken on the basis of the evaluation reports concerning each of the tools for the automated exchange of personal data. The reports are drafted once the Member States notify the General Secretariat of the Council "that they have implemented the obligations imposed on them under this decision" (Article 36(2)), and reply to the relevant questionnaires. In the cases of DNA, dactyloscopic and vehicle registration data, the evaluation mechanism includes an evaluation visit and a pilot run (Article 20 of Council Decision 2008/616/JHA and Chapter 4 of Annex thereto).[31]

The evaluation mechanism, currently ongoing, is not applicable however to those Member States sharing personal data under the framework of the Prum Treaty (Article 25(3) Council Decision 2008/615/JHA).

To support the Member States in the implementation of the necessary technical measures, initiatives such as the Mobile Competence Team and the Europol Helpdesk were set up by the Member States.

In accordance with Article 36(1), the deadline of the Member States for compliance with the provisions on automated data exchange regarding DNA, fingerprints and Vehicle Registration Data was on 26 August 2011. The implementation date was met by 12 Member States for the exchange of DNA profiles, by 9 Member States for the exchange of fingerprints and 9 Member States for the exchange of vehicle registration data. Some Member States did not meet the deadline due to legislative, financial or technical problems, the later including difficulties in obtaining financial support from ISEC fund, on insufficient number of experts participating in the evaluation visits, the high costs of the evaluation visits, and the lack of staff and financial means to set up the Europol Helpdesk. At the JHA meeting on 13 December 2011, the Council called upon the non-operational Member States to finalise as soon as possible the implementation process. It also invited the operational Member States to support them more actively, and carry out effective use of the Prüm databases for the exchange of information.

[31] The details of this evaluation procedure, which applies as from 13 October 2009, are set out in Council doc. 6661/2/09 REV 2 CRIMORG 25 ENFOPOL 39, as amended by doc. 10149/10 JAI 463 CRIMORG 103 ENFOPOL 145 ENFOCUSTOM 43. The details of the evaluation procedures are set out, for DNA data, in Council doc. 11899/2/10 REV 2 DAPIX 8 CRIMORG 141 ENFOPOL 203 + COR1; for dactyloscopic data in Council doc. 11898/2/10 REV 2 DAPIX 7 CRIMORG 140 ENFOPOL 202 + COR 1; for VRD in Council doc. 6661/1/09 REV 1 ADD 5 REV 2.

On the other hand, Article 21 of the Council Decision 2008/616/JHA envisageses the evaluation on regular bases of the administrative, technical and financial application of the automated data exchanges, when a particular attention should be paid to the automatic searching of vehicle registration data in cases of combating serious crime. Such an evaluation, based on the reports of the respective Member States, will be applicable to all Member States already applying Decision 2008/615/JHA at the time of the evaluation, and carried out with respect to the data categories for which data exchange has started among the Member States concerned.

The Council Decision 2008/615/JHA also placed an obligation on the Commission to submit a report to the Council, by 28 July 2012, on the implementation of this Decision accompanied by the proposals it deems necessary for any further development (Article 36(4)). The Report on the implementation of this Council Decision was published by the Commission in December 2012. It underlines that many Member States are not yet exchanging information through the Prüm system even though the deadline for transposition was 26 August 2011, and reminds those Member States of the option for the Commission to start infrindgement proceeding as from December 2014.[32]

The Council also issues regular information about the implementation of the Council Decisions on Prüm, including and overview of documents and procedures, overview of declarations, and an analysis of the implementation of automated data exchange.[33]

7.3 Criminal Records of Individuals from Other Member State. The European Criminal Records Information System (ECRIS)

7.3.1 Background

Criminal records are vital in many criminal investigations and proceedings. The existence of previous convictions may justify the adoption of deprivation of liberty as preventive measure against the suspect. At the end of a criminal proceeding, previous convictions may be taken into consideration as grounds for the aggravation of the penalty.

If the suspect is a citizen of another Member State who has not committed previous criminal offences in the States where he has been arrested, no criminal records will be found in national databases. However, he can be a serial serious offender having committed several crimes against the person in other countries.

---

[32] COM(2012) 732 final. Brussels, 7.12.2012.

[33] See Council document 5074/7/13 REV 7 JAI 6 DAPIX 1 ENFOPOL 1 CRIMORG 1.

The creation of an efficient mechanism enabling a Member State to get information on criminal records stored in other countries and consider such records in national criminal proceedings, has been a major concern for academics and legislators since the nineteenth century. At that time, prestigious institutions such as the Institute of International Law (Munich, 1883) and the Penitentiary Congress (Paris, 1895) promoted discussions on the possible recognition of legal effects of convictions issued in another country. To achieve this goal, academics were aware of the need to centralise at national level judicial convictions, and create a mechanism for the transmission of related information to the countries that needed it. It seems that the first suggestion for creating a central register of criminal records was made at the Penitentiary Congress of Washington in 1910, followed by the Conference for the Unification of Criminal Law of Rome in 1928.[34]

At the Ninth Congress of the International Association of Criminal Law (Paris, 1937) and the Twelfth Criminal and Penitentiary Congress (The Hague, 1950), prestigious academics discussed establishing contacts between the record offices of convictions separately maintained by the police and the judiciary, and proposed common rules for the creating of a central judicial register.[35]

Following these academic discussions, some bilateral and multilateral conventions on mutual legal assistance also introduced the need to exchange information on criminal records. The bilateral agreement signed between Germany and Belgium in 1879 established the obligation to report a criminal conviction to the relevant authorities of the convicted person's country of origin, thus initiating the application of the general rule that is still applicable today. With a wider scope, the Council of Europe Convention on Mutual Legal Assistance of 1959 regulated the transfer of criminal records on the basis of two guiding principles: firstly, the obligation of the Member States to transmit, at least once a year, criminal convictions of non-nationals to the State party concerned, and secondly, the obligation of the Member States to provide an answer to mutual legal assistance requests on criminal records.

Article 22 of the Council of Europe Convention on Mutual Legal Assistance of 1959 stated:

> Each contracting Party shall inform any other Party of all criminal convictions and subsequent measures in respect of nationals of the latter Party, entered in the judicial records. Ministries of Justice shall communicate such information to one another at least once a year. Where the person concerned is considered a national of two or more other Contracting Parties, the information shall be given to each of these Parties, unless the person is a national of the Party in the territory of which he was convicted.

Article 13 of the Convention established:

> 1. A requested Party shall communicate extracts from and information relating to judicial records, requested from it by the judicial authorities of a Contracting Party and needed in a criminal matter, to the same extent that these may be available to its own judicial authorities in [a] like case.

---

[34] *See* Quintano Ripolles (1957), p. 147.

[35] Quintano Ripolles (1957), p. 147.

2. In any case other than that provided for in paragraph 1 of this article the request shall be complied with in accordance with the conditions provided for by the law, regulations or practice of the requested Party.

However, many European countries had reservations about both legal provisions, making the exchange of information on criminal convictions less efficient in practice.[36]

Some decades later, in a European Union without internal borders, the need to exchange and recognise criminal records issued in another Member State become a top priority, especially after some cases, which appeared in mass media, of persons accused of child pornography who had committed such criminal offences in other member States. In line with the conclusions of the Tampere European Council of 15 and 16 October 1999, the Programme of measures to implement the principle of mutual recognition of decisions in criminal matters[37] included, in measure (3), the establishment of a standard form such as that drawn up for the Schengen bodies, translated into all the official languages of the European Union, for criminal record requests. In 2002, Denmark presented its initiative proposing the adoption of a Council Decision on increasing cooperation between European Union Member States on disqualifications.[38] The Council decided to continue working on a legal instrument with a broader scope than that applied to sexual offenders.

Five years later, the Hague Programme adopted by the European Council on 4 and 5 November 2004 called for a greater exchange of information from national conviction and disqualification databases. The Action Plan of the Council and the Commission to develop the Hague Programme also mentioned the need to improve information exchanges about criminal convictions.

In January 2005, the Commission presented the White paper on exchanges of information on convictions and the effects of such convictions in the European Union.[39] The paper examined the conditions governing circulation of information on convictions in the different Member States, and proposed an ambitious action programme to set up a computerised system of exchange of information on convictions using a standardised format.

In November 2005, the Council adopted Council Decision 2005/876/JHA of 21 November 2005 on the exchange of information extracted from criminal records.[40] The goal of this Decision was to facilitate the existing mechanisms for the transmission of information on criminal records, mainly Article 6(1) of the 2000 Convention, and to establish the specific right of a Member State's central authority to send a request for information extracted from its criminal records to the central authority of another Member State, in accordance with its national law.

---

[36] *See also* Council of Europe Recommendation No R(84) 10 on criminal records and rehabilitation of convicted persons.

[37] OJ C 12, 15.1.2001, p. 10.

[38] OJ C 223, 19.9.2002, p. 17.

[39] COM(2005) 10 final and SEC(2005) 63. Brussels, 25.1.2005.

[40] OJ L 322, 9.12.2005, p. 34.

7.3.2 Legal Framework

In 2009, the following three legal instruments were adopted:

- Council Framework Decision 2009/315/JHA of 26 February 2009 on the organisation and content of the exchange of information extracted from criminal records between Member States[41] (Council Framework Decision on criminal records). This Decision replaces Council Decision 2005/876/JHA of 21 November 2005 on the exchange of information extracted from criminal records;
- Council Decision 2009/31/JHA of 6 April 2009 on the establishment of the European Criminal Records Information System (ECRIS) in application of Article 11 of Framework Decision 2009/315/JHA[42]; and
- Council Framework Decision 2008/675/JHA of 24 July 2008 on taking account of convictions in the Member States of the European Union in the course of new criminal proceedings.[43]

The mechanism established in the EU Decisions listed above allows an investigating judge or prosecutor, through its central authority, to request information on a non-national through a de-centralised information system and a standardised form.

The Member States should have taken the necessary measures to comply with the provisions of the Council Framework Decision on criminal records by 27 April 2012, and with the Council Framework Decision on ECRIS by 7 April 2012.[44] However, the complexity of the task has required further time for appropriate implementation.

7.3.3 Main Elements of the System

7.3.3.1 The Central Authorities

Information extracted from criminal records is exchanged through the central authorities designated for this purpose by each Member State. Thus, the investigating judge or prosecutor who needs criminal records information from another Member State must contact his central authority, who, subsequently, will request the information from the central authority of the Member State of the person's nationality.

[41] OJ L 93, 7.4.2009, p. 23.

[42] OJ L 93, 7.4.2009, p. 33.

[43] OJ L 220, 15.8.2008, p. 32.

[44] Council Framework Decision 2008/675/JHA of 24 July 2008 on taking account of convictions in the Member States of the European Union in the course of new criminal proceedings. *See infra* Sect. 9.7.

The Member States have the obligation to inform the General Secretariat of the Council and the Commission of the designated central authority (or authorities). The General Secretariat of the Council provides this contact information to the Member States and Eurojust (Article 3(2) of Council Framework Decision on criminal records).

7.3.3.2 The Nationality of the Convicted Person

The criterion adopted for the storage and transmission of information on criminal records is the nationality of the convicted person. The system is, therefore, only useful for nationals of the Member States.

The system does not provide information on nationals from third States, even if they reside in a Member State and have been convicted in a criminal proceeding taking place within EU territory. Due to the complexities of the system for the exchange of information on criminal proceedings at EU level,[45] the Commission adopted a pragmatic approach and decided to limit the scope of the system to EU nationals. With respect to third States' nationals, other solutions are under consideration, *inter alia*, the creation of an index system.

7.3.3.3 The Member State in Which the Conviction Takes Place

The Member State in which a conviction is entered against a national of another Member State is responsible for transmitting this information, as well as any further alterations or deletions, to the Member State of the person's nationality.

The particular information to be transmitted by the convicting Member State is outlined in Article 11(1) of the Council Framework Decision on criminal convictions, establishing distinctions among obligatory, optional and additional information.

7.3.3.4 The Member State of the Person's Nationality

The Member State of the person's nationality is required to store and update all obligatory and optional information on the convictions of their nationals. They "may store" additional information on the convictions of their nationals transmitted from other Member States.

The central authority of the person's nationality is responsible for replying to requests for information extracted from criminal records made by the requesting Member State.

---

[45] *See* Commission working document on the feasibility of an index of third-country nationals convicted in the European Union, COM(2006) 359 final. Brussels, 4.7.2006.

7.3.3.5 The Requesting and Requested Member States

The competent judicial authority that, in the course of a criminal proceeding, needs information on criminal records for a national of another Member State must send the corresponding request first to its own central authority. This central authority, "in accordance with its national law", will submit the request to the central authority of the Member State of the person's nationality (requested Member State.

7.3.4 The Proceeding

The requests for information must be submitted using the form provided in the Annex to the Council Framework Decision on criminal records, in an official language of the requested Member State[46] (Article 6(4) and Article 10, first paragraph, of the Council Framework Decision thereof).

The Council has issued a Manual of Procedures to help the central authorities of the Member States complete in the form correctly.[47]

The central authority of the Member State from which the information is sought must provide the requested information "immediately and in any event within a period not exceeding ten working days from the date the request was received", using the form provided in the Annex to the Council Framework Decision on criminal records (Article 8(1)). The reply must be provided "in one of its official languages or in any other language accepted by both Member States" (Article 10, second paragraph).[48]

If additional information to identify the person involved is necessary, the requested Member State " shall immediately consult the requesting Member State with a view to providing a reply within 10 days from the date the additional information is received" (Article 8(1), second paragraph).

---

[46] Nevertheless, the third paragraph of Article 10 of the Council Framework Decision on criminal records allows the Member States, "at the time of the adoption of this Framework Decision or at a later date, [to] indicate, in a statement to the General Secretariat of the Council, which are the official languages of the institutions of the European Union that is accepts". The General Secretariat of the Council will disseminate this information accordingly.

[47] Last version of the Manual of Procedures can be found in Council document 8848/10 COPEN 104 EJN 9 EUROJUST 44, updating Council document 1120/2/08 REV2 COPEN 137 EJN 51 EUROJUST 68.

[48] *See* previous footnote.

7.3.5 The Computerised System

Council Decision 2009/316/JHA of 6 April 2009 on the establishment of ECRIS outlines a plan to build and develop a computerised, de-centralised exchange system for information on convictions among Member States.

The system neither creates a central database nor allows Member States' central authorities to directly access the information stored in another Member State's criminal records. Rather, it establishes a network connecting the domestic criminal conviction databases to each other, without replacing or introducing relevant modifications in such databases.[49] The system consists of two elements: interconnection software, and a common communication structure.

7.3.5.1 ECRIS Interconnection Software

Interconnection software will enable information exchanges between Member States' criminal record databases. Each Member State is responsible for covering its own costs arising from the implementation, administration, use and maintenance of both the interconnection software and the national databases (Articles 3(1)(a) and (8) of Council Decision on ECRIS).

7.3.5.2 Common Communication Structure

The Commission is responsible for the common communication structure, which has initially been called the Trans-European Service for Telematics between Administrations (S-TESTA) network, and is funded via the general budget of the European Union (Articles 3(1)(b), (5) and (6)).

To facilitate the implementation of ECRIS, Council Decision 2009/316/JHA requests that Member States and the Commission coordinate their work to establish "logging systems and procedures making it possible to monitor the functioning of ECRIS and the establishment of non-personal statistics", a common set of protocols and the creation of procedures to verify the conformity of national software applications with the provided technical specifications (Articles 6(2)(a), (b) and (c)).

7.3.6 Additional Measures

Council Decision 2009/316/JHA includes additional measures to make the standardised format a user-friendly tool for the exchange of information on criminal records. These additional measures include the tables of categories of offences and

[49] *See* Recital (10) of Council Decision on ECRIS.

categories of penalties and measures provided for in Annexes A and B, and the non-binding manual for practitioners referred to in Articles 5 and 6(2)(a) of Council Decision 2009/316/JHA.

7.3.6.1 Tables of Categories of Offences and Categories of Penalties

By providing the tables of categories of offences and categories of penalties the Council Decision hopes to overcome the obstacles caused by differences in the criminal systems of the Member States. The tables are expected to facilitate the automatic translation of requests, and ensure common understanding of the information provided. As expressed in Recital (14) of Council Decision 2009/316/JHA, both tables "are a tool aimed at helping the recipient to gain better understanding of the fact(s) and type of penalty(ies) or measure(s) contained in the information transmitted".

The Annexes to Council Decision 2009/316/JHA include a detailed list of possible offences (Annex A) and a list of categories of penalties and alternative measures that could be imposed on the convicted person by national courts (Annex B). Annex A also helps national authorities gain available information relating to the level of completion and the level of participation in the offence and, where applicable, to the existence of total or partial exemption from criminal responsibility or recidivism. Annex B contemplates the possibility of providing, where applicable, available information on the nature and/or conditions of execution of the penalty or measure imposed.

Each offence, penalty and alternative measure is accompanied by a code, which should be referred to in the standardised format, when the central authority transmits the information in its request to the appropriate Member State.

Among the implementing measures, Article 6(1) of Council Decision 2009/316/JHA also acknowledges the Council's ability to modify Annexes A and B, acting by qualified majority and after consulting the European Parliament.

7.3.6.2 Non-binding Manual for Practitioners

Another implementation measure in Article 6(2)(a) of Council Decision 2009/316/JHA is the non-binding manual for practitioners "addressing in particular the modalities of identification of offenders, as well as recording the common understanding of the categories of offences and penalties and measures listed respectively in Annexes A and B".

On the basis of the information provided for the Member States, the General Secretariat of the Council issued the initial draft of the non-binding manual for practitioners in March 2011. At the request of the majority of delegations, who considered the initial draft too complex, the Presidency submitted a simplified and shorter version in October of that year. At the time of writing this reduced version is being revised regularly by the General Secretariat of the Council.

7.4 Relevant Information Extracted from Other Databases

7.4.1 Customs Information System (CIS)

The Customs Information System (CIS) was created by Council Regulation (EC) No 515/97 of 13 March 1997 on mutual assistance between the administrative authorities of the Member States and cooperation between the latter and the Commission to ensure the correct application of the law on customs or agricultural matters.[50] The cited Council Regulation was amended in 2003[51] and 2008.[52]

Another relevant instrument governing CIS is the Council Decision 2009/917/JHA of 30 November 2009 on the use of information technology for customs purposes,[53] which has replaced three legal instruments: the Convention of 26 July 1995 on the use of information technology for customs purposes (CIS Convention),[54] the Protocol of 12 March 1999 on the scope of the laundering of proceeds in the cited Convention,[55] and the Protocol of 8 May 2003 regarding the creation of a customs file identification database.[56]

CIS centralises the information provided by Member States' customs administrations and helps them in the prevention, investigation and prosecution of infringements of Community legislation on customs and agriculture.

CIS includes data on goods; means of transport; businesses; people; trends in fraud; available competences; goods retained, seized or confiscated; and cash retained, seized or confiscated. It can be accessed by a limited number of national authorities in the Member States (national customs, taxation, agricultural, public health and police authorities). Europol and Eurojust have been able to access to the system since May 2011. CIS is managed by OLAF.[57]

The "*Fichier d'Indentification des Dossier d' Enquête*" (FIDE) is a database added to CIS to facilitate investigations carried out by the Commission and the Member States. It enables national authorities investigating one or more persons or businesses possibly involved in a fraud case to identify the competent authorities of other Member States that are investigating or have conducted investigations against the same individuals or companies, allowing them to coordinate their efforts. FIDES is, therefore, a register of individuals and companies, but does not reveal

---

[50] OJ L 82, 22.3.1997, p. 1.

[51] Council Regulation (EC) No 807/2003 of 14 April 2003 adapting to Decision 1999/468/EC the provisions relating to committees which assist the Commission in the exercise of its implementing powers laid down in Council instruments adopted in accordance with the consultation procedure (unanimity), OJ L 122, 16.5.2003.

[52] Regulation (EC) No 766/2008 of 9 July 2008, OJ L 218, 13.8.2008.

[53] OJ L 323, 10.12.2009, p. 20.

[54] OJ C 316, 27.11.1995.

[55] OJ C 91, 31.3.1999, p. 2.

[56] OJ C 139, 1.3.2003, p. 2.

[57] *See* Sect. 6.8 of this book.

details of the investigations' resulting discoveries. FIDES has been fully operational since 15 September 2008.[58]

7.4.2 *Visa Information System*

The Visa Information System (VIS) is a system for exchange of information on short-sta visas. It allows the implementation between the Member States of a common policy on visa regimes through the processing and exchange of data related to all applications of short stays to visit or transit the Schengen Area.

VIS has a complex legal framework,[59] mainly governed by Regulation (EC) No 767/2008 of 9 July 2008 concerning the VISA Information System (VIS) and the exchange of data between Member States on short-stay visas (VIS Regulation),[60] and Council Decision 2008/633/JHA of 23 June 2008 concerning access for consultation of the Visa Information System (VIS) by designated authorities of Member States and by Europol for the purposes of the prevention, detection and investigation of terrorist offences and of other serious criminal offences.[61] In accordance with the Council Decision of 22 July 2013, the designated authorities and Europol have access for consultation of the VIS System since 1 September 2013.[62]

VIS consists of a centralised system with a national section in each participating Member State, and a technical support function initially based in France and connected to all visa-issuing Schengen States and their external border crossing points. VIS is also expected to assist the Member States in examining asylum applications. VISA system is now handled by eu-LISA.

The system includes alphanumeric data, a digital photograph and fingerprints of the applicant, links to previous visa applications and to the application files of persons travelling together with the applicant (e.g., spouse and children).

---

[58] *Idem.*

[59] *See* http://ec.europa.eu/home-affairs/doc_centre/borders/borders_it_vis_en.htm.

[60] OJ L 218, 13.8.2008, p. 60.

[61] OJ L 218, 13.8.2008, p. 82. See Opinion of the European Data Protection Supervisor on the Proposal for a Council Decision concerning access for consultation of the Visa Information System (VIS) by the authorities of Member States responsible for internal security and by Europol for the purposes of the prevention, detection and investigation of terrorist offences and of other serious criminal offences (COM (2005) 600 final) (2006/C 97/03). In accordance with the Council Decision of 22 July 2013, the designated authorities of the Member States and Europol have access for consultation of the VIS System since 1 September 2013. OJ L 198, 23.7.2013, p. 45.

[62] OJ L 198, 23.7.2013, p. 45.

VIS is becoming operational in different regions around the world gradually. On 14 November 2013, VIS was deployed in the ninth region (Central Asia), tenth region (South-East Asia) and eleventh region (Palestine).[63]

One of the main concerns of the Member States is related to the non-optimal quality of data (both biometric and alphanumeric) introduced in the system by the consular authorities. Despite this issue, VIS is functioning well and, by 31 October 2013, VIS had processed 5.0 million Schengen visa applications and issued 4.2 million visas.[64]

7.4.3 Eurodac, for Law Enforcement Purposes

Eurodac was established by Council Regulation No 2725/2000 on 11 December 2000.[65] It is a centralised, automated identification system for comparing fingerprints of asylum seekers and certain categories of illegal immigrants, with the main goal of identifying the Member State responsible for examining individual asylum applications under the Dublin II Regulation.

Iceland, Norway and Switzerland also participate in the system, as they are part of the Dublin II Regulation.

Data provided by the Member States include fingerprints, EU country of origin, gender, place and date of the asylum application or the apprehension of the person, reference number, date when the person's fingerprints were taken, and the date that the data were transmitted to the Central Unit.

Comparison of the applicant's fingerprints to those stored in Eurodac permits the appropriate authorities to determine whether or not the asylum seeker has previously claimed asylum in another Member State, or entered EU territory unlawfully.

In 2008, the Commission proposed changes to Eurodac[66] intended to ensure more efficient support of the Dublin II Regulation, proper assessment of data protection concerns, and alignment of Eurodac's management framework with that of SIS II and VIS in light of the then future creation of the Agency for the operational management of large-scale IT systems.

Following the Parliament's legislative resolution and negotiations in the Council, the Commission adopted an amended proposal in September 2009, thus introducing the possibility that Member States' law enforcement authorities and Europol have access to Eurodac's central database to prevent, detect and investigate terrorist

[63] See Commission Implementing Decision of 8 November 2013 determining the date from which the Visa Information System (VIS) is to start operations in a ninth, a tenth and an eleventh region. OJ L 299, 9.11.2013, p. 52.

[64] Fourth bi-annual report on the functioning of the Schengen area (1 May–31 October 2013). COM(2013) 832 final. Brussels, 28.11.2013, p. 7.

[65] OJ L 316, 15.12.2000, p. 1.

[66] COM(2008) 825 final, SEC(2008) 2981 and SEC(2008) 2982. Brussels, 3.12.2008.

offences and other serious criminal offences. This potential access by law enforcement authorities and Europol to the information included in Eurodac was highly criticised.

Following the entry into force of the Treaty of Lisbon, a proposal for a Regulation on Eurodac (further amended by the Commission) was adopted by the Council on 26 June 2013.[67] It lays down the conditions under which Member States' designated authorities and Europol may request the comparison of fingerprint data with those stored in Eurodac for law enforcement purposes.

References

Burgess M (July 2007) The Prum Process: playing or abusing the system? Eur Sec Rev 34:1
Quintano Ripolles A (1957) Tratado de Derecho Penal Internacional e International Penal. Tomo II, Madrid, p 147

[67] Regulation (EU) No 603/2013 of 26 June 2013 on the establishment of 'Eurodac' for the comparison of fingerprints for the effective application of Regulation (EU) No 604/2013 establishing the criteria and mechanisms for determining the Member State responsible for examining an application for international protection lodged in one of the Member States by a third-country national or a stateless person and on requests for the comparison with Eurodac data by Member States' law enforcement authorities and Europol for law enforcement purposes, and amending Regulation (EU) No 1077/2011 establishing a European Agency for the operational management of large-scale IT systems in the area of freedom, security and justice (recast). OJ L 180, 29.6.2013, p. 1.

Chapter 8
Different Channels, Tools and Legal Instruments for the Exchange of Information at Police Level

8.1 Channels

The European Information Exchange Model (EIXM) refers to SIRENE, the Europol National Units and Interpol National Central Bureaux as the main channels for cross-border information exchange. Interpol National Central Bureaux[1] operates 24/7 in order to ensure appropriate exchange of information either with Interpol or bilaterally (with other country participating in the system) by using the I-24/7 communication tool developed by Interpol.

The EIXM encourages the Member States to use simultaneously or subsequently different channels in the context of the same cross-border operation or investigation:

> A criminal investigation can involve parallel or sequential use of more than one instrument. In a cross-border case of serious or organised crime, a person or object could be checked against both the Europol Information System and SIS, and where there are "hits" follow-up requests could be made via Europol or SIRENE channels, respectively. A biometric trace could be the subject of a Prüm exchange followed by a post-hit Swedish Initiative request using the SIENA tool.[2]

The existance of multiple channels has motivated the proposal for the setting up of Single Point of Contact (SPOC) for international police cooperation in the Member States. SPOCs would operate 24/7 and bring together its SIRENE Bureau, ENU and Interpol National Central Bureaux, and contact points for other channels.

The fact that each UE information system, database and (for some of them) channel is governed by different rules for the processing and protection of personal data might complicate the interaction of all of them in a particular operation and/or

The opinions expressed by the author are personal and do not necessary coincide with those of the institution she is working for.

[1] SIRENE has been mentioned in Sect. 7.2 and the Europol National Units in Sect. 4.3.

[2] COM(2012) 735 final, p. 6.

Á.G. Zarza (ed.), *Exchange of Information and Data Protection in Cross-border Criminal Proceedings in Europe*, DOI 10.1007/978-3-642-40291-3_8,

investigation. Hence a major harmonisation of the rules for the processing and protection of personal data stored in the EU information systems and databases might be consdiered to be a matter of high priority.

Police authorities may also exchange information directly, on the basis inter alia of the Council Framework Decision analysed in the next section.

8.2 The Council Framework Decision 2006/960/JHA on Exchange of Information and Intelligence Among the Police Authorities of the Member States

8.2.1 Legal Framework

Council Framework Decision 2006/960/JHA of 18 December 2006 on simplifying the exchange of information and intelligence between law enforcement authorities of the Member States of the European Union (Swedish Framework Decision) was adopted by the Council at its JHA meeting of 18 December 2006.[3] It entered into force on 30 December 2006, the day of its publication in the Official Journal of the European Union.[4] Member States should have implemented the necessary measures to comply with the provisions of this Framework Decision no later than 19 December 2008.[5]

The Swedish Framework Decision is also applicable to Iceland, Norway, Switzerland and Liechtenstein. For Iceland and Norway,[6] as well as Switzerland,[7] the Swedish Framework Decision constitutes a development of the provisions of the Schengen *acquis*.

---

[3] OJ L 386, 29.12.2006, p. 89.

[4] Article 13.

[5] Article 12(6). See Commission Staff Working Paper SEC(2011) 593 final. Brussels, 13.5.2011, "Operation of the Council Framework Decision 2006/960/JHA of 18 December 2006 (Swedish Initiative)".

[6] *See* Article 1 of Council Decision 1999/437/EC of 17 May 1999 on certain arrangements for the application of the Agreement concluded by the Council of the European Union and the Republic of Iceland and the Kingdom of Norway concerning the association of those two States with the implementation, application and development of the Schengen *acquis*, OJ L 386, 29.12.2006.

[7] *See* Agreement signed between the European Union, the European Community and the Swiss Confederation concerning the association of the Swiss Confederation with the implementation, application and development of the Schengen *acquis*, which fall within the area referred to in Article 1(H) of Decision 1999/437/EC read in conjunction with Article 4(1) of Decision 2004/860/EC (OJ L 370, 17.12.2004, p. 78) on the signing on behalf of the European Community and on the provisional application of certain provisions of that Agreement, and with Article 4(1) of Decision 2004/849/EC (OJ L 368, 15.12.2004, p. 26) on the signing on behalf of the European Union, and on the provisional application of certain provisions of that Agreement.

8.2.2 *Purpose and Scope*

The main objective of the Swedish Council Decision is to establish a common framework for rapid and effective exchanges of information and intelligence among law enforcement authorities of the Member States in order to support intelligence operations and criminal investigations.

The Swedish Framework Decision's main scope of application is the list of offences excluded from the control of double criminality in Article 2(2) of Council Framework Decision 2002/584/JHA on the European arrest warrant.[8]

The Swedish initiative covers *existing* information and intelligence; therefore, it does not establish any obligation for law enforcement authorities to gather and store new criminal data. The existing information and intelligence might be held by the law enforcement authorities or by public authorities or private entities and made available to law enforcement authorities without the need to adopt any coercive measures.

8.2.3 *Main Elements for the Exchange of Information*

8.2.3.1 The Request for Information

The law enforcement authority conducting a criminal operation or a criminal investigation in a Member State may request that the law enforcement authority of another Member State to provide certain information "for the purpose of detection, prevention or investigation of an offence where there are factual reasons to believe that relevant information and intelligence is available in another Member State".

The request for information should contain, at a minimum, the details set out in Annex B to the Swedish Framework Decision, including the underlying criminal activity giving rise to the request, the purpose for which the specific information and intelligence is sought, and the connection between the purpose and the person who is the subject of the information and intelligence (Article 5(1) and (3)).

The Swedish Framework Decision clearly advises law enforcement authorities to "refrain from requesting more information or intelligence, or setting narrower time frames than necessary for the purpose of the request" (Article 5(2)).

8.2.3.2 Channels and Language

Law enforcement authorities are required to use existing channels for the cross-border exchange of information and intelligence.

---

[8] OJ L 190, 18.7.2002, p. 1.

The language of the communication shall be agreed upon among the Member States concerned, based on the particular channel used.

Member States may nominate a contact person for urgent cases, whose details should be communicated to the General Secretariat of the Council (Article 6(1)).

8.2.3.3 Transmission of Information and Intelligence

The law enforcement authority that receives the request must provide the information or intelligence under the same conditions applicable to the exchange of information with other national law enforcement authorities, and within the strict deadlines established by the Swedish initiative.

In addition, the law enforcement authority that receives the request is only entitled to refuse requests for information or intelligence for those reasons expressly recognised in Article 10 of the Council Framework Decision.

Rules derived from the speciality rule apply when the information held by the law enforcement authority that receives the request was provided by another Member State or a third State.

Equivalent Access of Information

The transmission of information is based on the principle of "equivalent access", according to which information must be provided to requesting Member States under conditions no stricter than that applicable at national level. In particular, the exchange of information or intelligence cannot be subject to an agreement or authorisation by a judicial authority if the same information or intelligence is accessible by the national law enforcement authorities in an internal procedure without such agreement or authorisation (Article 3(3)).

Conversely, if a judicial authorisation or agreement to have access is needed at national level, the requested competent law enforcement authority "shall be obliged to ask the competent judicial authority for an agreement or authorisation to access and exchange the information sought" (Article 3(4)).

Time Limits

When delivering the requested information and intelligence, law enforcement authorities are subject to different deadlines depending upon the seriousness of the criminal activities being investigated and the urgency of the request.

For urgent requests concerning serious criminal offences included in the list of Article 2(2) of the Council Framework Decision on the European Arrest Warrant, the requested law enforcement authority should respond within a maximum of 8 h, provided that the information is held in a database directly accessible by a law enforcement authority.

For non-urgent requests for information and intelligence related to serious criminal offences (interpreted in the same manner as above), the requested authority should comply within 1 week if the requested information or intelligence is held in a database directly accessible by a law enforcement authority. In other cases, the information should be communicated to the requesting competent law enforcement authorities within 14 days.

If the law enforcement authority is not able to provide information within the deadline described above, he or she shall immediately provide reasons to the requesting authority using the form provided in Annex A of the Council Framework Decision. In urgent cases, "where the provision of the information or intelligence requested within the period of 8 hours would put a disproportionate burden on the requested law enforcement authority, the provision may be postponed, by no later than 3 days, and be immediately communicated to the requested law enforcement authority" (Articles 4(2) and (3)).

Grounds for Refusal

The law enforcement authority responding to a request may refuse to provide information or intelligence "if there are factual reasons to assume that the provision of the information or intelligence would (a) harm essential national security interests of the requested Member State; or (b) jeopardise the success of a current investigation or a criminal intelligence operation or the safety of individuals; or (c) clearly be disproportionate or irrelevant with regard to the purposes for which it has been requested".

The law enforcement authority could also refuse the exchange of information "where the request pertains to an offence punishable by a term of imprisonment of 1 year or less under the law of the requested Member State" (Articles 10(1) and (2)).

In cases where a judicial authorisation or an agreement is necessary, the law enforcement authority may refuse the request for information if such authorisation or agreement has not been given by the corresponding judicial authority (Article 10(3)).

Speciality Principle

Another Member State or third State could have provided the information held by the requested law enforcement authority under the speciality principle. In that case, the transmission of information "may only take place with the consent of the Member State or third country that provided the information or intelligence" (Article 3(5)).

8.2.3.4 Spontaneous Exchange of Information and Intelligence

The Swedish Framework Decision also contemplates the spontaneous exchange of information and intelligence between law enforcement authorities, in cases where there are "factual reasons to believe that the information and intelligence could assist in the detection, prevention or investigation of offences" included within the list of offences excluded from the double criminality check of the Council Framework Decision on the European arrest warrant (Article 7(1)).

In these cases, "the provision of information and intelligence shall be limited to what is deemed relevant and necessary for the successful detection, prevention or investigation of the crime or criminal activity in question" (Article 7(2)).

Chapter 9
Exchange of Information Between Judicial Authorities in Different Steps of Criminal Proceedings

9.1 In Order to Obtain Information and Documents, or to Undertake Certain Investigative Measures in Another Member State

A prosecutor or investigating judge conducting an investigation may need particular documents or different types of information located in another Member State. To obtain such information, the most relevant legal instrument applicable at present is the Convention of 2000 and its Protocol.

The Convention of 2000 ensures and promotes direct contacts between the requesting and requested Member States, as well as spontaneous exchange of information between them.

Article 6(1) first indent is as follows:

> Requests for mutual assistance and spontaneous exchange of information referred to in Article 7 shall be made in writing, or by any means capable of producing a written record under conditions allowing the receiving Member State to establish authenticity. Such requests shall be made directly between judicial authorities with territorial competence for initiating and executing them, and shall be returned through the same channels unless otherwise specified in this Article.

Regarding the spontaneous exchange of information, Article 7 Convention of 2000 states that "the providing authority may, pursuant to its national law, impose conditions on the use of such information by the receiving authority", in whose case "the receiving authority shall be bound by those conditions".

The opinions expressed by the author are personal and do not necessary coincide with those of the institution she is working for.

Á.G. Zarza (ed.), *Exchange of Information and Data Protection in Cross-border Criminal Proceedings in Europe*, DOI 10.1007/978-3-642-40291-3_9,

A particular provision related to the processing and protection of personal data exchanged in accordance with the Convention of 2000 has been introduced in its Article 23:

Article 23

Personal data protection

1. Personal data communicated under this Convention may be used by the Member State to which they have been transferred:
   (a) for the purpose of proceedings to which this Convention applies;
   (b) for other judicial and administrative proceedings directly related to proceedings referred to under point (a);
   (c) for preventing an immediate and serious threat to public security;
   (d) for any other purpose, only with the prior consent of the communicating Member State, unless the Member State concerned has obtained the consent of the data subject.
2. This Article shall also apply to personal data not communicated but obtained otherwise under this Convention.
3. In the circumstances of the particular case, the communicating Member State may require the Member State to which the personal data have been transferred to give information on the use made of the data.
4. Where conditions on the use of personal data have been imposed pursuant to Articles 7 (2), 18(5), 18(6) or 20(4), these conditions shall prevail. Where no such conditions have been imposed, this Article shall apply.
5. The provisions of Article 13(10) shall take precedence over this Article regarding information obtained under Article 13.

The added value of this legal provision in a legal instrument of judicial cooperation in criminal matters is not clear, if we take into consideration that the principles of legality and proportionally applicable in both judicial cooperation in criminal matters and national criminal proceedings will have the same result.

If the information needed is related to one or more bank accounts that the suspect holds or controls in other Member State, the judicial authority may issue a request for mutual legal assistance in application of Articles 1–3 (depending on the particular type of information or measure required), or a request for additional information in accordance with Article 4, of the Protocol to the Convention of 2000[1] (thereinafter referred as "the Protocol"). Once again, European Union law encourages the requested judicial authority to adopt an active and collaborative role in Article 5 of the Protocol:

> If the competent authority of the requested Member State in the course of the execution of a request for mutual assistance considers that is may be appropriate to undertake investigations not initially foreseen, or which could not be specified when the request was made, it

[1] Protocol established by the Council in accordance with Article 34 of the Treaty on European Union to the Convention on Mutual Assistance in Criminal Matters between the Member States of the European Union (OJ C 326, 21.11.2001, p. 2).

shall immediately inform the requesting authority accordingly in order to enable it to take further action.

The information gathered and exchanged in the framework of a Joint Investigation Team also deserves some attention. JITs are governed by Article 13 Convention of 2002 and by Council Framework Decision 2002/45/JHA of 13 June 2002.[2] They are set up for a specific purpose and a limited period to carry out criminal investigations in one or more of the Member States whose officials are participating in the team. One of the added value of a JIT is the ability to exchange information between its members without the need to issue and execute (as a general rule) requests for mutual assistance and/or orders for mutual recognition. In this respect, Article 1(9) CFrD of JITs states that:

> A member of the joint investigation team may, in accordance with his or her national law and within the limits of his or her competence, provide the team with information available in the Member State which has seconded him or her for the purpose of the criminal investigations conducted by the team.

Paragraph (10) of the same legal provision establishes the purposes under which the information lawfully obtained in a Member State may be used in another one.

It is worthily mentioned that, as a first step to replace the already described legal instruments of mutual legal assistance by new ones based on the principle of mutual recognition, the Council adopted in 2008 the Council Framework Decision 2008/978/JHA of 18 December 2008 on the European evidence warrant for the purpose of obtaining objects, documents and data for use in proceedings in criminal matters[3] (hereinafter, CFrD on EEW).

With this legal instruments, the investigating judge or prosecutor requiring criminal data available in another Member State may request the transmission of such data by issuing a form annexed to Council Framework Decision 2008/978/JHA. The executing judicial authority should facilitate such information "where the objects, documents or data are already in the possession of the executing authority before the EEW is issued" (Article 4(4)).

However, in practice, the EEW has not been widely applied by the judicial authorities, among other reasons, due to its reduced scope of application, which excludes the possibility of requiring the executing authority to (a) "conduct interviews, take statements or initiate other types of hearings involving suspects, witnesses, experts or any other party"; (b) "carry out bodily examinations or obtain bodily material or biometric data *directly from the body of any person*, including DNA samples or fingerprints"; (c) "obtain information in real time such as through the interception of telecommunications, covert surveillance or monitoring of bank accounts"; (d) "conduct analysis of existing objects, documents or data"; and (e) "obtain communications data retained by providers of a publicly available electronic communications service or a public communications network".

[2] OJ L 162, 20.6.2002, p. 1. See also Council Resolution of 26 February 2010 on a Model Agreement for setting up a Joint Investigation Team (JIT), OJ C 70, 19.3.2010, p. 1.

[3] OJ L 350, 30.12.2008, p. 72.

As result, when an investigation requires to undertake several investigative measures or needs different type of information from another Member State, the competent judicial authority has to apply different legal instruments and issue several requests for cooperation, some of them reflecting the principle of mutual recognition, others based on mutual legal assistance.

9.2 For the Purposes of Executing a European Arrest Warrant

As it has been mentioned in the previous section, the judicial authority conducting an investigation at national level that needs to have a suspect residing in another Member State arrested can send the corresponding European Arrest Warrant directly to the executing judicial authority.

To ensure the information is transmitted timely and efficiently, both judicial authorities can make use of different channels and mechanisms.

- If the location of the requested person is unknown or if for any other reason the issuing judicial authority cannot identify the competent executing judicial authority, "it shall make the requisite enquiries, including through the contact points of the European Judicial Network" (Article 10 CFrD on EAW).
- The EAW should be forwarded "by any secure means capable of producing written records under conditions allowing the executing Member State to establish authenticity" (Article 10(4) CFrD on EAW). In particular, the issuing judicial authority may:
  - Issue an alert for the requested person in SIS (Article 9(2) CFrD on EAW reproduced in the previous section);
  - As alternative to SIS, "the issuing judicial authority may call on Interpol to transmit a European Arrest Warrant" (Article 10(3) CFrD on EAW);
  - Effect the transmission "via the secure telecommunications system of the European Judicial Network" (Article 10(2) CFrD on EAW).

In many occasions, the transmission of a EAW is the first step of a close collaboration and, depending on the complexity of the case, frequent contacts and exchange of information between both judicial authorities:

- "All difficulties concerning the transmission or the authenticity of nay document needed for the execution of the European Arrest Warrant shall be dealt with by direct contacts between the judicial authorities involved (...)" (Article 10 (5) CFrD on EAW);
- If the judicial authority who has received the EAW is not competent to execute it, "shall inform the issuing judicial authority accordingly" (Article 10(6) CFrR on EAW);

- When the information transmitted is considered insufficient by the executing judicial authority, "it shall request that the necessary supplementary information (...) be furnished as a matter of urgency" (Article 15(2) CFrD on EAW); conversely, "the issuing judicial authority may at any time forward any additional useful information to the executing judicial authority" (Article 15 (3) CFrD on EAW);
- Where the EAW cannot be executed within the time limits laid down in Article 17 CFD on EAW, "the executing judicial authority shall immediately inform the issuing judicial authority thereof, giving the reasons for the delay" (Article, 17 (4));
- The conditions and duration of the temporary transfer of the requested person "shall be determined by mutual agreement between the issuing and executing judicial authorities" (Article 18(2) CFrD on EAW);
- Following the decision of surrender the suspect, the date should be agreed between the authorities concerned (Article 23(1) CFrD on EAW); when the surrender is prevented by circumstances beyond the control of any of the Member States, or if such surrender should be temporarily postponed for serious humanitarian reasons, the executing judicial authority shall immediately inform the issuing judicial authority and agree on a new surrender date (Article 23 (3) and (4) CFrD on EAW); the conditional surrender should be determined "by mutual agreement between the executing and the issuing judicial authorities" (Article 24 (2) CFrD on EAW);
- In order to deduct the period of detention served in the executing Member State from the total period of detention to be served in the issuing Member State, "all information concerning the duration of the detention of the requested person on the basis of the EAW shall be transmitted by the executing judicial authority (...):" (Article 26(2) CFrD on EAW).

Both Eurojust and EJN can provide assistance and support for the issuing and further steps related to the execution of an EAW. Hence, the National Members of Eurojust, in their capacity as national judicial authorities and in agreement with a competent national authority may issue, complete and execute EAW. In cases of multiple EAW for the same person, the judicial authority "may seek the advice of Eurojust" (Article 16(2) CFrD on EAW).

In these cases, the judicial authority requesting support and assistance needs to provide (to the Eurojust National Member, to the contact point of EJN) some details of the investigation, including personal data of the suspect.

9.3 With a View to the Adoption and Monitoring of Supervisory Measures Alternative to Provisional Detention

In some criminal investigations, the competent judicial authority may consider that the physical presence of the suspect in the Member State is not required (or not anymore), and therefore allow the suspect residing in another Member State, whilst awaiting trial, provided that some supervisory measures as an alternative to provisional detention are adopted in that Member State. In these situations, after the consent of the suspect to return to that Member State, the competent judicial authority may issue a decision on supervision measures and forward it to the competent authority of the Member State in which the person is lawfully and ordinarily residing. The Council Framework Decision 2009/829/JHA of 23 October 2009 on the application, between Member States of the European Union, of the principle of mutual recognition to decisions on supervision measures as an alternative to provisional detention (thereinafter, "CFrD on SM"), laid down the rules for the recognition and monitoring of such supervision measures, as well as the rules for the surrender of the person concerned in case of breach of these measures.

On the procedure for forwarding a decision on supervision measures together with the certificate, Article 10(2) of the cited Council Framework Decision states:

> The decision on supervision measures or a certified copy of it, together with the certificate, shall be forwarded by the competent authority in the issuing State directly to the competent authority in the executing State by any means which leaves a written record under conditions allowing the executing State to establish their authenticity. The original of the decision on supervision measures, or a certified copy of it, and the original of the certificate, shall be sent to the executing State if so requires. All official communications shall also be made directly between the said competent authorities.

If the competent authority in the executing Member State is unknown, the issuing authority "shall make all necessary inquiries, including via de contact points of the European Judicial Network" (Article 10(6) CFrD on SM).

Moreover, in the same spirit of mutual trust and close collaboration between the issuing and the executing judicial authority than the CFrD on EAW, the abovementioned legal instrument on supervision measures promotes and expressly refers to different situations requiring direct contacts and agreements between both judicial authorities:

- If the circumstances that motivated the adoption of this measure have changed, or if certain difficulties appear, "the competent authorities of the issuing and executing States shall consult each other so as to avoid, as far as possible, any discontinuance in the monitoring of the supervision order" (Article 11(3) CFrD on SM);
- When the decision on supervision cannot be adopted by the executing State within the timeframes laid down in Article 12 CFD on SM, "it shall immediately inform the competent authority in the issuing State, by any means of its

choosing, giving reasons for the delay and indicating how long it expects to take to issue a final decision" (Article 12(3) CFD on SM);

- Among the obligations of the authorities involved, the issuing judicial authority can be invited to provide information as to whether the monitoring of the supervisory measures is still needed in the circumstances of the particular case at hand. If so, "the competent authority in the issuing State shall, without delay, reply to such an invitation" (Article 19(1) CFD on SM). The later has also the obligation to "immediately notify the competent authority in the issuing State of any breach of a supervision measure" (Article 19(3) CFD on SM);
- The need of both judicial authorities to consult to each other is reiterated and regulated in detail in Article 22 CFrD on SM.

9.4 With the Aim of Freezing and Further Confiscating of Properties, and Securing Evidence. Execution of Financial Penalties

Within the framework of a criminal proceeding, the competent authority may issue an order for the freezing of criminal assets, to be recognised and executed in another Member State. A similar order may be issued with the aim of ensuring certain evidence located abroad. In both cases, the legal instrument applicable (the Council Framework Decision 2003/577/JHA of 22 July 2003 on the execution in the European Union of orders freezing property or evidence, CFrD on OFpe) is governed by the principle of mutual recognition and, as result, will be based on direct contacts between both judicial authorities.

In accordance with this principle, freezing orders and the corresponding certificates are transmitted by the issuing Member State to the executing one "by any means capable of producing a written record under conditions allowing the executing State to establish authenticity" (Article 4(1) CFD on OfPE). EJN can assist the issuing authority in the identification of the competent authority in the executing Member State (Article 4(3) CFrD on OfPE).

Direct contacts between both judicial authorities, with the support of other networks (EJN, ARO) and EU bodies (Eurojust) when necessary, continue during further steps in the execution procedure.

When executed, "a report on the execution of the freezing order shall be made forthwith to the competent authority in the issuing State by any means capable of producing a written record" and the decision itself should be communicated "as soon as possible and, whenever practicable, within 24 hours of receipt of the freezing order" (Article 5(1), third indent, and (3) CFrD on OfPE). Communication between both judicial authorities should continue in the course of the legal remedy than a third party may potentially bring to court. Moreover, "if the action is brought in the executing State, the judicial authority of the issuing State shall be informed thereof and of the grounds of the action, so that, it can submit the arguments that it deems necessary" (Article 11(3) CFrD on OfPE).

Being an order freezing a provisional measure, it should be accompanied or followed by a request for confiscation of the criminal assets and properties, or for transferring of evidence to the issuing Member State (Article 10(1) CFrD on OfPE).

When further confiscation has been requested or foreseen, the Council Framework Decision 2006/783/JHA of 6 October 2006 on the application of the principle of mutual recognition to confiscation orders (CFrD on CO) becomes applicable. As any other instrument inspired on mutual recognition, direct contacts and close collaboration between the issuing and executing judicial authorities are regulated and promoted (see in particular Articles 4(3) and (4) for the transmissions of orders; Article 8(5) regarding difficulties in execution; Article 9 on legal remedies; Article 10(3) and (4) in case of postponement of a confiscation order; Article 14(3) on further execution of a confiscation order; and Article 17 related to the information on the results of the execution of the Council Framework Decision 2006/783/JHA).

9.5 With the Purpose of Executing Judgments Imposing Custodial Sentences, Measures Involving Deprivation of Liberty, or Judgments and Probation Decisions with a View to the Supervision of Probation Measures and Alternative Sanctions

In accordance the Tampere conclusions, and in order to extend the principle of mutual recognition to the final judgements involving deprivation of liberty, or imposing probation measures and alternative sanctions, the JHA Council adopted the following two framework decisions in November 2008:

- The Council Framework Decision 2008/909/JHA of 27 November 2008 on the application of the principle of mutual recognition to judgments in criminal matters imposing custodial sentences or measures involving deprivation of liberty for the purpose of their enforcement in the European Union (CFrD on Deprivation of Liberty/DL).

  With this Council Decision, custodial sentences and final decisions imposing deprivation of liberty issued in a Member State can be forwarded (jointly with the corresponding certificate), to the Member State of the nationality of the sentenced person, or to the Member State in which the sentenced person has been legally residing continuously, with a view of their execution.

  This mechanism, mainly intended to facilitate the social rehabilitation of the sentenced persons, becomes applicable and is complementary to the decisions for non-execution of an EAW "issued for the purposes of execution of a custodial sentence or detention order, where the requested person is staying in, or is a national or a resident of the executing Member State and that State undertakes to execute the sentence or detention order in accordance with its domestic law" (Article 4(6) CFrD on EAW). It is also applicable in cases of execution of an EAW under the condition that the person, after being heard, is returned to the executing Member State in order to serve there the custodial sentence or detention order passed against him in the issuing Member State (Article 5(3) CFrD on EAW).

As mentioned in it Recital (8), "the forwarding of the judgment and the certificate to the executing State is subject to consultation between the competent authorities of the issuing and the executing State, and the consent of the competent authority of the executing State" (see also Article 5). The consultation among both judicial authorities is also foreseen in other steps of the execution proceeding (see inter alia Article 10 in cases of partial recognition and enforcement; Article 12(3) on the need the competent authorities of the issuing State in cases of delay; and Article 21 on the information to be given by the executing State).

- The Council Framework Decision 2008/947/JHA of 27 November 2008 on the application of the principle of mutual recognition to judgments and probation decisions with a view to the supervision of probation measures and alternative sanctions (CFrD on PMAS).

  The purpose of this legal instrument is to facilitate "the social rehabilitation of sentenced persons, improving the protection of victims and of the general public, and facilitating the application of suitable probation measures and alternative sanctions in cases of offenders not living in the State of conviction" (Article 1 (1) CFrD on PMAS). To this aim, the judicial authority of the issuing State should forward the judgment and, where applicable, the probation decision, accompanied by the corresponding certificate, directly to the issued Member State (Article 6 CFrD on PMAS).

  As any other instrument on mutual recognition analysed in previous sections, this Council Framework Decision states that any possible difficulty should be dealt directly between the competent authorities of the issuing and executing Member States. Article 15 CFrD on PMAS, on consultations between competent authorities, is as follow:

  > Where and whenever it is felt appropriate, competent authorities of the issuing State and of the executing State may consult each other with a view to facilitating the smooth and efficient application of this Framework Decision.[4]

9.6 With the Purpose of Executing Financial Penalties

Financial penalties imposed by judicial (also administrative) authorities of a Member State can be enforced in another by sending the judicial decision, together with the corresponding certificate, to the competent authority of the Member State in

[4] See also Article 9(4) in cases of withdrawal of the certificate by the issuing authority; Article 12 on time limits and possible delays.

which the person against whom a decision has been passed has property or income is normally resident (in the case of a legal person, where its seat is registered).

The Council Framework Decision 2005/214/JHA of 24 February 2005 on the application of the principle of mutual recognition to financial penalties, is also based on a constant dialogue and collaboration between the issuing and executing judicial authorities (see in particular Articles 4 and 14, the later related to the information from the executing State).

9.7 Taking Consideration of Criminal Convictions in a Further Criminal Proceedings of Another Member State

The principle of mutual recognition in criminal matters does not only ensure that judicial decisions issued in the course or as result of a national criminal proceeding should be directly executed in another Member State. It also allows taking consideration of the final conviction adopted in such national criminal proceeding, in the course of a different and independent criminal proceeding initiated in another Member State. In other words, the principle of mutual recognition allows taking consideration of criminal records in further and independent criminal proceedings undertaken in another Member State, by recognising to such criminal records equivalent legal effects.

The legal instrument applicable is the Council Framework Decision 2008/675/JHA of 24 July 2008 on taking account of convictions in the Member States of the European Union in the course of new criminal proceedings.[5] As stated in its Article 3(1), the information on previous criminal records can be obtained under applicable instruments on mutual assistance or on the exchange of information extracted from criminal records, as we have seen in this chapter, in the section devoted to ECRIS.

[5] OJ L 220, 15.8.2008, p. 32.

Chapter 10
Processing and Protection of Personal Data in the Framework of Police and Judicial Cooperation in Criminal Matters

10.1 Scope of DP Framework Decision

We have seen in other sections of this book[1] that each EU information system or database has been accompanied by its own set of provisions governing the processing and protection of personal data. In most of the cases these provisions constitute a complete and coherent set of rules covering all relevant aspects of data protection (data quality, data protection, data security, organisation of supervision and liability). In other cases, the legal provisions lay down some specificites for the processing and protection of personal data and state that, for any other aspect on this matter, the rules on the Convention 108 and the Recommendation No. R(87)15 on the use of personal data in the police sector apply.

In The Hague Programme, the European Council considered that the recognition and further developments of the principle of availability would increase notably the exchange of information among law enforcement authorities at all levels (not only through the existing EU information systems and databases) and concluded that a set of horizontal rules on this matter was necessary.[2] The *Council Framework Decision 2008/977/JHA on the protection of personal data processed in the framework of police and judicial cooperation in criminal matters*[3] (DP Framework Decision) was adopted with this horizontal approach. However, as mentioned previously, its scope of application was rather limited.[4]

The DP Framework Decision was not applicable to those EU information systems and databases having their own set of rules for the processing and protection of personal data, neither to the EU agencies and bodies having their own tailor-made set of rules on this matter (as Eurojust and Europol). For those legal systems and databases having specific rules complemented by the 108 Convention, the DP

---

[1] See Part IV, Chaps. 7 and 8 of this book.

[2] See Part II, Chap. 2, Sect. 2.2 of this book.

[3] OJ L 350, 30.12.2008, p. 60.

[4] See Part II, Chap. 2, Sect. 2.3.1 of this book.

Á.G. Zarza (ed.), *Exchange of Information and Data Protection in Cross-border Criminal Proceedings in Europe*, DOI 10.1007/978-3-642-40291-3_10,

Framework Decision applies subsidiarity. In the area of national security interests and specific intelligence activities, this Framework Decision was not applicable neither.

Conversely, the scope of application of the DP Framework Decision included "the processing of personal data in the framework of police and judicial cooperation in criminal matters" [Art. 1(1)]. Recital (2) states that:

> Common action in the field of police cooperation under Article 30(1)(b) of the Treaty on European Union and *common action on judicial cooperation in criminal matters under Article 31(1)(a) of the Treaty on European Union imply a need to process the relevant information* which should be subject to appropriate provisions on the protection of personal data.

The same approach is reiterated in Recital (5) according to which:

> The exchange of personal data within the framework of police and *judicial cooperation in criminal matters*, notably under the principle of availability of information as laid down in The Hague Programme, should be supported by clear rules enhancing mutual trust between the competent authorities (...).

Whilst the need to have clear rules for the exchange of information at police level seems to be noncontroversial, the extension to which such rules should be applicable by judges and prosecutors in the course of ongoing judicial investigations and criminal proceedings with a cross-border dimension is arguable.

10.2 Application of DP Framework Decision to Cross-Border Police Investigations

The need for clear rules for the processing and protection of personal data in the area of police cooperation seems to be obvious: no other rules are limiting the powers of law enforcement authorities to ensure the protection of fundamental rights of the individuals concerned by the access, processing, exchange of transmission of police information.

The situation is different in the context of judicial cooperation in criminal matters.

10.3 Overlapping of Certain Principles and Rights of DP Framework Decision with the Principles and Rights of Criminal Proceedings

The judicial authorities of the Member States do not exchange information in the same context than police authorities. Prosecutors and investigating judges request information, transmit the information requested, or clarify certain points of such requests in the framework of existing national criminal proceedings, and in accordance with both the legal instruments of judicial cooperation in criminal matters and the national Codes of criminal proceedings.

As we have seen in a previous section,[5] the legal instruments on judicial cooperation contain clear rules on the type of information that can be requests and the purposes for such requests. Although the principle of mutual recognition allows direct contacts between judicial authorities, it is clear that both the issuing and the executing judicial authority will not exchange information and personal data other than those mentioned in the legal instrument applicable, in accordance with the principle of legality, and will accommodate their requests to the importance of the criminal offence committed, in accordance with the principle of proportionality.

Hence, it seems that the principles of lawfulness and proportionality lay down in Art. 3(1) DP Framework Decision overlap with those applied on a day-to-day basis by the competent authorities of the Member States in the course of a cross-border judicial investigation and/or criminal proceeding. There would not be any need, then, to transpose such principles into the national legislations on judicial cooperation in criminal matters.

Art. 3(1) DP Framework Decision is as follows:

> Personal data may be collected y the competent authorities only for specified, explicit and legitimate purposes in the framework of their tasks and may be processed only for the same purpose for which data were collected. Processing of the data shall be lawful and adequate, relevant and not excessive in relation to the purposes for which they are collected.

Regardless of whether the information is exchanged through normal post or fax, or making use of a information system or database (SIS-II, EJN secure connection), the legality and proportionality principles governing judicial cooperation in criminal matters should prevail.

It can be argued that the principles of legality and proportionality are not well developed in the area of judicial cooperation in criminal matters. It is certainly true. It can be considered that the principle of mutual recognition has been developed more by practitioners than from a theoretical point of view, and that there is not yet in the EU a dogmatic and overall theoretical construction of this principle. The extended competences of the Court of Justice after the Treaty of Lisbon may contribute enormously to the development of a doctrine on the principles of legality and proportionality in the area of judicial cooperation in criminal matters, especially in relation to the legal instruments based on the principle of mutual recognition. However, the fact that these principles are not developed enough cannot have as a consequence that other set of rules (i.e., the principles of data protection) apply instead.

It is also true that, as far as judicial authorities are extracting information from certain databases (ECRIS) or transmitting their requests through others (SIS-II),

[5] See Part IV, Chap. 9 of this book.

the rules on data protection should be applicable in these cases. This is also true. The judicial authorities, as "users", should take in mind that these databases are subject to some administrative rules for the processing and protection of personal data. Therefore, as users of these databases, they should also comply with such rules. However, this cannot have as a consequence that the set of rules for the processing and protection of personal data, and not the legality and proportionality principles governing judicial cooperation in criminal matters, should be applicable by the judicial authorities of the Member States. As mentioned previously, the legality and proportionality principles governing judicial cooperation in criminal maters should prevail.

The situation is similar regarding the fundamental rights of the suspects and accused persons. As mentioned in other sections,[6] another good example of the overlapping between both set of rules is the right of the suspect to have access to the judicial file. In cross-border cases, experts on data protection will advice the suspect to request access to the judicial file in accordance with Art. 17(1) DP Framework Decision, which is as follows:

> (1) every data subject shall have the right to obtain, following requests made at reasonable intervals, without constraint and without excessive delay or expense:
>
> (a) at least a confirmation from the controller or from the national supervisory authority as to whether or not data relating to him have been transmitted or made available and information on the recipients or categories of recipients to whom the data have been disclosed and communication of the data undergoing processing, or
> (b) at least confirmation from the national supervisory authority that all necessary verifications have taken place.

It rather seems that, in the context of an ongoing investigation or prosecution with a cross-border dimension, Directive 2012/13/EU on the right to information in criminal proceedings[7] on the should apply.

This Directive recognises the right of information about the existence of a criminal investigation against a particular suspect or accused person (Arts. 3 and 6), the right of access to the materials of the case (Art. 7), and the right to challenge the information provided [Art. 8(2)].

The right of information in a criminal proceeding is inferred from the case-law of the European Court of Human Rights. According to this principle, suspects and accused persons must be informed, either orally or in writing, of the existence of an investigation or a criminal proceeding against them.

The information must be provided promptly, and at the latest before the first official interview of the suspect or accused person by the police or by another competent authority.

The suspects and accused persons who are arrested or detained should be also informed of the reasons for their arrest or detention, including the criminal act they

[6] See Part I, Chap. 1 of this book.

[7] OJ L 142, 1.6.2012, p. 1.

are suspected or accused of having committed [Art. 6(2)]. This right also applies to individuals subject to a European Arrest Warrant (Art. 1).

More detailed information on the accusation, including the nature and legal classification of the criminal offence, as well as the nature of participation by the accused person, must be provided "at the latest on submission of the merits of the accusation to a court" [Art. 6(3)].

The suspect and accused person must be kept informed of further steps of a criminal proceeding and until its conclusion, "which is understood to mean the final determination of the question whether the suspect or accused person has committed the criminal offence, including, where applicable, sentencing and the resolution of any appeal".

Any changes in the information given must be also communicated to the suspects or accused persons, if this necessary "to safeguard the fairness of the proceedings" [Art. 6(4)].

Recital (35) clarifies that, "where information is provided in accordance with this Directive, the competent authorities should take note of this in accordance with existing recording procedures under national law and should not be subject to any additional obligation to introduce new mechanisms or *to any additional administrative burden*". We could then understand that the information provided to the suspect excludes the obligation to inform him also in accordance with the administrative rules for the protection of personal data.

As per the right of access to the materials of the case, the Directive makes a distinction between the materials essential to challenging effectively the lawfulness of an arrest or detention, and the access to the material evidence.

The materials required to challenge effectively the lawfulness of an arrest or detention may include documents, photographs, audio and videorecording, among others. They should be made available to suspects or accused persons or to their lawyers at the latest before a competent judicial authority is called to decide upon the lawfulness of the arrest or detention.

Access to material evidence should be granted to the suspects and accused persons or their lawyers, in order to safeguard the fairness of the proceedings and to prepare the defense, in due time and at the latest upon submission of the merits o the accusation to the judgment of a court. "Where further material evidence comes into the possession of the competent authorities, access shall be granted to it in due time to allow for it to be considered".

The Directive also establishes certain limitations to the right of access to the materials of the case. Access may be refused "if such access may lead to a serious threat to the life or the fundamental rights of another person", or "if such refusal is strictly necessary to safeguard an important public interest, such as n case where access could prejudice an ongoing investigation or seriously harm the national security of the Member States in which the criminal proceedings are instituted" [Art. 7(4)].

Lastly, the Directive also recognises the right of the suspect "to challenge, in accordance with procedures in national law, the possible failure or refusal of the competent authorities to provide information in accordance with this Directive" [Art. 8(2)].

Hence, the abovementioned rights of information, access or rectification of personal data does not seem applicable when a formal criminal proceeding has started, neither when police investigations resulted in the arrest or detention of suspects and accused persons. In these situations, the rights to information about the accusation, the right of access to the materials of the case, and the right to challenge the information provided are applicable instead in the context of these criminal investigations and proceedings, by the competent law enforcement and judicial authorities.

This is the approach taken by the DP Framework Directive regarding the right of rectification in Art. 4(2), according to which:

> When the personal data are contained in a judicial decision or record related to the issuance of a judicial decision, the rectification, erasure or blocking shall be carried out in accordance with national rules of judicial proceedings.

When the Framework Decisions implementing the principle of mutual recognition were adopted, there was not a parallel set of fundamental rights protecting the suspects and accused persons. Again, the consequence of the lack of proper rules in the area of judicial cooperation cannot be extension of the scope of application of the rights on data protection. Moreover, the Commission has developed the roadmap, and we will have in a short period of time a complete set of fundamental rights protecting the suspects and accused persons.

10.4 Importance of Certain Principles and Guarantees on Data Protection in Court Proceedings

The application at administrative level and/or by police authorities of certain principles and safeguards on data protection ensures the admissibility in court as evidence of the information and personal data collected. Conversely, the lack of compliance of such principles and guarantees may compromise their legitimacy and have as result the inadmissibility as evidence of the information retrieved from these databases and information systems.

From this perspective, the principle of accuracy deserves especial attention.

In the framework of police investigations, not all the information collected will be accurate. In some situations, law enforcement authorities will gather only intelligence or mere suspicious about the movements of a criminal organisation. In other cases, the information can be more precise and include, for example, the names and home addresses of some members of the criminal organisation. Finally, when police investigation are close to an end, the information gathered can be very detailed and precised. When the three types of information are stored in databases, it is convenient to mark the level of accuracy of this information. This can be done by classifying the information in accordance to different levels, or accompanying the information with some comments allowing further assessing on its level of accuracy.

Moreover, information initially considered not very accurate can be further completed and updated with new data, thus making it more precise. In this respect, the Framework Decision states that "personal data shall be rectified if inaccurate and, where this is possible and necessary, completed or updated".

The specification of the levels or degrees of accuracy of the information gathered for law enforcement purposes is extremely important for judicial authorities conducting investigations and criminal proceedings, as it will allow them to assess the reliability of the information and data as evidence in court. In general, intelligence or mere suspicious about the movements of a criminal organisations are not enough to be assessed as evidence, whilst more precised and verified information would have more chances to be considered as reliable evidence.

Another relevant safeguard is the need to keep log and document of all the transmissions of personal data. Art. 10 DP Framework Decision is as follows:

> (1) All transmissions of personal data are to be logged or documented for the purposes of verification of the lawfulness of the data processing, self monitoring and ensuring proper data integrity and security.
>
> (2) Logs or documentation prepared under paragraphs 1 shall be communicated on request to the competent supervisory authority for the control of data protection. The competent supervisory authority shall use this information only for the control of data protection and for ensuring proper data processing as well as data integrity and security.

Logs and documentation can be extremely important for prosecutors, in order to assess the integrity of the information that will be used to prosecute the suspects of criminal offences, especially should integrity of the information extracted from a database be challenged by the defense lawyer.

In a further step, the tracing and documentation of the information can facilitate the role of the court in the admissibility and further assessment of the evidence based on information extracted from databases or information systems, or exchanged between law enforcement authorities.

For the same reason, the technical and organisational measures to protect personal data against accidental or unlawful destruction, alteration, unauthorised disclosure or access listed in Art. 22(2) will be most useful for prosecution purposes, and in order to bring to court the suspects and accused persons. Among other examples, this legal provision set up the need to implement measures designed to "prevent the unauthorised reading, copying, modification or removal of data media" [parr. (b)], also during "transfers of personal data or during transportation of data media" [parr. (h)], and to ensure "that stored data cannot be corrupted by means of a malfunctioning of the system".

Lastly, the non-observance of the time limits for erasure and review lay down in Arts. 5 and 9 DP Framework Decision could make difficult the admissibility as evidence of the information retrieved from this database or information system.

Chapter 11
Exchange of Information with Third States

11.1 Transmission to Third States of Information and Personal Data Stored by Private Companies

Most of private companies gather and process information and personal data for their own purposes. This is the case, among many other examples, of air carriers and banks. In both cases, experience has proven that such information and personal data, properly analysed by specialised law enforcement authorities at the right time, can be extremely useful for preventing criminal activities (e.g. terrorist attacks in air flights), identifing the movements and connections of criminal organisations operating across the world such (as those involved in trafficking of human beings), or detecting the transferring of the benefits of illegal activities.

Immediate after the terrorist attacks in New York and Washington in 2001, the United States adopted several internal laws compelling private companies to transfer huge amount of information to US specialised bodies for the purposes of preventing and fighting crime. From the perspective of the EU Member States, which all have a different understanding of privacy and data protection to the US, this action had a huge impact and obliged the EU institutions to start negotiations in order to ensure a proper balance between the need to fight against crime and the need to protect the fundamental rights of the citizens whose personal data are collected for private reasons but might then be transmitted to the law enforcement authorities of US. As result, different agreements have been signed between the EU and US (and with other third States) with regard to the transmission of information by private companies to US.

The opinions expressed by the author are personal and do not necessary coincide with those of the institution she is working for.

Á.G. Zarza (ed.), *Exchange of Information and Data Protection in Cross-border Criminal Proceedings in Europe*, DOI 10.1007/978-3-642-40291-3_11,

The practical application of such agreements generates a workflow between the private companies and US law enforcement authorities. When the processing of information by US authorities is relevant for the purposes of preventing or fighting crime in EU, the North-american authorities are obliged to transmit such information to the law enforcement and/or judicial authorities of the Member States, to Europol and/or to Eurojust. Also EU national competent authorities, Eurojust and Europol are empowered to send requests for information to US authorities. When such requests are sent by Eurojust or the judicial authorities of the Member States, they should be issued in accordance with the Agreement on mutual legal assistance between the European Union and the United States of America[1] and the bilateral agreements signed between the Member State(s) concerned and US.

11.2 The EU-US Agreement on the Processing and Transfer of Financial Messaging Data from EU to US for the purposes of the Terrorist Finance Tracking Programme (TFTP)

11.2.1 Background

After the terrorist attacks in Washington and New York on 11 September 2001, the USA approved the Terrorist Finance Tracking Program (TFTP). This program enabled the US Treasury Department to deliver subpoenas to the main provider of international financial payment messaging services in Europe, the Society for Worldwide Interbank Financial Telecommunication (SWIFT), to gain access to SWIFT's financial messaging data in support of its terrorism investigations.

After the adoption of the TFTP, SWIFT stored all relevant financial messages on two identical ("mirror") servers, one located in Europe and one in the USA. The financial messaging data of EU citizens carried over the SWIFT network was stored on the American server; this enabled the US Treasury Department to issue subpoenas against SWIFT.

In June 2006, the *New York Times* revealed the programme and SWIFT's decision to facilitate access to its data. In Europe, the matter raised major data protection concerns.

The Belgian Data Privacy Commission, the Article 29 Data Protection Working Party and the EDPS concluded that SWIFT's decision to make information accessible to the US Treasury Department was a breach of a Belgian law transposing Directive 95/46/EC.

The European Central Bank was asked whether or not it had failed to inform the relevant data protection authorities and national banks of the US practice of

[1] OJ L 181, 19.7.2003, p. 34.

accessing SWIFT's financial transaction data, or to use its power of moral persuasion against SWIFT in this matter.

The European Parliament, in its Resolution on SWIFT, the Passenger Name Record (PNR) Agreement and the transatlantic dialogue on these issues,[2] stated:

> (..) under clearly defined conditions, data generated in financial transactions *can be used exclusively for judicial investigative purposes in connection with suspicion of terrorism financing* and recalls that both the EC and US in their respective legislation (Regulation (EC) No 1781/2006 of the European Parliament and the Council of 15 November 2006 on information on the payer accompanying transfer of funds and the US Bank Secrecy Act) have implemented Financial Action Task Force (FATF) Recommendation VII.[3]

As a result of this criticism, the European Union negotiated a set of undertakings, based upon EU data protection rules, to be applied by the US Treasury Department when receiving and processing EU-originated data.[4]

In July 2007, SWIFT adhered to the "Safe Harbour" privacy principles[5] and adopted a SWIFT Personal Data Protection Policy. It also changed its network architecture, announced its intention to halt its practice of mirroring SWIFT message data in the EU and in the USA, and created an Operating Centre in Switzerland that began operations in 2009.

In light of these developments, the Belgian Data Privacy Commission's 2008 report expressed its satisfaction with the measures taken by SWIFT.

In 2008, the Commission also designated Mr Jean-Louis Bruguière to report on the safeguards adopted by SWIFT. Mr Bruguière published two reports (December 2008 and January 2010), and concluded that the US Treasury Department had complied with the undertakings agreed upon with the EU institutions.

At its 27 July 2009 meeting, the General Affairs and External Relations Council[6] approved "Guidelines for negotiations with the United States for an international agreement to make financial payment messaging data available to the US Treasury Department in order to prevent terrorism and terrorist financing".

---

[2] P6_TA(2007)0039.

[3] Recommendation VII FATF (wire transfers) is as follows:

> Countries should take measures to require financial institutions, including money laundering remitters, to include accurate and meaningful originator information (name, address and account number) on funds transfers and related messages that are sent, and the information should remain with the transfer or related message through the payment chain. Countries should take measures to ensure that financial institutions, including money remitters, conduct enhanced scrutiny of and monitor for suspicious activity funds transfers which do not contain complete originator information (name, address and account number).

[4] These undertakings, known as "TFTP Representations" were published at OJ C 166, 20.7.2007.

[5] *See* Commission Decision of 26 July 2000 pursuant to Directive 95/46/EC of the Parliament and of the Council on the adequacy of the protection provided by the Safe Harbour Privacy Principles and related frequently asked questions issued by the US Department of Commerce. Commission document 2000/520/EC, OJ L 215, 25.8.2000, p. 7.

[6] *See* Press Release 12353/09 (Presse 228), p. 21.

These guidelines and the subsequent Commission negotiations were interpreted as an interim solution, in light of the imminent entry into force of the Lisbon Treaty and the co-decision procedure established therein. On the basis of such Guidelines, a first draft of the Agreement between the European Union and the United States of America on the processing and transfer to Financial Messaging Data from the European Union to the United States of America for the purposes of the Terrorist Finance Tracking Programme (EU–US Agreement on TFTP) was not approved by the European Parliament. However, on 8 July 2011, the European Parliament gave its consent to a revised version of the Agreement.

11.2.2 Legal Framework

The EU–US Agreement on TFPT was concluded by Council Decision 2010/412/EU of 13 July 2010.[7] It entered into force on 1 August 2010, and is valid for a period of 5 years. It shall be automatically extended for subsequent periods of 1 year "unless one of the Parties notifies the other in writing through diplomatic channels, at least six (6) months in advance, of its intention not to extend this Agreement" (Article 23(2)).

11.2.3 Transmission of Information

11.2.3.1 Purpose

The main objective of the EU–US Agreement on TFTP is to ensure the transmission of financial records to the US Treasury Department, for the exclusive purpose of the prevention, investigation, detection or prosecution of terrorism or terrorism financing, of the "financial payments messages referring to financial transfers and related data stored in the territory of the EU *by providers of international financial payment messaging services*, that are jointly designated pursuant to this Agreement" (Article 1(1)(a)).

The "providers of international financial payment messaging services" are those identified in the Annex to the EU–US Agreement on TFTP. So far, only SWIFT has been included in this Annex; it can be updated, as necessary, by exchange of diplomatic notes.[8]

Conversely, the EU–US Agreement on TFTP establishes the conditions under which "relevant information obtained through the TFTP is provided to law

---

[7] OJ L 195, 27.7.2010, p. 5.

[8] Article 3 *in fine* of the Agreement, according to which "Any amendments to the Annex shall be duly published in the *Official Journal of the European Union*".

enforcement, public security, or counter terrorism authorities of Member States, or Europol or Eurojust, for the purpose of the prevention, investigation, detection, or prosecution of terrorism or terrorist financing" (Article 1(1)(b)).

11.2.3.2 Requests by US Treasury Department to Obtain Data from Designated Providers

The US Treasury Department is entitled to request, in accordance with US law, that the designated provider transmits any data necessary for the prevention, investigation, detection or prosecution of terrorism or terrorist financing that are stored in the territory of the European Union.

To reduce the scope of the requests, Article 4(2)(c) establishes that they should "be tailored as narrowly as possible in order to minimise the amount of data requested, taking due account of past and current terrorism risk analyses focused on message types and geography as well as perceived terrorism threats and vulnerabilities".

The request is sent directly to the designated provider. A copy is sent to Europol simultaneously to verify in an expedited manner whether the request complies with the requirements of the EU–US Agreement on TFTP. Europol will notify the designated provider accordingly.

After Europol confirms the request, the designated provider is obligated to provide the data directly to the US Treasury Department, and to keep a log of all data transmitted.

11.2.3.3 Spontaneous Provision of Information and EU Requests for TFTP Searches

The US Treasury Department must ensure the availability to Member States, Europol and Eurojust "of the information obtained through the TFTP that may contribute to the investigation, prevention, detection or prosecution by the European Union of terrorism or its financing" (Article 9).

Moreover, law enforcement authorities of the Member States (including public security and counter-terrorism authorities), Europol and Eurojust may request a search for relevant information obtained through the TFPT where there are "reasons to believe that a person or entity has a nexus to terrorism or its financing" (Article 10).

11.2.4 Data Protection Safeguards

The EU–US Agreement on TFTP contains several provisions regarding the principles and safeguards on data protection to be respected by both parties.

Article 5 regulates the safeguards to be applied by the US Treasury Department to the information obtained from the designated provider. A search of the provided data is only possible where there is pre-existing information or evidence indicating that the subject of the search might be connected to terrorism or its financing.

Searches and the reasons therefor must be recorded. Non-extracted data should be deleted within the strict periods regulated in Article 6. Onward transfers are only possible under the conditions established by Article 7.

With regard to citizens' data protection rights, their rights of access, rectification, erasure and blocking are regulated in Articles 15 and 16. In addition, the US Treasury Department is obligated to provide a public website with detailed information on the TFTP and its purposes, including contact details and the procedures available for the exercise of the rights recognised in Articles 15 and 16.[9]

11.2.5 Reports on the Joint Review of the Implementation of the EU–US Agreement on TFTP

As envisioned in Article 13 of the EU–US Agreement on TFTP, the first Report on the joint review of the implementation of the Agreement between the European Union and the United States of America on the processing and transfer of Financial Messaging Data from the European Union to the United States for the purposes of the Terrorism Finance Tracking Programme was issued on 17–18 February 2011.[10]

In general terms, the group of experts concluded:

> (…) all of the relevant elements of the Agreement have been implemented in accordance with its provisions, including the data protection provisions. The measures which have been taken to ensure such implementation by the US authorities are convincing, and in some cases go beyond what is required under the Agreement. In addition, the review team has been presented with convicting indications of the added value of the Terrorist Finance Tracking Programme (TFTP) to efforts to combat terrorism and its financing.[11]

Discussing the added value of the TFTP in combating terrorism, the group of experts pointed out that:

> (…) TFTP allows not only for the identification of new links between known terrorist suspects and the people to whom they transfer funds, but also for the discovery of other identifying information on such suspects, such as bank account numbers, addresses etc. One of the main reasons for the unique value of TFTP to preventing and combating terrorism and its financing is that it allows the identification of such links also in the absence of earlier information on the bank accounts for the terrorist suspects. Banking information in general is considered very important for these sorts of investigations, since the persons concerned have a clear interest in providing accurate information to ensure that the money gets to where it is intended to go. Bank transfers are considered a reliable and accurate indicator of a link between the person sending the money and the recipient - such links must then be further investigated to establish whether they are related to terrorism.

---

[9] www.treasury.gov/resource-center/terrorist-illicit-finance/Terrorist-Finance-Tracking/Pages/tftp.aspx.

[10] *See also* the Europol Report to the European Parliament, "Europol Activities in Relation to the TFTP Agreement. Information note to the European Parliament. 1 August 2010 - 1 April 2011".

[11] *See* p. 4.

A second report was issued in October 2012.[12]

In general terms, both group of experts focused recommendations on the following points:

- EU and US authorities should collect more feedback from the actors involved in the transferring and processing of financial messaging data in order to provide relevant information about the added value of the TFPT;
- Over the course of future reviews, both parties should provide more statistical information on the overall volume of the data provided and accessed;
- More accurate information (particularly classified information) should be provided to Europol in order to facilitate its verification work. Moreover, it is recommend that law enforcement authorities and Eurojust consider regard Europol as the EU's single reference point for issuing requests, and that a copy of the request sent directly to the US Treasure Department should be sent to Europol in a systematic and timely manner.
- The information available on the TFTP website should be improved, particularly by providing more information on the scope for rectification, erasure and blocking of information.

11.3 Agreements with US, Canada and Australia on the Processing and Transfer by Air Carriers of Passenger Name Record (PNR) Data

Passenger Name Record (PNR) data is a collection of unverified information provided by air passengers when booking and checking in flights, including travel dates, itinerary, contact details, name of the agency booking the flight, method of payment, seat number and baggage information, among others.[13] PNR data are collected and held by air carriers for operational purposes, and retained for a certain period of time for their own commercial purposes.

After the terrorist attacks in United States in September 2001, some countries (namely United States, Canada, Australia, United Kingdom) enacted national laws extending the periods for the retention of PNR data by airlines, and regulating the

[12] Report on the second joint review of the implementation of the Agreement between the European Union and the United States of America on the processing and transfer of Financial Messaging data from the European Union to the United States for the purposes of the Terrorist Finance Tracking Program. October 2012. SWD (2912) 454 final. Brussels, 14.12.2012.

[13] PNR data are different and wider in scope from Advance Passenger Information (API), the later being taken from the machine-readable part of a passport, and including the name, place of birth, nationality of the person, passport number and expiry date. API is regulated by the Directive 2004/82/EC of 29 August 2004, on the obligation of carriers to communicate passengers data (OJ L 261, 6.8.2004, p. 24), according to which this type of data should be made available to border control authorities for the purpose of improving border controls and combating irregular immigration.

obligation of such companies to transfer PNR data to law enforcement authorities for the purposes of preventing and fighting against terrorism.

It was judged that if the information stored by air carriers, carefully analysed by law enforcement authorities, can be an effective tool to prevent criminal activities, detect such activities in real time and take immediate action or, when a criminal activities have been committed, identify the criminals, and keep track of their movements and association so as to unravel criminal networks. As example, the assessment of PNR data can give an indication of the travel routes commonly used by an undercover group of human traffickers.

However, the practical application of these legal instruments by airlines operating flights from and to the territory of the Member States of the European Union generated two main concerns.

On the one hand, the existence of different standards for the processing of personal data by the Member States of the EU and by third States gave rise to serious doubts about the protection of privacy of the EU citizens providing PNR data. To face this challenge, the Commission started negotiations for agreements with US, Canada and Australia to establish the conditions under which air companies of the Member States could transfer PNR data to these countries.

On the other hand, the transfer of PNR data and its further analysis by law enforcement authorities of the Member States was not regulated at EU level. Together with United Kingdom, already mentioned, other Member States started developing their own PNR systems and laid down different rules for the periods of data retention, structure of the system, geographic scope, data protection and security, among other matters.

In the case of US, a first Agreement signed on 19 October 2006 was replaced by an Agreement signed on 23 July 2007,[14] which it has been provisionally applicable with the entry into force of the existing one, the Agreement between the US and EU on the use and transfer of Passenger Name Records to the US Department of Homeland Security (hereinafter, "EU–US PNR Agreement"), on 1st July 2012.[15] The provisional application of the Agreement of 2007 was due to the decision of the European Parliament to postpone its vote on the request for consent until a new agreement incorporating the main concerns raised by the Parliament were negotiated with US.[16]

[14] *See* Council Decision 2007/551/CFSP/JHA of 23 July 2007, OJ L 204, 4.8.2008, p. 16. On this Agreement, see Papakonstantinou (2009), p. 885.

[15] See Council Decision of 13 December 2011 on the signing, on behalf of the Union, of the Agreement between the United States of America and the European Union on the use and transfer of Passenger Name Records to the United States Department of Homeland Security (OJ L 215, 11.8.2012, p. 1).

[16] See European Parliament Resolution of 5 May 2010 on the launch of negotiations for PNR agreements with the United States, Australia and Canada (OJ C 81E, 15.3.2011, p. 70).

Like the current EU–US PNR Agreement, it regulates the conditions under which air carriers should provide to the US Department of Homeland Security (DHS) the PNR data listed in the Annex thereto. Such personal data can be only transferred and further processed by DHS for the purposes of preventing and fighting against terrorism and related criminal activities, terrorism financing, and other serious cross-border offences punishable by a sentence of imprisonment of 3 years or more.

PNR data should be transfered to DHS by using the "push" method, secure electronic means, and initially at 96 hours before the scheduled flight departure although DHS may also require a carrier, on a case-by-case basis, to provide PNR data between or after the regular timeframe.

DHS is responsible for the appropriate technical measures and organisational arrangements to protect personal data contained in PNR data against accidental, unlawful or unauthorised destruction, loss, disclosure, alteration, access, processing or use of such data.

Sensitive data provided by air carriers should be filtered and masked out, with two relevant exceptions. Firstly, where the life of an individual could be imperiled or seriously impaired (in that case, sensitive data can only be processed on a case-by-case basis and with the approval of a DHS senior manager). Secondly, sensitive data can be retained for the time specified in US law for the purpose of a specific investigation, prosecution or enforcement action.

The Agreement sets a data retention period of 10 years for transnational crime and 15 years for terrorism. After 6 months, personally identifiable PNR information should be masked out and, after 5 years, PNR data should be moved to a dormant database with additional controls.

The Agreement also contemplates the transferring of the analytical information obtained from PNR to the competent authorities of the Member States, as well as Europol and Eurojust, within the remit of their respective mandates and for the purposes of preventing, detecting, investigating and prosecuting terrorist and other serious of crime within the European Union.

Lastly, the EU–US Agreement has set out a review and evaluation mechanism that, among other matters, should seek information from US on the exchange of PNR information regarding EU citizens and residents in the territory of EU.[17]

On the other hand, the Agreement on the processing and transfer of Passenger Name Record (PNR) data by air carriers to the Australian Customs and Border Protection Service was signed on 29 September 2011 and entered into force on 1st June 2012. This Agreement replaced the previous one, dated on 2008, which was also applied provisionally after the Parliament decided to postpone its vote on the request for consent on both Agreements with US and Australia.

The arrangements with Canada consist of three instruments: a Commission "Adequacy Decision",[18] the "Commitments by the Canada Border Service

[17] See Annex to the Council Decision 2012/471/EU of 13 December 2011, p. 3.

[18] OJ L 91, 29.3.2006, p. 49.

Agency" (CBSA) annexed to this Decision,[19] and an International Agreement.[20] Negotiations for a new Agreement are on ongoing at the time of writing.

References

Hobbing P (September 2008) Tracing terrorists: the EU–Canada agreement in PNR matters. CEPS Special Report. Available at www.ceps.eu

Papakonstantinou V (2009) The PNR agreement and transatlantic anti-terrorist co-operation: no firm human rights framework on either side of the Atlantic. Common Mark Law Rev 46(3):885

[19] OJ L 91, 29.3.2006, p. 53.

[20] OJ L 82, 21.3.2006, p. 15. On this Agreement, see in detail Hobbing (2008).

Part V
New Developments

Chapter 12
Future Developments of the JHA Area

One of the legal provisions introduced by the Treaty of Lisbon into the Foundational Treaties was Article 68 TFEU, according to which "the European Council shall define the strategic guidelines for legislative and operational planning within the Area of Freedom, Security and Justice". In line with this legal provision the European Council, at its meeting on 27–28 June 2013, invited the incoming Presidencies of the EU to initiate a reflection process on the implementation of the Stockholm Programme and on the way forward.

The European Council expects to hold a discussion regarding the future development of the JHA Area at its meeting in June 2014 in order to define strategic guidelines for the period 2015–2019.

The preparatory works for that meeting have started. These preparatory works also intend to provide inputs for the Commission's Communication on the future of the JHA area to be issued in the first quarter of 2014.

Following a couple of discussion papers circulated by the Lithuanian Presidency at the Informal JHA meeting on 18–19 July 2013 in Vilnius,[1] a revised single document is serving as the basis for in-depth discussions during the meetings of CATS, COSI and SCIFA committees, as well as the Working Party on Civil Law Matters (General Questions).[2]

In this single document the Lithuanian Presidency of the EU has adopted a cautious approach. Taking in mind the current economic situation and limited financial resources, the next multi-annual would focus on the consolidation of the progress made in the JHA Area and, for those areas not developed as expected, on strategies to improve quality implementation.

Among other key priorities, the Lithuanian Presidency has underlined the importance of the JHA agencies "that are so vital in providing practical support

[1] Council doc. 13340/13 and 13341/13. Brussels, 5 September 2013.

[2] Council doc. 14898/13. Brussels, 16 October 2013.

Á.G. Zarza (ed.), *Exchange of Information and Data Protection in Cross-border Criminal Proceedings in Europe*, DOI 10.1007/978-3-642-40291-3_12,

to the competent authorities of the Member States",[3] creating and sharing professional knowledge and know-how, and building a European common culture.

It has also been highlighted that "the most recent scientific and technological achievements"[4] should contribute to the functioning of the Area of Freedom, Security and Justice of the EU, whilst at the same time respecting privacy and fundamental rights.

There is a lot to be done in order to improve collaboration among the EU agencies and practitioners. As we have seen in Chap. 3, the agencies with JHA competences have proposed new methods of working and for responding to serious cross-border crime. These methodologies go beyond the traditional mechanisms of police and judicial cooperation. As an example, Eurojust has proposed innovative methods for coordinating investigative measures to be adopted by different Member States to tackle a cross-border criminal organisation or network. Europol is seeking to encourage Member States to share intelligence and police information on new trends of criminality or particular networks for the purposes of preventing and fighting cross-border crime. Both agencies are very much committed to the setting up and running of Joint Investigations Teams. The regular use by practitioners of these new and innovative working methods and tools needs time to change habits, awareness of the added value of involving the agencies in national criminal investigations and proceedings. This needs practically orientated training courses. In these areas the use of new technologies needs to be explored further. As the Commission mentioned in its Communication on training, online training courses should be promoted in order to maximise training results at a reduced costs.

New technologies can also play a more relevant role in the transmission of information and requests for cooperation in the area of justice and home affairs. It is remarkable that, in twenty-first century, most of the originals of letters of request, European Arrest Warrants and other European orders are sent by ordinary post. A more expeditive channel for the transmission of these requests and orders would accelerate its execution enormously. This is one of the objectives of the e-Codex project developed by several Member States under the umbrella of e-Justice, which is analysed in another section of this chapter on new developments.

At the Council meeting on 5–6 December 2013, Ministers of Justice and Home Affairs held a discussion at political level on future developments in this area. Following this meeting, the contributions of the internal bodies of the Council have been compiled by the Lithuanian Presidency of the EU. They will serve as the basis for further discussions under the incoming Greek Presidency of the EU.

On the other hand, the challenges ahead for EU criminal law were also analysed at the Conference "Assises de la Justice. What role for Justice in the European Union?", organised by the Commission on 21 and 22 November 2013, in Brussels.[5]

---

[3] Council doc. 14898/13, p. 5.

[4] Council doc. 14898/13, p. 6.

[5] Information on this event is available at: http://ec.europa.eu/justice/events/assises-justice-2013/index_en.htm.

The discussion paper on EU criminal law highlighted the importance for practitioners to work together, exchange information in a fast and secure way, and obtain assistance from colleagues by making use of the existing tools and mechanisms, including Union bodies, networks, data-bases and Joint Investigation Teams. To overcome the existing difficulties derived from the fact that some of those mechanisms are not easily accessible or not used, the Commission has suggested "to further simplify these tools and make them more easily accessible to practitioners also thorough training schemes".[6]

Hence, there seem to be quality food for thought and further discussions in 2014, with a view to the adoption of the "Athens Programme".

[6] See "Discussion paper 2: EU Criminal Law" at: http://ec.europa.eu/justice/events/assises-justice-2013/files/criminal_law_en.pdf.

Chapter 13
The Eurojust Draft Regulation: Ten Relevant Points

In July of 2013, the Commission launched a legislative package based on Arts. 85 and 86 TFEU that included *inter alia* a proposal for the establishment of a European Union Agency for Criminal Justice Cooperation (Eurojust) (EJ draft Regulation).

This EU Agency, which will be the legal successor of the existing Eurojust[1] [Art. 1(2) EJ draft Regulation], will continue providing support and assistance in the "*coordination and cooperation between national investigating and prosecuting authorities in relation to serious crime affecting two or more Member States, or requiring a prosecution on common bases, on the basis of operations conducted and information supplied by the Member States' authorities and by Europol*" [Arts. 85(1) TFEU and 2(1) EJ draft Regulation].

The EJ draft Regulation proposes important changes in the structure and governance of Eurojust, its data protection regime, and the exchange of information and collaboration with EU partners, third States and international organisations and bodies. It also suggests some changes in the operational functions and powers of the National Members, and in the control of Eurojust's activities by the European Parliament. The most relevant aspects of the EJ draft Regulation have been summarised in the following ten points.[2]

[1] On Eurojust, see Chap. 3 of this book.

[2] On the EJ new Regulation, see more in detail Busuioca and Groenleerb (2013), p. 285: Coninsx (2013), p. 173: Monar (2013), p. 187: Petit Leclair (2012), p. 38: Wade (2013): Weyemberg (2011), p. 75. See also the following Eurojust reports **.

Á.G. Zarza (ed.), *Exchange of Information and Data Protection in Cross-border Criminal Proceedings in Europe*, DOI 10.1007/978-3-642-40291-3_13,

13.1 Legal Framework

In accordance with Art. 85(1) TFEU, the legal instrument proposed by the Commission is a Regulation. It means that this legal instrument will be binding in its entirety and directly applicable in the Member States in accordance with the Treaties (Art. 68 EJ draft Regulation), without the need of further implementation.

The direct application of the EJ draft Regulation has given rise to some concerns in the Member States, especially with regard to the minimum core of powers granted to the National Members in its Art. 8. As we will see in Sect. 13.4, the purpose of Art. 8 is to ensure that all Member States are empowered by the same set of powers, regardless the particularities of the national legal systems and traditions. As the future Regulation will be immediately applicable, the Member States will not have any room for manoeuvre recognised in Art. 9(a) EJ Decision (national safeguarding clause), which allows Member States to adapt the powers described in Arts. 9a–9f to their particularities of their respective legal systems.

On the other hand, the draft EJ Regulation includes a paragraph in Art. 1, according to which:

> In each of the Member States, Eurojust shall enjoy the most extensive legal capacity accorded to legal persons under their laws. It may, in particular, acquire and dispose of movable and immovable property and be party lo legal proceedings (parr. (3)).

The existing Art. 1 last indent of the EJ Decision, according to which "Eurojust shall have legal personality" seems to be more clear and better aligned with Art. 3(2) of the EPPO draft Regulation and Art. 64(1) of the EP draft Regulation. The existing wording will also avoid the risk to misunderstand the possibility of Eurojust to "be party to legal proceedings" as the Eurojust capacity to act independently in national criminal proceedings.

13.2 Mission and Competence

As mentioned, Art. 2(1) EJ draft Regulation has confirmed that Eurojust will continue supporting and strengthening

> coordination and cooperation between national investigating and prosecuting authorities in relation to serious crime affecting two or more Member States, or requiring a prosecution on common bases, on the basis of operations conducted and information supplied by the Member States' authorities and by Europol.

Although this paragraph reproduces literally Art. 85(1) TFEU, Art. 8 EJ new Regulation seems to go further than the existing supportive role of Eurojust, by conferring on the National Members the power of issuing and executing themselves any mutual legal assistance or mutual recognition request. We will back to this matter in Sect. 13.4.

On the other hand, guidance on the interpretation of certain expressions of Art. 2 EJ draft Regulation (for instance "requiring a prosecution on common bases; "on the basis of operations conducted (. . .) by Member States' authorities", exercise of Eurojust tasks "on its own initiative") would be useful in view of their practical application. To this aim, some recitals in the draft Regulation or some references in a future Explanatory report might be an option.

As regards the competence of Eurojust, Art. 3 EJ draft Regulation has reduced its scope at least in three directions:

- First, the general competence of Eurojust covers "the forms of crime listed in Annex 1". The list provided in the Annex seems to be quite reduced and does not correspond with the types of criminality listed in the EP draft Regulation, neither with the lists of types of crime excluding from the double criminality control in the legal instruments on mutual recognition in criminal matters.
- Second the competence of Eurojust is not extended to types of crime other than those included in the list "at the request of a competent authority of a Member State" [as the existing Art. 4(2) EJ Decision recognises]. This limitation could impede Eurojust involvement in investigations or prosecutions against new types or trends of criminality. It might also make difficult the Eurojust support in cases apparently involving not such serious types of crime but whose resolution would require the issuing, transmission or execution of complex letters of request and European Arrest Warrants.
- Third, Art. 3(1) excludes from Eurojust competence "the crimes for which the European Public Prosecutor's Office is competent". Taking in mind that the EPPO will most probably set up through enhanced cooperation, Eurojust competence should cover the crimes affecting the EU budget at least in respect of non-participating Member States.

On the other hand, in accordance with Art. 3(4) EJ draft Regulation, Eurojust is entitled to assist investigations and prosecutions affecting only one Member State and the Union, at the request of either a national authority of the Member State concerned or the Commission. Apart from cases related to the financial interests of the EU, which in the original are excluded from the scope of Eurojust, it is difficult to identify other types of criminality "affecting only one Member States and the Union" in relation to which the assistance of Eurojust may be required.

13.3 Operational Functions of Eurojust

The EJ draft Regulation has not exploited fully the tasks that might be conferred to Eurojust in light of Art. 85(1) TFEU, including "the initiation of criminal investigations", the proposal for "the initiation of prosecutions conducted by the competent national authorities" provided that "formal acts of judicial procedure shall be carried out by the competent national officials", the "coordination of investigations and prosecutions", and the "resolution of conflicts of jurisdiction" [parr. (c)].

The Commission might consider the possible enhancement of Eurojust role and tasks at a later stage, especially when the sixth round of mutual evaluations is completed.[3]

The "Operational functions of Eurojust" are listed in Art. 4 draft EJ Regulation, whilst the conditions for exercising such operational functions acting through one or more National Members or as a College are specified in Art. 5 EJ draft Regulation. The process for following-up of Eurojust requests and opinions in accordance with both legal provisions is however laid down in Art. 23 draft EJ Regulation: the importance of this legal provision and its close link with Arts. 4 and 5 might recommend its insertion immediate after Arts. 4 and 5. Another possibility would be the insertion of a new last paragraph, related to the follow-up of requests and opinions, in Art. 4 EJ draft Regulation.

The organisation of coordination meetings is expressly included in the type of logistical support that Eurojust can provide. In particular, Art. 4(3)(b) states that Eurojust may "supply logistical support, including assistance for translation, interpretation and the organisation of coordination meetings".

The complexity and importance of the coordination meetings[4] makes advisable a more detailed regulation of this Eurojust tool. The organisation and running of coordination meetings involve relevant matters from a national and European perspective, and a more specific legal framework is necessary.

As regards the follow-up actions from of the coordination meetings, a short reference of this possibility in the legal provision related to the follow-up of requests and opinions of Eurojust might help to improve the cooperation between Eurojust and the judicial authorities of the Member States when the support of Eurojust is still needed before a coordination meeting, as it happens in the majority of cases. This will also enable Eurojust to assess the results of the support provided.

The coordination centres should be also mentioned in Art. 4(3)(b), if not developed with certain details in a specific legal provision.

13.4 Powers of the National Members

The proposed legal provision related to the powers of the National Members (Art. 8 EJ draft Regulation) has raised two main concerns.

The first one is that, in accordance with Art. 8(1)(a), the National Members of Eurojust would be entrusted with issuing and executing mutual legal assistance or mutual recognition requests [Art. 8(1)(a) *in fine*], thus placing National Members a role that goes beyond the mere support and assistance to the national competent authorities facing problems during the issuing, transmission and execution of such requests and orders.

---

[3] On the sixth round of mutual evaluations, see Sect. 3.1 of this book. On the rounds of mutual evaluations by the Member States, see Gutiérrez Zarza (2006a), p. 159; and Gutiérrez Zarza (2006b), p. 99.

[4] On Eurojust coordination meetings, see Sect. 3.4.4 of this book.

The second concern is of a more general character. The rationale behind Art. 9 EJ draft Regulation is to ensure a common core of powers for all National Members. That was also one of the objectives of the Eurojust reform of 2009, however, at that time the common core of powers of Art. 9a–9f were attenuated with the insertion of a national safeguard clause in Art. 9a. Art. 8 EJ draft Regulation has not included a similar provision, most probably in order to avoid the existing geometric variable among the Member States. The absence of this clause and the legal nature of the proposal in its entirety (a Regulation of the EU) has raised some concerns among some Member States, who consider that the powers conferred by Art. 8, and especially the power of the National Members to "issue and execute" mutual legal assistance and mutual recognition requests is contrary to their legal systems and/or constitutional rules. As example, Ireland has decided not to exercise an opt in if this legal provision remains unchanged because "the powers contained in Art. 8 are incompatible with those exercise by a prosecutor in the Irish system".

Arts. 9a–9f EJ Decision were the result of several rounds of negotiation in order to find the most appropriate balance between a minimum set of powers granted to all National Members and the need to respect the national legal systems and particularities of the Member States. A similar intense debate among the Member States on the powers of National Members in light of Art. 8 EJ draft Regulation will most likely take place as well.

13.5 Governance

Some of the most relevant changes proposed by the EJ draft Regulation are related to the new structure and governance of Eurojust.

The new structure includes the National Members, the College, the Executive Board and the Administrative Director (Art. 6). The staff of Eurojust is not mentioned.

As regards the College, the distinction between its operational and management functions is expressly regulated in Art. 10(1). The strategic (horizontal) work of Eurojust is not reflected in the EJ draft Regulation.

As management board, the College is composed by all the National Members and two representatives of the Commission. The European Public Prosecutor, who will receive the agendas of all College meetings, is entitled to participate in such meetings, "without the right to vote, whenever issues are discussed which he or she considers to be of relevance for the functioning of the European Public Prosecutor's Office" [Art. 12(3)].

In accordance with the Common Approach of the EU decentralised Agencies,[5] the Executive Board is conceived as a new organ of Eurojust not involved in its

[5] Document is available at http://europa.eu/agencies/documents/joint_statement_and_common_approach_2012_en.pdf.

operational functions [Art. 16(1)] but focused on the preparation of discussions and decisions of the College as Management Board. This Executive Board will be also responsible for the adoption of an anti-fraud strategy and the implementing rules to the Staff Regulations, the follow-up of the internal and external audit reports, evaluations and investigations, including those of the European Data Protection Supervisor (EDPS) and the European Anti-Fraud Office (OLAF).

This Executive Board will be composed of the President and Vice-Presidents of the College, one representative of the Commission and one other member of the College. The Administrative Director will take part in the meetings of the Executive Board, but shall not have the right to vote [Art. 16(4)].

The European Public Prosecutor, who will receive the agendas of all Executive Board meetings, is entitled to participate in such meetings "without the right to vote, whenever issues are discussed which he or she considers to be of relevance for the functioning of the European Public Prosecutor's Office". He or she will have the possibility to address written opinions for Executive Board's response "in writing without undue delay" [Art. 16(8)].

The role of the Administrative Director will focus on the implementation of the administrative tasks assigned to Eurojust (Art. 18). The Administrative Director is also expressly recognised as the legal representative of Eurojust [Art. 18(3)].

The involvement of the European Parliament and, in certain manner, of the National Parliaments in the evaluation of Eurojust's activities deserves a short reference in this section.

In accordance with Art. 85(1) last paragraph TFEU, the Regulations adopted by the European Parliament and the Council in accordance with the ordinary legislative procedure "shall also determine arrangements for involving the European Parliament and national Parliaments in the evaluation of Eurojust's activities". In line with this provision, Art. 55(1) EJ draft Regulation has stipulated that the Eurojust Annual Report [and other relevant documents listed in parr. (3)] will be sent to the European Parliament and to the National Parliaments. Moreover, the President of the College could be requested to appear before the European Parliament "to discuss matters relating to Eurojust", including the presentation of the Annual Report, as long as the obligations of confidentiality and discretion are not compromised and discussions are not focused on the concrete actions in relations to specific operational cases [Art. 55(2)].

13.6 Access to National Databases and Information Systems

One of the powers conferred to the National Members is the access to some databases and information systems relevant for the purposes of investigating and prosecuting serious cross-border crime. In particular, Art. 9 EJ draft Regulation mentions "criminal records", "registers of arrested persons", "investigation registers", "DNA registers" and "other registers of public authorities of their Member States where such information is necessary to fulfil their tasks".

The proposed legal provision, which is quite similar to the existing Art. 9 EJ Decision, would be a good opportunity to reflect further on the possibility that the National Members might be able to accelerate the exchange of information and personal data stored in national databases that is needed in ongoing investigations and court proceedings in another Member State.

Access to national databases does not provide any added value to national investigations and criminal proceedings of the same Member State, simply because the national authorities of this Member State will have access to this information. Hence, it seems that the access to information of national databases (for example, on criminal records) will be useful for the judicial authorities of other Member States. This will be the case, for example of the criminal records a person who is being investigated in a Member State for cases of child abuses. In this situation, it does not seem very effective that, after checking the criminal records of this individual and extracting the relevant information by the National Member of Eurojust, a new and formal request should be made and executed through the central authorities designated by both Member States in accordance with Art. 3 ECRIS Framework Decision.[6] As anticipated, the drafting of this legal provision could be more ambitious, and explore further possibilities of the National Members of Eurojust as facilitators of the exchange of information extracted from national databases in cases involving Eurojust.

On the other hand, Art. 9(e) EJ Decision allows access to "other registers of public authorities". It might be useful to consider also the possibility of conferring access to, or at least be able to obtain the information contained in registers of private companies, including airlines, financial institutions or service providers, as soon as a judicial authorisation to get such information is not required. Otherwise, the National Members would have fewer powers to request information from private companies in EU Member States than the EU law enforcement authorities.

13.7 Exchange of Information Between Eurojust and the National Authorities of the Member States

No special changes have been introduced by the new legal provisions related to the exchange of information with the Member States and between the National Members.

---

[6] Council Framework Decision 2009/315/JHA of 28 February on the organisation and content of exchange of information extracted from criminal records between the Member States. OJ L 93, 7.4.2009, p. 23. On the ECRIS system, see Sect. 7.3 of this book.

The most relevant amendment seems to be the deletion of the list of criminal offences in relation to which the national authorities should provide information to Eurojust [Art. 13(4), (5), (6) and (7) EJ Decision]. In the EJ draft Regulation the equivalent legal provision [Art. 21(5)] is as follows:

> The national competent authorities shall inform their national members without undue delay of any case concerning crimes under the competence of Eurojust affecting at least three Member States and for which requests for or decisions on judicial cooperation, including those based on instruments giving effect to the principle of mutual recognition, have been transmitted to at least two Member States.

The simplification of the rules under which national authorities should sent information to Eurojust should be welcome. National authorities perceive paragraphs (4)–(7) of Art. 13 EJ Decision as quite complex and do not see the real added value of sending information to Eurojust in all the situations covered.

13.8 The CMS

The EJ proposal contains some major changes related to CMS. Firstly, Art. 40 states that Europol, under its mandate, will have "indirect access on the basis of a hit/no hit system to information provided to Eurojust" [parr (1)], "only for the purpose of identifying whether information available at Eurojust matches with information processed at Europol" [parr (2)]. As a kind of mirror provision has been introduced in the EP draft Regulation, according to which Europol should take all appropriate measures "to enable Eurojust and the European Anti-Fraud Office (OLAF) within their respective mandates, to have access to and be able to search all information that has been provided" [Art. 27(1)].

Secondly, the CMS will be available for use by the European Public Prosecutor's Office. The provisions on access to the Case Management System and the temporary work files of the EJ draft Regulation will apply *mutatis mutandis* to the EPPO. The EJ proposal is not clear enough on whether the EPPO will make use of the Eurojust CMS as such or if, inspired on this system, a new CMS will be set up by the EPPO, without prejudice of the possibility of the EPPO to have access to EJ CMS for the purposes of cross-referencing.

13.9 Processing and Protection of Personal Data

As previously mentioned, the EJ Proposal "particularises and complements Regulation (EC) No 45/2001 in as far as personal data processed by Eurojust for its operational tasks are concerned" [Art. 27(5) EJ Proposal]. With this approach, Article 27–37 introduces some particularities to the general framework of data protection for EU institutions and bodies set out by the abovementioned

Regulations. Therefore, the Commission has considered there is not a need for a specific and robust legal regime for the processing and protection of personal data at Eurojust—as the existing one—only certain particularities to the general framework are necessary.

In the particular field of Eurojust classified information, the security principles contained in the Commission's security rules for protecting European Union Classified Information (EUCI) and sensitive non-classified information, as set out in the Annex to the Commission Decision 2001/844/EC, ECSC, Euratom[7] (Art. 62 EJ Proposal), will be applicable.

13.9.1 Data Integrity and Accuracy

The EJ Proposal establishes an obligation on Eurojust to process personal data "in such a way that it can be established which authority provided the data or where the personal data has been retrieved from" [Art. 34(1)]. This will allow the identification of the sources from which the data has been retrieved and therefore facilitate requests and complaints for unauthorised, incorrect processing of data (Arts. 34 and 37 EJ Proposal).

The EJ proposal states some time limits for the storage of personal data in Eurojust CMS. Most of them are related to the state of investigations and prosecutions at national level and are based on the idea that, if national proceedings come to an end, there is no need for Eurojust to continue storing that information.

Art. 28(5) and (6) includes two provisions related to the retention periods that are also relevant for other purposes.

First, Art. 28(5) is as follows:

> Where a file contains non-automated and unstructured data, once the deadline for storage of the last item of automated data from the file has elapsed, all documents in the file shall be returned to the authority which supplied them and any copies shall be destroyed.

This paragraph is applicable for the (copies of the) documents extracted from the national judicial files which are sent to the National Members for the purposes of coordination and cooperation. Part of the information contained in those documents is extracted and introduced in CMS, but not the whole dossier sent to Eurojust (only the entities listed in Annex 2 of EJ draft Regulation). When the involvement of Eurojust in the case is not longer required, the personal data stored in CMS should be deleted, and the paper files provided by the judicial authorities returned to the authority which supplied them.

---

[7] OJ L 317, 3.12.2001, p. 1.

Second, Art. 28(6) states:

> Where Eurojust has coordinated an investigation or prosecution, the National Members concerned shall inform Eurojust and the other Member States concerned of all judicial decisions relating to the case which have become final in order, inter alia, that point (b) of paragraph 1 may be applied.

Point (b) of paragraph (1) refers to "the date on which the person has been acquitted and the judicial decision became final" as one of the criteria to take into consideration for limiting the storage of personal data in CMS. However, Art. 28(6) could also serve as legal basis enabling the National Members to request the national judicial authorities copy of the judicial decisions relating to the case which have become final.

13.9.2 Data Protection

As the EJ Council Decision in force, the EJ Proposal expressly recognises the right of access, rectification and erasure of personal data, and does not recognise the right of information. This omission should be welcome, as it will avoid any risk to disclosure information that should be keep confidential in accordance with the rules of criminal proceedings, on the basis of an equivalent provision to the existing Art. 9 EJ rules of procedure on DP.[8]

When the right of access is restricted, Art. 32(4) EJ draft Decision allows the possibility of omitting the principal reasons for that restriction, and the mere communication to the data subject that all necessary verifications by the European Data Protection Supervisor have taken place is suitable instead.

13.9.3 Data Security

On the other hand, the EJ proposal insists on the importance of keeping records of any collection, alteration, access, disclosure, combination or erasure of personal data used for operational purposes. As mentioned in previous sections, the logging and documentation of the activities related to the processing of personal data might become crucial to accredited data integrity and its further consideration as evidence in a trial. For this reason, the logs should be kept as long as national criminal proceedings are ongoing [and not to be deleted "after 18 months", as set up by Art. 29(1) EJ Proposal].

---

[8] Rules of procedure on the processing and protection of personal data at Eurojust. Text adopted unanimously by the College of Eurojust during the meeting of 21 October 2004 and approved by the Council on 24 February 2005. OJ C 68, 19.3.2005, p. 1.

13.10 Exchange of Information and Judicial Cooperation with EU Partners, Third States, and International Organisations and Bodies

The EJ Proposal has slightly changed the approach of the cooperation between Eurojust and its European and international partners. The changes are mainly related to the new legal framework governing the exchange of information processed by Eurojust, and the need to ensure a coherence between the Eurojust policy for transferring of personal data, and the policies of the Commission, the Council and the European External Action Service in this area.

As a result, the guiding principles for the exchange of information are as follows:

- Eurojust may exchange strategic information with EU partners, international organisations and bodies [Art. 38(1) and (2)]
- Eurojust may also *receive* operational information "as far as necessary for the performance of its tasks" [Art. 38(3).
- Eurojust is only entitled to transfer personal data to third countries, international organisations and bodies and third States "if this is necessary for preventing and combating crime that falls under Eurojust's competence and in accordance with this Regulation". Moreover, if the information was provided to Eurojust by a Member State, as a general rule Eurojust may seek that State's consent.
- EU partners, third States, international organisations and bodies may seek Eurojust's explicit consent before transferring any personal data that has been provided by Eurojust.

No special changes have been introduced in the relations between Eurojust and the EU networks with competences in criminal matters (Art. 39 EJ draft Regulation).

As regards Europol, as mentioned, the most relevant point is the obligation of Eurojust to take appropriate measures "to enable Europol, within its mandate, to have indirect access on the basis of a hit/no hit system to information provided by Eurojust" and to ensure that the information generating the hit may be shared.

Eurojust should also involve Europol in investigations and prosecutions requiring coordination, cooperation and support in accordance with the mandate of Europol [Art. 40(4) EJ draft Regulation].

As also mentioned, a particular provision is devoted to the relations with the EPPO (Art. 41 EJ draft Regulation).

The EJ Regulation reproduces the general principles guiding the relations between Eurojust and OLAF [Art. 42(2) and (3) EJ draft Regulation].

In relation to third States and international organisations, the proposed changes are aimed at ensuring the alignment of the external relation policy of the Eurojust with (1) the adequacy decisions issued by the Commission, and (2) the international agreements concluded between the Union and third States or international organisations in accordance with Art. 218 TFEU. Within this EU general framework, Eurojust is not expected to initiate ad hoc negotiations with third States or international organisations, neither its own verification mechanism for the level of adequacy of third States. It may, however, conclude working arrangements to implement the Union agreements or the Commission adequacy decisions. Subject to these working arrangements, Eurojust may post liaison magistrates to third countries [Art. 46(1) EJ draft Regulation].

In additional to this general framework for cooperation and exchange of information with third States, the EJ draft Regulation enables Eurojust to authorise the transfer of personal data to third States or international organisations on a case-by-case basis, under certain circumstances [see Art. 45(2)]. The College of Eurojust, in agreement with the EDPS, will be also entitled to authorise sets of transfers, for a period not exceeding one year renewable, under the same circumstances [Art. 45(3) EJ Proposal].

References

Busuioca M, Groenleerb M (2013) Beyond design: the evolution of Europol and Eurojust. Perspect Eur Polit Soc 14(3):285

Coninsx M (2013) Editorial of ERA Forum 2:173

Gutiérrez Zarza A (2006a) La evaluación de los Estados Miembros en el tercer Pilar de la Unión Europea: el caso particular de la Orden de Detención Europea (I). En Revista de Derecho y Proceso Penal 16:159

Gutiérrez Zarza A (2006b) Evaluation of the Member States in the third pillar of the European Union. The specific case of the European Arrest Warrant. In: Weyemberg A, De Biolley S (eds) Comment évaluer le droit penal européen? Instituut d'Etudes Europeennes, Belgium, p 99

Monar J (2013) Eurojust present and future role at the frontline of European Union criminal justice cooperation. ERA Forum 2:187

Petit Leclair S (2012) Justice et securité en Europe: Eurojust ou la creation d'un parquet europeen. Les Cahiers de la sécurité 20:38

Wade ML (2013) Judicial control: the CJEU and the future of Eurojust. ERA Forum 2

Weyemberg A (2011) The development of Eurojust: potential and limitations of Article 85 of the TFEU. N J Eur Crim Law 2(1):75

Chapter 14
The European Public Prosecutor's Office Draft Regulation: Ten Relevant Points

It is difficult to find another European body that has triggered so many policy discussions and in relation to which so many studies and articles have been issued as the European Public Prosecutor.[1]

Interest in this proposed EU body was regenerated with the entry into force of the Treaty of Lisbon, through the inclusion of a provision in the TFEU [Art. 86(1)] according to which a European Public Prosecutor's Office should be established "from Eurojust", and the presentation in July 2013 of a Commission proposal on the European Public Prosecutor's Office (EPPO draft Regulation).[2] The proposal was part of a legislative package including also a draft Regulation on Eurojust.[3]

The most relevant ten points of the EPPO draft Regulation have been summarised below.

---

[1] See the *Corpus Iuris introducing penal provisions for the purpose of the financial interests of the European Union*, coordinated by Prof. Delmas Marty (1997). A revised version of the Corpus Iuris, accompanied by an extensive comparative study on the potential impact of the setting up of an European Prosecutor on national prosecution systems is in *The implementation of the Corpus Iuris in the Member States*, coordinated by Prof. Delmas Marty and Vervaele (2000).

Following the entry into force of the Treaty of Lisbon, see De Angelis (2011), p. 43. Ligeti (2013).

[2] COM (2013) 534 final. Brussels, 17.7.2013.

See Caianiello (2013), p. 115; Da Costa Andrade (2013), p. 329 ; Editorial (2013), p. 121 ; ECBA (2013), p. 185; Espina Ramos (2011); Hamran and Szabova (2013), p. 40; Ligeti (2011a): Ligeti (2011b), p. 105. Ligeti and Simonato (2013); Mauro (2011), p. 743; Monar (2013), p. 339; Peers (2011), p. 858; Ruggieri (2013a), p. 109; and Ruggieri (2013b); Spencer (2011); Wade (2013), p. 439.

[3] On the EJ draft Regulation, see Chap. 13 of this handbook.

Á.G. Zarza (ed.), *Exchange of Information and Data Protection in Cross-border Criminal Proceedings in Europe*, DOI 10.1007/978-3-642-40291-3_14,

14.1 The Setting Up of the EPPO "from Eurojust"

One of the most controversial points of the EPPO has been, and still is, its relationship with Eurojust and, closely connected with this matter, whether the EPPO should be located in Luxembourg, in The Hague (and within Eurojust) or in any other place.

In 1965, a Decision of 8 April expressed the will of the Representatives of the Governments of the Member States to locate or transfer to Luxembourg any other Community institution or service, specially in the financial area, provided that its good functioning was ensured (Art. 10).[4]

Many things have happened since 1956, including the introduction of a particular provision in the Treaties of the EU, the so well known Article 86(1) TFEU, according to which the EPPO should be established "from Eurojust".

However the Commission, in its EPPO draft Regulation, has interpreted these two words ("from Eurojust") as the need to "establish links between them" [Recital (3)], and more in particular as to the need for the EPPO to "establish and maintain a special relationship with Eurojust based on close cooperation and the development of operational, administrative and management links between them" (Art. 57 EPPO draft Regulation).

Moreover, Recital (49) EPPO draft Regulation states that

> The representatives of the Member States, meeting at Head of State or Government level in Brussels on 13 December 2003 have determined the seat of the European Public Prosecutor's Office.

On 12–13 December 2003, the European Council adopted some Conclusions related to the seat of certain offices and agencies of the EU, and expressly agreed that "if a European Public Prosecutor's Office is established, its seat will be in Luxembourg in accordance with the cited Decision of 8 April 1965."[5]

This is contrary to the Commission proposal, according to which the EPPO will be located in The Hague and "within Eurojust".

---

[4] See Decision of the Representatives of the Governments of the Member States of 8 April 1965 related to the provisional location of certain institutions and services of the Communities (67/446/EEC) (67/30/Euratom), OJ 152, 13.7.197, p. 1. This Decision, which was part of the Merger Treaty of 1965, is only available in German, Dutch and French. French version is as follows:

> Les gouvernements des États membres sont disposés à installer ou à transférer à Luxembourg d'autres organismes et services communautaires, particuliérement dans le domaine financier, pour autant que leur bon fonctionement soit assuré.
>
> A cette fin, ils invitent la Commission à leur présenter chaque anné un rapport sur la situation existante en que qui concerne l'installation es organismes et services communaitaires et sur les possibilities de prendre de nouvelles mesures dans le sens de cette disposition en tenant compte des nécessités du boon fonctionement des Communautés.

[5] Council doc. 538/104 POLGEN 2. Brussels, 5 February 2004, p. 27.

14.2 The "Yellow Card" to the EPPO Draft Regulation

A relevant matter that came up in the autumn of 2013 was the compliance of the EPPO draft Proposal with the principles of subsidiarity and proportionality.

In accordance with Protocol (No. 2) on the application of the principles of subsidiarity and proportionality,[6] any new legislative initiative should contain "some assessment of the proposal's financial impact and, in the case of a directive, of its implications for the rules to be put in place by Member States", and provide the reasons (substantiated by qualitative and, whenever possible, quantitative indicators) " for concluding that a Union objective can be better achieved at Union level" (Art. 5).

On the principle of subsidiarity, Recital (5) EPPO draft Regulation considered that:

> (...) Since the objectives of this Regulation, namely the setting up of the European Public Prosecutor's Office, cannot be achieved by the Member States given the fragmentation of national prosecutions in the area of offences committed against the Union's financial interests and can therefore, by reason of the fact that the European Public Prosecutor's Office is to have exclusive competence to prosecute such offences, be better achieved at Union level, the Union may adopt measures, in accordance with the principle of subsidiarity as set out in Article 5 of the Treaty on European Union.

Regarding the principle of proportionality, Recital (6) EPPO draft Proposal mentioned that,

> As set out by Article 5 of the Treaty on European Union, this Regulation does not go beyond what is necessary in order to achieve these objectives and ensured that its impact on the legal orders and the institutional structures of the Member States is the least intrusive possible.

Also in line with (No. 2) (Art. 4), the Commission forwarded the EPPO draft Regulation to National parliaments in parallel to the Union legislator. Within 8 weeks from the date of the transmission, a number of 14 National chambers totaling 19 votes (14 were required) issued reasoned opinions stating that the EPPO proposal did not comply with the principle of subsidiarity.[7] In particular, opinions were issued by the Dutch Senate, Dutch House of Representatives, Czech Senate, Cyprus House of Representatives, UK House of Commons, UK House of Lords; Irish Parliament, Hungarian Parliament, Swedish Parliament, Romanian Chamber of Deputies, Slovenian Parliament, French Senate, and Maltese Parliament.

In general terms, the national parliaments considered that the objective of protecting the financial interests of the EU can be achieved by the Member States in cooperation with the existing EU bodies with competences in this field (OLAF, Europol, Eurojust). The UK House of Lords stated that "EU fraud could be effectively countered though the existing framework based on the criminal law systems of the Member States and co-ordination between them and the EU

---

[6] This Protocol was introduced by the Treaty of Lisbon and is annexed to the Treaties. OJ C 115, 9.5.2008, p. 206.

[7] See Council doc. 16624/13 Brussels, 28 November 2013.

institutions, strengthened if necessary".[8] The House of Lords and the Czech Senate[9] draw attention to the fact that the last reform of Eurojust has not yet been fully implemented and evaluated.

Some National parliaments concluded that the figures provided by the Commission in its impact assessment lacked credibility. Moreover, the Commission has proposed the setting up of an EPPO to ensure continuity in the protection of the financial interest of the EU in the territory of the EU, without bearing in mind that Denmark is automatically excluded by virtue of Protocol 22 and UK made clear that they will not be opting in to the proposal under the terms of Protocol 21.

A few National parliaments also expressed concerns because the setting up of an EPPO could imply a far-reaching impact on the constitutional systems of the Member States and of the structure and organisation of the national judiciary systems.[10] The Irish Parliament[11] and both the Senate and the House of Representatives of The Netherlands also considered criminal law to be primarily a national competence, and the investigations and prosecutions of all fraud related offences, including offences against the financial interests of the EU, to be primarily a duty of national authorities.[12]

The opinions issued by these National parliaments have resulted in a "yellow card" to the Commission Proposal of the EPPO. It is the second "yellow card" confronted by the Commission after the introduction of Protocol (No. 2) by the Treaty of Lisbon: the first one was issued in May 2012 with the occasion of the so call "Monti II" Proposal related to the right to take collective action within the context of the freedom of establishment and the freedom to provide services. According to this "yellow card" procedure the EU institution proposing the new legal instrument must review the draft and, after such review, may decide to maintain, amend or withdraw the draft, giving appropriate reasons for each decision.

In the first "yellow card", the Commission withdrew the proposal. In the "yellow card" of the EPPO, the Commission has decided to maintain the Proposal of the EPPO.

14.3 Structure and Governance

The draft Regulation proposes a decentralised integrated structure for the EPPO [Art. 3(1)],[13] which will be composed of the European Public Prosecutor, four Deputies, and at least one European Delegated Prosecutor located in each Member State (Art. 6).

---

[8] Council doc. 15656/13. Brussels, 14 November 2013.

[9] Council doc. 16030/1/13 REV 1. Brussels, 16 November 2013.

[10] Czech Senate (Council doc. 16030/1/13 REV 1, cit.) and Slovenian National Assembly (Council doc. 16010/13. Brussels, 13 November 2013).

[11] Council doc. 16023/13, Brussels, 13 November 2013.

[12] Council doc. 16042/13. Brussels, 13 November 2013.

[13] White (2013), p. 22.

The European Public Prosecutor and his four Deputies will integrate the nuclear structure of the EPPO, where all the important decisions will be taken in order to ensure consistency within the territory of the Union.

The most important feature of the delegates will be their integration into the prosecution systems of the Member States. To this aim the European Delegated Prosecutors will enjoy a "dual status": as members of a EU office and as national prosecutors empowered to carry out procedural activities with direct impact in national criminal proceedings. As result of the dual status, "they will receive remuneration from the EU budget and will be covered by the Staff Regulations".[14]

The nuclear structure of the EPPO will be supported by the necessary staff. The EPPO draft Regulation has foreseen that EPPO staff will come from OLAF's current resources and rely on the administrative support of Eurojust.

When necessary, additional resources may be allocated to the European Delegated Prosecutors.

The rules related to the independence and accountability of the EPPO, which are clearly stated in Art. 5 EPPO draft Regulation, have been drafted with special care. Both guarantees are crucial to ensure the legitimacy of the EPPO, the absence of any pressure against him and his team, and an efficient protection of the financial interest of the EU. Closely related to both guarantees, the rules for the appointment and dismissal of the EPPO are laid down in Articles 8 (concerning the European Public Prosecutor), 9 (concerning the Deputies) and 10 (relating the European delegated Prosecutors) EPPO draft Regulation.[15]

14.4 Competence

The scope of competence of the EPPO will cover "the criminal offences affecting the financial interests of the Union" [Arts. 4(1) and 12 EPPO draft Regulation]. Contrary to the *Corpus Iuris*, the EPPO draft Regulation does not include a specific set of rules on the criminal offences and sanctions to be applied by the EPPO: they are identified in the Proposal for a Directive on the fight against fraud to the Unions' financial interests by means of criminal law,[16] which will be complementary to the EPPO draft Regulation.

To this purpose, the territory of the Union's Member States must be considered a single legal area in which the European Public Prosecutor's Office may exercise its competence [Art. 25(1) P. EPPO]. This competence will also cover offences partially or wholly committed outside the territory of the Member States by one of their nationals, or by (staff) members of the European Union institutions and bodies.

[14] Explanatory Memorandum of the EPPO draft Regulation, p. 8.

[15] Conway (2013).

[16] COM(2012) 363 final. Brussels, 11.7.2012.

In the original, the "criminal offences affecting the financial interests of the Union" were of the exclusive competence of the EPPO: no other EU body would be competent to investigate, prosecute and bring to court these criminal offences. Considering that the EPPO will be set up most probably by enhanced cooperation among a reduced number of Member States of the EU, Eurojust should be competent to provide support and assistance at least in respect to those criminal offences affecting the non-participating Member States.[17]

Another relevant aspect, which will have important consequences in practice, is the "vis expansiva" of the EPPO for criminal offences in principle excluded from his scope of application which are however "inextricably linked" to the criminal offences detrimental to the financial interests of the EU. This will be a crucial point for the EPPO, as in practice will not be so easy to delimit the competences of the EPPO and of the national prosecutions services. In many cases, criminal offences affecting the EU budget are only the point of an iceberg,[18] or a single element of a complex case involving organised crime, corruption or other criminal offences in principle out of the competence of the EPPO. Being aware of the difficulties related to the ancillary competence of the EPPO, Art. 13 EPPO draft Regulation has foreseen a close dialogue with the national prosecution services in order to solve these situations.

The "vis expansiva" of the competence of the EPPO is also foreseen *de lege ferenda*. In accordance with Article 86(4) TFEU, Art. 74(1) EPPO draft Regulation contains a review clause according to which the evaluation report to be issued by the Commission by 5 years after the start of application of this Regulation "shall contain its findings on the feasibility and advisability of extending the competence of the European Public Prosecutor's Office to other criminal offences in accordance with Art. 86(4) TFEU". Another legal basis for extending the competences of the EPPO is provided for in Art. 74(1), according to which:

> The Commission shall submit legislative proposals to the European Parliament and the Council if it concludes that more detailed rules on the setting up of the European Public Prosecutor's Office, its functions or the procedure applicable to its activities are necessary. It may recommend to the European Council the extension of the competences of the European Public Prosecutor's Office in accordance with Art. 84(4) of the Treaty.

14.5 Tasks

The EPPO will be responsible "for investigating, prosecuting and bringing to judgment the perpetrators of, and accomplices in, the financial interests of the Union" [Art. 4(1) EPPO draft Regulation]. In particular, the tasks of the EPPO cover all the stages of the investigation and criminal proceedings: (1) the initiation and conduction of an investigation, including the request or order to carry out

---

[17] See Sect. 3.1 of this book.

[18] See Willliams (2013), p. 227–234.

investigation measures in the Member States, (2) the acts of prosecution, including the dismissal of the case, (3) the exercise of his functions in the competent courts of the Member States, including the presentation of evidence and requests for confiscation of properties related to, or proceeds derived from, an offence within the competence of the EPPO, and (4) any appeals before the national courts until the case has been finally disposed of [Art. 4(2) and (3) EPPO draft Regulation].

In relation to the abovementioned point (4), the EPPO is considered "as a national authority for the purpose of the judicial review of its acts of investigation and prosecution" and, as result, "national courts should be entrusted with the judicial review of all acts of investigation and prosecution of the European Public Prosecutor's Office which may be challenged" (Recital 37).

In accordance with Art. 267 TFEU,

> National Courts are able or, in certain circumstances, bound to refer to the Court of Justice questions for preliminary rulings on the interpretation or the validity of provisions of Union law, including this Regulation, which are relevant for the judicial review of the acts of investigation and prosecution of the European Public Prosecutor's Office. National courts should not be able to refer questions on the validity of the acts of the European Public Prosecutor's Office to the Court of Justice, since those acts should not be considered acts of a body of the Union for the purpose of judicial review (Recital 38)).

An analysis of the tasks of the EPPO in each step of the investigation and criminal proceedings would exceed the purpose of this publication. However, there are three elements related to the tasks of the EPPO that requires further attention.

The first element is the set of principles that will govern the performance of EPPO's tasks, and in particular the principles of legality and proportionality. On the principle of legality, Art. 11(3) states:

> Although the EPPO relies on the procedural rules of the Member States, there are also many aspects to lay down at EU level through the rules of procedure mentioned in Art. 11(3). Otherwise, the lack of appropriate and complete rules of procedure may result in an application of the rules on data protection instead, as it happens with OLAF.

As mentioned in other sections of this publication, formal investigations and criminal proceedings should be properly governed by their own set of rules (legality principle), including those limiting the investigative powers of law enforcement and judicial authorities by the proportionality principle. As expressly mentioned in the EPPO draft Regulation, "the actions of the European Public Prosecutor's Office shall be guided by the principle of proportionality" [Art. 11(2)], according to which the investigative measures listed in Art. 26(1) "shall not be ordered without reasonable grounds and if less intrusive means can achieve the same objective" [Art. 26(3)].

The second element to consider are the fundamental rights protecting suspects and accused persons. As anticipated in Art. 11(1), the EPPO draft Regulation has included a specific chapter on "Procedural safeguards" (Arts. 32–35) which recognises inter alia "the right to information and access to the case materials, as provided for in Directive 2012/13/EU of the European Parliament and of the Council" [Art. 32(2)(b)] "from the time that they are suspected of having committed an offence" and provided that, "once the indictment has been acknowledged by the competent national court, the suspect and accused persons' procedural rights shall be based on the national regime applicable in the relevant case" [Art. 32(3)]. Hence, the suspects and accused persons are protected by specific fundamental rights during the formal investigation and further steps of criminal proceedings: any overlapping of the data protection rules with those fundamental rights should be prevented.

The third element is related to the tasks of the European Data Protection Supervisor. As mentioned, the procedural acts of the EPPO are subject to judicial control before the national courts. The EDPS, in the exercise of its supervisory role, is not entitled to oversee such procedural acts: the jurisdictional power of national courts should prevail.

14.6 Exchange of Information with the National Competent Authorities

The investigation, prosecution and bringing to trial of criminal offences affecting the financial interests of the EU will generate a constant exchange of information between the European Public Prosecutor the European Delegated Prosecutors and most probably the law enforcement authorities of the Member States concerned, with the support—when necessary—of Europol.

For instance, this frequent exchange of information will ensure that the European Public Prosecutor is aware of the existence of any conduct which might constitute an offence within its competence and decide on the possible initiation of a criminal investigation. In that case, further exchange of information will enable the European Public Prosecutor to monitor the progress of the investigation and give the necessary instructions and guidelines to the European Delegated Prosecutors.

As a result of the investigation, the summary of the case, the draft indictment and the list of evidence submitted by the European Delegated Prosecutor(s) will allow the European Public Prosecutor to take a decision on the dismissal, transaction, or prosecution before national courts, or referral of the case back for further investigations. If a prosecution is to go ahead, the European Public Prosecutor will decide, "in close consultation with the European Delegated Prosecutor", the jurisdiction of trial and determine the competent national court.

In cases when the European Public Prosecutor has decided to conduct the investigation himself/herself, the European Delegated Prosecutor(s) of the Member State(s) concerned must be informed accordingly.

These are only some examples of a constant exchange of information that will continue in further steps of the criminal proceedings. As mentioned in the previous section of this book, the constant collaboration between the EPPO and the other actors involved in criminal investigations and proceedings for the protection of the financial interests of the EU should be governed by appropriate set of procedural rules.

14.7 The Case Management System

The Case Management System (CMS) is the IT tool regulated in Arts. 22–24 EPPO draft Proposal and the Annex thereto, to facilitate the management of the investigations and prosecutions conducted by the European Public Prosecutor and his Delegates. It is composed of temporary work files and an index.

The EPPO will be responsible for the management of the temporary work files and decide, on a case-by-case basis, whether to keep the temporary work file restricted or to give access to it.

The European Delegated Prosecutors may have access to the index (unless otherwise decided by the EPPO), the temporary work files related to investigations or prosecutions taking place in their Member State. For those investigations and prosecutions taking place in another Member State, access to the information of the temporary work file related to the Member State of the European Delegated Prosecutor will be granted (Art. 24).

It is unclear whether the EPPO CMS will be part of the CMS of Eurojust [as it seems to be in light of Art. 24(8) *in fine* EJ draft Regulation] or a separate system [as it is likely in accordance with Art. 22(1) EPPO draft Regulation].

The Annex to the EPPO draft Regulation contains a list of entities to be inserted in the CMS: with the sole exceptions provided for in Art. 37(2)–(4), no other personal data should be entered in the system.

14.8 Processing and Protection of Personal Data

According to Art. 37(5) EPPO draft Regulation, the processing and protection of personal data in the context of the operational activities of the EPPO is subject to Regulation (EC) No. 45/2001, which is particularised and complemented by some specific provisions of the EPPO draft Regulation: mainly by its Chapter VI (Arts. 37–47) and Arts. 56(3), (4) and (5), and 67.

As mentioned in previous sections, it is important to take in mind that the EPPO draft Regulation contains two parallel set of legal provisions governing the exchange of information and the rights of suspects and accused persons, namely the provisions on procedural law analysed in the previous section and the provisions for the processing and protection of personal data referred in the previous paragraph. In many occasions, both set of rules conflict to each other, as it is the case of the right of access of any data subject (Art. 42) vis a vis the right to information and access to case materials [Art. 2(b)]. The right of information to the database subject recognised in Regulation (EC) No. 45/2001 might also require further consideration, as it can compromise seriously ongoing investigations and prosecutions. The same applies to the right of information in cases of security breaches.

In other occasions the guarantees established by the data protection rules will ensure the accuracy and integrity of the information and data that will be further presented in court, thus facilitating their admissibility as evidence. Logging and documentation might be also extremely important in this context, although the obligation to delete data after 18 months, as set out in Art. 39(1) seems to be unrealistic taking into consideration the complexity of many cases affecting the financial interests of the EU and therefore the length of investigations and criminal proceedings in such cases.

Certainly, the interactions between both set of rules would require further reflection during the legislative process. This matter is especially important because the EPPO is a prosecution authority and, as such, should be primarily regulated by rules of criminal procedure, regardless the need to include some specific administrative rules on which type of information should be included in CMS and other related matters. In other words, the CMS and the channels for receiving and transmit information are "tools" at the disposal of the EPPO, who is however subject in his operational functions to the rules of criminal proceedings.

14.9 Exchange of Information and Cooperation with EU Partners

The special relationship and close cooperation between the EPPO and Eurojust proclaimed in Art. 57 EPPO draft Regulation is expressed in many other provisions of this Regulation.

At institutional level, "the European Public Prosecutor and the President of Eurojust shall meet on a regular basis to discuss issues of common concern" [Art. 41(1) EJ Proposal].

At management level, The EPPO will receive the agendas of the meetings of the College of Eurojust [Art. 12(3)] and of the Executive Board [Art. 16(7)]. It is entitled to address written opinions to the College, which must be respond "in writing without undue delay". In any case, such written opinions must be presented "whenever the College adopts the annual budget and work programme" [Art. 41(8) EJ Proposal]. The EPPO will also receive the agendas of the Executive Board of Eurojust, and is empowered to address written opinions to this Board [Art. 16(7)].

From an operational point of view, Eurojust may be associated with the activities of the EPPO "concerning cross-border or complex cases" when the investigations of the EPPO reveal elements falling outside the material or territorial competence of the EPPO. A complex case may exceed the material competence of the EPPO if it involves criminal offences other than those affecting the financial interests of the EU. A case may exceed the territorial competence of the EU if Member States other than those participating in the EPPO are affected by the criminal offences. In these cases, Eurojust and EPPO may exchange information, participate in the coordination of specific acts of investigation, among other possibilities. Eurojust may also play a relevant role in the identification of the national jurisdiction being in the best position to prosecute and bring to court criminal offences affecting the financial interests of the EU.

Request from EPPO must be treated by Eurojust "without undue delay" and, "where appropriate, as if they had been received from a national authority competent for judicial cooperation" [Art. 41(2) EJ draft Regulation].

As previously mentioned, the EPPO will have access "to a mechanism for automatic cross-checking of data in Eurojust's Case Management System". The purpose of this mechanism is enabling the EPPO to indentify whether information available at Eurojust matches with information processed by the EPPO. When a match is found, both bodies and the Member State(s) concerned will be informed accordingly. "In cases where the data was provided by a third State, Eurojust shall only inform that third party of the match found with the consent of the EPPO" [Art. 41(5) in fine EJ draft Regulation].

In order to support the cooperation required by the EPPO, Eurojust must make use "of the Eurojust National Coordination System (. . .) as well as the relations it has established with third countries, including liaison magistrates" [Art. 41(3) EJ Proposal].

Regarding the administrative links, the EPPO "shall rely on the support and resources of the administration of Eurojust". In the framework of an Agreement to be signed among both institutions, Eurojust will provide to the EPPO technical support in the preparation of the annual budget and other management documents, in staff recruitment and career-management, security services, IT services, financial management, accounting and audit services, among others [Art. 57(6) EPPO draft Regulation and Art. 41(7) EJ draft Regulation].

The relations with any other Union institutions, agencies and bodies, including Europol and OLAF are laid down briefly in Art. 58 EPPO draft Proposal. With respect to Europol, the cooperation between both EU bodies will entail the exchange of information and personal data "for the purposes for which it was provided" and with the possibility of further use only as far as such use "falls within the mandate of the body receiving the data", and subject to the prior authorisation of the body which provided the data [Art. 58(2)]. With respect to the Commission, including OLAF, an agreement setting out the modalities for cooperation might be signed between the Commission and the EPPO [Art. 58(3) EPPO draft Regulation].

14.10 Cooperation and Exchange of Information with Third States, International Organisations and Bodies

The modalities for cooperation between the EPPO and third States are regulated in Art. 59 EPPO draft Proposal, according to which the EPPO is entitled to designate contact points in third countries in order to facilitate cooperation [Art. 59(2)], and submit to the Council "proposals for the negotiation of agreements with one or more third countries regarding the cooperation between the European Public Prosecutor's Office and the competent authorities of these third countries" with regard to legal assistance in criminal matters and extradition [Art. 59(3)].

To ensure that the EPPO will benefit from the international agreements on legal assistance in criminal matters and of extradition signed by the Member States with third parties, each Member State should recognise the EPPO "as a competent authority" for the purpose of the implementation of such international agreements [Art. 59(4) EPPO draft Regulation].

Lastly, some legal provisions regulate the transfer of personal data to third countries and international organisations. However, provided that the EPPO will be a formal prosecution service who will always carry out its activities in the framework of criminal proceedings and therefore with the power to exchange information in the context of agreements of judicial cooperation, Art. 61 does not seem very convenient. The international agreements of judicial cooperation should be applicable instead, and exchange of information should only be authorised in the framework of particular investigations for particular purposes as laid down in such agreements on judicial cooperation.

References

Caianiello M (2013) The proposal for a regulation on the establishment of an European Public Prosecutor's Office: everything changes, or nothing changes? Eur J Crime Crim Law Crim Justice 2:115

Conway G (2013) Holding to account a possible European Public Prosecutor: supranational governance and accountability across diverse legal traditions. Crim Law Forum 3 (published online)

Da Costa Andrade AR (2013) O futuro da Cooperacao Judiciaria em Materia Penal: a criacao da Procuradoria Europeia (?) Debater a Europa 9:329

De Angelis F (2011) L'Espace Judiciaire Penal Europeen: Une Vision se concretise. Era Forum scripta iuris europaei 12:43 (Springer)

Delmas Marty M (1997) Corpus Iuris introducing penal provisions for the purpose of the financial interests of the European Union. Economica, Paris

Delmas Marty M, Vervaele J (2000) The implementation of the Corpus Iuris in the Member States. Intersentia, Utrecht

ECBA (2013) Cornerstones for a draft regulation on the establishment of a European Public Prosecutor's Office ("EPPO") in accordance with Article 86 par 1–3 TFEU. N J Eur Crim Law 1–2:185

Editorial (2013) Habemus EPPO! Eur Crim Law Rev 2:121

Espina Ramos J (2011) Towards a European Public Prosecutor's Office. The long and winding road. In: Klip A (ed) Substantive Criminal Law of the European Union. Antwerpen

Hamran L, Szabova E (2013) European Public Prosecutor's Office – Cui Bono? N J Eur Crim Law 1–2:40

Ligeti K (2011) The European Public Prosecutor's Office: which model? In: Klip A (ed) Substantive Criminal Law of the European Union. Antwerpen

Ligeti K (2011b) The European Public Prosecutor's office: how should the rules applicable to its procedures be determined? Eur Crim Law Rev 2:105

Ligeti K (ed) (2013) Toward a prosecutor for the European Union: a comparative analysis. Hart, Oxford

Ligeti K, Simonato M (2013) The European Public Prosecutor's Office: towards a truly European Prosecution Service. N J Eur Crim Law 1–2

Mauro C (2011) Vers un parquet europeen? La Semaine Juridique 26:743

Monar J (2013) Eurojust and the European Public Prosecutor perspective: from cooperation to integration in EU Criminal Justice? Perspect Eur Polit Soc 14(3):339

Peers S (2011) European Public Prosecutor. EU Justice and Home Affairs Law. Oxford University Press, Oxford, p 858

Ruggieri F (2013a) The future of the European Public Prosecutor's Office in the framework of Articles 85 and 86 TFEU. In: Ruggieri F (ed) Criminal proceedings, languages and the European Union. Springer, Heidelberg, p 109

Ruggieri F (2013b) Eurojust and the European Public Prosecutor's Office after the Lisbon Treaty. Transnational inquiries and the protection of fundamental rights in criminal proceedings: a study in Memory of Vottorio Grevi and Giovanni Tranchina. TMC Asser Press, The Hague

Spencer J (2011) Who's is afraid of the big, bad European Public Prosecutor? Camb Yearbook Eur Legal Stud 14

Wade ML (2013) A European Public Prosecutor: potential and pitfalls. Crime Law Soc Change 59(4):439

White S (2013) Towards a decentralised European Public Prosecutor's Office? N J Eur Crim Law 1–2:22

Willliams A (2013) Fighting fraud in the EU: a note on icebergs and evidence. ERA Forum 14:227–234

Chapter 15
The European Investigation Order Draft Directive

In 2012, a group of Member States presented a proposal for a Directive of the European Parliament and of the Council to create the European Investigation Order in criminal matters,[1] with the aim of replacing the existing instruments in this area with a comprehensive system for obtaining evidence in cross-border cases, based on the principle of mutual recognition in criminal matters.

The new approach proposed in this initiative is based on a single instrument, the European Investigation Order (EIO) which would be issued for the purposes of carrying out specific investigative measures in the executing Member State, gathering the resulting information and evidence and transmitting them to the issuing Member State. With an horizontal approach, the EIO will cover most of the investigative measures, except the setting up of Joint Investigation Teams (JITs) and the gathering and transmission of evidence within JITs.

The issues of data processing and protection of personal data have also been discussed during the negotiations on the EIO draft Directive, in the context of which different versions for a Recital on this matter have been suggested.

In the original draft, the Commission suggested introducing a recital making reference to the data protection principles of the Convention 108, its Protocol, and Framework Decision 2008/977/JHA, as follows[2]:

> The personal data processed in the context of the implementation of this Directive will be protected in accordance with the principles set out in the relevant instruments, including the Council of Europe Convention 108 of 28 January 1981 for the protection of individuals with regard to the automatic processing of personal data, the Additional Protocol to that Convention of 8 November 2001 and Council Framework Decision 2008/977/JHA of 27 November 2008 on the protection of personal data processed in the framework of police

[1] Initiative of the Kingdom of Belgium, the Republic of Bulgaria, the Republic of Estonia, the Kingdom of Spain, the Republic of Austria, the Republic of Slovenia and the Kingdom of Sweden for a Directive of the European Parliament and the Council regarding the European Investigation Order in criminal matters. Council document 9288/10 COPEN 117 EUROJUST 49 EJN 13 PARLNAT 13 CODEC 384. Brussels, 21 May 2010.

[2] Commission document C(2010) 5789 final. Brussels, 24.8.2010, p. 10.

Á.G. Zarza (ed.), *Exchange of Information and Data Protection in Cross-border Criminal Proceedings in Europe*, DOI 10.1007/978-3-642-40291-3_15,

> and judicial cooperation in criminal matters, as well as by the additional protection afforded by this Directive in line with Article 23 of the Convention on mutual assistance in criminal matters between the Member States of the European Union.

A simplified version of this paragraph was suggested in a later stage of negotiations, according to which:

> Personal data processed, when implementing this Directive, should be protected in accordance with the provisions on the protection of personal data processed in the framework of police and judicial cooperation in criminal matters and with relevant international instruments in this field.

As suggested in other sections of this book, the introduction of this type of legal provisions in legal instruments of judicial cooperation are not necessary. They do not add anything new and may lead to some confusion with regard to the rules applicable for the exchange of information between judicial authorities in the framework created for specific requests for judicial cooperation based on the principle of mutual recognition. The European Investigations Orders, as such, will be subject to the principles of legality and proportionality applicable in the area of judicial cooperation in criminal matters, and the fundamental rights of the suspects will be protected in accordance with the Directives issued by the Commission with the same purpose.

Chapter 16
Exchange of Information Through e-Justice Portal: The e-Codex Pilots

In the EU, "e-Justice" is a broad concept covering all matters related to the use of information and communication technologies in the areas of civil, criminal and administrative law. The aim is to ensure better access to Justice by EU citizens and practitioners, and strengthen cooperation between all the actors involved in judicial proceedings (including lawyers, notaries, prosecutors, judges).

The main tool for the achievement of its objectives is the e-Justice portal,[1] which was launched in 2010 and gradually expanded in accordance with the European e-Justice Action Plan 2009–2013[2] and the European e-Justice Roadmap.[3] This portal is conceived as a "one-stop (electronic) shop" for information related to a wide range of projects and initiatives developed by the Member States and the Commission to assist citizens, businesses, lawyers and judicial authorities in the clarification of legal questions and the resolution of cross-border cases and disputes.

e-Codex (e-Justice Communication via On-line Data Exchange) is one of the most challenging projects developed under the umbrella of e-Justice.[4] It is a large-scale project with the main goals of ensuring the interoperability of the information systems created by the Member States in the area of Justice, and developing common standards and tools allowing access and better use of that systems in cross-border cases.

e-Codex includes several pilots, some of them aimed at creating a first version of the technical requirements, common standards, legal amendments (if any), and methodology applicable for the exchange of formal requests on judicial cooperation in criminal matters among the judicial authorities of the issuing and executing

[1] https://e-justice.europa.eu/home.do.

[2] Council docum. 15315/08 JURINFO 71 JAI 612 JUSTCIV 239 COPEN 216.

[3] Council docum. 9714/1/10 REV 1 EJUSTICE 59.

[4] www.e-codex.en/home.html.

Á.G. Zarza (ed.), *Exchange of Information and Data Protection in Cross-border Criminal Proceedings in Europe*, DOI 10.1007/978-3-642-40291-3_16,

Member States. It offers the possibility of exchanging European Arrest Warrants, orders for freezing and further confiscation, financial penalties and other judicial decisions and official forms through a secure channel (and not by normal post, as it happens now in most of the cases) and will certainly facilitate and accelerate judicial investigations and further steps of criminal proceedings with a cross-border dimension.

Chapter 17
Processing and Protection of Personal Data in National Investigations and Criminal Proceedings

17.1 Scope of the DP draft Directive

On 25 January 2012, the Vice-President of the Commission and the holder of the justice portfolio Ms Reding proposed the comprehensive reform of the existing rules governing the processing and protection of personal data in EU.[1] The new EU legislative package included mainly a policy communication and two legislative proposals[2]:

- The Communication COM(2012) 9 final on "Safeguarding Privacy in a Connected World – A European Data Protection Framework for the 21st Century"[3];
- The Proposal for a Regulation on the protection of individuals with regard to the processing of personal data and on the free movement on such data (General DP Regulation)[4];
- The Proposal for a Directive on the protection of individuals with regard to the processing of personal data by competent authorities for the purposes of prevention, investigation, detection or prosecution of criminal offences or the execution of criminal penalties, and the free movement of such data (DP draft Directive).[5]

---

[1] See Press release of the European Commission, IP/12/46, p. 1. On this legislative package, see "Review of the EU Framework for Data Protection – the current state of play", video message of Peter Hustinx at the occasion of the Conference *Emerging Challenges in privacy Law: Australasian – EU perspectives,* Monash University, Melbourne, 24 February 2012, available at www.edps.europa.eu; Cullen and Gonié (2012), p. 117; Blume (2012), p. 130.

[2] See also the Impact Assessment of the Commission, Document SEC(2012) 72 final, Brussels, 25.1.2012; and the Executive Summary to the Impact Assessment, Document SEC(2012) 73 final, Brussels, 25.1.2012.

[3] Brussels, 25.1.2012.

[4] COM(2012) 11 final. Brussels, 25.1.2012.

[5] Document COM(2012) 10 final. 2012/0010 (COD). See also the Commission Staff Working Documents SEC(2012) 72 final and SEC(2012) 73 final.

Á.G. Zarza (ed.), *Exchange of Information and Data Protection in Cross-border Criminal Proceedings in Europe*, DOI 10.1007/978-3-642-40291-3_17,

The DP draft Directive was accompanied by the Report from the Commission based on Article 29(2) of the Council Framework Decision of 27 November 2008 on the protection of personal data processed in the framework of police and judicial cooperation in criminal matters.[6]

Three main challenges had given rise to the new package presented by the Commission: the increasing capabilities of modern technologies; the globalisation of data flows and the frequently transfer of personal data to third States, and "the growing appetite for personal data for reasons of public interest, in particular for public security matters".[7]

During the presentation of the new package, Ms Redding stressed the need to reinforce the protection of the fundamental rights of the citizens in an online environment, thus enhancing trust in the digital markets and promoting the movement of capital and increasing use of Internet by customers. In Ms Reding' words:

> The protection of personal data is a fundamental right for all Europeans, but citizens do not always feel in full control of their personal data. My proposals will help build trust in online services because people will be better informed about their rights and in more control of their information. The reform will accomplish this while making life easier and less costly for businesses. A strong, clear and uniform legal framework at EU level will help to unleash the potential of the Digital Single Market and foster economic growth, innovation and job creation.

The Commissioner also underlined that the new package was aimed at ensuring a comprehensive and coherent approach on data protection in the EU. This approach was not considered incompatible with the presentation of two different proposals (the General DP draft Regulation, the DP draft Directive), instead of a simple legal instrument.

Moreover, in the particular case of the DP draft Directive, its scope will not cover the processing of personal data "by the Union institutions, bodies, offices and agencies". This means that, among others, Eurojust and Europol will continue applying their corresponding set of rules of the processing and protection of personal data, whilst OLAF will continue developing its approach to the use of data under Regulation (EC) No. 45/2001 of 18 December 2000 on the protection of individuals with regard to the processing of personal data by the Community institutions and bodies and the free movement of such data.[8] Each EU information system and database set up for the purposes of preventing, investigating and prosecuting criminal offences (Prüm system, ECRIS system, SIS-II, VIS...) will continue governed by its own set of rules as well.

Another relevant and controversial aspect of the DP draft Directive is that it covers both cross-border and domestic processing of personal data. The extension of the EU data protection rules to the national investigations and proceedings has been a constant request by the experts on data protection in the past years,

[6] Document COM(2012) 12 final. See also the Commission Staff Working Document Annex accompanying the cited Report, document SEC(2012) 75 final.

[7] Cf. Reding (2011), p. 3.

[8] OJ L 8, 21.1.2001, p. 1.

especially during the negotiations and further implementation (by some Member States) of the Framework Decision 2008/977/JHA. The authors of the DP draft Directive have responded to this request, however, if finally approved, the national legislators will be faced with the challenge of achieving compatibility and aligning their traditional principles and rights of the criminal proceedings with the "new generation" set of principles and rights for the processing and protection of personal data. The task will not be easy. As we will see in the next sections, different principles and rights on data protection pay different roles in the context of investigations and criminal proceedings.

17.2 Application of DP Draft Directive to Police Investigations

As police authorities make an increased use of the new technologies, and in particular to the databases and information systems, the investigative methods of law enforcement authorities should comply with the rules for the processing and processing of personal data. No other rules regulate such intelligence and police investigative work at police level.

17.3 Overlapping of Certain Principles and Rights of the DP Draft Directive with the Principles and Rights of Criminal Proceedings

In the context of a formal investigation conducted by a prosecutor, as well as during court proceedings, however, the judicial authorities should comply with the principles and rights governing criminal proceedings, which are contained—in most of the Member States—in national codes and related legal provisions. The principles of legality and proportionality, and the fundamental rights of suspects and accused persons, should be fully respected.

The DP draft Directive regulates the principles of lawfulness and proportionality, as well as the right of access, rectification or deletion of personal data.

It seems, then, that both set of rules overlap.

The Council of Europe, the pioneer institution in the area of personal data, has stated that the principles and rules of criminal proceedings can have the same effects than those related to personal data:

> The provisions of national codes of criminal procedure require judicial authorities to accomplish their missions of prosecution or of judgement without explicit references to data processing or to a complete listing of specific purposes. In this respect, it must be acknowledged that the traditional provisions in codes of criminal procedure which were not drafted with data protection principles in mind can nevertheless fulfil the data protection requirements of Convention 108, in particular when they specify the purposes of the

activities of the judicial authorities, or even when they develop these activities more generally without providing a specific authorisation to set data processing.

With the same approach:

> Although national criminal codes are not specifically designed with data protection in mind, many of their rules, such as safeguards for accused personas, rules for collecting evidence, balance of interests in a fair trial, can have the same effects as data protection principles.[9]

Therefore, there is no reason to apply the principles and rights on data protection in the context of ongoing investigations and prosecutions: the rights of suspects and accused persons are already protected by the principles and rules of the criminal proceedings.

The principles of lawfulness means that personal data can only be processed in those cases expressly regulated by law. This principle is recognised in Article 4 (a) DP draft directive, according to which personal data must be processed fairly and "lawfully", and in Article 7, which is as follows:

> Member States shall provide that the processing of personal data is lawful only if and to the extend that processing is necessary:
>
> (a) for the performance of a task carried out by a competent authority, based on law for the purposes set out in Article 1(1); or
> (b) for compliance with a legal obligation to which the controller is subject; or
> (c) in order to protect the vital interests of the data subject or of another person; or
> (d) for the prevention of an immediate and serious threat to public security.

On this principle, the Council of Europe has concluded that there is no need to recognise such principles from the perspective on data protection when there an equivalent principle (the legality principle) is recognised in national criminal proceedings. In Council of Europe words:

> There is not need to create specific legal rules authorising the judicial authorities to process personal data, in every case, in order to fulfil the requirements of the lawfulness principle when provisions in criminal procedure codes already provide such rules.[10]

The same applies to the principle of proportionality,[11] which is embedded in the following principles lay down in Article 4 DP draft Directive:

> Member States shall provide that personal data must be:
> (...)
> (b) collected for specified, explicit and legitimate purposes, and not further processed in a way incompatible with those purposes;
> (c) adequate, relevant and not excessive in relation to the purposes for which they are processed
> (d) (...) every reasonable step must be taken to ensure that personal data that are inaccurate, having regard to the purpose for which they are processed, are erased or rectified without delay
> (...).

[9] 2002 Report of the Council of Europe de 2002, cit., paragraph (12).

[10] 2002 Report of the Council of Europe, cit., paragraph (14).

[11] On this principle, from a cross-border perspective, vid. Bachmaier Winter (2013), p. 85.

The principle of proportionality is one of the fundamental rights of criminal proceedings, and ensures a proper balance between the investigative measures to de adopted in a particular situation and the fundamental rights of the suspect and accused person. Again, there is a clear overlapping between both sets of objectives and there is no need to duplicate (by introducing specific data protection principles) in the criminal codes legal provisions that already exist.

The same applies to the right of access to personal data vis à vis the right of information in criminal proceedings. Experts on data protection will advise the suspect to exercise the right of access to information, whilst judicial authorities and lawyers will advise the suspect to exercise the right to be informed about the charges against him as provided for in the national codes of criminal proceedings.

The scope, limitations and modalities for exercising this fundamental right are extensively regulated in Arts, 12 to 14 DP new Directive. However, its Art. 17 states:

> Rights of the data subject in criminal investigations and proceedings
>
> Member States may provide that the rights of information, access, rectification, erasure and restriction of processing referred to in Articles 11 to 1 are carried out in accordance with national rules of judicial proceedings where the personal data are contained in a judicial decision or record processed in the course of criminal investigations and proceedings 2.

In other words, the implementation of Arts. 12–14 will not be necessary as soon as the Member State protect the right of the suspect to be informed of the investigation and to have access to the judicial files in accordance with the rules (or Code) of criminal proceedings.

This has been also the approach of the Council of Europe, according to whom:

> The right of the data subject to have access to his or her personal data is one of the best-known data protection principles. In the context of judicial data, access should be granted to any data subject who request access to the judicial file, whether on the basis of the provisions of criminal codes or on the basis of data protection legislation[12].

There are another two rights traditionally applicable in the area of data protection that should be applied, although, very carefully. These are the principles of information to the data subject (Art. 11 DP draft Directive) and the right of the individual to be notified in case of security breaches (Art. 28 thereto). As mentioned earlier, the individuals subject to a judicial investigation and/or criminal proceedings are protected by the fundamental rights recognised in the Code of criminal proceedings. These Codes also regulate the situations under which the exercise of this fundamental right can be delayed in order to protect ongoing investigative measures. Any information sent to the data subject, without regard to these caveats, in accordance with Arts. 11 or 28 in this context could have very unfortunate consequences.

[12] 2000 Report of the Council of Europe, cit., paragraph (45).

17.4 Inspiration of Certain Principles for Updating the Codes of Criminal Proceedings

The principle of retention of personal data (Art. 4 DP draft Directive) could serve as an inspiration to regulate the final destination of the judicial files. Many national codes of criminal procedure do not pay any attention to the future use and retention judicial files and dossiers after the closure of a criminal proceeding. Traditionally, it has been considered that the information contained in such dossiers could be needed in a further appeal or extraordinary revision of the judgment, or during its execution. As result, judicial files and dossiers are retained in old archives and warehouses for decades (or even centuries).

17.5 Importance of Certain Principles and Guarantees on Data Protection in Court Proceedings

Art. 4 DP draft Directive recognises the principles of data integrity and quality, by stating that data must be "accurate". Art. 6, on "different degrees of accuracy and reliability of personal data", states:

> 1. Member States shall ensure that, as far possible, the different categories of personal data undergoing processing are distinguished in accordance with their degree of accuracy and reliability.
> 2. Member States shall ensure that, as far as possible, personal data based on facts are distinguished from personal data based on personal assessments.

The integrity and quality of the information extracted from EU information systems and databases in order to be integrated in a judicial file is absolutely crucial. Integrity and accuracy ensure the appropriate admissibility and proper assessment as evidence of this type of information and personal data.

The retention of personal data beyond the limits laid down in the rules on data protection could also have consequences in court proceedings. It is not clear whether such information and personal data could be admissible as evidence in court. If not admissible, then the next question would be whether the inadmissibility could contaminate other types of information and evidence gathered as result of this initial retrieval of information. As in many other areas, the theory of the fruits of the poisonous tree can be subject to different interpretations.

Controllers must take appropriate technical and organisational measures to protect personal data against avoid accidental destruction, loss, unauthorised access and all other forms of unlawful processing. The security measures taken should reflect the nature of the risk and the level of potential harm, but some basic steps should be taken to safeguard all personal data.

The proposal for a new Directive regulates the "keeping of records" in Article 24, and the rules on data security on Articles 27–29.

Keeping records on the collection, alteration, consultation, disclosure, combination or erasure of the information processed, "for the purposes of verification of the lawfulness of the data processing, self-monitoring and for ensuring data integrity and data security" [Article 24(2)], could be crucial for assessing the reliability of the information stored as evidence in court. In certain types of crime (espionage, disclosure of confidential information) the keeping of records could be a crucial element for the identification of the perpetrator of the criminal offences and the collection of evidence against him.

References

Bachmaier Winter L (2013) The role of the proportionality principle in cross-border investigations involving fundamental rights. In: Ruggeri S (ed) Transnational inquiries and the protection of fundamental rights. Springer, Heidelberg, p 85

Blume P (2012) Will it be a better world? The proposed EU data protection regulation. Int Data Privacy Law 2(3):130

Cullen P, Gonié J (2012) 1995–2012: from a directive to a regulation, the Microsoft perspective. Int Data Privacy Law 2(3):117

Reding V (2011) The upcoming data protection reform for the European Union. Int Data Privacy Law 1(1):3

Chapter 18
Towards a EU Passenger Name Record (PNR) Scheme?

Following the first proposal on this matter presented by the Commission in 2007 (hereinafter, "previous proposal of 2007"),[1] after the entry force of the Treaty of Lisbon the Commission presented in April 2011 a *Proposal for a Directive on the use of Passenger Name Record data for the prevention, detection, investigation and prosecution of terrorist offences and serious crime*[2] (hereinafter, "proposal for a EU PNR scheme"). Following the general approach agreed at the JHA Council of 26–27 April 2012, at the time of writing this Proposal is awaiting its first reading at the European Parliament.

Compared to the previous proposal of 2007, the proposal for a EU PNR scheme has been much welcomed by the European Parliament, at least by its Rapporteur, who has agreed "which the vast majority of the Commission's approach to the transmission and use of PNR data" and considered the proposal "a sound platform for discussion in this house".[3]

---

[1] Proposal for a Council Framework Decision on the use of Passenger Name Record (PNR) data for law enforcement purposes. Doc COM(2007) 654 final, SEC(2007) 1422, and SEC(2007) 1453. The proposal was discussed in detail by the Council's internal bodies, and subject to comments by the European Parliament (see Resolution of November 2008 P6_TA(2008) 0561); the European Data Protection Supervisor (Opinion published at OJ C 100, 1.5.2008), the Article 29 Working Party on Data Protection (Opinion number 145 of 5.12.2007), and the Fundamental Rights Agency (available at http://fra.europa.eu/fraWebsite/attachments/FRA_opinion_PNR_en.pdf). The entry into force of the Lisbon Treaty obligated the Commission to reconsider the legal basis for the initial proposal. A comparative analysis between this proposal and the Agreements on PNR signed at that time with Canada and US can be found at Boehm (2010), p. 251.

On this proposal, and in particular its implications regarding human rights standards, see Brouwer (2009).

[2] COM(2011) 32 final. Brussels, 2.2.2011, SEC(2011) 132 final, and SEC(2011) 133 final.

[3] See draft Report on the proposal for a EU PNR scheme, Rapporteur Timothy Kirkhope, docum. 2011/0023(COD).

Á.G. Zarza (ed.), *Exchange of Information and Data Protection in Cross-border Criminal Proceedings in Europe*, DOI 10.1007/978-3-642-40291-3_18,

More sceptical, the EDPS has reiterated the lack of justification of the necessity of a European PNR scheme in addition to a number of other instruments allowing for the processing of personal data for law enforcement purposes. Moreover:

> the EDPS recalls that in his view, PNR data could certainly be necessary for law enforcement purposes in specific cases and meet data protection requirements. It is their use in a systematic and indiscriminate way, with regard to all passengers, which raises specific concerns.[4]

In general terms, the proposal for a EU PNR scheme regulates the transfer by airlines and further processing by the so-called "Passengers Information Units" (PIU) of PNR data provided by passengers of extra-EU flights to and from the Member States, for the purposes of prevention, detection, investigation and prosecution of terrorist offences and serious crime.

The scope of the proposal has been quite controversial. Firstly, its scope was initially limited to the transfer and further processing of PNR data provided by passengers of flights with origin or destination out of the territory of the European Union (extra-flights). The internal bodies of the Council extensively discussed whether the EU PNR scheme could also cover flights operating within the territory of the European Union, as some delegations suggested. As a compromise solution, it was agreed at the JHA Council of 26–27 April 2012 that the system would allow, but not oblige, Member States to collect PNR data also relating to "selected" intra-EU flights. On this point, the draft report of the European Parliament has declared to be convinced that "the inclusion of intra-EU flights would bring clear added value to any EU PNR scheme" and, although this would add to initial costs "there are clear benefits to their inclusion: uniform set up and strong security advantages".[5]

Secondly, while the proposal of the Commission covered "terrorist offences" and "serious crime" it gave the Member States the option to extend its scope of application to minor offences. As mentioned by the EPDS, the terms "serious crime" and "minor offences" are quite vague, thus giving the Member States the possibility to interpret them in very different manners. Hence,

> instead of leaving the faculty of narrowing the scope of application to Member States, the EDPS considers that the Proposal should explicitly list offences which should be included in its scope and those which should be excluded as they should be considered as minor and do not meet the proportionality test.[6]

On the other hand, the above-mentioned "Passenger Information Unit" (PIU) should be designated by each Member State as the authority responsible for collecting and further processing PNR data transmitted by air carriers using the

---

[4] See Opinion of the EDPS on the EU PNR scheme, OJ C 181, 22.6.2011, p. 24. See also Opinion of the Article 29 Working Party (WP 181, 5 April 2011) and FRA Opinion 1/2011 (Vienna, 14 June 2011). More critical, see Brouwer (2011).

[5] Draft Report of the European Parliament (Rapporteur: Timothy Kirkhope) on the EU PNR scheme, p. 32.

[6] Opinion of the EDPS on the EU PNR scheme, p. 27.

"push method", according to which air carriers should forward PNR data, by their own means, to the national authorities of the arrival or departures State.[7]

PIUs will process PNR data in a systematic manner, carrying out an assessment of the passengers prior to their scheduled arrival to or departure from the Member States in order to identify the persons who require further examination by the competent national authorities (law enforcement authorities expressly designated by the Member States) with a view to taking any appropriate action for the purpose of preventing, detecting, investigating and prosecuting terrorist offences and serious crime. PIUs can also process information on a case-by-case basis, to respond to requests issued from other competent authorities in specific cases.

When the PIUs consider that PNR data, or the results of the processing of such data, can be necessary for the prevention, detection, investigation or prosecution of terrorist offences or serious crime, this information should be transmitted to the corresponding competent authorities to the same Member State. The same information should be also "upon request" to the PIU of another Member State or, in cases or emergency, to the competent authorities of another Member State. Submitted to strict conditions, PNR data can also be transmitted to third States.[8]

The periods of data retention are also another controversial point of the proposal for a EU PNR scheme. The initial text of the Commission proposed a total retention period of 5 years, although after 30 days PNR data should be masked out (meaning that the data could only be consulted after a specific authorisation). At its JHA meeting in April 2012, the Council agreed to retain the overall retention period of 5 years, but to prolong the first period during which the data are fully accessible to 2 years, because some Member States considered 30 days too short from an operational point of view "as it may often be necessary to check very quickly – within a time span of a few hours- the travel history of a person who is automatically selected for further review".[9]

The proposal also includes specific provisions on the protection of personal data, according to which data subject should have the same rights of access, rectification, erasure and blocking, compensation, and judicial redress as those regulated by Council Framework Decision 2008/977/JHA. As it has been pointed out by the EDPS, the protection of personal data should not rely on the cited Council Framework Decision, as the later includes shortcomings, notably in terms of data subject's rights and transfers to third countries: a higher standard of safeguards, based on the principles of Directive 95/46/EC, should be developed in the Proposal".[10]

[7] In the proposal of 2007, the "push method" was combined with the "pull methods", the later allowing the national authorities to obtain PNR data by having direct access to the reservation systems of the air carriers.

[8] On this matter, more in detail, see Part IV, Chap. 11 of this publication.

[9] Press release, 3,162nd Council Meeting JHA. Council document 9197/12 PRESSE 172 PR CO 24, p. 8.

[10] Opinion of the EDPS on the EU PNR scheme, p. 30.

Last but not least, the proposal regulates the obligation of the PIUs to log or document every receipt, transfer and request of PNR data "for the purposes of verification of the lawfulness of the data processing, self-monitoring and ensuring proper data integrity and security of data processing". There can be no doubt about the added value of these logs for ensuring data integrity and its admissibility as evidence in court.[11]

References

Boehm F (2010) Tit for tat – Europe's revenge for the Canadian and US-American PNR systems? The envisaged European model of analysing flight passenger data. ERA Forum 11:251

Brouwer E (2009) The EU passenger name record system and human rights. Transferring passenger data or passenger freedom? CEPS working document no. 320, September 2009. Available at www.ceps.eu

Brouwer E (2011) Ignoring dissent and legality. The EU's proposal to share the personal information of all passengers. CEPS, June 2011. Available at www.ceps.eu

[11] On this matter, see more in detail Part IV, Chap. 10.

Chapter 19
Towards a Terrorism Finance Tracking System (TFTS) in the European Union?

As we have seen in Chap. 11, on 12 July 2010 the United States and the European Union concluded the Agreement on the processing and transfer to Financial Messaging Data from the European Union to the United States of America for the purposes of the Terrorist Finance Tracking Programme (EU–US Agreement on TFTP). The negotiations of that Agreement were quite difficult and controversial, including the reluctance of the European Parliament to authorise the massive transfer of personal data to a third country without strict guarantees to protect personal data of innocent individuals. The Parliament suggested that the Council should instruct the Commission to conduct a study on the legal and technical framework for extraction on data on the EU territory (instead of transferring bulk data directly to US).

As suggested by the European Parliament, on 13 July 2011 the Commission issued a Communication on the options available as regards the setting up of a Terrorist Finance Tracking System (TFTS) in the European Union.[1]

The Communication was presented in CATS meeting on 5–6 September 2011, where the Commission explained that going forward with this initiative would require the transfer of bulk data, and asked delegations for a clear position as to whether they wanted the Commission to proceed with the preparation of a legislative proposal on the matter. The EU Terrorism Coordinator and the Director of Europol stressed the importance of the TFTP mechanism to ensure EU security. Some delegations supported the initiative and some others expressed some concerns, and the majority of representatives requested further details from the Commission as to the exact operational, financial and legal aspects of a possible TFTS in Europe, including an impact assessment of the proposal which should cover, among

[1] "A European Terrorist Finance Tracking System: available options" COM(2011) 429 final.

Á.G. Zarza (ed.), *Exchange of Information and Data Protection in Cross-border Criminal Proceedings in Europe*, DOI 10.1007/978-3-642-40291-3_19,

others, the possible extension of the scope of the TFTS to serious threats to the internal security other than terrorism.[2]

At that CATS meeting, the Presidency announced its intention to have a discussion at Ministerial level about the real operational need and potential added value of establishing a TFTP in the European Union, as well as about the key outstanding issues that the Commission should address in its further preparatory works, including the above mentioned impact assessment. Discussions are ongoing on this matter at the time of writing.

[2] Council Document 14306/11 CATS 77 COMIX 575.

A. EUROPEAN UNION

1. Treaty on European Union

Published at OJ C 83, 30.3.2010, p. 15.

PREAMBLE

HIS MAJESTY THE KING OF THE BELGIANS, HER MAJESTY THE QUEEN OF DENMARK, THE PRESIDENT OF THE FEDERAL REPUBLIC OF GERMANY, THE PRESIDENT OF IRELAND, THE PRESIDENT OF THE HELLENIC REPUBLIC, HIS MAJESTY THE KING OF SPAIN, THE PRESIDENT OF THE FRENCH REPUBLIC, THE PRESIDENT OF THE ITALIAN REPUBLIC, HIS ROYAL HIGHNESS THE GRAND DUKE OF LUXEMBOURG, HER MAJESTY THE QUEEN OF THE NETHERLANDS, THE PRESIDENT OF THE PORTUGUESE REPUBLIC, HER MAJESTY THE QUEEN OF THE UNITED KINGDOM OF GREAT BRITAIN AND NORTHERN IRELAND[1]

(. . .)

RESOLVED to facilitate the free movement of persons, while ensuring the safety and security of their peoples, by establishing an area of freedom, security and justice, in accordance with the provisions of this Treaty and the Treaty on the Functionning of the European Union,

[1] The Republic of Bulgaria, the Czech Republic, the Republich of Estonia, the Republic of Cyprus, the Republic of Latvia, the Republic of Lithuania, the Republic of Hungary, the Republic of Malta, the Republic of Austria, the Republic of Poland, the Republic of Slovenia, the Slovak Republic, the Republic of Finland and the Kingdom of Sweden have since become members of the European Union.

Á.G. Zarza (ed.), *Exchange of Information and Data Protection in Cross-border Criminal Proceedings in Europe*, DOI 10.1007/978-3-642-40291-3,

See Article 3(3) TEU; Title V (Articles 67 to 89) of Part Three TFUE.

(. . .)
WHO, having exchanged their full powers, found in good and due form, have agreed as follows:

(. . .)

TITLE I – COMMON PROVISIONS

(. . .)

Article 3
(ex Article 2 TUE)

(. . .)
2. The Union shall offer its citizens an area of freedom, security and justice without internal frontiers, in which the free movement of persons is ensured in conjunction with appropriate measures with respect to external borders controls, asylum, immigration and the prevention and combating of crime.

See Article 3(3) TEU; Title V (Articles 67 to 89) of Part Three TFUE.

Article 6
(ex Article 6 TUE)

1. The Union recognises the rights, freedoms and principles set out in the Charter of Fundamental Rights of the European Union of 7 December 2000, as adapted at Strasbourg, on 12 December 2007, which shall have the same legal value as the Treaties.
The provisions of the Charter shall not extend in any way the competences of the Union as defined in the Treaties.
The rights, freedoms and principles in the Charter shall de interpreted in accordance with the general provisions in Title VII of the Charter governing its interpretation and application and with due regard to the explanations referred to in the Charter, that set out the sources of those provisions.

See Charter of Fundamental Rights of the European Union

2. The Union shall accede to the European Convention for the Protection of Human Rights and Fundamental Freedoms. Such accession shall not affect the Union's competences as defined in the Treaties.
3. Fundamental rights, as guaranteed by the European Convention for the Protection of Human Rights and Fundamental Freedoms and as they result from the constitutional traditions common to the Member States, shall constitute general principles of the Union's law.

See European Convention for the Protection of Human Rights and Fundamental Freedoms

(. . .)

2. Treaty on the Functioning of the European Union

Published at OJ C 83, 30.3.2010, p. 47

(*Extract*)

PART ONE – PRINCIPLES

Article 1

1. This Treaty organises the functioning of the Union and determines the areas of, delimitation of, and arrangements for exercising its competences.

TITLE 1 – CATEGORIES AND AREAS OF UNION COMPETENCE

Article 2

(...)

2. When the Treaties confer on the Union a competence shared with the Member States in a specific area, the Union and the Member States may legislate and adopt legally binding acts in that area. The Member States shall exercise their competence to the extent that the Union has not exercised its competence. The Member states shall again exercise their competence to the extent that the Union has decided to cease exercising its competence.

(...)

Article 4

(...)

2. Shared competences between the Union and the Member States applies in the following principal areas:

(...)

(j) area of freedom, security and justice;

(...)

TITLE II – PROVISIONS HAVING GENERAL APPLICATION

(...)

Article 16

(ex Article 286 TEC)

1. Everyone has the right to the protection of personal data concerning them.
2. The European Parliament and the Council, acting in accordance with the ordinary legislative procedure, shall lay down the rules relating to the protection of individuals with regard to the processing of personal data by Union institutions, bodies, offices and agencies, and by the Member States when carrying out activities which fall within the scope of Union law, and the rules relating to the free movement of such data. Compliance with these rules shall be subject to the control of independent authorities.

The rules adopted on the basis of this Article shall be without prejudice to the specific rules laid down in Article 39 of the Treaty on European Union.

(...)

PART THREE – UNION POLICIES AND INTERNAL ACTIONS

TITLE V – AREA OF FREEDOM, SECURITY AND JUSTICE

CHAPTER 1 – GENERAL PROVISIONS

Article 67

(ex Article 61 TEC and ex Article 29 TEU)

1. The Union shall constitute an area of freedom, security and justice with respect for fundamental rights and the different legal systems and traditions of the Member States.
2. It shall ensure the absence of internal border controls for persons and shall frame a common policy on asylum, immigration and external border control, based on solidarity between Member States, which is fair towards third-country nationals. For the purpose of this Title, stateless persons shall be treated as third-country nationals.
3. The Union shall endeavour to ensure a high level of security through measures to prevent and combat crime, racism and xenophobia, and through measures for coordination and cooperation between police and judicial authorities and other competent authorities, as well as through the mutual recognition of judgments in criminal matters and, if necessary, through the approximation of criminal laws.
4. The Union shall facilitate access to justice, in particular through the principle of mutual recognition of judicial and extrajudicial decisions in civil matters.

Article 76

The acts referred to in Chapters 4 and 5, together with the measures referred to in Article 74 which ensure administrative cooperation in the areas covered by these Chapters, shall be adopted:

(a) on a proposal from the Commission, or
(b) on the initiative of a quarter of the Member States.

(...)

CHAPTER 4 – JUDICIAL COOPERATION IN CRIMINAL MATTERS

Article 82

(ex Article 31 TEU)

1. Judicial cooperation in criminal matters in the Union shall be based on the principle of mutual recognition of judgments and judicial decisions and shall include the approximation of the laws and regulations of the Member States in the areas referred to in paragraph 2 and in Article 83.

The European Parliament and the Council, acting in accordance with the ordinary legislative procedure, shall adopt measures to:

(a) lay down rules and procedures for ensuring recognition throughout the Union of all forms of judgments and judicial decisions;
(b) prevent and settle conflicts of jurisdiction between Member States;
(c) support the training of the judiciary and judicial staff;
(d) facilitate cooperation between judicial or equivalent authorities of the Member States in relation to proceedings in criminal matters and the enforcement of decisions.

2. To the extent necessary to facilitate mutual recognition of judgments and judicial decisions and police and judicial cooperation in criminal matters having a cross-border dimension, the European Parliament and the Council may, by means of directives adopted in accordance with the ordinary legislative procedure, establish minimum rules. Such rules shall take into account the differences between the legal traditions and systems of the Member States.
They shall concern:

(a) mutual admissibility of evidence between Member States;
(b) the rights of individuals in criminal procedure;
(c) the rights of victims of crime;
(d) any other specific aspects of criminal procedure which the Council has identified in advance by a decision; for the adoption of such a decision, the Council shall act unanimously after obtaining the consent of the European Parliament.
Adoption of the minimum rules referred to in this paragraph shall not prevent Member States from maintaining or introducing a higher level of protection for individuals.

3. Where a member of the Council considers that a draft directive as referred to in paragraph 2 would affect fundamental aspects of its criminal justice system, it may request that the draft directive be referred to the European Council. In that case, the ordinary legislative procedure shall be suspended. After discussion, and in case of a consensus, the European Council shall, within four months of this suspension, refer the draft back to the Council, which shall terminate the suspension of the ordinary legislative procedure.
Within the same timeframe, in case of disagreement, and if at least nine Member States wish to establish enhanced cooperation on the basis of the draft directive concerned, they shall notify the European Parliament, the Council and the Commission accordingly. In such a case, the authorisation to proceed with enhanced cooperation referred to in Article 20(2) of the Treaty on European Union and Article 329(1) of this Treaty shall be deemed to be granted and the provisions on enhanced cooperation shall apply.

Article 83

(ex Article 31 TEU)

1. The European Parliament and the Council may, by means of directives adopted in accordance with the ordinary legislative procedure, establish minimum rules concerning the definition of criminal offences and sanctions in the areas of particularly serious crime with a cross-border dimension resulting from the nature or impact of such offences or from a special need to combat them on a common basis. These areas of crime are the following: terrorism, trafficking in human beings and sexual exploitation of women and children, illicit drug trafficking, illicit arms trafficking, money laundering, corruption, counterfeiting of means of payment, computer crime and organised crime.
On the basis of developments in crime, the Council may adopt a decision identifying other areas of crime that meet the criteria specified in this paragraph. It shall act unanimously after obtaining the consent of the European Parliament.
2. If the approximation of criminal laws and regulations of the Member States proves essential to ensure the effective implementation of a Union policy in an area which has been subject to harmonisation measures, directives may establish minimum rules with regard to the definition of criminal offences and sanctions in the area concerned. Such directives shall be adopted by the same ordinary or special legislative procedure as was followed for the adoption of the harmonisation measures in question, without prejudice to Article 76.
3. Where a member of the Council considers that a draft directive as referred to in paragraph 1 or 2 would affect fundamental aspects of its criminal justice system, it may request that the draft directive be referred to the European Council. In that case, the ordinary legislative procedure shall be suspended. After discussion, and in case of a consensus, the European Council shall, within four months of this suspension, refer the draft back to the Council, which shall terminate the suspension of the ordinary legislative procedure.
Within the same timeframe, in case of disagreement, and if at least nine Member States wish to establish enhanced cooperation on the basis of the draft directive concerned, they shall notify the European Parliament, the Council and the Commission accordingly. In such a case, the authorisation to proceed with enhanced cooperation referred to in Article 20(2) of the Treaty on European Union and Article 329(1) of this Treaty shall be deemed to be granted and the provisions on enhanced cooperation shall apply.

Article 84

The European Parliament and the Council, acting in accordance with the ordinary legislative procedure, may establish measures to promote and support the action of Member States in the field of crime prevention, excluding any harmonisation of the laws and regulations of the Member States.

Article 85

(ex Article 31 TEU)

1. Eurojust's mission shall be to support and strengthen coordination and cooperation between national investigating and prosecuting authorities in relation to serious crime affecting two or more Member States or requiring a prosecution on common bases, on the basis of operations conducted and information supplied by the Member States' authorities and by Europol.
In this context, the European Parliament and the Council, by means of regulations adopted in accordance with the ordinary legislative procedure, shall determine Eurojust's structure, operation, field of action and tasks. These tasks may include:

(a) the initiation of criminal investigations, as well as proposing the initiation of prosecutions conducted by competent national authorities, particularly those relating to offences against the financial interests of the Union;
(b) the coordination of investigations and prosecutions referred to in point (a);
(c) the strengthening of judicial cooperation, including by resolution of conflicts of jurisdiction and by close cooperation with the European Judicial Network.
These regulations shall also determine arrangements for involving the European Parliament and national Parliaments in the evaluation of Eurojust's activities.

2. In the prosecutions referred to in paragraph 1, and without prejudice to Article 86, formal acts of judicial procedure shall be carried out by the competent national officials.

Article 86

1. In order to combat crimes affecting the financial interests of the Union, the Council, by means of regulations adopted in accordance with a special legislative procedure, may establish a European Public Prosecutor's Office from Eurojust. The Council shall act unanimously after obtaining the consent of the European Parliament.
In the absence of unanimity in the Council, a group of at least nine Member States may request that the draft regulation be referred to the European Council. In that case, the procedure in the Council shall be suspended. After discussion, and in case of a consensus, the European Council shall, within four months of this suspension, refer the draft back to the Council for adoption.
Within the same timeframe, in case of disagreement, and if at least nine Member States wish to establish enhanced cooperation on the basis of the draft regulation concerned, they shall notify the European Parliament, the Council and the Commission accordingly. In such a case, the authorisation to proceed with enhanced cooperation referred to in Article 20(2) of the Treaty on European Union and Article 329(1) of this Treaty shall be deemed to be granted and the provisions on enhanced cooperation shall apply.
2. The European Public Prosecutor's Office shall be responsible for investigating, prosecuting and bringing to judgment, where appropriate in liaison with Europol, the perpetrators of, and accomplices in, offences against the Union's financial

interests, as determined by the regulation provided for in paragraph 1. It shall exercise the functions of prosecutor in the competent courts of the Member States in relation to such offences.
3. The regulations referred to in paragraph 1 shall determine the general rules applicable to the European Public Prosecutor's Office, the conditions governing the performance of its functions, the rules of procedure applicable to its activities, as well as those governing the admissibility of evidence, and the rules applicable to the judicial review of procedural measures taken by it in the performance of its functions.
4. The European Council may, at the same time or subsequently, adopt a decision amending paragraph 1 in order to extend the powers of the European Public Prosecutor's Office to include serious crime having a cross-border dimension and amending accordingly paragraph 2 as regards the perpetrators of, and accomplices in, serious crimes affecting more than one Member State. The European Council shall act unanimously after obtaining the consent of the European Parliament and after consulting the Commission.

CHAPTER 5 – POLICE COOPERATION

Article 87

(ex Article 30 TEU)

1. The Union shall establish police cooperation involving all the Member States' competent authorities, including police, customs and other specialised law enforcement services in relation to the prevention, detection and investigation of criminal offences.
2. For the purposes of paragraph 1, the European Parliament and the Council, acting in accordance with the ordinary legislative procedure, may establish measures concerning:

(a) the collection, storage, processing, analysis and exchange of relevant information;
(b) support for the training of staff, and cooperation on the exchange of staff, on equipment and on research into crime-detection;
(c) common investigative techniques in relation to the detection of serious forms of organised crime.

3. The Council, acting in accordance with a special legislative procedure, may establish measures concerning operational cooperation between the authorities referred to in this Article. The Council shall act unanimously after consulting the European Parliament.

In case of the absence of unanimity in the Council, a group of at least nine Member States may request that the draft measures be referred to the European Council. In that case, the procedure in the Council shall be suspended. After discussion, and in case of a consensus, the European Council shall, within four months of this suspension, refer the draft back to the Council for adoption.

Within the same timeframe, in case of disagreement, and if at least nine Member States wish to establish enhanced cooperation on the basis of the draft measures concerned, they shall notify the European Parliament, the Council and the Commission accordingly. In such a case, the authorisation to proceed with enhanced cooperation referred to in Article 20(2) of the Treaty on European Union and Article 329(1) of this Treaty shall be deemed to be granted and the provisions on enhanced cooperation shall apply.
The specific procedure provided for in the second and third subparagraphs shall not apply to acts which constitute a development of the Schengen *acquis*.

Article 88

(ex Article 30 TEU)

1. Europol's mission shall be to support and strengthen action by the Member States' police authorities and other law enforcement services and their mutual cooperation in preventing and combating serious crime affecting two or more Member States, terrorism and forms of crime which affect a common interest covered by a Union policy.
2. The European Parliament and the Council, by means of regulations adopted in accordance with the ordinary legislative procedure, shall determine Europol's structure, operation, field of action and tasks. These tasks may include:

(a) the collection, storage, processing, analysis and exchange of information, in particular that forwarded by the authorities of the Member States or third countries or bodies;
(b) the coordination, organisation and implementation of investigative and operational action carried out jointly with the Member States' competent authorities or in the context of joint investigative teams, where appropriate in liaison with Eurojust.

These regulations shall also lay down the procedures for scrutiny of Europol's activities by the European Parliament, together with national Parliaments.
3. Any operational action by Europol must be carried out in liaison and in agreement with the authorities of the Member State or States whose territory is concerned. The application of coercive measures shall be the exclusive responsibility of the competent national authorities.

Article 89

(ex Article 32 TEU)

The Council, acting in accordance with a special legislative procedure, shall lay down the conditions and limitations under which the competent authorities of the Member States referred to in Articles 82 and 87 may operate in the territory of another Member State in liaison and in agreement with the authorities of that State. The Council shall act unanimously after consulting the European Parliament.

(...)

TITLE II – FINANCIAL PROVISIONS

(...)

CHAPTER 6 – COMBATING FRAUD

Article 325

(ex Article 280 TEC)

1. The Union and the Member States shall counter fraud and any other illegal activities afecting the financial interests of the Union through measures to be taken in accordance with this Article, which shall act as deterrent and be such as to afford effective protection in the Member States, and in all the Union's institutions, bodies, offices and agencies.
2. Member States shal take the same measures to counter fraud afecting the ifnancial interests of the Union as they take to counter fraud affecting their own Financial interests.
3. Without prejudice to other provisions of the Treaties, the Member States shall coordinate their action aimed at protecting the financial interests of the Union against fraud. To this end they shall organise, together with the Commission, close and regular cooperation between the competent authorities.
4. The European Parliament and the Council, acting in accordance with the ordinary legislative procedure, after consulting the Court of Auditors, shall adopt the necessary measures in the fields of the prevention of and fight against fraud affecting the financial interests of the Union with a view to affording effective and equivalent protection in the Member States and in all the Union's institutions, bodies, offices and agencies.
5. The Commission, in cooperation with Member States, shall each year submit to the European Parliament and to the Council a report on the measures taken for the implementation of this Article.

3. Protocol (No 19) On the Schengen Acquis Integrated into the Framework of the European Union

THE HIGH CONTRACTING PARTIES,
NOTING that the Agreements on the gradual abolition of checks at common borders signed by some Member States of the European Union in Schengen on 14 June 1985 and on 19 June 1990, as well as related agreements and the rules adopted on the basis of these agreements, have been integrated into the framework of the European Union by the Treaty of Amsterdam of 2 October 1997,
DESIRING to preserve the Schengen *acquis*, as developed since the entry into force of the Treaty of Amsterdam, and to develop this *acquis* in order to contribute towards achieving the objective of offering citizens of the Union an area of freedom, security and justice without internal borders,
TAKING INTO ACCOUNT the special position of Denmark,
TAKING INTO ACCOUNT the fact that Ireland and the United Kingdom of Great Britain and Northern Ireland do not participate in all the provisions of the Schengen *acquis*; that provision should, however, be made to allow those Member States to accept other provisions of this *acquis* in full or in part,
RECOGNISING that, as a consequence, it is necessary to make use of the provisions of the Treaties concerning closer cooperation between some Member States,
TAKING INTO ACCOUNT the need to maintain a special relationship with the Republic of Iceland and the Kingdom of Norway, both States being bound by the provisions of the Nordic passport union, together with the Nordic States which are members of the European Union,
HAVE AGREED UPON the following provisions, which shall be annexed to the Treaty on European Union and to the Treaty on the Functioning of the European Union:

Article 1

The Kingdom of Belgium, the Republic of Bulgaria, the Czech Republic, the Kingdom of Denmark, the Federal Republic of Germany, the Republic of Estonia, the Hellenic Republic, the Kingdom of Spain, the French Republic, the Italian Republic, the Republic of Cyprus, the Republic of Latvia, the Republic of Lithuania, the Grand Duchy of Luxembourg, the Republic of Hungary, Malta, the Kingdom of the Netherlands, the Republic of Austria, the Republic of Poland, the Portuguese Republic, Romania, the Republic of Slovenia, the Slovak Republic, the Republic of Finland and the Kingdom of Sweden shall be authorised to establish closer cooperation among themselves in areas covered by provisions defined by the Council which constitute the Schengen *acquis*.
This cooperation shall be conducted within the institutional and legal framework of the European Union and with respect for the relevant provisions of the Treaties.

Article 2

The Schengen *acquis* shall apply to the Member States referred to in Article 1, without prejudice to Article 3 of the Act of Accession of 16 April 2003 or to Article 4 of the Act of Accession of 25 April 2005. The Council will substitute itself for the Executive Committee established by the Schengen agreements.

Article 3

The participation of Denmark in the adoption of measures constituting a development of the Schengen *acquis*, as well as the implementation of these measures and their application to Denmark, shall be governed by the relevant provisions of the Protocol on the position of Denmark.

Article 4

Ireland and the United Kingdom of Great Britain and Northern Ireland may at any time request to take part in some or all of the provisions of the Schengen *acquis*. The Council shall decide on the request with the unanimity of its members referred to in Article 1 and of the representative of the Government of the State concerned.

Article 5

1. Proposals and initiatives to build upon the Schengen *acquis* shall be subject to the relevant provisions of the Treaties.
In this context, where either Ireland or the United Kingdom has not notified the Council in writing within a reasonable period that it wishes to take part, the authorisation referred to in Article 329 of the Treaty on the Functioning of the European Union shall be deemed to have been granted to the Member States referred to in Article 1 and to Ireland or the United Kingdom where either of them wishes to take part in the areas of cooperation in question.
2. Where either Ireland or the United Kingdom is deemed to have given notification pursuant to a decision under Article 4, it may nevertheless notify the Council in writing, within three months, that it does not wish to take part in such a proposal or initiative. In that case, Ireland or the United Kingdom shall not take part in its adoption. As from the latter notification, the procedure for adopting the measure building upon the Schengen *acquis* shall be suspended until the end of the procedure set out in paragraphs 3 or 4 or until the notification is withdrawn at any moment during that procedure.
3. For the Member State having made the notification referred to in paragraph 2, any decision taken by the Council pursuant to Article 4 shall, as from the date of entry into force of the proposed measure, cease to apply to the extent considered necessary by the Council and under the conditions to be determined in a decision of the Council acting by a qualified majority on a proposal from the Commission. That decision shall be taken in accordance with the following criteria: the Council seek to retain the widest possible measure of participation of the Member State concerned without seriously affecting the practical operability of the various parts of the Schengen *acquis*, while respecting their coherence. The Commission shall

submit its proposal as soon as possible after the notification referred to in paragraph 2. The Council shall, if needed after convening two successive meetings, act within four months of the Commission proposal.
4. If, by the end of the period of four months, the Council has not adopted a decision, a Member State may, without delay, request that the matter be referred to the European Council. In that case, the European Council shall, at its next meeting, acting by a qualified majority on a proposal from the Commission, take a decision in accordance with the criteria referred to in paragraph 3.
5. If, by the end of the procedure set out in paragraphs 3 or 4, the Council or, as the case may be, the European Council has not adopted its decision, the suspension of the procedure for adopting the measure building upon the Schengen *acquis* shall be terminated. If the said measure is subsequently adopted any decision taken by the Council pursuant to Article 4 shall, as from the date of entry into force of that measure, cease to apply for the Member State concerned to the extent and under the conditions decided by the Commission, unless the said Member State has withdrawn its notification referred to in paragraph 2 before the adoption of the measure. The Commission shall act by the date of this adoption. When taking its decision, the Commission shall respect the criteria referred to in paragraph 3.

Article 6

The Republic of Iceland and the Kingdom of Norway shall be ass associated with the implementation of the Schengen *acquis* and its further development. Appropriate procedures shall be agreed to that effect in an Agreement to be concluded with those States by the Council, acting by the unanimity of its Members mentioned in Article 1. Such Agreement shall include provisions on the contribution of Iceland and Norway to any financial consequences resulting from the implementation of this Protocol.
A separate Agreement shall be concluded with Iceland and Norway by the Council, acting unanimously, for the establishment of rights and obligations between Ireland and the United Kingdom of Great Britain and Northern Ireland on the one hand, and Iceland and Norway on the other, in domains of the Schengen *acquis* which apply to these States.

Article 7

For the purposes of the negotiations for the admission of new Member States into the European Union, the Schengen *acquis* and further measures taken by the institutions within its scope shall be regarded as an *acquis* which must be accepted in full by all States candidates for admission.

4. Declarations Annexed to the Final Act of the Intergovernmental Conference Which Adopted the Treaty of Lisbon, Signed on 13 December 2007

OJ C 83, 30.3.2010, p. 345

A. Declarations concerning provisions of the Treaties

(. . .)

1. Declaration concerning the Charter of Fundamental Rights of the European Union

The Charter of Fundamental Rights of the European Union, which has legally binding force, confirms the fundamental rights guaranteed by the European Convention for the Protection of Human Rights and Fundamental Freedoms and as they result from the constitutional traditions common to the Member States.
The Charter does not extend the field of application of union law beyond the powers of the Union or establish any new power or task for the Union, or modify powers and tasks as defined by the Treaties.

2. Declaration on Article 6(2) of the Treaty on European Union

The Conference agrees that the Union's accession to the European Convention for the Protection of Human Rights and Fundamental Freedoms should eb arranged in such a way as to preserve the specific features of union law. In this connection, the Conference notes the existence of a regular dialoque between the Court of Justice of the European Union and the European Court of Human Rights; such dialogue could be reinforced when the Union accedes to that Convention.

(. . .)

20. Declaration on Article 16 of the Treaty on the Functioning of the European Union

The Conference declares that, whenever rules on protection of personal data to be adopted on the basis of Article 16 could have direct implications for national security, due account will have to be taken of the specific characteristics of the matter. It recalls that the legislation presently applicable (see in particular Directive 95/46/EC) includes specific derogations in this regard.

21. Declaration on the protection of personal data in the fields of judicial cooperation in criminal matters and police cooperation

The Conference acknowledges that specific rules on the protection of personal data and the free movement of such data in the fields of judicial cooperation in criminal matters and police cooperation base don Article 16 of the Treaty on the Functioning of the European Union may prove necessary because of the specific nature of these fields.

(...)

B. Declarations concerning Protocols annexed to the Treaties

See Declarations n. 44, 45, 46 and 47 related to Article 5 of the Protocol on the Schengen acquis integrated into the framework of the European Union.

(...)

5. Charter of Fundamental Rights of the European Union

(2000/C 364/01). Published at OJ C 83, 30.3.2010, p. 389.

(Extract)

Preamble

(...)

The Union contributes to the preservation and to the development of these common values while respecting the diversity of the cultures and traditions of the peoples of Europe as well as the national identities of the Member States and the organisation of their public authorities at national, regional and local levels; it seeks to promote balanced and sustainable development and ensures free movement of persons, services, goods and capital, and the freedom of establishment.

To this end, it is necessary to strengthen the protection of fundamental rights in the light of changes in society, scial progress and scientific and technological developments by making those rights more visible in a Charter.

This Charter reaffirms, with due regard for the powers and tasks of the Union and for the principle of subsidiarity, the rights as they result, in particular, from the constitutional traditions and international obligations common to the Member States, the European Convention for the Protection of Human Rights and Fundamental Freedoms, the Social Charters adopted by the union and by the Council of Europe and the case-law of the Court of Justice of the European Union and of the European Court of Human Rights. In this context the Charter will be interpreted by the courts of the Union and the Member States with due regard to the explanations prepared under the authority of the Praesidium of the Convention which drafted the Charter and updated under the responsibility of the Praesidium of the European Convention.

(...)

Article 7

Respect for private and family life

Every one has the right to respect for his or her private and family life, home and communications.

Article 8

Protection of personal data

1. Everyone has the right to the protection of personal data concerning him or her.
2. Such data must be processed fairly for specified purposes and on the basis of the consent of the person concernid or some other legitimate basis laid Doob by law. Everyone has the right of access to data which has been collected concerning him or her, and the right to have it rectified.

3. Compliance with these rules shall be subject to control by an independent authority.

(. . .)

Article 42

Right of access to documents

Any citizen of the Union, and any natural or legal person residing or having its registered office in a Member State, has a right of access to documents of the institutions, bodies, offices and agencies of the Union, whatever their medium.

(. . .)

TITLE VI

JUSTICE

Article 47

Right to an effective remedy and to a fair trial

Everyone whose rights and freedoms guaranteed by the law of the Union are violated has the right to an effective remedy before a tribunal in compliance with the conditions laid down in this Article.
Everyone is entitled to a fair and public hearing within a reasonable time by an independent and impartial tribunal previously established by law. Everyone shall have the possibility of being advised, defended and represented.
Legal aid shall be made available to those who lack sufficient resources in so far as such aid is necessary to ensure effective access to justice.

Article 48

Presumption of innocence and right of defence

1. Everyone who has been charged shall be presumed innocent until proved guilty according to law.
2. Respect for the rights of the defence of anyone who has been charged shall be guaranteed.

Article 49

Principles of legality and proportionality of criminal offences and penalties

1. No one shall be held guilty of any criminal offence on account of any act or omission which did not constitute a criminal offence under national law or international law at the time when it was committed. Nor shall a heavier penalty be imposed than the one that was applicable at the time the criminal offence was committed. If, subsequent to the commission of a criminal offence, the law provides for a lighter penalty, that penalty shall be applicable.
2. This Article shall not prejudice the trial and punishment of any person for any act or omission which, at the time when it was committed, was criminal according to the general principles recognised by the community of nations.
3. The severity of penalties must not be disproportionate to the criminal offence.

Article 50

Right not to be tried or punished twice in criminal proceedings for the same criminal offence

No one shall be liable to be tried or punished again in criminal proceedings for an offence for which he or she has already been finally acquitted or convicted within the Union in accordance with the law.

TITLE VII

GENERAL PROVISIONS GOVERNING THE INTERPRETATION AND APPLICATION OF THE CHARTER

(...)

Article 52

Scope and interpretation of rights and principles

1. Any limitation on the exercise of the rights and freedoms recognised by this Charter must be provided for by law and respect the essence of those rights and freedoms. Subject to the principle of proportionality, limitations may be made only if they are necessary and genuinely meet objectives of general interest recognised by the Union or the need to protect the rights and freedoms of others.
2. Rights recognised by this Charter for which provision is made in the Treaties shall be exercised under the conditions and within the limits defined by those Treaties.
3. In so far as this Charter contains rights which correspond to rights guaranteed by the Convention for the Protection of Human Rights and Fundamental Freedoms, the meaning and scope of those rights shall be the same as those laid down by the said Convention. This provision shall not prevent Union law providing more extensive protection.
4. In so far as this Charter recognises fundamental rights as they result from the constitutional traditions common to the Member States, those rights shall be interpreted in harmony with those traditions
5. The provisions of this Charter which contain principles may be implemented by legislative and executive acts taken by institutions, bodies, offices and agencies of the Union, and by acts of Member States when they are implementing Union law, in the exercise of their respective powers. They shall be judicially cognisable only in the interpretation of such acts and in the ruling on their legality.
6. Full account shall be taken of national laws and practices as specified in this Charter.
7. The explanations drawn up as a way of providing guidance in the interpretation of this Charter shall be given due regard by the courts of the Union and of the Member States.

***

The above text adapts the wording of the Charter proclaimed on 7 December 2000, and will replace it as from the date of entry into force of the Treaty of Lisbon.

6. The Stockholm Programme – An Open and Secure Europe Serving and Protecting Citizens

(2000/C 364/01). Published at OJ C 83, 30.3.2010, p. 389.

(*Extract*)

1. TOWARDS A CITIZENS' EUROPE IN THE AREA OF FREEDOM, SECURITY AND JUSTICE
(...)

1.1. Political priorities
(...)

Promoting citizenship and fundamental rights: European citizenship must become a tangible reality. The area of freedom, security and justice must, above all, be a single area in which fundamental rights and freedoms are protected. The enlargement of the Schengen area must continue. Respect for the human person and human dignity and for the other rights set out in the Charter of Fundamental Rights of the European Union and the European Convention for the protection of Human Rights and fundamental freedoms are core values. For example, the exercise of these rights and freedoms, in particular citizens' privacy, must be preserved beyond national borders, especially by protecting personal data. Allowance must be made for the special needs of vulnerable people. Citizens of the Union and other persons must be able to exercise their specific rights to the fullest extent within, and even, where relevant, outside the Union.

1.2. The tools

If the next multiannual programme is to be implemented successfully, the following tools are important.

(...)

1.2.6. Training

In order to foster a genuine European judicial and law enforcement culture, it is essential to step up training on Union-related issues and make it systematically accessible for all professions involved in the implementation of the area of freedom, security and justice. This will include judges, prosecutors, judicial staff, police and customs officers and border guards.
The objective of systematic European Training Schemes offered to all persons involved should be pursued. The ambition for the Union and its Member States

should be that a substantive number of professionals by 2015 will have participated in a European Training Scheme or in an exchange programme with another Member State, which might be part of training schemes that are already in place. For this purpose existing training institutions should in particular be used.
Member States have the primary responsibility in this respect, but the Union must give their efforts support and financial backing and also be able to have its own mechanisms to supplement national efforts. The European Council considers that EU and international cooperation aspects should be part of national curricula. For training of judges, prosecutors and judicial staff it is important to safeguard judicial independence while at the same time the emphasis should be placed on the European dimension for professionals that use European instruments frequently. CEPOL and Frontex should play a key role in training of law enforcement personnel and border guards with a view to ensuring a European dimension in training. Training of border guards and customs officers is of special importance with a view to fostering a common approach to an integrated border management. Solutions at European level could be sought, with a view to strengthening European Training Schemes. E-learning programmes and common training materials must also be developed to train professionals in the European mechanisms.
The European Council invites the Commission to:

– propose an Action Plan for raising substantially the level of European training schemes and exchange programmes systematically in the Union. The Plan should propose how to ensure that one third of all police involved in European police cooperation and half of the judges, prosecutors and judicial staff involved in European judicial cooperation as well as half of other professionals involved in European cooperation could be offered European Training Schemes,
– examine what could be defined as a European Training Scheme, and to suggest in the Action Plan how to develop this idea with a view to giving it a European dimension,
– set up specific "Erasmus"-style exchange programmes, which could involve non-Member States and in particular candidate countries and countries with which the Union has concluded Partnership and Cooperation Agreements,
– ensure that participation in joint courses, exercises and exchange programmes is decided on the basis of tasks and is not dependent on sector-specific criteria.

1.2.7. Communication

The achievements in the area of freedom, security and justice are generally of great importance to citizens, businesses and professionals. The European Council therefore calls on all Union institutions, in particular the Commission as well as on the Member States, to consider ways to better communicate to citizens and practitioners the concrete results of the policy in the area of freedom, security and justice. It asks the Commission to devise a strategy on how best to explain to citizens how they can benefit from the new tools and legal frameworks, for instance through the use of e-Justice and the e-Justice Portal.

1.2.8. Dialogue with civil society

The European Council encourages the Union institutions, within the framework of their competences, to hold an open, transparent and regular dialogue with representative associations and civil society. The Commission should put in place specific mechanisms, such as the European Justice Forum, to step up dialogue in areas where such mechanisms are appropriate.

1.2.9. Financing

The European Council emphasises that the Stockholm Programme should be financed within the headings and ceilings of the current financial framework. Many of the measures and actions in this programme can be implemented through a more effective use of existing instruments and funds.

The European Council notes that the current financial perspectives expire at the end of 2013. It underlines its intention to reflect the goals of the Stockholm Programme. This programme does not however prejudge the negotiations on the next financial perspective.

The European Council also considers that procedures for application to the financing programmes should, while taking account of the experience of Member States, be transparent, flexible, coherent and streamlined and made more easily accessible to administrations, established partners and practitioners through the active dissemination of clear guidelines, a mechanism for identifying partners and accurate programming. The European Council requests the Commission to examine appropriate means of achieving that goal.

Within the next financial perspectives, it should be examined how best to design the financial instruments in order to ensure a suitable support for operational projects developed outside the Union which enhance the Union's security, in particular in the field of fighting against organised crime and terrorism. Careful consideration should be given to ways and means to speed up the Union's reaction to urgent events in this area in terms of financial assistance and how to provide technical assistance for the global implementation of international conventions, such as those relating to terrorism.

1.2.10. Action Plan

In light of the Stockholm Programme, the European Council invites the Commission to present promptly an Action Plan in the first 6 months of 2010 to be adopted by the Council. This Action Plan will translate the aims and priorities of the Stockholm Programme into concrete actions with a clear timetable for adoption and implementation. It should include a proposal for a timetable for the transformation of instruments with a new legal basis.

2. PROMOTING CITIZENS' RIGHTS: A EUROPE OF RIGHTS

(...)

2.2. Full Exercise of the Right to Free Movement

(...)

As noted by the European Parliament, Schengen cooperation, which has removed internal border controls within much of the Union, is a major achievement in the area of freedom, security and justice. The European Council recalls its attachment to the further enlargement of the Schengen area. Provided that all requirements to apply the Schengen acquis have been fulfilled, the European Council calls on the Council, the European Parliament and the Commission to take all necessary measures to allow for the abolition of controls at internal borders with the remaining Member States that have declared their readiness to join the Schengen area without delay.
(...)
Obtaining a right of residence under Union law for the citizens of the Union and their family members is an advantage inherent in the exercise of the right to free movement. The purpose of that right is however not to circumvent immigration rules. Freedom of movement not only entails rights but also imposes obligations on those that benefit from it; abuses and fraud should be avoided. Member States should further safeguard and protect the right to free movement by working together, and with the Commission, to combat actions of a criminal nature with forceful and proportionate measures, with due regard to the applicable law.
The European Council therefore further invites the Commission to:

– monitor the implementation and application of these rules to avoid abuse and fraud,
– examine how best to exchange information, inter alia, on residence permits and documentation and how to assist Member States' authorities to tackle abuse of this fundamental right effectively.

With this aim in mind, Member States should also closely monitor the full and correct implementation of the existing acquis and tackle possible abuse and fraud of the right to free movement of persons and exchange information and statistics on such abuse and fraud. If systematic trends in abuse and fraud of the right to free movement are identified, Member States should report such trends to the Commission, which will suggest to the Council how these trends might be addressed through the most appropriate means.
(...)

2.5. Protecting citizen's Rights in the information society

When it comes to assessing the individual's privacy in the area of freedom, security and justice, the right to freedom is overarching. The right to privacy and the right to the protection of personal data are set out in the Charter of Fundamental Rights. The Union must therefore respond to the challenge posed by the increasing exchange of personal data and the need to ensure the protection of privacy. The Union must secure a comprehensive strategy to protect data within the Union and in its relations with other countries. In that context, it should promote the application of the principles set out in relevant Union instruments on data protection and the 1981 Council of Europe Convention for the Protection of Individuals with regards to Automatic Processing of Personal Data as well as promoting accession to that Convention. It must also foresee and regulate the circumstances in which interference by public authorities with the exercise of these rights is justified and also apply data protection principles in the private sphere.

The Union must address the necessity for increased exchange of personal data whilst ensuring the utmost respect for the protection of privacy. The European Council is convinced that the technological developments not only present new challenges to the protection of personal data, but also offer new possibilities to better protect personal data.

Basic principles such as purpose limitation, proportionality, legitimacy of processing, limits on storage time, security and confidentiality as well as respect for the rights of the individual, control by national independent supervisory authorities, and access to effective judicial redress need to be ensured and a comprehensive protection scheme must be established. These issues are also dealt with in the context of the Information Management Strategy for EU internal security referred to in Chapter 4.

The European Council invites the Commission to:

– evaluate the functioning of the various instruments on data protection and present, where necessary, further legislative and non-legislative initiatives to maintain the effective application of the above principles,
– propose a Recommendation for the negotiation of a data protection and, where necessary, data sharing agreements for law enforcement purposes with the United States of America, building on the work carried out by the EU-US High Level Contact Group on Information Sharing and Privacy and Personal Data Protection,
– consider core elements for data protection agreements with third countries for law enforcement purposes, which may include, where necessary, privately held data, based on a high level of data protection,
– improve compliance with the principles of data protection through the development of appropriate new technologies, improving cooperation between the public and private sectors, particularly in the field of research,
– examine the introduction of a European certification scheme for "privacy-aware" technologies, products and services,
– conduct information campaigns, in particular to raise awareness among the public.

On a broader front, the Union must be a driving force behind the development and promotion of international standards for personal data protection, based on relevant Union instruments on data protection and the 1981 Council of Europe Convention for the Protection of Individuals with regard to Automatic Processing of Personal Data, and in the conclusion of appropriate bilateral or multilateral instruments.

3. MAKING PEOPLE'S LIVES EASIER: A EUROPE OF LAW AND JUSTICE

(. . .)

3.2. Strengthening mutual trust

One of the consequences of mutual recognition is that rulings made at national level have an impact in other Member States, in particular in their judicial systems. Measures aimed at strengthening mutual trust are therefore necessary in order to take full advantage of these developments.
The Union should support Member States' efforts to improve the efficiency of their judicial systems by encouraging exchanges of best practice and the development of innovative projects relating to the modernisation of justice.

3.2.1. Training

Training of judges (including administrative courts), prosecutors and other judicial staff is essential to strengthen mutual trust (see also Chapter 1.2.6). The Union should continue to support and strengthen measures to increase training in line with Articles 81 and 82 TFEU.
(. . .)

4. A EUROPE THAT PROTECTS

(. . .)

4.2. Upgrading the tools for the job

Security in the Union requires an integrated approach where security professionals share a common culture, pool information as effectively as possible and have the right technological infrastructure to support them.

4.2.1. Forging a common culture

The European Council stresses the need to enhance mutual trust between all the professionals concerned at national and Union level. A genuine European law enforcement culture should be developed through exchange of experiences and good practice as well as the organisation of joint training courses and exercises in line with Chapter 1.2.6.
The European Council encourages Member States to devise mechanisms that gives incentives to professionals for taking up duties related to cross-border cooperation and thereby favour the creation of a Union-wide response at all levels.

4.2.2. Managing the flow of information

The European Council notes with satisfaction that developments over the past years in the Unon have led to a wide Choice and created an extensive toolbox for collecting, processing and sharing information between national authorities and other European players in the area of freedom, security and justice. The principle of availability will continue to give important impetus to this work.
The European Council acknowledges the need for coherence and consolidation in developing information management and exchange and invites the Council and the Commission to:

– implement the Information Management Strategy for EU internal security [4], which includes a strong data protection regime. Development must be coherent with the priorities set for the area of freedom, security and justice and the internal security strategy, supporting the business vision for law enforcement, judicial cooperation, border management and public protection.

In this context, the European Council invites the Commission to:

– assess the need for developing a European Information Exchange Model based on the evaluation of the current instruments, including Council Decision 2008/615/JHA of 23 June 2008 on the stepping up of cross-border cooperation, particularly in combating terrorism and cross-border crime and Council Decision 2008/616/JHA of 23 June 2008 on the implementation of Decision 2008/615/JHA (Prüm framework) and Council Framework Decision 2006/960/JHA of 18 December 2006 on simplifying the exchange of information and intelligence between law enforcement authorities of the Member States of the European Union (the so-called "Swedish Framework Decision"). These assessments will determine whether these instruments function as originally intended and meet the goals of the Information Management Strategy.

The Information Management Strategy for EU internal security is based on:

– business-driven development (a development of information exchange and its tools that is driven by law enforcement needs,
– a strong data protection regime consistent with the strategy for protection of personal data referred to in Chapter 2,
– a well targeted data collection, both to protect fundamental rights of citizens and to avoid an information overflow for the competent authorities,
– guiding principles for a policy on the exchange of information with third countries for law enforcement purposes,
– interoperability of IT systems ensuring full conformity with data protection and data security principles when developing such systems,
– a rationalisation of the different tools, including the adoption of a business plan for large IT systems,
– overall coordination, convergence and coherence.

The necessary Union and national structures need to be in place to ensure the implementation and management of the different information management tools. The European Council also calls for the establishment of an administration, as proposed by the Commission, having the competence and capacity to develop technically and manage large-scale IT systems in the area of freedom, security and justice, as referred to in the joint statements of the European Parliament, the Council and the Commission in December 2006 and October 2007. Possible additional tasks should be considered by the Council in the light of the Information Management Strategy.
Reflecting the discussions in the Council and the European Parliament, with a view to setting up an Union Passenger Names Record (PNR) system, the European Council calls upon the Commission:

– to propose an Union measure, that ensures a high level of data protection, on PNR for the purpose of preventing, detecting, investigating and prosecuting terrorist offences and serious crime, based on an impact assessment.

4.2.3. Mobilising the necessary technological tools

The European Council, while ensuring consistency with the strategy for protection of personal data referred to in Chapter 2, stresses the need for new technologies to keep pace with and promote the current trends towards mobility, while ensuring that people are safe, secure and free.
The European Council invites the Council, the Commission, the European Parliament, where appropriate, and the Member States to:

– draw up and implement policies to ensure a high level of network and information security throughout the Union and improve measures aimed at protection, security preparedness and resilience of critical infrastructure, including Information and Communication Technology (ICT) and services infrastructure,
– promote legislation that ensures a very high level of network security and allows faster reactions in the event of cyber attacks.

The European Council also invites the Council and the Commission to:

– ensure that the priorities of the internal security strategy are tailored to the real needs of users and focus on improving interoperability. Research and development in the field of security should be supported by public–private partnerships.

The European Council invites:

– the Member States to implement the European Criminal Records Information System (ECRIS) as soon as possible,
– the Commission to assess whether the networking of criminal records makes it possible to prevent criminal offences from being committed (for example through checks on access to certain jobs, particularly those relating to children), and whether it is possible to extend the exchange of information on supervision measures,
– the Commission to propose, in addition to ECRIS, a register of third-country nationals who have been convicted by the courts of the Member States.

The European Council recalls the need for ensuring consistency with the strategy for the protection of personal data and the business plan for setting up large scale IT systems as referred to in Chapter 2, and calls on the Commission to:

– make a feasibility study on the need for, and the added value of, setting up a European Police Records Index system (EPRIS) and to make a report to the Council in the course of 2012 on the issue,
– to reflect on how to further develop the use of existing databases for law enforcement purposes, while fully respecting data protection rules, so as to make full use of new technologies with a view to protecting the citizens,
– examine how best to promote that Member States' competent authorities can exchange information on travelling violent offenders including those attending sporting or large public events.

4.3. Effective policies

4.3.1. More effective European law enforcement cooperation

The prime objective of Union law enforcement cooperation is to combat forms of crime that have typically a cross-border dimension. Focus should not only be placed on combating terrorism and organised crime but also cross-border wide-spread crime that have a significant impact on the daily life of the citizens of the Union. Europol should become a hub for information exchange between the law enforcement authorities of the Member States, a service provider and a platform for law enforcement services.
The European Council encourages Member States' competent authorities to use the investigative tool of Joint Investigative Teams (JITs) as much as possible in appropriate cases. Europol and Eurojust should be systematically involved in major cross-border operations and informed when JITs are set up. The model agreement for setting up JITs should be updated. Europol and Eurojust should step up their cooperation further. Eurojust should ensure that its work is followed up at judicial level. Europol and Eurojust should expand their work with third countries especially by forging closer links with the regions and countries neighbouring the Union. Europol should work more closely with Common Security and Defence Policy (CSDP) police missions and help promote standards and good practice for European law enforcement cooperation in countries outside the Union. Cooperation with Interpol should be stepped up with a view to creating synergies and avoiding duplication.
The European Council invites the Commission, and, where appropriate, the Council and the High Representative of the Union for foreign affairs and security policy, to:

– examine how it could be ensured that Europol receives information from Member States law enforcement authorities so that the Member States can make full use of Europol capacities,

– examine how operational police cooperation could be stepped up, for example as regards incompatibility of communication systems and other equipment, use of undercover agents, and, where necessary, draw operational conclusions to that end,
– issue as soon as possible a reflection document on how best to ensure that the activities of Europol may be scrutinised and evaluated by the European Parliament, together with national parliaments in line with Articles 85 and 88 TFEU,
– consider developing a Police Cooperation Code which would consolidate existing instruments and, where necessary, amend and simplify them,
– make a proposal to the Council and the European Parliament to adopt a decision on the modalities of cooperation, including on exchange of information between Union agencies, in particular Europol, Eurojust and Frontex, which ensures data protection and security,

(...)

5. ACCESS TO EUROPE IN A GLOBALISED WORLD

5.1. Integrated Management of the external borders

(...)

The European Council also invites Member States and the Commission to explore how the different types of checks carried out at the external border can be better coordinated, integrated and rationalised with a view to the twin objective of facilitating access and improving security. Moreover, the potential of enhanced information exchange and closer cooperation between border guard authorities and other law enforcement authorities working inside the territory should be explored, in order to increase efficiency for all the parties involved and fight cross-border crime more effectively.
The European Council considers that technology can play a key role in improving and reinforcing the system of external border controls. The entry into operation of the Second generation Schengen Information System II (SIS II) and the roll-out of the Visa Information system (VIS) therefore remains a key objective and the European Council calls on the Commission and Member States to ensure that they now become fully operational in keeping with the timetables to be established for that purpose. Before creating new systems, an evaluation of these and other existing systems should be made and the difficulties encountered when they were set up should be taken into account. The setting up of an administration for large-scale IT systems could play a central role in the possible development of IT systems in the future.
The European Council is of the opinion that an electronic system for recording entry to and exit from Member States could complement the existing systems, in order to allow Member States to share data effectively while guaranteeing data protection rules. The introduction of the system at land borders deserves special

attention and the implications to infrastructure and border lines should be analysed before implementation.
The possibilities of new and interoperable technologies hold great potential for rendering border management more efficient as well as more secure but should not lead to discrimination or unequal treatment of passengers. This includes, inter alia, the use of gates for automated border control.
The European Council invites the Commission to:

– present proposals for an entry/exit system alongside a fast track registered traveller programme with a view to such a system becoming operational as soon as possible,
– to prepare a study on the possibility and usefulness of developing a European system of travel authorisation and, where appropriate, to make the necessary proposals,
– to continue to examine the issue of automated border controls and other issues connected to rendering border management more efficient.

5.2. Visa policy

The European Council believes that the entry into force of the Visa Code and the gradual roll-out of the VIS will create important new opportunities for further developing the common visa policy. That policy must also be part of a broader vision that takes account of relevant internal and external policy concerns. The European Council therefore encourages the Commission and Member States to take advantage of these developments in order to intensify regional consular cooperation by means of regional consular cooperation programmes which could include, in particular, the establishment of common visa application centres, where necessary, on a voluntary basis..

(. . .)

7. EUROPE IN A GLOBALISED WORLD – THE EXTERNAL DIMENSION OF FREEDOM, SECURITY AND JUSTICE

(. . .)

7.3. Continued thematic priorities with new tools

The European Council considers that the key thematic priorities identified in the previous strategy remain valid, i.e. the fight against terrorism, organised crime, corruption, drugs, the exchange of personal data in a secure environment and managing migration flows. The fight against trafficking in human beings and smuggling of persons needs to be stepped up.
Building on the Strategy for the external dimension of JHA: Global freedom, security and justice adopted in 2005 and other relevant acquis in this field, such

as the Global Approach to Migration, Union external cooperation should focus on areas where Union activity provides added value, in particular:

> (. . .)
> – Information exchange that flows securely, efficiently and with adequate data protection standards between the Union and third countries,
> (. . .)

The European Council invites the Commission to:

> – examine whether ad hoc cooperation agreements with specific third countries to be identified by the Council could be a way of enhancing the fight against trafficking in human beings and smuggling of persons and making proposals to that end. In particular, such agreements could involve full use of all leverage available to the Union, including the use of existing financing programmes, cooperation in the exchange of information, judicial cooperation and migration tools.

The threat of terrorism and organised crime remains high. It is therefore necessary to work with key strategic partners to exchange information while continuing to work on longer-term objectives such as measures to prevent radicalisation and recruitment, as well as the protection of critical infrastructures. Operational agreements by Eurojust, Europol, as well as working arrangements with Frontex, should be strengthened.de Eurojust y Europol, y los acuerdos de trabajo con Frontex deberían reforzarse.

7.4. Agreements with third countries

Protection of personal data is a core activity of the Union. There is a need for a coherent legislative framework for the Union for personal data transfers to third countries for law enforcement. A framework model agreement consisting of commonly applicable core elements of data protection could be created.

7.5. Geographical priorities and International organisations

(. . .)

Cooperation has been intensified with the USA in the past 10 years including on all matters relating to the area of freedom, security and justice. Regular Ministerial Troika and Senior officials' meetings are held under each Presidency. In line with what has been laid down in the "Washington Statement" adopted at the Ministerial Troika meeting in October 2009, the dialogue should continue and be deepened. Ongoing cooperation in the fight against terrorism and transnational crime, border security, visa policy, migration and judicial cooperation should be pursued. An agreement on the protection of personal data exchanged for law enforcement purposes needs to be negotiated and concluded rapidly. The Union and the USA will work together to complete visa-free travel between the USA and the Union as soon as possible and increase security for travellers. Joint procedures should be set

up for the implementation of the agreements on judicial cooperation, and regular consultations need to take place.
The Common Space for an area of freedom, security and justice and the new agreement currently under negotiation will provide the framework for intense and improved future cooperation with the Russian Federation. Building also on the outcomes of the bi-annual Permanent Partnership Councils on freedom, security and justice, the Union and Russia should continue to cooperate within the framework of the visa dialogue and on legal migration, while tackling illegal immigration, enhance common fight against organised crime and particularly operational cooperation, and improve and intensify judicial cooperation. An agreement, which should satisfy high standards of data protection, should be made with Eurojust as soon as possible. A framework agreement on information exchange should be concluded in that context. The visa dialogue must continue. The visa facilitation and readmission agreement should be implemented fully.

7. Communication from the Commission – Delivering an area of freedom, security and justice for Europe's citizens – Action Plan implementing the Stockholm Programme

Brussels, 20.4.2010
COM(2010) 171 final

(...)

2. Ensuring the protection of fundamental rights

The protection of the rights enshrined in the Charter of Fundamental Rights, which should become the compass for all EU law and policies, needs to be given full effect and its Rights made tangible and effective. The Commission will apply a "Zero Tolerance Policy" as regards violations of the Charter. The Commission will reinforce its mechanisms to ensure compliance with the Charter and report on it to the European Parliament and Council. In a global society characterised by rapid technological change where information Exchange knows no borders, it is particularly important that privacy must be preserved. The Union must ensure that the fundamental right to data protection is consistently applied. We need to strengthen the EU's stance in protecting the personal data of the individual in the context of all EU policies, including law enforcement and crime prevention as well as in our international relations.

(...)

4. Strengthening confidence in the European judicial area

(...)

The administration of justice must not be impeded by unjustifiable differences between the Member States' judicial systems: criminals should not be able to avoid prosecution and prison by crossing borders and exploiting differences between national legal systems. A solid common European procedural base is needed. A new and comprehensive system for obtaining evidence in cross-border cases and better exchange of information between Member States' authorities on offences committed are essential tools to developing a functioning area of freedom, security and justice. The Commission will prepare the establishment of a European Public Prosecutor's Office from Eurojust, with the responsibility to investigate, prosecute and bring to judgement offences against the Union's financial interests. In doing so, the Commission will further reflect on the cooperation with all the actors involved, including the European Anti-Fraud Office (OLAF).

5. Ensuring the security of Europe

(...)

An Internal Security Strategy, based upon the full respect of fundamental rights and on solidarity between Member States, will be implemented with care and firm resolve to face the growing cross-border challenges. It implies a coordinated approach to police cooperation, border management, criminal justice cooperation and civil protection. We need to address all the common security threats from terrorism and organised crime, to safety concerns related to man-made and natural disasters. Given the increasing use of new technologies, tackling efficiently those threats also requires a complementary policy ensuring the preparedness and resilience of Europe's networks and ICT infrastructure.

(. . .)

The establishment of a strategic agenda for the exchange of information requires an overview of existing data collection, processing and data-sharing systems, with a thorough assessment of their usefulness, efficiency, effectiveness, proportionality and their respect of the right to privacy. It should also lay the ground for a coherent development of all existing and future information systems.

(. . .)

We also need to remove all the obstacles in the way of effective law enforcement cooperation between Member States. EU agencies and bodies such as FRONTEX, Europol and Eurojust, as well as OLAF, have a crucial role to play. They must cooperate better and be given the powers and resources necessary to achieve their goals within clearly defined roles.

(. . .)

Smart use of modern technologies in border management to complement existing tools as a part of a risk management process can also make Europe more accessible to bona fIDE travellers and stimulate innovation among EU industries, thus contributing to Europe's prosperity and growth, and ensure the feeling of security of Union's citizens. The coming into operation of the SIS II and VIS systems will continue to be a high priority.

ANNEX

(. . .)

Protecting fundamental Rights in the information society		
Actions	Responsible party	Calendar
Communication on a new legal Framework for the protection of personal data alter the entry into forceo f the Lisbon Treaty	Commission	2010
New comprehensive legal framework for data protection	Commission	2010
Communication on privacy and trust in Digital Europe: ensuring citizen's confidence in mew services	Commission	2010
Recommendation to authorise the negotiation of a personal data protection agreement for law enforcement purposes with the United States of America	Commission	2010
Communication on core elements for personal data protection in agreements between the European Union and tirad countries for law enforcement purposes	Commission	2012

The benefits fro citizens of a European judicial area		
Providing easier access to justice		
Actions	Responsible party	Calendar
Opening of the European e-Justice Portal and preparation for future releases	Comission	2010
(. . .)		

Ensuring the security of Europe

Managing the flow of information		
Actions	Responsible party	Calendar
Communication on the overview on information collection and exchange	Commission	2010
Legislative proposal on a common EU approach to the use of passenger name record data for law enforcement purposes	Commission	2010
Communication on the transfer of APssenger Name Record (PNR) data to third countries	Commission	2010
Proposals for authorising the negotiation and negotiation of agreements on Passenger Name Record data between the European Union and relevant third countries	Commission	2010
Evaluation report of the application of the Data Retention Directive 2006/24/EC, if necessasry followwed by a proposal for revision	Commission	2010 2012
Report on the implementation of the Framework Decision 2006/960/JHA (Swedish initiative) on the Exchange of information between the law enrocement authorities	Commission	2011
Reporto n the implementation of the Decision 2008/615/JHA (Prüm Decision)on the interconnection of DNA, fingerprints and Vehicle information databases	Commission	2012

(continued)

Managing the flow of information		
Actions	Responsible party	Calendar
Communication on enhancing the traceability of users of pre-paid Communications services for law enforcement purposes	Commission	2012 2013
Green paper on commercial information relevant to law enforcement and information Exchange models	Commission	2012
Green paper on commercial information relevant to law enforcement and information Exchange models	Commission	2012
Police code, including the nodification of the main instruments of access to information	Commission	2014

Mobilising the necessary techonogical tools		
Actions	Responsible party	Timetable
Legislative proposal for a European register of convicted third countries nationals	Commission	2011
Proposals on implementing measures on the European Criminal Records Information System (ECRIS)	Commission	2011
Communication on the feasibility of setting up a EU Police Records Index System (EPRIS)	Commission	2012
Communication on possible measures to prmote the Exchange of information between Member States, including Europol, on violent travelling offenders in connection with major events	Commission	2012
Communication on ECRIS evaluation and on its future development extending it to Exchange information on supervision measures	Commission	2014

Effective policies		
More effective European law enforcement cooperation		
Actions	Responsible party	Timetable
(. . .)		
Proposal on information Exchange between Europol, Eurojust and Frontex	Commission	2011
(. . .)		
Communication on the improvement of customs and police cooperation in the EU, including refections on undercover officers, on Police Cooperation and Customs Centres, on an EU approach to Intelligence led policing, and on common actions to improbé operacional police cooperation: assessment of state of play and possible recommendations	Commission	2014
(. . .)		

Cyber crime and Network and Information Society

Actions	Responsible party	Timetable
Measures aiming at reinforced and high level Network and Information Security Policy, including legislative nitiatives such as the one on modernised Network and Information Security Agency (ENISA) as well as other mesaures allowingfaster reactions in the event of Cyber attacks	Council Commission	2010 (adopted)
Legislative proosal on attacks against information Systems	Commission	2010
Creation fo a cybercrime alert platform at European level	Europol Commision	2010
Develop a European model agreement on public private partnerships in the fight against cybercrime and for Cyber security	Commission	2011

Economic crime and corruption

Actions	Responsible party	Timetable
(...)		
Establishment of a sustainable institucional Framework for FIU.NET (EU Financial Intelligence Units Network), including possible database on suspicious transactions, following a feasibility study	Comisión	2013
(...)		

Access to Europe in a globalised world

Integrated Management of the external world

Actions	Responsible party	Timetable
(...)		
Development and entry into operation of the Schengen Information System II (SIS II)	Commission Member States	December 2011 or 2013, depending on the technical solution to be followed
Start operation of the Agency for the operacional Management of large-scale IT Systems in the area of freedom, security and justice		2012
Communication on the better cooperation, coordination, integration and rationalisaton of the different checks carried out at the external borders with a view to twin the objective of facilitating access and improving security	Commission	2012
Communication on the long term development of Frontex including the feasibility of the creation of a European system of border guards	Commission	2014
Use of the CRMS (Community Risk Management System) in order to exchange risk	Commission	Ongoing

(continued)

Access to Europe in a globalised world		
Integrated Management of the external world		
Actions	Responsible party	Timetable
information between customs offices at the border and further development of the common risk assessment criteria and standards for Management, security and safety at the external borders.		
(...)		

8. Directive 95/46/EC of the Parliament and the Council of 24 October 1995 on the protection of individuals with regard to the processing of personal data and on the free movement of such data

(2000/C 364/01). Published at OJ L 281, 23.11.1995, p. 31.

(*Extract*)

THE EUROPEAN PARLIAMENT AND THE COUNCIL OF THE EUROPEAN UNION

(. . .)

(13) Whereas the activities referred to in Titles V and VI of the Treaty on European Union regarding public safety, defence, State security or the acitivities of the State in the area of criminal laws fall outside the scope of Community law, without prejudice to the obligations incumbent upon Member States under Article 56 (2), Article 57 or Article 100a of the Treaty establishing the European Community; whereas the processing of personal data that is necessary to safeguard the economic well-being of the State does not fall within the scope of this Directive where such processing relates to State security matters;

(. . .)

HAVE ADOPTED THIS DIRECTIVE:

CHAPTER I GENERAL PROVISIONS

(. . .)

Article 3
Scope
(. . .)

2. This Directive shall not apply to the processing of personal data:

– in the course of an activity which falls outside the scope of Community law, such as those provided for by Titles V and VI of the Treaty on European Union and in any case to processing operations concerning public security, defence, State security (including the economic well-being of the State when the processing operation relates to State security matters) and the activities of the State in areas of criminal law,

(. . .)

B. COUNCIL OF EUROPE

1. European Convention for the Protection of Human Rights and Fundamental Freedoms

CETS No. 005.
Opening for signature in Rome on 4.11.1950.
Entry into force on 3.9.1953 (after 10 ratifications).
Signed by the 27 Member States of the European Union. Open for accession by the European Union
This Convention has been amended by Protocol No 14 (CETS No 194) as from the date of its entry into force on 1 June 2010.

(extract)

Article 7
Right to a fair trial

1. In the determination of his civil rights and obligations or of any criminal charge against him, everyone is entitled to a fair and public hearing within a reasonable time by an independent and impartial tribunal established by law. Judgment shall be pronounced publicly but the press and public may be excluded from all or part of the trial in the interest of morals, public order or national security in a democratic society, where the interests of juveniles or the protection of the private live of the parties so require, or to the extend strictly necessary in the opinion of the court in special circumstances where publicity would prejudice the interest of justice.
2. Everyone charged with a criminal offence shall be presumed innocent until proved guilty according to law.
3. Everyone charged with a criminal offence has the following minimum rights:

Á.G. Zarza (ed.), *Exchange of Information and Data Protection in Cross-border Criminal Proceedings in Europe*, DOI 10.1007/978-3-642-40291-3,

(a) to be informed promptly, in a language which he understands and in detail, of the nature and cause of the accusation against him;
(b) to have adequate time and facilities for the preparation of his defence;
(c) to defend himself in person or through legal assistance of his own choosing or, if he has not sufficient means to pay for legal assistance, to be given it free when the interest of justice so require;
(d) to examine or have examined witnesses against him and to obtain the attendance and examination of witnesses on his behalf under the same conditions as witnesses against him.
(e) to have the free assistance of an interpreter if he cannot understand or speak the language used in court.

Article 8
Right to respect for private and family life

1. Everyone has the right to respect for his private and family life, his home and his correspondence.
2. There shall be no interference by a public authority with the exercise of this right except such as is in aordance with the law and is necessary in a democratic society in the interests of national security, public safety or the economic well-being of the country, for the prevention of disorder or crime, for the protection of health or morals, or for the protection of the rights and freedoms of others.

2. Convention for the protection of individuals with regard to automatic processing of personal data (Convention 108)

CETS No. 108.
Opening for signature in Strasbourg on 28.1.1981
Entry into force on 1.10.1985 (after 5 ratifications).
Signed by the 27 Member States of the European Union.

Preamble
The member States of the Council of Europe, signatory hereto,
Considering that the aim of the Council of Europe is to achieve greater unity between its members, based in particular on respect for the rule of law, as well as human rights and fundamental freedoms;
Considering that it is desirable to extend the safeguards for everyone's rights and fundamental freedoms, and in particular the right to the respect for privacy, taking account of the increasing flow across frontiers of personal data undergoing automatic processing;

Reaffirming at the same time their commitment to freedom of information regardless of frontiers;
Recognising that it is necessary to reconcile the fundamental values of the respect for privacy and the free flow of information between peoples,
Have agreed as follows:

Chapter I – General provisions

Article 1 – Object and purpose

The purpose of this convention is to secure in the territory of each Party for every individual, whatever his nationality or residence, respect for his rights and fundamental freedoms, and in particular his right to privacy, with regard to automatic processing of personal data relating to him ("data protection").

Article 2 – Definitions

For the purposes of this convention:

a. "personal data" means any information relating to an identified or identifiable individual ("data subject");
b. "automated data file" means any set of data undergoing automatic processing;
c. "automatic processing" includes the following operations if carried out in whole or in part by automated means: storage of data, carrying out of logical and/or arithmetical operations on those data, their alteration, erasure, retrieval or dissemination;
d. "controller of the file" means the natural or legal person, public authority, agency or any other body who is competent according to the national law to decide what should be the purpose of the automated data file, which categories of personal data should be stored and which operations should be applied to them.

Article 3 – Scope

1. The Parties undertake to apply this convention to automated personal data files and automatic processing of personal data in the public and private sectors.
2. Any State or the European Union may, at the time of signature or when depositing its instrument of ratification, acceptance, approval or accession, or at any later time, give notice by a declaration addressed to the Secretary General of the Council of Europe:

a. that it will not apply this convention to certain categories of automated personal data files, a list of which will be deposited. In this list it shall not include, however, categories of automated data files subject under its domestic law to data protection provisions. Consequently, they shall amend this list by a new declaration whenever additional categories of automated personal data files are subjected to data protection provisions under their domestic law;
b. that they will also apply this convention to information relating to groups of persons, associations, foundations, companies, corporations and any other bodies

consisting directly or indirectly of individuals, whether or not such bodies possess legal personality;
c. that it will also apply this Convention to personal data files which are not processed automatically.

3. Any State or the European Communities which has extended the scope of this Convention by any of the declarations provided for in sub-paragraph 2.b or c above may give notice in the said declaration that such extensions shall apply only to certain categories of personal data files, a list of which will be deposited.
4. Any Party which has excluded certain categories of automated personal data files by a declaration provided for in sub-paragraph 2.a above may not claim the application of this convention to such categories by a Party which has not excluded them.
5. Likewise, a Party which has not made one or other of the extensions provided for in sub-paragraphs 2.b and c above may not claim the application of this convention on these points with respect to a Party which has made such extensions.
6. The declarations provided for in paragraph 2 above shall take effect from the moment of the entry into force of the convention with regard to the State or the European Union which has made them if they have been made at the time of signature or deposit of their instrument of ratification, acceptance, approval or accession, or three months after their receipt by the Secretary General of the Council of Europe if they have been made at any later time. These declarations may be withdrawn, in whole or in part, by a notification addressed to the Secretary General of the Council of Europe. Such withdrawals shall take effect three months after the date of receipt of such notification.

Chapter II – Basic principles for data protection

Article 4 – Duties of the Parties

1. Each Party shall take the necessary measures in its domestic law to give effect to the basic principles for data protection set out in this chapter.
2. These measures shall be taken at the latest at the time of entry into force of this convention in respect of that Party.

Article 5 – Quality of data

Personal data undergoing automatic processing shall be:

a. obtained and processed fairly and lawfully;
b. stored for specified and legitimate purposes and not used in a way incompatible with those purposes;
c. adequate, relevant and not excessive in relation to the purposes for which they are stored;
d. accurate and, where necessary, kept up to date;
e. preserved in a form which permits identification of the data subjects for no longer than is required for the purpose for which those data are stored.

Article 6 – Special categories of data

Personal data revealing racial origin, political opinions or religious or other beliefs, as well as personal data concerning health or sexual life, may not be processed automatically unless domestic law provides appropriate safeguards. The same shall apply to personal data relating to criminal convictions.

Article 7 – Data security

Appropriate security measures shall be taken for the protection of personal data stored in automated data files against accidental or unauthorised destruction or accidental loss as well as against unauthorised access, alteration or dissemination.

Article 8 – Additional safeguards for the data subject

Any person shall be enabled:

a. to establish the existence of an automated personal data file, its main purposes, as well as the identity and habitual residence or principal place of business of the controller of the file;
b. to obtain at reasonable intervals and without excessive delay or expense confirmation of whether personal data relating to him are stored in the automated data file as well as communication to him of such data in an intelligible form;
c. to obtain, as the case may be, rectification or erasure of such data if these have been processed contrary to the provisions of domestic law giving effect to the basic principles set out in Articles 5 and 6 of this convention;
d. to have a remedy if a request for confirmation or, as the case may be, communication, rectification or erasure as referred to in paragraphs b and c of this article is not complied with.

Article 9 – Exceptions and restrictions

1. No exception to the provisions of Articles 5, 6 and 8 of this convention shall be allowed except within the limits defined in this article.
2. Derogation from the provisions of Articles 5, 6 and 8 of this convention shall be allowed when such derogation is provided for by the law of the Party and constitutes a necessary measure in a democratic society in the interests of:

a. protecting State security, public safety, the monetary interests of the State or the suppression of criminal offences;
b. protecting the data subject or the rights and freedoms of others.

3. Restrictions on the exercise of the rights specified in Article 8, paragraphs b, c and d, may be provided by law with respect to automated personal data files used for statistics or for scientific research purposes when there is obviously no risk of an infringement of the privacy of the data subjects.

Article 10 – Sanctions and remedies

Each Party undertakes to establish appropriate sanctions and remedies for violations of provisions of domestic law giving effect to the basic principles for data protection set out in this chapter.

Article 11 – Extended protection

None of the provisions of this chapter shall be interpreted as limiting or otherwise affecting the possibility for a Party to grant data subjects a wider measure of protection than that stipulated in this convention.

Chapter III – Transborder data flows

Article 12 – Transborder flows of personal data and domestic law

1. The following provisions shall apply to the transfer across national borders, by whatever medium, of personal data undergoing automatic processing or collected with a view to their being automatically processed.
2. A Party shall not, for the sole purpose of the protection of privacy, prohibit or subject to special authorisation transborder flows of personal data going to the territory of another Party.
3. Nevertheless, each Party shall be entitled to derogate from the provisions of paragraph 2:

a. insofar as its legislation includes specific regulations for certain categories of personal data or of automated personal data files, because of the nature of those data or those files, except where the regulations of the other Party provide an equivalent protection;
b. when the transfer is made from its territory to the territory of a non-ing State through the intermediary of the territory of another Party, in order to avoid such transfers resulting in circumvention of the legislation of the Party referred to at the beginning of this paragraph.

Chapter IV – Mutual assistance

Article 13 – Co-operation between parties

1. The Parties agree to render each other mutual assistance in order to implement this convention.
2. For that purpose:

a. each Party shall designate one or more authorities, the name and address of each of which it shall communicate to the Secretary General of the Council of Europe;
b. each Party which has designated more than one authority shall specify in its communication referred to in the previous sub-paragraph the competence of each authority.

3. An authority designated by a Party shall at the request of an authority designated by another Party:

a. furnish information on its law and administrative practice in the field of data protection;
b. take, in conformity with its domestic law and for the sole purpose of protection of privacy, all appropriate measures for furnishing factual information relating to specific automatic processing carried out in its territory, with the exception however of the personal data being processed.

Article 14 – Assistance to data subjects resident abroad

1. Each Party shall assist any person resident abroad to exercise the rights conferred by its domestic law giving effect to the principles set out in Article 8 of this convention.
2. When such a person resides in the territory of another Party he shall be given the option of submitting his request through the intermediary of the authority designated by that Party.
3. The request for assistance shall contain all the necessary particulars, relating *inter alia* to:

a. the name, address and any other relevant particulars identifying the person making the request;
b. the automated personal data file to which the request pertains, or its controller;
c. the purpose of the request.

Article 15 – Safeguards concerning assistance rendered by designated authorities

1. An authority designated by a Party which has received information from an authority designated by another Party either accompanying a request for assistance or in reply to its own request for assistance shall not use that information for purposes other than those specified in the request for assistance.
2. Each Party shall see to it that the persons belonging to or acting on behalf of the designated authority shall be bound by appropriate obligations of secrecy or confidentiality with regard to that information.
3. In no case may a designated authority be allowed to make under Article 14, paragraph 2, a request for assistance on behalf of a data subject resident abroad, of its own accord and without the express consent of the person concerned.

Article 16 – Refusal of requests for assistance

A designated authority to which a request for assistance is addressed under Articles 13 or 14 of this convention may not refuse to comply with it unless:

a. the request is not compatible with the powers in the field of data protection of the authorities responsible for replying;
b. the request does not comply with the provisions of this convention;
c. compliance with the request would be incompatible with the sovereignty, security or public policy (ordre public) of the Party by which it was designated, or with the rights and fundamental freedoms of persons under the jurisdiction of that Party.

Article 17 – Costs and procedures of assistance

1. Mutual assistance which the Parties render each other under Article 13 and assistance they render to data subjects abroad under Article 14 shall not give rise to the payment of any costs or fees other than those incurred for experts and interpreters. The latter costs or fees shall be borne by the Party which has designated the authority making the request for assistance.
2. The data subject may not be charged costs or fees in connection with the steps taken on his behalf in the territory of another Party other than those lawfully payable by residents of that Party.
3. Other details concerning the assistance relating in particular to the forms and procedures and the languages to be used, shall be established directly between the Parties concerned.

Chapter V – Consultative Committee

Article 18 – Composition of the committee

1. A Consultative Committee shall be set up after the entry into force of this convention.
2. Each Party shall appoint a representative to the committee and a deputy representative. Any member State of the Council of Europe which is not a Party to the convention shall have the right to be represented on the committee by an observer.
3. The Consultative Committee may, by unanimous decision, invite any non-member State of the Council of Europe which is not a Party to the convention to be represented by an observer at a given meeting.

Article 19 – Functions of the committee

The Consultative Committee:

a. may make proposals with a view to facilitating or improving the application of the convention;
b. may make proposals for amendment of this convention in accordance with Article 21;
c. shall formulate its opinion on any proposal for amendment of this convention which is referred to it in accordance with Article 21, paragraph 3;
d. may, at the request of a Party, express an opinion on any question concerning the application of this convention.

Article 20 – Procedure

1. The Consultative Committee shall be convened by the Secretary General of the Council of Europe. Its first meeting shall be held within twelve months of the entry into force of this convention. It shall subsequently meet at least once every two years and in any case when one-third of the representatives of the Parties request its convocation.

2. A majority of representatives of the Parties shall constitute a quorum for a meeting of the Consultative Committee.
3. Every Party has a right to vote. Each State which is a Party to the Convention shall have one vote. Concerning questions witin their competence, the European Union exercise their right to vote and cast a number of votes equal to the number of Member States that are Parties to the Convention and have transferred their competencies to the European Union in the field concerned. In this case, those Member States of the European Union do not vote, and the other Member States may vote. The European Union do not vote when a question which does not fall within their competence if concerned.

Section (3) inserted to allow the accession of the European Communities (European Union), as approved by the Committee of Ministers in Strasbourg, on 15 June 1999. Sections (4) and (5) below renumbered accordingly.

4. After each of its meetings, the Consultative Committee shall submit to the Committee of Ministers of the Council of Europe a report on its work and on the functioning of the convention.
5. Subject to the provisions of this convention, the Consultative Committee shall draw up its own Rules of Procedure.

Chapter VI – Amendments

Article 21 – Amendments

1. Amendments to this convention may be proposed by a Party, the Committee of Ministers of the Council of Europe or the Consultative Committee.
2. Any proposal for amendment shall be communicated by the Secretary General of the Council of Europe to the member States of the Council of Europe, to the European Union, and to every non-member State which has acceded to or has been invited to accede to this Convention in accordance with the provisions of Article 23.
3. Moreover, any amendment proposed by a Party or the Committee of Ministers shall be communicated to the Consultative Committee, which shall submit to the Committee of Ministers its opinion on that proposed amendment.
4. The Committee of Ministers shall consider the proposed amendment and any opinion submitted by the Consultative Committee and may approve the amendment.
5. The text of any amendment approved by the Committee of Ministers in accordance with paragraph 4 of this article shall be forwarded to the Parties for acceptance.
6. Any amendment approved in accordance with paragraph 4 of this article shall come into force on the thirtieth day after all Parties have informed the Secretary General of their acceptance thereof.

Chapter VII – Final clauses

Article 22 – Entry into force

1. This convention shall be open for signature by the member States of the Council of Europe. It is subject to ratification, acceptance or approval. Instruments of ratification, acceptance or approval shall be deposited with the Secretary General of the Council of Europe.
2. This convention shall enter into force on the first day of the month following the expiration of a period of three months after the date on which five member States of the Council of Europe have expressed their consent to be bound by the convention in accordance with the provisions of the preceding paragraph.
3. In respect of any member State which subsequently expresses its consent to be bound by it, the convention shall enter into force on the first day of the month following the expiration of a period of three months after the date of deposit of the instrument of ratification, acceptance or approval.

Article 23 – Accession by non-member States or the European Union

1. After the entry into force of this Convention, the Committee of Ministers of the Council of Europe may invite any State not a member of the Council of Europe to accede to this convention by a decision taken by the majority provided for in Article 20.d of the Statute of the Council of Europe and by the unanimous vote of the representatives of the Contracting States entitled to sit on the committee.
2. The European Communities may accede to the Convention.
3. In respect of any acceding State, or of the European Union, the Convention shall enter into force on the first day of the month following the expiration of a period of three months after the date of deposit of the instrument of accession with the Secretary General of the Council of Europe.

Article 24 – Territorial clause

1. Any State or the European Union may at the time of signature or when depositing its instrument of ratification, acceptance, approval or accession, specify the territory or territories to which this Convention shall apply.
2. Any State or the European Communities may at any later date, by a declaration addressed to the Secretary General of the Council of Europe, extend the application of this convention to any other territory specified in the declaration. In respect of such territory the Convention shall enter into force on the first day of the month following the expiration of a period of three months after the date of receipt of such declaration by the Secretary General.

Article 25 – Reservations

No reservation may be made in respect of the provisions of this convention.

Article 26 – Denunciation

1. Any Party may at any time denounce this convention by means of a notification addressed to the Secretary General of the Council of Europe.
2. Such denunciation shall become effective on the first day of the month following the expiration of a period of six months after the date of receipt of the notification by the Secretary General.

Article 27 – Notifications

The Secretary General of the Council of Europe shall notify the member States of the Council of Europe, the European Union, and any State which has acceded to this convention of:

a. any signature;
b. the deposit of any instrument of ratification, acceptance, approval or accession;
c. any date of entry into force of this convention in accordance with Articles 22, 23 and 24;
d. any other act, notification or communication relating to this Convention.

In witness whereof the undersigned, being duly authorised thereto, have signed this Convention.
Done at Strasbourg, the 28th day of January 1981, in English and in French, both texts being equally authoritative, in a single copy which shall remain deposited in the archives of the Council of Europe. The Secretary General of the Council of Europe shall transmit certified copies to each member State of the Council of Europe and to any State invited to accede to this Convention.

3. Additional Protocol to the Convention 108 Regarding Supervisory Authorities and Transborder Data Flows

CETS No. 181
Opening for signature in Strasbourg on 8.11.2001.
Entry into force on 1.7.2004 (after 5 ratifications).
The following Member States have ratified the Protocol (date of the entry into force): Austria (1.8.2008); Bulgaria (1.11.2010); Cyprus (1.7.2004); Czech republic (1.7.2004); Estonia (1.11.2009); France (1.9.2007); Germany (1.7.2004); Hungary (1.9.2005); Ireland (1.9.2009); Latvia (1.3.2008); Lithuania (1.7.2004); Luxembourg (1.5.2007); the Netherlands (1.1.2005); Poland (1.11.2005); Portugal (1.5.2007); Romania (1.6.2006); Slovaquia (1.7.2004); Spain (1.10.2010) and Sweden (1.7.2004).
Open for signature by the European Union.

Preamble

The Parties to this additional Protocol to the Convention for the Protection of Individuals with regard to Automatic Processing of Personal Data, opened for signature in Strasbourg on 28 January 1981 (hereafter referred to as "the Convention");
Convinced that supervisory authorities, exercising their functions in complete independence, are an element of the effective protection of individuals with regard to the processing of personal data;
Considering the importance of the flow of information between peoples;
Considering that, with the increase in exchanges of personal data across national borders, it is necessary to ensure the effective protection of human rights and fundamental freedoms, and in particular the right to privacy, in relation to such exchanges of personal data,
Have agreed as follows:

Article 1 – Supervisory authorities

1. Each Party shall provide for one or more authorities to be responsible for ensuring compliance with the measures in its domestic law giving effect to the principles stated in Chapters II and III of the Convention and in this Protocol.
2. a. To this end, the said authorities shall have, in particular, powers of investigation and intervention, as well as the power to engage in legal proceedings or bring to the attention of the competent judicial authorities violations of provisions of domestic law giving effect to the principles mentioned in paragraph 1 of Article 1 of this Protocol.
b. Each supervisory authority shall hear claims lodged by any person concerning the protection of his/her rights and fundamental freedoms with regard to the processing of personal data within its competence.

3. The supervisory authorities shall exercise their functions in complete independence.
4. Decisions of the supervisory authorities, which give rise to complaints, may be appealed against through the courts.
5. In accordance with the provisions of Chapter IV, and without prejudice to the provisions of Article 13 of the Convention, the supervisory authorities shall co-operate with one another to the extent necessary for the performance of their duties, in particular by exchanging all useful information.

Article 2 – Transborder flows of personal data to a recipient which is not subject to the jurisdiction of a Party to the Convention

1. Each Party shall provide for the transfer of personal data to a recipient that is subject to the jurisdiction of a State or organisation that is not Party to the Convention only if that State or organisation ensures an adequate level of protection for the intended data transfer.
2. By way of derogation from paragraph 1 of Article 2 of this Protocol, each Party may allow for the transfer of personal data:

a. if domestic law provides for it because of:

– specific interests of the data subject, or
– legitimate prevailing interests, especially important public interests, or

b. if safeguards, which can in particular result from contractual clauses, are provided by the controller responsible for the transfer and are found adequate by the competent authorities according to domestic law.

Article 3 – Final provisions

1. The provisions of Articles 1 and 2 of this Protocol shall be regarded by the Parties as additional articles to the Convention and all the provisions of the Convention shall apply accordingly.
2. This Protocol shall be open for signature by States Signatories to the Convention. After acceding to the Convention under the conditions provided by it, the European Union may sign this Protocol. This Protocol is subject to ratification, acceptance or approval. A Signatory to this Protocol may not ratify, accept or approve it unless it has previously or simultaneously ratified, accepted or approved the Convention or has acceded to it. Instruments of ratification, acceptance or approval of this Protocol shall be deposited with the Secretary General of the Council of Europe.
3. a. This Protocol shall enter into force on the first day of the month following the expiry of a period of three months after the date on which five of its Signatories have expressed their consent to be bound by the Protocol in accordance with the provisions of paragraph 2 of Article 3.
b. In respect of any Signatory to this Protocol which subsequently expresses its consent to be bound by it, the Protocol shall enter into force on the first day of the

month following the expiry of a period of three months after the date of deposit of the instrument of ratification, acceptance or approval.

4. a. After the entry into force of this Protocol, any State which has acceded to the Convention may also accede to the Protocol.
b. Accession shall be effected by the deposit with the Secretary General of the Council of Europe of an instrument of accession, which shall take effect on the first day of the month following the expiry of a period of three months after the date of its deposit.

5. a. Any Party may at any time denounce this Protocol by means of a notification addressed to the Secretary General of the Council of Europe.
b. Such denunciation shall become effective on the first day of the month following the expiry of a period of three months after the date of receipt of such notification by the Secretary General.

6. The Secretary General of the Council of Europe shall notify the member States of the Council of Europe, the European Union and any other State which has acceded to this Protocol of:

a. any signature;
b. the deposit of any instrument of ratification, acceptance or approval;
c. any date of entry into force of this Protocol in accordance with Article 3;
d. any other act, notification or communication relating to this Protocol.

In witness whereof the undersigned, being duly authorised thereto, have signed this Protocol.
Done at Strasbourg, this 8th day of November 2001, in English and in French, both texts being equally authentic, in a single copy which shall be deposited in the archives of the Council of Europe. The Secretary General of the Council of Europe shall transmit certified copies to each member State of the Council of Europe, the European Union and any State invited to accede to the Convention.

4. Recommendation No R(87) 15 of the Committee of Ministers to Member States Regulating the Use of Personal Data in the Police Sector

The Committee of Ministers, under the terms of Article 15.b of the Statute of the Council of Europe,
Considering that the aim of the Council of Europe is to achieve a greater unity between its members;
Aware of the increasing use of automatically processed personal data ini the plice sector and of the possible benefits obtained through the use of computers and other technical means in this field;
Taking account also of concern about the possible threat to the privacy of the individual arising through the misuse of automated processing methods;
Recognising the need to balance the interests of society in the prevention and suppression of criminal offences and the maintenance of public order on the oe hand and the interests of the individual and his rights to privacy on the other;
Bearing in mind the provisions of the Convention for the Protection of Indiiduals with regard to Automatic Processing of Personal Data of 28 January 1981 and in particular the derogations permited under Article 9;
Aware also of the provisions of Article 8 of the Convention for the Protection of Human Rights and Fundamental Freedoms,
Recommends the governments of member states to:

– be guided in their domestic law and practice by the principles appended to this recommendation and
– ensure publicity for the provisions appended to this recommendation and in particular for the rights which its application confers on individuals.

Appendix to Recommendation No R(87) 15

Scope and definitions

The principles contained in this recommendation apply to the collection, storage, use and communication of personal data for police purposes which are the subject of automatic processing.
For the purposes of this recommendation, the expression "personal data" covers any information relating to an identified or identifiable individual. An individual shall not be regarded as "identifiable" if identification requires an unreasonable amount of time, cost and manpower.
The expression "for police purposes" covers all the tasks which the police authorities must perform for the prevention and suppression of criminal offences and the maintenance of public order.
The expression "responsible body" (controller of the file) denotes the authority, service or any other public body which is competent according to national law to

decide on the purpose of an automated file, the categories of personal data which must be stored and the operations which are to be applied to them.
A Member State may extend the principles contained in this recommendation to personal data not undergoing automatic processing.
Manual processing of data should not take place if the aim is to avoid the provisions of this recommendation.
A Member State smay extend the principles contained in this recommendation to data relating to groups of persons, associations, foundations, companies, corporations or any other body consisting directly or indirectly of individuals, whether or not such bodies possess legal personality.
The provisions of this recommendation should not be interpreted as limiting or otherwise affecting the possibility for a Member State to extend, where appropriate, certain of these principles to the collection, storage and use of personal data for purposes of state security.

Basis principles

Principle 1 – Control and notification

1.1. Each Member State should have an independent supervisory authority outside the police sector whichi should be responsible for ensuring respect for the principles contained in this recommendation.
1.2. New technical means for data processing may only be introduced if all reasonable measures have been taken to ensure that their use complies with the spirit of existing data protection legislation.
1.3. The responsible doby should consult the supervisory authorities in advance in any case where the introduction of automatic processing methods raises questions about the application of this recommendation.
1.4. Permanent automated files should eb notified to the supervisory authority. The notification should specify the nature of each file declared, the body responsible for its processing, its purposes, the tuype of data contained in the file and the persons to whocm the data are communicated.
Ad hoc files which have been set up at the time of particular inquiries should also be notified to the supervisory authorities either in accordance whith the conditions settled with the latter, taking account of the specific nature of these files, or ini accordance with national legislation.

Principle 2 – Collection of data

2.1. The collection of personal data for police purposes shoudl be limited to such as necessary for the prevention of a real danger or the suppresion of a specific criminal offence. Any exception to this provision should be the subject of specific national legislation.
2.2. Where data concerning an individual have been collected an stored without his knowledge, an unless the data are deleted, he should be informed, where applicable, that information is held about him as soon as the object of the police activities is no longer likely to be prejudiced.

2.3. The collection of data by technical surveillance of other automated measus should be provided for in specific provisions.
2.4. The collection of data on individuals solely on the basis that they have a particular racial origin, particular relisious convictions, sexual behaviour or political opinions or belong to particular movements or organisations which are not proscribed by law should be prohibited. The collection of data concerning these factors may only be carried out if absolutely necessary for the purposes of a particular inquiry.

Principle 3 – Storage of data

5.1. As far as possible, the storage of personal dat aofr police purposes shold be limited to accurate data and to such data as are necessary to allow police bodies to perform their lawful tasks within the framework of national law and their obligations arising from international law.
5.2. As far as possible, the different categories of data stored should be distinguished in accordance with their degree or accuracy or reliability and, in particular, data based on facts should be distinguished from data based on opinions or personal assessment.
5.3. Where data which have been collected for administrative purposes are to be stored permanently, they should be stored in a separate file. In any case, measures should be taken so that administrative data are not subject to rules applicable to police data.

Principle 4 – Use of data by the police

6. Subject to the principle 5, personal data collected and stored by the police for police purposes should be used exclusively for those purposes

Principle 5 – Communication of data

5.1. Communication with the police sector
The Communication of data between police bodies to be used for police purposes should only be permissible if there exists a legitimate interest for such communication within the framework of the legal powers of these bodies.
5.2. i. Communication to other public bodies
Communication of data to ther public bodies should only be permissible if, in a particular case:

a. There exist a clear legal obligation or authorisation, or with the authorisation of the supervisory authority, or if
b. These data are indispensable to the recipient to enable him to fulfil his own lawful task and pvided that the aim of the collection or processing to be carried out by the recicpients is not compatible with the original processing, and the legal oblications of the communicating body are not contrary to this.

ii. Furthermore, communication to other public bodies is exceptionally permissible if, in a particular case:

a. the communication is unboubtelly in the interest of the data subject and either the data subject has consented or circumstances as such as to allow a clear presumption of such consent, or if
b. the communication is necessary so as to prevent a serious and imminent danger.

5.3. i. Comunication to private parties
The communication of data to private parties should only be permissible if, ina particular cas, there exist a clear legal ogligation or authorisation, or which the authorisation of the supervisory authority.
ii. Communication to pricate parties is exceptionally permissible if, in a particular case:

a. the communication is undoubtedly in the interes of the data subject and either the data subject has consented or circumstances are such as to allow a clear presumption of such concsent, or if
b. the communication is necessary so as to prevent a serious and imminent danger.

5.4. International communication
Communication of data to foreign authorities ahold be restricted to police bodies. It should obly be permissible:

a. I there exists a clear legal providion under national or international law,
b. In the absence of such a provision, if the communication is necessary for the prevention of a serious and imminent danger or is necessary for the suppression of a serious criminal offence under ordinary law,
c. And provided that domestic regulations for the protection of the person is not prejudiced.

5.5. i. Request for communication
Subject to specific provisions contained in national legislation or in international agreements, requests for communication of ata should provide indications as to thebody or person requesting them as well as the reason for the request and its objective.
ii. Conditions for communication
As far as possible, the quality of data should be verified at the latest at the time of their communication. As far a spossible, in all communications of data, judicial decisions, as well as decisions not to prosecute, shold be indicated and data based on opinions or personal assessments checked at source before being communicated and their degree of accuracy or reliability indicated.
If it is discovered that the data are no longer accurate and up to date, they should not be communicated. If data which are no longer accurate or up to date have been communicated, the communicating body should inform as far aas possible all the recipens of the data of their non-conformity.

iii. Safeguards for communication

The data communicated to other public bodies, private parties and foreign authorities should not be used for purposes other than those specified in the request for communication.

Use of the data for other purposes should, without prejudice to paragraphs 5.2 to 5.4 of this principle, be made subject to the agreement of the communicating body.

5.6. Interconnection of files and on-line access to files

The interconnexion of files with files held for different purposes is subject to either of the following conditions:

a. the grant of an authorisation by the supervisory body for the purposes of an inquiry into a particular offence, or
b. in compliance with a clear legal provision.

Direct access/on-line access to a file shold only be allowed if it is in accordance with domestic legislation which should take account of Principles 3 to 6 of this recommendation.

Principle 6 – Publicity, right of access to police files, right of rectification and right of appeal

6.1. The supervisory authority should take measures so as to satisfy itself that the public is informed of the existence of files which are the subject of notification as well as of its rights in regard to these files. Implementation of this principle should take account of the specific nature of *ad hoc* files, in particular the need to avoid serous prejudice to the performance of a legal task of the police bodies.

6.2. The data subject should be able to abtain access to a police file at reasonable intervals and without excessive delay in accordance with the arrangements provided for by domestic law.

6.3. The data subject should be able to obtain, where appropriate, rectification of his data which are contained in a file.

Personal data which the exercise of the right of acces reveals to be inaccurate or whic are found to be excessive, inaccurate or irrelevant in application of any of the other principles contained in this recommendation should eb erased or corrected or else be the subject of a corrective statement added to the file.

Such erasure or corrective measures should be extended as far as possible to all documents accompanying the police file and, if not done immediately, should eb carried out, at the latest, at the time of subsequent processing of the data or of their next communication.

6.4. Exercise of the rights of access, rectification and erasure should only be restricted insofar as a restriction is indpeneisable for the performance of a legal task of the police or is necessary for the protection of the data subject or the rights and freedoms of others.

In the interest of the data subject, a written statement can be excluded by law for specific cases.

6.5. A refusal or a restriction of thise rights should be reasoned in writing. It should only be possible to refuse to communicate the reasons insofar as this is indispensable for the performance of a legal task of the police or is necessary for the protection of the rights and freedoms of others.

6.6. Where access is refused, the data subject should be able to appeal to the supervisory authority or to another independent body which shall satisfy itself that the refusal is well founded.

Principle 7 – Length of storage and updating of data

7.1 Measures should be taken so that personal data kept for police purposes are deleted if they are no longer necessary for the purposes for which they were stored.
For this purpose, consideration shall in particular be given to the following criteria: the need to retain data in the light of the conclusion of an inquiry into a particular case: a final decision, in particular an acquittal: rehabilitation, spent conviction" ammesties" the age of the data subject, particular categories of data.

7.2 Rules aimed at fixing storage periods for the different categories of personal data as well as regular checks on their wuality should be established in agreement with the supervisory authority or in accordance with domestic law.

Principle 8 – Data security

8. The responsible body should take all the necessary measures to ensure the appropriate physical and logical security of the data and prevent unauthorised access, communication or alteration.
The different characteristics and contens of files should, for this purpose, be taken into account.

C. EUROJUST, EUROPOL AND OLAF. EU NETWORKS FOR ADMINISTRATIVE, POLICE AND JUDICIAL COOPERATION IN CRIMINAL MATTERS

1. Council Decision 2002/187/JHA of 28 February 2002 Setting Up Eurojust with a View to Reinforcing the Fight Against Serious Crime as Amended by Council Decision 2003/659/JHA, and by Council Decision 2009/426/JHA of 16 December 2008 on the Strengthening of Eurojust

Consolidated version of the abovementioned Council Decision, prepared by the General Secretariat of the Council at the request of a number of delegations in July 2009 (Council document 14927/08 COPEN 200 EUROJUST 88 EJN 66).
The Council Decision 2002/187/JHA of 28 February 2002 setting up Eurojust with a view to reinforcing the fight against serious crime was published at OJ L 63, 6.3.2002, p. 1.
The Council Decision 2003/659/JHA of 18 June 2003 amending the Council Decision 2002/187/JHA was published at OJ L 245, 29.9.2003, p. 44.
The Council Decision 2009/426/JHA of 16 December 2008 on the strengthening of Eurojust was published at OJ L 138, 4.6.2009, p. 14

THE COUNCIL OF THE EUROPEAN UNION,

(. . .)

HAS DECIDED AS FOLLOWS:

Article 1 – Establishment and legal personality

This Decision establishes a unit, referred to as “Eurojust”, as a body of the Union. Eurojust shall have legal personality.

Á.G. Zarza (ed.), *Exchange of Information and Data Protection in Cross-border Criminal Proceedings in Europe*, DOI 10.1007/978-3-642-40291-3,

Article 2 – Composition of Eurojust

1. Eurojust shall have one national member seconded by each Member State in accordance with its legal system, who is a prosecutor, judge or police officer of equivalent competence.
2. Member States shall ensure continuous and effective contribution to the achievement by Eurojust of its objectives under Article 3. To fulfil those objectives:

(a) the national member shall be required to have his regular place of work at the seat of Eurojust;
(b) each national member shall be assisted by one deputy and by another person as an assistant. The deputy and the assistant may have their regular place of work at Eurojust. More deputies or assistants may assist the national member and may, if necessary and with the agreement of the College, have their regular place of work at Eurojust.

3. The national member shall have a position which grants him the powers referred to in this Decision in order to be able to fulfil his tasks.
4. National members, deputies and assistants shall be subject to the national law of their Member State as regards their status.
5. The deputy shall fulfil the criteria provided for in paragraph 1 and be able to act on behalf of or to substitute the national member. An assistant may also act on behalf of or substitute the national member if he fulfils the criteria provided for in paragraph 1.
6. Eurojust shall be linked to a Eurojust national coordination system in accordance with Article 12.
7. Eurojust shall have the possibility of posting liaison magistrates in third States in accordance with this Decision.
8. Eurojust shall, in accordance with this Decision, have a Secretariat headed by an Administrative Director.

Article 3 – Objectives

1. In the context of investigations and prosecutions, concerning two or more Member States, of criminal behaviour referred to in Article 4 in relation to serious crime, particularly when it is organised, the objectives of Eurojust shall be:

(a) to stimulate and improve the coordination, between the competent authorities of the Member States, of investigations and prosecutions in the Member States, taking into account any request emanating from a competent authority of a Member State and any information provided by any body competent by virtue of provisions adopted within the framework of the Treaties;
(b) to improve cooperation between the competent authorities of the Member States, in particular by facilitating the execution of requests for, and decisions on, judicial cooperation, including regarding instruments giving effects to the principle of mutual recognition;
(c) to support otherwise the competent authorities of the Member States in order to render their investigations and prosecutions more effective.

2. In accordance with the rules laid down by this Decision and at the request of a Member State's competent authority, Eurojust may also assist investigations and prosecutions concerning Orly that Member State and a non-Member State where an agreement establishing cooperation pursuant to Article 26a(2) has been concluded with the said State or where in a specific case there is an essential interest in providing such assistance.
3. In accordance with the rules laid down by this Decision and at the request either of a Member State's competent authority or of the Commission, Eurojust may also assist investigations and prosecutions concerning only that Member State and the Community.

Article 4 – Competences

1. The general competence of Eurojust shall cover:

(a) the types of crime and the offences in respect of which Europol is at all times competent to act[2];
(b) other offences committed together with the types of crime and the offences referred to in point (a).

2. For types of offences other than those referred to in §1, Eurojust may in addition, in accordance with its objectives, assist in investigations and prosecutions at the request of a competent authority of a Member State.

Article 5 – Tasks of Eurojust

1. In order to accomplish its objectives, Eurojust shall fulfil its tasks:

(a) through one or more of the national members concerned in accordance with Art. 6, or
(b) as a College in accordance with Art. 7:

(i) when so requested by one or more of the national members concerned by a case dealt with by Eurojust, or
(ii) when the case involves investigations or prosecutions which have repercussions at Union level or which might affect Member States other than those directly concerned, or
(iii) when a general question relating to the achievement of its objectives is involved, or
(iv) when otherwise provided for in this Decision.

2. When it fulfils its tasks, Eurojust shall indicate whether it is acting through one or more of the national members within the meaning of Art. 6 or as a College within the meaning of Art. 7.

[2] Council Decision of 6 April 2009 establishing the European Police office (Europol).

Article 5a – On-call coordination (OCC)

1. In order to fulfil its tasks in urgent cases, Eurojust shall put in place an On-Call Coordination (OCC) able to receive and process at all times requests referred to it. The OCC shall be contactable, through a single OCC contact point at Eurojust, on a 24 hour/7 day basis.
2. The OCC shall rely on one representative (OCC representative) per Member State who may be either the national member, his deputy, or an assistant entitled to replace the nacional member. The OCC representative shall be able to act on a 24 hour/7 day basis.
3. When in urgent cases a request for, or a decision on, judicial cooperation, including regarding instruments giving effect to the principle of mutual recognition, needs to be executed in one or more Member States, the requesting or issuing competent authority may forward it to the OCC. The OCC contact point shall immediately forward it to the OCC representative of the Member State from which the request originates and, if explicitly requested by the transmitting or issuing authority, to the OCC representatives of the Member States on the territory of which the request should be executed. These OCC representatives shall act without delay, in relation to the execution of the request in their Member State, through the exercise of tasks or powers available to them and referred to in Article 6 and Articles 9a to 9f.

Article 6 – Tasks of Eurojust acting through its national members

1. When Eurojust acts through its national members concerned, it:

   (a) may ask the competent authorities of the Member States concerned, giving its reasons, to:

      (i) undertake an investigation or prosecution of specific acts;
      (ii) accept that one of them may be in a better position to undertake an investigation or to prosecute specific acts;
      (iii) coordinate between the competent authorities of the Member States concerned;
      (iv) set up a joint investigation team in keeping with the relevant cooperation instruments;
      (v) provide it with any information that is necessary for it to carry out its tasks;
      (vi) take special investigative measures;
      (vii) take any other measure justified for the investigation or prosecution;

   (b) shall ensure that the competent authorities of the Member States concerned inform each other on investigations and prosecutions of which it has been informed;
   (c) shall assist the competent authorities of the Member States, at their request, in ensuring the best possible coordination of investigations and prosecutions;
   (d) shall give assistance in order to improve cooperation between the competent nacional authorities;

(e) shall cooperate and consult with the European Judicial Network, including making use of and contributing to the improvement of its documentary database;
(f) shall, in the cases referred to in Article 3(2) and (3) and with the agreement of the College, assist investigations and prosecutions concerning the competent authorities of only one Member State;

2. The Member States shall ensure that competent national authorities respond without undue delay to requests made under this Article.

Article 7 – Tasks of Eurojust acting as a college

1. When Eurojust acts as a College, it:

(a) may in relation to the types of crime and the offences referred to in Article 4 (1) ask the competent authorities of the Member States concerned, giving its reasons:

(i) to undertake an investigation or prosecution of specific acts;
(ii) to accept that one of them may be in a better position to undertake an investigation or to prosecute specific acts;
(iii) to coordinate between the competent authorities of the Member States concerned;
(iv) to set up a joint investigation team in keeping with the relevant cooperation instruments;
(v) to provide it with any information that is necessary for it to carry out its tasks;

(b) shall ensure that the competent authorities of the Member States inform each other of investigations and prosecutions of which it has been informed and which have repercussions at Union level or which might affect Member States other than those directly concerned;
(c) shall assist the competent authorities of the Member States, at their request, in ensuring the best possible coordination of investigations and prosecutions;
(d) shall give assistance in order to improve cooperation between the competent authorities of the Member States, in particular on the basis of Europol's analysis;
(e) shall cooperate and consult with the European Judicial Network, including making use of and contributing to the improvement of its documentary database;
(f) may assist Europol, in particular by providing it with opinions based on analyses carried out by Europol;
(g) may supply logistical support in the cases referred to in points (a), (c) and (d). Such logistical support may include assistance for translation, interpretation and the organisation of coordination meetings.

2. Where two or more national members can not agree on how to resolve a case of conflict of jurisdiction as regards the undertaking of investigations or prosecution pursuant to Article 6 and in particular Article 6(1)(c), the College shall be asked to issue a written non-binding opinion on the case, provided the matter could not be resolved through mutual agreement between the competent national authorities

concerned. The opinion of the College shall be promptly forwarded to the Member States concerned. This paragraph is without prejudice to paragraph 1(a)(ii).
3. Notwithstanding the provisions contained in any instruments adopted by the European Union regarding judicial cooperation, a competent authority may report to Eurojust recurrent refusals or difficulties concerning the execution of requests for, and decisions on, judicial cooperation, including regarding instruments giving effect to the principle of mutual recognition, and request the College to issue a written non-binding opinion on the matter, provided it could not be resolved through mutual agreement between the competent national authorities or through the involvement of the national members concerned. The opinion of the College shall be promptly forwarded to the Member States concerned.

Article 8 – Follow up to requests and opinions of Eurojust

If the competent authorities of the Member States concerned decide not to comply with a request referred to in Article 6(1)(a) or Article 7(1)(a) or decide not to follow a written opinion referred to in Article 7(2) and (3), they shall inform Eurojust without undue delay of their decision and of the reasons for it. Where it is not possible to give the reasons for refusing to comply with a request because to do so would harm essential national security interests or would jeopardise the safety of individuals, the competent authorities of the Member States may cite operational reasons.

Article 9 – National members

1. The length of a national member's term of office shall be at least four years. The Member State of origin may renew the term of office. The national member shall not be removed before the end of a term without informing the Council before the removal and indicating to it the reason therefore. Where a national member is President or Vice-President of Eurojust, his term of office as a member shall at least be such that he can fulfil his function as President or Vice-President for the full elected term.
2. All information exchanged between Eurojust and Member States shall be directed through the national member.
3. In order to meet Eurojust's objectives, the national member shall have at least equivalent access to, or at least be able to obtain the information contained in, the following types of registers of his Member State as would be available to him in his role as a prosecutor, Judge or police officer, whichever is applicable, at national level:

(a) criminal records;
(b) registers of arrested persons;
(c) investigation registers;
(d) DNA registers;
(e) other registers of his Member State where he deems this information necessary for him to be able to fulfil his tasks.

4. A national member may contact the competent authorities of his Member State directly.

Article 9a – Powers of the national member granted to him at national level

1. When a national member exercises the powers referred to in Articles 9b, 9c and 9d, he does so in his capacity as a competent national authority acting in accordance with national law and subject to the conditions laid down in this Article and Articles 9b to 9e. In the performance of his tasks the national member shall, where appropriate, make it known whenever he is acting in accordance with the powers granted to national members under this Article and Articles 9b, 9c and 9d.
2. Each Member State shall define the nature and extent of the powers it grants its nacional member as regards judicial cooperation in respect of that Member State. However, each Member State shall grant its national member at least the powers described in Article 9b and, subject to Article 9e, the powers described in Articles 9c and 9d, which would be available to him as a judge, prosecutor or police officer, whichever is applicable, at national level.
3. When appointing its national member and at any other time if appropriate, the Member State shall notify Eurojust and the General Secretariat of the Council of its decision regarding the implementation of paragraph 2 so that the latter can inform the other Member States. The Member States shall undertake to accept and recognise the prerogatives thus granted in so far as they are in conformity with international commitments.
4. Each Member State shall define the right for a national member to act in relation to foreign judicial authorities, in accordance with its international commitments.

Article 9b – Ordinary powers

1. National members, in their capacity as competent national authorities, shall be entitled to receive, transmit, facilitate, follow up and provide supplementary information in relation to the execution of requests for, and decisions on, judicial cooperation, including regarding instruments giving effect to the principle of mutual recognition. When powers referred to in this paragraph are exercised, the competent national authority shall be informed promptly.
2. In case of partial or inadequate execution of a request for judicial cooperation, nacional members, in their capacity as competent national authorities, shall be entitle d to ask the competent national authority of their Member State for supplementary measures in order for the request to be fully executed.

Article 9c – Powers exercised in agreement with a competent national authority

1. National members may, in their capacity as competent national authorities, in agreement with a competent national authority, or at its request and on a case-by-case basis, exercise the following powers:

(a) issuing and completing requests for, and decisions on, judicial cooperation, including regarding instruments giving effect to the principle of mutual recognition;
(b) executing in their Member State requests for, and decisions on, judicial cooperation, including regarding instruments giving effect to the principle of mutual recognition;

(c) ordering in their Member State investigative measures considered necessary at a coordination meeting organised by Eurojust to provide assistance to competent national authorities concerned by a concrete investigation and to which competent national authorities concerned with the investigation are invited to participate;
(d) authorising and coordinating controlled deliveries in their Member State.

2. Powers referred to in this Article shall, in principle, be exercised by a competent national authority.

Article 9d – Powers exercised in urgent cases

In their capacity as competent national authorities, national members shall, in urgent cases and in so far as it is not possible for them to identify or to contact the competent nacional authority in a timely manner, be entitled:

(a) to authorise and to coordinate controlled deliveries in their Member State;
(b) to execute, in relation to their Member State a request for, or a decision on, judicial cooperation, including regarding instruments giving effect to the principle of mutual recognition.

As soon as the competent national authority is identified or contacted, it shall be informed of the exercise of powers referred to in this Article.

Article 9e – Requests from national members where powers cannot be exercised

1. The national member, in his capacity as a competent national authority, shall be at least competent to submit a proposal to the authority competent for the carrying out of powers referred to in Articles 9c and 9d when granting such powers to the nacional member is contrary to:

(a) constitutional rules,
or
(b) fundamental aspects of the criminal justice system:

(i) regarding the division of powers between the police, prosecutors and judges,
(ii) regarding the functional division of tasks between prosecution authorities,
or
(iii) related to the federal structure of the Member State concerned.

2. Member States shall ensure that, in cases referred to in paragraph 1, the request issued by the national member be handled without undue delay by the competent national authority.

Article 9f – Participation of national members in joint investigation teams

National members shall be entitled to participate in joint investigation teams, including in their setting up, in accordance with Article 13 of the Convention on

Mutual Assistance in Criminal Matters between the Member States of the European Union or Council Framework Decision 2002/465/JHA of 13 June 2002 on joint investigation teams,[3] concerning their own Member State. However, Member States may make the participation of the national member subject to the agreement of the competent national authority.
National members, their deputies or their assistants, shall be invited to participate in any joint investigation team involving their Member State and for which Community funding is provided under the applicable financial instruments. Each Member State shall define whether the national member participates in the joint investigation team as a nacional competent authority or on behalf of Eurojust.

Article 10 – College

1. The College shall consist of all the national members. Each national member shall have one vote.
2. The Council shall, acting by a qualified majority, approve Eurojust's rules of procedure on a proposal from the College. The College shall adopt its proposal by a two-thirds majority alter consulting the Joint Supervisory Board provided for in Article 23 as regards the provisions on the processing of personal data. The provisions of the rules of procedure which concern the processing of personal data may be made the subject of separate approval by the Council.

See Rules of procedure of Eurojust (2002/C 286/01). OJ C 286, 22.11.2001, p. 1.

See Rules of procedure on the processing and protection of personal data at Eurojust. Adopted by the College of Eurojust at its meeting on 21 October 2004 and approved by the Council on 24 February 2005 (2005/C 68/01). OJ C 68, 19.3.2005, p. 1.

3. When acting in accordance with Art. 7(1)(a), (2) and (3), the College shall take its decisions by a two-thirds majority. Other decisions of the College shall be taken in accordance with the rules of procedure.

Article 11 – Role of the commission

1. The Commission shall be fully associated with the work of Eurojust, in accordance with Art. 36(2) of the Treaty. It shall participate in that work in the areas within its competence.
2. As regards work carried out by Eurojust on the coordination of investigations and prosecutions, the Commission may be invited to provide its expertise.

[3] OJ L 162, 20.6.2002, p. 1.

3. For the purpose of enhancing cooperation between Eurojust and the Commission, Eurojust may agree on necessary practical arrangements with the Commission.

Article 12 – Eurojust national coordination system

1. Each Member State shall designate one or more national correspondents for Eurojust.
2. Each Member State shall, before 04 June 2011, set up a Eurojust nacional coordination system to ensure coordination of the work carried out by:

(a) the national correspondents for Eurojust;
(b) the national correspondent for Eurojust for terrorism matters;
(c) the national correspondent for the European Judicial Network and up to three other contact points of the European Judicial Network;
(d) national members or contact points of the Network for Joint Investigation Teams and of the networks set up by Council Decision 2002/494/JHA of 13 June 2002 setting up a European network of contact points in respect of persons responsible for genocide, crimes against humanity and war crimes,[4] Council Decision 2007/845/JHA of 6 December 2007 concerning cooperation between Asset Recovery Offices of the Member States in the field of tracing and identification of proceeds from, or other property related to, crime[5] and by Council Decision 2008/852/JHA of 24 October 2008 on a contact-point network against corruption.[6]

3. The persons referred to in paragraphs 1 and 2 shall maintain their position and status under national law.
4. The national correspondents for Eurojust shall be responsible for the functioning of the Eurojust national coordination system. When several correspondents for Eurojust are designated, one of them shall be responsible for the functioning of the Eurojust national coordination system.
5. The Eurojust national coordination system shall facilitate, within the Member State, the carrying out of the tasks of Eurojust, in particular by:

(a) ensuring that the Case Management System referred to in Article 16 receives information related to the Member State concerned in an efficient and reliable manner;
(b) assisting in determining whether a case should be dealt with with the assistance of Eurojust or of the European Judicial Network;
(c) assisting the national member to identify relevant authorities for the execution of requests for, and decisions on, judicial cooperation, including regarding instruments giving effect to the principle of mutual recognition;
(d) maintaining close relations with the Europol National Unit.

---

[4] OJ L 167, 26.6.2002, p. 1.
[5] OJ L 332, 18.12.2007, p. 103.
[6] OJ L 301, 12.11.2008, p. 38.

6. In order to meet the objectives referred to in paragraph 5, persons referred to in paragraph 1 and paragraph 2(a), (b) and (c) shall, and persons referred to in paragraph 2(d) may, be connected to the Case Management System in accordance with this Article and Articles 16, 16a, 16b and 18 as well as with the Rules of Procedure of Eurojust. The connection to the Case Management System shall be at the charge of the general budget of the European Union.
7. Nothing in this Article shall be construed to affect direct contacts between competent judicial authorities as provided for in instruments on judicial cooperation, such as Article 6 of the Convention on Mutual Assistance in Criminal Matters between the Member States of the European Union. Relations between the national member and national correspondents shall not preclude direct contacts between the nacional member and his competent authorities.

Article 13 – Exchanges of information with the Member States and between national members

1. The competent authorities of the Member States shall exchange with Eurojust any information necessary for the performance of its tasks in accordance with Articles 4 and 5 as well as with the rules on data protection set out in this Decision. This shall at least include the information referred to in paragraphs 5, 6 and 7.
2. The transmission of information to Eurojust shall be interpreted as a request for the assistance of Eurojust in the case concerned only if so specified by a competent authority.
3. The national members of Eurojust shall be empowered to exchange any information necessary for the performance of the tasks of Eurojust, without prior authorisation, among themselves or with their Member State's competent authorities. In particular national members shall be promptly informed of a case which concerns them.
4. This Article shall be without prejudice to other obligations regarding the transmission of information to Eurojust, including Council Decision 2005/671/JHA of 20 September 2005 on the exchange of information and cooperation concerning terrorist offences.[7]
5. Member States shall ensure that national members are informed of the setting up of a joint investigation team, whether it is set up under Article 13 of the Convention on Mutual Assistance in Criminal Matters between the Member States of the European Union or under Framework Decision 2002/465/JHA2, and of the results of the work of such teams.
6. Member States shall ensure that their national member is informed without undue delay of any case in which at least three Member States are directly involved and for which requests for or decisions on judicial cooperation, including regarding instruments giving effect to the principle of mutual recognition, have been transmitted to at least two Member States and

[7] OJ L 105, 13.4.2006, 54.

(a) the offence involved is punishable in the requesting or issuing Member State by a custodial sentence or a detention order for a maximum period of at least five or six years, to be decided by the Member State concerned, and is included in the following list:

(i) trafficking in human beings;
(ii) sexual exploitation of children and child pornography;
(iii) drug trafficking;
(iv) trafficking in firearms, their parts and components and ammunition;
(v) corruption;
(vi) fraud affecting the financial interests of the European Communities;
(vii) counterfeiting of the euro;
(viii) money laundering;
(ix) attacks against information systems;

or
(b) there are factual indications that a criminal organisation is involved;
or
(c) there are indications that the case may have a serious cross-border dimension or repercussions at European Union level or that it might affect Member States other than those directly involved.

7. Member States shall ensure that their national member is informed of:

(a) cases where conflicts of jurisdiction have arisen or are likely to arise;
(b) controlled deliveries affecting at least three States, at least two of which are Member States;
(c) repeated difficulties or refusals regarding the execution of requests for, and decisions on, judicial cooperation, including regarding instruments living effect to the principle of mutual recognition.

8. National authorities shall not be obliged in a particular case to supply information if this would mean:

(a) harming essential national security interests; or
(b) jeopardising the safety of individuals.

9. This Article shall be without prejudice to conditions set in bilateral or multilateral agreements or arrangements between Member States and third countries including any conditions set by third countries concerning the use of information once supplied.
10. Information transmitted to Eurojust pursuant to paragraphs 5, 6 and 7 shall at least include, where available, the types of information contained in the list provided for in the Annex.
11. Information referred to in this Article shall be transmitted to Eurojust in a structured way.
12. By 04 June 20141, the Commission shall establish, on the basis of information transmitted by Eurojust, a report on the implementation of this Article,

accompanied by any proposal it may deem appropriate, including with a view to considering an amendment of paragraphs 5, 6 and 7 and the Annex.

Article 13 – Information provided by Eurojust to competent national authorities

1. Eurojust shall provide competent national authorities with information and feedback on the results of the processing of information, including the existence of links with cases already stored in the Case Management System.
2. Furthermore, where a competent national authority requests Eurojust to provide it with information, Eurojust shall transmit it in the timeframe requested by that authority.

Article 14 – Processing of personal data

1. Insofar as it is necessary to achieve its objectives, Eurojust may, within the framework of its competence and in order to carry out its tasks, process personal data, by automated means or in structured manual files.
2. Eurojust shall take the necessary measures to guarantee a level of protection for personal data at least equivalent to that resulting from the application of the principles of the Council of Europe Convention of 28 January 1981 and subsequent amendments thereto where they are in force in the Member States.
3. Personal data processed by Eurojust shall be adequate, relevant and not excessive in relation to the purpose of the processing, and, taking into account the information provided by the competent authorities of the Member States or other partners in accordance with Art. 13, 26 and 26a accurate and up-to-date. Personal data processed by Eurojust shall be processed fairly and lawfully.

Article 15 – Restrictions on the processing of personal data

1. When processing data in accordance with Article 14(1), Eurojust may process only the following personal data on persons who, under the national legislation of the Member States concerned are suspected of having committed or having taken part in a criminal offence in respect of which Eurojust is competent or who have been convicted of such an offence:

(a) surname, maiden name, given names and any alias or assumed names;
(b) date and place of birth;
(c) nationality;
(d) sex;
(e) place of residence, profession and whereabouts of the person concerned;
(f) social security numbers, driving licences, identification documents and passport data;
(g) information concerning legal persons if it includes information relating to identified or identifiable individuals who are the subject of a judicial investigation or prosecution;
(h) bank accounts and accounts with other financial institutions;

(i) description and nature of the alleged offences, the date on which they were committed, the criminal category of the offences and the progress of the investigations;
(j) the facts pointing to an international extension of the case;
(k) details relating to alleged membership of a criminal organisation;
(l) telephone numbers, e-mail addresses and data referred to in Article 2(2)(a) of Directive 2006/24/EC of the European Parliament and of the Council of 15 March 2006 on the retention of data generated or processed in connection with the provision of publicly available electronic communications services or of public Communications networks[8];
(m) vehicle registration data;
(n) DNA profiles established from the non-coding part of DNA, photographs and fingerprints.

2. When processing data in accordance with Art. 14(1), Eurojust may process only the following personal data on persons who, under the national legislation of the Member States concerned, are regarded as witnesses or victims in a criminal investigation or prosecution regarding one or more of the types of crime and the offences defined in Art. 4:

(a) surname, maiden name, given names and any alias or assumed names;
(b) date and place of birth;
(c) nationality;
(d) sex;
(e) place of residence, profession and whereabouts of the person concerned;
(f) the description and nature of the offences involving them, the date on which they were committed, the criminal category of the offences and the progress of the investigations.

3. However, in exceptional cases, Eurojust may also, for a limited period of time, process other personal data relating to the circumstances of an offence where they are immediately relevant to and included in ongoing investigations which Eurojust is helping to coordinate, provided that the processing of such specific data is in accordance with Articles 14 and 21. The Data Protection Officer referred to in Article17 shall be informed immediately of recourse to this paragraph. Where such other data refer to witnesses or victims within the meaning of paragraph 2, the decision to process them shall be taken jointly by at least two nacional members.
4. Personal data, processed by automated or other means, revealing racial or ethnic origin, political opinions, religious or philosophical beliefs, trade union membership, and data concerning health or sex life may be processed by Eurojust only when such data are necessary for the national investigations concerned as well as for coordination within Eurojust. The Data Protection Officer shall be informed immediately of recourse to this paragraph. Such data may not be processed in the

[8] OJ L 105, 13.4.2006, p. 54.

Index referred to in Art. 16(1). Where such other data refer to witnesses or victims within the meaning of paragraph 2, the decision to process them shall be taken by the College.

Article 16 – Case management system, index and temporary work files

1. In accordance with this Decision, Eurojust shall establish a Case Management System composed of temporary work files and of an index which contain personal and non-personal data.
2. The Case Management System shall be intended to:

(a) support the management and coordination of investigations and prosecutions for which Eurojust is providing assistance, in particular by the cross-referencing of information;
(b) facilitate access to information on ongoing investigations and prosecutions;
(c) facilitate the monitoring of lawfulness and compliance with the provisions of this Decision concerning the processing of personal data.

3. The Case Management System, in so far as this is in conformity with rules on data protection contained in this Decision, may be linked to the secure telecommunications connection referred to in Article 9 of Council Decision 2008/976/JHA of 16 December 2008 on the European Judicial Network.[9]
4. The index shall contain references to temporary work files processed within the framework of Eurojust and may contain no personal data other than those referred to in Article 15(1)(a) to (i), (k) and (m) and in Article 15(2).
5. In the performance of their duties in accordance with this Decision, the nacional members of Eurojust may process data on the individual cases on which they are working in a temporary work file. They shall allow the Data Protection Officer to have access to the work file. The Data Protection Officer shall be informed by the national member concerned of the opening of each new temporary work file that contains personal data.
6. For the processing of case related personal data, Eurojust may not establish any automated data file other than the Case Management System.

Article 16a – Functioning of temporary work files and the index

1. A temporary work file shall be opened by the national member concerned for every case with respect to which information is transmitted to him in so far as this transmission is in accordance with this Decision or with instruments referred to in Article 13(4). The national member shall be responsible for the management of the temporary work files which he has opened.
2. The national member who has opened a temporary work file shall decide, on a case-by-case basis, whether to keep the temporary work file restricted or to give access to it or to parts of it, where necessary to enable Eurojust to carry out its tasks, to other national members or to authorised Eurojust staff.

---

[9] OJ L 348, 24.12.2008, p. 130.

3. The national member who has opened a temporary work file shall decide which information related to this temporary work file shall be introduced in the index.

Article 16b – Access to the case management system at national level

1. Persons referred to in Article 12(2) in so far as they are connected to the Case Management System in accordance with Article 12(6) may only have access to:

(a) the index, unless the national member who has decided to introduce the data in the index expressly denied such access;
(b) temporary work files opened or managed by the national member of their Member State;
(c) temporary work files opened or managed by national members of other Member States and to which the national member of their Member States has received access unless the national member who opened or manages the temporary work file expressly denied such access.

2. The national member shall, within the limitations provided for in paragraph 1, decide on the extent of access to the temporary work files which is granted in his Member State to persons referred to in Article 12(2) in so far as they are connected to the Case Management System in accordance with Article 12(6).
3. Each Member State shall decide, after consultation with its national member, on the extent of access to the index which is granted in that Member State to persons referred to in Article 12(2) in so far as they are connected to the Case Management System in accordance with Article 12(6). Member States shall notify Eurojust and the General Secretariat of the Council of their decision regarding the implementation of this paragraph so that the latter can inform the other Member States.
However, persons referred to in Article 12(2), in so far as they are connected to the Case Management System in accordance with Article 12(6), shall at least have access to the index to the extent necessary to access the temporary work files to which they have been granted access in accordance with paragraph 2 of this Article.
4. By 04 June 2013, Eurojust shall report to the Council and the Commission on the implementation of paragraph 3. Each Member State shall consider, on the basis of that report, the opportunity to review the extent of access provided in accordance with paragraph 3.

Article 17 – Data protection officer

1. Eurojust shall have a specially appointed Data Protection Officer, who shall be a member of the staff. Within that framework, he or she shall be under the direct authority of the College.
In the performance of the duties referred to in this article, he shall act independently.
2. The Data Protection Officer shall in particular have the following tasks:

(a) ensuring, in an independent manner, lawfulness and compliance with the provisions of this Decision concerning the processing of personal data;

(b) ensuring that a written record of the transmission and receipt, for the purposes of Art. 19(3) in particular, of personal data is kept in accordance with the provisions to be laid down in the rules of procedure, under the security conditions laid down in Art. 22;
(c) ensuring that data subjects are informed of their rights under this Decision at their request.

3. In the performance of his tasks, the Data Protection Officer shall have access to all the data processed by Eurojust and to all Eurojust premises.
4. When he finds that in his view processing has not complied with this Decision, the Data Protection Officer shall:

(a) inform the College, which shall acknowledge receipt of the information;
(b) refer the matter to the JSB if the College has not resolved the non-compliance of the processing within a reasonable time.

Article 18 – Authorised access to personal data

Only national members, their deputies and their assistants referred to in Article 2 (2), persons referred to in Article 12(2) in so far as they are connected to the Case Management System in accordance with Article 12(6) and authorised Eurojust staff may, for the purpose of achieving Eurojust's objectives and within the limits provided for in Articles 16, 16a and 16b, have access to personal data processed by Eurojust.

Article 19 – Right of access to personal data

1. Every individual shall be entitled to have access to personal data concerning him processed by Eurojust under the conditions laid down in this article.
2. Any individual wishing to exercise his right to have access to data concerning him which are stored at Eurojust, or to have them checked in accordance with Art. 20, may make a request to that effect free of charge in the Member State of his choice, to the authority appointed for that purpose in that Member State, and that authority shall refer it to Eurojust without delay.
3. The right of any individual to have access to personal data concerning him or to have them checked shall be exercised in accordance with the laws and procedures of the Member State in which the individual has made his request. If, however, Eurojust can ascertain which authority in a State transmitted the data in question, that authority may require that the right of access be exercised in accordance with the rules of the law of that Member State.
4. Access to personal data shall be denied if:

(a) such access may jeopardise one of Eurojust's activities;
(b) such access may jeopardise any national investigation;
(c) such access may jeopardise the rights and freedoms of third parties.

5. The decision to grant this right of access shall take due account of the status, with regard to the data stored by Eurojust, of those individuals submitting the request.

6. The national members concerned by the request shall deal with it and reach a decision on Eurojust's behalf. The request shall be dealt with in full within three months of receipt. Where the members are not in agreement, they shall refer the matter to the College, which shall take its decision on the request by a two-thirds majority.
7. If access is denied or if no personal data concerning the applicant are processed by Eurojust, the latter shall notify the applicant that it has carried out checks, without giving any information which could reveal whether or not the applicant is known.
8. If the applicant is not satisfied with the reply given to his request, he may appeal against that decision before the JSB. The JSB shall examine whether or not the decision taken by Eurojust is in conformity with this Decision.
9. The competent law enforcement authorities of the Member States shall be consulted by Eurojust before a decision is taken. They shall subsequently be notified of its contents through the national members concerned.

Article 20 – Correction and deletion of personal data

1. In accordance with Art. 19(3), every individual shall be entitled to ask Eurojust to correct, block or delete data concerning him if they are incorrect or incomplete or if their input or storage contravenes this Decision.
2. Eurojust shall notify the applicant if it corrects, blocks or deletes the data concerning him. If the applicant is not satisfied with Eurojust's reply, he may refer the matter to the JSB within thirty days of receiving Eurojust's decision.
3. At the request of a MS's competent authorities, national member or national correspondent, if any, and under their responsibility, Eurojust shall, in accordance with its rules of procedure, correct or delete personal data being processed by Eurojust which were transmitted or entered by that Member State, its national member or its national correspondent. The Member States' competent authorities and Eurojust, including the national member or national correspondent, if any, shall in this context ensure that the principles laid down in Art. 14(2) and (3) and in Art. 15(4) are complied with.
4. If it emerges that personal data processed by Eurojust are incorrect or incomplete or that their input or storage contravenes the provisions of this Decision, Eurojust shall block, correct or delete such data.
5. In the cases referred to in §3 and 4, all the suppliers and addressees of such data shall be notified immediately. In accordance with the rules applicable to them, the addressees, shall then correct, block or delete those data in their own systems.

Article 21 – Time limits for the storage of personal data

1. Personal data processed by Eurojust shall be stored by Eurojust for only as long as is necessary for the achievement of its objectives.
2. The personal data referred to in Art. 14(1) which have been processed by Eurojust may not be stored beyond the first applicable among the following dates:

(a) the date on which prosecution is barred under the statute of limitations of all the Member States concerned by the investigation and prosecutions;

(aa) the date on which the person has been acquitted and the decision became final;

(b) three years after the date on which the judicial decision of the last of the Member States concerned by the investigation or prosecutions became final;
(c) the date on which Eurojust and the Member States concerned mutually established or agreed that it was no longer necessary for Eurojust to coordinate the investigation and prosecutions, unless there is an obligation to provide Eurojust with this information in accordance with Article 13(6) and (7) or according to instruments referred to in Article 13(4);
(d) three years after the date on which data were transmitted according to Article 13(6) and (7) or according to instruments referred to in Article 13(4).

3. (a) Observance of the storage periods referred to in paragraph 2(a),(b),(c) and (d) shall be reviewed constantly by appropriate automated processing. Nevertheless, a review of the need to store the data shall be carried out every three years after they were entered.
(b) When one of the storage deadlines referred to in paragraph 2(a), (b), (c) and (d) has expired, Eurojust shall review the need to store the data longer in order to enable it to achieve its objectives and it may decide by way of derogation to store those data until the following review. However, once prosecution is statute barred in all Member States concerned as referred to in paragraph 2(a), data may only be stored if they are necessary in order for Eurojust to provide assistance in accordance with this Decision.
(c) Where data has been stored by way of derogation pursuant to point (b) a review of the need to store those data shall take place every three years.

4. Where a file exists containing non-automated and unstructured data, once the deadline for storage of the last item of automated data from the file has elapsed all the documents in the file shall be returned to the authority which supplied them and any copies shall be destroyed.
5. Where Eurojust has coordinated an investigation or prosecutions, the national members concerned shall inform Eurojust and the other Member States concerned of all the judicial decisions relating to the case which have become final in order, inter alia, that § 2(b) may be applied.

Article 22 – Data security

1. Eurojust and, insofar as it is concerned by data transmitted from Eurojust, each Member State, shall, as regards the processing of personal data within the framework of this Decision, protect personal data against accidental or unlawful destruction, accidental loss or unauthorised disclosure, alteration and access or any other unauthorised form of processing.

2. The rules of procedure shall contain the technical measures and the organisational arrangements needed to implement this Decision with regard to data security and in particular measures designed to:

(a) deny unauthorised persons access to data processing equipment used for processing personal data;
(b) prevent the unauthorised reading, copying, modification or removal of data media;
(c) prevent the unauthorised input of data and the unauthorised inspection, modification or deletion of stored personal data;
(d) prevent the use of automated data processing systems by unauthorised persons using data communication equipment;
(e) ensure that persons authorised to use an automated data processing system only have access to the data covered by their access authorisation;
(f) ensure that it is possible to verify and establish to which bodies personal data are transmitted when data are communicated;
(g) ensure that it is subsequently possible to verify and establish which personal data have been input into automated data processing systems and when and by whom the data were input;
(h) prevent unauthorised reading, copying, modification or deletion of personal data Turing transfers of personal data or during transportation of data media.

Article 23 – Joint Supervisory Body (JSB)[10]

1. An independent JSB shall be established to monitor collectively the Eurojust activities referred to in Art. 14 to 22, 26, 26a and 27 in order to ensure that the processing of personal data is carried out in accordance with this Decision. In order to fulfil these tasks, the JSB shall be entitled to have full access to all files where such personal data are processed. Eurojust shall provide the JSB with all information from such files that it requests and shall assist that body in its tasks by every other means. The Joint Supervisory Body shall meet at least once in each half year. It shall also meet within the three months following the lodging of an appeal referred to in Article 19(8) or within three months following the date when a case was referred to it in accordance with Article 20(2). The Joint Supervisory Body may also be convened by its chairman when at least two Member States so request. In order to set up the JSB, each Member State, acting in accordance with its legal system, shall appoint a judge who is not a member of Eurojust, or, if its constitutional or national system so requires a person holding an office giving him sufficient independence, for inclusion on the list of judges who may sit on the JSB as members or ad hoc judges. No such appointment shall be for less than three years. Revocation of the appointment shall be governed by the principles for renoval applicable under the national law of the Member State of origin.

[10] Information on the Joint Supervisory Body of Eurojust is available at www.eurojust.europa.eu/jsb.htm.

Appointment and renoval shall be communicated to both the Council General Secretariat and Eurojust.
2. The JSB shall be composed of 3 permanent members and, as provided for in §4, ad hoc judges.
3. A judge appointed by a Member State shall become a permanent member after being elected by the plenary meeting of the persons appointed by the Member States in accordance with paragraph 1, and shall remain a permanent member for three years. Elections shall be held yearly for one permanent member of the Joint Supervisory Body by means of secret ballot.
The Joint Supervisory Body shall be chaired by the member who is in his third year of mandate after elections. Permanent members may be re-elected. Appointees wishing to be elected shall present their candidacy in writing to the Secretariat of the Joint Supervisory Body ten days before the meeting in which the election is to take place.
4. One or more ad hoc judges shall also have seats, but only for the duration of the examination of an appeal concerning personal data from the Member State which has appointed them.
4a. The JSB shall adopt in its rules of procedure measures necessary to implement paragraphs 3 and 4.

Cfr. Act of the Joint Supervisory Body of Eurojust of 23 June 2009 laying down its rules of procedure (adopted unanimously at the plenary meeting of the Joint Supervisory Body of Eurojust on 23 June 2009) (2010/C 182/03). OJ C 182, 7.7.2010, p. 3

The Rules of Procedure of the JSB are reproduced below in this handbook.

5. The composition of the JSB shall remain the same for the duration of an appeals procedure even if the permanent members have reached the end of their term of office pursuant to § 3.
6. Each member and ad hoc judge shall be entitled to one vote. In the event of a tied vote, the chairman shall have the casting vote.
7. The JSB shall examine appeals submitted to it in accordance with Art. 19(8) and Art. 20(2) and carry out controls in accordance with §1, first sub§, of this article. If the JSB considers that a decision taken by Eurojust or the processing of data by it is not compatible with this Decision, the matter shall be referred to Eurojust, which shall accept the decision of the JSB.
8. Decisions of the JSB shall be final and binding on Eurojust.
9. The persons appointed by the Member States in accordance with §1, third sub§, presided over by the chairman of the JSB, shall adopt internal rules of procedure which, for the purpose of the examination of appeals, lay down objective criteria for the appointment of the Body's members.

10. Secretariat costs shall be borne by the Eurojust budget. The secretariat of the JSB shall enjoy independence in the discharge of its function within the Eurojust secretariat. The Secretariat of the Joint Supervisory Body may rely upon the expertise of the secretariat established by Decision 2000/641/JHA1.
11. The members of the JSB shall be subject to the obligation of confidentiality laid down in Art. 25.

Article 24 – Liability for unauthorised or incorrect processing of data

1. Eurojust shall be liable, in accordance with the national law of the Member State where its headquarters are situated, for any damage caused to an individual which results from unauthorised or incorrect processing of data carried out by it.
2. Complaints against Eurojust pursuant to the liability referred to in §1 shall be heard by the courts of the Member State where its headquarters are situated.
3. Each Member State shall be liable, in accordance with its national law, for any damage caused to an individual, which results from unauthorised or incorrect processing carried out by it of data which were communicated to Eurojust.

Article 25 – Confidentiality

1. The national members, their deputies and their assistants referred to in Article 2 (2), Eurojust staff, national correspondents and the Data Protection Officer shall be bound by an obligation of confidentiality, without prejudice to Article 2(4).
2. The obligation of confidentiality shall apply to all persons and to all bodies called upon to work with Eurojust.
3. The obligation of confidentiality shall also apply after leaving office or employment or alter the termination of the activities of the persons referred to in § 1 and 2.
4. Without prejudice to Article 2(4), the obligation of confidentiality shall apply to all information received by Eurojust.

Article 25a – Cooperation with the European Judicial Network and other networks of the European Union involved in cooperation in criminal matters

1. Eurojust and the European Judicial Network shall maintain privileged relations with each other, based on consultation and complementarity, especially between the national member, the European Judicial Network contact points of the same Member State and the national correspondents for Eurojust and the European Judicial Network. In order to ensure efficient cooperation, the following measures shall be taken:

(a) national members shall, on a case-by-case basis, inform the European Judicial Network contact points of all cases which they consider the Network to be in a better position to deal with;
(b) the Secretariat of the European Judicial Network shall form part of the staff of Eurojust. It shall function as a separate unit. It may draw on the administrative resources of Eurojust which are necessary for the performance of the European Judicial Network's tasks, including for covering the costs of the plenary meetings of the Network. Where plenary meetings are held at the premises of the

Council in Brussels, the costs may only cover travel expenses and costs for interpretation. Where plenary meetings are held in the Member State holding the Presidency of the Council, the costs may only cover part of the overall costs of the meeting;
(c) European Judicial Network contact points may be invited on a case-by-case basis to attend Eurojust meetings.

2. Without prejudice to Article 4(1), the Secretariat of the Network for Joint Investigation Teams and of the network set up by Decision 2002/494/JHA shall form part of the staff of Eurojust. These secretariats shall function as separate units. They may draw on the administrative resources of Eurojust which are necessary for the performance of their tasks. Coordination between the secretariats shall be ensured by Eurojust.
This paragraph shall apply to the secretariat of any new network set up by a decision of the Council where that decision provides that the secretariat shall be provided by Eurojust.
3. The network set up by Decision 2008/852/JHA may request that Eurojust provide a secretariat to the network. If such request is made, paragraph 2 shall apply.

Article 26 – Relations with Community or Union related institutions, bodies and agencies

1. Insofar as is relevant for the performance of its tasks, Eurojust may establish and maintain cooperative relations with the institutions, bodies and agencies set up by, or on the basis of, the Treaties establishing the European Communities or the Treaty on European Union. Eurojust shall establish and maintain cooperative relations with at least:

(a) Europol;
(b) OLAF;
(c) the European Agency for the Management of Operational Cooperation at the External Borders of the Member States of the European Union (Frontex);
(d) the Council, in particular its Joint Situation Centre.

Eurojust shall also establish and maintain cooperative relations with the European Judicial Training Network.
2. Eurojust may conclude agreements or working arrangements with the entities referred to in paragraph 1. Such agreements or working arrangements may, in particular, concern the exchange of information, including personal data, and the secondment of liaison officers to Eurojust. Such agreements or working arrangements may only be concluded after consultation by Eurojust with the Joint Supervisory Body concerning the provisions on data protection and after the approval by the Council, acting by qualified majority. Eurojust shall inform the Council of any plans it has for entering into any such negotiations and the Council may draw any conclusions it deems appropriate.

See Agreement between Eurojust and Europol of 1.10.2009; Practical Agreement on arrangements of cooperation between Eurojust and OLAF signed of 24.9.2008; Memorandum of Understanding between Eurojust and the European Judicial Training Network signed of 7.2.2008.

See also the Memorandum of Understanding between Eurojust and CEPOL signed on 7.12. 2009

See Opinion of the Joint Supervisory Body on the revised agreement between Eurojust and Europol; Opinion of the Joint Supervisory Body on the draft accord on cooperation arrangements between Eurojust and OLAF

3. Prior to the entry into force of an agreement or arrangement as referred to in paragraph 2, Eurojust may directly receive and use information, including personal data, from the entities referred to in paragraph 1, in so far as this is necessary for the legitimate performance of its tasks, and it may directly transmit information, including personal data, to such entities, in so far as this is necessary for the legitimate performance of the recipient's tasks and in accordance with the rules on data protection provided in this Decision.

4. OLAF may contribute to Eurojust's work to coordinate investigations and prosecution procedures regarding the protection of the financial interests of the European Communities, either on the initiative of Eurojust or at the request of OLAF where the competent national authorities concerned do not oppose such participation.

5. For purposes of the receipt and transmission of information between Eurojust and OLAF, and without prejudice to Article 9, Member States shall ensure that the national members of Eurojust shall be regarded as competent authorities of the Member States solely for the purposes of Regulation (EC) No 1073/1999 and Council Regulation (Euratom) No 1074/1999 of 25 May 1999 concerning investigations conducted by the European Anti-Fraud Office (OLAF). The Exchange of information between OLAF and national members shall be without prejudice to the information which must be given to other competent authorities under those Regulations.

Article 26a – Relations with third States and organisations

1. In so far as is required for the performance of its tasks, Eurojust may establish and maintain cooperative relations with the following entities:

(a) third States;
(b) organisations such as:

(i) international organisations and their subordinate bodies governed by public law;
(ii) other bodies governed by public law which are based on an agreement between two or more States; and
(iii) the International Criminal Police Organisation (Interpol)

2. Eurojust may conclude agreements with the entities referred to in paragraph 1. Such agreements may, in particular, concern the exchange of information, including personal data, and the secondment of liaison officers or liaison magistrates to Eurojust. Such agreements may only be concluded after consultation by Eurojust with the Joint Supervisory Body concerning the provisions on data protection and after the approval by the Council, acting by qualified majority. Eurojust shall inform the Council of any plans it has for entering into any such negotiations and the Council may draw any conclusions it deems appropriate.

See the Agreement between Eurojust and Norway of 9 June 2004; Agreement between Eurojust and Iceland of 15.11.2005; Agreement between Eurojust and United States of America of 6 November 2006; Agreement between Eurojust and Croatia of 9 November 2007; Agreement between Eurojust and former Yugoslav Republic of Macedonia of 28.11.2008, and Agreement between Eurojust and Switzerland on 28.11.2008.

See also the Memorandum of Understanding between Eurojust and the Iberoamerican Network of International Legal Cooperation (IberRed) of 4.5.2009, and Memorandum of Understanding between Eurojust and the United Nations Office of Drugs and Crime of 26.2.2010.

The cited Agreements and Memorandums of Understanding are available at www.eurojust.europa.eu/official_documents/eju_agreements.htm

See Opinion of the draft agreement between Eurojust and Croatia; Opinion of the Joint Supervisory Body on the draft Agreement between Eurojust and the former Yugoslav Republic of Macedonia; Opion of the Joint Supervisory Body on the draft Agreement between Eurojust and Switzerland.

The cited opinions are available at www.eurojust.europa.eu/jsb-publications.htm

3. Agreements referred to in paragraph 2 containing provisions on the exchange of personal data may only be concluded if the entity concerned is subject to the Council of Europe Convention of 28 January 1981 or after an assessment confirming the existence of an adequate level of data protection ensured by that entity.

4. Agreements referred to in paragraph 2 shall include provisions on the monitoring of their implementation, including implementation of the rules on data protection.

5. Prior to the entry into force of the agreements referred to in paragraph 2, Eurojust may directly receive information, including personal data in so far as this is necessary for the legitimate performance of its tasks.
6. Prior to the entry into force of the agreements referred to in paragraph 2, Eurojust may under the conditions laid down in Article 27(1), directly transmit information, except for personal data, to these entities, in so far as this is necessary for the legitimate performance of the recipient's tasks.
7. Eurojust may, under the conditions laid down in Article 27(1), transmit personal data to the entities referred to in paragraph 1, where:

(a) this is necessary in individual cases for the purposes of preventing or combating criminal offences for which Eurojust is competent, and (b) Eurojust has concluded an agreement as referred to in paragraph 2 with the entity concerned which has entered into force and which permits the transmission of such data.

8. Any subsequent failure, or substantial likelihood of failure, on the part of the entibies referred to in paragraph 1 to meet the conditions referred to in paragraph 3, shall immediately be communicated by Eurojust to the Joint Supervisory Body and the Member States concerned. The Joint Supervisory Body may prevent the further exchange of personal data with the relevant entities until it is satisfied that adequate remedies have been provided.
9. However, even if the conditions referred to in paragraph 7 are not fulfilled, a nacional member may, acting in his capacity as a competent national authority and in conformity with the provisions of his own national law, by way of exception and with the sole aim of taking urgent measures to counter imminent serious danger threatening a person or public security, carry out an exchange of information involving personal data. The national member shall be responsible for the legality of authorising the communication. The national member shall keep a record of communications of data and of the grounds for such communications. The communication of data shall be authorised only if the recipient gives an undertaking that the data will be used only for the purpose for which they were communicated.

Article 27 – Transmission of data

1. Before Eurojust exchanges any information with the entities referred to in Article 26a, the national member of the Member State which submitted the information shall give his consent to the transfer of that information. In appropriate cases the national member shall consult the competent authorities of the Member States.
2. Eurojust shall be responsible for the legality of the transmission of data. Eurojust shall keep a record of all transmissions of data under Articles 26 and 26a and of the grounds for such transmissions. Data shall only be transmitted if the recipient gives an undertaking that the data will be used only for the purpose for which they were transmitted.

Article 27a – Liaison magistrates posted to third States

1. For the purpose of facilitating judicial cooperation with third States in cases in which Eurojust is providing assistance in accordance with this Decision, the

College may post liaison magistrates to a third State, subject to an agreement as referred to in Article 26a with that third State. Before negotiations are entered into with a third State, the Council, acting by qualified majority, shall give its approval. Eurojust shall inform the Council of any plans it has for entering into any such negotiations and the Council may draw any conclusions it deems appropriate.
2. The liaison magistrate referred to in paragraph 1 is required to have experience of working with Eurojust and adequate knowledge of judicial cooperation and how Eurojust operates. The posting of a liaison magistrate on behalf of Eurojust shall be subject to the prior consent of the magistrate and of his Member State.
3. Where the liaison magistrate posted by Eurojust is selected among national members, deputies or assistants:

(i) he shall be replaced in his function as a national member, deputy or assistant, by the Member State;
(ii) he ceases to be entitled to exercise the powers granted to him in accordance with Articles 9a to 9e.

4. Without prejudice to Article 110 of the Staff Regulations of Officials of the European Communities laid down by Regulation (EEC, Euratom, ECSC) No 259/681, the College shall draw up rules on the posting of liaison magistrates and adopt the necessary implementing arrangements in this respect in consultation with the Commission.
5. The activities of liaison magistrates posted by Eurojust shall be the subject of supervision by the Joint Supervisory Body. The liaison magistrates shall report to the College, which shall inform the European Parliament and the Council in the annual report and in an appropriate manner of their activities. The liaison magistrates shall inform national members and national competent authorities of all cases concerning their Member State.
6. Competent authorities of the Member States and liaison magistrates referred to in paragraph 1 may contact each other directly. In such cases, the liaison magistrate shall inform the national member concerned of such contacts.
7. The liaison magistrates referred to in paragraph 1 shall be connected to the Case Management System.

Article 27b – Requests for judicial cooperation to and from third States

1. Eurojust may, with the agreement of the Member States concerned, coordinate the execution of requests for judicial cooperation issued by a third State where these requests are part of the same investigation and require execution in at least two Member States. Requests referred to in this paragraph may also be transmitted to Eurojust by a competent national authority.
2. In case of urgency and in accordance with Article 5a, the OCC may receive and process requests referred to in paragraph 1 of this Article and issued by a third State which has concluded a cooperation agreement with Eurojust.
3. Without prejudice to Article 3(2), where requests for judicial cooperation, which relate to the same investigation and require execution in a third State, are made,

Eurojust may also, with the agreement of the Member States concerned, facilitate judicial cooperation with that third State.
4. Requests referred to in paragraphs 1, 2 and 3 may be transmitted through Eurojust if it is in conformity with the instruments applicable to the relationship between that third State and the European Union or the Member States concerned.

Article 27c – Liability other than liability for unauthorised or incorrect processing of data

1. Eurojust's contractual liability shall be governed by the law applicable to the contract in question.
2. In the case of non-contractual liability, Eurojust shall, independently of any liability under Article 24, make good any damage caused through the fault of the College or the staff of Eurojust in the performance of their duties in so far as it may be imputed to them and regardless of the different procedures for claiming damages which exist under the law of the Member States.
3. Paragraph 2 shall also apply to damage caused through the fault of a nacional member, a deputy or an assistant in the performance of his duties. However, when he is acting on the basis of the powers granted to him pursuant to Articles 9a to 9e, his Member State of origin shall reimburse Eurojust the sums which Eurojust has paid to make good such damage.
4. The injured party shall have the right to demand that Eurojust refrain from taking, or cease, any action.
5. The national courts of the Member States competent to deal with disputes involving Eurojust's liability as referred to in this Article shall be determined by reference to Council Regulation (EC) No 44/2001 of 22 December 2000 on jurisdiction and the recognition and enforcement of judgments in civil and commercial matters.[11]

Article 28 – Organisation and operation

1. The College shall be responsible for the organisation and operation of Eurojust.
2. The College shall elect a President from among the national members and may, if it considers it necessary, elect at most two Vice-Presidents. The result of the election shall be submitted to the Council acting by qualified majority, for its approval.
3. The President shall exercise his duties on behalf of the College and under its authority, direct its work and monitor the daily management ensured by the Administrative Director. The rules of procedure shall specify the cases in which his decisions or actions shall require prior authorisation or a report to the College.
4. The term of office of the President shall be three years. He may be re-elected once. The term of office of any Vice-President(s) shall be governed by the rules of procedure.
5. Eurojust shall be assisted by a secretariat headed by an Administrative Director.

[11] OJ L 12, 16.1.2001, p. 1.

6. Eurojust shall exercise over its staff the powers devolved to the Appointing Authority. The College shall adopt appropriate rules for the implementation of this § in accordance with the rules of procedure.

(...)

Article 39 – Access to documents

On the basis of a proposal by the Administrative Director, the College shall adopt rules for access to Eurojust documents, taking account of the principles and limits stated in Regulation (EC) No 1049/2001 of the European Parliament and of the Council of 30 May 2001 regarding public access to European Parliament, Council and Commission documents

Article 39a – EU classified information

Eurojust shall apply the security principles and minimum standards set out in Council Decision 2001/264/EC of 19 March 2001 adopting the Council's security regulations[12] in the management of EU classified information.

(...)

Article 43 – Taking of effect

This Decision shall take effect on the day of its publication in the Official Journal of the European Union.
Done at Brussels
For the Council
The President

[12] OJ L 101, 11.4.2001, p. 1.

ANNEX

List referred to in Article 13(10) setting out the minimum types of information to be transmitted, where available, to Eurojust pursuant to Article 13(5), (6) and (7)

1. For situations referred to in Article 13(5):

   (a) participating Member States,
   (b) type of offences concerned,
   (c) date of the agreement setting up the team,
   (d) planned duration of the team, including modification of this duration,
   (e) details of the leader of the team for each participating Member State,
   (f) short summary of the results of the joint investigation teams.

2. For situations referred to in Article 13(6):

   (a) data which identify the person, group or entity that is the object of a criminal investigation or prosecution,
   (b) Member States concerned,
   (c) the offence concerned and its circumstances,
   (d) data related to the requests for, or decisions on, judicial cooperation including regarding instruments giving effect to the principle of mutual recognition, which are issued, including:

      (i) date of the request,
      (ii) requesting or issuing authority,
      (iii) requested or executing authority,
      (iv) type of request (measures requested),
      (v) whether or not the request has been executed, and if not on what grounds.

3. For situations referred to in Article 13(7)(a):

   (a) Member States and competent authorities concerned,
   (b) data which identify the person, group or entity that is the object of a criminal investigation or prosecution,
   (c) the offence concerned and its circumstances.

4. For situations referred to in Article 13(7)(b):

   (a) Member States and competent authorities concerned,
   (b) data which identify the person, group or entity that is the object of a criminal investigation or prosecution,
   (c) type of delivery,
   (d) type of offence in connection with which the controlled delivery is carried out.

5. For situations referred to in Article 13(7)(c):

   (a) requesting or issuing State,
   (b) requested or executing State,
   (c) description of the difficulties."

EUROJUST TEMPLATE

for the transmission of information ex Article 13(5) to (7) of the Eurojust Decision [1]

version 2.0

To be submitted to your National Desk at Eurojust and re-submitted if relevant updates are available.

No additional investigation is required in order to fill in the form. Only currently available information is expected.

The fields in gray colour are optional fields.

A) GENERAL INFORMATION

1. Originating Member State

2. National file reference number(s)

3. Authority responsible for the case

   Name

   Street

   City

   Responsible person

4. Authority responsible for the transmission of the information to Eurojust (if different from the above)

5. Has Eurojust already been involved in this case (e.g. through an earlier template or request for assistance)? YES NO

6. Do you intend to request the assistance of Eurojust?

7. Do you intend to attach a file? YES NO

B) SPECIFIC INFORMATION

(click on the relevant item to expand)

+ **Joint Investigation Teams - Article 13(5)**

[1] The template is based on Council Decision 2009/426/JHA of 16 December 2008 and Annex I thereto (hereinafter referred to as the "Eurojust Decision").

2. Council Decision 2009/371/JHA of 9 April 2009 Establising the European Police Office (Europol)[13]

THE COUNCIL OF THE EUROPEAN UNION,

(. . .)

HAS DECIDED AS FOLLOWS:

CHAPTER I

ESTABLISHMENT AND TASKS

Article 1

Establishment

1. This Decision replaces the provisions of the Convention based on Article K.3 of the Treaty on European Union, on the establishment of a European Police Office (Europol Convention).
Europol shall have its seat in The Hague, the Netherlands.
2. Europol, as referred to in this Decision, shall be regarded as the legal successor of Europol, as established by the Europol Convention.
3. Europol shall liaise with a single national unit in each Member State, to be established or designated in accordance with Article 8.

Article 2

Legal capacity

1. Europol shall have legal personality.
2. In each Member State Europol shall enjoy the most extensive legal and contractual capacity accorded to legal persons under that Member State's law. Europol may, in particular, acquire and dispose of movable and immovable property and may be a party to legal proceedings.
3. Europol shall be empowered to conclude a Headquarters Agreement with the Kingdom of the Netherlands.

Article 3

Objective

The objective of Europol shall be to support and strengthen action by the competent authorities of the Member States and their mutual cooperation in preventing and combating organised crime, terrorism and other forms of serious crime affecting two or more Member States.

---

[13] OJ L 121, 15.5.2009, p. 37.

For the purposes of this Decision, "competent authorities" shall mean all public bodies existing in the Member States which are responsible under national law for preventing and combating criminal offences.

Article 4

Competence

1. Europol's competence shall cover organised crime, terrorism and other forms of serious crime as listed in the Annex affecting two or more Member States in such a way as to require a common approach by the Member States owing to the scale, significance and consequences of the offences.
2. On a recommendation by the Management Board, the Council shall lay down its priorities for Europol, taking particular account of strategic analyses and threat assessments prepared by Europol.
3. Europol's competence shall also cover related criminal offences. The following offences shall be regarded as related criminal offences:

(a) criminal offences committed in order to procure the means of perpetrating acts in respect of which Europol is competent;
(b) criminal offences committed in order to facilitate or carry out acts in respect of which Europol is competent;
(c) criminal offences committed to ensure the impunity of acts in respect of which Europol is competent.

Article 5

Tasks

1. Europol shall have the following principal tasks:

(a) to collect, store, process, analyse and exchange information and intelligence;
(b) to notify the competent authorities of the Member States without delay via the national unit referred to in Article 8 of information concerning them and of any connections identified between criminal offences;
(c) to aid investigations in the Member States, in particular by forwarding all relevant information to the national units;
(d) to ask the competent authorities of the Member States concerned to initiate, conduct or coordinate investigations and to suggest the setting up of joint investigation teams in specific cases;
(e) to provide intelligence and analytical support to Member States in connection with major international events;
(f) to prepare threat assessments, strategic analyses and general situation reports relating to its objective, including organised crime threat assessments.

2. The tasks referred to in paragraph 1 shall include providing support to Member States in their tasks of gathering and analysing information from the Internet in order to assist in the identification of criminal activities facilitated by or committed using the Internet.

3. Europol shall have the following additional tasks:

(a) to develop specialist knowledge of the investigative procedures of the competent authorities of the Member States and to provide advice on investigations;
(b) to provide strategic intelligence to assist and promote the efficient and effective use of the resources available at national and Union level for operational activities and the support of such activities.

4. Additionally, in the context of its objective under Article 3, Europol may, in accordance with the staffing and budgetary resources at its disposal and within the limits set by the Management Board, assist Member States through support, advice and research in the following areas:

(a) the training of members of their competent authorities, where appropriate in cooperation with the European Police College;
(b) the organisation and equipment of those authorities by facilitating the provision of technical support between the Member States;
(c) crime prevention methods;
(d) technical and forensic methods and analysis, and investigative procedures.

5. Europol shall also act as the Central Office for combating euro counterfeiting in accordance with Council Decision 2005/511/JHA of 12 July 2005 on protecting the euro against counterfeiting, by designating Europol as the Central Office for combating euro counterfeiting.[14] Europol may also encourage the coordination of measures carried out in order to fight euro counterfeiting by the competent authorities of the Member States or in the context of joint investigation teams, where appropriate in liaison with Union entities and third States' bodies. Upon request, Europol may financially support investigations of euro counterfeiting.

Article 6

Participation in joint investigation teams

1. Europol staff may participate in supporting capacity in joint investigation teams, including such teams set up in accordance with Article 1 of Council Framework Decision 2002/465/JHA of 13 June 2002 on joint investigation teams,[15] in accordance with Article 13 of the Convention of 29 May 2000 on mutual assistance in criminal matters between the Member States of the European Union,[16] or in accordance with Article 24 of the Convention of 18 December 1997 on mutual assistance and cooperation between customs administrations,[17] in so far as those teams are investigating criminal offences in respect of which Europol is competent under Article 4 of this Decision.

[14] OJ L 185, 16.7.2005, p. 35.
[15] OJ L 162, 20.6.2002, p. 1.
[16] OJ C 197, 12.7.2000, p. 3.
[17] OJ C 24, 23.1.1998, p. 2.

Europol staff may, within the limits provided for by the law of the Member States in which a joint investigation team is operating and in accordance with the arrangement referred to in paragraph 2, assist in all activities and exchange information with all members of the joint investigation team, in accordance with paragraph 4. They shall not, however, take part in the taking of any coercive measures.
2. The administrative implementation of participation by Europol staff in a joint investigation team shall be laid down in an arrangement between the Director and the competent authorities of the Member States participating in the joint investigation team, with the involvement of the national units. The rules governing such arrangements shall be determined by the Management Board.
3. The rules referred to in paragraph 2 shall specify the conditions under which Europol staff are placed at the disposal of the joint investigation team.
4. In accordance with the arrangement referred to in paragraph 2, Europol staff may liaise directly with members of a joint investigation team and provide members and seconded members of the joint investigation team, in accordance with this Decision, with information from any of the components of the information processing systems referred to in Article 10. In the event of such direct liaison, Europol shall at the same time inform the national units of the Member States represented in the team as well as those of the Member States which provided the information thereof.
5. Information obtained by a Europol staff member while part of a joint investigation team may, with the consent and under the responsibility of the Member State which provided the information, be included in any of the components of the information processing systems referred to in Article 10 under the conditions laid down in this Decision.
6. During the operations of a joint investigation team, Europol staff shall, with respect to offences committed against or by them, be subject to the national law of the Member State of operation applicable to persons with comparable functions.

Article 7

Requests by Europol for the initiation of criminal investigations

1. Member States shall deal with any request by Europol to initiate, conduct or coordinate investigations in specific cases and shall give such requests due consideration. The Member States shall inform Europol whether the investigation requested will be initiated.
2. Before making a request for the initiation of criminal investigations, Europol shall inform Eurojust accordingly.
3. If the competent authorities of the Member State decide not to comply with a request made by Europol, they shall inform Europol of their decision and of the reasons therefor unless they are unable to give their reasons because:

(a) to do so would harm essential national security interests; or
(b) to do so would jeopardise the success of investigations under way or the safety of individuals.

4. Replies to requests by Europol for the initiation, conduct or coordination of investigations in specific cases and information for Europol concerning the results of investigations shall be forwarded through the competent authorities of the Member States in accordance with the rules laid down in this Decision and the relevant national legislation.

Article 8

National units

1. Each Member State shall establish or designate a national unit responsible for carrying out the tasks set out in this Article. An official shall be appointed in each Member State as the head of the national unit.
2. The national unit shall be the only liaison body between Europol and the competent authorities of the Member States. Member States, however, may allow direct contacts between designated competent authorities and Europol subject to conditions determined by the Member State in question, including prior involvement of the national unit.
The national unit shall at the same time receive from Europol any information exchanged in the course of direct contacts between Europol and designated competent authorities. Relations between the national unit and the competent authorities shall be governed by national law, and in particular, the relevant national constitutional requirements.
3. Member States shall take the measures necessary to ensure that their national units are able to fulfil their tasks and, in particular, have access to relevant national data.
4. The national units shall:

(a) supply Europol on their own initiative with the information and intelligence necessary for it to carry out its tasks;
(b) respond to Europol's requests for information, intelligence and advice;
(c) keep information and intelligence up to date;
(d) evaluate information and intelligence in accordance with national law for the competent authorities and transmit that material to them;
(e) issue requests for advice, information, intelligence and analysis to Europol;
(f) supply Europol with information for storage in its databases;
(g) ensure compliance with the law in every exchange of information between themselves and Europol.

5. Without prejudice to the Member States' discharging the responsibilities incumbent upon them with regard to the maintenance of law and order and the safeguarding of internal security, a national unit shall not in any particular case be obliged to supply information or intelligence if that would entail:

(a) harming essential national security interests;
(b) jeopardising the success of a current investigation or the safety of individuals; or
(c) disclosing information relating to organisations or specific intelligence activities in the field of State security.

6. The costs incurred by the national units in communications with Europol shall be borne by the Member States and, apart from the costs of connection, shall not be charged to Europol.
7. The heads of the national units shall meet on a regular basis to assist Europol on operational matters, on their own initiative or at the request of the Management Board or the Director, in particular to:

(a) consider and develop proposals that will improve Europol's operational effectiveness and encourage commitment from Member States;
(b) evaluate the reports and analyses drafted by Europol in accordance with Article 5(1)(f) and develop measures in order to help to implement their findings;
(c) provide support in the establishment of joint investigation teams involving Europol in accordance with Article 5(1)(d) and Article 6.

Article 9

Liaison officers

1. Each national unit shall second at least one liaison officer to Europol. Except as otherwise stipulated in specific provisions of this Decision, liaison officers shall be subject to the national law of the seconding Member State.
2. Liaison officers shall constitute the national liaison bureaux at Europol and shall be instructed by their national units to represent the interests of the latter within Europol in accordance with the national law of the seconding Member State and the provisions applicable to the administration of Europol.
3. Without prejudice to Article 8(4) and (5), liaison officers shall:

(a) provide Europol with information from the seconding national unit;
(b) forward information from Europol to the seconding national unit;
(c) cooperate with Europol staff by providing information and giving advice; and
(d) assist in the exchange of information from their national units with the liaison officers of other Member States under their responsibility in accordance with national law. Such bilateral exchanges may also cover crimes outwith the competence of Europol, as far as allowed by national law.

4. Article 35 shall apply mutatis mutandis to the activities of liaison officers.
5. The rights and obligations of liaison officers in relation to Europol shall be determined by the Management Board.
6. Liaison officers shall enjoy the privileges and immunities necessary for the performance of their tasks in accordance with Article 51(2).
7. Europol shall ensure that liaison officers are fully informed of and associated with all of its activities, as far as that is compatible with their position.
8. Europol shall provide Member States free of charge with the necessary premises in the Europol building and adequate support for the performance of the activities of their liaison officers. All other costs which arise in connection with the secondment of liaison officers shall be borne by the seconding Member State, including the costs

of equipment for liaison officers, unless the Management Board recommends otherwise in specific cases when drawing up Europol's budget.

CHAPTER II

INFORMATION PROCESSING SYSTEMS

Article 10

Information processing

1. In so far as it is necessary for the achievement of its objectives, Europol shall process information and intelligence, including personal data, in accordance with this Decision. Europol shall establish and maintain the Europol Information System referred to in Article 11 and the analysis work files referred to in Article 14. Europol may also establish and maintain other systems processing personal data set up in accordance with paragraphs 2 and 3 of this Article.
2. The Management Board, acting on a proposal from the Director after having taken into account the possibilities offered by existing Europol information processing systems and after consulting the Joint Supervisory Body, shall decide on the establishment of a new system processing personal data. That Management Board decision shall be submitted to the Council for approval.
3. The Management Board decision referred to in paragraph 2 shall determine the conditions and limitations under which Europol may establish the new system processing personal data. The Management Board decision may allow processing of personal data relating to the categories of persons referred to in Article 14(1), but not the processing of personal data revealing racial or ethnic origin, political opinions, religious or philosophical beliefs or trade-union membership and the processing of data concerning health or sex life. The Management Board decision shall ensure that the measures and principles referred to in Articles 18, 19, 20, 27, 29 and 35 are properly implemented. In particular, the Management Board decision shall define the purpose of the new system, access to and the use of the data, as well as time limits for the storage and deletion of the data.
4. Europol may process data for the purpose of determining whether such data are relevant to its tasks and can be included in the Europol Information System referred to in Article 11, in the analysis work files referred to in Article 14 or in other systems processing personal data established in accordance with paragraphs 2 and 3 of this Article. The Management Board, acting on a proposal from the Director and after consulting the Joint Supervisory Body, shall determine the conditions relating to the processing of such data, in particular with respect to access to and the use of the data, as well as time limits for the storage and deletion of the data that may not exceed six months, having due regard to the principles referred to in Article 27. That Management Board decision shall be submitted to the Council for approval.

Article 11

Europol Information System

1. Europol shall maintain the Europol Information System.
2. Europol shall ensure compliance with the provisions of this Decision governing operation of the Europol Information System. It shall be responsible for the proper working of the Europol Information System in technical and operational respects and shall, in particular, take all measures necessary to ensure that the measures referred to in Articles 20, 29, 31 and 35 regarding the Europol Information System are properly implemented.
3. The national unit in each Member State shall be responsible for communication with the Europol Information System. It shall, in particular, be responsible for the security measures referred to in Article 35 in respect of the data-processing equipment used within the territory of the Member State in question, for the review provided for in Article 20 and, in so far as required under the laws, regulations, administrative provisions and procedures of that Member State, for the proper implementation of this Decision in other respects.

Article 12

Content of the Europol Information System

1. The Europol Information System may be used to process only such data as are necessary for the performance of Europol's tasks. The data input shall relate to:

(a) persons who, in accordance with the national law of the Member State concerned, are suspected of having committed or having taken part in a criminal offence in respect of which Europol is competent or who have been convicted of such an offence;
(b) persons regarding whom there are factual indications or reasonable grounds under the national law of the Member State concerned to believe that they will commit criminal offences in respect of which Europol is competent.

2. Data relating to the persons referred to in paragraph 1 may include only the following particulars:

(a) surname, maiden name, given names and any alias or assumed name;
(b) date and place of birth;
(c) nationality;
(d) sex;
(e) place of residence, profession and whereabouts of the person concerned;
(f) social security numbers, driving licences, identification documents and passport data; and
(g) where necessary, other characteristics likely to assist in identification, including any specific objective physical characteristics not subject to change such as dactyloscopic data and DNA profile (established from the non-coding part of DNA).

3. In addition to the data referred to in paragraph 2, the Europol Information System may also be used to process the following particulars concerning the persons referred to in paragraph 1:

(a) criminal offences, alleged criminal offences and when, where and how they were (allegedly) committed;
(b) means which were or may be used to commit those criminal offences including information concerning legal persons;
(c) departments handling the case and their filing references;
(d) suspected membership of a criminal organisation;
(e) convictions, where they relate to criminal offences in respect of which Europol is competent;
(f) inputting party.

These data may also be input when they do not yet contain any references to persons. Where Europol inputs the data itself, as well as when it gives its filing reference, it shall also indicate the source of the data.
4. Additional information held by Europol or national units concerning the persons referred to in paragraph 1 may be communicated to any national unit or Europol should either so request. National units shall do so in compliance with their national law.
Where the additional information concerns one or more related criminal offences as defined in Article 4(3), the data stored in the Europol Information System shall be marked accordingly to enable national units and Europol to exchange information concerning the related criminal offences.
5. If proceedings against the person concerned are definitively dropped or if that person is definitively acquitted, the data relating to the case in respect of which either decision has been taken shall be deleted.

Article 13

Use of the Europol Information System

1. National units, liaison officers, the Director, Deputy Directors and duly empowered Europol staff shall have the right to input data directly into the Europol Information System and retrieve them from it. Data may be retrieved by Europol where that is necessary for the performance of its tasks in a particular case. Retrieval by the national units and liaison officers shall be effected in accordance with the laws, regulations, administrative provisions and procedures of the accessing party, subject to any additional provisions laid down in this Decision.
2. Only the party which has input data may modify, correct or delete such data. Where another party has reason to believe that data as referred to in Article 12 (2) are incorrect or wishes to supplement them, it shall immediately inform the inputting party. The inputting party shall examine such information without delay and if necessary modify, supplement, correct or delete the data immediately.
3. Where the system contains data as referred to in Article 12(3) concerning a person, any party may input additional data as referred to in that provision. Where

there is an obvious contradiction between the data input, the parties concerned shall consult each other and reach agreement.
4. Where a party intends to delete altogether data as referred to in Article 12 (2) which it has input concerning a person and data as referred to in Article 12 (3) in respect of the same person have been input by other parties, responsibility in terms of data-protection legislation pursuant to Article 29(1) and the right to modify, supplement, correct and delete such data pursuant to Article 12(2) shall be transferred to the next party to have input data as referred to in Article 12(3) on that person. The party intending to delete shall inform the party to which responsibility in terms of data protection is transferred of its intention.
5. Responsibility for the permissibility of retrieval from, input into and modifications within the Europol Information System shall lie with the retrieving, inputting or modifying party. It must be possible to identify that party. The communication of information between national units and the competent authorities of the Member States shall be governed by national law.
6. In addition to the national units and persons referred to in paragraph 1, competent authorities designated to that effect by the Member States may also query the Europol Information System. However, the result of the query shall indicate only whether the data requested are available in the Europol Information System. Further information may then be obtained via the national unit.
7. Information concerning the competent authorities designated in accordance with paragraph 6, including subsequent modifications, shall be transmitted to the General Secretariat of the Council, which shall publish the information in the Official Journal of the European Union.

Article 14

Analysis work files

1. Where this is necessary for the performance of its tasks, Europol may store, modify, and use data concerning criminal offences in respect of which it is competent, including data on the related criminal offences referred to in Article 4 (3), in analysis work files. The analysis work files may contain data on the following categories of persons:

(a) persons as referred to in Article 12(1);
(b) persons who might be called on to testify in investigations in connection with the offences under consideration or in subsequent criminal proceedings;
(c) persons who have been the victims of one of the offences under consideration or with regard to whom certain facts give reason to believe that they could be the victims of such an offence;
(d) contacts and associates; and
(e) persons who can provide information on the criminal offences under consideration.

The processing of personal data revealing racial or ethnic origin, political opinions, religious or philosophical beliefs or trade-union membership and the processing of

data concerning health or sex life shall not be permitted unless strictly necessary for the purposes of the file concerned and unless such data supplement other personal data already input in that file. The selection of a particular group of persons solely on the basis of the abovementioned sensitive data, in breach of the aforementioned rules with regard to purpose, shall be prohibited.
The Council, acting by qualified majority after consulting the European Parliament, shall adopt implementing rules for analysis work files prepared by the Management Board, which shall previously have obtained the opinion of the Joint Supervisory Body, containing additional details, in particular with regard to the categories of personal data referred to in this Article, to the security of the data concerned and to the internal supervision of their use.
2. Analysis work files shall be opened for the purposes of analysis defined as the assembly, processing or use of data with the aim of assisting criminal investigations. Each analysis project shall entail the establishment of an analysis group closely associating the following participants:

(a) analysts and other Europol staff designated by the Director;
(b) liaison officers and/or experts from the Member States supplying the information or concerned by the analysis within the meaning of paragraph 4.

Only analysts shall be authorised to input data into the file concerned and modify such data. All participants in the analysis group may retrieve data from the file.
3. At the request of Europol or on their own initiative, national units shall, subject to Article 8(5), communicate to Europol all the information which it may require for the purpose of a particular analysis work file. Member States shall communicate such data only where processing thereof for the purposes of preventing, analysing or combating offences is also authorised by their national law. Depending on their degree of urgency, data from designated competent authorities may be routed directly to the analysis work file in accordance with Article 8(2).
4. If an analysis is of a general nature and of a strategic type, all Member States, through liaison officers and/or experts, shall be fully associated in the findings thereof, in particular through the communication of reports drawn up by Europol.
If the analysis bears on specific cases not concerning all Member States and has a direct operational aim, representatives of the following Member States shall participate therein:

(a) Member States which were the source of the information giving rise to the decision to open the analysis work file, or those which are directly concerned by that information, and Member States subsequently invited by the analysis group to take part in the analysis because they are also becoming concerned;
(b) Member States which learn from consulting the index function referred to in Article 15 that they need to be informed and assert that need to know under the conditions laid down in paragraph 5 of this Article.

5. The need to be informed may be claimed by authorised liaison officers. Each Member State shall nominate and authorise a limited number of such liaison officers.

A liaison officer shall claim the need to be informed as provided for in point (b) of the second subparagraph of paragraph 4 by means of a written reasoned statement approved by the authority to which he is subordinate in his Member State and forwarded to all the participants in the analysis. He shall then be associated automatically in the analysis in progress.
If an objection is raised in the analysis group, automatic association shall be deferred until the completion of a conciliation procedure, which shall comprise three stages as follows:

(a) the participants in the analysis shall endeavour to reach agreement with the liaison officer claiming the need to be informed. They shall have no more than eight days for that purpose;
(b) if no agreement is reached, the heads of the national units concerned and the Director shall meet within three days and try to reach agreement;
(c) if the disagreement persists, the representatives of the parties concerned on the Management Board shall meet within eight days. If the Member State concerned does not waive its need to be informed, association of that Member State shall be decided on by consensus.

6. The Member State communicating an item of data to Europol shall be the sole judge of the degree of its sensitivity and variations thereof and shall be entitled to determine the conditions for the handling of the data. Any dissemination or operational use of data communicated shall be decided on by the Member State that communicated the data to Europol. If it cannot be determined which Member State communicated the data to Europol, the decision on dissemination or operational use of data shall be taken by the participants in the analysis. A Member State or an associated expert joining an analysis in progress may not, in particular, disseminate or use the data without the prior agreement of the Member States initially concerned.
7. By way of derogation from paragraph 6, in cases in which Europol finds, after the time of inclusion of data in an analysis work file, that those data relate to a person or object on which data submitted by another Member State or third party were already input in the file, the Member State or third party concerned shall be informed immediately of the link identified, in accordance with Article 17.
8. Europol may invite experts from the entities referred to in Articles 22(1) or 23 (1) to be associated with the activities of an analysis group, where:

(a) an agreement or working arrangement such as referred to in Articles 22(2) and 23(2) which contains appropriate provisions on the exchange of information, including the transmission of personal data, and on the confidentiality of exchanged information, is in force between Europol and the entity concerned;
(b) the association of the experts from the entity is in the interest of the Member States;
(c) the entity is directly concerned by the analysis work; and
(d) all participants agree on the association of the experts from the entity with the activities of the analysis group.

Under the conditions laid down in points (b), (c) and (d) of the first subparagraph, Europol shall invite experts of the European Anti-Fraud Office to be associated with the activities of the analysis group if the analysis project concerns fraud or any other illegal activities affecting the financial interests of the European Communities.
The association of experts from an entity with the activities of an analysis group shall be subject to an arrangement between Europol and the entity. The rules governing such arrangements shall be determined by the Management Board.
Details of the arrangements between Europol and entities shall be sent to the Joint Supervisory Body, which may address any comments it deems necessary to the Management Board.

Article 15

Index function

1. An index function shall be created by Europol for the data stored in the analysis work files.
2. The Director, the Deputy Directors, duly empowered Europol staff, liaison officers and duly empowered members of national units shall have the right to access the index function. The index function shall be such that it is clear to the person using it, from the data being consulted, whether an analysis work file contains data which are of interest for the performance of the tasks of the person using the index function.
3. Access to the index function shall be defined in such a way that it is possible to determine whether or not an item of information is stored in an analysis work file, but not to establish connections or further conclusions regarding the content of the file.
4. The Management Board shall define the detailed procedures for the design of the index function, including the conditions of access to the index function, after obtaining the advice of the Joint Supervisory Body.

Article 16

Order opening an analysis work file

1. For every analysis work file, the Director shall specify in an order opening the file:

(a) the file name;
(b) the purpose of the file;
(c) the groups of persons concerning whom data are stored;
(d) the nature of the data to be stored and personal data revealing racial or ethnic origin, political opinions, religious or philosophical beliefs or trade-union membership and data concerning health or sex life which are strictly necessary;
(e) the general context leading to the decision to open the file;
(f) the participants in the analysis group at the time of opening the file;
(g) the conditions under which the personal data stored in the file may be communicated, to which recipients and under what procedure;
(h) the time limits for examination of the data and the duration of storage;
(i) the method of establishment of the audit log.

2. The Management Board and the Joint Supervisory Body shall immediately be informed by the Director of the order opening the file or any subsequent change in the particulars referred to in paragraph 1 and shall receive the dossier. The Joint Supervisory Body may address any comments it deems necessary to the Management Board. The Director may request the Joint Supervisory Body to do that within a specified period of time.
3. The analysis work file shall be retained for a maximum period of three years. Before the expiry of that three-year period, Europol shall review the need for the continuation of the file. When it is strictly necessary for the purpose of the file, the Director may order the continuation of the file for a further period of three years. The Management Board and the Joint Supervisory Body shall immediately be informed by the Director of the elements in the file justifying the strict need for its continuation. The Joint Supervisory Body shall address any comments it deems necessary to the Management Board. The Director may request the Joint Supervisory Body to do that within a specified period of time.
4. At any time the Management Board may instruct the Director to amend an opening order or to close an analysis work file. The Management Board shall decide on what date any such amendment or closure will take effect.

CHAPTER III

COMMON PROVISIONS ON INFORMATION PROCESSING

Article 17

Duty to notify

Without prejudice to Article 14(6) and (7), Europol shall promptly notify the national units and, if the national units so request, their liaison officers of any information concerning their Member State and of connections identified between criminal offences in respect of which Europol is competent under Article 4. Information and intelligence concerning other serious crime of which Europol becomes aware in the course of its duties may also be communicated.

Article 18

Provisions on control of retrievals

Europol shall establish, in cooperation with the Member States, appropriate control mechanisms to allow the verification of the legality of retrievals from any of its automated data files used to process personal data and to allow Member States access to the audit logs on request. The data thus collected shall be used only for the purpose of such verification by Europol and the supervisory bodies referred to in Articles 33 and 34 and shall be deleted after 18 months, unless the data are further required for ongoing control. The Management Board shall decide on the details of such control mechanisms after consulting the Joint Supervisory Body.

Article 19

Rules on the use of data

1. Personal data retrieved from any of Europol's data processing files or communicated by any other appropriate means shall be transmitted or used only by the competent authorities of the Member States in order to prevent and combat crimes in respect of which Europol is competent, and to prevent and combat other serious forms of crime. Europol shall use the data only for the performance of its tasks.
2. If, in the case of certain data, the communicating Member State or the communicating third State or third body stipulates particular restrictions on use to which such data is subject in that Member State, third State or third body, such restrictions shall also be complied with by the user of the data except in the specific case where national law lays down that the restrictions on use be waived for judicial authorities, legislative bodies or any other independent body set up under the law and made responsible for supervising the national competent authorities. In such cases, the data shall be used only after consultation of the communicating Member State the interests and views of which shall be taken into account as far as possible.
3. Use of the data for other purposes or by authorities other than the national competent authorities shall be possible only after consultation of the Member State which transmitted the data in so far as the national law of that Member State permits.

Article 20

Time limits for the storage and deletion of data

1. Europol shall hold data in data files only for as long as is necessary for the performance of its tasks. The need for continued storage shall be reviewed no later than three years after the input of data. Review of data stored in the Europol Information System and their deletion shall be carried out by the inputting unit. Review of data stored in other Europol data files and their deletion shall be carried out by Europol. Europol shall automatically inform the Member States three months in advance of the expiry of the time limits for reviewing the storage of data.
2. During the review, the units referred to in the third and fourth sentences of paragraph 1 may decide on the continued storage of data until the following review which shall take place after another period of three years if that is still necessary for the performance of Europol's tasks. If no decision is taken on the continued storage of data, those data shall be deleted automatically.
3. Where a Member State deletes from its national data files data communicated to Europol which are stored in other Europol data files, it shall inform Europol accordingly. In such cases, Europol shall delete the data unless it has further interest in them, based on intelligence that is more extensive than that possessed by the communicating Member State. Europol shall inform the Member State concerned of the continued storage of such data.

4. Such data shall not be deleted if this would damage the interests of a data subject who requires protection. In such cases, the data shall be used only with the consent of the data subject.

Article 21

Access to data from other information systems

In so far as Europol is entitled under Union, international or national legal instruments to gain computerised access to data from other information systems, of national or international nature, Europol may retrieve personal data by such means if that is necessary for the performance of its tasks. The applicable provisions of such Union, international or national legal instruments shall govern access to and the use of this data by Europol, in so far as they provide for stricter rules on access and use than those of this Decision.

CHAPTER IV

RELATIONS WITH PARTNERS

Article 22

Relations with Union or Community institutions, bodies, offices and agencies

1. In so far as it is relevant to the performance of its tasks, Europol may establish and maintain cooperative relations with the institutions, bodies, offices and agencies set up by, or on the basis of, the Treaty on European Union and the Treaties establishing the European Communities, in particular:

(a) Eurojust;
(b) the European Anti-Fraud Office (OLAF)[18];
(c) the European Agency for the Management of Operational Cooperation at the External Borders of the Member States of the European Union (Frontex)[19];
(d) the European Police College (CEPOL);
(e) the European Central Bank;
(f) the European Monitoring Centre for Drugs and Drug Addiction (EMCDDA).[20]

2. Europol shall conclude agreements or working arrangements with the entities referred to in paragraph 1. Such agreements or working arrangements may concern the exchange of operational, strategic or technical information, including personal data and classified information. Any such agreement or working arrangement may

[18] Commission Decision 1999/352/EC, ECSC, Euratom of 28 April 1999 establishing the European Anti-fraud Office (OLAF) (OJ L 136, 31.5.1999, p. 20

[19] Council Regulation EC) No 2007/2004 of 26 October 2004 establishing a European Agency for the Management of Operational Cooperation at the External Borders of the Member States of the European Union (OJ L 349, 25.11.2004, p. 1).

[20] Regulation (EC) No 1920/2006 of the European Parliament and of the Council of 12 December 2006 on the European Monitoring Centre for Drugs and Drug Addiction (OJ L 376, 27.12.2006, p. 1).

be concluded only after approval by the Management Board which shall previously have obtained, as far as it concerns the exchange of personal data, the opinion of the Joint Supervisory Body.
3. Before the entry into force of the agreement or working arrangement referred to in paragraph 2, Europol may directly receive and use information, including personal data, from the entities referred to in paragraph 1, in so far as that is necessary for the legitimate performance of its tasks, and it may, under the conditions laid down in Article 24(1), directly transmit information, including personal data, to such entities, in so far as that is necessary for the legitimate performance of the recipient's tasks.
4. Transmission by Europol of classified information to the entities referred to in paragraph 1 shall be permissible only in so far as agreement on confidentiality exists between Europol and the recipient.

Article 23

Relations with third States and organisations

1. In so far as it is necessary for the performance of its tasks, Europol may also establish and maintain cooperative relations with:

(a) third States;
(b) organisations such as:
(i) international organisations and their subordinate bodies governed by public law;
(ii) other bodies governed by public law which are set up by, or on the basis of, an agreement between two or more States; and
(iii) the International Criminal Police Organisation (Interpol).

2. Europol shall conclude agreements with the entities referred to in paragraph 1 which have been put on the list referred to in Article 26(1)(a). Such agreements may concern the exchange of operational, strategic or technical information, including personal data and classified information, if transmitted via a designated contact point identified by the agreement referred to in paragraph 6(b) of this Article. Such agreements may be concluded only after the approval by the Council, which shall previously have consulted the Management Board and, as far as it concerns the exchange of personal data, obtained the opinion of the Joint Supervisory Body via the Management Board.
3. Before the entry into force of the agreements referred to in paragraph 2, Europol may directly receive and use information, including personal data and classified information, in so far as that is necessary for the legitimate performance of its tasks.
4. Before the entry into force of the agreements referred to in paragraph 2, Europol may, under the conditions laid down in Article 24(1), directly transmit information other than personal data and classified information to the entities referred to in paragraph 1 of this Article, in so far as that is necessary for the legitimate performance of the recipient's tasks.

5. Europol may, under the conditions laid down in Article 24(1), directly transmit information other than personal data and classified information to the entities referred to in paragraph 1 of this Article which are not on the list referred to in Article 26(1)(a), in so far as that is absolutely necessary in individual cases for the purposes of preventing or combating criminal offences in respect of which Europol is competent.
6. Europol may, under the conditions laid down in Article 24(1), transmit to the entities referred to in paragraph 1 of this Article:

(a) personal data and classified information, where that is necessary in individual cases for the purposes of preventing or combating criminal offences in respect of which Europol is competent; and
(b) personal data, where Europol has concluded with the entity concerned an agreement as referred to in paragraph 2 of this Article which permits the transmission of such data on the basis of an assessment of the existence of an adequate level of data protection ensured by that entity.

7. Transmission by Europol of classified information to the entities referred to in paragraph 1 shall be permissible only in so far as agreement on confidentiality exists between Europol and the recipient.
8. By way of derogation from paragraphs 6 and 7 and without prejudice to Article 24(1), Europol may transmit personal data and classified information which it holds to the entities referred to in paragraph 1 of this Article where the Director considers the transmission of the data to be absolutely necessary to safeguard the essential interests of the Member States concerned within the scope of Europol's objectives or in the interests of preventing imminent danger associated with crime or terrorist offences. The Director shall in all circumstances consider the data-protection level applicable to the body in question with a view to balancing that data-protection level and those interests. The Director shall inform the Management Board and the Joint Supervisory Body as soon as possible of his or her decision and of the basis of the assessment of the adequacy of the level of data protection afforded by the entities concerned.
9. Before the transmission of personal data in accordance with paragraph 8, the Director shall assess the adequacy of the level of data protection afforded by the entities concerned, taking into account all the circumstances relevant to the transmission of personal data, in particular:

(a) the nature of the data;
(b) the purpose for which the data is intended;
(c) the duration of the intended processing;
(d) the general or specific data-protection provisions applying to the entity;
(e) whether or not the entity has agreed to specific conditions required by Europol concerning the data.

Article 24

Transmission of data

1. If the data concerned were transmitted to Europol by a Member State, Europol shall transmit them to the entities referred to in Article 22(1) and Article 23(1) only with that Member State's consent. The Member State concerned may give its prior consent, in general terms or subject to specific conditions, to such transmission. Such consent may be withdrawn at any time.
If the data were not transmitted by a Member State, Europol shall satisfy itself that transmission of those data is not liable to:

(a) obstruct the proper performance of the tasks in respect of which a Member State is competent;
(b) jeopardise the security or public order of a Member State or otherwise prejudice its general welfare.

2. Europol shall be responsible for the legality of the transmission of data. Europol shall keep a record of all transmissions of data under this Article and of the grounds for such transmissions. Data shall be transmitted only if the recipient gives an undertaking that the data will be used only for the purpose for which they were transmitted.

Article 25

Information from private parties and private persons

1. For the purpose of this Decision:

(a) "private parties" shall mean entities and bodies established under the law of a Member State or a third State, especially companies and firms, business associations, non-profit organisations and other legal persons governed by private law, which do not fall under Article 23(1);
(b) "private persons" shall mean all natural persons.

2. In so far as it is necessary for the legitimate performance of its tasks, Europol may process information, including personal data, from private parties under the conditions laid down in paragraph 3.
3. Personal data from private parties may be processed by Europol under the following conditions:

(a) Personal data from private parties which are established under the law of a Member State may be processed by Europol only if they are transmitted via the national unit of that Member State in accordance with its national law. Europol may not contact private parties in the Member States directly in order to retrieve information.
(b) Personal data from private parties which are established under the law of a third State with which Europol has, in accordance with Article 23, concluded a cooperation agreement allowing for the exchange of personal data may be transmitted to

Europol only via the contact point of that State as identified by, and in accordance with, the cooperation agreement in force.
(c) Personal data from private parties which are established under the law of a third State with which Europol has no cooperation agreement allowing for the exchange of personal data may be processed by Europol only if:

(i) the private party concerned is on the list referred to in Article 26(2); and
(ii) Europol and the private party concerned have concluded a memorandum of understanding on the transmission of information, including personal data, confirming the legality of the collection and transmission of the personal data by that private party and specifying that the personal data transmitted may be used only for the legitimate performance of Europol's tasks. Such a memorandum of understanding may be concluded only after approval by the Management Board which shall previously have obtained the opinion of the Joint Supervisory Body.

If the transmitted data affect interests of a Member State, Europol shall immediately inform the national unit of the Member State concerned.
4. In addition to the processing of data from private parties in accordance with paragraph 3, Europol may directly retrieve and process data, including personal data, from publicly available sources, such as media and public data and commercial intelligence providers, in accordance with the data-protection provisions of this Decision. In accordance with Article 17, Europol shall forward all relevant information to the national units.
5. Information, including personal data, from private persons may be processed by Europol if it is received via a national unit in accordance with national law or via the contact point of a third State with which Europol has concluded a cooperation agreement in accordance with Article 23. If Europol receives information, including personal data, from a private person residing in a third State with which Europol has no cooperation agreement, Europol may forward it only to the Member State or the third State concerned with which Europol has concluded a cooperation agreement in accordance with Article 23. Europol may not contact private persons directly in order to retrieve information.
6. Personal data transmitted to or retrieved by Europol under paragraph 3(c) of this Article may only be processed for the purpose of their inclusion in the Europol Information System referred to in Article 11 and the analysis work files referred to in Article 14 or other systems processing personal data established in accordance with Article 10(2) and (3) if those data are related to other data already entered in one of the aforementioned systems or if they are related to a previous query by a national unit within one of the aforementioned systems.
The responsibility for data processed by Europol, which have been transmitted under the conditions laid down in paragraph 3(b) and (c) and paragraph 4 of this Article, and for the information transmitted via the contact point of a third State with which Europol has concluded a cooperation agreement in accordance with Article 23, shall lie with Europol in accordance with Article 29(1)(b).
7. The Director shall submit a comprehensive report to the Management Board on the application of this Article two years after the date of application of this

Decision. On the advice of the Joint Supervisory Body or on its own initiative, the Management Board may take any measure deemed appropriate in accordance with Article 37(9)(b).

Article 26

Implementing rules governing Europol's relations

1. The Council, acting by qualified majority after consulting the European Parliament, shall:

(a) determine, in a list, the third States and organisations referred to in Article 23 (1) with which Europol shall conclude agreements. The list shall be prepared by the Management Board and reviewed when necessary; and
(b) adopt implementing rules governing the relations of Europol with the entities referred to in Articles 22(1) and 23(1), including the exchange of personal data and classified information. The implementing rules shall be prepared by the Management Board which shall previously have obtained the opinion of the Joint Supervisory Body.

2. The Management Board shall draw up and review, when necessary, a list determining the private parties with which Europol may conclude memoranda of understanding in accordance with Article 25(3)(c)(ii) and adopt rules governing the content of and the procedure for the conclusion of such memoranda of understanding after obtaining the opinion of the Joint Supervisory Body.

CHAPTER V

DATA PROTECTION AND DATA SECURITY

Article 27

Standard of data protection

Without prejudice to specific provisions of this Decision, Europol shall take account of the principles of the Council of Europe Convention for the Protection of Individuals with regard to Automatic Processing of Personal Data of 28 January 1981 and of Recommendation No R (87) 15 of the Committee of Ministers of the Council of Europe of 17 September 1987. Europol shall observe those principles in the processing of personal data, inter alia, in respect of automated and non-automated data held in the form of data files, especially any structured set of personal data accessible in accordance with specific criteria.

Article 28

Data Protection Officer

1. The Management Board shall appoint, on the proposal of the Director, a Data Protection Officer who shall be a member of the staff. In the performance of his or her duties, he or she shall act independently.
2. The Data Protection Officer shall in particular have the following tasks:

(a) ensuring, in an independent manner, lawfulness and compliance with the provisions of this Decision concerning the processing of personal data, including the processing of personal data relating to Europol staff;
(b) ensuring that a written record of the transmission and receipt of personal data is kept in accordance with this Decision;
(c) ensuring that data subjects are informed of their rights under this Decision at their request;
(d) cooperating with Europol staff responsible for procedures, training and advice on data processing;
(e) cooperating with the Joint Supervisory Body;
(f) preparing an annual report and communicating that report to the Management Board and to the Joint Supervisory Body.

3. In the performance of his or her tasks, the Data Protection Officer shall have access to all the data processed by Europol and to all Europol premises.
4. If the Data Protection Officer considers that the provisions of this Decision concerning the processing of personal data have not been complied with, he or she shall inform the Director, requiring him or her to resolve the non-compliance within a specified time.
If the Director does not resolve the non-compliance of the processing within the specified time, the Data Protection Officer shall inform the Management Board and shall agree with the Management Board a specified time for a response.
If the Management Board does not resolve the non-compliance of the processing within the specified time, the Data Protection Officer shall refer the matter to the Joint Supervisory Body.
5. The Management Board shall adopt further implementing rules concerning the Data Protection Officer. Those implementing rules shall in particular concern selection and dismissal, tasks, duties and powers and safeguards for the independence of the Data Protection Officer.

Article 29

Responsibility in data protection matters

1. The responsibility for data processed at Europol, in particular as regards the legality of the collection, the transmission to Europol and the input of data, as well as their accuracy, their up-to-date nature and verification of the storage time limits, shall lie with:

(a) the Member State which input or otherwise communicated the data;
(b) Europol in respect of data communicated to Europol by third parties, including data communicated by private parties in accordance with Article 25(3)(b) and (c) and Article 25(4) as well as data communicated via the contact point of a third State with which Europol has concluded a cooperation agreement in accordance with Article 23 or which result from analyses conducted by Europol.

2. Data which have been transmitted to Europol but have not yet been input in one of Europol's data files shall remain under the data-protection responsibility of the

party transmitting the data. Europol shall, however, be responsible for ensuring the security of the data in accordance with Article 35(2) in that until such data have been input in a data file, they may be accessed only by authorised Europol staff for the purpose of determining whether they can be processed at Europol, or by authorised officials of the party which supplied the data. If Europol, after appraising them, has reason to assume that data supplied are inaccurate or no longer up-to-date, it shall inform the party which supplied the data.
3. In addition, subject to other provisions in this Decision, Europol shall be responsible for all data processed by it.
4. If Europol has evidence that data input into one of its systems referred to in Chapter II are factually incorrect or have been unlawfully stored, it shall inform the Member State or other party involved accordingly.
5. Europol shall store data in such a way that it can be established by which Member State or third party they were transmitted or whether they are the result of an analysis by Europol.

Article 30

Individual's right of access

1. Any person shall be entitled, at reasonable intervals, to obtain information on whether personal data relating to him or her are processed by Europol and to have such data communicated to him or her in an intelligible form, or checked, in all cases under the conditions laid down in this Article.
2. Any person wishing to exercise his or her rights under this Article may make a request to that effect without excessive costs in the Member State of his or her choice to the authority appointed for that purpose in that Member State. That authority shall refer the request to Europol without delay, and in any case within one month of receipt.
3. The request shall be answered by Europol without undue delay and in any case within three months of its receipt by Europol in accordance with this Article.
4. Europol shall consult the competent authorities of the Member States concerned before deciding on its response to a request under paragraph 1. A decision on access to data shall be conditional upon close cooperation between Europol and the Member States directly concerned by the communication of such data. In any case in which a Member State objects to Europol's proposed response, it shall notify Europol of the reasons for its objection.
5. The provision of information in response to a request under paragraph 1 shall be refused to the extent that such refusal is necessary to:

(a) enable Europol to fulfil its tasks properly;
(b) protect security and public order in the Member States or to prevent crime;
(c) guarantee that any national investigation will not be jeopardised;
(d) protect the rights and freedoms of third parties.

When the applicability of an exemption is assessed, the interests of the person concerned shall be taken into account.

6. If the provision of information in response to a request under paragraph 1 is refused, Europol shall notify the person concerned that it has carried out checks, without giving any information which might reveal to him or her whether or not personal data concerning him or her are processed by Europol.
7. Any person shall have the right to request the Joint Supervisory Body, at reasonable intervals, to check whether the manner in which his or her personal data have been collected, stored, processed and used by Europol is in compliance with the provisions of this Decision concerning the processing of personal data. The Joint Supervisory Body shall notify the person concerned that it has carried out checks, without giving any information which might reveal to him or her whether or not personal data concerning him or her are processed by Europol.

Article 31

Data subject's right to correction and deletion of data

1. Any person shall have the right to ask Europol to correct or delete incorrect data concerning him or her. If it emerges, either on the basis of the exercise of this right or otherwise, that data held by Europol which have been communicated to it by third parties or which are the result of its own analyses are incorrect or that their input or storage is in breach of this Decision, Europol shall correct or delete such data.
2. If data that are incorrect or processed in breach of this Decision were transmitted directly to Europol by Member States, the Member States concerned shall correct or delete such data in collaboration with Europol.
3. If incorrect data were transmitted by another appropriate means or if the errors in the data supplied by Member States are due to faulty transmission or were transmitted in breach of this Decision or if they result from their being input, taken over or stored in an incorrect manner or in breach of this Decision by Europol, Europol shall correct or delete the data in collaboration with the Member States concerned.
4. In the cases referred to in paragraphs 1, 2 and 3, the Member States or third parties which have received the data shall be notified forthwith. The recipient Member States and the third parties shall also correct or delete those data. Where deletion is not possible, the data shall be blocked to prevent any future processing.
5. The data subject making the request shall be informed by Europol in writing without undue delay and in any case within three months that data concerning him or her have been corrected or deleted.

Article 32

Appeals

1. In its reply to a request for a check, for access to data, or for correction and deletion of data, Europol shall inform the person making the request that if he or she is not satisfied with the decision, he or she may appeal to the Joint Supervisory Body. Such person may also refer the matter to the Joint Supervisory Body if there has been no response to his or her request within the time limit laid down in Article 30 or 31.

2. If the person making the request lodges an appeal to the Joint Supervisory Body, the appeal shall be examined by that body.
3. Where an appeal relates to a decision as referred to in Article 30 or 31, the Joint Supervisory Body shall consult the national supervisory bodies or the competent judicial body in the Member State which was the source of the data or the Member State directly concerned. The decision of the Joint Supervisory Body, which may extend to a refusal to communicate any information, shall be taken in close cooperation with the national supervisory body or competent judicial body.
4. Where an appeal relates to access to data input by Europol in the Europol Information System or data stored in the analysis work files or in any other system established by Europol for the processing of personal data pursuant to Article 10 and where objections from Europol persist, the Joint Supervisory Body shall be able to overrule such objections only by a majority of two thirds of its members after having heard Europol and the Member State or Member States referred to in Article 30(4). If there is no such majority, the Joint Supervisory Body shall notify the person making the request of the refusal, without giving any information which might reveal the existence of any personal data concerning that person.
5. Where an appeal relates to the checking of data input by a Member State in the Europol Information System or of data stored in the analysis work files or in any other system established by Europol for the processing of personal data pursuant to Article 10, the Joint Supervisory Body shall ensure that the necessary checks have been carried out correctly in close cooperation with the national supervisory body of the Member State which has input the data. The Joint Supervisory Body shall notify the person making the request that it has carried out the checks, without giving any information which might reveal the existence of any personal data concerning that person.
6. Where an appeal relates to the checking of data input by Europol in the Europol Information System or of data stored in the analysis work files or in any other system established by Europol for the processing of personal data pursuant to Article 10, the Joint Supervisory Body shall ensure that the necessary checks have been carried out by Europol. The Joint Supervisory Body shall notify the person making the request that it has carried out the checks, without giving any information which might reveal the existence of any personal data concerning that person.

Article 33

National supervisory body

1. Each Member State shall designate a national supervisory body with the task to monitor independently, in accordance with its national law, the permissibility of the input, the retrieval and any communication to Europol of personal data by the Member State concerned and to examine whether such input, retrieval or communication violates the rights of the data subject. For that purpose, the national supervisory body shall have access, at the national unit or at liaison officers' premises, to the data input by the Member State in the Europol Information System

or in any other system established by Europol for the processing of personal data pursuant to Article 10 in accordance with the relevant national procedures.
For the purpose of exercising their supervisory function, national supervisory bodies shall have access to the offices and documents of their respective liaison officers at Europol.
In addition, in accordance with the relevant national procedures, the national supervisory bodies shall supervise the activities of national units and the activities of liaison officers, in so far as such activities are of relevance to the protection of personal data. They shall also keep the Joint Supervisory Body informed of any actions they take with respect to Europol.
2. Any person shall have the right to request the national supervisory body to ensure that the input or communication to Europol of data concerning him or her in any form and the consultation of the data by the Member State concerned are lawful.
This right shall be exercised in accordance with the national law of the Member State in which the request is made.

Article 34

Joint Supervisory Body

1. An independent Joint Supervisory Body shall be set up to review, in accordance with this Decision, the activities of Europol in order to ensure that the rights of the individual are not violated by the storage, processing and use of the data held by Europol. In addition, the Joint Supervisory Body shall monitor the permissibility of the transmission of data originating from Europol. The Joint Supervisory Body shall be composed of a maximum of two members or representatives, where appropriate assisted by alternates, of each of the independent national supervisory bodies, having the necessary abilities and appointed for five years by each Member State. Each delegation shall be entitled to one vote.
The Joint Supervisory Body shall choose a chairman from among its members.
In the performance of their duties, the members of the Joint Supervisory Body shall not receive instructions from any other body.
2. Europol shall assist the Joint Supervisory Body in the performance of the latter's tasks. In doing so, it shall in particular:

(a) supply the information the Joint Supervisory Body requests and give it access to all documents and paper files as well as to the data stored in its data files;
(b) allow the Joint Supervisory Body free access at all times to all its premises;
(c) implement the Joint Supervisory Body's decisions on appeals.

3. The Joint Supervisory Body shall be competent to examine questions relating to implementation and interpretation in connection with Europol's activities as regards the processing and use of personal data, to examine questions relating to checks carried out independently by the national supervisory bodies of the Member States or relating to the exercise of the right of access, and to draw up harmonised proposals for common solutions to existing problems.

4. If the Joint Supervisory Body identifies any violations of the provisions of this Decision in the storage, processing or use of personal data, it shall make any complaints it deems necessary to the Director and shall request him to reply within a specified time limit. The Director shall keep the Management Board informed of the entire procedure. If it is not satisfied with the response given by the Director to its request, the Joint Supervisory Body shall refer the matter to the Management Board.
5. For the fulfilment of its tasks and to contribute to the improvement of consistency in the application of the rules and procedures for data processing, the Joint Supervisory Body shall cooperate as necessary with other supervisory authorities.
6. The Joint Supervisory Body shall draw up activity reports at regular intervals. Such reports shall be forwarded to the European Parliament and to the Council. The Management Board shall have the opportunity to make comments, which shall be attached to the reports.
The Joint Supervisory Body shall decide whether or not to publish its activity report, and, if it decides to do so, shall determine how it should be published.
7. The Joint Supervisory Body shall adopt its rules of procedure by a majority of two thirds of its members and shall submit them to the Council for approval. The Council shall act by qualified majority.
8. The Joint Supervisory Body shall set up an internal committee comprising one qualified representative from each Member State with the right to vote. The committee shall have the task of examining the appeals provided for in Article 32 by all appropriate means. Should they so request, the parties, assisted by their advisers if they so wish, shall be heard by the committee. The decisions taken in this context shall be final as regards all the parties concerned.
9. The Joint Supervisory Body may set up one or more other committees in addition to the one referred to in paragraph 8.
10. The Joint Supervisory Body shall be consulted on that part of Europol's budget which concerns it. Its opinion shall be annexed to the draft budget in question.
11. The Joint Supervisory Body shall be assisted by a secretariat, the tasks of which shall be defined in the rules of procedure.

Article 35

Data security

1. Europol shall take the necessary technical and organisational measures to ensure the implementation of this Decision. Measures shall be considered necessary where the effort they involve is proportionate to the objective they are designed to achieve in terms of protection.
2. In respect of automated data processing at Europol, each Member State and Europol shall implement measures designed to:

(a) deny unauthorised persons access to data-processing equipment used for processing personal data (equipment access control);
(b) prevent the unauthorised reading, copying, modification or removal of data media (data media control);

(c) prevent the unauthorised input of data and the unauthorised inspection, modification or deletion of stored personal data (storage control);
(d) prevent the use of automated data-processing systems by unauthorised persons using data-communication equipment (user control);
(e) ensure that persons authorised to use an automated data-processing system have access only to the data covered by their access authorisation (data access control);
(f) ensure that it is possible to verify and establish to which bodies personal data may be or have been transmitted using data communication equipment (communication control);
(g) ensure that it is possible to verify and establish which personal data have been input into automated data-processing systems and when and by whom the data were input (input control);
(h) prevent the unauthorised reading, copying, modification or deletion of personal data during transfers of personal data or during the transportation of data media (transport control);
(i) ensure that installed systems may, in the event of interruption, be restored immediately (recovery);
(j) ensure that the functions of the system perform without fault, that the appearance of faults in the functions is immediately reported (reliability) and that stored data cannot be corrupted by system malfunctions (integrity).

(. . .)

CHAPTER VII

CONFIDENTIALITY ISSUES

Article 40

Confidentiality

1. Europol and the Member States shall take appropriate measures to protect information subject to the requirement of confidentiality which is obtained by or exchanged with Europol pursuant to this Decision. To that end the Council, acting by qualified majority after consulting the European Parliament, shall adopt appropriate rules on confidentiality prepared by the Management Board. Those rules shall include provisions concerning the cases in which Europol may exchange information subject to the requirement of confidentiality with third parties.
2. Where Europol intends to entrust persons with a sensitive activity, Member States shall undertake to arrange, at the request of the Director, for security screening of their own nationals to be carried out in accordance with their national provisions and to provide each other with mutual assistance for that purpose. The relevant authority under national provisions shall inform Europol only of the results of the security screening. Those results shall be binding on Europol.
3. Each Member State and Europol may entrust the processing of data at Europol only to those persons who have had special training and undergone security screening. The Management Board shall adopt rules for the security clearance of

Europol staff. The Director shall regularly inform the Management Board on the state of security screening of Europol staff.

Article 41

Obligation of discretion and confidentiality

1. The members of the Management Board, the Director, the Deputy Directors, employees of Europol and liaison officers shall refrain from any action and any expression of opinion which might be harmful to Europol or prejudice its activities.
2. The members of the Management Board, the Director, the Deputy Directors, employees of Europol and liaison officers, as well as any other person under a particular obligation of discretion or confidentiality, shall be bound not to disclose any facts or information which come to their knowledge in the performance of their duties or the exercise of their activities to any unauthorised person or to the public. This shall not apply to facts or information too insignificant to require confidentiality. The obligation of discretion and confidentiality shall apply even after the termination of office or employment, or after the termination of activities. Notification of the particular obligation referred to in the first sentence shall be given by Europol together with a warning of the legal consequences of any infringement. A written record shall be drawn up of such notification.
3. The members of the Management Board, the Director, the Deputy Directors, employees of Europol and liaison officers, as well as other persons under the obligation provided for in paragraph 2, shall not give evidence in or outside a court or make any statements on any facts or information which come to their knowledge in the performance of their duties or the exercise of their activities without reference to the Director or, in the case of the Director himself, to the Management Board.
The Management Board or the Director, depending on the case, shall approach the judicial body or any other competent body with a view to ensuring that the necessary measures under the national law applicable to the body approached are taken.
Such measures may either be to adjust the procedures for giving evidence in order to ensure the confidentiality of the information or, provided that the national law concerned so permits, to refuse to make any communication concerning data in so far as it is vital for the protection of the interests of Europol or of a Member State.
Where a Member State's legislation provides for the right to refuse to give evidence, persons referred to in paragraph 2 asked to give evidence shall be required to obtain permission to do so. Permission shall be granted by the Director or, in the case of evidence to be given by the Director, by the Management Board.
Where a liaison officer is asked to give evidence concerning information he receives from Europol, such permission shall be given after the agreement of the Member State responsible for the officer concerned has been obtained. The obligation to seek permission to give evidence shall apply even after the termination of office or employment or after the termination of activities.

Furthermore, if the possibility exists that the evidence may extend to information and knowledge which a Member State has communicated to Europol or which clearly involves a Member State, the position of that Member State concerning the evidence shall be sought before permission is granted.
Permission to give evidence may be refused only in so far as that is necessary to protect the overriding interests of Europol or of a Member State or Member States that need protection.
4. Each Member State shall treat any infringement of the obligation of discretion or confidentiality laid down in paragraphs 2 and 3 as a breach of the obligations imposed by its law on official or professional secrets or its provisions for the protection of classified material.
It shall ensure that the rules and provisions concerned also apply to its own employees who have contact with Europol in the course of their work.

(. . .)

CHAPTER IX

MISCELLANEOUS PROVISIONS

Article 45

Rules concerning access to Europol documents

On the basis of a proposal by the Director, and not later than six months after the date of application of this Decision, the Management Board shall adopt rules concerning access to Europol documents, taking into account the principles and limits set out in Regulation (EC) No 1049/2001 of the European Parliament and of the Council of 30 May 2001 regarding public access to European Parliament, Council and Commission documents.[21]

Article 46

EU classified information

Europol shall apply the security principles and minimum standards set out in Council Decision 2001/264/EC of 19 March 2001 adopting the Council's security regulations[22] regarding EU classified information.

(. . .)

Article 48

Informing the European Parliament

The Presidency of the Council, the Chairperson of the Management Board and the Director shall appear before the European Parliament at its request to discuss

[21] OJ L 145, 31.5.2001, p. 43.
[22] OJ L 101, 11.4.2001, p. 1.

matters relating to Europol taking into account the obligations of discretion and confidentiality.

Article 49

Combating fraud

The rules laid down by Regulation (EC) No 1073/1999 of the European Parliament and of the Council of 25 May 1999 concerning investigations conducted by the European Anti-Fraud Office (OLAF)[23] shall apply to Europol. On the basis of the proposal by the Director, and not later than six months after the date of application of this Decision, the Management Board shall adopt the implementing measures necessary, which may exclude operational data from the scope of OLAF's investigations.

(. . .)

Article 52

Liability for unauthorised or incorrect data processing

1. Each Member State shall be liable, in accordance with its national law, for any damage caused to an individual as a result of legal or factual errors in data stored or processed at Europol. Only the Member State in which the event which gave rise to the damage occurred shall be the subject of an action for compensation on the part of the injured party, who shall apply to the courts having jurisdiction under the national law of the Member State concerned. A Member State may not plead that another Member State or Europol had transmitted inaccurate data in order to avoid its liability under its national legislation vis-à-vis an injured party.
2. If the legal or factual errors referred to in paragraph 1 occurred as a result of the erroneous communication of data or of failure to comply with the obligations laid down in this Decision on the part of one or more Member States or as a result of unauthorised or incorrect storage or processing by Europol, Europol or the other Member State in question shall be bound to reimburse, on request, for the amounts paid as compensation pursuant to paragraph 1 unless the data were used in breach of this Decision by the Member State in the territory of which the damage was caused.
3. Any dispute between the Member State that has paid the compensation pursuant to paragraph 1 and Europol or another Member State over the principle or the amount of the reimbursement shall be referred to the Management Board, which shall settle the matter by a majority of two thirds of its members.

(. . .)

[23] OJ L 136, 31.5.1999, p. 1.

Article 54

Liability with regard to Europol's participationin joint investigation teams

1. The Member State in the territory of which damage is caused by Europol staff operating in accordance with Article 6 in that Member State during their assistance in operational measures shall make good such damage under the conditions applicable to damage caused by its own officials.
2. Unless otherwise agreed by the Member State concerned, Europol shall reimburse in full any sums that that Member State has paid to the victims or persons entitled on their behalf for damage referred to in paragraph 1. Any dispute between that Member State and Europol over the principle or the amount of the reimbursement shall be referred to the Management Board, which shall settle the matter.

(. . .)

CHAPTER XI

FINAL PROVISIONS

Article 61

Transposition

The Member States shall ensure that their national law conforms to this Decision by the date of application of this Decision.

Article 62

Replacement

This Decision replaces the Europol Convention and the Protocol on the privileges and immunities of Europol, the members of its organs, the Deputy Directors and employees of Europol as of the date of application of this Decision.

Article 63

Repeal

Unless otherwise provided in this Decision, all measures implementing the Europol Convention shall be repealed with effect from the date of application of this Decision.

Article 64

Entry into force and application

1. This Decision shall enter into force on the 20th day following its publication in the Official Journal of the European Union.
2. It shall apply from 1 January 2010 or the date of application of the Regulation referred to in Article 51(1), whichever is the later.
However, the second subparagraph of Article 57(2) and Articles 59, 60 and 61 shall apply from the date of entry into force of this Decision.

Done at Luxembourg, 6 April 2009.
For the Council
The President

ANNEX

List of other forms of serious crime which Europol is competent to deal with in accordance with Article 4(1):

- unlawful drug trafficking,
- illegal money-laundering activities,
- crime connected with nuclear and radioactive substances,
- illegal immigrant smuggling,
- trafficking in human beings,
- motor vehicle crime,
- murder, grievous bodily injury,
- illicit trade in human organs and tissue,
- kidnapping, illegal restraint and hostage taking,
- racism and xenophobia,
- organised robbery,
- illicit trafficking in cultural goods, including antiquities and works of art,
- swindling and fraud,
- racketeering and extortion,
- counterfeiting and product piracy,
- forgery of administrative documents and trafficking therein,
- forgery of money and means of payment,
- computer crime,
- corruption,
- illicit trafficking in arms, ammunition and explosives,
- illicit trafficking in endangered animal species,
- illicit trafficking in endangered plant species and varieties,
- environmental crime,
- illicit trafficking in hormonal substances and other growth promoters.

With regard to the forms of crime listed in Article 4(1) for the purposes of this Decision:

(a) "crime connected with nuclear and radioactive substances" means the criminal offences listed in Article 7(1) of the Convention on the Physical Protection of Nuclear Material, signed at Vienna and New York on 3 March 1980, and relating to the nuclear and/or radioactive materials defined in Article 197 of the Treaty establishing the European Atomic Community and in Council Directive 96/29/

Euratom of 13 May 1996 laying down basic safety standards for the protection of the health of workers and the general public against the dangers arising from ionizing radiation[24];
(b) "illegal immigrant smuggling" means activities intended deliberately to facilitate, for financial gain, the entry into, residence or employment in the territory of the Member States, contrary to the rules and conditions applicable in the Member States;
(c) "trafficking in human beings" means the recruitment, transportation, transfer, harbouring or receipt of persons, by means of the threat or use of force or other forms of coercion, of abduction, of fraud, of deception, of the abuse of power or of a position of vulnerability or of the giving or receiving of payments or benefits to achieve the consent of a person having control over another person, for the purpose of exploitation. Exploitation shall include, as a minimum, the exploitation of the prostitution of others or other forms of sexual exploitation, the production, sale or distribution of child-pornography material, forced labour or services, slavery or practices similar to slavery, servitude or the removal of organs;
(d) "motor vehicle crime" means the theft or misappropriation of motor vehicles, lorries, semi-trailers, the loads of lorries or semi-trailers, buses, motorcycles, caravans and agricultural vehicles, works vehicles and the spare parts for such vehicles, and the receiving and concealing of such objects;
(e) "illegal money-laundering activities" means the criminal offences listed in Article 6(1) to (3) of the Council of Europe Convention on Laundering, Search, Seizure and Confiscation of the Proceeds from Crime, signed in Strasbourg on 8 November 1990;
(f) "unlawful drug trafficking" means the criminal offences listed in Article 3(1) of the United Nations Convention of 20 December 1988 against Illicit Traffic in Narcotic Drugs and Psychotropic Substances and in the provisions amending or replacing that Convention.

The forms of crime referred to in Article 4 and in this Annex shall be assessed by the competent authorities of the Member States in accordance with the law of the Member States to which they belong.

[24] OJ L 159, 29.6.1996, p. 1.

3. 1999/352/EC, ECSC, Euratom: Commission Decision of 28 April 1999 establishing the European Anti-Fraud Office (OLAF), as amended by Council Decision 2013/478/EU of 27 September 2013

Article 1

Establishment of the Office

A European Anti-fraud Office (OLAF), hereinafter referred to as "the Office", is hereby established.

Article 2

Tasks of the Office

1. The Office shall exercise the Commission's powers to carry out external administrative investigations for the purpose of strengthening the fight against fraud, corruption and any other illegal activity adversely affecting the Union's financial interests, as well as any other act or activity by operators in breach of Union's provisions.
The Office shall be responsible for carrying out internal administrative investigations intended:

(a) to combat fraud, corruption and any other illegal activity adversely affecting the Community's financial interests,
(b) to investigate serious facts linked to the performance of professional activities which may constitute a breach of obligations by officials and servants of the Communities likely to lead to disciplinary and, in appropriate cases, criminal proceedings or an analogous breach of obligations by Members of the institutions and bodies, heads of the bodies or members of staff of the institutions and bodies not subject to the Staff Regulations of Officials of the European Communities and the Conditions of Employment of Other Servants of the Communities.

The Office shall exercise the Commission's powers as they are defined in the provisions established in the framework of the Treaties, and subject to the limits and conditions laid down therein.
The Office may be entrusted with investigations in other areas by the Commission or by the other institutions or bodies.
2. The Office shall be responsible for providing the Commission's support in cooperating with the Member States in the area of the fight against fraud. This includes support to improve the protection of the euro against counterfeiting through training and technical assistance.
3. The Office shall be responsible for the activity of developing a concept for the fight against fraud as referred to in paragraph 1. This may include taking part in the

activities of international bodies and associations specialised in the fight against fraud and corruption for the purpose, in particular, of exchanging best practices.
4. The Office shall be responsible for the preparation of legislative and regulatory initiatives of the Commission with the objective of fraud prevention as referred to in paragraph 1, and on the protection of the euro against counterfeiting.
5. The Office shall be responsible for any other operational activity of the Commission in relation to the fight against fraud as referred to in paragraph 1, and in particular:

(a) developing the necessary infrastructure;
(b) ensuring the collection and analysis of information;
(c) giving technical support, in particular in the area of training, to the other institutions or bodies as well as to the competent national authorities.

6. The Office shall be in direct contact with the police and judicial authorities.
7. The Office shall represent the Commission, at service level, in the forums concerned, in the fields covered by this Article.

Article 3

Independence of the investigative function

The Office shall exercise the powers of investigation referred to in Article 2(1) in complete independence. In exercising these powers, the Director-General of the Office shall neither seek nor take instructions from the Commission, any government or any other institution or body.

Article 4

Supervisory Committee

A Supervisory Committee shall be established, the composition and powers of which shall be laid down by the Community legislature. This Committee shall be responsible for the regular monitoring of the discharge by the Office of its investigative function.

Article 5

Director-General

1. The Office shall be headed by a Director-General. The Director-General shall be appointed by the Commission, in accordance with the procedure specified in paragraph 2. The term of office of the Director-General shall be seven years and shall not be renewable.
The Director General shall be responsible for the Office's conduction of investigations.
2. In order to appoint a new Director-General, the Commission shall publish a call for applications in the Official Journal of the European Union. Such publication shall take place at the latest six months before the end of the term of office of the Director-General in office. After a favourable opinion has been given by the Supervisory Committee on the selection procedure applied by the Commission,

the Commission shall draw up a list of suitably qualified candidates. After consultations with the European Parliament and the Council, the Commission shall appoint the Director-General.

3. The Commission shall exercise, with regard to the Director-General, the powers conferred on the appointing authority. Any decision on initiating disciplinary proceedings against the Director-General under Article 3, paragraph 1, point (c) of Annex IX to the Staff Regulations shall be taken by reasoned decision of the Commission, after consulting the Supervisory Committee. The decision shall be communicated for information to the European Parliament, the Council and the Supervisory Committee.

Article 6

Operation of the Office

1. The Director of the Office shall exercise, with regard to the staff of the Office, the powers of the appointing authority and of the authority empowered to conclude contracts of employment delegated to him. He shall be permitted to sub-delegate those powers. In accordance with the Conditions of Employment of Other Servants, he shall lay down the conditions and detailed arrangements for recruitment, in particular as to the length of contracts and their renewal.

2. After consulting the Supervisory Committee, the Director-General shall send the Director-General for budgets a preliminary draft budget to be entered in the annex concerning the Office to the Commission section of the general budget of the European Union.

3. Director-General shall act as authorising officer for implementation of the appropriations entered in the annex concerning the Office to the Commission section of the general budget of the European Union and the appropriations entered under the anti-fraud budget headings for which powers are delegated to him in the internal rules on implementation of the general budget. He shall be permitted to sub-delegate his powers to staff members subject to the Staff Regulations of Officials or Conditions of Employment of Other Servants in accordance with the abovementioned internal rules.

4. Commission decisions concerning its internal organisation shall apply to the Office in so far as they are compatible with the provisions concerning the Office adopted by the Community legislator, with this Decision and with the detailed rules implementing it.

Article 7

Effective date

This Decision shall take effect on the date of the entry into force of the European Parliament and Council Regulation (EC) concerning investigations carried out by the European Anti-fraud Office.

Done at Brussels, 28 April 1999.
For the Commission
The President

3.bis. Regulation (EU, EURATOM) No 883/2013 of 11 September concerning investigations conducted by the European Anti-Fraud Office (OLAF) and repealing Regulation (EC) No 1073/1999 of the European Parliament and of the Council and Council Regulation (Euratom) No 1074/1999

See Position (EU) No 2/2013 of the Council at first reading, adopted by the Council on 26 February 2013, Commission Statements, and Statement by the European Parliament, the Council and the Commission at OJ C 89E, 27.03.2013, p. 1.

THE EUROPEAN PARLIAMENT AND THE COUNCIL OF THE EUROPEAN UNION,

(...)

HAVE ADOPTED THIS REGULATION:

Article 1

Objectives and tasks

1. In order to step up the fight against fraud, corruption and any other illegal activity affecting the financial interests of the European Union and of the European Atomic Energy Community (hereinafter referred to collectively, when the context so requires, as "the Union"), the European Anti-Fraud Office established by Decision 1999/352/EC, ECSC, Euratom ("the Office") shall exercise the powers of investigation conferred on the Commission by:

   (a) the relevant Union acts; and
   (b) the relevant cooperation and mutual assistance agreements concluded by the Union with third countries and international organisations.

2. The Office shall provide the Member States with assistance from the Commission in organising close and regular cooperation between their competent authorities in order to coordinate their action aimed at protecting the financial interests of the Union against fraud. The Office shall contribute to the design and development of methods of preventing and combating fraud, corruption and any other illegal activity affecting the financial interests of the Union. The Office shall promote and coordinate, with and among the Member States, the sharing of operational experience and best procedural practices in the field of the protection of the financial interests of the Union, and shall support joint anti-fraud actions undertaken by Member States on a voluntary basis.
3. This Regulation shall apply without prejudice to:

   (a) Protocol (No 7) on the privileges and immunities of the European Union attached to the Treaty on European Union and to the Treaty on the Functioning of the European Union;

(b) the Statute for Members of the European Parliament;
(c) the Staff Regulations;
(d) Regulation (EC) No 45/2001.

4. Within the institutions, bodies, offices and agencies established by, or on the basis of, the Treaties ("institutions, bodies, offices and agencies"), the Office shall conduct administrative investigations for the purpose of fighting fraud, corruption and any other illegal activity affecting the financial interests of the Union. To that end, it shall investigate serious matters relating to the discharge of professional duties constituting a dereliction of the obligations of officials and other servants of the Union liable to result in disciplinary or, as the case may be, criminal proceedings, or an equivalent failure to discharge obligations on the part of members of institutions and bodies, heads of offices and agencies or staff members of institutions, bodies, offices or agencies not subject to the Staff Regulations (hereinafter collectively referred to as "officials, other servants, members of institutions or bodies, heads of offices or agencies, or staff members").
5. For the application of this Regulation, competent authorities of the Member States and institutions, bodies, offices or agencies may establish administrative arrangements with the Office. Those administrative arrangements may concern, in particular, the transmission of information and the conduct of investigations.

Article 2

Definitions

For the purposes of this Regulation:

(1) "financial interests of the Union" shall include revenues, expenditures and assets covered by the budget of the European Union and those covered by the budgets of the institutions, bodies, offices and agencies and the budgets managed and monitored by them;
(2) "irregularity" shall mean "irregularity" as defined in Article 1(2) of Regulation (EC, Euratom) No 2988/95;
(3) "fraud, corruption and any other illegal activity affecting the financial interests of the Union" shall have the meaning applied to those words in the relevant Union acts;
(4) "administrative investigations" ("investigations") shall mean any inspection, check or other measure undertaken by the Office in accordance with Articles 3 and 4, with a view to achieving the objectives set out in Article 1 and to establishing, where necessary, the irregular nature of the activities under investigation; those investigations shall not affect the powers of the competent authorities of the Member States to initiate criminal proceedings;
(5) "person concerned" shall mean any person or economic operator suspected of having committed fraud, corruption or any other illegal activity affecting the financial interests of the Union and who is therefore subject to investigation by the Office;
(6) "economic operator" shall have the meaning applied to that term by Regulation (EC, Euratom) No 2988/95 and Regulation (Euratom, EC) No 2185/96;

(7) "administrative arrangements" shall mean arrangements of a technical and/or operational nature concluded by the Office, which may in particular aim at facilitating the cooperation and the exchange of information between the parties thereto, and which do not create additional legal obligations.

Article 3

External investigations

1. The Office shall exercise the power conferred on the Commission by Regulation (Euratom, EC) No 2185/96 to carry out on-the-spot checks and inspections in the Member States and, in accordance with the cooperation and mutual assistance agreements and any other legal instrument in force, in third countries and on the premises of international organisations.
   As part of its investigative function, the Office shall carry out the checks and inspections provided for in Article 9(1) of Regulation (EC, Euratom) No 2988/95 and in the sectoral rules referred to in Article 9(2) of that Regulation in the Member States and, in accordance with the cooperation and mutual assistance agreements and any other legal instrument in force, in third countries and on the premises of international organisations.
2. With a view to establishing whether there has been fraud, corruption or any other illegal activity affecting the financial interests of the Union in connection with a grant agreement or decision or a contract concerning Union funding, the Office may, in accordance with the provisions and procedures laid down by Regulation (Euratom, EC) No 2185/96, conduct on-the-spot checks and inspections on economic operators.
3. During on-the-spot checks and inspections, the staff of the Office shall act, subject to the Union law applicable, in compliance with the rules and practices of the Member State concerned and with the procedural guarantees provided for in this Regulation.
   At the request of the Office, the competent authority of the Member State concerned shall provide the staff of the Office with the assistance needed in order to carry out their tasks effectively, as specified in the written authorisation referred to in Article 7(2). If that assistance requires authorisation from a judicial authority in accordance with national rules, such authorisation shall be applied for.
   The Member State concerned shall ensure, in accordance with Regulation (Euratom, EC) No 2185/96, that the staff of the Office are allowed access, under the same terms and conditions as its competent authorities and in compliance with its national law, to all information and documents relating to the matter under investigation which prove necessary in order for the on-the-spot checks and inspections to be carried out effectively and efficiently.
4. Member States shall, for the purposes of this Regulation, designate a service ("the anti-fraud coordination service") to facilitate effective cooperation and exchange of information, including information of an operational nature, with the Office. Where appropriate, in accordance with national law, the anti-fraud

coordination service may be regarded as a competent authority for the purposes of this Regulation.

5. During an external investigation, the Office may have access to any relevant information, including information in databases, held by the institutions, bodies, offices and agencies, connected with the matter under investigation, where necessary in order to establish whether there has been fraud, corruption or any other illegal activity affecting the financial interests of the Union. For that purpose Article 4(2) and (4) shall apply.
6. Where, before a decision has been taken whether or not to open an external investigation, the Office handles information which suggests that there has been fraud, corruption or any other illegal activity affecting the financial interests of the Union, it may inform the competent authorities of the Member States concerned and, where necessary, the competent Commission services.

   Without prejudice to the sectoral rules referred to in Article 9(2) of Regulation (EC, Euratom) No 2988/95, the competent authorities of the Member States concerned shall ensure that appropriate action is taken, in which the Office may take part, in compliance with national law. Upon request, the competent authorities of the Member States concerned shall inform the Office of the action taken and of their findings on the basis of information as referred to in the first subparagraph of this paragraph.

(. . .)

Article 5. Opening of investigations

1. The Director-General may open an investigation when there is a sufficient suspicion, which may also be based on information provided by any third party or anonymous information, that there has been fraud, corruption or any other illegal activity affecting the financial interests of the Union. The decision by the Director-General whether or not to open an investigation shall take into account the investigation policy priorities and the annual management plan of the Office established in accordance with Article 17(5). That decision shall also take into account the need for efficient use of the Office's resources and for proportionality of the means employed. With regard to internal investigations, specific account shall be taken of the institution, body, office or agency best placed to conduct them, based, in particular, on the nature of the facts, the actual or potential financial impact of the case, and the likelihood of any judicial follow-up.
2. The decision to open an external investigation shall be taken by the Director-General, acting on his own initiative or following a request from a Member State concerned or any institution, body, office or agency of the Union.

   The decision to open an internal investigation shall be taken by the Director-General, acting on his own initiative or following a request from the institution, body, office or agency within which the investigation is to be conducted or from a Member State.

3. While the Director-General is considering whether or not to open an internal investigation following a request as referred to in paragraph 2, and/or while the Office is conducting an internal investigation, the institutions, bodies, offices or agencies concerned shall not open a parallel investigation into the same facts, unless agreed otherwise with the Office.
4. Within two months of receipt by the Office of a request as referred to in paragraph 2, a decision whether or not to open an investigation shall be taken. It shall be communicated without delay to the Member State, institution, body, office or agency which made the request. Reasons shall be given for a decision not to open an investigation. If, on the expiry of that period of two months, the Office has not taken any decision, the Office shall be deemed to have decided not to open an investigation.

   Where an official, other servant, member of an institution or body, head of office or agency, or staff member, acting in accordance with Article 22a of the Staff Regulations, provides information to the Office relating to a suspected fraud or irregularity, the Office shall inform that person of the decision whether or not to open an investigation in relation to the facts in question.
5. If the Director-General decides not to open an internal investigation, he may without delay send any relevant information to the institution, body, office or agency concerned for appropriate action to be taken in accordance with the rules applicable to that institution, body, office or agency. The Office shall agree with that institution, body, office or agency, if appropriate, on suitable measures to protect the confidentiality of the source of that information and shall, if necessary, ask to be informed of the action taken.
6. If the Director-General decides not to open an external investigation, he may without delay send any relevant information to the competent authorities of the Member State concerned for action to be taken where appropriate, in accordance with its national rules. Where necessary, the Office shall also inform the institution, body, office or agency concerned.

Article 6

Access to information in databases prior to the opening of an investigation

1. Prior to the opening of an investigation, the Office shall have the right of access to any relevant information in databases held by the institutions, bodies, offices or agencies when this is indispensable in order to assess the basis in fact of allegations. That right of access shall be exercised within the time-limit, to be set by the Office, required for a prompt assessment of the allegations. In exercising that right of access, the Office shall respect the principles of necessity and proportionality.
2. The institution, body, office or agency concerned shall sincerely cooperate by allowing the Office to obtain any relevant information under conditions to be specified in the decisions adopted under Article 4(1).

Article 7

Investigations procedure

1. The Director-General shall direct the conduct of investigations on the basis, where appropriate, of written instructions. Investigations shall be conducted under his direction by the staff of the Office designated by him.
2. The staff of the Office shall carry out their tasks on production of a written authorisation showing their identity and their capacity. The Director-General shall issue such authorisation indicating the subject matter and the purpose of the investigation, the legal bases for conducting the investigation and the investigative powers stemming from those bases.
3. The competent authorities of the Member States shall, in conformity with national rules, give the necessary assistance to enable the staff of the Office to fulfil their tasks effectively.

   The institutions, bodies, offices and agencies shall ensure that their officials, other servants, members, heads and staff members provide the necessary assistance to enable the staff of the Office to fulfil their tasks effectively.
4. Where an investigation combines external and internal elements, Articles 3 and 4 shall apply respectively.
5. Investigations shall be conducted continuously over a period which must be proportionate to the circumstances and complexity of the case.
6. Where investigations show that it might be appropriate to take precautionary administrative measures to protect the financial interests of the Union, the Office shall without delay inform the institution, body, office or agency concerned of the investigation in progress. The information supplied shall include the following:

   (a) the identity of the official, other servant, member of an institution or body, head of office or agency, or staff member concerned and a summary of the facts in question;
   (b) any information that could assist the institution, body, office or agency concerned in deciding whether it is appropriate to take precautionary administrative measures in order to protect the financial interests of the Union;
   (c) any special measures of confidentiality recommended, in particular in cases entailing the use of investigative measures falling within the competence of a national judicial authority or, in the case of an external investigation, within the competence of a national authority, in accordance with the national rules applicable to investigations.

   The institution, body, office or agency concerned may at any time decide to take, in close cooperation with the Office, any appropriate precautionary measures, including measures for the safeguarding of evidence, and shall inform the Office without delay of such decision.
7. Where necessary, it shall be for the competent authorities of the Member States, at the Office's request, to take the appropriate precautionary measures under their national law, in particular measures for the safeguarding of evidence.

8. If an investigation cannot be closed within 12 months after it has been opened, the Director-General shall, at the expiry of that 12-month period and every six months thereafter, report to the Supervisory Committee, indicating the reasons and the remedial measures envisaged with a view to speeding up the investigation.

Article 8

Duty to inform the Office

1. The institutions, bodies, offices and agencies shall transmit to the Office without delay any information relating to possible cases of fraud, corruption or any other illegal activity affecting the financial interests of the Union.
2. The institutions, bodies, offices and agencies and, in so far as their national law allows, the competent authorities of the Member States shall, at the request of the Office or on their own initiative, transmit to the Office any document or information they hold which relates to an ongoing investigation by the Office.
3. The institutions, bodies, offices and agencies and, in so far as their national law allows, the competent authorities of the Member States shall transmit to the Office any other document or information considered pertinent which they hold relating to the fight against fraud, corruption and any other illegal activity affecting the financial interests of the Union.

Article 9

Procedural guarantees

1. In its investigations the Office shall seek evidence for and against the person concerned. Investigations shall be conducted objectively and impartially and in accordance with the principle of the presumption of innocence and with the procedural guarantees set out in this Article.
2. The Office may interview a person concerned or a witness at any time during an investigation. Any person interviewed shall have the right to avoid self-incrimination.

   The invitation to an interview shall be sent to a person concerned with at least 10 working days' notice. That notice period may be shortened with the express consent of the person concerned or on duly reasoned grounds of urgency of the investigation. In the latter case, the notice period shall not be less than 24 hours. The invitation shall include a list of the rights of the person concerned, in particular the right to be assisted by a person of his choice.

   The invitation to an interview shall be sent to a witness with at least 24 hours' notice. That notice period may be shortened with the express consent of the witness or on duly reasoned grounds of urgency of the investigation.

   The requirements referred to in the second and third subparagraphs shall not apply to the taking of statements in the context of on-the-spot checks and inspections.

   Where, in the course of an interview, evidence emerges that a witness may be a person concerned, the interview shall be ended. The procedural rules provided for in this paragraph and in paragraphs 3 and 4 shall immediately apply. That witness shall be informed forthwith of his rights as a person concerned and shall receive, upon request, a copy of the records of any statements made by him in the past. The Office may not use that person's past statements against him without giving him first the opportunity to comment on those statements.

The Office shall draw up a record of the interview and give the person interviewed access to it so that the person interviewed may either approve the record or add observations. The Office shall give the person concerned a copy of the record of the interview.

3. As soon as an investigation reveals that an official, other servant, member of an institution or body, head of office or agency, or staff member may be a person concerned, that official, other servant, member of an institution or body, head of office or agency, or staff member shall be informed to that effect, provided that this does not prejudice the conduct of the investigation or of any investigative proceedings falling within the remit of a national judicial authority.
4. Without prejudice to Articles 4(6) and 7(6), once the investigation has been completed and before conclusions referring by name to a person concerned are drawn up, that person shall be given the opportunity to comment on facts concerning him.

   To that end, the Office shall send the person concerned an invitation to comment either in writing or at an interview with staff designated by the Office. That invitation shall include a summary of the facts concerning the person concerned and the information required by Articles 11 and 12 of Regulation (EC) No 45/2001, and shall indicate the time-limit for submitting comments, which shall not be less than 10 working days from receipt of the invitation to comment. That notice period may be shortened with the express consent of the person concerned or on duly reasoned grounds of urgency of the investigation. The final investigation report shall make reference to any such comments.

   In duly justified cases where it is necessary to preserve the confidentiality of the investigation and/or entailing the use of investigative proceedings falling within the remit of a national judicial authority, the Director-General may decide to defer the fulfilment of the obligation to invite the person concerned to comment.

   In cases referred to in Article 1(2) of Annex IX to the Staff Regulations, failure on the part of the institution, body, office or agency to respond within one month to the request of the Director-General for deferral of the fulfilment of the obligation to invite the person concerned to comment shall be deemed to constitute a reply in the affirmative.
5. Any person interviewed shall be entitled to use any of the official languages of the institutions of the Union. However, officials or other servants of the Union may be required to use an official language of the institutions of the Union of which they have a thorough knowledge.

Article 10

Confidentiality and data protection

1. Information transmitted or obtained in the course of external investigations, in whatever form, shall be protected by the relevant provisions.
2. Information transmitted or obtained in the course of internal investigations, in whatever form, shall be subject to professional secrecy and shall enjoy the protection afforded by the rules applicable to the Union institutions.
3. The institutions, bodies, offices or agencies concerned shall ensure that the confidentiality of the investigations conducted by the Office is respected, together with the legitimate rights of the persons concerned, and, where judicial proceedings have been initiated, that all national rules applicable to such proceedings have been adhered to.
4. The Office may designate a Data Protection Officer in accordance with Article 24 of Regulation (EC) No 45/2001.
5. The Director-General shall ensure that any information provided to the public is given neutrally and impartially, and that its disclosure respects the confidentiality of investigations and complies with the prnciples set out in this Article and in Article 9(1).

   In accordance with the Staff Regulations, staff of the Office shall refrain from any unauthorised disclosure of information received in the line of duty, unless that information has already been made public or is accessible to the public, and shall continue to be bound by that obligation after leaving the service.

Article 11

Investigation report and action to be taken following investigations

1. On completion of an investigation by the Office, a report shall be drawn up, under the authority of the Director-General. That report shall give an account of the legal basis for the investigation, the procedural steps followed, the facts established and their preliminary classification in law, the estimated financial impact of the facts established, the respect of the procedural guarantees in accordance with Article 9 and the conclusions of the investigation.

   The report shall be accompanied by recommendations of the Director-General on whether or not action should be taken. Those recommendations shall, where appropriate, indicate any disciplinary, administrative, financial and/or judicial action by the institutions, bodies, offices and agencies and by the competent authorities of the Member States concerned, and shall specify in particular the estimated amounts to be recovered, as well as the preliminary classification in law of the facts established.
2. In drawing up such reports and recommendations, account shall be taken of the national law of the Member State concerned. Reports drawn up on that basis shall constitute admissible evidence in administrative or judicial proceedings of the Member State in which their use proves necessary, in the same way and under the same conditions as administrative reports drawn up by national administrative inspectors. They shall be subject to the same evaluation rules as

those applicable to administrative reports drawn up by national administrative inspectors and shall have the same evidentiary value as such reports.

3. Reports and recommendations drawn up following an external investigation and any relevant related documents shall be sent to the competent authorities of the Member States concerned in accordance with the rules relating to external investigations and, if necessary, to the competent Commission services.
4. Reports and recommendations drawn up following an internal investigation and any relevant related documents shall be sent to the institution, body, office or agency concerned. That institution, body, office or agency shall take such action, in particular of a disciplinary or legal nature, as the results of the internal investigation warrant, and shall report thereon to the Office, within a time-limit laid down in the recommendations accompanying the report, and, in addition, at the request of the Office.
5. Where the report drawn up following an internal investigation reveals the existence of facts which could give rise to criminal proceedings, that information shall be transmitted to the judicial authorities of the Member State concerned.
6. At the request of the Office, the competent authorities of the Member States concerned shall, in due time, send to the Office information on action taken, if any, following the transmission by the Director-General of his recommendations in accordance with paragraph 3, and following the transmission by the Office of any information in accordance with paragraph 5.
7. Without prejudice to paragraph 4, if, on completion of an investigation, no evidence has been found against the person concerned, the Director-General shall close the investigation regarding that person and inform that person within 10 working days.
8. Where an informant who has provided the Office with information leading or relating to an investigation so requests, the Office may notify that informant that the investigation has been closed. The Office may, however, refuse any such request if it considers that it is such as to prejudice the legitimate interests of the person concerned, the effectiveness of the investigation and of the action to be taken subsequent thereto, or any confidentiality requirements.

Article 12

Exchange of information between the Office and the competent authorities of the Member States

1. Without prejudice to Articles 10 and 11 of this Regulation and to the provisions of Regulation (Euratom, EC) No 2185/96, the Office may transmit to the competent authorities of the Member States concerned information obtained in the course of external investigations in due time to enable them to take appropriate action in accordance with their national law.
2. Without prejudice to Articles 10 and 11, the Director-General shall transmit to the judicial authorities of the Member State concerned information obtained by the Office, in the course of internal investigations, concerning facts which fall within the jurisdiction of a national judicial authority.

In accordance with Article 4 and without prejudice to Article 10, the Director-General shall also transmit to the institution, body, office or agency concerned the information referred to in the first subparagraph of this paragraph, including the identity of the person concerned, a summary of the facts established, their preliminary classification in law and the estimated impact on the financial interests of the Union.

Article 9(4) shall apply.

3. The competent authorities of the Member State concerned shall, without prejudice to their national law, inform the Office in due time, on their own initiative or at the request of the Office, of the action taken on the basis of the information transmitted to them under this Article.
4. The Office may provide evidence in proceedings before national courts and tribunals in conformity with national law and the Staff Regulations.

Article 13

Cooperation of the Office with Eurojust and Europol

1. Within its mandate to protect the financial interests of the Union, the Office shall cooperate, as appropriate, with Eurojust and with the European Police Office (Europol). Where necessary in order to facilitate that cooperation, the Office shall agree with Eurojust and Europol on administrative arrangements. Such working arrangements may concern exchange of operational, strategic or technical information, including personal data and classified information and, on request, progress reports.

   Where this may support and strengthen coordination and cooperation between national investigating and prosecuting authorities, or where the Office has forwarded to the competent authorities of the Member States information giving grounds for suspecting the existence of fraud, corruption or any other illegal activity affecting the financial interests of the Union in the form of serious crime, it shall transmit relevant information to Eurojust, within the mandate of Eurojust.
2. The competent authorities of the Member States concerned shall be informed, in a timely manner, by the Office in cases where information provided by them is transmitted by the Office to Eurojust or Europol.

Article 14

Cooperation with third countries and international organisations

1. Administrative arrangements may be agreed, as appropriate, by the Office with competent authorities in third countries and with international organisations. The Office shall coordinate its action as appropriate with the competent Commission services and with the European External Action Service, in particular before agreeing such arrangements. Such arrangements may concern exchange of operational, strategic or technical information, including, on request, progress reports.

2. The Office shall inform the competent authorities of the Member States concerned before information provided by them is transmitted by the Office to competent authorities in third countries or to international organisations.

   The Office shall keep a record of all transmissions of personal data, including the grounds for such transmissions, in accordance with Regulation (EC) No 45/2001.

(. . .)

4. Council Decision 2000/642/JHA of 17 October 2000 concerning arrangements for cooperation between Financial Intelligence Units of the Member States in respect of exchanging information

Article 1

1. Member States shall ensure that FIUs, set up or designated to receive disclosures of financial information for the purpose of combating money laundering shall cooperate to assemble, analyse and investigate relevant information within the FIU on any fact which might be an indication of money laundering in accordance with their national powers.

2. For the purposes of paragraph 1, Member States shall ensure that FIUs exchange, spontaneously or on request and either in accordance with this Decision or in accordance with existing or future memoranda of understanding, any available information that may be relevant to the processing or analysis of information or to investigation by the FIU regarding financial transactions related to money laundering and the natural or legal persons involved.

3. Where a Member State has designated a police authority as its FIU, it may supply information held by that FIU to be exchanged pursuant to this Decision to an authority of the receiving Member State designated for that purpose and being competent in the areas mentioned in paragraph 1.

Article 2

1. Member States shall ensure that, for the purposes of this Decision, FIUs shall be a single unit for each Member State and shall correspond to the following definition:

'Acentral, national unit which, in order to combat money laundering, is responsible for receiving (and to the extent permitted, requesting), analysing and disseminating to the competent authorities, disclosures of financial information which concern suspected proceeds of crime or are required by national legislation or regulation'.

2. In the context of paragraph 1, a Member State may establish a central unit for the purpose of receiving or transmitting information to or from decentralised agencies.

3. Member States shall indicate the unit which is an FIU within the meaning of this Article. They shall notify this information to the General Secretariat of the Council in writing. This notification does not affect the current relations concerning cooperation between the FIUs.

Article 3

Member States shall ensure that the performance of the functions of the FIUs under this Decision shall not be affected by their internal status, regardless of whether they are administrative, law enforcement or judicial authorities.

Article 4

1. Each request made under this Decision shall be accompanied by a brief statement of the relevant facts known to the requesting FIU. The FIU shall specify in the request how the information sought will be used.

2. When a request is made in accordance with this Decision, the requested FIU shall provide all relevant information, including available financial information and requested law enforcement data, sought in the request, without the need for a formal letter of request under applicable conventions or agreements between Member States.

3. An FIU may refuse to divulge information which could lead to impairment of a criminal investigation being conducted in the requested Member State or, in exceptional circumstances, where divulgation of the information would be clearly disproportionate to the legitimate interests of a natural or legal person or the Member State concerned or would otherwise not be in accordance with fundamental principles of national law. Any such refusal shall be appropriately explained to the FIU requesting the information.

Article 5

1. Information or documents obtained under this Decision are intended to be used for the purposes laid down in Article 1(1).

2. When transmitting information or documents pursuant to this Decision, the transmitting FIU may impose restrictions and conditions on the use of information for purposes other than those stipulated in paragraph 1. The receiving FIU shall comply with any such restrictions and conditions.

3. Where a Member State wishes to use transmitted information or documents for criminal investigations or prosecutions for the purposes laid down in Article 1(1), the transmitting Member State may not refuse its consent to such use unless it does so on the basis of restrictions under its national law or conditions referred to in Article 4(3). Any refusal to grant consent shall be appropriately explained.

4. FIUs shall undertake all necessary measures, including security measures, to ensure that information submitted under this Decision is not accessible by any other authorities, agencies or departments.

5. The information submitted will be protected, in conformity with the Council of Europe Convention of 28 January 1981 for the Protection of Individuals with regard to Automatic Processing of Personal Data and taking account of Recommendation No R(87)15 of 15 September 1987 of the Council of Europe Regulating the Use of Personal Data in the Police Sector, by at least the same rules of confidentiality and protection of personal data as those that apply under the national legislation applicable to the requesting FIU.

Article 6

1. FIUs may, within the limits of the applicable national law and without a request to that effect, exchange relevant information.

2. Article 5 shall apply in relation to information forwarded under this Article.

Article 7

Member States shall provide for, and agree on, appropriate and protected channels of communication between FIUs.

Article 8

This Decision shall be implemented without prejudice to the Member States' obligations towards Europol, as they have been laid down in the Europol Convention.

5. Council Decision 2007/845/JHA of 6 December 2007 concerning cooperation between Asset Recovery Offices of the Member States in the field of tracing and identification of proceeds from, and other properties related to, crime.

Article 1
Asset Recovery Offices

1. Each Member State shall set up or designate a national Asset Recovery Office, for the purposes of the facilitation of the tracing and identification of proceeds of crime and other crime related property which may become the object of a freezing, seizure or confiscation order made by a competent judicial authority in the course of criminal or, as far as possible under the national law of the Member State concerned, civil proceedings.
2. Without prejudice to paragraph 1, a Member State may, in conformity with its national law, set up or designate two Asset Recovery Offices. Where a Member State has more than two authorities charged with the facilitation of the tracing and identification of proceeds of crime, it shall nominate a maximum of two of its Asset Recovery Offices as contact point(s).
3. Member States shall indicate the authorities which are the national Asset Recovery Offices within the meaning of this Article. They shall notify this information and any subsequent changes to the General Secretariat of the Council in writing. This notification shall not preclude other authorities which are charged with the facilitation of the tracing and identification of proceeds of crime from exchanging information under Articles 3 and 4 with an Asset Recovery Office of another Member State.

Article 2
Cooperation between Asset Recovery Offices

1. Member States shall ensure that their Asset Recovery Offices cooperate with each other for the purposes set out in Article 1(1), by exchanging information and best practices, both upon request and spontaneously.
2. Member States shall ensure that this cooperation is not hampered by the status of the Asset Recovery Offices under national law, regardless of whether they form part of an administrative, law enforcement or a judicial authority.

Article 3
Exchange of information between Asset Recovery Offices on request

1. An Asset Recovery Office of a Member State or other authorities in a Member State charged with the facilitation of the tracing and identification of proceeds of crime may make a request to an Asset Recovery Office of another Member State for information for the purposes set out in Article 1(1). To that end it shall rely on Framework Decision 2006/960/JHA and on the rules adopted in implementation thereof.

2. When filling out the form provided for under Framework Decision 2006/960/JHA, the requesting Asset Recovery Office shall specify the object of and the reasons for the request and the nature of the proceedings. It shall also provide details on property targeted or sought (bank accounts, real estate, cars, yachts and other high value items) and/or the natural or legal persons presumed to be involved (e.g. names, addresses, dates and places of birth, date of registration, shareholders, headquarters). Such details shall be as precise as possible.

Article 4
Spontaneous exchange of information between Asset Recovery Offices

1. Asset Recovery Offices or other authorities charged with the facilitation of the tracing and identification of proceeds of crime may, within the limits of the applicable national law and without a request to that effect, exchange information which they consider necessary for the execution of the tasks of another Asset Recovery Office in pursuance of purpose set out in Article 1(1).
2. Article 3 shall apply to the exchange of information under this Article *mutatis mutandis*.

Article 5
Data protection

1. Each Member State shall ensure that the established rules on data protection are applied also within the procedure on exchange of information provided for by this Decision.
2. The use of information which has been exchanged directly or bilaterally under this Decision shall be subject to the national data protection provisions of the receiving Member State, where the information shall be subject to the same data protection rules as if they had been gathered in the receiving Member State. The personal data processed in the context of the application of this Decision shall be protected in accordance with the Council of Europe Convention of 28 January 1981 for the Protection of Individuals with regard to Automatic Processing of Personal Data, and, for those Member States which have ratified it, the Additional Protocol of 8 November 2001 to that Convention, regarding Supervisory Authorities and Transborder Data Flows. The principles of Recommendation No R(87) 15 of the Council of Europe Regulating the Use of Personal Data in the Police Sector should also be taken into account when law enforcement authorities handle personal data obtained under this Decision.

Article 6
Exchange of best practices
Member States shall ensure that the Asset Recovery Offices shall exchange best practices concerning ways to improve the effectiveness of Member States' efforts in tracing and identifying proceeds from, and other property related to, crime which may become the object of a freezing, seizure or confiscation order by a competent judicial authority.

6. Council Regulation (EU) No 904/2010 of 7 October 2010 on administrative cooperation and combating fraud in the field of value added tax

CHAPTER X
EUROFISC

Article 33

1. In order to promote and facilitate multilateral cooperation in the fight against VAT fraud, this Chapter establishes a network for the swift exchange of targeted information between Member States hereinafter called 'Eurofisc'.
2. Within the framework of Eurofisc, Member States shall:

(a) establish a multilateral early warning mechanism for combating VAT fraud;
(b) coordinate the swift multilateral exchange of targeted information in the subject areas in which Eurofisc will operate (hereinafter 'Eurofisc working fields');
(c) coordinate the work of the Eurofisc liaison officials of the participating Member States in acting on warnings received.

Article 34

1. Member States shall participate in the Eurofisc working fields of their choice and may also decide to terminate their participation therein.
2. Member States having chosen to take part in a Eurofisc working field shall actively participate in the multilateral exchange of targeted information between all participating Member States.
3. Information exchanged shall be confidential, as provided for in Article 55.

Article 35

The Commission shall provide Eurofisc with technical and logistical support. The Commission shall not have access to the information referred to in Article 1, which may be exchanged over Eurofisc.

Article 36

1. The competent authorities of each Member State shall designate at least one Eurofisc liaison official. Eurofisc liaison officials shall be competent officials within the meaning of Article 2(1)(c) and shall carry out the activities referred to in Article 33(2). They shall remain answerable only to their national administrations.
2. The liaison officials of the Member States participating in a particular Eurofisc working field (hereinafter 'participating Eurofisc liaison officials') shall designate a coordinator (hereinafter 'Eurofisc working field coordinator'), among the participating Eurofisc liaison officials, for a limited period of time. Eurofisc working field coordinators shall:

(a) collate the information received from the participating Eurofisc liaison officials and make all information available to the other participating Eurofisc liaison officials. The information shall be exchanged by electronic means;
(b) ensure that the information received from the participating Eurofisc liaison officials is processed, as agreed by the participants in the working field, and make the result available to the participating Eurofisc liaison officials;
(c) provide feedback to the participating Eurofisc liaison officials.

Article 37

Eurofisc working field coordinators shall submit an annual report of the activities of all working fields to the Committee referred to in Article 58(1).

7. Council Decision 2008/976/JHA of 16 December 2008 on the European Judicial Network

Article 1
Creation
The network of judicial contact points set up between the Member States under Joint Action 98/428/JHA, hereinafter referred to as the 'European Judicial Network', shall continue to operate in accordance with the provisions of this Decision.

Article 2
Composition

1. The European Judicial Network shall be made up, taking into account the constitutional rules, legal traditions and internal structure of each Member State, of the central authorities responsible for international judicial cooperation and the judicial or other competent authorities with specific responsibilities within the context of international cooperation.
2. One or more contact points of each Member State shall be established in accordance with its internal rules and internal division of responsibilities, care being taken to ensure effective coverage of the whole of its territory.
3. Each Member State shall appoint, among the contact points, a national correspondent for the European Judicial Network.
4. Each Member State shall appoint a tool correspondent for the European Judicial Network.
5. Each Member State shall ensure that its contact points have functions in relation to judicial cooperation in criminal matters and adequate knowledge of a language of the European Union other than its own national language, bearing in mind the need to be able to communicate with the contact points in the other Member States.
6. Where the liaison magistrates referred to in Council Joint Action 96/277/JHA of 22 April 1996 concerning a framework for the exchange of liaison magistrates to improve judicial cooperation between the Member States of the European Union (1) have been appointed in a Member State and have duties analogous to those assigned by Article 4 of this Decision to the contact points, they shall be linked to the European Judicial Network and to the secure telecommunications connection pursuant to Article 9 of this Decision by the Member State appointing the liaison magistrate in each case, in accordance with the procedures to be laid down by that Member State.
7. The Commission shall designate a contact point for those areas falling within its sphere of competence.
8. The European Judicial Network shall have a Secretariat which shall be responsible for the administration of the Network.

Article 3
Manner of operation of the Network
The European Judicial Network shall operate in particular in the following three ways:

(a) it shall facilitate the establishment of appropriate contacts between the contact points in the various Member States in order to carry out the functions laid down in Article 4;
(b) it shall organise periodic meetings of the Member States representatives in accordance with the procedures laid down in Articles 5 and 6;
(c) it shall constantly provide a certain amount of up-to-date background information, in particular by means of an appropriate telecommunications network, under the procedures laid down in Articles 7, 8 and 9.

Article 4
Functions of contact points

1. The contact points shall be active intermediaries with the task of facilitating judicial cooperation between Member States, particularly in actions to combat forms of serious crime. They shall be available to enable local judicial authorities and other competent authorities in their own Member State, contact points in the other Member States and local judicial and other competent authorities in the other Member States to establish the most appropriate direct contacts. They may if necessary travel to meet other Member States contact points, on the basis of an agreement between the administrations concerned.
2. The contact points shall provide the local judicial authorities in their own Member State, the contact points in the other Member States and the local judicial authorities in the other Member States with the legal and practical information necessary to enable them to prepare an effective request for judicial cooperation or to improve judicial cooperation in general.
3. At their respective level the contact points shall be involved in and promote the organisation of training sessions on judicial cooperation for the benefit of the competent authorities of their Member State, where appropriate in cooperation with the European Judicial Training Network.
4. The national correspondent, in addition to his tasks as a contact point referred to in paragraphs 1 to 3, shall in particular:

(a) be responsible, in his Member State, for issues related to the internal functioning of the Network, including the coordination of requests for information and replies issued by the competent national authorities;
(b) be the main person responsible for the contacts with the Secretariat of the European Judicial Network including the participation in the meetings referred to in Article 6;
(c) where requested, give an opinion concerning the appointment of new contact points.

5. The European Judicial Network tool correspondent, who may also be a contact point referred to in paragraphs 1 to 4, shall ensure that the information related to his Member State and referred to in Article 7 is provided and updated in accordance with Article 8.

Article 5
Purposes and venues of the plenary meetings of contact points

1. The purposes of the plenary meetings of the European Judicial Network, to which at least three contact points per Member State shall be invited, shall be as follows:

(a) to allow the contact points to get to know each other and exchange experience, particularly concerning the operation of the Network;
(b) to provide a forum for discussion of practical and legal problems encountered by the Member States in the context of judicial cooperation, in particular with regard to the implementation of measures adopted by the European Union.

2. The relevant experience acquired within the European Judicial Network shall be passed on to the Council and the Commission to serve as a basis for discussion of possible legislative changes and practical improvements in the area of international judicial cooperation.
3. Meetings referred to in paragraph 1 shall be organised regularly and at least three times a year. Once a year, the meeting may be held on the premises of the Council in Brussels or on the premises of Eurojust in The Hague. Two contact points per Member States shall be invited to meetings organised on the premises of the Council and at Eurojust. Other meetings may be held in the Member States, to enable the contact points of all the Member States to meet authorities of the host Member State other than its contact points and visit specific bodies in that Member State with responsibilities in the context of international judicial cooperation or of combating certain forms of serious crime. The contact points participate in these meetings at their own expense.

Article 6
Meetings of the correspondents

1. The European Judicial Network national correspondents shall meet on an *ad hoc* basis, at least once a year and as its members deem appropriate, at the invitation of the national correspondent of the Member State which holds the Presidency of the Council, which shall also take account of the Member States wishes for the correspondents to meet. During these meetings, administrative matters related to the Network shall in particular be discussed.
2. The European Judicial Network tool correspondents shall meet on an *ad hoc* basis, at least once a year and as its members deem appropriate, at the invitation of the tool correspondent of the Member State which holds the Presidency of the Council. The meetings shall deal with the issues referred to in Article 4(5).

Article 7

Content of the information disseminated within the European Judicial Network

The Secretariat of the European Judicial Network shall make the following information available to contact points and competent judicial authorities:

(a) full details of the contact points in each Member State with, where necessary, an explanation of their responsibilities at national level;
(b) an information technology tool allowing the requesting or issuing authority of a Member State to identify the competent authority in another Member State to receive and execute its request for, and decisions on, judicial cooperation, including regarding instruments giving effect to the principle of mutual recognition;
(c) concise legal and practical information concerning the judicial and procedural systems in the Member States;
(d) the texts of the relevant legal instruments and, for conventions currently in force, the texts of declarations and reservations.

Article 8

Updating of information

1. The information distributed within the European Judicial Network shall be constantly updated.
2. It shall be each Member State's individual responsibility to check the accuracy of the data contained in the system and to inform the Secretariat of the European Judicial Network as soon as data on one of the four points referred to in Article 7 need to be amended.

Article 9

Telecommunication tools

1. The Secretariat of the European Judicial Network shall ensure that the information provided under Article 7 is made available on a website which is constantly updated.
2. The secure telecommunications connection shall be set up for the operational work of the contact points of the European Judicial Network. The setting up of the secure telecommunications connection shall be at the charge of the general budget of the European Union. The setting up of the secure telecommunications connection shall make possible the flow of data and of requests for judicial cooperation between Member States.
3. The secure telecommunications connection referred to in paragraph 2 may also be used for their operational work by the national correspondents for Eurojust, national correspondents for Eurojust for terrorist matters, the national members of Eurojust and liaison magistrates appointed by Eurojust. It may be linked to the Case Management System of Eurojust referred to in Article 16 of Decision 2002/187/JHA.
4. Nothing in this Article shall be construed to affect direct contacts between competent judicial authorities as provided for in instruments on judicial

cooperation, such as Article 6 of the Convention on Mutual Assistance in Criminal Matters between the Member States of the European Union.

Article 10
Relationship between the European Judicial Network and Eurojust
The European Judicial Network and Eurojust shall maintain privileged relations with each other, based on consultation and complementarity, especially between the contact points of a Member State, the Eurojust national member of the same Member State and the national correspondents for the European Judicial Network and Eurojust. In order to ensure efficient cooperation, the following measures shall be taken:

(a) the European Judicial Network shall make available to Eurojust the centralised information indicated in Article 7 and the secure telecommunications connection set up under Article 9;
(b) the contact points of the European Judicial Network shall, on a case-by-case basis, inform their own national member of all cases which they deem Eurojust to be in a better position to deal with;
(c) the national members of Eurojust may attend meetings of the European Judicial Network at the invitation of the latter.

D. EU INFORMATION SYSTEMS, DATABASES AND CHANNELS FOR THE EXCHANGE OF INFORMATION

1. Council Decision 2008/615/JHA on the stepping up of cross-border cooperation, particularly in combating terrorism and cross-border crime

Article 1
Aim and scope
By means of this Decision, the Member States intend to step up cross-border cooperation in matters covered by Title VI of the Treaty, particularly the exchange of information between authorities responsible for the prevention and investigation of criminal offences. To this end, this Decision contains rules in the following areas:

(a) provisions on the conditions and procedure for the automated transfer of DNA profiles, dactyloscopic data and certain national vehicle registration data (Chapter 2);
(b) provisions on the conditions for the supply of data in connection with major events with a cross-border dimension (Chapter 3);
(c) provisions on the conditions for the supply of information in order to prevent terrorist offences (Chapter 4);
(d) provisions on the conditions and procedure for stepping up cross-border police cooperation through various measures (Chapter 5).

CHAPTER 2

ONLINE ACCESS AND FOLLOW-UP REQUESTS

SECTION 1

DNA profiles

Article 2

Establishment of national DNA analysis files

1. Member States shall open and keep national DNA analysis files for the investigation of criminal offences. Processing of data kept in those files, under this

Á.G. Zarza (ed.), *Exchange of Information and Data Protection in Cross-border Criminal Proceedings in Europe*, DOI 10.1007/978-3-642-40291-3,

Decision, shall be carried out in accordance with this Decision, in compliance with the national law applicable to the processing.
2. For the purpose of implementing this Decision, the Member States shall ensure the availability of reference data from their national DNA analysis files as referred to in the first sentence of paragraph 1. Reference data shall only include DNA profiles established from the non-coding part of DNA and a reference number. Reference data shall not contain any data from which the data subject can be directly identified. Reference data which is not attributed to any individual (unidentified DNA profiles) shall be recognisable as such.
3. Each Member State shall inform the General Secretariat of the Council of the national DNA analysis files to which Articles 2 to 6 apply and the conditions for automated searching as referred to in Article 3(1) in accordance with Article 36.

Article 3
Automated searching of DNA profiles

1. For the investigation of criminal offences, Member States shall allow other Member States' national contact points as referred to in Article 6, access to the reference data in their DNA analysis files, with the power to conduct automated searches by comparing DNA profiles. Searches may be conducted only in individual cases and in compliance with the requesting Member State's national law.
2. Should an automated search show that a DNA profile supplied matches DNA profiles entered in the receiving Member State's searched file, the national contact point of the searching Member State shall receive in an automated way the reference data with which a match has been found. If no match can be found, automated notification of this shall be given.

Article 4
Automated comparison of DNA profiles

1. For the investigation of criminal offences, the Member States shall, by mutual consent, via their national contact points, compare the DNA profiles of their unidentified DNA profiles with all DNA profiles from other national DNA analysis files' reference data. Profiles shall be supplied and compared in automated form. Unidentified DNA profiles shall be supplied for comparison only where provided for under the requesting Member State's national law.
2. Should a Member State, as a result of the comparison referred to in paragraph 1, find that any DNA profiles supplied match any of those in its DNA analysis files, it shall, without delay, supply the other Member State's national contact point with the reference data with which a match has been found.

Article 5
Supply of further personal data and other information
Should the procedures referred to in Articles 3 and 4 show a match between DNA profiles, the supply of further available personal data and other information relating to the reference data shall be governed by the national law, including the legal assistance rules, of the requested Member State.

Article 6
National contact point and implementing measures

1. For the purposes of the supply of data as referred to in Articles 3 and 4, each Member State shall designate a national contact point. The powers of the national contact points shall be governed by the applicable national law.
2. Details of technical arrangements for the procedures set out in Articles 3 and 4 shall be laid down in the implementing measures as referred to in Article 33.

Article 7
Collection of cellular material and supply of DNA profiles
Where, in ongoing investigations or criminal proceedings, there is no DNA profile available for a particular individual present within a requested Member State's territory, the requested Member State shall provide legal assistance by collecting and examining cellular material from that individual and by supplying the DNA profile obtained, if:

(a) the requesting Member State specifies the purpose for which this is required;
(b) the requesting Member State produces an investigation warrant or statement issued by the competent authority, as required under that Member State's law, showing that the requirements for collecting and examining cellular material would be fulfilled if the individual concerned were present within the requesting Member State's territory; and
(c) under the requested Member State's law, the requirements for collecting and examining cellular material and for supplying the DNA profile obtained are fulfilled.

SECTION 2

Dactyloscopic data

Article 8
Dactyloscopic data

For the purpose of implementing this Decision, Member States shall ensure the availability of reference data from the file for the national automated fingerprint identification systems established for the prevention and investigation of criminal offences.
Reference data shall only include dactyloscopic data and a reference number. Reference data shall not contain any data from which the data subject can be directly identified. Reference data which is not attributed to any individual (unidentified dactyloscopic data) must be recognisable as such.

Article 9
Automated searching of dactyloscopic data

1. For the prevention and investigation of criminal offences, Member States shall allow other Member States' national contact points, as referred to in Article 11, access to the reference data in the automated fingerprint identification systems

which they have established for that purpose, with the power to conduct automated searches by comparing dactyloscopic data. Searches may be conducted only in individual cases and in compliance with the requesting Member State's national law.
2. The confirmation of a match of dactyloscopic data with reference data held by the Member State administering the file shall be carried out by the national contact point of the requesting Member State by means of the automated supply of the reference data required for a clear match.

Article 10
Supply of further personal data and other information
Should the procedure referred to in Article 9 show a match between dactyloscopic data, the supply of further available personal data and other information relating to the reference data shall be governed by the national law, including the legal assistance rules, of the requested Member State.

Article 11
National contact point and implementing measures

1. For the purposes of the supply of data as referred to in Article 9, each Member State shall designate a national contact point. The powers of the national contact points shall be governed by the applicable national law.
2. Details of technical arrangements for the procedure set out in Article 9 shall be laid down in the implementing measures as referred to in Article 33.

SECTION 3

Vehicle registration data

Article 12
Automated searching of vehicle registration data

1. For the prevention and investigation of criminal offences and in dealing with other offences coming within the jurisdiction of the courts or the public prosecution service in the searching Member State, as well as in maintaining public security, Member States shall allow other Member States' national contact points, as referred to in paragraph 2, access to the following national vehicle registration data, with the power to conduct automated searches in individual cases:

(a) data relating to owners or operators; and
(b) data relating to vehicles.

Searches may be conducted only with a full chassis number or a full registration number. Searches may be conducted only in compliance with the searching Member State's national law.
2. For the purposes of the supply of data as referred to in paragraph 1, each Member State shall designate a national contact point for incoming requests. The powers of the national contact points shall be governed by the applicable national law. Details

of technical arrangements for the procedure shall be laid down in the implementing measures as referred to in Article 33.

CHAPTER 3

MAJOR EVENTS

Article 13
Supply of non-personal data

For the prevention of criminal offences and in maintaining public order and security for major events with a cross-border dimension, in particular for sporting events or European Council meetings, Member States shall, both upon request and of their own accord, in compliance with the supplying Member State's national law, supply one another with any non-personal data required for those purposes.

Article 14
Supply of personal data

1. For the prevention of criminal offences and in maintaining public order and security for major events with a cross-border dimension, in particular for sporting events or European Council meetings, Member States shall, both upon request and of their own accord, supply one another with personal data if any final convictions or other circumstances give reason to believe that the data subjects will commit criminal offences at the events or pose a threat to public order and security, in so far as the supply of such data is permitted under the supplying Member State's national law.
2. Personal data may be processed only for the purposes laid down in paragraph 1 and for the specified events for which they were supplied. The data supplied must be deleted without delay once the purposes referred to in paragraph 1 have been achieved or can no longer be achieved. The data supplied must in any event be deleted after not more than a year.

Article 15
National contact point
For the purposes of the supply of data as referred to in Articles 13 and 14, each Member State shall designate a national contact point. The powers of the national contact points shall be governed by the applicable national law.

(. . .)

CHAPTER 6

GENERAL PROVISIONS ON DATA PROTECTION

Article 24
Definitions and scope

1. For the purposes of this Decision:

(a) 'processing of personal data' shall mean any operation or set of operations which is performed upon personal data, whether or not by automatic means, such as

collection, recording, organisation, storage, adaptation or alteration, sorting, retrieval, consultation, use, disclosure by supply, dissemination or otherwise making available, alignment, combination, blocking, erasure or destruction of data. Processing within the meaning of this Decision shall also include notification of whether or not a hit exists;
(b) 'automated search procedure' shall mean direct access to the automated files of another body where the response to the search procedure is fully automated;
(c) 'referencing' shall mean the marking of stored personal data without the aim of limiting their processing in future;
(d) 'blocking' shall mean the marking of stored personal data with the aim of limiting their processing in future.

2. The following provisions shall apply to data which are or have been supplied pursuant to this Decision, save as otherwise provided in the preceding Chapters.

Article 25
Level of data protection

1. As regards the processing of personal data which are or have been supplied pursuant to this Decision, each Member State shall guarantee a level of protection of personal data in its national law at least equal to that resulting from the Council of Europe Convention for the Protection of Individuals with regard to Automatic Processing of Personal Data of 28 January 1981 and its Additional Protocol of 8 November 2001 and in doing so, shall take account of Recommendation No R (87) 15 of 17 September 1987 of the Committee of Ministers of the Council of Europe to the Member States regulating the use of personal data in the police sector, also where data are not processed automatically.
2. The supply of personal data provided for under this Decision may not take place until the provisions of this Chapter have been implemented in the national law of the territories of the Member States involved in such supply. The Council shall unanimously decide whether this condition has been met.
The supply of personal data as provided for in this Decision has already started pursuant to the Treaty of 27 May 2005 between the Kingdom of Belgium, the Federal Republic of Germany, the Kingdom of Spain, the French Republic, the Grand Duchy of Luxembourg, the Kingdom of the Netherlands and the Republic of Austria on the stepping up of cross-border cooperation, particularly in combating terrorism, cross-border crime and illegal migration (Prüm Treaty).

Article 26
Purpose

1. Processing of personal data by the receiving Member State shall be permitted solely for the purposes for which the data have been supplied in accordance with this Decision. Processing for other purposes shall be permitted solely with the prior authorisation of the Member State administering the file and subject only to the national law of the receiving Member State. Such authorisation may be granted

provided that processing for such other purposes is permitted under the national law of the Member State administering the file.
2. Processing of data supplied pursuant to Articles 3, 4 and 9 by the searching or comparing Member State shall be permitted solely in order to:

(a) establish whether the compared DNA profiles or dactyloscopic data match;
(b) prepare and submit a police or judicial request for legal assistance in compliance with national law if those data match;
(c) record within the meaning of Article 30.

The Member State administering the file may process the data supplied to it in accordance with Articles 3, 4 and 9 solely where this is necessary for the purposes of comparison, providing automated replies to searches or recording pursuant to Article 30. The supplied data shall be deleted immediately following data comparison or automated replies to searches unless further processing is necessary for the purposes mentioned under points (b) and (c) of the first subparagraph.
3. Data supplied in accordance with Article 12 may be used by the Member State administering the file solely where this is necessary for the purpose of providing automated replies to search procedures or recording as specified in Article 30. The data supplied shall be deleted immediately following automated replies to searches unless further processing is necessary for recording pursuant to Article 30. The searching Member State may use data received in a reply solely for the procedure for which the search was made.

Article 27
Competent authorities

Personal data supplied may be processed only by the authorities, bodies and courts with responsibility for a task in furtherance of the aims mentioned in Article 26. In particular, data may be supplied to other entities only with the prior authorisation of the supplying Member State and in compliance with the law of the receiving Member State.

Article 28
Accuracy, current relevance and storage time of data

1. The Member States shall ensure the accuracy and current relevance of personal data. Should it transpire ex officio or from a notification by the data subject, that incorrect data or data which should not have been supplied have been supplied, this shall be notified without delay to the receiving Member State or Member States. The Member State or Member States concerned shall be obliged to correct or delete the data. Moreover, personal data supplied shall be corrected if they are found to be incorrect. If the receiving body has reason to believe that the supplied data are incorrect or should be deleted the supplying body shall be informed forthwith.
2. Data, the accuracy of which the data subject contests and the accuracy or inaccuracy of which cannot be established shall, in accordance with the national law of the Member States, be marked with a flag at the request of the data subject. If a flag exists, this may be removed subject to the national law of the Member States

and only with the permission of the data subject or based on a decision of the competent court or independent data protection authority.
3. Personal data supplied which should not have been supplied or received shall be deleted. Data which are lawfully supplied and received shall be deleted:

(a) if they are not or no longer necessary for the purpose for which they were supplied; if personal data have been supplied without request, the receiving body shall immediately check if they are necessary for the purposes for which they were supplied;
(b) following the expiry of the maximum period for keeping data laid down in the national law of the supplying Member State where the supplying body informed the receiving body of that maximum period at the time of supplying the data.

Where there is reason to believe that deletion would prejudice the interests of the data subject, the data shall be blocked instead of being deleted in compliance with national law. Blocked data may be supplied or used solely for the purpose which prevented their deletion.

Article 29
Technical and organisational measures to ensure data protection and data security

1. The supplying and receiving bodies shall take steps to ensure that personal data is effectively protected against accidental or unauthorised destruction, accidental loss, unauthorised access, unauthorised or accidental alteration and unauthorised disclosure.
2. The features of the technical specification of the automated search procedure are regulated in the implementing measures as referred to in Article 33 which guarantee that:

(a) state-of-the-art technical measures are taken to ensure data protection and data security, in particular data confidentiality and integrity;
(b) encryption and authorisation procedures recognised by the competent authorities are used when having recourse to generally accessible networks; and
(c) the admissibility of searches in accordance with Article 30(2), (4) and (5) can be checked.

Article 30
Logging and recording: special rules governing automated and non-automated supply

1. Each Member State shall guarantee that every nonautomated supply and every non-automated receipt of personal data by the body administering the file and by the searching body is logged in order to verify the admissibility of the supply.
Logging shall contain the following information:

(a) the reason for the supply;
(b) the data supplied;
(c) the date of the supply; and
(d) the name or reference code of the searching body and of the body administering the file.

2. The following shall apply to automated searches for data based on Articles 3, 9 and 12 and to automated comparison pursuant to Article 4:

(a) only specially authorised officers of the national contact points may carry out automated searches or comparisons. The list of officers authorised to carry out automated searches or comparisons shall be made available upon request to the supervisory authorities referred to in paragraph 5 and to the other Member States;
(b) each Member State shall ensure that each supply and receipt of personal data by the body administering the file and the searching body is recorded, including notification of whether or not a hit exists. Recording shall include the following information:

(i) the data supplied;
(ii) the date and exact time of the supply; and
(iii) the name or reference code of the searching body and of the body administering the file.

The searching body shall also record the reason for the search or supply as well as an identifier for the official who carried out the search and the official who ordered the search or supply.

3. The recording body shall immediately communicate the recorded data upon request to the competent data protection authorities of the relevant Member State at the latest within four weeks following receipt of the request. Recorded data may be used solely for the following purposes:

(a) monitoring data protection;
(b) ensuring data security.

4. The recorded data shall be protected with suitable measures against inappropriate use and other forms of improper use and shall be kept for two years. After the conservation period the recorded data shall be deleted immediately.
5. Responsibility for legal checks on the supply or receipt of personal data lies with the independent data protection authorities or, as appropriate, the judicial authorities of the respective Member States. Anyone can request these authorities to check the lawfulness of the processing of data in respect of their person in compliance with national law. Independently of such requests, these authorities and the bodies responsible for recording shall carry out random checks on the lawfulness of supply, based on the files involved.
The results of such checks shall be kept for inspection for 18 months by the independent data protection authorities. After this period, they shall be immediately deleted. Each data protection authority may be requested by the independent data protection authority of another Member State to exercise its powers in accordance with national law. The independent data protection authorities of the Member States shall perform the inspection tasks necessary for mutual cooperation, in particular by exchanging relevant information.

Article 31
Data subjects' rights to information and damages

1. At the request of the data subject under national law, information shall be supplied in compliance with national law to the data subject upon production of proof of his identity, without unreasonable expense, in general comprehensible terms and without unacceptable delays, on the data processed in respect of his person, the origin of the data, the recipient or groups of recipients, the intended purpose of the processing and, where required by national law, the legal basis for the processing.
Moreover, the data subject shall be entitled to have inaccurate data corrected and unlawfully processed data deleted. The Member States shall also ensure that, in the event of violation of his rights in relation to data protection, the data subject shall be able to lodge an effective complaint to an independent court or a tribunal within the meaning of Article 6(1) of the European Convention on Human Rights or an independent supervisory authority within the meaning of Article 28 of Directive 95/46/EC of the European Parliament and of the Council of 24 October 1995 on the protection of individuals with regard to the processing of personal data and on the free movement of such data (1) and that he is given the possibility to claim for damages or to seek another form of legal compensation. The detailed rules for the procedure to assert these rights and the reasons for limiting the right of access shall be governed by the relevant national legal provisions of the Member State where the data subject asserts his rights.
2. Where a body of one Member State has supplied personal data under this Decision, the receiving body of the other Member State cannot use the inaccuracy of the data supplied as grounds to evade its liability vis-à-vis the injured party under national law. If damages are awarded against the receiving body because of its use of inaccurate transfer data, the body which supplied the data shall refund the amount paid in damages to the receiving body in full.

Article 32
Information requested by the Member States

The receiving Member State shall inform the supplying Member State on request of the processing of supplied data and the result obtained.

2. Council Decision 2008/616/JHA of 23 June 2008 on the implementation of Council Decision 2008/615/JHA

Article 1

Aim

The aim of this Decision is to lay down the necessary administrative and technical provisions for the implementation of Decision 2008/615/JHA, in particular as regards the automated exchange of DNA data, dactyloscopic data and vehicle registration data, as set out in Chapter 2 of that Decision, and other forms of cooperation, as set out in Chapter 5 of that Decision.

Article 2

Definitions

For the purposes of this Decision:

(a) 'search' and 'comparison', as referred to in Articles 3, 4 and 9 of Decision 2008/615/JHA, mean the procedures by which it is established whether there is a match between, respectively, DNA data or dactyloscopic data which have been communicated by one Member State and DNA data or dactyloscopic data stored in the databases of one, several, or all of the Member States;
(b) 'automated searching', as referred to in Article 12 of Decision 2008/615/JHA, means an online access procedure for consulting the databases of one, several, or all of the Member States;
(c) 'DNA profile' means a letter or number code which represents a set of identification characteristics of the noncoding part of an analysed human DNA sample, i.e. the particular molecular structure at the various DNA locations (loci);
(d) 'non-coding part of DNA' means chromosome regions not genetically expressed, i.e. not known to provide for any functional properties of an organism;
(e) 'DNA reference data' mean DNA profile and reference number;
(f) 'reference DNA profile' means the DNA profile of an identified person;
(g) 'unidentified DNA profile' means the DNA profile obtained from traces collected during the investigation of criminal offences and belonging to a person not yet identified;
(h) 'note' means a Member State's marking on a DNA profile in its national database indicating that there has already been a match for that DNA profile on another Member State's search or comparison;
(i) 'dactyloscopic data' mean fingerprint images, images of fingerprint latents, palm prints, palm print latents and templates of such images (coded minutiae), when they are stored and dealt with in an automated database;
(j) 'vehicle registration data' mean the data-set as specified in Chapter 3 of the Annex to this Decision;
(k) 'individual case', as referred to in Article 3(1), second sentence, Article 9(1), second sentence and Article 12(1) of Decision 2008/615/JHA, means a single investigation or prosecution file. If such a file contains more than one DNA profile,

or one piece of dactyloscopic data or vehicle registration data, they may be transmitted together as one request.

CHAPTER 2

COMMON PROVISIONS FOR DATA EXCHANGE

Article 3

Technical specifications

Member States shall observe common technical specifications in connection with all requests and answers related to searches and comparisons of DNA profiles, dactyloscopic data and vehicle registration data. These technical specifications are laid down in the Annex to this Decision.

Article 4

Communications network

The electronic exchange of DNA data, dactyloscopic data and vehicle registration data between Member States shall take place using the Trans European Services for Telematics between Administrations (TESTA II) communications network and further developments thereof.

Article 5

Availability of automated data exchange

Member States shall take all necessary measures to ensure that automated searching or comparison of DNA data, dactyloscopic data and vehicle registration data is possible 24 hours a day and seven days a week. In the event of a technical fault, the Member States' national contact points shall immediately inform each other and shall agree on temporary alternative information exchange arrangements in accordance with the legal provisions applicable. Automated data exchange shall be re-established as quickly as possible.

Article 6

Reference numbers for DNA data and dactyloscopic data The reference numbers referred to in Article 2 and Article 8 of Decision 2008/615/JHA shall consist of a combination of the following:

(a) a code allowing the Member States, in the case of a match, to retrieve personal data and other information in their databases in order to supply it to one, several or all of the Member States in accordance with Article 5 or Article 10 of Decision 2008/615/JHA;
(b) a code to indicate the national origin of the DNA profile or dactyloscopic data; and
(c) with respect to DNA data, a code to indicate the type of DNA profile.

CHAPTER 3

DNA DATA

Article 7

Principles of DNA data exchange

1. Member States shall use existing standards for DNA data exchange, such as the European Standard Set (ESS) or the Interpol Standard Set of Loci (ISSOL).
2. The transmission procedure, in the case of automated searching and comparison of DNA profiles, shall take place within a decentralised structure.
3. Appropriate measures shall be taken to ensure confidentiality and integrity for data being sent to other Member States, including their encryption.
4. Member States shall take the necessary measures to guarantee the integrity of the DNA profiles made available or sent for comparison to the other Member States and to ensure that these measures comply with international standards such as ISO 17025.
5. Member States shall use Member State codes in accordance with the ISO 3166-1 alpha-2 standard.

Article 8

Rules for requests and answers in connection with DNA data

1. A request for an automated search or comparison, as referred to in Articles 3 or 4 of Decision 2008/615/JHA, shall include only the following information:

(a) the Member State code of the requesting Member State;
(b) the date, time and indication number of the request;
(c) DNA profiles and their reference numbers;
(d) the types of DNA profiles transmitted (unidentified DNA profiles or reference DNA profiles); and
(e) information required for controlling the database systems and quality control for the automatic search processes.

2. The answer (matching report) to the request referred to in paragraph 1 shall contain only the following information:

(a) an indication as to whether there were one or more matches (hits) or no matches (no hits);
(b) the date, time and indication number of the request;
(c) the date, time and indication number of the answer;
(d) the Member State codes of the requesting and requested Member States;
(e) the reference numbers of the requesting and requested Member States;
(f) the type of DNA profiles transmitted (unidentified DNA profiles or reference DNA profiles);
(g) the requested and matching DNA profiles; and
(h) information required for controlling the database systems and quality control for the automatic search processes.

3. Automated notification of a match shall only be provided if the automated search or comparison has resulted in a match of a minimum number of loci. This minimum is set out in Chapter 1 of the Annex to this Decision.
4. The Member States shall ensure that requests comply with declarations issued pursuant to Article 2(3) of Decision 2008/615/JHA. These declarations shall be reproduced in the Manual referred to in Article 18(2) of this Decision.

Article 9

Transmission procedure for automated searching of unidentified DNA profiles in accordance with Article 3 of Decision 2008/615/JHA

1. If, in a search with an unidentified DNA profile, no match has been found in the national database or a match has been found with an unidentified DNA profile, the unidentified DNA profile may then be transmitted to all other Member States' databases and if, in a search with this unidentified DNA profile, matches are found with reference DNA profiles and/or unidentified DNA profiles in other Member States' databases, these matches shall be automatically communicated and the DNA reference data transmitted to the requesting Member State; if no matches can be found in other Member States' databases, this shall be automatically communicated to the requesting Member State.
2. If, in a search with an unidentified DNA profile, a match is found in other Member States' databases, each Member State concerned may insert a note to this effect in its national database.

Article 10

Transmission procedure for automated search of reference DNA profiles in accordance with Article 3 of Decision 2008/615/JHA
If, in a search with a reference DNA profile, no match has been found in the national database with a reference DNA profile or a match has been found with an unidentified DNA profile, this reference DNA profile may then be transmitted to all other Member States' databases and if, in a search with this reference DNA profile, matches are found with reference DNA profiles and/or unidentified DNA profiles in other Member States' databases, these matches shall be automatically communicated and the DNA reference data transmitted to the requesting Member State; if no matches can be found in other Member States' databases, it shall be automatically communicated to the requesting Member State.

Article 11

Transmission procedure for automated comparison of unidentified DNA profiles in accordance with Article 4 of Decision 2008/615/JHA

1. If, in a comparison with unidentified DNA profiles, matches are found in other Member States' databases with reference DNA profiles and/or unidentified DNA profiles, these matches shall be automatically communicated and the DNA reference data transmitted to the requesting Member State.

2. If, in a comparison with unidentified DNA profiles, matches are found in other Member States' databases with unidentified DNA profiles or reference DNA profiles, each Member State concerned may insert a note to this effect in its national database.

CHAPTER 4

DACTYLOSCOPIC DATA

Article 12

Principles for the exchange of dactyloscopic data

1. The digitalisation of dactyloscopic data and their transmission to the other Member States shall be carried out in accordance with the uniform data format specified in Chapter 2 of the Annex to this Decision.
2. Each Member State shall ensure that the dactyloscopic data it transmits are of sufficient quality for a comparison by the automated fingerprint identification systems (AFIS).
3. The transmission procedure for the exchange of dactyloscopic data shall take place within a decentralised structure.
4. Appropriate measures shall be taken to ensure the confidentiality and integrity of dactyloscopic data being sent to other Member States, including their encryption.
5. The Member States shall use Member State codes in accordance with the ISO 3166-1 alpha-2 standard.

Article 13

Search capacities for dactyloscopic data

1. Each Member State shall ensure that its search requests do not exceed the search capacities specified by the requested Member State. Member States shall submit declarations as referred to in Article 18(2) to the General Secretariat of the Council in which they lay down their maximum search capacities per day for dactyloscopic data of identified persons and for dactyloscopic data of persons not yet identified.
2. The maximum numbers of candidates accepted for verification per transmission are set out in Chapter 2 of the Annex to this Decision.

Article 14

Rules for requests and answers in connection with dactyloscopic data

1. The requested Member State shall check the quality of the transmitted dactyloscopic data without delay by a fully automated procedure. Should the data be unsuitable for an automated comparison, the requested Member State shall inform the requesting Member State without delay.
2. The requested Member State shall conduct searches in the order in which requests are received. Requests shall be processed within 24 hours by a fully automated procedure. The requesting Member State may, if its national law so prescribes, ask for accelerated processing of its requests and the requested Member State shall conduct these searches without delay. If deadlines cannot be met for

reasons of force majeure, the comparison shall be carried out without delay as soon as the impediments have been removed.

CHAPTER 5

VEHICLE REGISTRATION DATA

Article 15

Principles of automated searching of vehicle registration data

1. For automated searching of vehicle registration data Member States shall use a version of the European Vehicle and Driving Licence Information System (Eucaris) software application especially designed for the purposes of Article 12 of Decision 2008/615/JHA, and amended versions of this software.
2. Automated searching of vehicle registration data shall take place within a decentralised structure.
3. The information exchanged via the Eucaris system shall be transmitted in encrypted form.
4. The data elements of the vehicle registration data to be exchanged are specified in Chapter 3 of the Annex to this Decision.
5. In the implementation of Article 12 of Decision 2008/615/JHA, Member States may give priority to searches related to combating serious crime.

Article 16

Costs
Each Member State shall bear the costs arising from the administration, use and maintenance of the Eucaris software application referred to in Article 15(1).

Article 18

Annex and Manual

1. Further details concerning the technical and administrative implementation of Decision 2008/615/JHA are set out in the Annex to this Decision.
2. A Manual shall be prepared and kept up to date by the General Secretariat of the Council, comprising exclusively factual information provided by the Member States through declarations made pursuant to Decision 2008/615/JHA or this Decision or through notifications made to the General Secretariat of the Council. The Manual shall be in the form of a Council Document.

Article 19

Independent data protection authorities
Member States shall, in accordance with Article 18(2) of this Decision, inform the General Secretariat of the Council of the independent data protection authorities or the judicial authorities as referred to in Article 30(5) of Decision 2008/615/JHA.

Article 20

Preparation of decisions as referred to in Article 25(2) of Decision 2008/615/JHA

1. The Council shall take a decision as referred to in Article 25(2) of Decision 2008/615/JHA on the basis of an evaluation report which shall be based on a questionnaire.
2. With respect to the automated data exchange in accordance with Chapter 2 of Decision 2008/615/JHA, the evaluation report shall also be based on an evaluation visit and a pilot run that shall be carried out when the Member State concerned has informed the General Secretariat in accordance with the first sentence of Article 36 (2) of Decision 2008/615/JHA.
3. Further details of the procedure are set out in Chapter 4 of the Annex to this Decision.

Article 21

Evaluation of the data exchange

1. An evaluation of the administrative, technical and financial application of the data exchange pursuant to Chapter 2 of Decision 2008/615/JHA, and in particular the use of the mechanism of Article 15(5), shall be carried out on a regular basis. The evaluation shall relate to those Member States already applying Decision 2008/615/JHA at the time of the evaluation and shall be carried out with respect to the data categories for which data exchange has started among the Member States concerned. The evaluation shall be based on reports of the respective Member States.
2. Further details of the procedure are set out in Chapter 4 of the Annex to this Decision.

Article 22

Relationship with the Implementing Agreement of the Prum Treaty For the Member States bound by the Prum Treaty, the relevant provisions of this Decision and the Annex hereto once fully implemented shall apply instead of the corresponding provisions contained in the Implementing Agreement of the Prum Treaty. Any other provisions of the Implementing Agreement shall remain applicable between the contracting parties of the Prüm Treaty.

Article 23

Implementation
Member States shall take the necessary measures to comply with the provisions of this Decision within the periods referred to in Article 36(1) of Decision 2008/615/JHA.

Article 24

Application
This Decision shall take effect 20 days following its publication in the Official Journal of the European Union.

Annex

CHAPTER 1: Exchange of DNA-Data

1. *DNA related forensic issues, matching rules and algorithms*

1.1. *Properties of DNA-profiles*

The DNA profile may contain 24 pairs of numbers representing the alleles of 24 loci which are also used in the DNA-procedures of Interpol. The names of these loci are shown in the following table:

The seven grey loci in the top row are both the present European Standard Set (ESS) and the Interpol Standard Set of Loci (ISSOL).

Inclusion Rules:

The DNA-profiles made available by the Member States for searching and comparison as well as the DNA-profiles sent out for searching and comparison must contain at least six full designated (1) loci and may contain additional loci or blanks depending on their availability. The reference DNA profiles must contain at least six of the seven ESS of loci. In order to raise the accuracy of matches, all available alleles shall be stored in the indexed DNA profile database and be used for searching and comparison. Each Member State should implement as soon as practically possible any new ESS of loci adopted by the EU.
Mixed profiles are not allowed, so that the allele values of each locus will consist of only two numbers, which may be the same in the case of homozygosity at a given locus.

1.2. Matching rules

The comparison of two DNA-profiles will be performed on the basis of the loci for which a pair of allele values is available in both DNA-profiles. At least six full designated loci (exclusive of amelogenin) must match between both DNA-profiles before a hit response is provided.
A full match (Quality 1) is defined as a match, when all allele values of the compared loci commonly contained in the requesting and requested DNA-profiles are the same. A near match is defined as a match, when the value of only one of all the compared alleles is different in the two DNA profiles (Quality 2, 3 and 4). A near match is only accepted if there are at least six full designated matched loci in the two compared DNA profiles.
The reason for a near match may be:
— a human typing error at the point of entry of one of the DNA-profiles in the search request or the DNAdatabase,
— an allele-determination or allele-calling error during the generation procedure of the DNA-profile.

1.3. Reporting rules

Both full matches, near matches and ‘no hits’ will be reported.

The matching report will be sent to the requesting national contact point and will also be made available to the requested national contact point (to enable it to estimate the nature and number of possible follow-up requests for further available personal data and other information associated with the DNA-profile corresponding to the hit in accordance with Articles 5 and 10 of Decision 2008/615/JHA).

3. Council Framework Decision 2009/315/JHA of 26 February 2009 on the organization and content of the exchange of information extracted from the criminal record between Member States[25]

Article 1 – Objective

The purpose of this Framework Decision is:

(a) to define the ways in which a Member State where a conviction is handed down against a national of another Member State (the "convicting Member State") transmits the information on such a conviction to the Member State of the convicted person's nationality (the "Member State of the person's nationality");
(b) to define storage obligations for the Member State of the person's nationality and to specify the methods to be followed when replying to a request for information extracted from criminal records;
(c) to lay down the framework for a computerised system of exchange of information on convictions between Member States to be built and developed on the basis of this Framework Decision and the subsequent decision referred to in Article 11.[26]

Article 2 – Definitions

For the purposes of this Framework Decision:

(a) "conviction" means any final decision of a criminal court against a natural person in respect of a criminal offence, to the extent these decisions are entered in the criminal record of the convicting Member State;
(b) "criminal proceedings" means the pre-trial stage, the trial stage itself and the execution of the conviction;
(c) "criminal record" means the national register or registers recording convictions in accordance with national law.

Article 3 – Central authority

1. For the purposes of this Framework Decision, each Member State shall designate a central authority. However, for the transmission of information under Article 4 and for replies under Article 7 to requests referred to in Article 6, Member States may designate one or more central authorities.
2. Each Member State shall inform the General Secretariat of the Council and the Commission of the central authority or authorities designated in accordance with paragraph 1. The General Secretariat of the Council shall notify the Member States and Eurojust of this information.

---

[25] OJ L 93, 7.4.2009, p. 23.
[26] OJ C 53, 3.3.2005, p. 1.

Article 4 – Obligations of the convicting Member State

1. Each Member State shall take the necessary measures to ensure that all convictions handed down within its territory are accompanied, when provided to its criminal record, by information on the nationality or nationalities of the convicted person if he is a national of another Member State.
2. The central authority of the convicting Member State shall, as soon as possible, inform the central authorities of the other Member States of any convictions handed down within its territory against the nationals of such other Member States, as entered in the criminal record.
If it is known that the convicted person is a national of several Member States, the relevant information shall be transmitted to each of these Member States, even if the convicted person is a national of the Member State within whose territory he was convicted.
3. Information on subsequent alteration or deletion of information contained in the criminal record shall be immediately transmitted by the central authority of the convicting Member State to the central authority of the Member State of the person's nationality.
4. Any Member State which has provided information under paragraphs 2 and 3 shall communicate to the central authority of the Member State of the person's nationality, on the latter's request in individual cases, a copy of the convictions and subsequent measures as well as any other information relevant thereto in order to enable it to consider whether they necessitate any measure at national level.

Article 5 – Obligations of the Member State of the person's nationality

1. The central authority of the Member State of the person's nationality shall store all information in accordance with Article 11(1) and (2) transmitted under Article 4 (2) and (3), for the purpose of retransmission in accordance with Article 7.
2. Any alteration or deletion of information transmitted in accordance with Article 4(3) shall entail identical alteration or deletion by the Member State of the person's nationality regarding information stored in accordance with paragraph 1 of this Article for the purpose of retransmission in accordance with Article 7.
3. For the purpose of retransmission in accordance with Article 7 the Member State of the person's nationality may only use information which has been updated in accordance with paragraph 2 of this Article.

Article 6 – Request for information on convictions

1. When information from the criminal record of a Member State is requested for the purposes of criminal proceedings against a person or for any purposes other than that of criminal proceedings, the central authority of that Member State may, in accordance with its national law, submit a request to the central authority of another Member State for information and related data to be extracted from the criminal record.
2. When a person asks for information on his own criminal record, the central authority of the Member State in which the request is made may, in accordance with its national law, submit a request to the central authority of another Member State

for information and related data to be extracted from the criminal record, provided the person concerned is or was a resident or a national of the requesting or requested Member State.

3. Once the time limit set out in Article 11(7) has elapsed, whenever a person asks the central authority of a Member State other than the Member State of the person's nationality for information on his own criminal record, the central authority of the Member State in which the request is made shall submit a request to the central authority of the Member State of the person's nationality for information and related data to be extracted from the criminal record in order to be able to include such information and related data in the extract to be provided to the person concerned.

4. All requests from the central authority of a Member State for information extracted from the criminal record shall be submitted using the form set out in the Annex.

Article 7 – Reply to a request for information on convictions

1. When information extracted from the criminal record is requested under Article 6 from the central authority of the Member State of the person's nationality for the purposes of criminal proceedings, that central authority shall transmit to the central authority of the requesting Member State information on:

(a) convictions handed down in the Member State of the person's nationality and entered in the criminal record;
(b) any convictions handed down in other Member States which were transmitted to it after 27 April 2012, in application of Article 4, and stored in accordance with Article 5(1) and (2);
(c) any convictions handed down in other Member States which were transmitted to it by 27 April 2012, and entered in the criminal record;
(d) any convictions handed down in third countries and subsequently transmitted to it and entered in the criminal record.

2. When information extracted from the criminal record is requested under Article 6 from the central authority of the Member State of the person's nationality for any purposes other than that of criminal proceedings, that central authority shall in respect of convictions handed down in the Member State of the person's nationality and of convictions handed down in third countries, which have been subsequently transmitted to it and entered in its criminal record, reply in accordance with its national law.

In respect of information on convictions handed down in another Member State, which have been transmitted to the Member State of the person's nationality, the central authority of the latter Member State shall in accordance with its national law transmit to the requesting Member State the information which has been stored in accordance with Article 5 (1) and (2) as well as the information which has been transmitted to that central authority by 27 April 2012, and has been entered in its criminal record.

When transmitting the information in accordance with Article 4, the central authority of the convicting Member State may inform the central authority of the Member

State of the person's nationality that the information on convictions handed down in the former Member State and transmitted to the latter central authority may not be retransmitted for any purposes other than that of criminal proceedings. In this case, the central authority of the Member State of the person's nationality shall, in respect of such convictions, inform the requesting Member State which other Member State had transmitted such information so as to enable the requesting Member State to submit a request directly to the convicting Member State in order to receive information on these convictions.
3. When information extracted from the criminal record is requested from the central authority of the Member State of the person's nationality by a third country, the Member State of the person's nationality may reply in respect of convictions transmitted by another Member State only within the limitations applicable to the transmission of information to other Member States in accordance with paragraphs 1 and 2.
4. When information extracted from the criminal record is requested under Article 6 from the central authority of a Member State other than the Member State of the person's nationality, the requested Member State shall transmit information on convictions handed down in the requested Member State and on convictions handed down against third country nationals and against stateless persons contained in its criminal record to the same extent as provided for in Article 13 of the European Convention on Mutual Assistance in Criminal Matters.
5. The reply shall be made using the form set out in the Annex. It shall be accompanied by a list of convictions, as provided for by national law.

Article 8 – Deadlines for replies

1. Replies to the requests referred to in Article 6(1) shall be transmitted by the central authority of the requested Member State to the central authority of the requesting Member State immediately and in any event within a period not exceeding ten working days from the date the request was received, as provided for by its national law, rules or practice, using the form set out in the Annex.
When the requested Member State requires further information to identify the person involved in the request, it shall immediately consult the requesting Member State with a view to providing a reply within ten working days from the date the additional information is received.
2. Replies to the request referred to in Article 6(2) shall be transmitted within twenty working days from the date the request was received.

Article 9 – Conditions for the use of personal data

1. Personal data provided under Article 7(1) and (4) for the purposes of criminal proceedings may be used by the requesting Member State only for the purposes of the criminal proceedings for which it was requested, as specified in the form set out in the Annex.
2. Personal data provided under Article 7(2) and (4) for any purposes other than that of criminal proceedings may be used by the requesting Member State in accordance with its national law only for the purposes for which it was requested

and within the limits specified by the requested Member State in the form set out in the Annex.
3. Notwithstanding paragraphs 1 and 2, personal data provided under Article 7(1), (2) and (4) may be used by the requesting Member State for preventing an immediate and serious threat to public security.
4. Member States shall take the necessary measures to ensure that personal data received from another Member State under Article 4, if transmitted to a third country in accordance with Article 7(3), is subject to the same usage limitations as those applicable in a requesting Member State in accordance with paragraph 2 of this Article. Member States shall specify that personal data, if transmitted to a third country for the purposes of a criminal proceeding, may be further used by that third country only for the purposes of criminal proceedings.
5. This Article does not apply to personal data obtained by a Member State under this Framework Decision and originating from that Member State.

Article 10 – Languages

When submitting a request referred to in Article 6(1), the requesting Member State shall transmit to the requested Member State the form set out in the Annex in the official language or one of the official languages of the latter Member State.
The requested Member State shall reply either in one of its official languages or in any other language accepted by both Member States.
Any Member State may, at the time of the adoption of this Framework Decision or at a later date, indicate, in a statement to the General Secretariat of the Council, which are the official languages of the institutions of the European Union that it accepts. The General Secretariat of the Council shall notify the Member States of this information.

Article 11 – Format and other ways of organising and facilitating exchanges of information on convictions

1. When transmitting information in accordance with Article 4(2) and (3), the central authority of the convicting Member State shall transmit the following information:

(a) information that shall always be transmitted, unless, in individual cases, such information is not known to the central authority (obligatory information):

(i) information on the convicted person (full name, date of birth, place of birth (town and State), gender, nationality and – if applicable – previous name (s));
(ii) information on the nature of the conviction (date of conviction, name of the court, date on which the decision became final);
(iii) information on the offence giving rise to the conviction (date of the offence underlying the conviction and name or legal classification of the offence as well as reference to the applicable legal provisions); and
(iv) information on the contents of the conviction (notably the sentence as well as any supplementary penalties, security measures and subsequent decisions modifying the enforcement of the sentence);

(b) information that shall be transmitted if entered in the criminal record (optional information):

(i) the convicted person's parents' names;
(ii) the reference number of the conviction;
(iii) the place of the offence; and
(iv) disqualifications arising from the conviction;

(c) information that shall be transmitted, if available to the central authority (additional information):

(i) the convicted person's identity number, or the type and number of the person's identification document;
(ii) fingerprints, which have been taken from that person; and
(iii) if applicable, pseudonym and/or alias name(s).

In addition, the central authority may transmit any other information concerning convictions entered in the criminal record.

2. The central authority of the Member State of the person's nationality shall store all information of the types listed in points (a) and (b) of paragraph 1, which it has received in accordance with Article 5(1) for the purpose of retransmission in accordance with Article 7. For the same purpose it may store the information of the types listed in point (c) of the first subparagraph and in the second subparagraph of paragraph 1.
3. Until the time limit set out in paragraph 7 has elapsed, central authorities of Member States which have not carried out the notification referred to in paragraph 6 shall transmit all information in accordance with Article 4, requests in accordance with Article 6, replies in accordance with Article 7 and other relevant information by any means capable of producing a written record under conditions allowing the central authority of the receiving Member State to establish the authenticity thereof.

   Once the time limit set out in paragraph 7 of this Article has elapsed, central authorities of Member States shall transmit such information electronically using a standardised format.
4. The format referred to in paragraph 3 and any other means of organising and facilitating exchanges of information on convictions between central authorities of Member States shall be set up by the Council in accordance with the relevant procedures of the Treaty on the European Union by 27 April 2012.

   Other such means include:

(a) defining all means by which understanding and automatically translating transmitted information may be facilitated;
(b) defining the means by which information may be exchanged electronically, particularly as regards the technical specification to be used and, if need be, any applicable exchange procedures;
(c) possible alterations to the form set out in the Annex.

5. If the mode of transmission referred to in paragraphs 3 and 4 is not available, the first subparagraph of paragraph 3 shall remain applicable for the entire period of such unavailability.
6. Each Member State shall carry out the necessary technical alterations to be able to use the standardised format and electronically transmit it to other Member States. It shall notify the Council of the date from which it will be able to carry out such transmissions.
7. Member States shall carry out the technical alterations referred to in paragraph 6 within three years from the date of adoption of the format and the means by which information on convictions may be exchanged electronically.

Article 12 – Relationship to other legal instruments

1. In relations between the Member States, this Framework Decision supplements the provisions of Article 13 of the European Convention on Mutual Assistance in Criminal Matters, its additional Protocols of 17 March 1978 and 8 November 2001, the Convention on Mutual Assistance in Criminal Matters between the Member States of the European Union and its Protocol of 16 October 2001.[27]
2. For the purposes of this Framework Decision, Member States shall waive the right to rely among themselves on their reservations to Article 13 of the European Convention on Mutual Assistance in Criminal Matters.
3. Without prejudice to their application in relations between Member States and third States, this Framework Decision replaces in relations between Member States which have taken the necessary measures to comply with this Framework Decision and ultimately with effect from 27 April 2012 the provisions of Article 22 of the European Convention on Mutual Assistance in Criminal Matters, as supplemented by Article 4 of said Convention's additional Protocol of 17 March 1978.
4. Decision 2005/876/JHA is hereby repealed.
5. This Framework Decision shall not affect the application of more favourable provisions in bilateral or multilateral agreements between Member States.

Article 13 – Implementation

1. Member States shall take the necessary measures to comply with the provisions of this Framework Decision by 27 April 2012.
2. Member States shall transmit to the General Secretariat of the Council and to the Commission the text of the provisions transposing into their national law the obligations imposed on them under this Framework Decision.
3. On the basis of that information the Commission shall, by 27 April 2015, present a report to the European Parliament and the Council on the application of this Framework Decision, accompanied if necessary by legislative proposals.

[27] OJ C 326, 21.11.2001, p. 1.

Article 14 – Entry into force

This Framework Decision shall enter into force on the 20th day following its publication in the Official Journal of the European Union.

Done at Brussels, 26 February 2009.
For the Council
The President

L 93/30 EN Official Journal of the European Union 7.4.2009

ANNEX

Form referred to in Articles 6, 7, 8, 9 and 10 of the Council Framework Decision 2009/315/JHA on the organisation and content of the exchange of information extracted from the criminal record between Member States

Request for information extracted from the criminal record

Members States are to consult the Manual of Procedures for assistance in filling in this form correctly

(a) Information on the requesting Member State:

Member State:

Central authority(ies):

Contact person:

Telephone (with STD code):

Fax (with STD code):

E-mail address:

Correspondence address:

File reference, if known:

(b) Information on the identity of the person concerned by the request (*):

Full name (forenames and all surnames)

Previous names:

Pseudonym and/or alias, if any:

Gender: M ☐ F ☐

Nationality:

Date of birth (in figures: dd/mm/yyyy):

Place of birth (town and State):

Father's name:

Mother's name:

Residence or known address:

Person's identity number or type and number of the person's identification document:

Fingerprints:

Other available identification information:

(*) To facilitate the identification of the person as much information as possible is to be provided.

7.4.2009 EN Official Journal of the European Union L 93/31

(c) Purpose of the request:

Please tick the appropriate box

(1) ☐ criminal proceedings (please identify the authority before which the proceedings are pending and, if available, the case reference number) ....

....

(2) ☐ request outside the context of criminal proceedings (please identify the authority before which the proceedings are pending and, if available, the case reference number, while ticking the relevant box):

(i) ☐ from a judicial authority ....

....

(ii) ☐ from a competent administrative authority ....

....

(iii) ☐ from the person concerned for information on own criminal record ....

....

Purpose for which the information is requested:

Requesting authority:

☐ the person concerned does not consent for this information to be divulged (if the person concerned was asked for its consent in accordance with the law of the requesting Member State).

Contact person for any further information needed:

Name:

Telephone:

E-mail address:

Other information (e.g. urgency of the request):

Reply to the request

Information relating to the person concerned

Please tick the appropriate box

The undersigned authority confirms that:

☐ there is no information on convictions in the criminal record of the person concerned

☐ there is information on convictions entered in the criminal record of the person concerned; a list of convictions is attached

☐ there is other information entered in the criminal record of the person concerned; such information is attached (optional)

☐ there is information on convictions entered in the criminal record of the person concerned but the convicting Member State intimated that the information about these convictions may not be retransmitted for any purposes other than that of criminal proceedings. The request for more information may be sent directly to .... (please indicate the convicting Member State)

☐ in accordance with the national law of the requested Member State, requests made for any purposes other than that of criminal proceedings may not be dealt with.

L 93/32 EN Official Journal of the European Union 7.4.2009

Contact person for any further information needed: Name: Telephone: E-mail address: Other information (limitations of use of the data concerning requests outside the context of criminal proceedings): Please indicate the number of pages attached to the reply form:
Done at on Signature and official stamp (if appropriate): Name and position/organisation:

If appropriate, please attach a list of convictions and send the complete package to the requesting Member State. It is not necessary to translate the form or the list into the language of the requesting Member State.

4. Council Decision 2009/316/JHA of 6 April 2009 on the establishment of the European Criminal Records Information System (ECRIS) in application of Article 11 of Framework Decision 2009/315/JHA[28]

THE COUNCIL OF THE EUROPEAN UNION,

(. . .)

HAS DECIDED AS FOLLOWS:

Article 1

Subject matter
This Decision establishes the European Criminal Records Information System (ECRIS).
This Decision also establishes the elements of a standardised format for the electronic exchange of information extracted from criminal records between the Member States, in particular as regards information on the offence giving rise to the conviction and information on the content of the conviction, as well as other general and technical implementation means related to organising and facilitating the exchange of information.

Article 2

Definitions
For the purposes of this Decision, the definitions laid down in Framework Decision 2009/315/JHA shall apply.

Article 3

European Criminal Records Information System (ECRIS)

1. ECRIS is a decentralised information technology system based on the criminal records databases in each Member State. It is composed of the following elements:

   (a) an interconnection software built in compliance with a common set of protocols enabling the exchange of information between Member States' criminal records databases;
   (b) a common communication infrastructure that provides an encrypted network.

2. This Decision is not aimed at establishing any centralised criminal records database. All criminal records data shall be stored solely in databases operated by the Member States.

---

[28] OJ L 93, 7.4.2009, p. 33.

3. Central authorities of the Member States referred to in Article 3 of Framework Decision 2009/315/JHA shall not have direct online access to criminal records databases of other Member States. The best available techniques identified together by Member States with the support of the Commission shall be employed to ensure the confidentiality and integrity of criminal records information transmitted to other Member States.
4. The interconnection software and databases storing, sending and receiving information extracted from criminal records shall operate under the responsibility of the Member State concerned.
5. The common communication infrastructure shall be the S-TESTA communications network. Any further developments thereof or any alternative secure network shall ensure that the common communication infrastructure in place continues to meet the conditions set out in paragraph 6.
6. The common communication infrastructure shall be operated under the responsibility of the Commission, and shall fulfil the security requirements and thoroughly respond to the needs of ECRIS.
7. In order to ensure the efficient operation of ECRIS, the Commission shall provide general support and technical assistance, including the collection and drawing up of statistics referred to in Article 6(2)(b)(i) and the reference implementation software.
8. Notwithstanding the possibility of using the European Union financial programmes in accordance with the applicable rules, each Member State shall bear its own costs arising from the implementation, administration, use and maintenance of its criminal records database and the interconnection software referred to in paragraph 1.

The Commission shall bear the costs arising from the implementation, administration, use, maintenance and future developments of the common communication infrastructure of ECRIS, as well as the implementation and future developments of the reference implementation software.

Article 4

Format of transmission of information

1. When transmitting information in accordance with Article 4(2) and (3) and Article 7 of Framework Decision 2009/315/JHA relating to the name or legal classification of the offence and to the applicable legal provisions, Member States shall refer to the corresponding code for each of the offences referred to in the transmission, as provided for in the table of offences in Annex A. By way of exception, where the offence does not correspond to any specific sub-category, the "open category" code of the relevant or closest category of offences or, in the absence of the latter, an "other offences" code, shall be used for that particular offence.

   Member States may also provide available information relating to the level of completion and the level of participation in the offence and, where applicable, to the existence of total or partial exemption from criminal responsibility or to recidivism.

2. When transmitting information in accordance with Article 4(2) and (3) and Article 7 of Framework Decision 2009/315/JHA relating to the contents of the conviction, notably the sentence as well as any supplementary penalties, security measures and subsequent decisions modifying the enforcement of the sentence, Member States shall refer to the corresponding code for each of the penalties and measures referred to in the transmission, as provided for in the table of penalties and measures in Annex B. By way of exception, where the penalty or measure does not correspond to any specific sub-category, the "open category" code of the relevant or closest category of penalties and measures or, in the absence of the latter, an "other penalties and measures" code, shall be used for that particular penalty or measure.

   Member States shall also provide, where applicable, available information relating to the nature and/or conditions of execution of the penalty or measure imposed as provided for in the parameters of Annex B. The parameter "non-criminal ruling" shall be indicated only in cases where information on such a ruling is provided on a voluntary basis by the Member State of nationality of the person concerned, when replying to a request for information on convictions.

Article 5

Information on national offences and penalties and measures

1. The following information shall be provided by the Member States to the General Secretariat of the Council, with a view in particular to drawing up the non-binding manual for practitioners referred to in Article 6(2)(a):

   (a) the list of national offences in each of the categories referred to in the table of offences in Annex A. The list shall include the name or legal classification of the offence and reference to the applicable legal provisions. It may also include a short description of the constitutive elements of the offence;
   (b) the list of types of sentences, possible supplementary penalties and security measures and possible subsequent decisions modifying the enforcement of the sentence as defined in national law, in each of the categories referred to in the table of penalties and measures in Annex B. It may also include a short description of the specific penalty or measure.

2. The lists and descriptions referred to in paragraph 1 shall be regularly updated by Member States. Updated information shall be sent to the General Secretariat of the Council.
3. The General Secretariat of the Council shall communicate to the Member States and to the Commission the information received pursuant to this Article.

Article 6

Implementing measures

1. The Council, acting by a qualified majority and after consulting the European Parliament, shall adopt any modifications of Annexes A and B as may be necessary.

2. The representatives of the relevant departments of the administrations of the Member States and the Commission shall inform and consult one another within the Council with a view to:

   (a) drawing up a non-binding manual for practitioners setting out the procedure for the exchange of information through ECRIS, addressing in particular the modalities of identification of offenders, as well as recording the common understanding of the categories of offences and penalties and measures listed respectively in Annexes A and B;
   (b) coordinating their action for the development and operation of ECRIS, concerning in particular:

      (i) the establishment of logging systems and procedures making it possible to monitor the functioning of ECRIS and the establishment of non-personal statistics relating to the exchange through ECRIS of information extracted from criminal records;
      (ii) the adoption of technical specifications of the exchange, including security requirements, in particular the common set of protocols;
      (iii) the establishment of procedures verifying the conformity of the national software applications with the technical specifications.

Article 7

Report
The Commission services shall regularly publish a report concerning the exchange, through ECRIS, of information extracted from the criminal record based in particular on the statistics referred to in Article 6(2)(b)(i). This report shall be published for the first time one year after submitting the report referred to in Article 13(3) of Framework Decision 2009/315/JHA.

Article 8

Implementation and time limits

1. Member States shall take the necessary measures to comply with the provisions of this Decision by 7 April 2012.
2. Member States shall use the format specified in Article 4 and comply with the means of organising and facilitating exchanges of information laid down in this Decision from the date notified in accordance with Article 11(6) of Framework Decision 2009/315/JHA.

Article 9

Taking of effect
This Decision shall take effect on the day of its publication in the Official Journal of the European Union.

Done at Luxembourg, 6 April 2009.
For the Council
The President
J. Pospíšil

Code	Categories and sub-categories of offences
0401 00	Trafficking in human beings for the purposes of labour or services exploitation
0402 00	Trafficking in human beings for the purposes of the exploitation of the prostitution of others or other forms of sexual exploitation
0403 00	Trafficking in human beings for the purposes of organ or human tissue removal
0404 00	Trafficking in human beings for the purpose of slavery, practices similar to slavery or servitude
0405 00	Trafficking in human beings for the purposes of labour or services exploitation of a minor
0406 00	Trafficking in human beings for the purposes of the exploitation of the prostitution of minors or other forms of their sexual exploitation
0407 00	Trafficking in human beings for the purposes of organ or human tissue removal of a minor
0408 00	Trafficking in human beings for the purpose of slavery, practices similar to slavery or servitude of a minor
0500 00 open category	**Illicit trafficking** (1) **and other offences related to weapons, firearms, their parts and components, ammunition and explosives**
0501 00	Illicit manufacturing of weapons, firearms, their parts and components, ammunition and explosives
0502 00	Illicit trafficking of weapons, firearms, their parts and components ammunition and explosives at national level (2)
0503 00	Illicit exportation or importation of weapons, firearms, their parts and components, ammunition and explosives
0504 00	Unauthorised possession or use of weapons, firearms, their parts and components, ammunition and explosives
0600 00 open category	**Environmental crime**
0601 00	Destroying or damaging protected fauna and flora species
0602 00	Unlawful discharges of polluting substances or ionising radiation into air, soil or water
0603 00	Offences related to waste, including hazardous waste
0604 00	Offences related to illicit trafficking (1) in protected fauna and flora species or parts thereof
0605 00	Unintentional environmental offences
0700 00 open category	**Offences related to drugs or precursors, and other offences against public health**
0701 00	Offences related to illicit trafficking (3) in narcotic drugs, psychotropic substances and precursors not exclusively for own personal consumption
0702 00	Illicit consumption of drugs and their acquisition, possession, manufacture or production exclusively for own personal consumption

Code	Categories and sub-categories of offences
0703 00	Aiding or inciting others to use narcotic drugs or psychotropic substances illicitly
0704 00	Manufacture or production of narcotic drugs not exclusively for personal consumption
0800 00 open category	**Crimes against the person**
0801 00	Intentional killing
0802 00	Aggravated cases of intentional killing (4)
0803 00	Unintentional killing
0804 00	Intentional killing of a new-born by his/her mother
0805 00	Illegal abortion
0806 00	Illegal euthanasia
0807 00	Offences related to committing suicide
0808 00	Violence causing death
0809 00	Causing grievous bodily injury, disfigurement or permanent disability
0810 00	Unintentionally causing grievous bodily injury, disfigurement or permanent disability
0811 00	Causing minor bodily injury
0812 00	Unintentionally causing minor bodily injury
0813 00	Exposing to danger of loss of life or grievous bodily injury
0814 00	Torture
0815 00	Failure to offer aid or assistance
0816 00	Offences related to organ or tissue removal without authorisation or consent
0817 00	Offences related to illicit trafficking (3) in human organs and tissue
0818 00	Domestic violence or threat
0900 00 open category	**Offences against personal liberty, dignity and other protected interests, including racism and xenophobia**
0901 00	Kidnapping, kidnapping for ransom, illegal restraint
0902 00	Unlawful arrest or deprivation of liberty by public authority
0903 00	Hostage-taking
0904 00	Unlawful seizure of an aircraft or ship
0905 00	Insults, slander, defamation, contempt

Code	Categories and sub-categories of offences
0906 00	Threats
0907 00	Duress, pressure, stalking, harassment or aggression of a psychological or emotional nature
0908 00	Extortion
0909 00	Aggravated extortion
0910 00	Illegal entry into private property
0911 00	Invasion of privacy other than illegal entry into private property
0912 00	Offences against protection of personal data
0913 00	Illegal interception of data or communication
0914 00	Discrimination on grounds of gender, race, sexual orientation, religion or ethnic origin
0915 00	Public incitement to racial discrimination
0916 00	Public incitement to racial hatred
0917 00	Blackmail
1000 00 open category	**Sexual offences**
1001 00	Rape
1002 00	Aggravated rape (*) other than rape of a minor
1003 00	Sexual assault
1004 00	Procuring for prostitution or sexual act
1005 00	Indecent exposure
1006 00	Sexual harassment
1007 00	Soliciting by a prostitute
1008 00	Sexual exploitation of children
1009 00	Offences related to child pornography or indecent images of minors
1010 00	Rape of a minor
1011 00	Sexual assault of a minor
1100 00 open category	**Offences against family law**
1101 00	Illicit sexual relations between close family members
1102 00	Polygamy

Code	Categories and sub-categories of offences
1400 00 open category	**Tax and customs offences**
1401 00	Tax offences
1402 00	Customs offences
1500 00 open category	**Economic and trade related offences**
1501 00	Bankruptcy or fraudulent insolvency
1502 00	Breach of accounting regulation, embezzlement, concealment of assets or unlawful increase in a company's liabilities
1503 00	Violation of competition rules
1504 00	Laundering of proceeds from crime
1505 00	Active or passive corruption in the private sector
1506 00	Revealing a secret or breaching an obligation of secrecy
1507 00	'Insider trading'
1600 00 open category	**Offences against property or causing damage to goods**
1601 00	Unlawful appropriation
1602 00	Unlawful appropriation or diversion of energy
1603 00	Fraud, including swindling
1604 00	Dealing in stolen goods
1605 00	Illicit trafficking (*) in cultural goods, including antiques and works of art
1606 00	Intentional damage or destruction of property
1607 00	Unintentional damage or destruction of property
1608 00	Sabotage
1609 00	Offences against industrial or intellectual property
1610 00	Arson
1611 00	Arson causing death or injury to persons
1612 00	Forest arson
1700 00 open category	**Theft offences**

Code	Categories and sub-categories of offences
1701 00	Theft
1702 00	Theft after unlawful entry into property
1703 00	Theft, using violence or weapons, or using threat of violence or weapons against person
1704 00	Forms of aggravated theft which do not involve use of violence or weapons, or use of threat of violence or weapons, against persons.
1800 00 open category	**Offences against information systems and other computer-related crime**
1801 00	Illegal access to information systems
1802 00	Illegal system interference
1803 00	Illegal data interference
1804 00	Production, possession, dissemination of or trafficking in computer devices or data enabling commitment of computer-related offences
1900 00 open category	**Forgery of means of payment**
1901 00	Counterfeiting or forging currency, including the euro
1902 00	Counterfeiting of non-cash means of payment
1903 00	Counterfeiting or forging public fiduciary documents
1904 00	Putting into circulation/using counterfeited or forged currency, non-cash means of payment or public fiduciary documents
1905 00	Possession of a device for the counterfeiting or forgery of currency or public fiduciary documents
2000 00 open category	**Falsification of documents**
2001 00	Falsification of a public or administrative document by a private individual
2002 00	Falsification of a document by a civil servant or a public authority
2003 00	Supply or acquisition of a forged public or administrative document; supply or acquisition of a forged document by a civil servant or a public authority
2004 00	Using forged public or administrative documents
2005 00	Possession of a device for the falsification of public or administrative documents
2006 00	Forgery of private documents by a private individual
2100 00 open category	**Offences against traffic regulations**
2101 00	Dangerous driving
2102 00	Driving under the influence of alcohol or narcotic drugs

L 93/46 EN Official Journal of the European Union 7.4.2009

ANNEX B

Common table of penalties and measures categories referred to in Article 4

Code	Categories and sub-categories of offences
1000 open category	**Deprivation of freedom**
1001	Imprisonment
1002	Life imprisonment
2000 open category	**Restriction of personal freedom**
2001	Prohibition from frequenting some places
2002	Restriction to travel abroad
2003	Prohibition to stay in some places
2004	Prohibition from entry to a mass event
2005	Prohibition to enter in contact with certain persons through whatever means
2006	Placement under electronic surveillance (1)
2007	Obligation to report at specified times to a specific authority
2008	Obligation to stay/reside in a certain place
2009	Obligation to be at the place of residence on the set time
2010	Obligation to comply with the probation measures ordered by the court, including the obligation to remain under supervision
3000 open category	**Prohibition of a specific right or capacity**
3001	Disqualification from function
3002	Loss/suspension of capacity to hold or to be appointed to public office
3003	Loss/suspension of the right to vote or to be elected
3004	Incapacity to contract with public administration
3005	Ineligibility to obtain public subsidies
3006	Cancellation of the driving licence (2)
3007	Suspension of driving licence
3008	Prohibition to drive certain vehicles
3009	Loss/suspension of the parental authority
3010	Loss/suspension of right to be an expert in court proceedings/witness under oath/juror
3011	Loss/suspension of right to be a legal guardian (3)
3012	Loss/suspension of right of decoration or title
3013	Prohibition to exercise professional, commercial or social activity
3014	Prohibition from working or activity with minors
3015	Obligation to close an establishment
3016	Prohibition to hold or to carry weapons
3017	Withdrawal of a hunting/fishing license

7.4.2009 EN Official Journal of the European Union L 93/47

Code	Categories and sub-categories of offences
3018	Prohibition to issue cheques or to use payment/credit cards
3019	Prohibition to keep animals
3020	Prohibition to possess or use certain items other than weapons
3021	Prohibition to play certain games/sports
4000 open category	**Prohibition or expulsion from territory**
4001	Prohibition from national territory
4002	Expulsion from national territory
5000 open category	**Personal obligation**
5001	Submission to medical treatment or other forms of therapy
5002	Submission to a social-educational programme
5003	Obligation to be under the care/control of the family
5004	Educational measures
5005	Socio-judicial probation
5006	Obligation of training/working
5007	Obligation to provide judicial authorities with specific information
5008	Obligation to publish the judgment
5009	Obligation to compensate for the prejudice caused by the offence
6000 open category	**Penalty on personal property**
6001	Confiscation
6002	Demolition
6003	Restoration
7000 open category	**Placing in an institution**
7001	Placing in a psychiatric institution
7002	Placing in a detoxification institution
7003	Placing in an educational institution
8000 open category	**Financial penalty**
8001	Fine
8002	Day-fine [4]
8003	Fine for the benefit of a special recipient [5]
9000 open category	**Working penalty**
9001	Community service or work
9002	Community service or work accompanied with other restrictive measures

L 93/48 EN Official Journal of the European Union 7.4.2009

Code	Categories and sub-categories of offences
10000 open category	**Military penalty**
10001	Loss of military rank (6)
10002	Expulsion from professional military service
10003	Military imprisonment
11000 open category	**Exemption/deferment of sentence/penalty, warning**
12000 open category	**Other penalties and measures**

(1) Fixed or mobile placement.
(2) Reapplication in order to obtain a new driving licence is necessary.
(3) Legal guardian for a person who is legally incompetent or for a minor.
(4) Fine expressed in daily units.
(5) E.g.: for an institution, association, foundation or a victim.
(6) Military demotion.

Parameters (to be specified where applicable)	
ø	Penalty
m	Measure
a	Suspended penalty/measure
b	Partially suspended penalty/measure
c	Suspended penalty/measure with probation/supervision
d	Partially suspended penalty/measure with probation/supervision
e	Conversion of penalty/measure
f	Alternative penalty/measure imposed as principal penalty
g	Alternative penalty/measure imposed initially in case of non-respect of the principal penalty
h	Revocation of suspended penalty/measure
i	Subsequent formation of an overall penalty
j	Interruption of enforcement/postponement of the penalty/measure (1)
k	Remission of the penalty
l	Remission of the suspended penalty
n	End of penalty
o	Pardon
p	Amnesty
q	Release on parole (liberation of a person before end of the sentence under certain conditions)
r	Rehabilitation (with or without the deletion of penalty from criminal records)
s	Penalty or measure specific to minors
t	Non-criminal ruling (2)

(1) Does not lead to avoidance of enforcement of penalty.
(2) This parameter will be indicated only when such information is provided in reply to the request received by the Member State of nationality of the person concerned.

5. Council Framework Decision 2006/960/JHA of 18 December 2006 on simplifying the exchange of information and intelligence between law enforcement authorities of the Member States of the European Union

TITLE I
SCOPE AND DEFINITIONS

Article 1
Objective and scope

1. The purpose of this Framework Decision is to establish the rules under which Member States' law enforcement authorities may exchange existing information and intelligence effectively and expeditiously for the purpose of conducting criminal investigations or criminal intelligence operations.
2. This Framework Decision shall be without prejudice to bilateral or multilateral agreements or arrangements between Member States and third countries and to instruments of the European Union on mutual legal assistance or mutual recognition of decisions regarding criminal matters, including any conditions set by third countries concerning the use of information once supplied.
3. This Framework Decision covers all information and/or intelligence as defined in Article 2(d). It does not impose any obligation on the part of the Member States to gather and store information and intelligence for the purpose of providing it to the competent law enforcement authorities of other Member States.
4. This Framework Decision does not impose any obligation on the part of the Member States to provide information and intelligence to be used as evidence before a judicial authority nor does it give any right to use such information or intelligence for that purpose. Where a Member State has obtained information or intelligence in accordance with this Framework Decision, and wishes to use it as evidence before a judicial authority, it has to obtain consent of the Member State that provided the information or intelligence, where necessary under the national law of the Member State that provided the information or intelligence, through the use of instruments regarding judicial cooperation in force between the Member States. Such consent is not required where the requested Member State has already given its consent for the use of information or intelligence as evidence at the time of transmittal of the information or intelligence.
5. This Framework Decision does not impose any obligation to obtain any information or intelligence by means of coercive measures, defined in accordance with national law, in the Member State receiving the request for information or intelligence. With their national law, provide information or intelligence previously obtained by means of coercive measures.
6. This Framework Decision shall not have the effect of modifying the obligation to respect fundamental rights and fundamental legal principles as enshrined in Article 6 of the Treaty on European Union and any obligations incumbent on law enforcement authorities in this respect shall remain unaffected.

Article 2
Definitions
For the purposes of this Framework Decision:

(a) 'competent law enforcement authority': a national police, customs or other authority that is authorised by national law to detect, prevent and investigate offences or criminal activities and to exercise authority and take coercive measures in the context of such activities. Agencies or units dealing especially with national security issues are not covered by the concept of competent law enforcement authority. Every Member State shall, by 18 December 2007, state in a declaration deposited with the General Secretariat of the Council which authorities are covered by the concept of 'competent law enforcement authority'. Such a declaration may be modified at any time.
(b) 'criminal investigation': a procedural stage within which measures are taken by competent law enforcement or judicial authorities, including public prosecutors, with a view to establishing and identifying facts, suspects and circumstances regarding one or several identified concrete criminal acts;
(c) 'criminal intelligence operation': a procedural stage, not yet having reached the stage of a criminal investigation, within which a competent law enforcement authority is entitled by national law to collect, process and analyse information about crime or criminal activities with a view to establishing whether concrete criminal acts have been committed or may be committed in the future;
(d) 'information and/or intelligence':

    (i) any type of information or data which is held by law enforcement authorities; and
    (ii) any type of information or data which is held by public authorities or by private entities and which is available to law enforcement authorities without the taking of coercive measures, in accordance with Article 1(5).

(e) 'offences referred to in Article 2(2) of the Framework Decision 2002/584/JHA on the European arrest warrant (1)' (hereinafter referred to as 'offences referred to in Article 2(2) of the Framework Decision 2002/584/JHA'): offences under national law which correspond to or are equivalent to those referred to in that provision.

TITLE II
EXCHANGE OF INFORMATION AND INTELLIGENCE
Article 3
Provision of information and intelligence

1. Member States shall ensure that information and intelligence can be provided to the competent law enforcement authorities of other Member States in accordance with this Framework Decision.
2. Information and intelligence shall be provided at the request of a competent law enforcement authority, acting in accordance with the powers conferred upon it by national law, conducting a criminal investigation or a criminal intelligence operation.

3. Member States shall ensure that conditions not stricter than those applicable at national level for providing and requesting information and intelligence are applied for providing information and intelligence to competent law enforcement authorities of other Member States. In particular, a Member State shall not subject the exchange, by its competent law enforcement authority with a competent law enforcement authority of another Member State, of information or intelligence which in an internal procedure may be accessed by the requested competent law enforcement authority without a judicial agreement or authorisation, to such an agreement or authorisation.
4. Where the information or intelligence sought may, under the national law of the requested Member State, be accessed by the requested competent law enforcement authority only pursuant to an agreement or authorisation of a judicial authority, the requested competent law enforcement authority shall be obliged to ask the competent judicial authority for an agreement or authorisation to access and exchange the information sought. The competent judicial authority of the requested Member State shall apply the same rules for its decision, without prejudice to Article 10(1) and (2), as in a purely internal case. Obtained from another Member State or from a third country and is subject to the rule of speciality, its transmission to the competent law enforcement authority of another Member State may only take place with the consent of the Member State or third country that provided the information or intelligence.

Article 4
Time limits for provision of information and intelligence

1. Member States shall ensure that they have procedures in place so that they can respond within at most eight hours to urgent requests for information and intelligence regarding offences referred to in Article 2(2) of Framework Decision 2002/584/JHA, when the requested information or intelligence is held in a database directly accessible by a law enforcement authority.
2. If the requested competent law enforcement authority is unable to respond within eight hours, it shall provide reasons for that on the form set out in Annex A. Where the provision of the information or intelligence requested within the period of eight hours would put a disproportionate burden on the requested law enforcement authority, it may postpone the provision of the information or intelligence. In that case the requested law enforcement authority shall immediately inform the requesting law enforcement authority of this postponement and shall provide the requested information or intelligence as soon as possible, but not later than within three days. The use made of the provisions under this paragraph shall be reviewed by 19 December 2009.
3. Member States shall ensure that for non-urgent cases, requests for information and intelligence regarding offences referred to in Article 2(2) of Framework Decision 2002/584/JHA should be responded to within one week if the requested information or intelligence is held in a database directly accessible by a law enforcement authority. If the requested competent law enforcement authority is unable to respond within one week, it shall provide reasons for that on the form set out in Annex A.

4. In all other cases, Member States shall ensure that the information sought is communicated to the requesting competent law enforcement authority within 14 days. If the requested competent law enforcement authority is unable to respond within 14 days, it shall provide reasons for that on the form set out in Annex A.

Article 5
Requests for information and intelligence

1. Information and intelligence may be requested for the purpose of detection, prevention or investigation of an offence where there are factual reasons to believe that relevant information and intelligence is available in another Member State. The request shall set out those factual reasons and explain the purpose for which the information and intelligence is sought and the connection between the purpose and the person who is the subject of the information and intelligence.
2. The requesting competent law enforcement authority shall refrain from requesting more information or intelligence or setting narrower time frames than necessary for the purpose of the request.
3. Requests for information or intelligence shall contain at least the information set out in Annex B.

Article 6
Communication channels and language

1. Exchange of information and intelligence under this Framework Decision may take place via any existing channels for international law enforcement cooperation. The language used for the request and the exchange of information shall be the one applicable for the channel used. Member States shall, when making their declarations in accordance with Article 2(a), also provide the General Secretariat of the Council with details of the contacts to which requests may be sent in cases of urgency. These details may be modified at any time. The General Secretariat of the Council shall communicate to the Member States and the Commission the declarations received.
2. Information or intelligence shall also be exchanged with Europol in accordance with the Convention based on Article K.3 of the Treaty on European Union, on the establishment of a European Police Office (Europol Convention) (1) and with Eurojust in accordance with the Council Decision 2002/187/JHA of 28 February 2002 setting up Eurojust with a view to reinforcing the fight against serious crime (2), insofar as the exchange refers to an offence or criminal activity within their mandate.

Article 7
Spontaneous exchange of information and intelligence

1. Without prejudice to Article 10, the competent law enforcement authorities shall, without any prior request being necessary, provide to the competent law enforcement authorities of other Member States concerned information and intelligence in cases where there are factual reasons to believe that the information and

intelligence could assist in the detection, prevention or investigation of offences referred to in Article 2(2) of Framework Decision 2002/584/JHA. The modalities of such spontaneous exchange shall be regulated by the national law of the Member States providing the information.

2. The provision of information and intelligence shall be limited to what is deemed relevant and necessary for the successful detection, prevention or investigation of the crime or criminal activity in question.

Article 8
Data protection

1. Each Member State shall ensure that the established rules on data protection provided for when using the communication channels referred to in Article 6 (1) are applied also within the procedure on exchange of information and intelligence provided for by this Framework Decision.
2. The use of information and intelligence which has been exchanged directly or bilaterally under this Framework Decision shall be subject to the national data protection provisions of the receiving Member State, where the information and intelligence shall be subject to the same data protection rules as if they had been gathered in the receiving Member State. The personal data processed in the context of the implementation of this Framework Decision shall be protected in accordance with the Council of Europe Convention of 28 January 1981 for the Protection of Individuals with regard to Automatic Processing of Personal Data, and, for those Member States which have ratified it, the Additional Protocol of 8 November 2001 to that Convention, regarding Supervisory Authorities and Transborder Data Flows. The principles of Recommendation No. R(87) 15 of the Council of Europe Regulating the Use of Personal Data in the Police Sector should also be taken into account when law enforcement authorities handle personal data obtained under this Framework Decision.
3. Information and intelligence provided under this Framework Decision may be used by the competent law enforcement authorities of the Member State to which it has been provided solely for the purposes for which it has been supplied in accordance with this Framework Decision or for preventing an immediate and serious threat to public security; processing for other purposes shall be permitted solely with the prior authorisation of the communicating Member State and subject to the national law of the receiving Member State. The authorisation may be granted insofar as the national law of the communicating Member State permits.
4. When providing information and intelligence in accordance with this Framework Decision, the providing competent law enforcement authority may pursuant to its national law impose conditions on the use of the information and intelligence by the receiving competent law enforcement authority. Conditions may also be imposed on reporting the result of the criminal investigation or criminal intelligence operation within which the exchange of information and intelligence has taken place. The receiving competent law enforcement authority shall be bound by such conditions, except in the specific case where national law lays down that

the restrictions on use be waived for judicial authorities, legislative bodies or any other independent body set up under the law and made responsible for supervising the competent law enforcement authorities. In such cases, the information and intelligence may only be used after prior consultation with the communicating Member State whose interests and opinions must be taken into account as far as possible. The receiving Member State may, in specific cases, be requested by the communicating Member State to give information about the use and further processing of the transmitted information and intelligence.

Article 9
Confidentiality
The competent law enforcement authorities shall take due account, in each specific case of exchange of information or intelligence, of the requirements of investigation secrecy. To that end the competent law enforcement authorities shall, in accordance with their national law, guarantee the confidentiality of all provided information and intelligence determined as confidential.

Article 10
Reasons to withhold information or intelligence

1. Without prejudice to Article 3(3), a competent law enforcement authority may refuse to provide information or intelligence only if there are factual reasons to assume that the provision of the information or intelligence would:

   (a) harm essential national security interests of the requested Member State; or
   (b) jeopardise the success of a current investigation or a criminal intelligence operation or the safety of individuals; or
   (c) clearly be disproportionate or irrelevant with regard to the purposes for which it has been requested.

2. Where the request pertains to an offence punishable by a term of imprisonment of one year or less under the law of the requested Member State, the competent law enforcement authority may refuse to provide the requested information or intelligence.
3. The competent law enforcement authority shall refuse to provide information or intelligence if the competent judicial authority has not authorised the access and exchange of the information requested pursuant to Article 3(4).

TITLE III
FINAL PROVISIONS
Article 11
Implementation

1. Member States shall take the necessary measures to comply with the provisions of this Framework Decision before 19 December 2006.
2. Member States shall transmit to the General Secretariat of the Council and to the Commission the text of the provisions transposing into their national laws the obligations imposed on them under this Framework Decision. On the basis of

this and other information provided by the Member States on request, the Commission shall, before 19 December 2006, submit a report to the Council on the operation of this Framework Decision. The Council shall before 19 December 2006 assess the extent to which Member States have complied with the provisions of this Framework Decision.

Article 12
Relation to other instruments

1. The provisions of Article 39(1), (2) and (3) and of Article 46 of the Convention Implementing the Schengen Agreement (1), in as far as they relate to exchange of information and intelligence for the purpose of conducting criminal investigations or criminal intelligence operations as provided for by this Framework Decision, shall be replaced by the provisions of this Framework Decision.
2. The Decision of the Schengen Executive Committee of 16 December 1998 on cross-border police cooperation in the area of crime prevention and detection (SCH/Com-ex (98) 51 rev 3) (2) and the Decision of the Schengen Executive Committee of 28 April 1999 on the improvement of police cooperation in preventing and detecting criminal offences (SCH/Com-ex (99) 18) (3) are hereby repealed.
3. Member States may continue to apply bilateral or multilateral agreements or arrangements in force when this Framework Decision is adopted in so far as such agreements or arrangements allow the objectives of this Framework Decision to be extended and help to simplify or facilitate further the procedures for exchanging information and intelligence falling within the scope of this Framework Decision.
4. Member States may conclude or bring into force bilateral or multilateral agreements or arrangements after this Framework Decision has come into force in so far as such agreements or arrangements allow the objectives of this Framework Decision to be extended and help to simplify or facilitate further the procedures for exchanging information and intelligence falling within the scope of this Framework Decision.
5. The agreements and arrangements referred to in paragraphs 3 and 4 may in no case affect relations with Member States which are not parties to them.
6. Member States shall no later than 19 December 2006, notify the Council and the Commission of the existing agreements and arrangements referred to in paragraph 3 which they wish to continue applying.
7. Member States shall also notify the Council and the Commission of any new agreement or arrangement as referred to in paragraph 4, within three months of their signature or, for those instruments which had already been signed before the adoption of this Framework Decision, their entry into force.

E. LEGAL INSTRUMENTS ON JUDICIAL COOPERATION IN CRIMINAL MATTERS

1. Convention on Mutual Assistance in Criminal Matters between the Member States of the European Union (2000 Convention)

Article 6
Transmission of requests for mutual assistance

1. Requests for mutual assistance and spontaneous exchanges of information referred to in Article 7 shall be made in writing, or by any means capable of producing a written record under conditions allowing the receiving Member State to establish authenticity. Such requests shall be made directly between judicial authorities with territorial competence for initiating and executing them, and shall be returned through the same channels unless otherwise specified in this Article.

   Any information laid by a Member State with a view to proceedings before the courts of another Member State within the meaning of Article 21 of the European Mutual Assistance Convention and Article 42 of the Benelux Treaty may be the subject of direct communications between the competent judicial authorities.
2. Paragraph 1 shall not prejudice the possibility of requests being sent or returned in specific cases:

   (a) between a central authority of a Member State and a central authority of another Member State; or
   (b) between a judicial authority of one Member State and a central authority of another Member State.

3. Notwithstanding paragraph 1, the United Kingdom and Ireland, respectively, may, when giving the notification provided for in Article 27(2), declare that requests and communications to it, as specified in the declaration, must be sent via its central authority. These Member States may at any time by a further declaration limit the scope of such a declaration for the purpose of giving greater

Á.G. Zarza (ed.), *Exchange of Information and Data Protection in Cross-border Criminal Proceedings in Europe*, DOI 10.1007/978-3-642-40291-3,

effect to paragraph 1. They shall do so when the provisions on mutual assistance of the Schengen Implementation Convention are put into effect for them.

Any Member State may apply the principle of reciprocity in relation to the declarations referred to above.

4. Any request for mutual assistance may, in case of urgency, be made via the International Criminal Police Organisation (Interpol) or any body competent under provisions adopted pursuant to the Treaty on European Union.
5. Where, in respect of requests pursuant to Articles 12, 13 or 14, the competent authority is a judicial authority or a central authority in one Member State and a police or customs authority in the other Member State, requests may be made and answered directly between these authorities. Paragraph 4 shall apply to these contacts.
6. Where, in respect of requests for mutual assistance in relation to proceedings as envisaged in Article 3(1), the competent authority is a judicial authority or a central authority in one Member State and an administrative authority in the other Member State, requests may be made and answered directly between these authorities.
7. Any Member State may declare, when giving the notification provided for in Article 27(2), that it is not bound by the first sentence of paragraph 5 or by paragraph 6 of this Article, or both or that it will apply those provisions only under certain conditions which it shall specify. Such a declaration may be withdrawn or amended at any time.
8. The following requests or communications shall be made through the central authorities of the Member States:

   (a) requests for temporary transfer or transit of persons held in custody as referred to in Article 9 of this Convention, in Article 11 of the European Mutual Assistance Convention and in Article 33 of the Benelux Treaty;
   (b) notices of information from judicial records as referred to in Article 22 of the European Mutual Assistance Convention and Article 43 of the Benelux Treaty. However, requests for copies of convictions and measures as referred to in Article 4 of the Additional Protocol to the European Mutual Assistance Convention may be made directly to the competent authorities.

Article 7
Spontaneous exchange of information

1. Within the limits of their national law, the competent authorities of the Member States may exchange information, without a request to that effect, relating to criminal offences and the infringements of rules of law referred to in Article 3 (1), the punishment or handling of which falls within the competence of the receiving authority at the time the information is provided.
2. The providing authority may, pursuant to its national law, impose conditions on the use of such information by the receiving authority.
3. The receiving authority shall be bound by those conditions.

(. . .)

TITLE IV
Article 23
Personal data protection

1. Personal data communicated under this Convention may be used by the Member State to which they have been transferred:
   (a) for the purpose of proceedings to which this Convention applies;
   (b) for other judicial and administrative proceedings directly related to proceedings referred to under point (a);
   (c) for preventing an immediate and serious threat to public security;
   (d) for any other purpose, only with the prior consent of the communicating Member State, unless the Member State concerned has obtained the consent of the data subject.
2. This Article shall also apply to personal data not communicated but obtained otherwise under this Convention.
3. In the circumstances of the particular case, the communicating Member State may require the Member State to which the personal data have been transferred to give information on the use made of the data.
4. Where conditions on the use of personal data have been imposed pursuant to Articles 7(2), 18(5)(b), 18(6) or 20(4), these conditions shall prevail. Where no such conditions have been imposed, this Article shall apply.
5. The provisions of Article 13(10) shall take precedence over this Article regarding information obtained under Article 13.

2. Protocol to the 2000 Convention

Article 1
Request for information on bank accounts

1. Each Member State shall, under the conditions set out in this Article, take the measures necessary to determine, in answer to a request sent by another Member State, whether a natural or legal person that is the subject of a criminal investigation holds or controls one or more accounts, of whatever nature, in any bank located in its territory and, if so, provide all the details of the identified accounts.
   The information shall also, if requested and to the extent that it can be provided within a reasonable time, include accounts for which the person that is the subject of the proceedings has powers of attorney.
2. The obligation set out in this Article shall apply only to the extent that the information is in the possession of the bank keeping the account.
3. The obligation set out in this Article shall apply only if the investigation concerns:

- an offence punishable by a penalty involving deprivation of liberty or a detention order of a maximum period of at least four years in the requesting State and at least two years in the requested State, or
- an offence referred to in Article 2 of the 1995 Convention on the Establishment of a European Police Office (Europol Convention), or in the Annex to that Convention, as amended, or
- to the extent that it may not be covered by the Europol Convention, an offence referred to in the 1995 Convention on the Protection of the European Communities' Financial Interests, the 1996 Protocol thereto, or the 1997 Second Protocol thereto.

4. The authority making the request shall, in the request:

   - state why it considers that the requested information is likely to be of substantial value for the purpose of the investigation into the offence,
   - state on what grounds it presumes that banks in the requested Member State hold the account and, to the extent available, which banks may be involved,
   - include any information available which may facilitate the execution of the request.

5. Member States may make the execution of a request according to this Article dependent on the same conditions as they apply in respect of requests for search and seizure.
6. The Council may decide, pursuant to Article 34(2)(c) of the Treaty of European Union, to extend the scope of paragraph 3.

Article 2
Requests for information on banking transactions

1. On request by the requesting State, the requested State shall provide the particulars of specified bank accounts and of banking operations which have been carried out during a specified period through one or more accounts specified in the request, including the particulars of any sending or recipient account.
2. The obligation set out in this Article shall apply only to the extent that the information is in the possession of the bank holding the account.
3. The requesting Member State shall in its request indicate why it considers the requested information relevant for the purpose of the investigation into the offence.
4. Member States may make the execution of a request according to this Article dependent on the same conditions as they apply in respect of requests for search and seizure.

Article 3
Requests for the monitoring of banking transactions

1. Each Member State shall undertake to ensure that, at the request of another Member State, it is able to monitor, during a specified period, the banking

operations that are being carried out through one or more accounts specified in the request and communicate the results thereof to the requesting Member State.
2. The requesting Member State shall in its request indicate why it considers the requested information relevant for the purpose of the investigation into the offence.
3. The decision to monitor shall be taken in each individual case by the competent authorities of the requested Member State, with due regard for the national law of that Member State.
4. The practical details regarding the monitoring shall be agreed between the competent authorities of the requesting and requested Member States.

Article 4
Confidentiality
Each Member State shall take the necessary measures to ensure that banks do not disclose to the bank customer concerned or to other third persons that information has been transmitted to the requesting State in accordance with Articles 1, 2 or 3 or that an investigation is being carried out.

Article 5
Obligation to inform
If the competent authority of the requested Member State in the course of the execution of a request for mutual assistance considers that it may be appropriate to undertake investigations not initially foreseen, or which could not be specified when the request was made, it shall immediately inform the requesting authority accordingly in order to enable it to take further action.

Article 6
Additional requests for mutual assistance

1. Where the competent authority of the requesting Member State makes a request for mutual assistance which is additional to an earlier request, it shall not be required to provide information already provided in the initial request. The additional request shall contain information necessary for the purpose of identifying the initial request.
2. Where, in accordance with the provisions in force, the competent authority which has made a request for mutual assistance participates in the execution of the request in the requested Member State, it may, without prejudice to Article 6 (3) of the 2000 Mutual Assistance Convention, make an additional request directly to the competent authority of the requested Member State while present in that State.

Article 7
Banking secrecy
A Member State shall not invoke banking secrecy as a reason for refusing any cooperation regarding a request for mutual assistance from another Member State.

Article 8
Fiscal offences

1. Mutual assistance may not be refused solely on the ground that the request concerns an offence which the requested Member State considers a fiscal offence.
2. If a Member State has made the execution of a request for search and seizure dependent on the condition that the offence giving rise to the request is also punishable under its law, this condition shall be fulfilled, with regard to offences referred to in paragraph 1, if the offence corresponds to an offence of the same nature under its law.

   The request may not be refused on the ground that the law of the requested Member State does not impose the same kind of tax or duty or does not contain a tax, duty, customs and exchange regulation of the same kind as the law of the requesting Member State.
3. Article 50 of the Schengen Implementation Convention is hereby repealed.

Article 9
Political offences

1. For the purposes of mutual legal assistance between Member States, no offence may be regarded by the requested Member State as a political offence, an offence connected with a political offence or an offence inspired by political motives.
2. Each Member State may, when giving the notification referred to in Article 13 (2), declare that it will apply paragraph 1 only in relation to:

   (a) the offences referred to in Articles 1 and 2 of the European Convention on the Suppression of Terrorism of 27 January 1977; and
   (b) offences of conspiracy or association, which correspond to the description of behaviour referred to in Article 3(4) of the Convention of 27 September 1996 relating to extradition between the Member States of the European Union, to commit one or more of the offences referred to in Articles 1 and 2 of the European Convention on the Suppression of Terrorism.

3. Reservations made pursuant to Article 13 of the European Convention on the Suppression of Terrorism shall not apply to mutual legal assistance between Member States.

Article 10
Forwarding refusals to the Council and involvement of Eurojust

1. If a request is refused on the basis of:

   – Article 2(b) of the European Mutual Assistance Convention or Article 22(2) (b) of the Benelux Treaty, or
   – Article 51 of the Schengen Implementation Convention or Article 5 of the European Mutual Assistance Convention, or

- Article 1(5) or Article 2(4) of this Protocol, and the requesting Member State maintains its request, and no solution can be found, the reasoned decision to refuse the request shall be forwarded to the Council for information by the requested Member State, for possible evaluation of the functioning of judicial cooperation between Member States.

2. The competent authorities of the requesting Member State may report to Eurojust, once it has been established, any problem encountered concerning the execution of a request in relation to the provisions referred to in paragraph 1 for a possible practical solution in accordance with the provisions laid down in the instrument establishing Eurojust.

3. Council Framework Decision 2002/584/JHA of 13 June 2002 on the European Arrest Warrant and the surrender procederes between Member States

THE COUNCIL OF THE EUROPEAN UNION,

(...)

HAS ADOPTED THIS FRAMEWORK DECISION:

CHAPTER 1

GENERAL PRINCIPLES

Article 1

Definition of the European arrest warrant and obligation to execute it

1. The European arrest warrant is a judicial decision issued by a Member State with a view to the arrest and surrender by another Member State of a requested person, for the purposes of conducting a criminal prosecution or executing a custodial sentence or detention order.
2. Member States shall execute any European arrest warrant on the basis of the principle of mutual recognition and in accordance with the provisions of this Framework Decision.
3. This Framework Decision shall not have the effect of modifying the obligation to respect fundamental rights and fundamental legal principles as enshrined in Article 6 of the Treaty on European Union.

(...)

Article 8

Content and form of the European arrest warrant

1. The European arrest warrant shall contain the following information set out in accordance with the form contained in the Annex:

   (a) the identity and nationality of the requested person;
   (b) the name, address, telephone and fax numbers and e-mail address of the issuing judicial authority;
   (c) evidence of an enforceable judgment, an arrest warrant or any other enforceable judicial decision having the same effect, coming within the scope of Articles 1 and 2;
   (d) the nature and legal classification of the offence, particularly in respect of Article 2;
   (e) a description of the circumstances in which the offence was committed, including the time, place and degree of participation in the offence by the requested person;

(f) the penalty imposed, if there is a final judgment, or the prescribed scale of penalties for the offence under the law of the issuing Member State;
(g) if possible, other consequences of the offence.

2. The European arrest warrant must be translated into the official language or one of the official languages of the executing Member State. Any Member State may, when this Framework Decision is adopted or at a later date, state in a declaration deposited with the General Secretariat of the Council that it will accept a translation in one or more other official languages of the Institutions of the European Communities.

CHAPTER 2

SURRENDER PROCEDURE

Article 9

Transmission of a European arrest warrant

1. When the location of the requested person is known, the issuing judicial authority may transmit the European arrest warrant directly to the executing judicial authority.
2. The issuing judicial authority may, in any event, decide to issue an alert for the requested person in the Schengen Information System (SIS).
3. Such an alert shall be effected in accordance with the provisions of Article 95 of the Convention of 19 June 1990 implementing the Schengen Agreement of 14 June 1985 on the gradual abolition of controls at common borders. An alert in the Schengen Information System shall be equivalent to a European arrest warrant accompanied by the information set out in Article 8(1).

For a transitional period, until the SIS is capable of transmitting all the information described in Article 8, the alert shall be equivalent to a European arrest warrant pending the receipt of the original in due and proper form by the executing judicial authority.

Article 10

Detailed procedures for transmitting a European arrest warrant

1. If the issuing judicial authority does not know the competent executing judicial authority, it shall make the requisite enquiries, including through the contact points of the European Judicial Network (1), in order to obtain that information from the executing Member State.
2. If the issuing judicial authority so wishes, transmission may be effected via the secure telecommunications system of the European Judicial Network.
3. If it is not possible to call on the services of the SIS, the issuing judicial authority may call on Interpol to transmit a European arrest warrant.
4. The issuing judicial authority may forward the European arrest warrant by any secure means capable of producing written records under conditions allowing the executing Member State to establish its authenticity.

5. All difficulties concerning the transmission or the authenticity of any document needed for the execution of the European arrest warrant shall be dealt with by direct contacts between the judicial authorities involved, or, where appropriate, with the involvement of the central authorities of the Member States.
6. If the authority which receives a European arrest warrant is not competent to act upon it, it shall automatically forward the European arrest warrant to the competent authority in its Member State and shall inform the issuing judicial authority accordingly.

(. . .)

Article 15

Surrender decision

1. The executing judicial authority shall decide, within the time-limits and under the conditions defined in this Framework Decision, whether the person is to be surrendered.
2. If the executing judicial authority finds the information communicated by the issuing Member State to be insufficient to allow it to decide on surrender, it shall request that the necessary supplementary information, in particular with respect to Articles 3 to 5 and Article 8, be furnished as a matter of urgency and may fix a time limit for the receipt thereof, taking into account the need to observe the time limits set in Article 17.
3. The issuing judicial authority may at any time forward any additional useful information to the executing judicial authority.

(. . .)

Article 17

Time limits and procedures for the decision to execute the European arrest warrant

1. A European arrest warrant shall be dealt with and executed as a matter of urgency.
2. In cases where the requested person consents to his surrender, the final decision on the execution of the European arrest warrant should be taken within a period of 10 days alter consent has been given.
3. In other cases, the final decision on the execution of the European arrest warrant should be taken within a period of 60 days after the arrest of the requested person.
4. Where in specific cases the European arrest warrant cannot be executed within the time limits laid down in paragraphs 2 or 3, the executing judicial authority shall immediately inform the issuing judicial authority thereof, giving the reasons for the delay. In such case, the time limits may be extended by a further 30 days.
5. As long as the executing judicial authority has not taken a final decision on the European arrest warrant, it shall ensure that the material conditions necessary for effective surrender of the person remain fulfilled.

6. Reasons must be given for any refusal to execute a European arrest warrant.
7. Where in exceptional circumstances a Member State cannot observe the time limits provided for in this Article, it shall inform Eurojust, giving the reasons for the delay. In addition, a Member State which has experienced repeated delays on the part of another Member State in the execution of European arrest warrants shall inform the Council with a view to evaluating the implementation of this Framework Decision at Member State level.

(. . .)

Article 18

Situation pending the decision

1. Where the European arrest warrant has been issued for the purpose of conducting a criminal prosecution, the executing judicial authority must:
   (a) either agree that the requested person should be heard according to Article 19;
   (b) or agree to the temporary transfer of the requested person.
2. The conditions and the duration of the temporary transfer shall be determined by mutual agreement between the issuing and executing judicial authorities.
3. In the case of temporary transfer, the person must be able to return to the executing Member State to attend hearings concerning him or her as part of the surrender procedure.

Article 23

Time limits for surrender of the person

1. The person requested shall be surrendered as soon as possible on a date agreed between the authorities concerned.
2. He or she shall be surrendered no later than 10 days after the final decision on the execution of the European arrest warrant.
3. If the surrender of the requested person within the period laid down in paragraph 2 is prevented by circumstances beyond the control of any of the Member States, the executing and issuing judicial authorities shall immediately contact each other and agree on a new surrender date. In that event, the surrender shall take place within 10 days of the new date thus agreed.
4. The surrender may exceptionally be temporarily postponed for serious humanitarian reasons, for example if there are substantial grounds for believing that it would manifestly endanger the requested person's life or health. The execution of the European arrest warrant shall take place as soon as these grounds have ceased to exist. The executing judicial authority shall immediately inform the issuing judicial authority and agree on a new surrender date. In that event, the surrender shall take place within 10 days of the new date thus agreed.
5. Upon expiry of the time limits referred to in paragraphs 2 to 4, if the person is still being held in custody he shall be released.

(. . .)

Article 24

Postponed or conditional surrender

1. The executing judicial authority may, after deciding to execute the European arrest warrant, postpone the surrender of the requested person so that he or she may be prosecuted in the executing Member State or, if he or she has already been sentenced, so that he or she may serve, in its territory, a sentence passed for an act other than that referred to in the European arrest warrant.
2. Instead of postponing the surrender, the executing judicial authority may temporarily surrender the requested person to the issuing Member State under conditions to be determined by mutual agreement between the executing and the issuing judicial authorities. The agreement shall be made in writing and the conditions shall be binding on all the authorities in the issuing Member State.

Article 26

Deduction of the period of detention served in the executing Member State

1. The issuing Member State shall deduct all periods of detention arising from the execution of a European arrest warrant from the total period of detention to be served in the issuing Member State as a result of a custodial sentence or detention order being passed.
2. To that end, all information concerning the duration of the detention of the requested person on the basis of the European arrest warrant shall be transmitted by the executing judicial authority or the central authority designated under Article 7 to the issuing judicial authority at the time of the surrender.

4. Council Framework Decision 2003/577/JHA of 22July 2003 on the execution in the European Union of orders freezing property or evidence

Article 1

Objective

The purpose of the Framework Decision is to establish the rules under which a Member State shall recognise and execute in its territory a freezing order issued by a judicial authority of another Member State in the framework of criminal proceedings.
It shall not have the effect of amending the obligation to respect the fundamental rights and fundamental legal principles as enshrined in Article 6 of the Treaty.

(...)

Article 4

Transmission of freezing orders

1. A freezing order within the meaning of this Framework Decision, together with the certificate provided for in Article 9, shall be transmitted by the judicial authority which issued it directly to the competent judicial authority for execution by any means capable of producing a written record under conditions allowing the executing State to establish authenticity.
2. The United Kingdom and Ireland, respectively, may, before the date referred to in Article 14(1), state in a declaration that the freezing order together with the certificate must be sent via a central authority or authorities specified by it in the declaration. Any such declaration may be modified by a further declaration or withdrawn any time. Any declaration or withdrawal shall be deposited with the General Secretariat of the Council and notified to the Commission. These Member States may at any time by a further declaration limit the scope of such a declaration for the purpose of giving greater effect to paragraph 1. They shall do so when the provisions on mutual assistance of the Convention implementing the Schengen Agreement are put into effect for them.
3. If the competent judicial authority for execution is unknown, the judicial authority in the issuing State shall make all necessary inquiries, including via the contact points of the European Judicial Network (1), in order to obtain the information from the executing State.
4. When the judicial authority in the executing State which receives a freezing order has no jurisdiction to recognise it and take the necessary measures for its execution, it shall, *ex officio*, transmit the freezing order to the competent judicial authority for execution and shall so inform the judicial authority in the issuing State which issued it.

Article 5

Recognition and immediate execution

1. The competent judicial authorities of the executing State shall recognise a freezing order, transmitted in accordance with Article 4, without any further formality being required and shall forthwith take the necessary measures for its immediate execution in the same way as for a freezing order made by an authority of the executing State, unless that authority decides to invoke one of the grounds for non-recognition or nonexecution provided for in Article 7 or one of the grounds for postponement provided for in Article 8.

   Whenever it is necessary to ensure that the evidence taken is valid and provided that such formalities and procedures are not contrary to the fundamental principles of law in the executing State, the judicial authority of the executing State shall also observe the formalities and procedures expressly indicated by the competent judicial authority of the issuing State in the execution of the freezing order.

   A report on the execution of the freezing order shall be made forthwith to the competent authority in the issuing State by any means capable of producing a written record.
2. Any additional coercive measures rendered necessary by the freezing order shall be taken in accordance with the applicable procedural rules of the executing State.
3. The competent judicial authorities of the executing State shall decide and communicate the decision on a freezing order as soon as possible and, whenever practicable, within 24 hours of receipt of the freezing order.

Article 10

Subsequent treatment of the frozen property

1. The transmission referred to in Article 4:

   (a) shall be accompanied by a request for the evidence to be transferred to the issuing State; or
   (b) shall be accompanied by a request for confiscation requiring either enforcement of a confiscation order that has been issued in the issuing State or confiscation in the executing State and subsequent enforcement of any such order; or
   (c) shall contain an instruction in the certificate that the property shall remain in the executing State pending a request referred to in (a) or (b). The issuing State shall indicate in the certificate the (estimated) date for submission of this request. Article 6(2) shall apply.

2. Requests referred to in paragraph 1(a) and (b) shall be submitted by the issuing State and processed by the executing State in accordance with the rules applicable to mutual assistance in criminal matters and the rules applicable to international cooperation relating to confiscation.

3. However, by way of derogation from the rules on mutual assistance referred to in paragraph 2, the executing State may not refuse requests referred to under paragraph 1(a) on grounds of absence of double criminality, where the requests concern the offences referred to in Article 3(2) and those offences are punishable in the issuing State by a prison sentence of at least three years.

Article 11

Legal remedies

1. Member States shall put in place the necessary arrangements to ensure that any interested party, including bona fide third parties, have legal remedies without suspensive effect against a freezing order executed pursuant to Article 5, in order to preserve their legitimate interests; the action shall be brought before a court in the issuing State or in the executing State in accordance with the national law of each.
2. The substantive reasons for issuing the freezing order can be challenged only in an action brought before a court in the issuing State.
3. If the action is brought in the executing State, the judicial authority of the issuing State shall be informed thereof and of the grounds of the action, so that it can submit the arguments that it deems necessary. It shall be informed of the outcome of the action.
4. The issuing and executing States shall take the necessary measures to facilitate the exercise of the right to bring an action mentioned in paragraph 1, in particular by providing adequate information to interested parties.
5. The issuing State shall ensure that any time limits for bringing an action mentioned in paragraph 1 are applied in a way that guarantees the possibility of an effective legal remedy for the interested parties.

5. Council Framework Decision 2008/909/JHA of 27 November 2008 on the application of the principle of mutual recognition to judgements and probation decisions with a view to the supervision of probation measures and alternative sanctions

Article 3

Purpose and scope

1. The purpose of this Framework Decision is to establish the rules under which a Member State, with a view to facilitating the social rehabilitation of the sentenced person, is to recognise a judgment and enforce the sentence.
2. This Framework Decision shall apply where the sentenced person is in the issuing State or in the executing State.
3. This Framework Decision shall apply only to the recognition of judgments and the enforcement of sentences within the meaning of this Framework Decision. The fact that, in addition to the sentence, a fine and/or a confiscation order has been imposed, which has not yet been paid, recovered or enforced, shall not prevent a judgment from being forwarded.

   The recognition and enforcement of such fines and confiscation orders in another Member State shall be based on the instruments applicable between the Member States, in particular Council Framework Decision 2005/214/JHA of 24 February 2005 on the application of the principle of mutual recognition to financial penalties (1) and Council Framework Decision 2006/783/JHA of 6 October 2006 on the application of the principle of mutual recognition to confiscation orders (2).
4. This Framework Decision shall not have the effect of modifying the obligation to respect fundamental rights and fundamental legal principles as enshrined in Article 6 of the Treaty on European Union.

CHAPTER II

RECOGNITION OF JUDGMENTS AND ENFORCEMENT OF SENTENCES

Article 4

Criteria for forwarding a judgment and a certificate to another Member State

1. Provided that the sentenced person is in the issuing State or in the executing State, and provided that this person has given his or her consent where required under Article 6, a judgment, together with the certificate for which the standard form is given in Annex I, may be forwarded to one of the following Member States:

   (a) the Member State of nationality of the sentenced person in which he or she lives; or

(b) the Member State of nationality, to which, while not being the Member State where he or she lives, the sentenced person will be deported, once he or she is released from the enforcement of the sentence on the basis of an expulsion or deportation order included in the judgment or in a judicial or administrative decision or any other measure taken consequential to the judgment; or
(c) any Member State other than a Member State referred to in (a) or (b), the competent authority of which consents to the forwarding of the judgment and the certificate to that Member State.

2. The forwarding of the judgment and the certificate may take place where the competent authority of the issuing State, where appropriate after consultations between the competent authorities of the issuing and the executing States, is satisfied that the enforcement of the sentence by the executing State would serve the purpose of facilitating the social rehabilitation of the sentenced person.
3. Before forwarding the judgment and the certificate, the competent authority of the issuing State may consult, by any appropriate means, the competent authority of the executing State. Consultation shall be obligatory in the cases referred to in paragraph 1(c). In such cases the competent authority of the executing State shall promptly inform the issuing State of its decision whether or not to consent to the forwarding of the judgment.
4. During such consultation, the competent authority of the executing State may present the competent authority of the issuing State with a reasoned opinion, that enforcement of the sentence in the executing State would not serve the purpose of facilitating the social rehabilitation and successful reintegration of the sentenced person into society.

   Where there has been no consultation, such an opinion may be presented without delay after the transmission of the judgment and the certificate. The competent authority of the issuing State shall consider such opinion and decide whether to withdraw the certificate or not.
5. The executing State may, on its own initiative, request the issuing State to forward the judgment together with the certificate. The sentenced person may also request the competent authorities of the issuing State or of the executing State to initiate a procedure for forwarding the judgment and the certificate under this Framework Decision. Requests made under this paragraph shall not create an obligation of the issuing State to forward the judgment together with the certificate.

   Shall adopt measures, in particular taking into account the purpose of facilitating social rehabilitation of the sentenced person, constituting the basis on which their competent authorities have to take their decisions whether or not to consent to the forwarding of the judgment and the certificate in cases pursuant to paragraph 1(c).
6. Each Member State may, either on adoption of this Framework Decision or later, notify the General Secretariat of the Council that, in its relations with other Member States that have given the same notification, its prior consent under

paragraph 1(c) is not required for the forwarding of the judgment and the certificate:

(a) if the sentenced person lives in and has been legally residing continuously for at least five years in the executing State and will retain a permanent right of residence in that State, and/or
(b) if the sentenced person is a national of the executing State in cases other than those provided for in paragraph 1(a) and (b).

In cases referred to in point (a), permanent right of residence shall mean that the person concerned:

— has a right of permanent residence in the respective Member State in accordance with the national law implementing Community legislation adopted on the basis of Article 18, 40, 44 and 52 of the Treaty establishing the European Community, or
— possesses a valid residence permit, as a permanent or longterm resident, for the respective Member State, in accordance with the national law implementing Community legislation adopted on the basis of Article 63 of the Treaty establishing the European Community, as regards Member States to which such Community legislation is applicable, or in accordance with national law, as regards Member States to which it is not.

Article 5

Forwarding of the judgment and the certificate

1. The judgment or a certified copy of it, together with the certificate, shall be forwarded, by the competent authority of the issuing State directly to the competent authority of the executing State by any means which leaves a written record under conditions allowing the executing State to establish its authenticity. The original of the judgment, or a certified copy of it, and the original of the certificate, shall be sent to the executing State if it so requires. All official communications shall also be made directly between the said competent authorities.
2. The certificate, shall be signed, and its content certified as accurate, by the competent authority of the issuing State.
3. The issuing State shall forward the judgment together with the certificate to only one executing State at any one time.
4. If the competent authority of the executing State is not known to the competent authority of the issuing State, the latter shall make all necessary inquiries, including via the Contact points of the European Judicial Network set up by Council Joint Action 98/428/JHA (1), in order to obtain the information from the executing State.
5. When an authority of the executing State which receives a judgment together with a certificate has no competence to recognise it and take the necessary measures for its enforcement, it shall, ex officio, forward the judgment together

with the certificate to the competent authority of the executing State and inform the competent authority of the issuing State accordingly.

Article 10

Partial recognition and enforcement

1. If the competent authority of the executing State could consider recognition of the judgment and enforcement of the sentence in part, it may, before deciding to refuse recognition of the judgment and enforcement of the sentence in whole, consult the competent authority of the issuing State with a view to finding an agreement, as provided for in paragraph 2.
2. The competent authorities of the issuing and the executing States may agree, on a case-by-case basis, to the partial recognition and enforcement of a sentence in accordance with the conditions set out by them, provided such recognition and enforcement does not result in the aggravation of the duration of the sentence. In the absence of such agreement, the certificate shall be withdrawn.

Article 12

Decision on the enforcement of the sentence and time limits

1. The competent authority in the executing State shall decide as quickly as possible whether to recognise the judgment and enforce the sentence and shall inform the issuing State thereof, including of any decision to adapt the sentence in accordance with Article 8(2) and (3).
2. Unless a ground for postponement exists under Article 11 or Article 23(3), the final decision on the recognition of the judgment and the enforcement of the sentence shall be taken within a period of 90 days of receipt of the judgment and the certificate.
3. When in exceptional cases it is not practicable for the competent authority of the executing State to comply with the period provided for in paragraph 2, it shall without delay inform the competent authority of the issuing State by any means, giving the reasons for the delay and the estimated time needed for the final decision to be taken.

Article 20

Information from the issuing State

1. The competent authority of the issuing State shall forthwith inform the competent authority of the executing State of any decision or measure as a result of which the sentence ceases to be enforceable immediately or within a certain period of time.
2. The competent authority of the executing State shall terminate enforcement of the sentence as soon as it is informed by the competent authority of the issuing State of the decision or measure referred to in paragraph 1.

Article 21

Information to be given by the executing State

The competent authority of the executing State shall without delay inform the competent authority of the issuing State by any means which leaves a written record:

(a) of the forwarding of the judgment and the certificate to the competent authority responsible for its execution in accordance with Article 5(5);
(b) of the fact that it is in practice impossible to enforce the sentence because after transmission of the judgment and the certificate to the executing State, the sentenced person cannot be found in the territory of the executing State, in which case there shall be no obligation on the executing State to enforce the sentence;
(c) of the final decision to recognise the judgment and enforce the sentence together with the date of the decision;
(d) of any decision not to recognise the judgment and enforce the sentence in accordance with Article 9, together with the reasons for the decision;
(e) of any decision to adapt the sentence in accordance with Article 8(2) or (3), together with the reasons for the decision;
(f) of any decision not to enforce the sentence for the reasons referred to in Article 19(1) together with the reasons for the decision;
(g) of the beginning and the end of the period of conditional release, where so indicated in the certificate by the issuing State;
(h) of the sentenced person's escape from custody;
(i) of the enforcement of the sentence as soon as it has been completed.

6. Council Framework Decision 2008/947/JHA of 27 November 2008 on the application of the principle of mutual recognition to judgements and probation decisions with a view to the supervision o probation measures and alternative sanctions

Article 1

Objectives and scope

1. This Framework Decision aims at facilitating the social rehabilitation of sentenced persons, improving the protection of victims and of the general public, and facilitating the application of suitable probation measures and alternative sanctions, in case of offenders who do not live in the State of conviction.
   With a view to achieving these objectives, this Framework Decision lays down rules according to which a Member State, other than the Member State in which the person concerned has been sentenced, recognises judgments and, where applicable, probation decisions and supervises probation measures imposed on the basis of a judgment, or alternative sanctions contained in such a judgment, and takes all other decisions relating to that judgment, unless otherwise provided for in this Framework Decision.
2. This Framework Decision shall apply only to:
   (a) the recognition of judgments and, where applicable, probation decisions;
   (b) the transfer of responsibility for the supervision of probation measures and alternative sanctions;
   (c) all other decisions related to those under (a) and (b); as described and provided for in this Framework Decision.
3. This Framework Decision shall not apply to:
   (a) the execution of judgments in criminal matters imposing custodial sentences or measures involving deprivation of liberty which fall within the scope of Framework Decision 2008/909/JHA;
   (b) recognition and execution of financial penalties and confiscation orders which fall within the scope of Council Framework Decision 2005/214/JHA of 24 February 2005 on the application of the principle of mutual recognition to financial penalties (1) and Council Framework Decision 2006/783/JHA of 6 October 2006 on the application of the principle of mutual recognition to confiscation orders (2).
4. This Framework Decision shall not have the effect of modifying the obligation to respect fundamental rights and fundamental legal principles as enshrined in Article 6 of the Treaty on European Union.

Article 6

Procedure for forwarding a judgment and, where applicable, a probation decision

1. When, in application of Article 5(1) or (2), the competent authority of the issuing State forwards a judgment and, where applicable, a probation decision to another Member State, it shall ensure that it is accompanied by a certificate, the standard form for which is set out in Annex I.
2. The judgment and, where applicable, the probation decision, together with the certificate referred to in paragraph 1, shall be forwarded by the competent authority of the issuing State directly to the competent authority of the executing State by any means which leaves a written record under conditions allowing the executing State to establish their authenticity. The original of the judgment and, where applicable, the probation decision, or certified copies thereof, as well as the original of the certificate, shall be sent to the competent authority of the executing State if it so requires. All official communications shall also be made directly between the said competent authorities.
3. The certificate referred to in paragraph 1 shall be signed and its content certified as accurate by the competent authority of the issuing State.
4. Apart from the measures and sanctions referred to in Article 4(1), the certificate referred to in paragraph 1 of this Article shall include only such measures or sanctions as notified by the executing State in accordance with Article 4(2).
5. The competent authority of the issuing State shall forward the judgment and, where applicable, the probation decision, together with the certificate referred to in paragraph 1 only to one executing State at any one time.
6. If the competent authority of the executing State is not known to the competent authority of the issuing State, the latter shall make all necessary inquiries, including via the contact points of the European Judicial Network created by Council Joint Action 98/428/JHA (1), in order to obtain the information from the executing State.
7. When an authority of the executing State which receives a judgment and, where applicable, a probation decision, together with the certificate referred to in paragraph 1, has no competence to recognise it and take the ensuing necessary measures for the supervision of the probation measure or alternative sanction, it shall, *ex officio*, forward it to the competent authority and shall without delay inform the competent authority of the issuing State accordingly by any means which leaves a written record.

Article 12

Time limit

1. The competent authority of the executing State shall decide as soon as possible, and within 60 days of receipt of the judgment and, where applicable, the probation decision, together with the certificate referred to in Article 6(1), whether or not to recognise the judgment and, where applicable, the probation decision and assume responsibility for supervising the probation measures or

alternative sanctions. It shall immediately inform the competent authority of the issuing State, by any means which leaves a griten record, of its decision.

2. When in exceptional circumstances it is not possible for the competent authority of the executing State to comply with the time limit provided for in paragraph 1, it shall immediately inform the competent authority of the issuing State by any means, giving the reasons for the delay and indicating the estimated time needed for the final decision to be taken.

7. Council Framework Decision 2005/214/JHA of 24 February 2005 on the application of the principle of mutual recognition to financial penalties (extract)

Article 1

Definitions

For the purposes of this Framework Decision:

(a) 'decision' shall mean a final decision requiring a financial penalty to be paid by a natural or legal person where the decision was made by:

  (i) a court of the issuing State in respect of a criminal offence under the law of the issuing State;
  (ii) an authority of the issuing State other than a court in respect of a criminal offence under the law of the issuing State, provided that the person concerned has had an opportunity to have the case tried by a court having jurisdiction in particular in criminal matters;
  (iii) an authority of the issuing State other than a court in respect of acts which are punishable under the national law of the issuing State by virtue of being infringements of the rules of law, provided that the person concerned has had an opportunity to have the case tried by a court having jurisdiction in particular in criminal matters;
  (iv) a court having jurisdiction in particular in criminal matters, where the decision was made regarding a decision as referred to in point (iii);

(b) 'financial penalty' shall mean the obligation to pay:

  (i) a sum of money on conviction of an offence imposed in a decision;
  (ii) compensation imposed in the same decision for the benefit of victims, where the victim may not be a civil party to the proceedings and the court is acting in the exercise of its criminal jurisdiction;
  (iii) a sum of money in respect of the costs of court or administrative proceedings leading to the decision;
  (iv) a sum of money to a public fund or a victim support organisation, imposed in the same decision.

  A financial penalty shall not include:

  — orders for the confiscation of instrumentalities or proceeds of crime,
  — orders that have a civil nature and arise out of a claim for damages and restitution and which are enforceable in accordance with Council Regulation (EC) No 44/2001 of 22 December 2000 on jurisdiction and the

recognition and enforcement of judgments in civil and commercial matters (1);

(c) 'issuing State' shall mean the Member State in which a decision within the meaning of this Framework Decision was delivered;
(d) 'executing State' shall mean the Member State to which a decision has been transmitted for the purpose of enforcement

(. . .)

Article 4

Transmission of decisions and recourse to the central authority

1. A decision, together with a certificate as provided for in this Article, may be transmitted to the competent authorities of a Member State in which the natural or legal person against whom a decision has been passed has property or income, is normally resident or, in the case of a legal person, has its registered seat.
2. The certificate, the standard form for which is given in the Annex, must be signed, and its contents certified as accurate, by the competent authority in the issuing State.
3. The decision or a certified copy of it, together with the certificate, shall be transmitted by the competent authority in the issuing State directly to the competent authority in the executing State by any means which leaves a written record under conditions allowing the executing State to establish its authenticity. The original of the decision, or a certified copy of it, and the original of the certificate, shall be sent to the executing State if it so requires. All official communications shall also be made directly between the said competent authorities.
4. The issuing State shall only transmit a decision to one executing State at any one time.
5. If the competent authority in the executing State is not known to the competent authority in the issuing State, the latter shall make all necessary inquiries, including via the contact points of the European Judicial Network (2) in order to obtain the information from the executing State.
6. When an authority in the executing State which receives a decision has no jurisdiction to recognise it and take the necessary measures for its execution, it shall, *ex officio*, transmit the decision to the competent authority and shall inform the competent authority in the issuing State accordingly.
7. The United Kingdom and Ireland, respectively, may state in a declaration that the decision together with the certificate must be sent via its central authority or authorities specified by it in the declaration. These Member States may at any

time by a further declaration limit the scope of such a declaration for the purpose of giving greater effect to paragraph 3. They shall do so when the provisions on mutual assistance of the Schengen Implementation Convention are put into effect for them. Any declaration shall be deposited with the General Secretariat of the Council and notified to the Commission.

(...)

Article 14

Information from the executing State

The competent authority of the executing State shall without delay inform the competent authority of the issuing State by any means which leaves a written record:

(a) of the transmission of the decision to the competent authority, according to Article 4(6);
(b) of any decision not to recognise and execute a decision, according to Articles 7 or 20(3), together with the reasons for the decision;
(c) of the total or partial non-execution of the decision for the reasons referred to in Article 8, Article 9(1) and (2), and Article 11(1);
(d) of the execution of the decision as soon as the execution has been completed;
(e) of the application of alternative sanction, according to Article 10.

Article 15

Consequences of transmission of a decision

1. Subject to paragraph 2, the issuing State may not proceed with the execution of a decision transmitted pursuant to Article 4.
2. The right of execution of the decision shall revert to the issuing State:

   (a) upon it being informed by the executing State of the total or partial non-execution or the non-recognition or the nonenforcement of the decision in the case of Article 7, with the exception of Article 7(2)(a), in the case of Article 11(1), and in the case of Article 20(3); or
   (b) when the executing State has been informed by the issuing State that the decision has been withdrawn from the executing State pursuant to Article 12.

3. If, after transmission of a decision in accordance with Article 4, an authority of the issuing State receives any sum of money which the sentenced person has paid voluntarily in respect of the decision, that authority shall inform the competent authority in the executing State without delay. Article 9(2) shall apply.

8. Council Framework Decision 2008/675/JHA of 24 July 2008 on taking into acount convictions in the Member States of the European Union in the course of new criminal proceedings

Article 1

Subject matter

1. The purpose of this Framework Decision is to determine the conditions under which, in the course of criminal proceedings in a Member State against a person, previous convictions handed down against the same person for different facts in other Member States, are taken into account.
2. This Framework Decision shall not have the effect of amending the obligation to respect the fundamental rights and fundamental legal principles as enshrined in Article 6 of the Treaty.

Article 2

Definitions

For the purposes of this Framework Decision "conviction" means any final decision of a criminal court establishing guilt of a criminal offence.

Article 3

Taking into account, in the course of new criminal proceedings, a conviction handed down in another Member State

1. Each Member State shall ensure that in the course of criminal proceedings against a person, previous convictions handed down against the same person for different facts in other Member States, in respect of which information has been obtained under applicable instruments on mutual legal assistance or on the exchange of information extracted from criminal records, are taken into account to the extent previous national convictions are taken into account, and that equivalent legal effects are attached to them as to previous national convictions, in accordance with national law.
2. Paragraph 1 shall apply at the pre-trial stage, at the trial stage itself and at the time of execution of the conviction, in particular with regard to the applicable rules of procedure, including those relating to provisional detention, the definition of the offence, the type and level of the sentence, and the rules governing the execution of the decision.
3. The taking into account of previous convictions handed down in other Member States, as provided for in paragraph 1, shall not have the effect of interfering with, revoking or reviewing previous convictions or any decision relating to their execution by the Member State conducting the new proceedings.

4. In accordance with paragraph 3, paragraph 1 shall not apply to the extent that, had the previous conviction been a national conviction of the Member State conducting the new proceedings, the taking into account of the previous conviction would, according to the national law of that Member State, have had the effect of interfering with, revoking or reviewing the previous conviction or any decision relating to its execution.
5. If the offence for which the new proceedings being conducted was committed before the previous conviction had been handed down or fully executed, paragraphs 1 and 2 shall not have the effect of requiring Member States to apply their national rules on imposing sentences, where the application of those rules to foreign convictions would limit the judge in imposing a sentence in the new proceedings.

However, the Member States shall ensure that in such cases their courts can otherwise take into account previous convictions handed down in other Member States.

Article 4

Relation to other legal instruments
This Framework Decision shall replace Article 56 of the European Convention of 28 May 1970 on the International Validity of Criminal Judgments as between the Member States parties to that Convention, without prejudice to the application of that Article in relations between the Member States and third countries.

Article 5

Implementation

1. Member States shall take the necessary measures to comply with the provisions of this Framework Decision by 15 August 2010.
2. Member States shall communicate to the General Secretariat of the Council and to the Commission the text of the provisions transposing into their national law the obligations imposed on them under this Framework Decision.
3. On the basis of that information the Commission shall, by 15 August 2011, present a report to the European Parliament and the Council on the application of this Framework Decision, accompanied if necessary by legislative proposals.

Article 6

Entry into force

This Framework Decision shall enter into force on the day of its publication in the Official Journal of the European Union.

Done at Brussels, 24 July 2008.
For the Council
The President

9. Council Framework Decision 2008/977/JHA of 27 November 2008 on the protection of personal data processed in the framework of police and judicial cooperation in criminal matters[29]

THE COUNCIL OF THE EUROPEAN UNION,

(. . .)

HAS ADOPTED THIS FRAMEWORK DECISION:

Article 1

Purpose and scope

1. The purpose of this Framework Decision is to ensure a high level of protection of the fundamental rights and freedoms of natural persons, and in particular their right to privacy, with respect to the processing of personal data in the framework of police and judicial cooperation in criminal matters, provided for by Title VI of the Treaty on European Union, while guaranteeing a high level of public safety.
2. In accordance with this Framework Decision, Member States shall protect the fundamental rights and freedoms of natural persons, and in particular their right to privacy when, for the purpose of the prevention, investigation, detection or prosecution of criminal offences or the execution of criminal penalties, personal data:

   (a) are or have been transmitted or made available between Member States;
   (b) are or have been transmitted or made available by Member States to authorities or to information systems established on the basis of Title VI of the Treaty on European Union; or
   (c) are or have been transmitted or made available to the competent authorities of the Member States by authorities or information systems established on the basis of the Treaty on European Union or the Treaty establishing the European Community.

3. This Framework Decision shall apply to the processing of personal data wholly or partly by automatic means, and to the processing otherwise than by automatic means, of personal data which form part of a filing system or are intended to form part of a filing system.
4. This Framework Decision is without prejudice to essential national security interests and specific intelligence activities in the field of national security.
5. This Framework Decision shall not preclude Member States from providing, for the protection of personal data collected or processed at national level, higher safeguards than those established in this Framework Decision.

[29] OJ L 350, 30.12.2008, p. 60.

Article 2

Definitions

For the purposes of this Framework Decision:

(a) "personal data" mean any information relating to an identified or identifiable natural person ("data subject"); an identifiable person is one who can be identified, directly or indirectly, in particular by reference to an identification number or to one or more factors specific to his physical, physiological, mental, economic, cultural or social identity;
(b) "processing of personal data" and "processing" mean any operation or set of operations which is performed upon personal data, whether or not by automatic means, such as collection, recording, organisation, storage, adaptation or alteration, retrieval, consultation, use, disclosure by transmission, dissemination or otherwise making available, alignment or combination, blocking, erasure or destruction;
(c) "blocking" means the marking of stored personal data with the aim of limiting their processing in future;
(d) "personal data filing system" and "filing system" mean any structured set of personal data which are accessible according to specific criteria, whether centralised, decentralised or dispersed on a functional or geographical basis;
(e) "processor" means any body which processes personal data on behalf of the controller;
(f) "recipient" means any body to which data are disclosed;
(g) "the data subject's consent" means any freely given specific and informed indication of his wishes by which the data subject signifies his agreement to personal data relating to him being processed;
(h) "competent authorities" mean agencies or bodies established by legal acts adopted by the Council pursuant to Title VI of the Treaty on European Union, as well as police, customs, judicial and other competent authorities of the Member States that are authorised by national law to process personal data within the scope of this Framework Decision;
(i) "controller" means the natural or legal person, public authority, agency or any other body which alone or jointly with others determines the purposes and means of the processing of personal data;
(j) "referencing" means the marking of stored personal data without the aim of limiting their processing in future;
(k) "to make anonymous" means to modify personal data in such a way that details of personal or material circumstances can no longer or only with disproportionate investment of time, cost and labour be attributed to an identified or identifiable natural person.

Article 3

Principles of lawfulness, proportionality and purpose

1. Personal data may be collected by the competent authorities only for specified, explicit and legitimate purposes in the framework of their tasks and may be processed only for the same purpose for which data were collected. Processing of the data shall be lawful and adequate, relevant and not excessive in relation to the purposes for which they are collected.
2. Further processing for another purpose shall be permitted in so far as:

   (a) it is not incompatible with the purposes for which the data were collected;
   (b) the competent authorities are authorised to process such data for such other purpose in accordance with the applicable legal provisions; and
   (c) processing is necessary and proportionate to that other purpose.

The competent authorities may also further process the transmitted personal data for historical, statistical or scientific purposes, provided that Member States provide appropriate safeguards, such as making the data anonymous.

Article 4

Rectification, erasure and blocking

1. Personal data shall be rectified if inaccurate and, where this is possible and necessary, completed or updated.
2. Personal data shall be erased or made anonymous when they are no longer required for the purposes for which they were lawfully collected or are lawfully further processed. Archiving of those data in a separate data set for an appropriate period in accordance with national law shall not be affected by this provision.
3. Personal data shall be blocked instead of erased if there are reasonable grounds to believe that erasure could affect the legitimate interests of the data subject. Blocked data shall be processed only for the purpose which prevented their erasure.
4. When the personal data are contained in a judicial decision or record related to the issuance of a judicial decision, the rectification, erasure or blocking shall be carried out in accordance with national rules on judicial proceedings.

Article 5

Establishment of time limits for erasure and review

Appropriate time limits shall be established for the erasure of personal data or for a periodic review of the need for the storage of the data. Procedural measures shall ensure that these time limits are observed.

Article 6

Processing of special categories of data

The processing of personal data revealing racial or ethnic origin, political opinions, religious or philosophical beliefs or trade-union membership and the processing of data concerning health or sex life shall be permitted only when this is strictly necessary and when the national law provides adequate safeguards.

Article 7

Automated individual decisions

A decision which produces an adverse legal effect for the data subject or significantly affects him and which is based solely on automated processing of data intended to evaluate certain personal aspects relating to the data subject shall be permitted only if authorised by a law which also lays down measures to safeguard the data subject's legitimate interests.

Article 8

Verification of quality of data that are transmitted or made available

1. The competent authorities shall take all reasonable steps to provide that personal data which are inaccurate, incomplete or no longer up to date are not transmitted or made available. To that end, the competent authorities shall, as far as practicable, verify the quality of personal data before they are transmitted or made available. As far as possible, in all transmissions of data, available information shall be added which enables the receiving Member State to assess the degree of accuracy, completeness, up-to-dateness and reliability. If personal data were transmitted without request the receiving authority shall verify without delay whether these data are necessary for the purpose for which they were transmitted.
2. If it emerges that incorrect data have been transmitted or data have been unlawfully transmitted, the recipient must be notified without delay. The data must be rectified, erased, or blocked without delay in accordance with Article 4.

Article 9

Time limits

1. Upon transmission or making available of the data, the transmitting authority may in line with the national law and in accordance with Articles 4 and 5, indicate the time limits for the retention of data, upon the expiry of which the recipient must erase or block the data or review whether or not they are still needed. This obligation shall not apply if, at the time of the expiry of these time limits, the data are required for a current investigation, prosecution of criminal offences or enforcement of criminal penalties.

2. Where the transmitting authority has not indicated a time limit in accordance with paragraph 1, the time limits referred to in Articles 4 and 5 for the retention of data provided for under the national law of the receiving Member State shall apply.

Article 10

Logging and documentation

1. All transmissions of personal data are to be logged or documented for the purposes of verification of the lawfulness of the data processing, self-monitoring and ensuring proper data integrity and security.
2. Logs or documentation prepared under paragraph 1 shall be communicated on request to the competent supervisory authority for the control of data protection. The competent supervisory authority shall use this information only for the control of data protection and for ensuring proper data processing as well as data integrity and security.

Article 11

Processing of personal data received from or made available by another Member State

Personal data received from or made available by the competent authority of another Member State may, in accordance with the requirements of Article 3(2), be further processed only for the following purposes other than those for which they were transmitted or made available:

(a) the prevention, investigation, detection or prosecution of criminal offences or the execution of criminal penalties other than those for which they were transmitted or made available;
(b) other judicial and administrative proceedings directly related to the prevention, investigation, detection or prosecution of criminal offences or the execution of criminal penalties;
(c) the prevention of an immediate and serious threat to public security; or
(d) any other purpose only with the prior consent of the transmitting Member State or with the consent of the data subject, given in accordance with national law.

The competent authorities may also further process the transmitted personal data for historical, statistical or scientific purposes, provided that Member States provide appropriate safeguards, such as, for example, making the data anonymous.

Article 12

Compliance with national processing restrictions

1. Where, under the law of the transmitting Member State, specific processing restrictions apply in specific circumstances to data exchanges between competent authorities within that Member State, the transmitting authority shall inform the recipient of such restrictions. The recipient shall ensure that these processing restrictions are met.

2. When applying paragraph 1, Member States shall not apply restrictions regarding data transmissions to other Member States or to agencies or bodies established pursuant to Title VI of the Treaty on European Union other than those applicable to similar national data transmissions.

Article 13

Transfer to competent authorities in third States or to international bodies

1. Member States shall provide that personal data transmitted or made available by the competent authority of another Member State may be transferred to third States or international bodies, only if:

   (a) it is necessary for the prevention, investigation, detection or prosecution of criminal offences or the execution of criminal penalties;
   (b) the receiving authority in the third State or receiving international body is responsible for the prevention, investigation, detection or prosecution of criminal offences or the execution of criminal penalties;
   (c) the Member State from which the data were obtained has given its consent to transfer in compliance with its national law; and
   (d) the third State or international body concerned ensures an adequate level of protection for the intended data processing.

2. Transfer without prior consent in accordance with paragraph 1(c) shall be permitted only if transfer of the data is essential for the prevention of an immediate and serious threat to public security of a Member State or a third State or to essential interests of a Member State and the prior consent cannot be obtained in good time. The authority responsible for giving consent shall be informed without delay.
3. By way of derogation from paragraph 1(d), personal data may be transferred if:

   (a) the national law of the Member State transferring the data so provides because of:

      (i) legitimate specific interests of the data subject; or
      (ii) legitimate prevailing interests, especially important public interests; or

   (b) the third State or receiving international body provides safeguards which are deemed adequate by the Member State concerned according to its national law.

4. The adequacy of the level of protection referred to in paragraph 1(d) shall be assessed in the light of all the circumstances surrounding a data transfer operation or a set of data transfer operations. Particular consideration shall be given to the nature of the data, the purpose and duration of the proposed processing operation or operations, the State of origin and the State or international body of final destination of the data, the rules of law, both general and sectoral, in force in the third State or international body in question and the professional rules and security measures which apply.

Article 14

Transmission to private parties in Member States

1. Member States shall provide that personal data received from or made available by the competent authority of another Member State may be transmitted to private parties only if:

   (a) the competent authority of the Member State from which the data were obtained has consented to transmission in compliance with its national law;
   (b) no legitimate specific interests of the data subject prevent transmission; and
   (c) in particular cases transfer is essential for the competent authority transmitting the data to a private party for:

      (i) the performance of a task lawfully assigned to it;
      (ii) the prevention, investigation, detection or prosecution of criminal offences or the execution of criminal penalties;
      (iii) the prevention of an immediate and serious threat to public security; or
      (iv) the prevention of serious harm to the rights of individuals.

2. The competent authority transmitting the data to a private party shall inform the latter of the purposes for which the data may exclusively be used.

Article 15

Information on request of the competent authority

The recipient shall, on request, inform the competent authority which transmitted or made available the personal data about their processing.

Article 16

Information for the data subject

1. Member States shall ensure that the data subject is informed regarding the collection or processing of personal data by their competent authorities, in accordance with national law.
2. When personal data have been transmitted or made available between Member States, each Member State may, in accordance with the provisions of its national law referred to in paragraph 1, ask that the other Member State does not inform the data subject. In such case the latter Member State shall not inform the data subject without the prior consent of the other Member State.

Article 17

Right of access

1. Every data subject shall have the right to obtain, following requests made at reasonable intervals, without constraint and without excessive delay or expense:

   (a) at least a confirmation from the controller or from the national supervisory authority as to whether or not data relating to him have been transmitted or

made available and information on the recipients or categories of recipients to whom the data have been disclosed and communication of the data undergoing processing; or
(b) at least a confirmation from the national supervisory authority that all necessary verifications have taken place.

2. The Member States may adopt legislative measures restricting access to information pursuant to paragraph 1(a), where such a restriction, with due regard for the legitimate interests of the person concerned, constitutes a necessary and proportional measure:

   (a) to avoid obstructing official or legal inquiries, investigations or procedures;
   (b) to avoid prejudicing the prevention, detection, investigation and prosecution of criminal offences or for the execution of criminal penalties;
   (c) to protect public security;
   (d) to protect national security;
   (e) to protect the data subject or the rights and freedoms of others.

3. Any refusal or restriction of access shall be set out in writing to the data subject. At the same time, the factual or legal reasons on which the decision is based shall also be communicated to him. The latter communication may be omitted where a reason under paragraph 2(a) to (e) exists. In all of these cases the data subject shall be advised that he may appeal to the competent national supervisory authority, a judicial authority or to a court.

Article 18

Right to rectification, erasure or blocking

1. The data subject shall have the right to expect the controller to fulfil its duties in accordance with Articles 4, 8 and 9 concerning the rectification, erasure or blocking of personal data which arise from this Framework Decision. Member States shall lay down whether the data subject may assert this right directly against the controller or through the intermediary of the competent national supervisory authority. If the controller refuses rectification, erasure or blocking, the refusal must be communicated in writing to the data subject who must be informed of the possibilities provided for in national law for lodging a complaint or seeking judicial remedy. Upon examination of the complaint or judicial remedy, the data subject shall be informed whether the controller acted properly or not. Member States may also provide that the data subject shall be informed by the competent national supervisory authority that a review has taken place.
2. If the accuracy of an item of personal data is contested by the data subject and its accuracy or inaccuracy cannot be ascertained, referencing of that item of data may take place.

Article 19

Right to compensation

1. Any person who has suffered damage as a result of an unlawful processing operation or of any act incompatible with the national provisions adopted pursuant to this Framework Decision shall be entitled to receive compensation for the damage suffered from the controller or other authority competent under national law.
2. Where a competent authority of a Member State has transmitted personal data, the recipient cannot, in the context of its liability vis-à-vis the injured party in accordance with national law, cite in its defence that the data transmitted were inaccurate. If the recipient pays compensation for damage caused by the use of incorrectly transmitted data, the transmitting competent authority shall refund to the recipient the amount paid in damages, taking into account any fault that may lie with the recipient.

Article 20

Judicial remedies

Without prejudice to any administrative remedy for which provision may be made prior to referral to the judicial authority, the data subject shall have the right to a judicial remedy for any breach of the rights guaranteed to him by the applicable national law.

Article 21

Confidentiality of processing

1. Any person who has access to personal data which fall within the scope of this Framework Decision may process such data only if that person is a member of, or acts on instructions of, the competent authority, unless he is required to do so by law.
2. Persons working for a competent authority of a Member State shall be bound by all the data protection rules which apply to the competent authority in question.

Article 22

Security of processing

1. Member States shall provide that the competent authorities must implement appropriate technical and organisational measures to protect personal data against accidental or unlawful destruction or accidental loss, alteration, unauthorised disclosure or access, in particular where the processing involves the transmission over a network or the making available by granting direct automated access, and against all other unlawful forms of processing, taking into account in particular the risks represented by the processing and the nature of the data to be protected. Having regard to the state of the art and the cost of their

implementation, such measures shall ensure a level of security appropriate to the risks represented by the processing and the nature of the data to be protected.

2. In respect of automated data processing each Member State shall implement measures designed to:

   (a) deny unauthorised persons access to data-processing equipment used for processing personal data (equipment access control);
   (b) prevent the unauthorised reading, copying, modification or removal of data media (data media control);
   (c) prevent the unauthorised input of data and the unauthorised inspection, modification or deletion of stored personal data (storage control);
   (d) prevent the use of automated data-processing systems by unauthorised persons using data communication equipment (user control);
   (e) ensure that persons authorised to use an automated data-processing system only have access to the data covered by their access authorisation (data access control);
   (f) ensure that it is possible to verify and establish to which bodies personal data have been or may be transmitted or made available using data communication equipment (communication control);
   (g) ensure that it is subsequently possible to verify and establish which personal data have been input into automated data-processing systems and when and by whom the data were input (input control);
   (h) prevent the unauthorised reading, copying, modification or deletion of personal data during transfers of personal data or during transportation of data media (transport control);
   (i) ensure that installed systems may, in case of interruption, be restored (recovery);
   (j) ensure that the functions of the system perform, that the appearance of faults in the functions is reported (reliability) and that stored data cannot be corrupted by means of a malfunctioning of the system (integrity).

3. Member States shall provide that processors may be designated only if they guarantee that they observe the requisite technical and organisational measures under paragraph 1 and comply with the instructions under Article 21. The competent authority shall monitor the processor in those respects.
4. Personal data may be processed by a processor only on the basis of a legal act or a written contract.

Article 23

Prior consultation

Member States shall ensure that the competent national supervisory authorities are consulted prior to the processing of personal data which will form part of a new filing system to be created where:

(a) special categories of data referred to in Article 6 are to be processed; or
(b) the type of processing, in particular using new technologies, mechanism or procedures, holds otherwise specific risks for the fundamental rights and freedoms, and in particular the privacy, of the data subject.

Article 24

Penalties

Member States shall adopt suitable measures to ensure the full implementation of the provisions of this Framework Decision and shall in particular lay down effective, proportionate and dissuasive penalties to be imposed in case of infringements of the provisions adopted pursuant to this Framework Decision.

Article 25

National supervisory authorities

1. Each Member State shall provide that one or more public authorities are responsible for advising and monitoring the application within its territory of the provisions adopted by the Member States pursuant to this Framework Decision. These authorities shall act with complete independence in exercising the functions entrusted to them.
2. Each authority shall in particular be endowed with:

   (a) investigative powers, such as powers of access to data forming the subject matter of processing operations and powers to collect all the information necessary for the performance of its supervisory duties;
   (b) effective powers of intervention, such as, for example, that of delivering opinions before processing operations are carried out, and ensuring appropriate publication of such opinions, of ordering the blocking, erasure or destruction of data, of imposing a temporary or definitive ban on processing, of warning or admonishing the controller, or that of referring the matter to national parliaments or other political institutions;
   (c) the power to engage in legal proceedings where the national provisions adopted pursuant to this Framework Decision have been infringed or to bring this infringement to the attention of the judicial authorities. Decisions by the supervisory authority which give rise to complaints may be appealed against through the courts.

3. Each supervisory authority shall hear claims lodged by any person concerning the protection of his rights and freedoms in regard to the processing of personal data. The person concerned shall be informed of the outcome of the claim.
4. Member States shall provide that the members and staff of the supervisory authority are bound by the data protection provisions applicable to the competent authority in question and, even after their employment has ended, are to be subject to a duty of professional secrecy with regard to confidential information to which they have access.

Article 26

Relationship to agreements with third States

This Framework Decision is without prejudice to any obligations and commitments incumbent upon Member States or upon the Union by virtue of bilateral and/or multilateral agreements with third States existing at the time of adoption of this Framework Decision.

In the application of these agreements, the transfer to a third State of personal data obtained from another Member State, shall be carried out while respecting Article 13(1)(c) or (2), as appropriate.

Article 27

Evaluation

1. Member States shall report to the Commission by 27 November 2013 on the national measures they have taken to ensure full compliance with this Framework Decision, and particularly with regard to those provisions that already have to be complied with when data is collected. The Commission shall examine in particular the implications of those provisions for the scope of this Framework Decision as laid down in Article 1(2).
2. The Commission shall report to the European Parliament and the Council within one year on the outcome of the evaluation referred to in paragraph 1, and shall accompany its report with any appropriate proposals for amendments to this Framework Decision.

Article 28

Relationship to previously adopted acts of the Union

Where in acts, adopted under Title VI of the Treaty on European Union prior to the date of entry into force of this Framework Decision and regulating the exchange of personal data between Member States or the access of designated authorities of Member States to information systems established pursuant to the Treaty establishing the European Community, specific conditions have been introduced as to the use of such data by the receiving Member State, these conditions shall take precedence over the provisions of this Framework Decision on the use of data received from or made available by another Member State.

Article 29

Implementation

1. Member States shall take the necessary measures to comply with the provisions of this Framework Decision before 27 November 2010.
2. By the same date Member States shall transmit to the General Secretariat of the Council and to the Commission the text of the provisions transposing into their national law the obligations imposed on them under this Framework Decision, as well as information on the supervisory authorities referred to in Article 25. On

the basis of a report established using this information by the Commission, the Council shall, before 27 November 2011, assess the extent to which Member States have complied with the provisions of this Framework Decision.

Article 30

Entry into force

This Framework Decision shall enter into force on the 20th day following its publication in the Official Journal of the European Union.

F. EXCHANGE OF INFORMATION WITH THIRD STATES

1. Agreement between the European Union and the United States of America on the processing and transfer of Financial Messaging Data from the European Union to the United States for the purposes of the Terrorist Finance Tracking Program (extract)

Published at OJ L 215, 11.8.2012, p. 5
Date of signature: 14.12.2011
Date of entry into force: 01.07.2012.
See Council Decision of 13 July 2010 on the conclusion of the Agreement between the European Union and the United States of America on the processing and transfer of Financial Messaging Data from the European Union to the United States for the purposes of the Terrorist Finance Tracking Program. OJ L 195, 27.07.2010, p. 3.

THE EUROPEAN UNION,

of the one part, and

THE UNITED STATES OF AMERICA,

of the other part,

Together hereinafter referred to as "the Parties",

(. . .)

HAVE AGREED AS FOLLOWS:

Á.G. Zarza (ed.), *Exchange of Information and Data Protection in Cross-border Criminal Proceedings in Europe*, DOI 10.1007/978-3-642-40291-3,

Article 1

Purpose of Agreement

1. The purpose of this Agreement is to ensure, with full respect for the privacy, protection of personal data, and other conditions set out in this Agreement, that:

   (a) financial payment messages referring to financial transfers and related data stored in the territory of the European Union by providers of international financial payment messaging services, that are jointly designated pursuant to this Agreement, are provided to the U.S. Treasury Department for the exclusive purpose of the prevention, investigation, detection, or prosecution of terrorism or terrorist financing; and
   (b) relevant information obtained through the TFTP is provided to law enforcement, public security, or counter terrorism authorities of Member States, or Europol or Eurojust, for the purpose of the prevention, investigation, detection, or prosecution of terrorism or terrorist financing.

2. The United States, the European Union, and its Member States shall take all necessary and appropriate measures within their authority to carry out the provisions and achieve the purpose of this Agreement.

Article 2

Scope of application

Conduct pertaining to terrorism or terrorist financing
This Agreement applies to the obtaining and use of financial payment messaging and related data with a view to the prevention, investigation, detection, or prosecution of:

(a) acts of a person or entity that involve violence, or are otherwise dangerous to human life or create a risk of damage to property or infrastructure, and which, given their nature and context, are reasonably believed to be committed with the aim of:

   (i) intimidating or coercing a population;
   (ii) intimidating, compelling, or coercing a government or international organisation to act or abstain from acting; or
   (iii) seriously destabilising or destroying the fundamental political, constitutional, economic, or social structures of a country or an international organisation;

(b) a person or entity assisting, sponsoring, or providing financial, material, or technological support for, or financial or other services to or in support of, acts described in subparagraph (a);
(c) a person or entity providing or collecting funds, by any means, directly or indirectly, with the intention that they should be used or in the knowledge that they are to be used, in full or in part, in order to carry out any of the acts described in subparagraphs (a) or (b); or

(d) a person or entity aiding, abetting, or attempting acts described in subparagraphs (a), (b), or (c).

Article 3

Ensuring provision of data by Designated Providers
The Parties, jointly and individually, shall ensure, in accordance with this Agreement and in particular Article 4, that entities jointly designated by the Parties under this Agreement as providers of international financial payment messaging services (Designated Providers) provide to the U.S. Treasury Department requested financial payment messaging and related data which are necessary for the purpose of the prevention, investigation, detection, or prosecution of terrorism or terrorist financing (Provided Data). The Designated Providers shall be identified in the Annex to this Agreement and may be updated, as necessary, by exchange of diplomatic notes. Any amendments to the Annex shall be duly published in the Official Journal of the European Union.

Article 4

U.S. Requests to obtain data from Designated Providers

1. For the purposes of this Agreement, the U.S. Treasury Department shall serve production orders (Requests), under authority of U.S. law, upon a Designated Provider present in the territory of the United States in order to obtain data necessary for the purpose of the prevention, investigation, detection, or prosecution of terrorism or terrorist financing that are stored in the territory of the European Union.
2. The Request (together with any supplemental documents) shall:
   (a) identify as clearly as possible the data, including the specific categories of data requested, that are necessary for the purpose of the prevention, investigation, detection, or prosecution of terrorism or terrorist financing;
   (b) clearly substantiate the necessity of the data;
   (c) be tailored as narrowly as possible in order to minimise the amount of data requested, taking due account of past and current terrorism risk analyses focused on message types and geography as well as perceived terrorism threats and vulnerabilities, geographic, threat, and vulnerability analyses; and
   (d) not seek any data relating to the Single Euro Payments Area.
3. Upon service of the Request on the Designated Provider, the U.S. Treasury Department shall simultaneously provide a copy of the Request, with any supplemental documents, to Europol.
4. Upon receipt of the copy, Europol shall verify as a matter of urgency whether the Request complies with the requirements of paragraph 2. Europol shall notify the Designated Provider that it has verified that the Request complies with the requirements of paragraph 2.
5. For the purposes of this Agreement, once Europol has confirmed that the Request complies with the requirements of paragraph 2, the Request shall have

binding legal effect as provided under U.S. law, within the European Union as well as the United States. The Designated Provider is thereby authorised and required to provide the data to the U.S. Treasury Department.

6. The Designated Provider shall thereupon provide the data (i.e., on a "push basis") directly to the U.S. Treasury Department. The Designated Provider shall keep a detailed log of all data transmitted to the U.S. Treasury Department for the purposes of this Agreement.
7. Once the data have been provided pursuant to these procedures, the Designated Provider shall be deemed to have complied with this Agreement and with all other applicable legal requirements in the European Union related to the transfer of such data from the European Union to the United States.
8. Designated Providers shall have all administrative and judicial redress available under U.S. law to recipients of U.S. Treasury Department Requests.
9. The Parties shall jointly coordinate with regard to the technical modalities necessary to support the Europol verification process.

Article 5

Safeguards applicable to the processing of Provided Data
General obligations

1. The U.S. Treasury Department shall ensure that Provided Data are processed in accordance with the provisions of this Agreement. The U.S. Treasury Department shall ensure the protection of personal data by means of the following safeguards, which shall be applied without discrimination, in particular on the basis of nationality or country of residence.
2. Provided Data shall be processed exclusively for the prevention, investigation, detection, or prosecution of terrorism or its financing.
3. The TFTP does not and shall not involve data mining or any other type of algorithmic or automated profiling or computer filtering.

   Data security and integrity

4. To prevent unauthorised access to or disclosure or loss of the data or any unauthorised form of processing:

   (a) Provided Data shall be held in a secure physical environment, stored separately from any other data, and maintained with high-level systems and physical intrusion controls;
   (b) Provided Data shall not be interconnected with any other database;
   (c) access to Provided Data shall be limited to analysts investigating terrorism or its financing and to persons involved in the technical support, management, and oversight of the TFTP;
   (d) Provided Data shall not be subject to any manipulation, alteration, or addition; and
   (e) no copies of Provided Data shall be made, other than for disaster recovery back-up purposes.

Necessary and proportionate processing of data

5. All searches of Provided Data shall be based upon pre-existing information or evidence which demonstrates a reason to believe that the subject of the search has a nexus to terrorism or its financing.
6. Each individual TFTP search of Provided Data shall be narrowly tailored, shall demonstrate a reason to believe that the subject of the search has a nexus to terrorism or its financing, and shall be logged, including such nexus to terrorism or its financing required to initiate the search.
7. Provided Data may include identifying information about the originator and/or recipient of a transaction, including name, account number, address, and national identification number. The Parties recognise the special sensitivity of personal data revealing racial or ethnic origin, political opinions, or religious or other beliefs, trade union membership, or health and sexual life (sensitive data). In the exceptional circumstance that extracted data were to include sensitive data, the U.S. Treasury Department shall protect such data in accordance with the safeguards and security measures set forth in this Agreement and with full respect and taking due account of their special sensitivity.

Article 6

Retention and deletion of data

1. During the term of this Agreement, the U.S. Treasury Department shall undertake an ongoing and at least annual evaluation to identify non-extracted data that are no longer necessary to combat terrorism or its financing. Where such data are identified, the U.S. Treasury Department shall permanently delete them as soon as technologically feasible.
2. If it transpires that financial payment messaging data were transmitted which were not requested, the U.S. Treasury Department shall promptly and permanently delete such data and shall inform the relevant Designated Provider.
3. Subject to any earlier deletion of data resulting from paragraphs 1, 2, or 5, all non-extracted data received prior to 20 July 2007 shall be deleted not later than 20 July 2012.
4. Subject to any earlier deletion of data resulting from paragraphs 1, 2, or 5, all non-extracted data received on or after 20 July 2007 shall be deleted not later than five (5) years from receipt.
5. During the term of this Agreement, the U.S. Treasury Department shall undertake an ongoing and at least annual evaluation to assess the data retention periods specified in paragraphs 3 and 4 to ensure that they continue to be no longer than necessary to combat terrorism or its financing. Where any such retention periods are determined to be longer than necessary to combat terrorism or its financing, the U.S. Treasury Department shall reduce such retention periods, as appropriate.
6. Not later than three years from the date of entry into force of this Agreement, the European Commission and the U.S. Treasury Department shall prepare a joint report regarding the value of TFTP Provided Data, with particular emphasis on

the value of data retained for multiple years and relevant information obtained from the joint review conducted pursuant to Article 13. The Parties shall jointly determine the modalities of this report.

7. Information extracted from Provided Data, including information shared under Article 7, shall be retained for no longer than necessary for specific investigations or prosecutions for which they are used.

Article 7

Onward transfer

Onward transfer of information extracted from the Provided Data shall be limited pursuant to the following safeguards:

(a) only information extracted as a result of an individualised search as described in this Agreement, in particular Article 5, shall be shared;
(b) such information shall be shared only with law enforcement, public security, or counter terrorism authorities in the United States, Member States, or third countries, or with Europol or Eurojust, or other appropriate international bodies, within the remit of their respective mandates;
(c) such information shall be shared for lead purposes only and for the exclusive purpose of the investigation, detection, prevention, or prosecution of terrorism or its financing;
(d) where the U.S. Treasury Department is aware that such information involves a citizen or resident of a Member State, any sharing of the information with the authorities of a third country shall be subject to the prior consent of competent authorities of the concerned Member State or pursuant to existing protocols on such information sharing between the U.S. Treasury Department and that Member State, except where the sharing of the data is essential for the prevention of an immediate and serious threat to public security of a Party to this Agreement, a Member State, or a third country. In the latter case the competent authorities of the concerned Member State shall be informed of the matter at the earliest opportunity;
(e) in sharing such information, the U.S. Treasury Department shall request that the information shall be deleted by the recipient authority as soon as it is no longer necessary for the purpose for which it was shared; and
(f) each onward transfer shall be duly logged.

Article 8

Adequacy

Subject to ongoing compliance with the commitments on privacy and protection of personal data set out in this Agreement, the U.S. Treasury Department is deemed to ensure an adequate level of data protection for the processing of financial payment messaging and related data transferred from the European Union to the United States for the purposes of this Agreement.

Article 9

Spontaneous provision of information

1. The U.S. Treasury Department shall ensure the availability, as soon as practicable and in the most expedient manner, to law enforcement, public security, or counter terrorism authorities of concerned Member States, and, as appropriate, to Europol and Eurojust, within the remit of their respective mandates, of information obtained through the TFTP that may contribute to the investigation, prevention, detection, or prosecution by the European Union of terrorism or its financing. Any follow-on information that may contribute to the investigation, prevention, detection, or prosecution by the United States of terrorism or its financing shall be conveyed back to the United States on a reciprocal basis and in a reciprocal manner.
2. In order to facilitate the efficient exchange of information, Europol may designate a liaison officer to the U.S. Treasury Department. The modalities of the liaison officer's status and tasks shall be decided jointly by the Parties.

Article 10

EU requests for TFTP searches

Where a law enforcement, public security, or counter terrorism authority of a Member State, or Europol or Eurojust, determines that there is reason to believe that a person or entity has a nexus to terrorism or its financing as defined in Articles 1 to 4 of Council Framework Decision 2002/475/JHA, as amended by Council Framework Decision 2008/919/JHA and Directive 2005/60/EC, such authority may request a search for relevant information obtained through the TFTP. The U.S. Treasury Department shall promptly conduct a search in accordance with Article 5 and provide relevant information in response to such requests.

Article 11

Cooperation with future equivalent EU system

1. During the course of this Agreement, the European Commission will carry out a study into the possible introduction of an equivalent EU system allowing for a more targeted transfer of data.
2. If, following this study, the European Union decides to establish an EU system, the United States shall cooperate and provide assistance and advice to contribute to the effective establishment of such a system.
3. Since the establishment of an EU system could substantially change the context of this Agreement, if the European Union decides to establish such a system, the Parties should consult to determine whether this Agreement would need to be adjusted accordingly. In that regard, U.S. and EU authorities shall cooperate to ensure the complementariness and efficiencies of the U.S. and EU systems in a manner that further enhances the security of citizens of the United States, the European Union, and elsewhere. In the spirit of this cooperation, the Parties shall actively pursue, on the basis of reciprocity and appropriate safeguards, the cooperation of any relevant international financial payment messaging service providers which are based in their respective territories for the purposes of ensuring the continued and effective viability of the U.S. and EU systems.

Article 12

Monitoring of safeguards and controls

1. Compliance with the strict counter terrorism purpose limitation and the other safeguards set out in Articles 5 and 6 shall be subject to monitoring and oversight by independent overseers, including by a person appointed by the European Commission, with the agreement of and subject to appropriate security clearances by the United States. Such oversight shall include the authority to review in real time and retrospectively all searches made of the Provided Data, the authority to query such searches and, as appropriate, to request additional justification of the terrorism nexus. In particular, independent overseers shall have the authority to block any or all searches that appear to be in breach of Article 5.
2. The oversight described in paragraph 1 shall be subject to regular monitoring, including of the independence of the oversight described in paragraph 1, in the framework of the review foreseen in Article 13. The Inspector General of the U.S. Treasury Department will ensure that the independent oversight described in paragraph 1 is undertaken pursuant to applicable audit standards.

Article 13

Joint review

1. At the request of one of the Parties and at any event after a period of six (6) months from the date of entry into force of this Agreement, the Parties shall jointly review the safeguards, controls, and reciprocity provisions set out in this Agreement. The review shall be conducted thereafter on a regular basis, with additional reviews scheduled as necessary.
2. The review shall have particular regard to (a) the number of financial payment messages accessed, (b) the number of occasions on which leads have been shared with Member States, third countries, and Europol and Eurojust, (c) the implementation and effectiveness of this Agreement, including the suitability of the mechanism for the transfer of information, (d) cases in which the information has been used for the prevention, investigation, detection, or prosecution of terrorism or its financing, and (e) compliance with data protection obligations specified in this Agreement. The review shall include a representative and random sample of searches in order to verify compliance with the safeguards and controls set out in this Agreement, as well as a proportionality assessment of the Provided Data, based on the value of such data for the investigation, prevention, detection, or prosecution of terrorism or its financing. Following the review, the European Commission will present a report to the European Parliament and the Council on the functioning of this Agreement, including the areas mentioned in this paragraph.
3. For the purposes of the review, the European Union shall be represented by the European Commission, and the United States shall be represented by the U.S. Treasury Department. Each Party may include in its delegation for the review experts in security and data protection, as well as a person with judicial experience. The European Union review delegation shall include

representatives of two data protection authorities, at least one of which shall be from a Member State where a Designated Provider is based.
4. For the purposes of the review, the U.S. Treasury Department shall ensure access to relevant documentation, systems, and personnel. The Parties shall jointly determine the modalities of the review.

Article 14

Transparency — providing information to the data subjects

The U.S. Treasury Department shall post on its public website detailed information concerning the TFTP and its purposes, including contact information for persons with questions. In addition, it shall post information about the procedures available for the exercise of the rights described in Articles 15 and 16, including the availability of administrative and judicial redress as appropriate in the United States regarding the processing of personal data received pursuant to this Agreement.

Article 15

Right of access

1. Any person has the right to obtain, following requests made at reasonable intervals, without constraint and without excessive delay, at least a confirmation transmitted through his or her data protection authority in the European Union as to whether that person's data protection rights have been respected in compliance with this Agreement, after all necessary verifications have taken place, and, in particular, whether any processing of that person's personal data has taken place in breach of this Agreement.
2. Disclosure to a person of his or her personal data processed under this Agreement may be subject to reasonable legal limitations applicable under national law to safeguard the prevention, detection, investigation, or prosecution of criminal offences, and to protect public or national security, with due regard for the legitimate interest of the person concerned.
3. Pursuant to paragraph 1, a person shall send a request to his or her European national supervisory authority, which shall transmit the request to the Privacy Officer of the U.S. Treasury Department, who shall make all necessary verifications pursuant to the request. The Privacy Officer of the U.S. Treasury Department shall without undue delay inform the relevant European national supervisory authority whether personal data may be disclosed to the data subject and whether the data subject's rights have been duly respected. In the case that access to personal data is refused or restricted pursuant to the limitations referred to in paragraph 2, such refusal or restriction shall be explained in writing and provide information on the means available for seeking administrative and judicial redress in the United States.

Article 16

Right to rectification, erasure, or blocking

1. Any person has the right to seek the rectification, erasure, or blocking of his or her personal data processed by the U.S. Treasury Department pursuant to this

Agreement where the data are inaccurate or the processing contravenes this Agreement.

2. Any person exercising the right expressed in paragraph 1 shall send a request to his or her relevant European national supervisory authority, which shall transmit the request to the Privacy Officer of the U.S. Treasury Department. Any request to obtain rectification, erasure, or blocking shall be duly substantiated. The Privacy Officer of the U.S. Treasury Department shall make all necessary verifications pursuant to the request and shall without undue delay inform the relevant European national supervisory authority whether personal data have been rectified, erased, or blocked, and whether the data subject's rights have been duly respected. Such notification shall be explained in writing and provide information on the means available for seeking administrative and judicial redress in the United States.

Article 17

Maintaining the accuracy of information

1. Where a Party becomes aware that data received or transmitted pursuant to this Agreement are not accurate, it shall take all appropriate measures to prevent and discontinue erroneous reliance on such data, which may include supplementation, deletion, or correction of such data.
2. Each Party shall, where feasible, notify the other if it becomes aware that material information it has transmitted to or received from the other Party under this Agreement is inaccurate or unreliable.

Article 18

Redress

1. The Parties shall take all reasonable steps to ensure that the U.S. Treasury Department and any relevant Member State promptly inform one another, and consult with one another and the Parties, if necessary, where they consider that personal data have been processed in breach of this Agreement.
2. Any person who considers his or her personal data to have been processed in breach of this Agreement is entitled to seek effective administrative and judicial redress in accordance with the laws of the European Union, its Member States, and the United States, respectively. For this purpose and as regards data transferred to the United States pursuant to this Agreement, the U.S. Treasury Department shall treat all persons equally in the application of its administrative process, regardless of nationality or country of residence. All persons, regardless of nationality or country of residence, shall have available under U.S. law a process for seeking judicial redress from an adverse administrative action.

Article 19

Consultation

1. The Parties shall, as appropriate, consult each other to enable the most effective use to be made of this Agreement, including to facilitate the resolution of any dispute regarding the interpretation or application of this Agreement.

2. The Parties shall take measures to avoid the imposition of extraordinary burdens on one another through application of this Agreement. Where extraordinary burdens nonetheless result, the Parties shall immediately consult with a view to facilitating the application of this Agreement, including the taking of such measures as may be required to reduce pending and future burdens.
3. The Parties shall immediately consult in the event that any third party, including an authority of another country, challenges or asserts a legal claim with respect to any aspect of the effect or implementation of this Agreement.

Article 20

Implementation and non-derogation

1. This Agreement shall not create or confer any right or benefit on any person or entity, private or public. Each Party shall ensure that the provisions of this Agreement are properly implemented.
2. Nothing in this Agreement shall derogate from existing obligations of the United States and Member States under the Agreement on Mutual Legal Assistance between the European Union and the United States of America of 25 June 2003 and the related bilateral mutual legal assistance instruments between the United States and Member States.

Article 21

Suspension or termination

1. Either Party may suspend the application of this Agreement with immediate effect, in the event of breach of the other Party's obligations under this Agreement, by notification through diplomatic channels.
2. Either Party may terminate this Agreement at any time by notification through diplomatic channels. Termination shall take effect six (6) months from the date of receipt of such notification.
3. The Parties shall consult prior to any possible suspension or termination in a manner which allows a sufficient time for reaching a mutually agreeable resolution.
4. Notwithstanding any suspension or termination of this Agreement, all data obtained by the U.S. Treasury Department under the terms of this Agreement shall continue to be processed in accordance with the safeguards of this Agreement, including the provisions on deletion of data.

Article 22

Territorial application

1. Subject to paragraphs 2 to 4, this Agreement shall apply to the territory in which the Treaty on European Union and the Treaty on the Functioning of the European Union are applicable and to the territory of the United States.
2. This Agreement will only apply to Denmark, the United Kingdom, or Ireland if the European Commission notifies the United States in writing that Denmark, the United Kingdom, or Ireland has chosen to be bound by this Agreement.

3. If the European Commission notifies the United States before the entry into force of this Agreement that it will apply to Denmark, the United Kingdom, or Ireland, this Agreement shall apply to the territory of such State on the same day as for the other EU Member States bound by this Agreement.
4. If the European Commission notifies the United States after the entry into force of this Agreement that it applies to Denmark, the United Kingdom, or Ireland, this Agreement shall apply to the territory of such State on the first day of the month following receipt of the notification by the United States.

Article 23

Final provisions

1. This Agreement shall enter into force on the first day of the month after the date on which the Parties have exchanged notifications indicating that they have completed their internal procedures for this purpose.
2. Subject to Article 21, paragraph 2, this Agreement shall remain in force for a period of five (5) years from the date of its entry into force and shall automatically extend for subsequent periods of one (1) year unless one of the Parties notifies the other in writing through diplomatic channels, at least six (6) months in advance, of its intention not to extend this Agreement.

Done at Brussels, on 28 June 2010, in two originals, in the English language. This Agreement shall also be drawn up in the Bulgarian, Czech, Danish, Dutch, Estonian, Finnish, French, German, Greek, Hungarian, Italian, Latvian, Lithuanian, Maltese, Polish, Portuguese, Romanian, Slovak, Slovenian, Spanish, and Swedish languages. Upon approval by both Parties, these language versions shall be considered equally authentic.

2. Agreement between the United States of America and the European Union on the use and transfer of passenger name records to the United States Department of Homeland Security

Published at OJ L 215, 11.8.2012, p. 5
Date of signature: 14.12.2011
Date of entry into force: 01.07.2012.
See Council Decision of 13 December 2011 on the signing on behalf of the Union of the Agreement thereto. OJ L 215, 11.8.2012, p. 1.

THE UNITED STATES OF AMERICA,

hereinafter referred to also as 'the United States', and

THE EUROPEAN UNION,

hereinafter referred to also as 'the EU',

together hereinafter referred to as 'the Parties',

(. . .)

HEREBY AGREE:

CHAPTER I – GENERAL PROVISIONS

Article 1 – Purpose

1. The purpose of this Agreement is to ensure security and to protect the life and safety of the public.
2. For this purpose, this Agreement sets forth the responsibilities of the Parties with respect to the conditions under which PNR may be transferred, processed and used, and protected.

Article 2 – Scope

1. PNR, as set forth in the Guidelines of the International Civil Aviation Organisation, shall mean the record created by air carriers or their authorised agents for each journey booked by or on behalf of any passenger and contained in carriers' reservation systems, departure control systems, or equivalent systems providing similar functionality (collectively referred to in this Agreement as 'reservation systems'). Specifically, as used in this Agreement, PNR consists of the data types set forth in the Annex to this Agreement ('Annex').
2. This Agreement shall apply to carriers operating passenger flights between the European Union and the United States.
3. This Agreement shall also apply to carriers incorporated or storing data in the European Union and operating passenger flights to or from the United States.

Article 3 – Provision of PNR

The Parties agree that carriers shall provide PNR contained in their reservation systems to DHS as required by and in accordance with DHS standards and consistent with this Agreement. Should PNR transferred by carriers include data beyond those listed in the Annex, DHS shall delete such data upon receipt.

Article 4 – Use of PNR

1. The United States collects, uses and processes PNR for the purposes of preventing, detecting, investigating, and prosecuting:

   (a) Terrorist offences and related crimes, including:

      (i) Conduct that —

         1. involves a violent act or an act dangerous to human life, property, or infrastructure; and
         2. appears to be intended to —

            a. intimidate or coerce a civilian population;
            b. influence the policy of a government by intimidation or coercion; or
            c. affect the conduct of a government by mass destruction, assassination, kidnapping, or hostage-taking;

      (ii) Activities constituting an offence within the scope of and as defined in applicable international conventions and protocols relating to terrorism;
      (iii) Providing or collecting funds, by any means, directly or indirectly, with the intention that they should be used or in the knowledge that they are to be used, in full or in part, in order to carry out any of the acts described in subparagraphs (i) or (ii);
      (iv) Attempting to commit any of the acts described in subparagraphs (i), (ii), or (iii);
      (v) Participating as an accomplice in the commission of any of the acts described in subparagraphs (i), (ii), or (iii);
      (vi) Organising or directing others to commit any of the acts described in subparagraphs (i), (ii), or (iii);
      (vii) Contributing in any other way to the commission of any of the acts described in subparagraphs (i), (ii), or (iii);
      (viii) Threatening to commit an act described in subparagraph (i) under circumstances which indicate that the threat is credible;

   (b) Other crimes that are punishable by a sentence of imprisonment of three years or more and that are transnational in nature.
   A crime is considered as transnational in nature in particular if:

      (i) it is committed in more than one country;
      (ii) it is committed in one country but a substantial part of its preparation, planning, direction or control takes place in another country;

(iii) it is committed in one country but involves an organised criminal group that engages in criminal activities in more than one country;
(iv) it is committed in one country but has substantial effects in another country; or
(v) it is committed in one country and the offender is in or intends to travel to another country.

2. PNR may be used and processed on a case-by-case basis where necessary in view of a serious threat and for the protection of vital interests of any individual or if ordered by a court.
3. PNR may be used and processed by DHS to identify persons who would be subject to closer questioning or examination upon arrival to or departure from the United States or who may require further examination.
4. Paragraphs 1, 2, and 3 shall be without prejudice to domestic law enforcement, judicial powers, or proceedings, where other violations of law or indications thereof are detected in the course of the use and processing of PNR.

CHAPTER II – SAFEGUARDS APPLICABLE TO THE USE OF PNR

Article 5 – Data security

1. DHS shall ensure that appropriate technical measures and organisational arrangements are implemented to protect personal data and personal information contained in PNR against accidental, unlawful or unauthorised destruction, loss, disclosure, alteration, access, processing or use.
2. DHS shall make appropriate use of technology to ensure data protection, security, confidentiality and integrity. In particular, DHS shall ensure that:

(a) encryption, authorisation and documentation procedures recognised by competent authorities are applied. In particular, access to PNR shall be secured and limited to specifically authorised officials;
(b) PNR shall be held in a secure physical environment and protected with physical intrusion controls; and
(c) a mechanism exists to ensure that PNR queries are conducted consistent with Article 4.

3. In the event of a privacy incident (including unauthorised access or disclosure), DHS shall take reasonable measures to notify affected individuals as appropriate, to mitigate the risk of harm of unauthorised disclosures of personal data and information, and to institute remedial measures as may be technically practicable.
4. Within the scope of this Agreement, DHS shall inform without undue delay the relevant European authorities about cases of significant privacy incidents involving PNR of EU citizens or residents resulting from accidental or unlawful destruction or accidental loss, alteration, unauthorised disclosure or access, or any unlawful forms of processing or use.
5. The United States confirms that effective administrative, civil, and criminal enforcement measures are available under US law for privacy incidents. DHS may take disciplinary action against persons responsible for any such privacy

incident, as appropriate, to include denial of system access, formal reprimands, suspension, demotion, or removal from duty.

6. All access to PNR, as well as its processing and use, shall be logged or documented by DHS. Logs or documentation shall be used only for oversight, auditing, and system maintenance purposes or as otherwise required by law.

Article 6 – Sensitive data

1. To the extent that PNR of a passenger as collected includes sensitive data (i.e. personal data and information revealing racial or ethnic origin, political opinions, religious or philosophical beliefs, trade union membership, or data concerning the health or sex life of the individual), DHS shall employ automated systems to filter and mask out sensitive data from PNR. In addition, DHS shall not further process or use such data, except in accordance with paragraphs 3 and 4.
2. DHS shall provide to the European Commission within 90 days of the entry into force of this Agreement a list of codes and terms identifying sensitive data that shall be filtered out.
3. Access to, as well as processing and use of, sensitive data shall be permitted in exceptional circumstances where the life of an individual could be imperilled or seriously impaired. Such data may be exclusively accessed using restrictive processes on a case-by-case basis with the approval of a DHS senior manager.
4. Sensitive data shall be permanently deleted not later than 30 days from the last receipt of PNR containing such data by DHS. However, sensitive data may be retained for the time specified in US law for the purpose of a specific investigation, prosecution or enforcement action.

Article 7 – Automated individual decisions

The United States shall not make decisions that produce significant adverse actions affecting the legal interests of individuals based solely on automated processing and use of PNR. rsonal data and information, and to institute remedial measures as may be technically practicable.

Article 8 – Retention of data

1. DHS retains PNR in an active database for up to five years. After the initial six months of this period, PNR shall be depersonalised and masked in accordance with paragraph 2 of this Article. Access to this active database shall, unless otherwise permitted by this Agreement, be restricted to a limited number of specifically authorised officials.
2. To achieve depersonalisation, personally identifiable information contained in the following PNR data types shall be masked out:

   (a) name(s);
   (b) other names on PNR;
   (c) all available contact information (including originator information);
   (d) general remarks, including other supplementary information (OSI), special service information (SSI), and special service request (SSR); and
   (e) any collected Advance Passenger Information System (APIS) information.

3. After this active period, PNR shall be transferred to a dormant database for a period of up to ten years. This dormant database shall be subject to additional controls, including a more restricted number of authorised personnel, as well as a higher level of supervisory approval required before access. In this dormant database, PNR shall not be repersonalised except in connection with law enforcement operations and then only in connection with an identifiable case, threat or risk. As regards the purposes as set out in Article 4(1)(b), PNR in this dormant database may only be repersonalised for a period of up to five years.
4. Following the dormant period, data retained must be rendered fully anonymised by deleting all data types which could serve to identify the passenger to whom PNR relate without the possibility of repersonalisation.
5. Data that are related to a specific case or investigation may be retained in an active PNR database until the case or investigation is archived. This paragraph is without prejudice to data retention requirements for individual investigation or prosecution files.
6. The Parties agree that, within the framework of the evaluation as provided for in Article 23(1), the necessity of a 10-year dormant period of retention will be considered.

Article 9 – Non-discrimination

The United States shall ensure that the safeguards applicable to processing and use of PNR under this Agreement apply to all passengers on an equal basis without unlawful discrimination.

Article 10 – Transparency

1. DHS shall provide information to the travelling public regarding its use and processing of PNR through:

   (a) publications in the Federal Register;
   (b) publications on its website;
   (c) notices that may be incorporated by the carriers into contracts of carriage;
   (d) statutorily required reporting to Congress; and
   (e) other appropriate measures as may be developed.

2. DHS shall publish and provide to the EU for possible publication its procedures and modalities regarding access, correction or rectification, and redress procedures.
3. The Parties shall work with the aviation industry to encourage greater visibility to passengers at the time of booking on the purpose of the collection, processing and use of PNR by DHS, and on how to request access, correction and redress.

Article 11 – Access for individuals

1. In accordance with the provisions of the Freedom of Information Act, any individual, regardless of nationality, country of origin, or place of residence is entitled to request his or her PNR from DHS. DHS shall timely provide such PNR subject to the provisions of paragraphs 2 and 3 of this Article.

2. Disclosure of information contained in PNR may be subject to reasonable legal limitations, applicable under US law, including any such limitations as may be necessary to safeguard privacy-protected, national security, and law enforcement sensitive information.
3. Any refusal or restriction of access shall be set forth in writing and provided to the requesting individual on a timely basis. Such notification shall include the legal basis on which information was withheld and shall inform the individual of the options available under US law for seeking redress.
4. DHS shall not disclose PNR to the public, except to the individual whose PNR has been processed and used or his or her representative, or as required by US law.

Article 12 – Correction or rectification for individuals

1. Any individual regardless of nationality, country of origin, or place of residence may seek the correction or rectification, including the possibility of erasure or blocking, of his or her PNR by DHS pursuant to the processes described in this Agreement.
2. DHS shall inform, without undue delay, the requesting individual in writing of its decision whether to correct or rectify the PNR at issue.
3. Any refusal or restriction of correction or rectification shall be set forth in writing and provided to the requesting individual on a timely basis. Such notification shall include the legal basis of such refusal or restriction and shall inform the individual of the options available under US law for seeking redress.

Article 13 – Redress for individuals

1. Any individual regardless of nationality, country of origin, or place of residence whose personal data and personal information has been processed and used in a manner inconsistent with this Agreement may seek effective administrative and judicial redress in accordance with US law.
2. Any individual is entitled to seek to administratively challenge DHS decisions related to the use and processing of PNR.
3. Under the provisions of the Administrative Procedure Act and other applicable law, any individual is entitled to petition for judicial review in US federal court of any final agency action by DHS. Further, any individual is entitled to petition for judicial review in accordance with applicable law and relevant provisions of:

   (a) the Freedom of Information Act;
   (b) the Computer Fraud and Abuse Act;
   (c) the Electronic Communications Privacy Act; and
   (d) other applicable provisions of US law.

4. In particular, DHS provides all individuals an administrative means (currently the DHS Traveller Redress Inquiry Program (DHS TRIP)) to resolve travel-related inquiries including those related to the use of PNR. DHS TRIP provides a redress process for individuals who believe they have been delayed or prohibited from boarding a commercial aircraft because they were wrongly identified as a

threat. Pursuant to the Administrative Procedure Act and Title 49, United States Code, Section 46110, any such aggrieved individual is entitled to petition for judicial review in US federal court from any final agency action by DHS relating to such concerns.

Article 14 – Oversight

1. Compliance with the privacy safeguards in this Agreement shall be subject to independent review and oversight by Department Privacy Officers, such as the DHS Chief Privacy Officer, who:

   (a) have a proven record of autonomy;
   (b) exercise effective powers of oversight, investigation, intervention, and review; and
   (c) have the power to refer violations of law related to this Agreement for prosecution or disciplinary action, when appropriate.

   They shall, in particular, ensure that complaints relating to non-compliance with this Agreement are received, investigated, responded to, and appropriately redressed. These complaints may be brought by any individual, regardless of nationality, country of origin, or place of residence.
2. In addition, application of this Agreement by the United States shall be subject to independent review and oversight by one or more of the following entities:

   (a) the DHS Office of Inspector General;
   (b) the Government Accountability Office as established by Congress; and
   (c) the US Congress.

   Such oversight may be manifested in the findings and recommendations of public reports, public hearings, and analyses.

CHAPTER III – MODALITIES OF TRANSFERS

Article 15 – Method of PNR transmission

1. For the purposes of this Agreement, carriers shall be required to transfer PNR to DHS using the 'push' method, in furtherance of the need for accuracy, timeliness and completeness of PNR.
2. Carriers shall be required to transfer PNR to DHS by secure electronic means in compliance with the technical requirements of DHS.
3. Carriers shall be required to transfer PNR to DHS in accordance with paragraphs 1 and 2, initially at 96 hours before the scheduled flight departure and additionally either in real time or for a fixed number of routine and scheduled transfers as specified by DHS.
4. In any case, the Parties agree that all carriers shall be required to acquire the technical ability to use the 'push' method not later than 24 months following entry into force of this Agreement.
5. DHS may, where necessary, on a case-by-case basis, require a carrier to provide PNR between or after the regular transfers described in paragraph 3. Wherever carriers are unable, for technical reasons, to respond timely to requests under this Article in accordance with DHS standards, or, in exceptional circumstances in

order to respond to a specific, urgent, and serious threat, DHS may require carriers to otherwise provide access.

Article 16 – Domestic sharing

1. DHS may share PNR only pursuant to a careful assessment of the following safeguards:
   (a) Exclusively as consistent with Article 4;
   (b) Only with domestic government authorities when acting in furtherance of the uses outlined in Article 4;
   (c) Receiving authorities shall afford to PNR equivalent or comparable safeguards as set out in this Agreement; and
   (d) PNR shall be shared only in support of those cases under examination or investigation and pursuant to written understandings and US law on the exchange of information between domestic government authorities.
2. When transferring analytical information obtained from PNR under this Agreement, the safeguards set forth in paragraph 1 of this Article shall be respected.

Article 17 – Onward transfer

1. The United States may transfer PNR to competent government authorities of third countries only under terms consistent with this Agreement and only upon ascertaining that the recipient's intended use is consistent with those terms.
2. Apart from emergency circumstances, any such transfer of data shall occur pursuant to express understandings that incorporate data privacy protections comparable to those applied to PNR by DHS as set out in this Agreement.
3. PNR shall be shared only in support of those cases under examination or investigation.
4. Where DHS is aware that PNR of a citizen or a resident of an EU Member State is transferred, the competent authorities of the concerned Member State shall be informed of the matter at the earliest appropriate opportunity.
5. When transferring analytical information obtained from PNR under this Agreement, the safeguards set forth in paragraphs 1 to 4 shall be respected.

Article 18 – Police, law enforcement and judicial cooperation

1. Consistent with existing law enforcement or other information-sharing agreements or arrangements between the United States and any EU Member State or Europol and Eurojust, DHS shall provide to competent police, other specialised law enforcement or judicial authorities of the EU Member States and Europol and Eurojust within the remit of their respective mandates, as soon as practicable, relevant, and appropriate, analytical information obtained from PNR in those cases under examination or investigation to prevent, detect, investigate, or prosecute within the European Union terrorist offences and related crimes or transnational crime as described in Article 4(1)(b).
2. A police or judicial authority of an EU Member State, or Europol or Eurojust, may request, within its mandate, access to PNR or relevant analytical information obtained from PNR that are necessary in a specific case to prevent, detect,

investigate, or prosecute within the European Union terrorist offences and related crimes or transnational crime as described in Article 4(1)(b). DHS shall, subject to the agreements and arrangements noted in paragraph 1 of this Article, provide such information.

3. Pursuant to paragraphs 1 and 2 of this Article, DHS shall share PNR only following a careful assessment of the following safeguards:

   (a) Exclusively as consistent with Article 4;
   (b) Only when acting in furtherance of the uses outlined in Article 4; and
   (c) Receiving authorities shall afford to PNR equivalent or comparable safeguards as set out in this Agreement.

4. When transferring analytical information obtained from PNR under this Agreement, the safeguards set forth in paragraphs 1 to 3 of this Article shall be respected.

CHAPTER IV – IMPLEMENTING AND FINAL PROVISIONS

Article 19 – Adequacy

In consideration of this Agreement and its implementation, DHS shall be deemed to provide, within the meaning of relevant EU data protection law, an adequate level of protection for PNR processing and use. In this respect, carriers which have provided PNR to DHS in compliance with this Agreement shall be deemed to have complied with applicable legal requirements in the EU related to the transfer of such data from the EU to the United States.

Article 20 – Reciprocity

1. The Parties shall actively promote the cooperation of carriers within their respective jurisdictions with any PNR system operating or as may be adopted in the other's jurisdiction, consistent with this Agreement.
2. Given that the establishment of an EU PNR system could have a material effect on the Parties' obligations under this Agreement, if and when an EU PNR system is adopted, the Parties shall consult to determine whether this Agreement would need to be adjusted accordingly to ensure full reciprocity. Such consultations shall in particular examine whether any future EU PNR system would apply less stringent data protection standards than those provided for in this Agreement, and whether, therefore, this Agreement should be amended.

Article 21 – Implementation and non-derogation

1. This Agreement shall not create or confer, under US law, any right or benefit on any person or entity, private or public. Each Party shall ensure that the provisions of this Agreement are properly implemented.
2. Nothing in this Agreement shall derogate from existing obligations of the United States and EU Member States, including under the Agreement on Mutual Legal Assistance between the European Union and the United States of 25 June 2003

and the related bilateral mutual legal assistance instruments between the United States and EU Member States.

Article 22 – Notification of changes in domestic law

The Parties shall advise each other regarding the enactment of any legislation that materially affects the implementation of this Agreement.

Article 23 – Review and evaluation

1. The Parties shall jointly review the implementation of this Agreement one year after its entry into force and regularly thereafter as jointly agreed. Further, the Parties shall jointly evaluate this Agreement four years after its entry into force.
2. The Parties shall jointly determine in advance the modalities and terms of the joint review and shall communicate to each other the composition of their respective teams. For the purpose of the joint review, the European Union shall be represented by the European Commission, and the United States shall be represented by DHS. The teams may include appropriate experts on data protection and law enforcement. Subject to applicable laws, participants in the joint review shall be required to have appropriate security clearances and to respect the confidentiality of the discussions. For the purpose of the joint review, DHS shall ensure appropriate access to relevant documentation, systems, and personnel.
3. Following the joint review, the European Commission shall present a report to the European Parliament and the Council of the European Union. The United States shall be given an opportunity to provide written comments which shall be attached to the report.

Article 24 – Resolution of disputes and suspension of agreement

1. Any dispute arising from the implementation of this Agreement, and any matters related thereto, shall give rise to consultations between the Parties, with a view to reaching a mutually agreeable resolution, including providing an opportunity for either Party to cure within a reasonable time.
2. In the event that consultations do not result in a resolution of the dispute, either Party may suspend the application of this Agreement by written notification through diplomatic channels, with any such suspension to take effect 90 days from the date of such notification, unless the Parties otherwise agree to a different effective date.
3. Notwithstanding any suspension of this Agreement, all PNR obtained by DHS pursuant to this Agreement prior to its suspension shall continue to be processed and used in accordance with the safeguards of this Agreement.

Article 25 – Termination

1. Either Party may terminate this Agreement at any time by written notification through diplomatic channels.
2. Termination shall take effect 120 days from the date of such notification, unless the Parties otherwise agree to a different effective date.

3. Prior to any termination of this Agreement, the Parties shall consult each other in a manner which allows sufficient time for reaching a mutually agreeable resolution.
4. Notwithstanding any termination of this Agreement, all PNR obtained by DHS pursuant to this Agreement prior to its termination shall continue to be processed and used in accordance with the safeguards of this Agreement.

Article 26 – Duration

1. Subject to Article 25, this Agreement shall remain in force for a period of seven years from the date of its entry into force.
2. Upon the expiry of the period set forth in paragraph 1 of this Article, as well as any subsequent period of renewal under this paragraph, the Agreement shall be renewed for a subsequent period of seven years unless one of the Parties notifies the other in writing through diplomatic channels, at least twelve months in advance, of its intention not to renew the Agreement.
3. Notwithstanding the expiration of this Agreement, all PNR obtained by DHS under the terms of this Agreement shall continue to be processed and used in accordance with the safeguards of this Agreement. Similarly, all PNR obtained by DHS under the terms of the Agreement between the United States of America and the European Union on the processing and transfer of passenger name record (PNR) data by air carriers to the United States Department of Homeland Security (DHS), signed at Brussels and Washington, 23 and 26 July 2007, shall continue to be processed and used in accordance with the safeguards of that Agreement.

Article 27 – Final provisions

1. This Agreement shall enter into force on the first day of the month after the date on which the Parties have exchanged notifications indicating that they have completed their internal procedures for this purpose.
2. This Agreement, as of the date of its entry into force, shall supersede the 23 and 26 July 2007 Agreement.
3. This Agreement will only apply to the territory of Denmark, the United Kingdom or Ireland, if the European Commission notifies the United States in writing that Denmark, the United Kingdom or Ireland has chosen to be bound by this Agreement.
4. If the European Commission notifies the United States before the entry into force of this Agreement that it will apply to the territory of Denmark, the United Kingdom or Ireland, this Agreement shall apply to the territory of the relevant State on the same day as for the other EU Member States bound by this Agreement.
5. If the European Commission notifies the United States before the entry into force of this Agreement that it will apply to the territory of Denmark, the United Kingdom or Ireland, this Agreement shall apply to the territory of the relevant State on the first day following receipt of the notification by the United States.

Done at Brussels this fourteenth day of December in the year two thousand and eleven, in two originals.

Pursuant to EU law, this Agreement shall also be drawn up by the EU in the Bulgarian, Czech, Danish, Dutch, Estonian, Finnish, French, German, Greek, Hungarian, Italian, Latvian, Lithuanian, Maltese, Polish, Portuguese, Romanian, Slovak, Slovenian, Spanish and Swedish languages.

For the European Union For the United States of America

ANNEX
PNR DATA TYPES

1. PNR record locator code
2. Date of reservation/issue of ticket
3. Date(s) of intended travel
4. Name(s)
5. Available frequent flier and benefit information (i.e. free tickets, upgrades, etc.)
6. Other names on PNR, including number of travellers on PNR
7. All available contact information (including originator information)
8. All available payment/billing information (not including other transaction details linked to a credit card or account and not connected to the travel transaction)
9. Travel itinerary for specific PNR
10. Travel agency/travel agent
11. Code share information
12. Split/divided information
13. Travel status of passenger (including confirmations and check-in status)
14. Ticketing information, including ticket number, one-way tickets and automated ticket fare quote
15. All baggage information
16. Seat information, including seat number
17. General remarks including OSI, SSI and SSR information
18. Any collected APIS information
19. All historical changes to the PNR listed under points 1 to 18